T0213575

Lecture Notes in Computer Science 9887

Commenced Publication in 1973
Founding and Former Series Editors:
Gerhard Goos, Juris Hartmanis, and Jan van Leeuwen

More information about this series at http://www.springer.com/series/7407

Alessandro E.P. Villa · Paolo Masulli
Antonio Javier Pons Rivero (Eds.)

Artificial Neural Networks and Machine Learning – ICANN 2016

25th International Conference on Artificial Neural Networks
Barcelona, Spain, September 6–9, 2016
Proceedings, Part II

 Springer

Editors
Alessandro E.P. Villa
University of Lausanne
Lausanne
Switzerland

Antonio Javier Pons Rivero
Universitat Politècnica de Catalunya
Terrrassa
Spain

Paolo Masulli
University of Lausanne
Lausanne
Switzerland

ISSN 0302-9743   ISSN 1611-3349   (electronic)
Lecture Notes in Computer Science
ISBN 978-3-319-44780-3   ISBN 978-3-319-44781-0   (eBook)
DOI 10.1007/978-3-319-44781-0

Library of Congress Control Number: 2016948233

LNCS Sublibrary: SL1 – Theoretical Computer Science and General Issues

Printed on acid-free paper

This Springer imprint is published by Springer Nature
The registered company is Springer International Publishing AG Switzerland

Preface

It is our honor and our pleasure to present this two-volume proceedings of the 25th International Conference on Artificial Networks (ICANN 2016) held during September 6–9, 2016, in Barcelona, Spain, and organized by the Universitat Politècnica de Catalunya and the Universitat Pompeu Fabra. The annual ICANN is the flagship conference of the European Neural Network Society (ENNS). After 25 editions, it is clear that ICANN's is a story of success. The field has grown and matured during all these years and the conference series has maintained its rank among the most prestigious conferences in the world. A special social gathering brought together all ENNS members to celebrate its 25th anniversary. Professor Teuvo Kohonen was the first president of ENNS serving the term 1990–1992. The office was then taken by John G. Taylor, Errki Oja, Wlodek Duch, and Alessandro Villa, who comes to the end of his last term. A new president of ENNS was elected and Barcelona is a very appropriate location for this anniversary edition. It has a long tradition in neuroscience going back to Santiago Ramón y Cajal, more than one century ago, who, after moving to the University of Barcelona, made his pioneering neuroanatomical studies in this city. We are sure that such a nice environment and intense program of activities will leave a positive trace in our memories.

The field of artificial neural networks evolved tremendously in the past quarter of a century, but the goal to bring together researchers from two worlds, i.e., information sciences and neurosciences, is still fresh and necessary. The conference gathers people not only from Europe but also from the rest of the globe. The 25th ICANN united presenters from 42 countries from all continents. ICANN 2016 was tightly organized in partnership with ENNS. This governance has been guided by not-for-profit procedures that allowed us to keep very low congress fees compared with international standards. Moreover, we consolidated the practice of offering a subscription to ENNS to all ICANN delegates who present a scientific communication.

The Scientific and Reviewing Committee selected 169 contributions, after a peer-review process of 227 submissions, which are published in these two proceedings volumes. The variety of topics covered by all these contributions proves the maturity and, at the same time, the vitality of the field of artificial neural networks. Besides, this year, we introduced short extended abstract contributions in order to encourage top-level scholars to join the conference without the need to submit a full paper. This opportunity appeared very attractive also to researchers who are interested in presenting results that could not justify a full paper submission. Hence, the implementation of this scheme eventually produced 122 full papers and 47 short extended abstracts.

The type of submission was not the ultimate criterion in assigning the submitters to an oral or a poster presentation. Papers were equally good and attributed to 94 oral and 75 poster presentations following, in the vast majority of the cases, the preference expressed by the authors. The proceedings of the 47 short presentations have been grouped together following the rules of the Publisher. Oral presentations were divided into 18 sessions following the usual dual track, initially intended as the brain-inspired computing track and machine-learning research track. As in the past editions the dual track became track A and track B, because many papers presented an interdisciplinary approach and track C for the posters. In addition, ICANN had eight plenary talks by internationally renowned speakers, in particular one lecture sponsored by ENNS, the John G. Taylor Memorial Lecture given by Errki Oja, past president of ENNS. Several satellite workshops completed the intensive program of ICANN 2016.

This scientific event would not have been possible without the participation of many people. We want to thank everyone who contributed, in one way or another, to the success of the conference and the publication of the proceedings. We want to express our deepest gratitude to the members of the Executive Committee of the ENNS, who have accepted the proposal of Barcelona organizing the event. We are grateful for the work of the Scientific and Reviewing Committee and all reviewers who worked under strong time constraints during the compilation of the proceedings. The conference would have been impossible without the contribution of all members of the Organizing Committees. We want to thank the outstanding work by the ENNS, UPC, and UPF personnel. We want to thank, particularly, the work of Paolo Masulli, Lara Escuain, and Daniel Malagarriga. The conference would not have been a reality without the help of Caroline Kleinheny. Finally, we would like to thank Anna Kramer, Frank Holzwarth, and Alfred Hofmann from Springer for their help with the tough publication project. We acknowledge, too, all authors who contributed to the volumes and shared their ideas during the conference. We are sure that the papers appearing in these volumes will contribute to the field of artificial neural networks with many new and inspiring ideas that will help other concepts flourish in the future.

July 2016

Alessandro E.P. Villa
Paolo Masulli
Antonio Javier Pons Rivero

Organization

General Chair

Antonio Javier Pons Rivero   Universitat Politècnica de Catalunya, Spain

Honorary Chair

Alessandro E.P. Villa   University of Lausanne, Switzerland

Local Co-chairs

Jordi Garcia-Ojalvo   Universitat Pompeu Fabra, Spain
Paul F.M.J. Verschure   ICREA-Universitat Pompeu Fabra, Spain

Communications Chair

Paolo Masulli   University of Lausanne, Switzerland

Registration Chair

Caroline Kleinheny   ENNS Secretariat, Switzerland

Scientific and Reviewing Committee

Javier Martín Buldú   Center for Biomedical Technology, Spain
Jérémie Cabessa   Université Panthéon-Assas - Paris 2, France
Joan Cabestany   Universitat Politècnica de Catalunya, Spain
Stephen Coombes   University of Nottingham, UK
José R. Dorronsoro   Universidad Autónoma de Madrid, Spain
Jordi Garcia-Ojalvo   Universitat Pompeu Fabra, Spain
Petia Georgieva   University of Aveiro, Portugal
Barbara Hammer   Bielefeld University, Germany
Petia Koprinkova-Hristova   Bulgarian Academy of Sciences, Bulgaria
Věra Kůrková   Czech Academy of Sciences, Czech Republic
Alessandra Lintas   University of Lausanne, Switzerland
Francesco Masulli   University of Genoa, Italy
Paolo Masulli   University of Lausanne, Switzerland
Claudio Mirasso   IFISC, Spain
Juan Manuel Moreno   Universitat Politècnica de Catalunya, Spain
    Arostegui
Günther Palm   Universität Ulm, Germany

Jaakko Peltonen	Aalto University Helsinki, Finland
Antonio Javier Pons Rivero	Universitat Politècnica de Catalunya, Spain
Jordi Soriano	Universitat de Barcelona, Spain
Paul F.M.J. Verschure	ICREA-Universitat Pompeu Fabra, Spain
Alessandro E.P. Villa	University of Lausanne, Switzerland

Program and Workshop Committee

Grégoire Montavon	Technische Universität Berlin, Germany
Antonio Javier Pons Rivero	Universitat Politècnica de Catalunya, Spain
Jordi Soriano	Universitat de Barcelona, Spain
Paul F.M.J. Verschure	ICREA-Universitat Pompeu Fabra, Spain

Secretariat and Communications

Ana Calle	Universitat Politècnica de Catalunya, Spain
Lara Escuain-Poole	Universitat Politècnica de Catalunya, Spain
Caroline Kleinheny	ENNS Secretariat, Switzerland
Daniel Malagarriga	Universitat Politècnica de Catalunya, Spain
Paolo Masulli	University of Lausanne, Switzerland

ENNS Travel Grant Committee

Barbara Hammer	Bielefeld University, Germany
Antonio Javier Pons Rivero	Universitat Politècnica de Catalunya, Spain
Alessandro E.P. Villa	University of Lausanne, Switzerland

Additional Reviewers

Amr Abdullatif	University of Genoa, Italy
Takeshi Abe	Okinawa Institute of Science and Technology Graduate University, Japan
Waqas Waseem Ahmed	Universitat Politècnica de Catalunya, Spain
Hisanao Akima	Tohoku University, Japan
Tetiana Aksenova	CEA, France
Carlos M. Alaíz	KU Leuven, Belgium
Bruno Apolloni	University of Milan, Italy
Daniel Araújo	Universidade Federal do Rio Grande do Norte, Brazil
Yoshiyuki Asai	Okinawa Institute of Science and Technology Graduate University, Japan
Pragathi Priyadharsini Balasubramani	Indian Institute of Technology, India
Alessandro Barardi	Universitat Politècnica de Catalunya, Spain
Pablo Barros	University of Hamburg, Germany
Lluís A. Belanche	Universitat Politècnica de Catalunya, Spain
Alexandre Bernardino	IST University of Lisbon, Portugal

Monji Kherallah	University of Sfax, Tunisia
Stefanos Kollias	NTUA, Greece
Petia Koprinkova-Hristova	Bulgarian Academy of Sciences, Bulgaria
Irena Koprinska	University of Sydney, Australia
Kostadin Koroutchev	UAM, Spain
Maciej Kusy	Rzeszow University of Technology, Poland
Markus Kächele	University of Ulm, Germany
Věra Kůrková	Czech Academy of Sciences, Czech Republic
Alessandra Lintas	University of Lausanne, Switzerland
Sheng Luo	Hasso Plattner Institute, Germany
Rania Maalej	National Engineering School of Sfax, Tunisia
Maciej Majewski	Koszalin University of Technology, Poland
Daniel Malagarriga	Universitat Politècnica de Catalunya, Spain
Thomas Martinetz	University of Lübeck, Germany
Paolo Masulli	University of Lausanne, Switzerland
Francesco Masulli	University of Genoa, Italy
Fernanda Matias	Universidade Federal de Alagoas, Brazil
Maurizio Mattia	Istituto Superiore di Sanità, Italy
Corrado Mencar	University of Bari A. Moro, Italy
Claudio Mirasso	IFISC, Spain
Juan Manuel Moreno Arostegui	Universitat Politècnica de Catalunya, Spain
Javier Márquez Ruiz	Universidad Pablo de Olavide Seville, Spain
Taishin Nomura	Osaka University, Japan
Dimitri Nowicki	National Academy of Science of Ukraine, Ukraine
Adil Omari	Universidad Autónoma de Madrid, Spain
Silvia Ortin	IFISC, Spain
Sebastian Otte	University of Tuebingen, Germany
Günther Palm	Universität Ulm, Germany
Juan Pardo	Universidad CEU Cardenal Herrera, Spain
Jaakko Peltonen	Aalto University Helsinki, Finland
Ernesto Pereda	University of La Laguna, Spain
Luis Pesquera	Instituto de Física de Cantabria, Spain
Gordon Pipa	University of Osnabrück, Germany
Angel Ricardo Plastino	Universidad del Noroeste de la Provincia de Buenos Aires, UNNOBA-Conicet, Argentina
Antonio Javier Pons Rivero	Universitat Politècnica de Catalunya, Spain
Yifat Prut	Hebrew University, Israel
Irene Rodriguez-Lujan	Universidad Autónoma de Madrid, Spain
João Rosa	Universidade de São Paulo, Brazil
Stefano Rovetta	University of Genoa, Italy
Ariel Ruiz-Garcia	Coventry University, UK
Vicent Sala	MCIA Research Center - UPC, Spain
Maria V. Sanchez-Vives	ICREA-IDIBAPS Barcelona, Spain
Friedhelm Schwenker	University of Ulm, Germany
Sugandha Sharma	University of Waterloo, Canada

Contents – Part II

Classification and Forecasting

Recognition and Navigation

Short Papers

Contents – Part I

Networks and Dynamics

Higher Nervous Functions

Learning Foundations

Short Papers

Deep Learning

Video Description Using Bidirectional Recurrent Neural Networks

Álvaro Peris[1]([✉]), Marc Bolaños[2,3], Petia Radeva[2,3],
and Francisco Casacuberta[1]

[1] PRHLT Research Center, Universitat Politècnica de València, Valencia, Spain
{lvapeab,fcn}@prhlt.upv.es
[2] Universitat de Barcelona, Barcelona, Spain
{marc.bolanos,petia.ivanova}@ub.edu
[3] Computer Vision Center, Bellaterra, Spain

Abstract. Although traditionally used in the machine translation field, the encoder-decoder framework has been recently applied for the generation of video and image descriptions. The combination of Convolutional and Recurrent Neural Networks in these models has proven to outperform the previous state of the art, obtaining more accurate video descriptions. In this work we propose pushing further this model by introducing two contributions into the encoding stage. First, producing richer image representations by combining object and location information from Convolutional Neural Networks and second, introducing Bidirectional Recurrent Neural Networks for capturing both forward and backward temporal relationships in the input frames.

Keywords: Video description · Neural Machine Translation · Birectional Recurrent Neural Networks · LSTM · Convolutional Neural Networks

1 Introduction

Automatic generation of image descriptions is a recent trend in Computer Vision that represents an interesting, but difficult task. This has been possible due to the dramatic advances in Convolutional Neural Network (CNN) models that allowed to outperform the state-of-the-art algorithms in many computer vision problems: object recognition, object detection, activity recognition, etc. Generating descriptions of videos represents an even more challenging task that could lead to multiple applications (e.g. video indexing and retrieval, movie description for multimedia applications or for blind people or human-robot interaction).

However, the problem of video description generation has several properties that make it specially difficult. Besides the significant amount of image information to analyze, videos may have a variable number of images and can be described with sentences of different length. Furthermore, the descriptions of videos use to be high-level summaries that not necessarily are expressed in

© Springer International Publishing Switzerland 2016
A.E.P. Villa et al. (Eds.): ICANN 2016, Part II, LNCS 9887, pp. 3–11, 2016.
DOI: 10.1007/978-3-319-44781-0_1

terms of the objects, actions and scenes observed in the images. There are many open research questions in this field requiring deep video understanding. Some of them are how to efficiently extract important elements from the images (e.g. objects, scenes, actions), to define the local (e.g. fine-grained motion) and global spatio-temporal information, determine the salient content worth to describe, and generate the final video description. All these specific questions need the attention of computer vision, machine translation and natural language understanding communities in order to be solved.

In this work, we propose to enrich the state-of-the-art architecture using bidirectional neural networks for modeling relationships in two temporal directions. Furthermore, we test the inclusion of supplementary features, which help to detect contextual information from the scene where the video takes place.

2   Related Work

Although the problem of video captioning recently appeared thanks to the new learning capabilities offered by Deep Learning techniques, the general pipeline adopted in these works resembles the traditional encoder-decoder methodology used in Machine Translation (MT). The main difference is that, in the encoder step, instead of generating a compact representation of the source language sentence, we generate a representation of the images belonging to the video.

MT aims to automatically translate text or speech from a source to a target language. Within the last decades, the prevailing approach is the statistical one [5]. The application of connectionist models in the area has drawn much the attention of researchers in the last years. Moreover, a new approach to MT has been recently proposed: the so-called Neural Machine Translation, where the translation process is carried out by a means of a large Recurrent Neural Network (RNN) [9]. These systems rely on the encoder-decoder framework: an encoder RNN produces a compact representation of an input sentence in the source language, and the decoder RNN takes this representation and generates the corresponding target language sentence. Both RNNs usually make use of gated units, such as the popular Long Short-term Memory (LSTM) [4], in order to cope with long-term relationships.

The recent reintroduction of Deep Learning in the Computer Vision field through CNNs [6], has allowed to obtain new and richer image representations compared to the traditional hand-crafted ones. These networks have demonstrated to be a powerful tool to extract feature representations for several kinds of computer vision problems like on objects [8] or scenes [15] recognition. Thanks to the CNNs ability to serve as knowledge transfer mechanisms, they have also been usually used as feature extractors.

The majority of the works devoted to generate textual descriptions from single images also follow the encoder-decoder architecture. In the encoding stage, they apply a combination of CNN and LSTM for describing the input image. In the decoding stage, an LSTM is in charge of receiving the image information and generating, word by word, a final description of the image [12].

The problem of video captioning is similar. Seminal works applied methodologies inspired by classical MT [7]. Nevertheless, more recent works following the encoder-decoder approach, obtained state-of-the-art performances [11,13].

We present a new methodology for natural language video description that makes use of deeper structures and a double-way analysis of the input video. We propose to use as a base architecture the one introduced in [13]. On the top of it, our contributions are twofold. First, we produce richer image representations by combining complementary CNNs for detecting objects and contextual information from the input images. Second, we introduce a Bidirectional LSTM (BLSTM) network in the encoding stage, which has the ability to learn forward and backward long-term relationships on the input sequence.

3 Methodology

An overview of our proposal is depicted in Fig. 1. We propose an encoder-decoder approach consisting of four stages, using both CNNs and LSTMs for describing images and for modeling their temporal relationship, respectively.

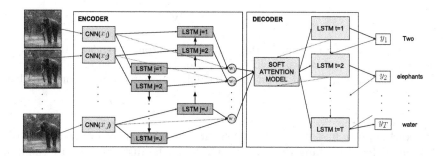

Fig. 1. General scheme of our proposed methodology. (Color figure online)

First (blue in the scheme), we apply two state of the art CNN models for extracting complementary features on each of the raw images from the video.

Second (red in the scheme), considering we need to describe the actions performed in consecutive frames, we apply a BLSTM for capturing temporal relationships and complementary information by taking a look at the action in a forward and in a backward manner.

Third (yellow in the scheme), the two output vectors from forward and backward LSTM models of the previous step are concatenated together with the CNN output for each image and are fed to a soft attention model in the decoder. This model decides on which parts of the input video should focus for emitting the next word, considering the description generated so far.

Fourth (green in the scheme), an LSTM network generates the video caption from the representation obtained in previous stages. The variable-length caption is obtained word by word, using a softmax function on the top of the LSTM.

3.1   Encoder

Given the video description problem, in the encoding stage we need to properly characterize the video for (1) understanding which kind of objects and structures appear in the images, and (2) modeling their relationships and actions along time.

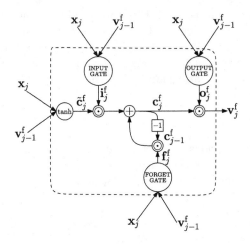

Fig. 2. Forward layer LSTM unit for the encoder. The output depends on the previous hidden state $(\mathbf{v}_{j-1}^{f})$ and the current feature vector from the video extracted by the CNN $(\mathbf{x}_j)$. Input, output and forget gates module the amount of information that flows across the unit.

For tackling the first part of the problem, several kinds of pretrained CNNs may be used for describing the images, which can be distinguished by the different architectures or by the different datasets used for training. Although an extended comparison and combinations of models could be used for applying this characterization, we propose combining object and context-related information. For this purpose we use the GoogleNet architecture [10] separately trained on two datasets, one for objects (ILSVRC dataset [8]), and the other for scenes (Places 205 [15]). The combination of these two kinds of data can inform about the objects appearing and their surroundings, being ideal for the problem at hand. Note that, given the nature of this task, an explicit object or scene segmentation is not required. Additionally, we must note that the features extracted are a representation of the whole image, which means that are not suitable for extracting spatial-related information. For a given video, the CNNs generate a sequence $\mathbf{V}_c$ of J d-dimensional feature vectors, $\mathbf{x}_1,\ldots,\mathbf{x}_J$ with $\mathbf{x}_j \in \mathbb{R}^d$ for $1 \leq j \leq J$, where J is the number of frames in the video.

To solve the second problem, a BLSTM processes the sequence $\mathbf{V}_c$, generating a new sequence $\mathbf{V}_{bi} = \mathbf{v}_1,\ldots,\mathbf{v}_J$ of J vectors. BLSTM networks are composed of two independent LSTM layers namely, forward and backward. Both layers are analogue, but the latter processes the input sequence reversed in time.

LSTM networks have, in addition to the classical hidden state, a memory state. Let $\mathbf{v}_j^f$ be the forward layer hidden state at the time-step j, and let $\mathbf{c}_j^f$ be its memory state. The hidden state $\mathbf{v}_j^f$ is computed as $\mathbf{c}_j^f$ controlled by an output gate $\mathbf{o}_j^f$. The current memory state depends on an updated memory state, and on the previous memory state, $\mathbf{c}_{j-1}^f$, respectively modulated by the forget and input gates, $\mathbf{f}_j^f$ and $\mathbf{i}_j^f$. The updated memory state $\tilde{\mathbf{c}}_j^f$ is obtained by applying a logistic non-linear function to the input and the previous hidden state. Each LSTM gate has associated two weight matrices, accounting for the input and the previous hidden state. Such matrices must be estimated on a training set. Figure 2 shows an illustration of an LSTM unit. The same architecture applies to the backward layer, but dependencies flow from the next time-step to the previous one. Since forward and backward layers are independent, they have different weight matrices to estimate.

Each feature vector $\mathbf{v}_j$ computed by the BLSTM results as the concatenation of the forward and backward hidden states: $\mathbf{v}_j = [\mathbf{v}_j^f; \mathbf{v}_j^b] \in \mathbb{R}^{2 \cdot D}$ for $1 \leq j \leq J$, being D the size of each forward and backward hidden state.

Finally, the encoder combines the sequences $\mathbf{V}_c$ and $\mathbf{V}_{bi}$ by concatenating the vectors from the CNN and from the BLSTM, producing a final sequence $\mathbf{V}$ of J feature vectors $\mathbf{w}_1, \ldots, \mathbf{w}_J$, $\mathbf{w}_j = [\mathbf{x}_j; \mathbf{v}_j] \in \mathbb{R}^{d+2 \cdot D}$ for $1 \leq j \leq J$.

3.2   Decoder

The decoder is an LSTM network, which acts as a language model, conditioned by the information provided by the encoder. This network is equipped with an attention mechanism [1,13]: a soft alignment model, implemented as a single-layered perceptron, that helps the decoder to know *where* to look at for generating each output word. Given the sequence $\mathbf{V}$ generated by the encoder, at each decoding time-step t the attention mechanism weights the J feature vectors and

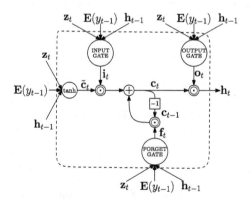

Fig. 3. Decoder LSTM unit. The output depends on the previous hidden state ($\mathbf{h}_t$), the word embedding of the previously generated word ($\mathbf{E}(y_{t-1})$) and the context vector provided by the attention mechanism ($\mathbf{z}_t$).

combines them into a single context vector $\mathbf{z}_t \in \mathbb{R}^{d+2 \cdot D}$. Considering that each of our feature vectors describes the scene in a different temporal moment, our dynamic attention mechanism acts as a learnable saliency mechanism applied along time, which is able to weight and emphasize the information of different frames.

The decoder LSTM is defined similarly to the forward layer from the encoder, but it takes into account the previously generated word and the context vector from the attention mechanism, in addition to its previous hidden state. The last word representation is provided by a word embedding matrix $\mathbf{E} \in \mathbb{R}^{m \times V}$, being m the size of the word embedding and V the size of the vocabulary. $\mathbf{E}$ is estimated together with the rest of the model parameters.

A probability distribution over the vocabulary of output words is defined from the hidden state $\mathbf{h}_t$, by means of a softmax function. This function represents the conditional probability of a word given an input video $\mathbf{V}$ and its history (the previously generated words): $p(y_t|y_1, \ldots, y_{t-1}, \mathbf{V})$. Following [9], a beam-search method is used to find the caption with highest conditional probability.

4   Results

In this section we describe the datasets and metrics used for evaluating and comparing our model to the video captioning state of the art.

4.1   Dataset

The **Microsoft Research Video Description Corpus** (MSVD) [2] is a dataset composed of 1970 open domain clips collected from YouTube and annotated using a crowd sourcing platform. Each video has a variable number of captions, written by different users. We used the splits made by [11,13], separating the dataset in 1200 videos for training, 100 for validation and the remaining 670 for testing. During training, the clips and each of their captions were treated separately, accounting for a total of more than $80,000$ training samples.

4.2   Evaluation Metrics

In order to evaluate and compare the results of the different models we used the standardized COCO-Caption evaluation package [3], which provides several metrics for text description comparison. We used three main metrics, all of them presented from 0 (minimum quality) to 100 (maximum quality):

BLEU: this metric compares the ratio of n-gram structures that are shared between the system hypotheses and the reference sentences.

METEOR: it computes the F1 score of precision and recall between hypotheses and references.

CIDEr: similarly to BLEU, it computes the number of matching n-grams, but penalizes any n-gram frequently found in the whole training set.

4.3 Experimental Results

On all the tests we used a batch size of 64, the learning rate was automatically set by the Adadelta [14] method and, as the authors in [13] reported, we applied a frame subsampling, picking only one image every 26 frames for reducing the computational load. The parameters of the network were randomly initialized. An evaluation on the validation set was performed every 1000 updates. The learning process was stopped when the reported error increased after 5 evaluations.

For each configuration we run 10 experiments. At each of them, we randomly set the value of the critical model hyperparameters. Such hyperparameters and their tested ranges are $m \in [300, 700]$, $|\mathbf{h}_t| \in [1000, 3000]$. When using the BLSTM encoder, we performed an additional selection on $|\mathbf{v}_j| \in [100, 2100]$.

Table 1. Text generation results for each model on the MSVD dataset. The results below the horizontal line are our proposals.

Model	BLEU [%]	METEOR [%]	CIDEr [%]
Objects[a]	51.5	32.5	66.0
Objects + BLSTM	**53.6**	**32.6**	66.4
Objects + Scenes	52.6	32.5	67.0
Objects + Scenes + BLSTM	52.8	31.3	**67.2**

[a]Model from [13] only with *Object* features evaluated on our system.

For each configuration, the best model with respect to the BLEU measure on the validation set was selected. In Table 1 we report the results of the best models on the test set. The first row correspond to the result obtained with our system with the object features from [13]. The configurations reported below the horizontal line are our proposals, where *Scenes* indicates we use scene-related features concatenated to *Objects* and *BLSTM* denotes the use of the additional BLSTM encoder.

5 Discussion and Conclusions

Analyzing the obtained results, a clear improvement trend can be derived when applying the BLSTM as a temporal inference mechanism. The BLSTM addition when using *Objects* features allows to improve the result on all metrics, obtaining a benefit of more than 2 BLEU points. Adding scenes-related features also slightly improves the result, although it is not as remarkable as the BLSTM improvement. The combination of *Objects*+*Scenes*+BLSTM offers the best CIDEr performance, nevertheless, this result is slightly below the *Objects*+BLSTM one on the other metrics. This behaviour is probably due to the significant increase on the number of parameters to learn. It should be investigated whether the reduction of the number of parameters by reducing the size of the CNN features, or the use of larger datasets could lead to further improvements.

In conclusion, we have presented a new methodology for natural language video description that takes profit from a bidirectional analysis of the input sequence. This architecture has the ability to infer information from data not only in a past-to-future fashion, but also in the future-to-past direction. Which means that its hidden state will incorporate more confident information, being even more evident in the initial frames where otherwise the result would only take into account a short time-span. On the other hand, the use of a bidirectional model yields doubling the number of parameters on the encoder, which will increase the computational time and the amount of data needed to train the model. Although, in order to extract further conclusions, the presented architecture should be tested on more datasets. Additionally, the use of complementary object and scene-related image features has proven to obtain a richer video representation. The improvements have allowed the method to outperform the state-of-the-art results in the problem at hand.

These results suggest that deep structures help to transfer the knowledge from the input sequence of frames to the output natural language caption. Hence, the next step to take must delve into the application of deeper modeling structures: 3D CNNs allow the recognition of actions and may solve some of the ambiguities existing in the tested methods, which only cope with object and scenes recognition. An additional future step should study the inclusion of spatio-temporal attention models for better coping with the nature of natural videos.

Acknowledgments. This work was partially founded by TIN2015-66951-C2-1-R, SGR 1219, PrometeoII/2014/030 and by a travel grant by the R-MIPRCV network. P. Radeva is partially supported by an ICREA Academia2014 grant. We acknowledge NVIDIA for the donation of a GPU used in this work.

References

1. Bahdanau, D., Cho, K., Bengio, Y.: Neural machine translation by jointly learning to align and translate. In: Proceedings of the International Conference on Learning Representations, arXiv:1409.0473 (2015)
2. Chen, D.L., Dolan, W.B.: Collecting highly parallel data for paraphrase evaluation. In: Proceedings of the 49th Annual Meeting of the Association for Computational Linguistics, vol. 1, pp. 190–200 (2011)
3. Chen, X., Fang, H., Lin, T.-Y., Vedantam, R., Gupta, S., Dollár, P., Zitnick, C.L.: Microsoft COCO captions: data collection and evaluation server. arXiv preprint arXiv:1504.00325 (2015)
4. Hochreiter, S., Schmidhuber, J.: Long short-term memory. Neural Comput. **9**(8), 1735–1780 (1997)
5. Koehn, P.: Statistical Machine Translation. Cambridge University Press, New York (2010)
6. Krizhevsky, A., Sutskever, I., Hinton, G.E.: ImageNet classification with deep convolutional neural networks. In: Advances in Neural Information Processing Systems, pp. 1097–1105 (2012)

7. Rohrbach, M., Qiu, W., Titov, I., Thater, S., Pinkal, M., Schiele, B.: Translating video content to natural language descriptions. In: Proceedings of the IEEE International Conference on Computer Vision and Pattern Recognition, pp. 433–440 (2013)
8. Russakovsky, O., Deng, J., Hao, S., Krause, J., Satheesh, S., Ma, S., Huang, Z., Karpathy, A., Khosla, A., Bernstein, M., Berg, A.C., Fei-Fei, L.: ImageNet large scale visual recognition challenge. Int. J. Comput. Vision **115**(3), 211–252 (2015)
9. Sutskever, I., Vinyals, O., Le, Q.V.: Sequence to sequence learning with neural networks. Adv. Neural Inf. Process. Syst. **27**, 3104–3112 (2014)
10. Szegedy, C., Liu, W., Jia, Y., Sermanet, P., Reed, S., Anguelov, D., Erhan, D., Vanhoucke, V., Rabinovich, A.: Going deeper with convolutions. In: Proceedings of the IEEE Conference on Computer Vision and Pattern Recognition, pp. 1–9 (2015)
11. Venugopalan, S., Rohrbach, M., Donahue, J., Mooney, R., Darrell, T., Saenko, K.: Sequence to sequence-video to text. In: Proceedings of the IEEE International Conference on Computer Vision, pp. 4534–4542 (2015)
12. Vinyals, O., Toshev, A., Bengio, S., Erhan, D.: Show and tell: a neural image caption generator. In: Proceedings of the IEEE Conference on Computer Vision and Pattern Recognition, pp. 3156–3164 (2015)
13. Yao, L., Torabi, A., Cho, K., Ballas, N., Pal, C., Larochelle, H., Courville, A.: Describing videos by exploiting temporal structure. In Proceedings of the IEEE International Conference on Computer Vision, pp. 4507–4515 (2015)
14. Zeiler, M.D.: ADADELTA: an adaptive learning rate method. arXiv preprint arXiv:1212.5701 (2012)
15. Zhou, B., Lapedriza, A., Xiao, J., Torralba, A., Oliva, A.: Learning deep features for scene recognition using places database. In: Advances in Neural Information Processing Systems, pp. 487–495 (2014)

Tactile Convolutional Networks for Online Slip and Rotation Detection

Martin Meier[✉], Florian Patzelt, Robert Haschke, and Helge J. Ritter

Neuroinformatics Group,
Center of Excellence Cognitive Interaction Technology (CITEC),
Bielefeld University, Bielefeld, Germany
{mmeier,fpatzelt,rhaschke,helge}@techfak.uni-bielefeld.de

Abstract. We present a deep convolutional neural network which is capable to distinguish between different contact states in robotic manipulation tasks. By integrating spatial and temporal tactile sensor data from a piezo-resistive sensor array through deep learning techniques, the network is not only able to classify the contact state into stable versus slipping, but also to distinguish between rotational and translation slippage. We evaluated different network layouts and reached a final classification rate of more than 97%. Using consumer class GPUs, slippage and rotation events can be detected within 10 ms, which is still feasible for adaptive grasp control.

1 Introduction

In autonomous robotic manipulation tasks, for example grasping and placing objects, estimating the stability of the object in hand plays a major role. Objects may slip out of the manipulator. This can lead to a state in the desired action sequence from which the system cannot recover easily. Due to occlusions, vision-based systems can hardly keep track of the state of objects hold in manipulators and are therefore of limited usefulness when it comes to detecting loss of grasp stability. For that reason, the loss of an object can only be detected after such events already occurred. Humans perceive the onset of slippage by sensing high-frequency micro-vibrations through specialized nerves (Pacinian corpuscle) in the skin [4].

One possibility for early detection of slippage events in robotic systems is the integration of tactile sensing capabilities directly into robotic manipulators. By having human like sensing skills, the system should be able to directly evaluate the contact state during interactions. Compared to imaging technologies where standards are established for data acquisition and representation, current tactile sensors posses a large variety of data acquisition techniques, which can be either based on electric [12], optic [15] or acoustic [6] effects. For example the authors in [2] discuss eight different technologies which are based on these three effects and are used in current state of the art tactile sensors. For a detailed technical overview the interested reader is referred to [2].

© Springer International Publishing Switzerland 2016
A.E.P. Villa et al. (Eds.): ICANN 2016, Part II, LNCS 9887, pp. 12–19, 2016.
DOI: 10.1007/978-3-319-44781-0_2

The work presented in [13] used support vector machines and random forests to detect object slippage with a BioTac [6] sensor. The BioTac sensor offers multiple modalities such as 19 electrodes to measure local contacts with a sampling rate of 100 Hz, thermal sensors and two pressure transducers, one for low (up to 100 Hz) and one for high (up to 2.2 kHz) frequencies, respectively. The features comprised all raw sensor values, where the high frequency component is supplied as a time series of the last 22 sensor readings which makes up for half of the feature vector. With these features used as input for a random forest, a $F_{score} > 0.75$ has been achieved in the evaluation. To predict slippage of held objects, the authors of [14] took an approach where they first learned friction properties based on data acquired from a force/torque sensor with Gaussian process regression. In [11], also a BioTac sensor is used to classify slip with a multilayer perceptron (MLP), but in contrast to [13], the authors used a sequence of 100 samples of the electrodes without utilizing the high frequency sensor. With this time series as input for a MLP, a classification rate of 80 % was achieved. The same type of tactile sensor utilized in this work was already used in [8] for a binary stable- vs. slip-classification. Here, the authors used a Fourier transformation over the whole sensor array with varying window sizes to predict slip velocity. They were able to achieve low mean squared errors of 0.04. These approaches have in common, that they rely on the classification of time series to detect slip events.

In areas outside of the scope of tactile sensing, convolutional neural networks (CNNs) have been successfully applied to time series classification tasks, for example in speech recognition. In [7], the authors evaluated the performance of convolutional networks compared to deep neural networks (DNNs), Gaussian mixture model (GMM) and Hidden markov model (HMM) approaches for large speech recognition tasks. The data was preprocessed by extracting mel-frequency cepstrum coefficients (MFCC) [3], a filter technique that resemble human auditory perception by using a logarithmic scale for pitch and loudness of the signal. With these frequency features as input for CNNs, the deep networks outperformed GMM and HMM approaches on different datasets. The authors in [1] evaluated the efficiency of a deep neural networks with and without convolutional layers in a similar speech recognition task and reported an increase of 6 to 10 % in the relative classification rate for CNNs compared to DNNs. By using CNNs in conjunction with short time Fourier transforms of brain waves recorded with an EEG, the authors in [10] could distinguish different types of musical rhythms perceived by their subjects.

The approach to employ time series data in slip detection tasks and the performance of convolutional architectures suggests, that CNNs are an appropriate choice to achieve a more fine grained classification of slippage events, in our case to not only distinguish between stick and slip condition, but also to approach the task of dividing the slip events further into translational and rotational events. In the following section, we will first outline the sensing technology used in our approach. Afterwards the employed convolutional architectures will be described, evaluated and discussed.

Fig. 1. Objects used for the evaluation and experimental setup for data recording. Two KuKa LWR robots with attached tactile sensors (light orange) holding a glass. The fingertip shaped sensor touching the glass from above is used to detect the onset of slippage for data labeling purposes. (Color figure online)

2   Sensor Properties and Data Acquisition

We recorded data by holding three different objects, a cardboard cylinder, a remote and a drinking glass, between two piezo-resistive tactile sensor arrays[1] [9], where each sensor array was attached to a 7 degree of freedom KuKa LWR robotic arm. An image showing the objects used for training and evaluation and the robot arms holding a drinking glass is shown in Fig. 1. The Myrmex sensor consists of a printed circuit board (PCB) with 16×16 taxels, each with a spatial dimension of 5×5 mm. Each taxel measures the change of resistance between two electrodes that is induced by a piezo-resistive foam covering the PCB layer. The change in resistance is digitized via a 12 bit analog-digital converter. The data of all taxels is sampled at a rate of up to 1.9 kHz and transmitted to the host PC via standard USB video protocol. An example of a single frame of the sensor data while holding a cylindrical cardboard box and the change over time of a single cell is shown in Fig. 2.

2.1   Data Recording

With three different objects, a total of 64 trials have been recorded for the three classification classes, namely a stable state, translational and rotational slip. We used two Myrmex sensors to hold the objects, each attached to the robot arm's end-effector as a "large" fingertip. The sensors were sampled with a rate

---

[1] Called *Myrmex* hereafter.

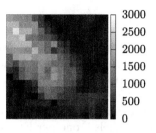

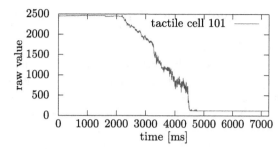

(a) Sensor response while holding a cardboard cylinder.

(b) Response of a single cell close to the center of the sensor for a whole trial.

Fig. 2. An image representation of the raw sensor data for a single frame is shown on the left. The right panel shows the raw value of a single cell over a whole trial.

of 1 kHz. The overall duration of these trials was 662.8 s, leading to a total of ≈ 1.3 M recorded sensor frames. To generate the slip events, we placed the objects between the sensors and let the robots exert varying forces (between 1 and 20 N) onto the objects, then moving the robotic arms slowly apart from each other. By manually placing the object during grasping we could induce either translational or rotational slip events: Translational slip events were generated by placing the center of mass directly above the center of contact. For the rotational slip events, the center of mass was placed horizontally shifted with respect to the center of contact.

2.2 Data Labeling

Acquiring ground-truth labels for the onset of slippage is a demanding task. For example, the authors in [13] hand labeled data based on video recordings of the trials while in [11] an inertial measurement unit was attached to the sliding object to provide a reference of the onset of slip events. The results from [11] actually suggest, that incipient slippage can be detected even before such traditional sensors as IMUs detect a motion of the object.

In our experiments we automated the labeling task of the data by placing a third tactile sensor, using the same piezo-resistive principle, in contact with the object, touching it from above. For technical reasons, this sensor could only be sampled with a rate of 500 Hz, but the signals were synchronized with the grasping Myrmex sensors. The onset of slippage was detected by evaluating the contact forces measured with the third sensor. We set the onset of slippage to the time when the sum of contacts on the third sensor started to decrease. The end of the trial was determined by the point in time when no more contacts were detected on the sensors holding the object. The sequence was labeled as rotational or translational slip, respectively, depending on the initial manual placement of the object.

3   Convolutional Tactile Networks

The properties of our sensor, the spatial arrangement of tactile cells combined with a high sampling frequency, suggest to use an approach similar to other time series classification techniques. By calculating a short-time Fourier transformation over a certain window size for each tactile sensor cell, we obtain a spatially arranged stack of Fourier coefficients which resembles the structure of RGB color images, but with an increased amount of channels – one per Fourier coefficient. On each of the channels we apply convolution and pooling layers to learn filters for each of the frequency bins. The output of these filters is fed into a fully connected layer, which is finally connected to a softmax layer for the classification. A convolution filter of width w and height h calculates the activation a at position i, j by multiplying the input activations $x_{i+k,j+l}$ from a previous layer with weights $W_{k,l}$ and is defined by Eq. 1 as

$$a_{i,j} = \sigma(\sum_{k=0}^{w-1} \sum_{l=0}^{h-1} W_{k,l} x_{i+k,j+l}) \tag{1}$$

where $\sigma()$ is a activation function, for example tanh(). A max pooling layer simply applies a $\max(0, x)$ function to a given input area of size $w \times h$.

The spatial arrangement of the frequency bins has an additional benefit for the classification task. For example in cases of translational slip, all active tactile sensor cells should have a similar amplitude whereas in cases of rotational slip, the amplitudes should differ because of increasing accelerations with respect to the distance of the center of rotation. After initial tests with different filter sizes in the convolution and pooling layers, we decided to investigate the three architectures described in Table 1 in detail since larger filter sizes turned out to decreased the classification performance slightly.

Table 1. Network architectures used in the evaluation. Here *conv 3 × 3* is a convolution layer with a kernel size of 3 × 3. *pool 2 × 2* is a max pooling layer and *fc 512* is a fully connected layer with 512 neurons.

#	Network architecture
1	conv 3 × 3 → pool 2 × 2 → fc 512
2	conv 3 × 3 → pool 2 × 2 → conv 3 × 3 → pool 2 × 2 → fc 512
3	conv 3 × 3 → pool 2 × 2 → conv 3 × 3 → pool 2 × 2 → fc 1024

4   Evaluation

To evaluate the proposed network architectures, we preprocessed the raw data by computing short time Fourier transformations for each of the tactile cells. We chose a window size of 64 ms for the STFTs, with a small shift of 8 ms.

That is, receiving tactile data at 1 kHz, the net generates classification results at a rate of 125 Hz. Additionally, the raw images were cropped to in include only the innermost 12×12 tactile cells of the sensor. This was necessary due to false-positives occurring at the borders, caused by the mechanical mounting of the foam. The raw data we recorded has another drawback with respect to practical applications. The sensor orientation was fixed throughout the recordings and gravity was the only acting force to create slippage events. Thus the slippage and rotation only occurred in one direction. We therefore augmented the dataset by rotating the raw data with 12 different angles, reaching from zero to 330° in steps of 30°, before calculating the short time Fourier transformation, which improves the generalization to other end-effector poses. Because stable states are overrepresented in the dataset, we sub-sampled the raw data to obtain an equal number of raw samples for the three classes. After the rotation and sub sampling process, we have a total of ≈ 2.1 M data samples of dimension ($12 \times 12 \times 32$) containing Fourier amplitudes. Fourier phases were not considered.

Before training, we split the dataset and kept 20 % of the available data samples as a test set for evaluating the proposed networks architectures. The data samples in the dataset were stored in an alternating fashion with respect to the labels to assure an even distribution of the three classes in the training and test set. We tested two conditions for the networks described in Table 1, one considering all frequency components and one applying a 60 Hz high pass filter, to explicitly remove low frequency vibrations from the robot arms before training. Already the smallest network with only one convolution and pooling layer achieves an accuracy of more than 91 %. Here the high pass filter increases the accuracy by 1.6 %. Adding a second Convolution and pooling block increases the classification accuracy further to nearly 98 %, when a high pass filter is included. For the case with the high pass filtered input data, we carried out an additional ten-fold cross-validation to confirm the results more thoroughly. Therefore, we split the dataset in ten chunks of equal size, created a training set from nine of the ten chunks and used the remaining chunk for testing. This was done with each of the ten chunks as test data. Table 3 shows a confusion matrix of the test accuracy for each network. The cells contain the average percentage over the ten runs and confirm the previous results from Table 2.

An example of the training behavior of network 3 with respect to test accuracy and loss is shown in Fig. 3. The network converges towards the final test accuracy after around 700000 iterations, where an iteration in this case is the batch processing of 64 samples of Fourier transformed data.

Table 2. Test accuracy for the networks from Table 1 with and without high pass filter. The last column shows the average time for a single forward pass.

#	Accuracy w/o filter	Acc. with high pass	Time fwd pass
1	91.01 %	92.65 %	0.29 ms
2	96.12 %	96.5 %	0.44 ms
3	97.45 %	97.89 %	0.43 ms

Table 3. Confusion matrices for the cross-validation of all networks with high pass filtered data. The letters s, t and r indicate the classes for stable, translational and rotational slip, respectively.

input	prediction				prediction				prediction		
	s	t	r		s	t	r		s	t	r
s	90.79%	5.83%	3.38%	s	95.73%	2.54%	1.73%	s	97.57%	1.41%	1.02%
t	2.13%	92.58%	5.29%	t	1.26%	96.37%	2.37%	t	0.68%	97.73%	1.58%
r	2.15%	3.17%	94.68%	r	0.97%	1.56%	97.47%	r	0.51%	0.93%	98.56%

(a) Network 1.   (b) Network 2.   (c) Network 3.

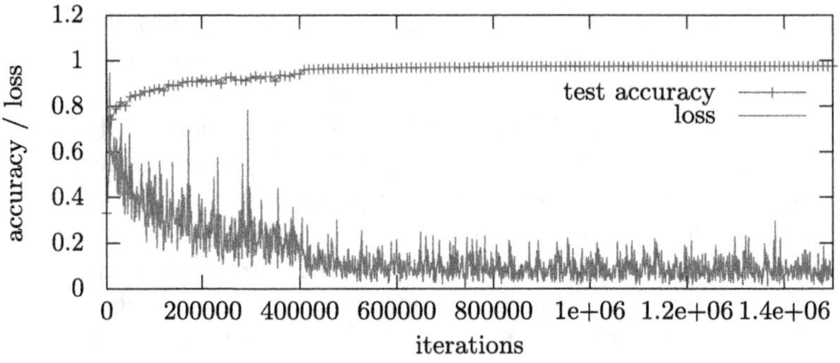

Fig. 3. Test accuracy and loss during training of network 3 from Table 3. One iteration in this figure is the batch processing of 64 samples.

5   Discussion

We presented an approach to detect translational and rotational slippage events in robot manipulation tasks. To our knowledge, using neural networks to discriminate between rotational and translational slip in addition to stable states has not been done before, since recent state of the art techniques only used a binary slip/non slip detection. We achieved state of the art classification results of more than 97 % by utilizing a convolutional neural network approach in conjunction with short time series of the sensor data. Using a consumer grade GPU for parallelization, the classification and preprocessing is fast enough to be integrated in real world robot controllers, for example for online grasp force adaptation. An interesting next step will be to transfer the work presented in this paper to the fingertip sensor [5], shown in Fig. 1, which we used for automatic labeling.

Acknowledgments. The research leading to these results has received funding from the European Community's Framework Programme Horizon 2020 – under grant agreement No 644938 – SARAFun and was supported by the Cluster of Excellence Cognitive Interaction Technology 'CITEC' (EXC 277) at Bielefeld University, which is funded by the German Research Foundation (DFG).

References

1. Abdel-Hamid, O., Mohamed, A.-R., Jiang, H., Deng, L., Penn, G., Yu, D.: Convolutional neural networks for speech recognition. IEEE/ACM Trans. Audio Speech Lang. Process. **22**(10), 1533–1545 (2014)
2. Dahiya, R.S., Valle, M.: Tactile sensing technologies. Robotic Tactile Sensing, pp. 79–136. Springer, Netherlands (2013)
3. Davis, S.B., Mermelstein, P.: Comparison of parametric representations for monosyllabic word recognition in continuously spoken sentences. IEEE Trans. Acoust. Speech Signal Process. **28**(4), 357–366 (1980)
4. Johansson, R., Westling, G.: Signals in tactile afferents from the fingers eliciting adaptive motor responses during precision grip. Exp. Brain Res. **66**(1), 141–154 (1987)
5. Koiva, R., Zenker, M., Schurmann, C., Haschke, R., Ritter, H.J.: A highly sensitive 3D-shaped tactile sensor. In: 2013 IEEE/ASME International Conference on Advanced Intelligent Mechatronics (AIM), pp. 1084–1089. IEEE (2013)
6. Lin, C.H., Erickson, T.W., Fishel, J.A., Wettels, N., Loeb, G.E.: Signal processing and fabrication of a biomimetic tactile sensor array with thermal, force and microvibration modalities. In: ROBIO, pp. 129–134 (2009)
7. Sainath, T.N. Mohamed, A.-R., Kingsbury, B., Ramabhadran, B.: Deep convolutional neural networks for LVCSR. In: 2013 IEEE International Conference on Acoustics, Speech and Signal Processing (ICASSP), pp. 8614–8618. IEEE (2013)
8. Schöpfer, M., Schürmann, C., Pardowitz, M., Ritter, H.: Using a piezo-resistive tactile sensor for detection of incipient slippage. In: 2010 41st International Symposium on Robotics (ISR) and 2010 6th German Conference on Robotics (ROBOTIK), pp. 1–7. VDE (2010)
9. Schürmann, C., Haschke, R., Ritter, H.: Modular high speed tactile sensor system with video interface. In: Tactile Sensing in Humanoids – Tactile Sensors and Beyond@ IEEE-RAS Conference on Humanoid Robots (Humanoids) (2009)
10. Stober, S., Cameron, D.J., Grahn, J.A.: Using convolutional neural networks to recognize rhythm stimuli from electroencephalography recordings. In: Advances in Neural Information Processing Systems, pp. 1449–1457 (2014)
11. Su, Z., Hausman, K., Chebotar, Y., Molchanov, A., Loeb, G.E., Sukhatme, G.S., Schaal, S.: Force estimation and slip detection/classification for grip control using a biomimetic tactile sensor. In: 2015 IEEE-RAS 15th International Conference on Humanoid Robots (Humanoids), pp. 297–303. IEEE (2015)
12. Teshigawara, S., Tsutsumi, T., Shimizu, S., Suzuki, Y., Ming, A., Ishikawa, M., Shimojo, M.: Highly sensitive sensor for detection of initial slip and its application in a multi-fingered robot hand. In: 2011 IEEE International Conference on Robotics and Automation (ICRA), pp. 1097–1102. IEEE (2011)
13. Veiga, F., van Hoof, H., Peters, J., Hermans, T.: Stabilizing novel objects by learning to predict tactile slip. In: 2015 IEEE/RSJ International Conference on Intelligent Robots and Systems (IROS), pp. 5065–5072. IEEE (2015)
14. Vina, B., Francisco, E., Bekiroglu, Y., Smith, C., Karayiannidis, Y., Kragic, D.: Predicting slippage and learning manipulation affordances through gaussian process regression. In: 2013 13th IEEE-RAS International Conference on Humanoid Robots (Humanoids), pp. 462–468. IEEE (2013)
15. Yuan, W., Li, R., Srinivasan, M.A., Adelson, E.H.: Measurement of shear and slip with a GelSight tactile sensor. In: 2015 IEEE International Conference on Robotics and Automation (ICRA), pp. 304–311. IEEE (2015)

DeepPainter: Painter Classification Using Deep Convolutional Autoencoders

Omid E. David[1(✉)] and Nathan S. Netanyahu[1,2]

[1] Department of Computer Science, Bar-Ilan University, Ramat-Gan, Israel
mail@omiddavid.com, nathan@cs.biu.ac.il
[2] Center for Automation Research, University of Maryland, College Park, MD, USA
nathan@cfar.umd.edu

Abstract. In this paper we describe the problem of painter classification, and propose a novel approach based on deep convolutional autoencoder neural networks. While previous approaches relied on image processing and manual feature extraction from paintings, our approach operates on the raw pixel level, without any preprocessing or manual feature extraction. We first train a deep convolutional autoencoder on a dataset of paintings, and subsequently use it to initialize a supervised convolutional neural network for the classification phase.

The proposed approach substantially outperforms previous methods, improving the previous state-of-the-art for the 3-painter classification problem from 90.44 % accuracy (previous state-of-the-art) to 96.52 % accuracy, i.e., a 63 % reduction in error rate.

1 Introduction

Art forgery, which dates back more than two thousand years, has played a key role in the development of painting authentication. This task has been usually performed manually by art experts who have dedicated their lives to this profession. Their expertise amounted to using various characteristics other than what the human eye can see, including chemical analysis, spectrometry, and infrared or X-ray imaging. The infamous Vermeer forgery [12] attests, perhaps, most vividly to the challenges presented by painting authentication. Han van Meegeren used historical canvasses and managed to deceive art experts into believing that his painting was an authentic Vermeer. Only after being charged with treason and sentenced to death for selling another (forged) Vermeer, did he confess and was forced to create another painting to prove himself innocent of treason. A more recent case of painting authenticity involves the Pollock paintings found a decade ago in a storage locker in Wainscott, NY. The authenticity of these paintings was compromised on the basis of computer analysis of the paintings' fractal dimension [14]. This claim was subsequently disputed by analyzing childlike drawings that supposedly have the same fractal dimension as the Pollock paintings [3].

In this paper we address the closely related problem of painting classification, i.e., the task of assigning a specific artist to a given painting (from a dataset of paintings by several artists). Note that the image authentication problem can

A.E.P. Villa et al. (Eds.): ICANN 2016, Part II, LNCS 9887, pp. 20–28, 2016.
DOI: 10.1007/978-3-319-44781-0_3

be viewed as a binary image classification problem (i.e., determine whether or not a given painting was painted by a certain artist). Recent developments for both problem types have focused on preprocessing techniques of reducing the high dimensionality of visual data to low-dimensional representations which can be manipulated towards image understanding.

Levy *et al.* [9,10] applied feature extraction to paintings using generic image processing (IP) functions (e.g., fractal dimension, Fourier spectra coefficients, texture coefficients, etc.), and restricted Boltzmann machines (RBM), followed by genetic algorithms (GA)-based learning of the weights of a weighted nearest neighbor (WNN) classifier [13]. Their approach achieved 90.44 % classification accuracy for the 3-painter classification problem.

In this paper we present the problem of painter classification and briefly survey recent research that has been conducted in the field. We then present our novel approach, which uses convolutional autoencoders (CAE) instead of image processing based feature extraction. We subsequently use the trained CAE to initialize a convolutional neural network (CNN) for supervised training on specific painters. The results demonstrate a substantial improvement over previous methods, improving the accuracy to 96.52 %. This sets a new state-of-the-art for the painter classification problem.

2   Background

Image authentication is the task of determining whether or not a given painting was painted by a specific artist. The related task addressed by us, though, is image classification, i.e., the task of determining the artist of a given painting (from a certain group of artists). The input to our problem consists of painting images of the group of artists (several paintings of each artist), and our objective is to automatically classify a given painting. One of the difficulties in solving this problem is that we cannot define a certain set of rules that the painting has to conform to in order to classify it to the subgroup corresponding to the correct artist. For this reason, computer vision techniques which are capable of identifying shapes and objects in an image are not sufficiently effective for solving the problem.

Formerly there have been attempts to harness the strength of image analysis tools to classify historical art paintings into categories of artists or genres. Levy *et al.* [9] used GA-based WNN with a set of 78 prevalent image features for classifying paintings by Rembrandt, Renoir, and van Gogh, obtaining 80 % classification accuracy. In their later work [10], they augmented their approach by also adding 20 features using restricted Boltzmann machines (RBM) [2], improving the classification accuracy to 90.44 %.

Herik and Postma [15] surveyed image features relevant to the historic art domain and concluded that neural network techniques combined with domain knowledge were most suitable to the task of automatic image classification. Under-drawing strokes in infrared reflectograms were analyzed by Kammerer *et al.* [4] in order to classify how and by what tools paintings are painted. Natural language processing techniques using a naive-Bayes classifier and the coefficients of a discrete cosine transform (DCT) were used by Keren [5] in order to classify local features in an image. Kroner *et al.* [7] classified drawings by using image histograms and pattern recognition methods.

The above past research focused on specific image processing features tailored for specific datasets (such as ink paintings, infrared reflectograms, or black and white sketches). This domain-specific knowledge facilitates the exploitation of various characteristics of the painting-specific domain.

In the next section we present our convolutional autoencoder based approach, which does not incorporate any domain-specific knowledge, and in fact is operating solely on the raw pixel level.

3   Feature Extraction Using Convolutional Autoencoders

3.1   Convolutional Neural Networks

In recent years convolutional neural networks (CNN) [1,6,8] have outperformed conventional image processing methods in all computer vision related tasks they have been applied to. The architecture of a CNN typically includes several components which are stacked on top of each other: the convolutional layer, the max-pooling layer, which subsamples the data (e.g., for each 2×2 region selects only the maximum value, thus resulting in four times reduction in size), and finally a classification layer (and usually several fully connected layers before the classification layer). Figure 1 shows a typical CNN,

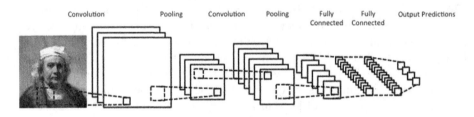

Fig. 1. Typical architecture of a convolutional neural network.

Standards CNNs are usually used in a supervised framework, where a large training dataset (typically including at least many thousands of images per class) is available. Thus, using CNNs for end-to-end painter classification is problematic, due to a smaller number of training samples available per painter (usually from a few tens of paintings to at most a few hundred paintings for more prolific painters).

3.2   Autoencoders

Where small number of training samples are available, unsupervised pretraining has proven highly effective [2,16]. Unsupervised training methods using neural networks involve either the use of restricted Boltzmann machines (RBM) [2] which are trained using contrastive divergence, or autoencoders [16] which are training using standard backpropagation.

The basic principle for all methods involves receiving an input $\mathbf{x}$ and mapping it to a latent representation $\mathbf{h}$, using a function $\mathbf{h} = \sigma(Wx + b)$, where σ is a nonlinear activation function, W is a matrix of weights between the two layers, and b is bias. The autoencoder then tries to reconstruct the original input by $\mathbf{y} = \sigma(W'h + b')$. Thus, each training sample x_i is first mapped to a hidden layer h_i and then reconstructed to y_i. The autoencoder is trained using backpropagation to reduce this reconstruction error.

3.3   Convolutional Autoencoders

The principles behind convolutional neural networks and autoencoders can be combined to produce convolutional autoencoders (CAE). Several approaches involving the combination of these methods have been explored in the past, and here we use a CAE architecture along the lines presented in [11,17,18].

In order to use CNNs as autoencoders, for each convolutional layer, a corresponding deconvolutional layer should be constructed. Additionally, max-pooling layers result in loss of information, and so an unpooling layer should try to approximately restore the original values. Note that the subsampling due to max-pooling in fact operates as a strong regularizer.

Deconvolution layers can either be equal but transposed to the original convolution layers, or learned from scratch. Often both approaches work equally well in practice. This is similar to standard autoencoders where the weights of the decoder layer W' can either be learned from scratch, or set to the transpose of the encoder layer ($W' = W^T$), this is referred to as *tied weights*.

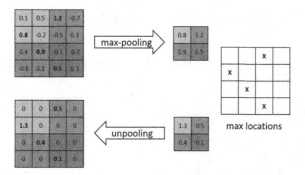

Fig. 2. Pooling and unpooling layers. For each pooling layer, the max locations are stored. These locations are then used in unpooling layer.

Several methods have been applied in the past for the unpooling operation [11,17,18]. Here we employ the method used in [18], where during pooling, the location of maximum value is stored, such that during unpooling the value is restored in that location, and the other locations are set to zero. Figure 2 illustrates unpooling, and Fig. 3 shows a complete convolutional autoencoder structure.

After training a CAE, we can remove the unpooling and deconvolution components, and use the convolution and pooling components to initialize a supervised CNN, by adding a fully connected layer followed by a classification layer.

4   CAE and CNN for Painter Classification

For unsupervised training of CAE, we use a randomly selected set of 5,000 paintings from the Webmuseum (webmuseum.meulie.net/wm). The images have 24-bit color depth with varying resolutions averaged approximately at 1000×1000 pixels, and compressed as JPEG formatted files. We have resampled the images and normalized them to 256×256 pixels. The goal here is to train the CAE to find features that are specifically useful for paintings, which have a more specific color and composition range in comparison to real-world images.

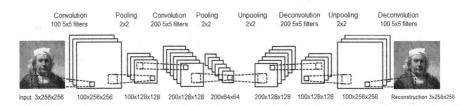

Fig. 3. Illustration of convolutional autoencoder. In this example the CAE comprises two convolution layers and their two corresponding deconvolution layers, and two max-pooling layers and their corresponding unpooling layers.

Our CAE contains the following layers (see Fig. 3). The convolution filter sizes are always of size 5×5.

1. the input layer consists of the raw image (resampled to 256×256 pixels) in three channels (R, G, and B)
2. convolutional layer of size $100 \times 256 \times 256$
3. max-pooling layer of size 2×2
4. convolutional layer of size $200 \times 128 \times 128$
5. max-pooling layer of size 2×2
6. unpooling layer of size 2×2
7. deconvolutional layer of size $200 \times 128 \times 128$
8. unpooling layer of size 2×2
9. deconvolutional layer of size $100 \times 256 \times 256$

The learning rate starts from 0.01 and is multiplied by 0.98 after each epoch. In order to further encourage the CAE to find meaningful features, we randomly remove 20 % of the pixels for the images per epoch. The concept here is similar to that of denoising autoencoders [16] which outperform traditional autoencoders.

The supervised classification benchmark is identical to that used by Levy *et al.* [9,10] in their experiments. It consists of $(3 \times 40 =)$ 120 digital reproductions of paintings by Rembrandt, Renoir, and van Gough, downloaded from the Webmuseum. The Appendix contains the painting titles of the images used in our experiments.

Having trained a CAE, we can now remove the decoder components (items 6 to 9 in the above list) and use the CAE for initializing a supervised CNN. On top of these components due to CNN, we add two fully connected layers of size 400 and 200, followed by a softmax output unit of size three (since there are three painters in the benchmark). The cross entropy loss is used.

The full CNN contains the following layers (see Fig. 1):

1. the input layer consists of the raw image (resampled to 256×256 pixels) in three channels (R, G, and B)
2. convolutional layer with 100 5×5 filters per input channel
3. max-pooling layer of size 2×2
4. convolutional layer with 200 5×5 filters per map
5. max-pooling layer of size 2×2
6. fully connected layer of size 400
7. fully connected layer of size 200
8. output softmax layer of size 3

To make our results directly comparable to those of Levy *et al.* [9,10], we conducted 10-fold cross validation, where in each of 10 runs 90 % of the data is used for training, and 10 % for validation.

Table 1. Classification accuracy for several previous methods and our CAE based method. The results are the average over 10-fold cross validation.

Feature extraction method	Supervised learning method	Accuracy
Image Processing	Nearest Neighbor	65.71 %
Image Processing	SVM	68.33 %
Image Processing	Genetic Algorithm	78.33 %
RBM	Nearest Neighbor	64.41 %
RBM	SVM	77.50 %
RBM	Genetic Algorithm	73.92 %
Image Processing + RBM	Nearest Neighbor	68.71 %
Image Processing + RBM	SVM	71.66 %
Image Processing + RBM	Genetic Algorithm	90.44 %
Convolutional Autoencoder	**CNN**	**96.52%**

After performing 10 such training and validation runs, the average accuracy obtained for our CNN over the validation set is 96.52 %. This represents a 63 % reduction in error rate in comparison to the previous state-of-the-art on this benchmark, which stood at 90.44 %.

Table 1 provides a summary of the classification accuracies obtained by previous methods and our method.

5   Conclusion

Automatic painter classification has gained much attention over the past decades, and much progress has been made with regards to both relevant preprocessing techniques and classification algorithms. Still, the problem of painter classification remains a complex task that requires more sophisticated techniques.

The results presented in this paper show that deep learning methods can be effectively employed for painter classification. Specifically, our results show that convolutional autoencoders are capable of extracting meaningful information from paintings, and combined with supervised convolutional networks, we managed to substantially improve the previous state-of-the-art, from 90.44 % accuracy (previous state-of-the-art) to 96.52 % accuracy, i.e., a 63 % reduction in error rate.

Appendix

This appendix lists the $(40 \times 3) = 120$ titles of the paintings experimented with by van Gogh, Rembrandt, and Renoir.

Table 2. Bigrams frequency.

#	van Gogh	Rembrandt	Renoir
1	bandaged-ear	abraham	apres-bain
2	berceuse	anslo	baigneuses
3	cordeville	aristotle-homer	bathers-1887
4	corridor-asylum	artemis	bathers-1918
5	cypress-star	bathing-river	bougival
6	cypresses	bathsheba	canoeist
7	flower-beds-holland	belshazzar	chocquet
8	green-vineyard	children	city
9	green-wheat-field	danae	country
10	house-ploughman	david	dancer
11	mme-trabuc	descent	durieux
12	mr-trabuc	emmaus	flowers

(continued)

Table 2. (*continued*)

#	van Gogh	Rembrandt	Renoir
13	old-mill	hendrickje	gabrielle
14	old-vineyard	holy-family	girl-seated
15	olive-alpilles	jan-six	jugglers
16	olive-trees	magn-glass	lady-piano
17	orchard-bloom-poplars	meditation	laundress
18	orchard-plum-trees	mill	loge
19	poppies	music-party	lucie-berard
20	red-vineyard	nicolaes-tulp	near-lake
21	reminiscences	old-man	fournaise
22	road-menders	ostrich	horsewoman
23	roulin	potiphar	meadow
24	self-1	prodigal-son	moulin-galette
25	self-2	raising-lazarus	nini
26	self-easel	.1640	parapluies
27	self-gauguin	.1661	premiere-sortie
28	self-orsay	.1669	promenade
29	self-whitney	.night-watch	ride
30	skull-cigarette	return-prodigal-son	romain-lacaux
31	sun-cloud	ruts	sisley-wife
32	threatening-skies	samson	women
33	trees-asylum	scholar	seashore
34	trees-ivy-asylum	self-1629	seated-bather
35	village-stairs	self-1634	sewing
36	wheat-field	self-1660	sisley
37	wheat-rising-sun	slaughtered-ox	swing
38	willows	staalmeesters	terrace
39	peasant	stofells	watercan
40	woman-arles	tobias	woman-veil

References

1. Behnke, S.: Hierarchical Neural Networks for Image Interpretation. LNCS, vol. 2766, pp. 1–13. Springer, Heidelberg (2003)
2. Hinton, G.E., Osindero, S., Teh, Y.W.: A fast learning algorithm for deep belief nets. Neural Comput. **18**(7), 1527–1554 (2006)
3. Jones-Smith, K., Mathur, H.: Fractal analysis: revisiting Pollock's drip paintings. Nature **444**(7119), E9–E10 (2006)

4. Kammerer, P., Lettner, M., Zolda, E., Sablatnig, R.: Identification of drawing tools by classification of textural and boundary features of strokes. Pattern Recogn. Lett. **28**(6), 710–718 (2007)
5. Keren, D.: Painter identification using local features and naive Bayes. In: Proceedings of the IEEE International Conference on Pattern Recognition, vol. 2, pp. 474–477 (2002)
6. Krizhevsky, A., Sutskever, I., Hinton, G.: Imagenet classification with deep convolutional neural networks. In: Bartlett, P., Pereira, F.C.N., Burges, C.J.C., Bottou, L., Weinberger, K.Q. (eds.) Advances in Neural Information Processing Systems, vol. 25, pp. 1106–1114 (2012)
7. Kroner, S., Lattner, A.: Authentication of free hand drawings by pattern recognition methods. In: Proceedings of the IEEE 14th International Conference on Pattern Recognition, vol. 1, pp. 462–464 (1998)
8. LeCun, Y., Bottou, L., Bengio, Y., Haffner, P.: Gradient-based learning applied to document recognition. Proc. IEEE **86**(11)
9. Levy, E., David, O.E., Netanyahu, N.S.: Painter classification using genetic algorithms. In: IEEE Congress on Evolutionary Computation, pp. 3027–3034 (2013)
10. Levy, E., David, O.E., Netanyahu, N.S.: Genetic algorithms and deep learning for automatic painter classification. In: ACM Genetic and Evolutionary Computation Conference, pp. 1143–1150 (2014)
11. Masci, J., Meier, U., Cireşan, D., Schmidhuber, J.: Stacked convolutional autoencoders for hierarchical feature extraction. In: Honkela, T. (ed.) ICANN 2011, Part I. LNCS, vol. 6791, pp. 52–59. Springer, Heidelberg (2011)
12. Phillips, D.: How do forgers deceive art critics? In: Gregory, R., Harris, J., Heard, P., Rose, D. (eds.) The Artful Eye, pp. 372–388. Oxford University Press (1995)
13. Siedlecki, W., Sklansky, J.: A note on genetic algorithms for large-scale feature selection. Pattern Recogn. Lett. **10**(5), 335–347 (1989)
14. Taylor, R.P., Guzman, R., Martin, T.P., Hall, G.D.R., Micolich, A.P., Jonas, D., Scannell, B.C., Fairbanks, M.S., Marlow, C.A.: Authenticating Pollock paintings using fractal geometry. Pattern Recogn. Lett. **28**(6), 695–702 (2007)
15. van den Herik, H.J., Postma, E.O.: Discovering the visual signature of painters. In: Kasabov, N. (ed.) Future Directions for Intelligent Systems and Information Sciences, pp. 129–147. Physica-Verlag, Heidelberg (2000)
16. Vincent, P., Larochelle, H., Bengio, Y., Manzagol, P.A.: Extracting and composing robust features with denoising autoencoders. In: 25th International Conference on Machine Learning, ICML, pp. 1096–1103 (2008)
17. Zeiler, M.D., Fergus, R.: Visualizing and understanding convolutional networks. In: Fleet, D., Pajdla, T., Schiele, B., Tuytelaars, T. (eds.) ECCV 2014, Part I. LNCS, vol. 8689, pp. 818–833. Springer, Heidelberg (2014)
18. Zeiler, M.D., Taylor, G.W., Fergus, R.: Adaptive deconvolutional networks for mid and high level feature learning. In: International Conference on Computer Vision, ICCV, pp. 2018–2025 (2011)

Revisiting Deep Convolutional Neural Networks for RGB-D Based Object Recognition

Lorand Madai-Tahy[(✉)], Sebastian Otte, Richard Hanten, and Andreas Zell

Cognitive Systems Group, University of Tuebingen,
Sand 1, 72076 Tuebingen, Germany
lorand.madai@gmail.com

Abstract. In this paper we reinvestigate Deep Convolutional Neural Networks (DCNNs) for RGB-D based object recognition. A previously proposed method in which DCNNs are pretrained on a large-scale RGB database and just fine-tuned to process colorized depth images is taken up and extended. We introduce and analyse multiple solutions to improve depth colorization and propose a new method for depth colorization based on surface normals. We show that our improvements increase the classification accuracy significantly, such that we can present new state-of-the-art results for the Washington RGB-D dataset. Our results also indicate that classification using only surface normals without RGB images outperforms classification using pure RGB images, which is to our knowledge a novel discovery in the field of DCNNs.

Keywords: Deep learning · Deep Convolutional Neural Networks · Fusion networks · Object recognition · RGB-D · Surface normals

1 Introduction

In the recent past, Deep Convolutional Neural Networks (DCNNs) have been used in RGB color image classification tasks with great success. First research investigations in the field of DCNNs incorporating also depth information, as provided by pervasively used RGB-D sensors, were proposed. However, to successfully train well generalizing DCNNs, very large databases of labeled training examples are required. While there are rich databases containing pure RGB data as, e.g., ImageNet [6], available databases for RGB-D images are quite rare and up to now not that large. Nonetheless, a very interesting approach to deal with this issue was addressed by Eitel et al. in [8]. Basically, their approach follows the idea of colorizing the depth channel of an RGB-D image, i.e., transforming it into a separate RGB image that can then be processed by a DCNN originally trained on a large-scale RGB database. More concretely, they reused and duplicated the feature extraction layers of a pre-trained DCNN, where the first network processes the RGB part and the second network processes the colorized depth part separately. Only in the last layer before the output layer these two processing pipelines are fused. This well elaborated design achieved the so far best

© Springer International Publishing Switzerland 2016
A.E.P. Villa et al. (Eds.): ICANN 2016, Part II, LNCS 9887, pp. 29–37, 2016.
DOI: 10.1007/978-3-319-44781-0_4

published state-of-the-art results for a category classification task on the Washington RGB-D dataset [11]. Even though the proposed approach demonstrated a great potential, one of its shortcomings is the way how the depth channel is colorized. When thinking of incorporating depth information for object recognition with DCNNs, a promising approach could be to use estimated surface normals, which should in principle provide local structure information better than pure depth images with absolute relations. However, in [8] it was pointed out that in the overall system simply mapping the entire range of depth values onto the jet color map was not inferior to other methods, including the use of surface normals as proposed earlier in [5]. But these results appeared surprising and were against our assumption. Hence, we re-investigated the approach in [8], while focusing on a more sophisticated colorization technique, which is mainly the aim of this paper. Thereby, our research contributions are as follows: First, we introduce and analyse multiple solutions to improve depth colorization. Second, we propose a new method for depth colorization based on surface normals. Third, we show that our improvements increase the classification accuracy significantly, such that we can present new state-of-the-art results for the Washington RGB-D dataset. Finally, our results also show that for object databases with objects of significantly different shapes, classification using only surface normals without RGB channels may outperform classification using pure RGB images, which is to our knowledge a novel discovery in the field of DCNNs. Nonetheless, the combination of RGB and depth still performs best.

2   Methodology

2.1   Deep Neural Network Architecture

In the study of Eitel et al. [8] the presented two-stream DNN approach incorporates processing RGB and depth images, whereas RGB and (colorized) depth images are processed separately through several layers and only combined in the end using a fully connected layer for fusion and one softmax layer for classification. The overall network architecture of this work, which is refered to as FusionNet, is depicted in Fig. 1. Each stream (RGB and depth) consists of layers based on the CaffeNet [7], which is a variation of the AlexNet [10]. More precisely, a stream consists of an input layer, 5 convolution layers, two fully connected layers and a softmax layer with pooling layers after the first, second and fifth convolution layer. For the FusionNet the softmax layers are removed and replaced by a fully connected layer that fuses both streams, followed by a softmax layer.

2.2   Dataset

The Washington dataset [11] consists of 51 different object classes, e.g. apple, with image sets of several individual objects belonging to each class, e.g. green apple or red apple, which are referred to as instances. For every RGB image there

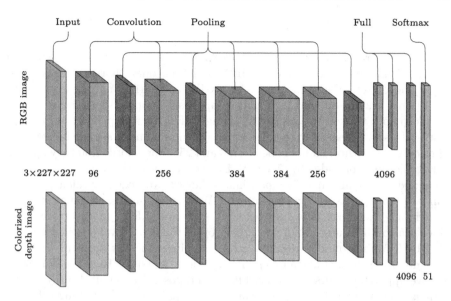

Input   Convolution   Pooling   Full   Softmax

RGB image

3×227×227   96   256   384   384   256   4096

Colorized depth image

4096   51

Fig. 1. Picture of the FusionNet architecture as used in [8]. Each horizontal block represents a layer of the network. Blue layers are part of the RGB stream, green layers are part of the depth stream. Each stream is a CaffeNet without its classification layer. Gray layers fuse both streams together and do classification based on the combined information. (Color figure online)

is a corresponding depth image in which the distance from the camera is stored in millimeters for every pixel. To enable the network to work with the dataset, the images need to be of a square shape and match a specific size. As in [8], for squaring of the Washington dataset images we used border replication, which means replicating the pixels of the longer sides of an image until it is squared (see Fig. 2). We resized all images to 256 × 256.

Fig. 2. Border replication for squaring dataset images. The outer pixels of the longer side are replicated along the axis of the shorter side until the entire image is quadratic.

3   Experimental Setup

There are several approaches for color-coding depth maps, such as calculating and colorizing surface normals [5], HHA, which encodes "horizontal disparity, height above ground, and the angle the pixel's local surface normal makes with the inferred gravity direction" [9] and an approach proposed by Eitel et al. [8], in which depth values are colorized applying a JET color map. They normalized depth values with respect to the maximum and minimum value of an image to be represented as natural numbers between 0 and 255. For colorization they applied a JET color map provided by OpenCV. But normalization only considering minimum and maximum values is suboptimal. Thus we proceeded by calculating the standard score for every raw depth value. We then applied a clipping function, constricting the range of values between -1.5 and 1.5 to catch outliers. We added 1.5 to all values and divided them by 3. Finally, all values where multiplied by 255 and rounded to allow color mapping. Another problem was that every depth image contains missing information stored as 0. To tackle this problem, we applied a recursive median filter as proposed by Lai et al. in [11]. The median filter is applied on missing values only considering non-missing values in its kernel. We applied the filter recursively until there were no missing values left. Figure 3 shows the results after applying different kinds of image modification. It is apparent that standardizing alone improves the visual outcome of color mapping. Reconstructing missing values makes it even more homogeneous. Although colorization using color mapping created good results overall, we thought there were two main problems with that approach. Firstly, the more space is covered by the depth map, the more the color map is spread across the area, leaving less color diversity to the actual object (see Fig. 4). Consequently the final colorization of an object also depends on the absolute distance from the camera and can be very different from image to image. Secondly, there does not seem to appear much information about the actual structure of the object. Given this observation, our goal was to find a better colorization method to create more consistent information. We therefore calculated and colorized the surface normals for every pixel, which better represent form and surface structure. We calculate the gradients for each pixel in horizontal (x-axis) and vertical direction (y-axis) using the Sobel operator. We define two 3D vectors a, b in direction of the z-axis with calculated gradients. We can calculate the surface normal n by calculating the cross product of a and b. As n has 3 dimensions, we map each of the three values of the surface normal $(x, y, z)^T$ to a corresponding RGB channel, namely, $x \rightarrow R$, $y \rightarrow G$, $z \rightarrow B$. Due to construction we have $x, y \in [-1, 1]$ and $z \in [0, 1]$. As RGB channels consist of natural numbers between 0 and 255, we calculate r, g and b according to $(r, g, b) = \left(\lfloor \frac{x+1}{2} \cdot 255 \rfloor, \lfloor \frac{y+1}{2} \cdot 255 \rfloor, \lfloor z \cdot 255 \rfloor \right)$. Figure 5 shows the result of calculating and colorizing surface normals in comparison to color mapping after standardization/normalization and color mapping. Although structural information seems to be more present with surface normals than after JET color mapping, there are also bigger patches of a slight pinkish color due to depth data inaccuracy. To achieve a more homogeneous image we designed a 'unique box blur' filter to fill up areas between colorized lines, such that the

Fig. 3. Comparison of color map colorization showing improvements over the original approach using colormapping alone (second image). From left to right, the first three images show colorization results after jet colormapping without and with standardization. Images four to six show the same with prior missing value reconstruction. (Color figure online)

Fig. 4. Results after colorization using simple color mapping vary greatly depending on the covered spatial area of the image. Maximum distance in the left image is 3.12 m compared to 0.80 m in the right image. (Color figure online)

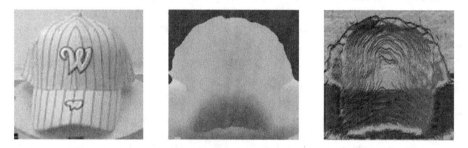

Fig. 5. Images of a cap in RGB (left), after jet colormapping with standardization and missing value reconstruction (middle) and surface normals (right). (Color figure online)

result is a homogeneous transition between colors. For a depth point p_{ij} with the indices (i, j) of a depth map D we define a matrix A such that the matrix contains all pixels surrounding p_{ij} according to a kernel size. Let L_A be a list storing all values of A. We remove all duplicates in L_A and calculate the mean value m of L_A. To make sure that mostly points are changed that are in fact part of a same-value area we add the constraint that $L_{A_{unique}}$ must not have more entries than the amount of entries in our kernel multiplied by a threshold factor t. For this experiment we chose $t = 0.5$. We assign $p_{ij} = m$. Results are shown in Fig. 6.

For training and evaluation of the FusionNet we used the experimental setup and sampling method presented in [11]. Hence, we sub-sampled our data base taking only every fifth image of the preprocessed RGB-D dataset. From this subset we excluded a random instance of every class from the training data base and added it to a testing data base. This whole process was repeated 10

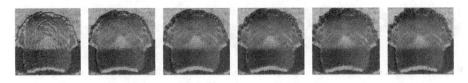

Fig. 6. Surface normal images after multiple iterations of unique box blur applied on a depth map. The procedure eliminates the discontinuities induced by the 3D sensor. (Color figure online)

times to measure average performance. Stream weights were initialized with the values of a CaffeNet model pre-trained on the ImageNet dataset. In this work, the model available in [7] was used. We then fine-tuned each stream separately, using the corresponding images from the modified Washington RGB-D dataset. As in [8] each stream was fine-tuned over 30000 iterations with learning rate of 0.01 which was reduced to 10^{-3} after 20000 iterations with a mini-batch size of 128. Training consisted of 30 epochs with a mini-batch size of 256 for each input stream, initial learning rate 0.01, which dropped after about 67 % by a factor of 0.1, momentum factor of 0.9 and weight decay of $2 \cdot 10^{-4}$. As suggested in [8], for FusionNet training the weights of the individual stream layers were fixed by setting their learning rate multiplier to 0.

4   Results and Discussion

Table 1 shows the accuracy of the FusionNet on the test set in comparison to other approaches. We see that improving color mapping improves the performance of the depth stream and the overall FusionNet. Furthermore, we see that the FusionNet using our surface normal method achieves an accuracy of 94.0 % on the test set, which is, to or knowledge, the best result achieved on this classification task to date. In Fig. 7 we show RGB images of an apple, a cap and two bowls and their corresponding colorized surface normal images. There are two things we think are important. First, for objects with distinct shapes there is often more structural information in surface normal images than in RGB images. For instance, the apple on the RGB image appears like a dark area, the surface normal image in contrast contains much information about the apple shape. We can make similar observations on the cap images. It is surprising that with suitable computed surface normals the classification accuracy on the Washington RGB-D data set is higher based on depth data alone (88.0 %) than on RGB data (84.7 %). Second, similarly shaped objects of different color may more easily be classified as one class based on surface normals than on color. For example, the two bowls in Fig. 7 which are very different in color become very similar in the surface normal image because their local shape structure is comparable. It makes sense to assume that this helps to classify an unseen instance of that object category, which should also share those structural characteristics, even if it is different in color.

Table 1. Classification rate [%] on the test set of the Washington RGB-D dataset [11].

Method	RGB	Depth	RGB-D
Nonlinear SVM [11]	74.5 ± 3.1	64.7 ± 2.2	83.9 ± 3.5
HKDES [3]	76.1 ± 2.2	75.7 ± 2.6	84.1 ± 2.2
Kernel Desc. [4]	77.7 ± 1.9	78.8 ± 2.7	86.2 ± 2.1
CKM Desc. [2]	N/A	N/A	86.4 ± 2.3
CNN-RNN [13]	80.8 ± 4.2	78.9 ± 3.8	86.8 ± 3.3
Upgraded HMP [5]	82.4 ± 3.1	81.2 ± 2.3	87.5 ± 2.9
CaRFs [1]	N/A	N/A	88.1 ± 2.4
CNN Features [12]	83.1 ± 2.0	N/A	89.4 ± 1.3
FusionNet Eitel et al. (HHA) [8]	84.1 ± 2.7	83.0 ± 2.7	91.0 ± 1.9
FusionNet Eitel et al. (jet) [8]	84.1 ± 2.7	83.8 ± 2.7	91.3 ± 1.4
FusionNet (jet)[a]	84.7 ± 3.7	81.8 ± 2.7	91.2 ± 1.6
FusionNet (improved jet)[a]	84.7 ± 3.7	82.9 ± 3.3	92.1 ± 2.0
FusionNet (surface normals)[a]	**84.7 ± 3.7**	**88.0 ± 2.5**	**94.0 ± 2.4**

[a]This paper.

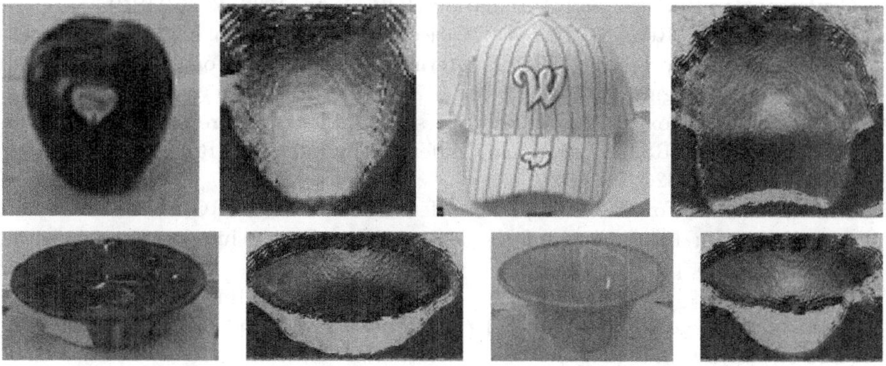

Fig. 7. Examples of RGB images and corresponding surface normal images demonstrating the advantage of colorized surface normals in terms of emphasizing local structures. (Color figure online)

5 Conclusion

Deep neural networks are one of the most powerful machine learning architectures nowadays, particularly for a broad range of image recognition tasks. Eitel et al. proposed a promising deep convolutional neural network design for RGB-D data processing (FusionNet) and an effective way of color-coding depth information. As the performance of a neural network strongly depends on the data we train it with, we modified the training input of the FusionNet in two ways:

We improved Eitel et al.'s depth colorization method, combining standard values with a recursive median filter for reconstructing missing depth information, which increased accuracy considerably. Secondly, we proposed an alternative colorization method based on the calculation of surface normals, which significantly increased category classification precision even further. These are, to our knowledge, the best results on the Washington RGB-D dataset to date. Moreover, we showed that category recognition based on surface normals can outperform recognition based on RGB images alone, if the objects have distinctive shapes and diverse colors. As to our knowledge this is a new finding, we presented an analysis of why that is the case, giving examples to demonstrate that under the above assumptions surface normals hold better information about object categories than RGB images.

References

1. Asif, U., Bennamoun, M., Sohel, F.: Efficient RGB-D object categorization using cascaded ensembles of randomized decision trees. In: IEEE International Conference on Robotics and Automation, ICRA 2015, pp. 1295–1302 (2015)
2. Blum, M., Springenberg, J., Wuelfing, J., Riedmiller, M.: A learned feature descriptor for object recognition in RGB-D data. In: Proceedings of the IEEE International Conference on Robotics and Automation (ICRA), pp. 1298–1303 (2012)
3. Bo, L., Lai, K., Ren, X., Fox, D.: Object recognition with hierarchical kernel descriptors. In: Proceedings of IEEE International Conference on Computer Vision and Pattern Recognition (CVPR), pp. 1729–1736 (2011)
4. Bo, L., Ren, X., Fox, D.: Depth kernel descriptors for object recognition. In: Proceedings of IEEE/RSJ International Conference on Intelligent Robots and Systems (IROS), pp. 821–826 (2011)
5. Bo, L., Ren, X., Fox, D.: Unsupervised feature learning for RGB-D based object recognition. In: Proceedings of the International Symposium on Experimental Robtics (ISER), pp. 387–402 (2012)
6. Deng, J., Dong, W., Socher, R., Li, L., Li, K., Fei-Fei, L.: Imagenet: a large-scale hierarchical image database. In: IEEE Computer Vision and Pattern Recognition (CVPR), pp. 248–255 (2009)
7. Donahue, J.: Caffenet. https://github.com/BVLC/caffe/tree/master/models/bvlc_reference_caffenet. Accessed 26 Feb 2016
8. Eitel, A., Springenberg, J.T., Spinello, L., Riedmiller, M., Burgaard, W.: Multimodal deep learning for robust RGB-D object recognition. In: IROS Conference, pp. 681–687 (2015)
9. Gupta, S., Girshick, R., Arbeláez, P., Malik, J.: Learning rich features from RGB-D images for object detection and segmentation. In: Fleet, D., Pajdla, T., Schiele, B., Tuytelaars, T. (eds.) ECCV 2014, Part VII. LNCS, vol. 8695, pp. 345–360. Springer, Heidelberg (2014)
10. Krizhevsky, A., Sutskever, I., Hinton, G.E.: Imagenet classification with deep convolutional neural networks. Adv. Neural Inf. Process. Syst. **25**, 1106–1114 (2012)
11. Lai, K., Bo, L., Ren, X., Fox, D.: A large-scale hierarchical multi-view RGB-D object dataset. In: Proceedings of the IEEE International Conference on Robotics, pp. 1817–1824 (2011)

12. Schwarz, M., Schulz, H., S.B.: RGB-D object recognition and pose estimation based on pre-trained convolutional neural network features. In: IEEE International Conference on Robotics and Automation (ICRA), pp. 1329–1335 (2015)
13. Socher, R., Huval, B., Bhat, B., Manning, C., Ng, A.: Convolutional-recursive deep learning for 3D object classification. Adv. Neural Inf. Process. Syst. (NIPS) **25**, 656–664 (2012)

Deep Learning for Emotion Recognition in Faces

Ariel Ruiz-Garcia[✉], Mark Elshaw, Abdulrahman Altahhan,
and Vasile Palade

Faculty of Engineering, Environment and Computing, School of Computing,
Electronics and Mathematics, Coventry University, Priory Street,
Coventry CV1 5FB, UK
ariel.ruizgarcia@coventry.ac.uk

Abstract. Deep Learning (DL) has shown real promise for the classification efficiency for emotion recognition problems. In this paper we present experimental results for a deeply-trained model for emotion recognition through the use of facial expression images. We explore two Convolutional Neural Network (CNN) architectures that offer automatic feature extraction and representation, followed by fully connected softmax layers to classify images into seven emotions. The first architecture explores the impact of reducing the number of deep learning layers and the second splits the input images horizontally into two streams based on eye and mouth positions. The first proposed architecture produces state of the art results with an accuracy rate of 96.93 % and the second architecture with split input produces an average accuracy rate of 86.73 %, respectively.

Keywords: Deep learning · Convolution neural networks · Emotion recognition · Empathic robots

1 Introduction

It has long been suggested that emotions are an important aspect of everyday life and essential for effective human-to-human interactions [1]. There has been a growing focus on improving interaction between humans and machines by allowing this to happen in a natural manner [2]. One way to enable this natural interaction is to allow the machine to recognise the emotional state of the user, empathise with them and create appropriate responses [3]. For example, a social robot would be able to encourage a cancer patient to take their medication in a more efficient manner if it could understand the emotional state of the patient. In this work we present experimental results on emotion recognition through the use of facial expressive images, a first step towards the development of an emphatic robot.

Humans express emotions through facial expressions, therefore automated emotional recognition systems have relied on these to recognise emotions. Various intelligent techniques have been used to perform emotion recognition from

© Springer International Publishing Switzerland 2016
A.E.P. Villa et al. (Eds.): ICANN 2016, Part II, LNCS 9887, pp. 38–46, 2016.
DOI: 10.1007/978-3-319-44781-0_5

faces such as Hidden Markov Models [4], State Vector Machines [5] and neural networks [6, 7]. We have recently seen in the development of the use of deep learning (DL) for neural networks to perform classification [8–14]. This paper will explore two architectures for Convolutional Neural Networks (CNN) to achieve deep learning classification of emotional states: Happy, Sad, Angry, Surprise, Fear, Disgust, and Neutral, from facial expressive images. These architectures will firstly, explore the impact on reducing the number of deep learning layers and secondly, the use of a novel image representation approach that splits the input images and makes use of two deep learning streams. The structure of the paper is as follows: Section 2 gives a brief description of the background on existing work; Sect. 3 describes the experimental methodology employed; Sect. 4 reports the results obtained. The succeeding section provides conclusions to the paper including future work.

2   Human Emotion Recognition - Previous Approaches

Human emotion recognition mechanisms, whether psychological or neurological, often rely on facial features to detect or recognize a specific emotion. However, the creation of a robot that can recognise emotions from images raises a number of difficulties. For example, using good quality images with enough relevant emotion-related information is often difficult due to the high computational costs imposed by big data processing and imminent changes in the environment [15]. One efficient way to overcome the former is by surveying the environment in an explorative stage and then quickly extract important features for this environment through Deep Learning, which can then be used to train a controller to achieve a specific task [15]. In order to overcome the high computational costs imposed by big visual sensory data, Altahhan [15] introduced a model that utilizes double deep learning for feature representation and action learning.

In this paper we focus on facial expression images due to the greater amount of emotion related information they contain. This approach exploits facial features such as the mouth, eyes, eyebrows and nose to classify people images as having a specific emotion. Khashman [16] proposed a neural network architecture which includes a pair of emotional neurons to account for anxiety levels. Additionally, global pattern averaging is applied in order to reduce the size of the input image over a tenfold. Khashman [16] reports an accuracy rate of 87.78 % for the proposed architecture. Another common approach to emotion recognition is making use of facial feature point localization. Sohail, and Bhattacharya [17] presented a method which includes identifying eleven different points and measuring the distances between these. This method requires reconstructing a representation of a neutral face to use as reference. Once a feature vector is obtained, this is inputted to a neural network which produces an average recognition rate of 92 %. A similar feature extraction method has been introduced by Hewahi and Baraka [18] in which they extract 28 features which describe the distances between certain points. They also consider ethnic group as an input factor while building the recognition model; a backpropagation neural network, and have reported an accuracy rate of 83.3 %. Gabor filter is also one of the most popular methods in image-processing due to its ability to detect edges and remark salient features, and due to its resemblance to the perception in the human visual system [19]. Ahsan et al. [19] have used a combination of Gabor filter with Local Transitional Pattern together with an SVM to successfully classify facial expression images, obtaining an average accuracy rate of 95 %. Chelali and Djeradi [20] have proposed a similar approach which relies on the magnitude vector produced by Gabor filter.

Most of the approaches described above produce state of the art results for the first stage of the problem we aim to solve: emotion recognition. However, they lack the capacity to create an approach that represents and selects the salient features in an autonomous manner. This issue can conveniently be solved by employing Deep Learning (DL) techniques as done by Altahhan [15]. DL offers an outstanding alternative to prescribed feature extraction and representation. More precisely, Convolution Neural Networks (CNN) have the ability to autonomously create a vector of salient features while at the same time reducing dimensionality space by having fewer parameters than fully connected networks with the same number of layers. Levi and Hassner [8] use different image representations, including Local Binary Pattern features, as input to a number of CNN ensembles in order to boost recognition performance. Ouellet [9] presented a deep CNN to extract relevant features from still images and then classify them as seven different emotions using a Support Vector Machine. The author reports a recognition rate of 94.4 % after training with 1.2 million images. Researchers at Google Inc. have proposed a 22 layer network, omitting five pooling layers, architecture called GoogLeNet [10]. This architecture has set a state of the art benchmark for classification and detection in the ImageNet Large-Scale Visual Recognition Challenge 2014 and has inspired a number of other architectures [10]. Another architecture for large scale recognition is proposed by Krizhevsky et al. [11]. Burkert et al. [12] presented an architecture with a pair of parallel feature extraction blocks consisting of Convolutional, Pooling, and rectified linear unit (ReLU) Layers. The authors achieved an average 99.6 % accuracy rate on the CKP dataset.

3   Methodology

3.1   Emotional Face Corpus

The emotion recognition from faces using CNN in this paper used the Karolinska directed Emotional faces database (KDEF) [21]. It contains a set with 70 individuals: 35 males and 35 females, all between 20 and 30 years old, each displaying seven different emotional expressions in five different angles. In our experiments we only use front angle images; a subset of 980 images. All images were taken under a con-trolled environment: subjects wore uniform T-Shirt colours, faces were centred with a grid, and eyes and mouths were positioned in fixed image coordinates [21]. To speed up training, face images were extracted, grey-scaled and resized to 100 by 100 as shown in Fig. 1 below. Our training set contained

Fig. 1. Sample extracted face images from the KDEF database [21]. Subject 07 displaying seven emotions: sad, surprised, neutral, happy, fear, disgust, angry.

98 randomly selected front angle images per emotion, giving us a total of 686 input samples. Our testing set contained 42 images per emotion and thus a total of 294 training samples.

3.2 Architectures

Since our aim is to explore biologically inspired neural architectures we decided to employ CNN for feature extraction and representation given that they are inspired by animal vision cortex [13]. These models are well known for their ability to extract salient features and for being faster than traditional models such as Multilayer Perceptron (MLP) networks due to a smaller number of parameters required for training. This paper explores two main architectures for the CNN to identify the number of deep learning layers that best represent the images and the impact of a split input stream representation for the architecture structure. Figure 2 illustrates a detailed description.

The architectures we propose are made up of convolution, rectified linear unit (ReLU), max pooling, and local response normalization (LRN) layers followed by one fully connected layer and one softmaxloss layer for classification. The convolutional layers incorporate constraints and achieve some degree of shift and deformation invariance using local receptive fields, shared weights, and spatial subsampling [13]. Their output can be summarized as:

$$C(x_{u,v}) = (x+a)^n = \sum_{i=-\frac{n}{2}}^{\frac{n}{2}} \sum_{j=-\frac{m}{2}}^{\frac{m}{2}} f_k(i,j) x_{u-i,v-j}. \tag{1}$$

where f_k is the filter with a kernel size $n \times m$, applied to the input x. In our models n is always the same as m. The convolutional layers in the first network use 60, 90, 120, and 240 filters respectively. Whereas the split input model learns 60, 90, and 120 filters. Given that ReLU functions marginally reduce training times in deep convolutional networks [11], every output of a convolutional layer in our models is shaped by a ReLU function. Given an input value x, ReLU output is given by:

$$f(x) = \max\{0, x\}. \tag{2}$$

The input is further reduced with max pooling layers. Let x_i be the input and m be the size of the filter, then the output of the max pooling layers is calculated as:

$$M(x_i) = \max\left\{x_{i+k,i+l} \big| |k| \le \frac{m}{2}, |l| \le \frac{m}{2} k, l \in \mathbb{N}\right\}. \tag{3}$$

a)

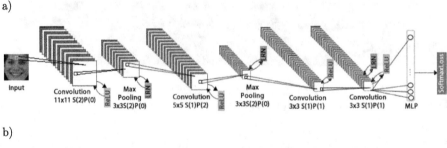

b)

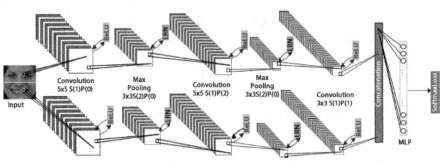

Fig. 2. (a) CNN with reduced deep learning layer, (b) Network with split input; S defines the stride size and P the padding. Face images from subject 07 in KDEF database [21].

Moreover, all spatial locations of the output of some of the pooling layers and ReLU layers are uniformly normalized using the Local Response Normalization (LRN) operator. Let k be the output channel, and $G(k) \subset \{1, 2, , D\}$ represent a corresponding subset of input channels, the output of LRN is calculated as follows:

$$y_{ijk} = x_{ijkz} \left(k + \alpha \sum_{t \in G(k)} x_{ijt}^2 \right)^{-\beta}. \tag{4}$$

Furthermore, our models use a fully connected layer which in term is an MLP. Let σ represent a sigmoid activation function, then the output of the hidden layer is computed by:

$$F(x) = \sigma(W * x). \tag{5}$$

Finally, the last layer in our models employs a *softmaxloss* operator which in turn is a combination of the softmax operator followed by the log-loss operator. Given the class ground-truth c, softmaxloss output is computed by:

$$y = -\sum_{ij} \left(x_{ijc} - \log \sum_{d=1}^{D} e^{x_{ijd}} \right). \tag{6}$$

The training process for both architectures was the same: the learning rate for filters and biases was initially set to 1.0 and dynamically adjusted down to 0.00001 over 1000 epochs, whereas the momentum was set to 0.9. The input vector was down-sampled by convolution and pooling layers using a sliding window with stride of 2.

4   Results and Discussion

After training for 15, 500, epochs the first model achieved its best performance producing an accuracy rate of 96.93 % on the testing set, not far from the results obtained by Burkert et al. [12]. Further training with the same parameters seems to cause overfitting. The second architecture proposed splits the image horizontally in half and feeds each half to a corresponding sub architecture to be processed in parallel. Each sub-architecture learns a representation of different face parts: in the case of the first half the salient features highlighted are the areas around the eyes whereas the second half highlights the area surrounding the mouth. The translation invariant features obtained from each subnetwork are then recombined for classification. This model with split input has been training for just 5, 280 epochs and has already achieved state of the art performance with an accuracy rate of 86.73 %. Table 1 illustrates the confusion matrices for both models; as it can be observed both networks achieved a higher performance rate when classifying facial images illustrating happy emotions. It is evident that both of our models misclassify neutral faces the most. This might be due to the similarity of this emotion with all the others, especially with sadness. As it can be observed in Fig. 1 above there is not a big difference between these two expressions and neutral has previously been defined as the basic human emotion [17] which implies that all other emotions are developed from this.

Table 1. Left: first network confusion matrix, right: split input network confusion matrix. A: angry; D: disgust; F: fear; H: happy; N: neutral; Sa: sad; Su: surprised.

	A	D	F	H	N	Sa	Su		A	D	F	H	N	Sa	Su
A	42	0	0	0	0	0	0	A	40	1	1	0	0	0	0
D	0	40	0	1	0	1	0	D	1	32	1	3	0	3	1
F	0	1	39	1	0	0	1	F	1	2	37	0	0	0	2
H	0	0	0	42	0	0	0	H	2	0	0	42	0	0	0
N	0	1	0	0	39	2	0	N	1	2	1	0	32	5	1
Sa	0	1	0	0	0	41	0	Sa	0	3	2	1	0	36	0
Su	0	0	1	0	0	0	41	Su	0	0	3	0	0	0	39

We have explored in this paper two new CNN architectures that create state of the art results. Our first architecture has achieved such performance with a reduced number of layers as opposed to the model proposed by [12]. Although second model, which uses two deep learning streams, has produced lower performance it has only been training for a fraction of the time that the first one was trained for. Moreover, this network has already outperformed the performance of the first model at 5000 epochs. We attribute this increase in performance to the split input around the mouth and eye areas; since these two are determining key factors for emotion recognition, each network ensemble learns to extract only of these salient features, thus having to do lesser weight modifications.

Beyond the neuroscientific and biological aspect, human emotions allow us to connect and share experiences with other people regardless of background. This cognitive process is vital for human-human interactions and could improve human-robot interactions. Our research aims to contribute to solving this issue by proposing a neural architecture that can allow a robotic machine to recognise a user's emotional state. To this day, empirical models such as Support Vector Machines seem to be the dominant classifiers in emotion recognition through facial expression images due to their high performance rate. However, the performance of these classifiers heavily relies on the image preprocessing techniques applied on the images. CNN, on the other hand, have the ability to extract and learn features autonomously. Our second architecture contains similar properties to that proposed by [12], however our model uses less parameters and less layers, being marginally faster and therefore more suitable for online learning.

5 Conclusion

To the best of our knowledge we are the first to propose an architecture for emotion recognition which splits the image into two sections in order to extract features with different parameters. This approach uses two network ensembles to extract salient features from around the mouth and eye areas. The model seems to take advantage of the most salient features, which are essential for emotion recognition. This approach has produced promising results and will therefore be improved in future work.

We hope that our research brings social robots a step closer to been fully accepted by society. The results reported above illustrate a fundamental initial step towards achieving this goal by providing us with a method for self-organised or autonomous feature extraction and representation learnt explicitly for emotion recognition. However, despite the high recognition performance achieved in the experiments we conducted, we have to take into consideration the fact that the training and testing datasets contain images of similar quality and taken under controlled environments. Future work will address the ability of the architectures developed to compensate for light and angle variations. In this manner, the number of layers and parameters will be adjusted accordingly in order to achieve the same performance results in real environments. Given the promise shown by the architecture with a split input, future work will look at its performance with the input being split into more sections or with random patches.

Future work will look at the development of an associative architecture to be combined with the proposed CNN. Additionally, future work will explore the possibility of using a multimodal approach and incorporate other inputs such as: speech signals, body language, heart rate readings, etc. into our model in order to obtain a comprehensive representation of the emotions and better recognition rates. Reinforcement learning techniques will be explored to allow the robot to learn which responses improve the interaction process with the user.

References

1. Lewis, M., Haviland-Jones, J., Barrett, L.: Handbook of Emotions. Guilford Press, New York (2008)
2. Chavhan, A., Chavan, S., Dahe, S., Chibhade, S.: A neural network approach for real time emotion recognition. IJARCCE **4**(3), 259–263 (2015)
3. Han, K., Yu, D., Tashev, I.: Speech emotion recognition using deep neural network and extreme learning machine. In: Interspeech, pp. 223–227 (2014)
4. Cohen, I., Garg, A., Huang, T.: Emotion recognition from facial expressions using multi-level HMM. In: Neural Information Processing Systems, vol. 2 (2000)
5. Sarnarawickrame, K., Mindya, S.: Facial expression recognition using active shape models and support vector machines. In: 2013 International Conference on Advances in ICT for Emerging Regions (ICTer), pp. 51–55 (2013)
6. Boughrara, H., Chtourou, M., Ben Amar, C., Chen, L.: Facial expression recognition based on a mlp neural network using constructive training algorithm. Multimed. Tools Appl. **75**, 709–731 (2014)
7. Kahou, S., Michalski, V., Konda, K., Memisevic, R., Pal, C.: Recurrent neural networks for emotion recognition in video. In: Proceedings of the 2015 ACM on International Conference on Multimodal Interaction (ICMI 2015), pp. 467–474 (2015)
8. Levi, G., Hassner, T.: Emotion recognition in the wild via convolutional neural networks and mapped binary patterns. In: Proceedings of the 2015 ACM on International Conference on Multimodal Interaction (ICMI 2015), pp. 503–510 (2015)
9. Ouellet, S.: Realtime emotion recognition for gaming using deep convolutional network features. CoRR. abs/1408.3750 (2014)
10. Szegedy, C., Lui, W., Jia, Y., Sermanet, P., Reed, S., Auguelov, D., Erhan, D., Vanhoucke, V., Rabinovich, A.: Going deeper with convolutions. In: Proceedings of the IEEE Conference on Computer Vision and Pattern Recognition, pp. 1–19 (2014)
11. Krizhevsky, A., Sutskever, I., Hinton, G.: Imagenet classification with deep convolutional neural networks. Adv. Neural Inf. Process. Syst. **25**, 1106–1114 (2012)
12. Burkert, P., Trier, F., Afzal, M.Z., Dengel, A., Liwicki, M.: DeXpression: Deep Convolutional Neural Network for Expression Recognition. CoRR. abs/1509.05371 (2015)
13. Lawrence, S., Giles, C., Tsoi, A.C., Back, A.: Face recognition: a convolutional neural network approach. IEEE Trans. Neural Netw. **8**, 98–113 (1997)
14. Brosch, T., Tam, R.: Efficient training of convolutional deep belief networks in the frequency domain for application to high-resolution 2D and 3D images. Neural Computation. **27**, 211–227 (2015)
15. Altahhan, A.: Navigating a robot through big visual sensory data. Procedia Comput. Sci. **53**, 478–485 (2015)
16. Khashman, A.: Application of an emotional neural network to facial recognition. Neural Comput. Appl. **18**, 309–320 (2008)
17. Sohail, A., Bhattacharya, P.: Classifying facial expressions using level set method based lip contour detection and multi-class support vector machines. Int. J. Pattern Recogn. Artif. Intell. **25**, 835–862 (2011)
18. Hewahi, N., Baraka, A.: Impact of ethnic group on human emotion recognition using backpropagation neural network. Broad Res. Artif. Intell. Neurosci. **2**, 20–27 (2011)

19. Ahsan, T., Jabid, T., Chong, U.: Facial expression recognition using local transitional pattern on gabor filtered facial images. IETE Tech Rev. **30**, 47 (2013)
20. Chelali, F., Djeradi, A.: Face recognition using MLP and RBF neural network with Gabor and discrete wavelet transform characterization: a comparative study. Math. Prob. Eng. **2015**, 116 (2015)
21. Lundqvist, D., Flykt, A., Ahman, A.: The Karolinska Directed Emotional Faces - KDEF. CD ROM from Department of Clinical Neuroscience, Psychology section, Karolinska Institutet (1998). ISBN 91-630-7164-9

Extracting Muscle Synergy Patterns from EMG Data Using Autoencoders

Martin Spüler[1]([✉]), Nerea Irastorza-Landa[2], Andrea Sarasola-Sanz[2], and Ander Ramos-Murguialday[2,3]

[1] Computer Science Department, University of Tübingen, Tübingen, Germany
spueler@informatik.uni-tuebingen.de
[2] Institute of Medical Psychology and Behavioral Neurobiology,
University of Tübingen, Tübingen, Germany
[3] TECNALIA, Health Technologies Department, San Sebastian, Spain

Abstract. Muscle synergies can be seen as fundamental building blocks of motor control. Extracting muscle synergies from EMG data is a widely used method in motor related research. Due to the linear nature of the methods commonly used for extracting muscle synergies, those methods fail to represent agonist-antagonist muscle relationships in the extracted synergies. In this paper, we propose to use a special type of neural networks, called autoencoders, for extracting muscle synergies. Using simulated data and real EMG data, we show that autoencoders, contrary to commonly used methods, allow to capture agonist-antagonist muscle relationships, and that the autoencoder models have a significantly better fit to the data than others methods.

Keywords: Electromyography (EMG) · Neural network · Matrix factorization · Extensor-flexor muscles

1 Introduction

Muscle synergies can be seen as fundamental building blocks of motor control [1]. As the human body contains more muscles than joints, the motor control problem (planning a movement) is ill-posed as there are infinite possibilities to perform a given task (e.g. arm movement to reach an object). To simplify movement control, muscle synergies describe the activation pattern for multiple muscles, which are co-active during a specific task. By controlling the muscle synergies, instead of each muscle separately, the motor control problem is reduced to only few degrees of freedom. Results supporting this theory have been found in a variety of species ranging from *Aplysia* to humans [1].

Agonist-antagonist relationships are an example for very basic synergy control. These relationships play a crucial role in extensor/flexor muscles like biceps and triceps, which are located on the opposite sides of the same joint. During contraction of the agonist muscle, the opposing muscle group (antagonist) needs to be inhibited to prevent working against the agonist muscles. It has been shown

A.E.P. Villa et al. (Eds.): ICANN 2016, Part II, LNCS 9887, pp. 47–54, 2016.
DOI: 10.1007/978-3-319-44781-0_6

that this inhibition can even happen at a spinal level (Ia inhibitory interneurons) [2] and plays a major role in movement control [3].

Muscle synergies are usually extracted out of electromyography (EMG) data, which is obtained by placing electrodes on the muscles and recording the electrical activity. To extract the synergies, different matrix factorization algorithms (e.g. PCA, ICA) can be used with non-negative matrix factorization (NNMF) being the most commonly used and established method. As inhibition of muscle activity can not directly be observed in EMG data, linear methods in general have difficulty to extract agonist-antagonist relationships. In the case of non-negative matrix factorization, it is essentially impossible to model any muscle inhibition due to the non-negative properties of the method.

While there are approaches to capture agonist-antagonist synergies by creating a physical model of the affected joints [4], we propose the use of autoencoders, a special type of artificial neural network [5], for an unsupervised extraction of muscle synergies from EMG data. In the following, we show that it allows to capture agonist-antagonist relationships in muscle synergies and that the obtained synergy models have a better fit than the models extracted by commonly used methods.

2   Methods

2.1   Autoencoder for Muscle Synergy Extraction

Autoencoders are a special type of neural network, which encode a lower-dimensional representation of the input space [5]. Assuming an n-dimensional input space and m-dimensional representation (with $m < n$), the autoencoder consists of n input units, fully connected to m hidden units, which are also fully connected to n output units (see Fig. 1). Given a specific dataset, the network is trained to show the same activation at the output units, as is given at the input units. As the low-dimensional hidden layer is between the input and output layer, the left part of the network acts as encoder, encoding the input as a lower-dimensional representation, while the right part acts as a decoder to decode the original data from the lower-dimensional representation.

When applying an autoencoder to EMG data to extract synergies, the number of input and output units has to be equal to the number of EMG channels. The number of hidden units is determined by the number of synergies one wants to extract. The network is then trained with the EMG data for the input and output units. After training, the activity at the hidden units represents the synergies. While the encoding part of the network is used to extract synergies from the EMG data, the decoding part reconstructs the individual muscle activity from the synergies. The weights of the connections in the decoding part represent the level of participation for each muscle in a given synergy.

2.2   Methods for Extraction of Muscle Synergies

To evaluate the use of autoencoders for the extraction of muscle synergies, we compared the use of autoencoders to other methods frequently used for the

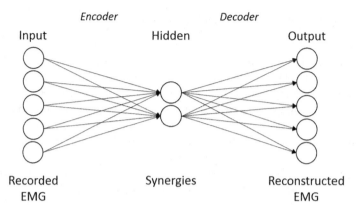

Fig. 1. Visualization of the autoencoder used for extraction of muscle synergies. Shown are 5 input and output neurons corresponding to 5 EMG channels and 2 hidden neurons corresponding to 2 synergies.

extraction of muscle synergies [6]. All methods used in this work are shortly explained in the following:

Autoencoder (AEnc) As explained above, autoencoders were used for extraction of muscle synergy patterns. A logistic sigmoid function was used as transfer function for the encoder and decoder part of the network. For training the autoencoder, the mean squared error was minimized including an L2-regularization with $\lambda = 0.001$.

Non-negative Matrix Factorization (NNMF) is an algorithm, where a matrix V is factorized into two matrices W and H, so that all matrices have no negative elements. NNMF was found to work well for extracting muscle synergies [6], however the non-negative property of the method prevents the method from finding agonist-antagonist muscle relationships.

Principal Component Analysis (PCA) is a computational method that separates a multivariate dataset into components. The separated components are orthogonal to each other and sorted by decreasing variance. For the extraction of muscle synergies, PCA is also used, but was shown to perform worse than ICA and NNMF [6].

Independent Component Analysis (ICA) is another computational method for separating statistically independent components from multiple mixed signals [7]. In this work, the FastICA implementation was used, which allows to extract a specified number of components. ICA was also found to work well for extracting muscle synergies [6].

2.3   Evaluation on Simulated Data

To demonstrate the use of autoencoders for the extraction of muscle synergies, we created a simulated dataset. For this dataset we assumed two muscles in an agonist-antagonist relationship. The data was modeled similar to the activation patterns of biceps and triceps during elbow extension/flexion [8]. A sinusoidal movement was assumed consisting of only one synergy with a sinusoidal pattern. During extension one of the muscles was inhibited, while during flexion the other muscle was inhibited. This behavior was reflected in the muscle weights being positive for one, and being negative for the other muscle.

All methods were applied on the simulated data, to evaluate how well the different methods capture this agonist-antagonist relation.

2.4   Extracting Muscle Synergies from Real EMG Data

To evaluate the different methods on real EMG data, we used EMG data from 9 subjects (2 sessions per subject), performing a reaching movement with the right arm. EMG was recorded with 6 surface EMG electrodes placed over different muscles of the right upper limb including biceps, triceps and frontal and posterior deltoid muscles. More information about the EMG data and the design of the experimental task can be found in [9,10]. As biceps/triceps and frontal/posterior deltoid muscles are known agonist-antagonist pairs in upper limb movements [11] we hope to find those relationships in the extracted synergies.

Extraction of synergies was not done directly on the raw EMG data, instead waveform length was extracted as feature for muscle activation. Waveform length (WL) [12], is the cumulative length of the waveform over the time segment. If x_t is the amplitude of the EMG channel at time t, the waveform length can be calculated with the following equation:

$$WL = \sum_{n=1}^{N-1} |x_{n+1} - x_n| \tag{1}$$

Before extracting the waveform length, the EMG signal was bandpass filtered between 10 Hz and 500 Hz and a 50 Hz notch filter was applied to filter out power line noise. The filtered EMG data was rectified and then the waveform length was extracted. WL was computed on an 200 ms window which was shifted in 50 ms steps over the EMG data.

2.5   Evaluation on Real EMG Data

The four previously described methods (AEnc, NNMF, PCA, ICA) were tested on real EMG data to evaluate which of the methods is best suited for the task of extracting muscle synergies.

3 Results

3.1 Evaluation on Simulated Data

The results for the evaluation on the simulated dataset can be seen in Fig. 2. While NNMF and ICA fail to capture the agonist-antagonist relationship in the simulated data, PCA models this relationship, but does not allow for a proper reconstruction. Training an autoencoder on the simulated data gave the best result and reconstructed muscle activity was closest to the original. It should be noted that the scaling of the synergy, as well as the muscle weights differ between the used methods. However, the absolute size of the scale is irrelevant for the extraction of muscle synergies and only the relative differences are important.

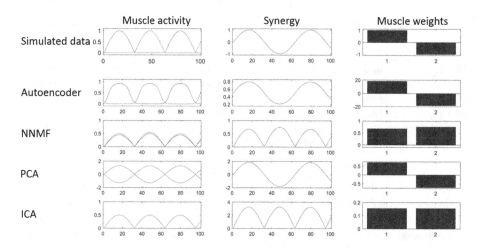

Fig. 2. Results for the different methods on simulated data. Simulated data contained one synergy with two muscles. Muscles were modeled as agonist (blue muscle with positive weight) and antagonist (red muscle with negative weight). Displayed is the synergy (middle), the muscles weights (right) and the muscle activity (left) which is reconstructed from the synergies and the weights. The simulated data is shown at the top. Below is the reconstruction of the synergies by applying different methods on the simulated data. (Color figure online)

3.2 Evaluation on Real EMG Data

To see how well autoencoder and the other methods work on real data, they were applied to EMG data from 9 subjects. Figure 3 shows an exemplary result of an autoencoder applied to the data from one subject. It can be clearly seen that the agonist-antagonist relationships between biceps and triceps, as well as between the deltoid muscles are properly modeled in the second synergy, which resembles the muscle activity for the forward/backward part of the reaching

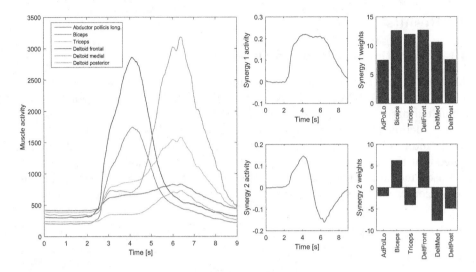

Fig. 3. Example of autoencoder applied to the EMG data from subject 1 performing a reaching movement (moving arm forward and backward). The average muscle activity during a reaching movement is shown on the left. On the right side, the results of the autoencoder applied to the data for the extraction of two synergies is shown. While the first synergy shows a general activation pattern, the second synergy clearly shows the agonist-antagonist relationships during forward and backward movement.

movement. The first synergy resembles the general muscle activity involved in the arm movement (compared to a relaxed state).

To see how well the models generated by the different methods fit the data, we compared the reconstructed data with the original data and calculated the explained variance (R^2) as a measure of how well the model fits the data. Results for a different number of synergies can be seen in Table 1. As the aim of using such methods for muscle synergy extraction is the reduction of the input space, especially the results with a low number of reconstructed synergies are important. For 1 and 2 reconstructed synergies, autoencoder performs significantly

Table 1. Explained variance (R^2) of the original data compared to the data reconstructed using muscle synergy models generated by the different methods for a varying number of reconstructed muscle synergies. Highest values are marked bold.

Method	Number of synergies					
	1	2	3	4	5	6
AEnc	**0.57**	**0.84**	**0.91**	**0.95**	0.96	0.97
NNMF	0.52	0.80	0.91	0.94	0.93	**1.00**
PCA	0.48	0.80	0.90	0.94	**0.99**	1.00
ICA	0.09	0.19	0.32	0.48	0.70	**1.00**

better than the other methods ($p < 0.001$, Wilcoxon signed rank test). For 3 and 4 synergies it performs better, but not significantly ($p > 0.05$), while PCA performs best with 5 reconstructed synergies. When using 6 reconstructed synergies the other methods achieve a perfect reconstruction, which is trivial as the number of synergies equals the number of EMG channels. Due to the non-linear transfer functions, autoencoder does not achieve a perfect reconstruction in this case, but would likewise be able to if linear transfer functions were used.

4 Discussion and Conclusion

Commonly used methods for the extraction of muscle synergies like PCA, ICA and especially NNMF fail to properly extract agonist-antagonist muscle relationships from EMG data. As these agonist-antagonist muscle relationships play a crucial role in motor control we proposed the use of autoencoders for the extraction of muscle synergies. Based on simulated data and on real EMG data we could show that autoencoders properly capture agonist-antagonist muscle relationships. As the reduction of components is the main motivation behind the extraction of muscle synergies, it is important that the methods work well with a low number of synergies. In these cases, autoencoders generate models for synergy extraction that fit significantly better to the data than the other methods.

As the inhibition of the antagonist muscle during agonist movement is not directly observable from the EMG data, linear methods (and especially non-negative factorization methods) are not able to properly capture these relationships. With autoencoder as a non-linear method we have shown that it is nevertheless possible to extract agonist-antagonist muscle relationships.

While the reduction of components is one of the goals, the question of how many synergies are involved in a movement is still an open issue. Tresch et al. [6] used a method based on the changes of explained variance when increasing the number of synergies to determine the correct number of synergies. Such a method could likewise be used to find the optimal number of synergies when using autoencoder. Due to space reasons, this topic hasn't been investigated in this paper, but it should be expected that a lower number of synergies is optimal for autoencoder, since they allow to model agonist-antagonist relationships as one synergy instead of describing agonist and antagonist activity as separate components.

As the extraction of muscle synergies has become an important method for investigating movement control (e.g. in stroke patients [13]) and has even been suggested to improve the control of brain-computer interfaces [14], the ability to properly model agonist-antagonist muscle relationships using autoencoders should hopefully foster research in these areas.

Acknowledgments. This work was supported by the *Baden-Württemberg Stiftung* (GRUENS), the *Deutsche Forschungsgemeinschaft* (DFG; SP 1533/2-1) and the German Ministry of Education and Research (MOTOR-BIC; FKZ 136W0053). Andrea Sarasola-Sanz and Nerea Irastorza-Landa are supported by the La Caixa-DAAD and Basque Government scholarships respectively.

References

1. Bizzi, E., Cheung, V.C.K.: The neural origin of muscle synergies. Front. Comput. Neurosci. **7**(51) (2013)
2. Nishimaru, H., Kakizaki, M.: The role of inhibitory neurotransmission in locomotor circuits of the developing mammalian spinal cord. Acta Physiol. **197**(2), 83–97 (2009)
3. Crone, C.: Reciprocal inhibition in man. Danish Med. Bull. **40**(5), 571–581 (1993)
4. Hirai, H., Miyazaki, F., Naritomi, H., Koba, K., Oku, T., Uno, K., Uemura, M., Nishi, T., Kageyama, M., Krebs, H.I.: On the origin of muscle synergies: invariant balance in the co-activation of agonist and antagonist muscle pairs. Front. Bioeng. Biotechnol. **3**(192) (2015)
5. Bengio, Y.: Learning deep architectures for ai. Found. Trends® Mach. Learn. **2**(1), 1–127 (2009)
6. Tresch, M.C., Cheung, V.C.K., d'Avella, A.: Matrix factorization algorithms for the identification of muscle synergies: evaluation on simulated and experimental data sets. J. Neurophysiol. **95**(4), 2199–2212 (2006)
7. Hyvärinen, A., Oja, E.: Independent component analysis: algorithms and applications. Neural Netw. **13**(4), 411–430 (2000)
8. Gordon, J., Ghez, C.: EMG patterns in antagonist muscles during isometric contraction in man: relations to response dynamics. Exp. Brain Res. **55**(1), 167–171 (1984)
9. Sarasola-Sanz, A., Irastorza-Landa, N., Shiman, F., Lopez-Larraz, E., Spüler, M., Birbaumer, N., Ramos-Murguialday, A.: EMG-based multi-joint kinematics decoding for robot-aided rehabilitation therapies. In: 2015 IEEE International Conference on Rehabilitation Robotics (ICORR), pp. 229–234. IEEE (2015)
10. Shiman, F., Irastorza-Landa, N., Sarasola-Sanz, A., Spüler, M., Birbaumer, N., Ramos-Murguialday, A.: Towards decoding of functional movements from the same limb using EEG. In: 2015 37th Annual International Conference of the IEEE Engineering in Medicine and Biology Society (EMBC), pp. 1922–1925. IEEE (2015)
11. Gowland, C., Basmajian, J.V., Plews, N., Burcea, I., et al.: Agonist and antagonist activity during voluntary upper-limb movement in patients with stroke. Phys. Ther. **72**(9), 624–633 (1992)
12. Phinyomark, A., Chujit, G., Phukpattaranont, P., Limsakul, C., Hu, H.: A preliminary study assessing time-domain EMG features of classifying exercises in preventing falls in the elderly. In: 2012 9th International Conference on Electrical Engineering/Electronics, Computer, Telecommunications and Information Technology (ECTI-CON), pp. 1–4, May 2012
13. Roh, J., Rymer, W.Z., Perreault, E.J., Yoo, S.B., Beer, R.F.: Alterations in upper limb muscle synergy structure in chronic stroke survivors. J. Neurophysiol. **109**(3), 768–781 (2013)
14. Vinjamuri, R., Weber, D.J., Mao, Z.-H., Collinger, J.L., Degenhart, A.D., Kelly, J.W., Boninger, M.L., Tyler-Kabara, E.C., Wang, W.: Toward synergy-based brain-machine interfaces. IEEE Trans. Inf Technol. Biomed. **15**(5), 726–736 (2011)

Integration of Unsupervised and Supervised Criteria for Deep Neural Networks Training

Francisco Zamora-Martínez[✉], Javier Muñoz-Almaraz, and Juan Pardo

Departamento de Ciencias Físicas, Matemáticas y de la Computación,
Universidad CEU Cardenal Herrera, Alfara del Patriarca, 46115 Valencia, Spain
{francisco.zamora,malmaraz,juaparal}@uchceu.es

Abstract. Training Deep Neural Networks has been a difficult task for a long time. Recently diverse approaches have been presented to tackle these difficulties, showing that deep models improve the performance of shallow ones in some areas like signal processing, signal classification or signal segmentation, whatever type of signals, e.g. video, audio or images. One of the most important methods is greedy layer-wise unsupervised pre-training followed by a fine-tuning phase. Despite the advantages of this procedure, it does not fit some scenarios where real time learning is needed, as for adaptation of some time-series models. This paper proposes to couple both phases into one, modifying the loss function to mix together the unsupervised and supervised parts. Benchmark experiments with MNIST database prove the viability of the idea for simple image tasks, and experiments with time-series forecasting encourage the incorporation of this idea into on-line learning approaches. The interest of this method in time-series forecasting is motivated by the study of predictive models for domotic houses with intelligent control systems.

Keywords: Deep learning · Stacked auto-encoders · Supervised learning · Time-series forecasting

1 Introduction

Deep Neural Networks (DNNs) training has been an open problem for a long time, mainly due to of the gradient vanishing problem [3,5]. These difficulties have been presented in literature several times [2,3,6,10,11] and recently it has been found that deep models are advantageous over shallow ones for such tasks like image or audio processing.

Greedy layer-wise pre-training have been presented as a solution to train multilayer perceptrons with many layers of non-linearities [2]. This method employs a pre-training phase where every layer of the deep model is initialized following an unsupervised criterion [2,6]. Other ideas have been presented previously to solve similar problems in recurrent neural networks [11]. This pre-training phase takes leverage over other approaches due to the huge amount of unsupervised data available on the internet, which are suitable for initialization of these deep models. However, in certain tasks the system needs to be installed at unknown

© Springer International Publishing Switzerland 2016
A.E.P. Villa et al. (Eds.): ICANN 2016, Part II, LNCS 9887, pp. 55–62, 2016.
DOI: 10.1007/978-3-319-44781-0_7

environments or under low-resource specifications. Therefore, sequential or online learning is required to train a model from *scratch* in real time under these circumstances. Besides, when unsupervised data are not available, pre-training stage complicates the pipeline forcing to train the model twice: pre-training initialization and fine-tuning stage.

Even more, an integrated approach would benefit from learning jointly a feature space transformation with discriminative properties in contrast with unsupervised pre-training [18]. Recently, the use of Rectified Linear Units (ReLUs) or other piece-wise linear activation functions are being studied to tackle DNNs training but pre-training is still relevant.

The present paper proposes to mix together unsupervised and supervised goals into one differentiable function, in such a way that a set of mixing coefficients can control the focus during training, paying more attention into the unsupervised part during first training iterations and moving gradually to an almost pure supervised training criterion. This paper studies empirical evidence of mix coefficients effect in MNIST benchmark and in a time-series forecasting problem. The interest of this method in time-series forecasting is motivated by its ability to train deep predictive models in unknown environments, e.g. domotic houses with intelligent control systems. For this particular scenario, the model can be estimated in real time while the control system is working in its final location [8,14] to capture the patterns of environmental, energetic and human behavior signals for energy efficiency purposes.

The proposed joint loss approach is directly related with [18], where a similar technique is presented for training of deep auto-encoders. However, in [18] authors proposed to train a deep auto-encoder following a mixed loss function, but the supervised classifier training is performed in a second stage. This difference is really important because different mixing coefficients and update algorithms are required when both supervised and unsupervised are coupled into the same loss function. Another similar work has been done in Sect. 9 of [12] where the authors propose a one stage approach not obtaining good results, most importantly due to sub-optimal result when mixing together the unsupervised and supervised losses, requiring a final fine-tune phase for optimality. Updating mix coefficients properly would solve optimality problem stated by [12].

2   Stacked Denoising Auto-Encoders and Deep Neural Networks

A Denoising Auto-Encoder (DAE) is a model designed to take a noisy input $\tilde{\mathbf{x}}$ and to reconstruct as output its clean version $\mathbf{x}$. A perturbation function is defined as $\tilde{\mathbf{x}} = \rho(\mathbf{x})$ which takes the vector $\mathbf{x}$ and randomly corrupts it. The DAE can be formalized as $\hat{\mathbf{x}} = A(\tilde{\mathbf{x}}; \boldsymbol{\theta}) = g \circ f(\tilde{\mathbf{x}})$ being $f(\mathbf{x}) = s(\mathbf{W}\mathbf{x} + \mathbf{b}_e)$ the encoder function, $g(\mathbf{h}) = s(\mathbf{W}^{\mathsf{T}}\mathbf{h} + \mathbf{b}_d)$ the decoder function, $\boldsymbol{\theta} = \{\mathbf{W}, \mathbf{b}_e, \mathbf{b}_d\}$, and $\mathbf{W}$, $\mathbf{b}_e$, $\mathbf{b}_d$ the weight matrix and bias vectors respectively.

Stacking together several DAEs, it is possible to build up a Stacked Denoising Auto-Encoder (SDAE) composing all encoder and decoder functions, e.g. for two layers of DAEs $\hat{\mathbf{x}} = g_1 \circ g_2 \circ f_2 \circ f_1 \circ \rho(\mathbf{x})$. Overfitting problems are avoided by the denoising objective and by adding a regularization term to the loss function. The empirical risk of SDAE for a given pattern $\mathbf{x}$ would be $L_u(A(\mathbf{x}; \boldsymbol{\theta}), \mathbf{x}) + \epsilon \Omega(\boldsymbol{\theta})$ being $L_u(\mathbf{x}; \boldsymbol{\theta})$ the unsupervised loss function, ϵ the regularization penalty term and $\Omega(\boldsymbol{\theta})$ the regularization function (usually the squared 2-norm of $\boldsymbol{\theta}$). Assuming logistic activation functions in SDAE, the loss function would be the cross-entropy, but different ones will be needed depending on the distribution of each DAE input/output features.

It is difficult to train a deep neural model for a supervised task because of the several non-linear layers and the vanishing gradient problem. To overcome this issue, usually the model is pre-trained in a greedy layer-wise fashion [2,12], learning locally each of the i-th DAEs, and finally the DNN model is built stacking all encoder functions and pushing on top a supervised layer. Formally, the DNN is described by the function $\hat{\mathbf{y}} = F(\mathbf{x}; \boldsymbol{\theta}) = \mathbf{h}^{(H+1)}$ being $\mathbf{h}^{(i)} = s(\mathbf{W}_i^{\mathsf{T}} \mathbf{h}^{(i-1)} + \mathbf{b}_i)$ for $1 \leq i \leq H+1$ the activation of every layer in the DNN. The DNN is fine-tuned $F(\mathbf{x}; \boldsymbol{\theta})$ to minimize the regularized empirical risk using a given loss function and the given $\mathcal{D}$ data set: $R(\boldsymbol{\theta}, \mathcal{D}) = \frac{1}{|\mathcal{D}|} \sum_{(\mathbf{x},\mathbf{y}) \in \mathcal{D}} L_s(F(\mathbf{x}; \boldsymbol{\theta}), \mathbf{y}) + \epsilon \Omega(\boldsymbol{\theta})$ being L_s the supervised loss function, usually cross-entropy loss function for classification tasks or mean square loss for regression tasks.

3   Integration of Unsupervised and Supervised Criteria

Joining together unsupervised and supervised loss functions it can be formalized an empirical risk equation which can be minimized for satisfying both goals. The mixing of this combination is controlled by a vector $\boldsymbol{\lambda} = \langle \lambda_0, \lambda_1, \ldots, \lambda_H \rangle$ with $H+1$ components, being λ_0 the coefficient for supervised criterion, and the remaining H coefficients for unsupervised criteria of each hidden layer. $\boldsymbol{\lambda}^{(t)}$ denotes the vector value at time step t. Formally, the DNN can be trained to minimize the following regularized empirical risk:

$$R(\boldsymbol{\theta}, \mathcal{D}) = \frac{1}{|\mathcal{D}|} \sum_{(\mathbf{x},\mathbf{y}) \in \mathcal{D}} \left[\lambda_0^{(t)} L_s(F(\mathbf{x}; \boldsymbol{\theta}), \mathbf{y}) + \sum_{k=1}^{H} \lambda_k^{(t)} U^{(k)} \right] + \epsilon \Omega(\boldsymbol{\theta}) \qquad (1)$$

$$U^{(k)} = L_u(A_k(\rho(\mathbf{h}^{(k-1)}); \theta), \mathbf{h}^{(k-1)}) \quad \text{for } 1 \leq k \leq H \qquad (2)$$

$$\lambda_k \geq 0 \qquad (3)$$

being $h^{(0)} = \mathbf{x}$, L_s the supervised loss, L_u the unsupervised loss for hidden layers and $A_k(\rho(h^{(k-1)}); \theta)$ the DAE encoder/decoder architecture. For simplicity, unsupervised models $A_k(\cdot)$ receive the same $\boldsymbol{\theta}$ as the supervised model $F(\cdot)$, however each unsupervised model requires only the bias vector and weight matrix related with k layer and the additional bias vector needed for the reconstruction of the output layer. This formalization can be specialized straightforward into the greedy layer-wise pre-training algorithm updating $\boldsymbol{\lambda}^{(t)}$ in a proper way.

The update policy for $\boldsymbol{\lambda}^{(t)}$ mix coefficients is very important to ensure model convergence and performance. At every time t, each component of $\boldsymbol{\lambda}^{(t)}$ should be updated, starting with high values of unsupervised loss during first training iterations but leading close to zero in the long term, so supervised goal dominates at the end of the training procedure.

This paper proposes the Greedy Exponential Decay (GED) policy, which essentially fixes supervised loss coefficient to a constant value ($\lambda_0^{(t)} = 1$) and updates the remaining coefficients employing an exponential decay function. Therefore, the unsupervised loss coefficients are initialized to a given constant Λ and their value is calculated following this rule $\lambda_k^{(t)} = \Lambda\gamma^t$ for $k > 0$, being γ the exponential decay term. Notice that γ^t is γ powers t. Notice that other policies are possible and will be studied in future extensions of this paper.

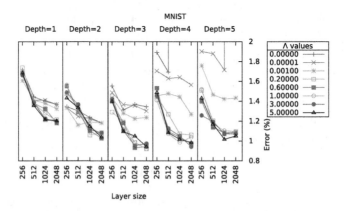

Fig. 1. Grid search results for GED algorithm in MNIST database. A grid with different values for initial mix Λ and layer sizes has been evaluated. For clarity purposes, the plot only shows a subset of all combinations large enough to observe trend in both hyper-parameters.

4   Experimental Evaluation

The GED method has been evaluated in two different tasks. First, MNIST dataset has been used to benchmark the method and to study its sensitivity for different hyper-parameters. Second, an indoor temperature forecasting task, taken from SML2010 UCI data set [1,15], has been employed to study the effect of this method for training time-series models. In all the experiments, ADADELTA algorithm [17] has been chosen as gradient descent optimizer, using a decay factor of $\gamma = 0.95$ and an epsilon of $\epsilon = 10^{-6}$. L2 regularization has been applied only to weights at the top layer (not biases) and fixed to $\epsilon = 0.01$. The algorithm has been implemented using APRIL-ANN toolkit [16], particularly its implementation of automatic differentiation.

4.1   MNIST Benchmark

In order to compare the proposed method with other literature approaches, experiments with the well-known MNIST data set [7] have been conducted. MNIST data set is an isolated digit classification task composed originally of 50000 training samples, 10000 for validation and 12000 for test. Different variations of this original data set are available, increasing the task difficulty. All variation data sets are formed by 10000 training samples, 2000 samples for validation and 50000 test samples. This paper conducts experiments with original MNIST and MNIST-basic variation.

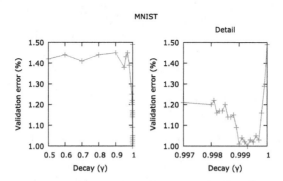

Fig. 2. Sensitivity of GED policy to decay γ hyper-parameter for a three layers DNN with 2048 neurons at each layer.

Training has been performed in mini-batches and monitored every two mini-batches. Training performance is measured using the empirical risk Eq. (1) averaged over the number of examples in two mini-batches, and validation performance is monitored by computing classification error (i.e. zero-one loss function) over the whole validation dataset. A 20 % masking noise has been used as perturbation for MNIST experiments.

Hyperopt [4] library have been used to perform automatic optimization of different hyper-parameters (learning rate, momentum, ...) for a DNN with three layers of 1024 neurons. After this step, a grid search has been conducted to evaluate the effect of Λ initial mix, layer sizes and model depth. Figure 1 shows the result of this grid search procedure. The figure shows that higher values of initial mix Λ are needed to achieve good performance, but values between of $\Lambda \in [0.2, 5.0]$ have very similar performance. The best classification error on validation set has been 1.01 %, achieved by a model with three layers of 2048 neurons and $\Lambda = 0.2$. In all cases decay term has been fixed to $\gamma = 0.999$.

Figure 2 shows the sensitivity of GED to different values of decay parameter γ. It can be observed a narrow range where sensitivity in this hyper-parameter is really increased, requiring a value of $\gamma \approx 0.999$ to ensure good performance. This behavior can be explained due to the effect of decaying speed in the importance of unsupervised loss. When γ approaches to 0 unsupervised training is negligible.

Table 1. Test error (%) plus its 95 % confidence interval in MNIST and MNIST-basic variation data sets. The proposed GED method uses a model with 3 hidden layers of 2048 neurons. For comparison purposes, SAE-3 and SDAE-3 results have been taken from [13] and SDAE-3J has been taken from [18].

Data set	SAE-3	SDAE-3	SDAE-3J	GED (proposed method)
MNIST	$1.40_{\pm0.23}$	$1.28_{\pm0.22}$	$1.10_{\pm0.21}$	$1.22_{\pm0.22}$
basic	$3.46_{\pm0.16}$	$2.84_{\pm0.15}$	$2.65_{\pm0.14}$	$2.72_{\pm0.14}$

For $\gamma = 1$, unsupervised training remains constant. And values of $\gamma \approx 0.999$ lead to a smooth and slow decaying of unsupervised loss effect, whose importance is negligible after approximately 10000 iterations. We conjecture that a value of γ close to $1/|\mathcal{D}|$ can be a good starting point to run a small grid search optimization of its value. Table 1 shows the test results of the proposed method, observing that its performance is equivalent to SDAE-3 results and better than the baseline SAE-3 in both benchmark data sets.

4.2 SML2010 Indoor Temperature Forecasting Task

This task is motivated by the application of predictive models to assist in energy efficiency problems. Indoor temperature data of the SML2010 data set from UCI machine learning repository [1,15] has been used to validate in laboratory the benefits of the proposed method. The data set contains 2016 training temperature points, 672 validation points and 672 test points. Every point is a 15 min average of temperature data. Trend have been removed applying first order differentiation to temperature series. A model with 48 inputs (12 h) and 12 output predictions (next 3 h) have been trained employing a sliding window to traverse the data set. For time-series task, the perturbation noise is a combination of Gaussian noise with $\sigma^2 = 0.01$ and a 10 % masking noise. In this case, the input layer DAE uses MSE as loss function, and internal hidden layers are logistic units, so cross-entropy loss function is required. Validation and test set performance has been measured by using Mean Absolute Error (MAE).

A grid search have been performed to optimize model hyper-parameters, so models with two to four layers, with $\{16, 32, 64, 128, 512, 1024\}$ neurons at each layer and with $\Lambda = \{0, 1\}$ have been tested.[1] The validation MAE result of this grid search is shown at Table 2. It is observed that the convergence of bigger networks is not attained when $\Lambda = 0$, while using higher values it achieves good performance even with large networks. Moving block bootstrap test [9] for pairwise data has been performed to compute statistical significance using 95 % confidence intervals, showing that for more than 3 hidden layers $\Lambda = 1$ improves the $\Lambda = 0$ baseline in almost all studied cases. This experimentation has been extended up to 10 layers DNNs with 64 hidden units to test the robustness of the method, observing a validation MAE which relies between 0.1274 to 0.1331.

---

[1] Note that $\Lambda = 0$ is equivalent to training without the proposed integrated method.

Table 2. Validation set MAE for a subset of the grid search combinations of number of layers (depth) and layer size for DNNs in SML2010 temperature forecasting task. In bold face are shown combinations where the $\Lambda = 1$ improves $\Lambda = 0$ result with statistically significant difference with a confidence of 95 % in a pairwise test.

Depth	Size	MAE $\Lambda = 0$	MAE $\Lambda = 1$
2	32	0.1298	0.1312
2	64	0.1292	0.1289
2	128	0.1300	0.1271
2	512	0.1320	0.1289
3	32	0.1322	**0.1266**
3	64	0.1350	**0.1257**
3	128	0.1308	0.1292
3	512	0.6160	**0.1312**
4	32	0.1352	**0.1295**
4	64	0.1341	0.1301
4	128	0.6159	**0.1293**
4	512	0.6164	**0.1352**

The final test set results, for the 3 layers model with 64 neurons, are 0.1269 when $\Lambda = 0$ and 0.1177 when $\Lambda = 1$, being their difference statistically significant under the stated bootstrap test [9].

5   Conclusions

This paper has presented a technique for integration of unsupervised and supervised criteria in order to perform training of DNNs in one phase, showing results equivalent to state-of-the-art greedy layer-wise unsupervised pre-training plus a fine-tuning stage. This integrated approach has been formalized in terms of a λ vector whose coefficients should be updated to follow a slow transition from a state with predominance of unsupervised criterion to a state of almost pure supervised criterion. This approach has been validated with MNIST benchmark and SML2010 temperature forecasting task. Time-series forecasting results motivate a thorough study introducing this approach into real time systems where the convergence of deep models is not always guaranteed. Improved techniques of updating the weights λ is the objective of future research. The effect of this integrated approach into gradients evolution during training is another open question which requires a more detailed study. A priori the proposed combination of unsupervised (auto-encoders) and supervised learning could be more effective than well known greedy layer-wise pre-training, because conditioning of unsupervised features to be discriminative by integration of the supervised goal, however, this remains an open question.

Acknowledgments. This work has been financed by the local government of *Generalitat Valenciana* under project GV/2015/088 and *Universidad CEU Cardenal Herrera*.

References

1. Bache, K., Lichman, M.: UCI machine learning repository (2016). http://archive. ics.uci.edu/ml
2. Bengio, Y., Lamblin, P., Popovici, D., Larochelle, H.: Greedy layer-wise training of deep networks. In: NIPS 2006, pp. 153–160. MIT Press (2007)
3. Bengio, Y., Simard, P., Frasconi, P.: Learning long-term dependencies with gradient descent is difficult. IEEE Trans. Neural Netw. **5**(2), 157–166 (1994)
4. Bergstra, J., Komer, B., Eliasmith, C., Yamins, D., Cox, D.D.: Hyperopt: a python library for model selection and hyperparameter optimization. Comp. Sci. Discov. **8**(1) (2015)
5. Glorot, X., Bengio, Y.: Understanding the difficulty of training deep feedforward neural networks. In: International Conference on AI and Statistics, pp. 249–256 (2010)
6. LeCun, Y., Bengio, Y., Hinton, G.: Deep learning. Nature **521**, 436–444 (2015)
7. Lecun, Y., Cortes, C.: The MNIST database of handwritten digits (1998). http:// yann.lecun.com/exdb/mnist/
8. Pardo, J., Zamora-Martínez, F., Botella-Rocamora, P.: Addendum: Pardo, J.; Zamora-Martínez, F.; Botella-Rocamora, P. online learning algorithm for time series forecasting suitable for low cost wireless sensor networks nodes. Sensors 2015, 15, 9277–9304. Senors **15**(7), 16831 (2015)
9. Politis, D.N., Romano, J.P.: The stationary bootstrap. J. Am. Stat. Assoc. **89**(428), 1303–1313 (1994)
10. Schmidhuber, J.: Deep learning in neural networks: an overview. Neural Netw. **61**, 85–117 (2015)
11. Schmidhuber, J.: Learning complex, extended sequences using the principle of history compression. Neural Comput. **4**(2), 234–242 (1992)
12. Vincent, P., Larochelle, H., Bengio, Y., Manzagol, P.A.: Extracting and composing robust features with denoising autoencoders. In: ICML, pp. 1096–1103 (2008)
13. Vincent, P., Larochelle, H., Lajoie, I., Bengio, Y., Manzagol, P.A.: Stacked denoising autoencoders: learning useful representations in a deep network with a local denoising criterion. J. Mach. Learn. Res. **11**, 3371–3408 (2010)
14. Zamora-Martínez, F., Romeu, P., Botella-Rocamora, P., Pardo, J.: On-line learning of indoor temperature forecasting models towards energy efficiency. Energ. Build. **83**, 162–172 (2014)
15. Zamora-Martínez, F., Romeu-Guallart, P., Pardo, J.: SML2010 data set (2014). https://archive.ics.uci.edu/ml/datasets/SML2010
16. Zamora-Martínez, F., España-Boquera, S., Gorbe-Moya, J., Pastor-Pellicer, J., Palacios-Corella, A.: APRIL-ANN toolkit, a pattern recognizer in Lua with artificial neural networks (2013). https://github.com/pakozm/april-ann
17. Zeiler, M.D.: Adadelta: an adaptive learning rate method (2012). arXiv preprint: arXiv:1212.5701
18. Zhou, Y., Arpit, D., Nwogu, I., Govindaraju, V.: Is Joint Training Better for Deep Auto-Encoders? ArXiv e-prints (2015)

Layer-Wise Relevance Propagation for Neural Networks with Local Renormalization Layers

Alexander Binder[1]([✉]), Grégoire Montavon[2], Sebastian Lapuschkin[3],
Klaus-Robert Müller[2,4], and Wojciech Samek[3]([✉])

[1] ISTD Pillar, Singapore University of Technology and Design, Singapore, Singapore
alexander_binder@sutd.edu.sg
[2] Machine Learning Group, Technische Universität Berlin, Berlin, Germany
[3] Machine Learning Group, Fraunhofer Heinrich Hertz Institute, Berlin, Germany
wojciech.samek@hhi.fraunhofer.de
[4] Department of Brain and Cognitive Engineering, Korea University,
Seoul, South Korea

Abstract. Layer-wise relevance propagation is a framework which allows to decompose the prediction of a deep neural network computed over a sample, e.g. an image, down to relevance scores for the single input dimensions of the sample such as subpixels of an image. While this approach can be applied directly to generalized linear mappings, product type non-linearities are not covered. This paper proposes an approach to extend layer-wise relevance propagation to neural networks with local renormalization layers, which is a very common product-type non-linearity in convolutional neural networks. We evaluate the proposed method for local renormalization layers on the CIFAR-10, Imagenet and MIT Places datasets.

Keywords: Neural networks · Image classification · Interpretability

1 Introduction

Artificial neural networks enjoy increasing popularity for image classification tasks. They have shown excellent performance in large scale competitions [4]. One reason is the ability to train neural networks with millions of training samples by parallelizing them on GPU hardware. This allows to use numbers of training samples which match the large number of parameters in deep neural networks. However, understanding what region of the image is important for a classification decision, is still an open question for neural networks, as well as for many other non-linear models. The work of [1] proposed Layer-wise Relevance Propagation (LRP) as a solution for explaining what pixels of an image are relevant for reaching a classification decision. This was done for neural networks, bag of word models [2,10], and in a subsequent work [5], for Fisher vectors.

This paper proposes an approach to extend LRP to neural networks with non-linearities beyond the commonly used neural network formulation. One example of such nonlinearities are local renormalization layers which can not be handled

© Springer International Publishing Switzerland 2016
A.E.P. Villa et al. (Eds.): ICANN 2016, Part II, LNCS 9887, pp. 63–71, 2016.
DOI: 10.1007/978-3-319-44781-0_8

by standard LRP [1]. The presented approach is based on first (or higher) order Taylor expansion. We consider a classification setup with real-valued outputs. A classifier f is a mapping of an input space $f : X \rightarrow \mathbb{R}$ such that $f(x) > 0$ denotes the presence of the class.

2   Layer-Wise Relevance Propagation for Neural Networks

In the following we consider neural networks consisting of layers of neurons. The output x_j of a neuron j is a non-linear activation function g as given by

$$x_j = g\Big(\sum_i w_{ij} x_i + b\Big) \tag{1}$$

Given an image x and a classifier f the aim of layer-wise relevance propagation is to assign each pixel p of x a pixel-wise relevance score $R_p^{(1)}$ such that

$$f(x) \approx \sum_p R_p^{(1)} \tag{2}$$

Pixels p with $R_p^{(1)} < 0$ contain evidence against the presence of a class, while $R_p^{(1)} > 0$ is considered as evidence for the presence of a class. These pixel-wise relevance scores can be visualized as an image called *heatmap* (see Fig. 1 for examples). Obviously, many possible such decompositions exist which satisfy Eq. 2. The work of [1] yield pixel-wise decompositions which are consistent with evaluation measures [8] and human intuition.

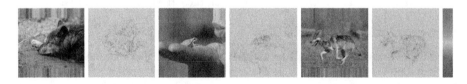

Fig. 1. Pixel-wise decompositions for classes wolf, frog and wolf using a neural network pretrained for the 1000 classes of the ILSVRC challenge.

Assume that we know the relevance $R_j^{(l+1)}$ of a neuron j at network layer $l+1$ for the classification decision $f(x)$, then we like to decompose this relevance into messages $R_{i \leftarrow j}^{(l,l+1)}$ sent to those neurons i at the layer l which provide inputs to neuron j such that Eq. 3 holds.

$$R_j^{(l+1)} = \sum_{i \in (l)} R_{i \leftarrow j}^{(l,l+1)} \tag{3}$$

We can then define the relevance of a neuron i at layer l by summing all messages from neurons at layer $l+1$ as in Eq. 4

$$R_i^{(l)} = \sum_{j \in (l+1)} R_{i \leftarrow j}^{(l,l+1)} \tag{4}$$

Equations 3 and 4 define the propagation of relevance from layer $l+1$ to layer l. The relevance of the output neuron at layer M is $R_1^{(M)} = f(x)$. The pixel-wise scores are the resulting relevances of the input neurons $R_d^{(1)}$.

The work in [1] established two formulas for computing the messages $R_{i \leftarrow j}^{(l,l+1)}$. The first formula called ϵ-rule is given by

$$R_{i \leftarrow j}^{(l,l+1)} = \frac{z_{ij}}{z_j + \epsilon \cdot \text{sign}(z_j)} R_j^{(l+1)} \qquad (5)$$

with $z_{ij} = (w_{ij}x_i)^p$ and $z_j = \sum_{k:w_{kj} \neq 0} z_{kj}$. The variable ϵ is a "stabilizer" term whose purpose is to avoid numerical degenerations when z_j is close to zero, and which is chosen to be small. The second formula called β-rule is given by

$$R_{i \leftarrow j}^{(l,l+1)} = \left((1 + \beta) \frac{z_{ij}^+}{z_j^+} - \beta \frac{z_{ij}^-}{z_j^-} \right) R_j^{(l+1)} \qquad (6)$$

where the positive and negative weighted activations are treated separately. The variable β controls how much inhibition is incorporated in the relevance redistribution. A fairly large value for β (e.g. $\beta = 1$) leads to sharper heatmaps. In both formulas the message $R_{i \leftarrow j}^{(l,l+1)}$ has the following structure

$$R_{i \leftarrow j}^{(l,l+1)} = v_{ij} R_j^{(l+1)} \quad \text{with} \quad \sum_i v_{ij} = 1 \qquad (7)$$

The meaningfulness of the resulting pixel-wise decomposition for the input layer $R_d^{(1)}$ comes from the fact that the terms v_{ij} are derived from the weighted activations $w_{ij}x_i$ of the input neurons. Note that layer-wise relevance propagation does not use gradients in contrast to backpropagation during the training phase. For full details on layer-wise relevance propagation the reader is referred to [1].

3   Extending LRP to Local Renormalization Layers

We consider a general neuron j whose pooling and activation does not fit into the structure given by Eq. 1, and consequently, intuition for a possible redistribution formula is lacking. In this paper we propose a strategy for such neurons, based on the Taylor expansion of its activation function. A Taylor-based approach was used in [6] for decomposing ReLU neurons by exploiting their local linearity. Here, we consider instead fully nonlinear neurons.

Suppose we can define for each neuron i input to neuron j a term v_{ij} which is derived from its activation x_i such that $\sum_i v_{ij} = 1$. Then we can define a message $R_{i \leftarrow j}^{(l,l+1)} = v_{ij} R_j^{(l+1)}$. Such messages were used in Eqs. 5 and 6 where the weighting v_{ij} was chosen to depend on the weighted activations of neuron i: $v_{ij} = c (w_{ij}x_i)^p$ and $v_{ij} = c_1 z_{ij}^+ + c_2 z_{ij}^-$, respectively. For differentiable neurons, such weighting can be obtained by performing a first order Taylor expansion. Let $x_j = g(x_{h_1}, \ldots, x_{h_n})$ be a nonlinear activation function. Then, by Taylor expansion at some reference point $(\tilde{x}_{h_1}, \ldots, \tilde{x}_{h_n})$, we get

$$x_j \approx g(\widetilde{x}_{h_1}, \ldots, \widetilde{x}_{h_n}) + \sum_{i \leftarrow j} \frac{\partial g}{\partial x_{h_i}} (\widetilde{x}_{h_1}, \ldots, \widetilde{x}_{h_n})(x_{h_i} - \widetilde{x}_{h_i}). \tag{8}$$

Elements of the sum can be assigned to incoming neurons, and the zero-order term can be redistributed equally between them, leading to the decomposition

$$\forall_{i \leftarrow j} : \; z_{ij} = \frac{1}{n} g(\widetilde{x}_{h_1}, \ldots, \widetilde{x}_{h_n}) + \frac{\partial g}{\partial x_{h_i}} (\widetilde{x}_{h_1}, \ldots, \widetilde{x}_{h_n})(x_{h_i} - \widetilde{x}_{h_i}) \tag{9}$$

of the neuron activation onto its input neurons. Local renormalization layers have been shown to improve the performance in deep neural networks [4]. Consider the local renormalization y_k of a neuron x_k by the set of its surrounding neurons $\{x_1, \ldots, x_n\}$ as

$$y_k(x_1, \ldots, x_n) = \frac{x_k}{(1 + b \sum_{i=1}^{n} x_i^2)^c} \tag{10}$$

This interaction can be modeled by a layer in the network that has an activation function as given in Eq. 10. Local renormalization layers represent a non-linearity which cannot be tackled exactly by LRP as introduced in [1], however the strategy proposed above can be applied.

One choice to be made is the point at which to perform the Taylor expansion. There are two apparent candidates, firstly the actual input to the renormalization layer $z_1 = (x_1, \ldots, x_n)$ and, secondly, the input corresponding to the case when only the neuron k fires which is to be normalized $z_2 = (0, \ldots \ldots, 0, x_k, 0, \ldots, 0)$. The partial derivative of y at z_2 is zero for all variables x_i with $i \neq k$ due to

$$\frac{\partial y_k}{\partial x_j} = \frac{\delta_{kj}}{(1 + b \sum_{i=1}^{n} x_i^2)^c} - 2bc \frac{x_k x_j}{(1 + b \sum_{i=1}^{n} x_i^2)^{c+1}} \tag{11}$$

This implies that the Taylor approximation has no off-diagonal contribution.

$$y_k(z_1) \approx y_k(z_2) + 0 = \frac{x_k}{(1 + b x_k^2)^c} \tag{12}$$

Therefore we apply the Taylor series around the point z_1:

$$y_k(z_2) \approx y_k(z_1) + \nabla y_k(z_1) \cdot (z_2 - z_1) \tag{13}$$

$$\Rightarrow y_k(z_1) \approx y_k(z_2) + \nabla y_k(z_1) \cdot (z_1 - z_2) \tag{14}$$

$$\Rightarrow y_k(z_1) \approx \frac{x_k}{(1 + b x_k^2)^c} - 2bc \sum_{j:j \neq k} \frac{x_k x_j^2}{(1 + b \sum_{i=1}^{n} x_i^2)^{c+1}} \tag{15}$$

This weighting satisfies the following qualitative properties: for the neuron input x_k which is to be normalized, the sign of the relevance is kept. For suppressing neighboring neurons x_i, $i \neq k$, the sign of the relevance can be flipped in line with their suppressing property. The absolute value of the relevance received by the suppressing neurons is proportional to the square of their input. In the limits $c \to 0$ and $b \to 0$, the local renormalization converges against the identity, and the approximation recovers the identity. A baseline to compare against is to treat the normalization as constant. In that case the weights v_{ij} for the relevance propagation in Eq. 3 become a zero one vector, the relevance is propagated only to that neuron which is to be normalized: $v_{ij} = 1$ if and only if i is the neuron which is to be normalized by neuron j.

4 Experiments

We need to define a measure for meaningfulness and quality of a pixel-wise decomposition in order to evaluate the various strategies to compute it. Here we use an idea from [8]: A pixel p is considered highly relevant for the classification score $f(x)$ of the image x if modifying it by assigning it a random RGB value $\tilde{x}(p)$, and classifying the modified image $\bar{x}_p = x \setminus \{x(p)\} \cup \{\tilde{x}(p)\}$ results in a strong decrease of the real-valued classification score $f(\bar{x}_p)$. This idea can be extended by sequentially modifying pixels from the most relevant to the least relevant. The result is a graph of the prediction score $f(\bar{x})$ as a function of the number of modified pixels. An example for some sequences which will be explained below is shown in Fig. 2. We can use these graphs to evaluate the meaningfulness of a pixel-wise decomposition.

In the first experiment we compare the measure when flipping highest-scoring pixels first, against flipping pixels in random order, and against flipping lowest scoring pixels first. If the classifier is able to identify pixels that are important for classification, then flipping highest scoring pixels first should result in the fastest decaying curve, while flipping lowest scoring pixels first should result in the slowest decrease. Figure 2 tests this property on the CIFAR-10 dataset [3] which consists of 50000 images of size 32×32 drawn from 10 object classes. Scores are averaged over the 5000 images of the test set of CIFAR-10 for a classifier in which local renormalization layers are treated as the identity during computation of pixel-wise scores. Experiments corroborate that flipping highest scoring pixels

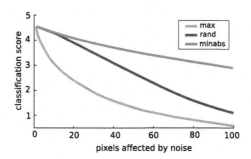

Fig. 2. Decrease of classification score as pixels are sequentially replaced by random noise on the CIFAR-10 dataset. Red curve: pixels with highest pixel-wise scores are flipped first. Blue curve: pixels are flipped in random order. Green curve: least relevant pixels are flipped first. A similar comparison for Imagenet is found in [8]. (Color figure online)

first results in the fastest decrease of the prediction score on average over the test set. The decrease is sharper compared to random flipping, or flipping lowest scoring pixels first.

In a second experiment we compare which treatment of the local renormalization layer is best to identify those pixels that are most relevant for classifying an image. The two tested approaches for treating the local renormalization are (1) like it would be the identity, (2) by first order Taylor expansion as given by Eq. 15. These approaches are furthermore tested when used in conjunction with the two methods proposed by [1], namely, the ϵ-rule in Eq. 5 with a fixed value of the numerical stabilizer ϵ, and the β-rule shown in Eq. 6, with fixed β.

Table 1. Comparison of different types of LRN layer treatments for two approaches of computing pixel-wise scores for CIFAR-10. Lower scores are better.

Rule for basic layers	Rule for normalization layers	AUC score
Eqs. 4, 5, $\epsilon = 0.01$	identity	37.10
Eqs. 4, 5, $\epsilon = 0.01$	first-order Taylor	35.47
Eqs. 4, 6, $\beta = 1$	identity	56.13
Eqs. 4, 6, $\beta = 1$	first-order Taylor	53.82

We measure the quality of heatmaps by perturbing highest pixels first and computing the area under the curve (AUC). Lower AUC averaged over a large number of images indicates a better identification of pixel relevance by the heatmap. Results on CIFAR-10 are shown in Table 1. We observe that in all cases using first order Taylor in normalization layers improves the heatmap AUC score. This shows its effectiveness for dealing with non-linear neuron layers.

Table 2. Comparison of different types of heatmap computations for Imagenet and MIT Places. We use the shortcut notation Δ_a^b for expressing $\text{AUC}_a - \text{AUC}_b$. Thus, a negative value indicates that the method produces better heatmaps with parameter a than with parameter b. Note that ϵ refers to Eqs. 4 and 5; β refers to Eqs. 4 and 6.

Dataset	Methods	$\Delta_{\epsilon=1}^{\epsilon=0.01}$	$\Delta_{\epsilon=0.01}^{\epsilon=100}$	$\Delta_{\epsilon=100}^{\beta=1}$	$\Delta_{\beta=1}^{\beta=0}$
Imagenet	identity	−21.29	2.75	−42.61	−49.07
	Taylor	−12.29	−41.75	−34.44	−50.76
MIT Places	identity	−20.19	12.91	−14.55	−49.37
	Taylor	−11.65	−22.55	−8.82	−48.7

We perform the same experiments also with Imagenet [7] and MIT Places [12] datasets, each time evaluating results for 5000 images from their respective unlabeled test sets. Note that computing a heatmap requires only a predicted

Table 3. Impact of using the Taylor method in various settings. Negative value indicates that using the Taylor expansion for the local renormalization is better in AUC terms (i.e. heatmaps are more representative of the importance of each pixel).

Dataset	Methods	$\epsilon = 1$	$\epsilon = 0.01$	$\epsilon = 100$	$\beta = 1$	$\beta = 0$
Imagenet	$\text{AUC}_{\text{Taylor}} - \text{AUC}_{\text{identity}}$	-35.84	-26.84	8.47	0.29	1.98
MIT Places	$\text{AUC}_{\text{Taylor}} - \text{AUC}_{\text{identity}}$	-33.13	-24.59	5.34	-0.39	-1.06

class label, not a ground truth. We evaluated results for the parameter settings $\beta = 0$, $\beta = 1$ in Eq. 6 and $\epsilon = 0.01$, $\epsilon = 1$, $\epsilon = 100$ in Eq. 5. Table 2 shows the difference of AUC between variants of LRP, when using either the identity or the Taylor expansion for local renormalization layers. We observe the following ordering starting with the lowest (best) AUC: $\epsilon = 1$, $\epsilon = 0.01$, $\epsilon = 100$, $\beta = 1$, $\beta = 0$. This order holds independent of whether we consider Imagenet or MIT places, when using Taylor for local renormalization layers. When using identity

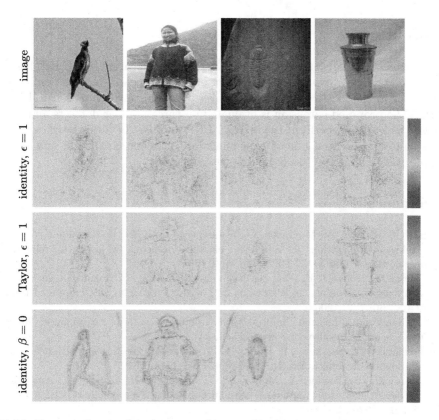

Fig. 3. Top row shows original unwarped image. Remaining rows show heatmaps produced by various parameters of the LRP method.

instead of Taylor, the order remain the same, except for $\epsilon = 100$ and $\epsilon = 0.01$ that are swapped. This is by itself an interesting result demonstrating that use of Taylor in the normalization layer does not disrupt the overall properties of relevance propagation techniques. For a comparison to other approaches such as heatmaps based on deconvolutions [11], or backpropagated gradients [9] we refer to [8].

Table 3 shows the difference of AUC between Taylor and identity for local renormalization layers, for various choices of datasets and LRP parameters. We observe that for the parameters with best AUC ($\epsilon = 1$ and $\epsilon = 0.01$), using Taylor expansion for representing local renormalization layers further improves the AUC scores. For the remaining choices the results are on par or slightly worse. This is consistent with the interpretation of large values of ϵ as smoothing out small contributions. It is also consistent with the observation that $\beta = 1$ and $\beta = 0$ yield both smooth heatmaps in general. Heatmaps for some parameters of interest are shown in Fig. 3. Taylor with $\epsilon = 1$ has both high pixel selectivity and low noise, which in agreement with its measured superiority in the quantitative experiments.

5   Conclusion

We have presented an extension of layer-wise relevance propagation (LRP) based on first-order Taylor expansions for product-type nonlinearities. Such nonlinearities occur in the local renormalization layers of deep convolutional neural networks. The proposed extension is evaluated on three popular datasets and it is shown to clearly outperform the original LRP method. In future work we will investigate the potential gain of using higher order Taylor expansions, and apply the method to a larger class of neural network layers.

References

1. Bach, S., Binder, A., Montavon, G., Klauschen, F., Müller, K.-R., Samek, W.: On pixel-wise explanations for non-linear classifier decisions by layer-wise relevance propagation. PLOS ONE **10**(7), e0130140 (2015)
2. Csurka, G., Dance, C.R., Fan, L., Willamowski, J., Bray, C.: Visual categorization with bags of keypoints. In: Workshop on Statistical Learning in Computer Vision, ECCV, pp. 1–22 (2004)
3. Krizhevsky, A.: Learning multiple layers of features from tiny images (2009). http://www.cs.toronto.edu/~kriz/cifar.html
4. Krizhevsky, A., Sutskever, I., Hinton, G.E.: Imagenet classification with deep convolutional neural networks. In: NIPS, pp. 1106–1114 (2012)
5. Lapuschkin, S., Binder, A., Montavon, G., Müller, K.-R., Samek, W.: Analyzing classifiers: fisher vectors and deep neural networks. In: Proceedings of IEEE CVPR, pp. 2912–2920 (2016)
6. Montavon, G., Bach, S., Binder, A., Samek, W., Müller, K.-R.: Explaining nonlinear classification decisions with deep taylor decomposition. CoRR, abs/1512.02479 (2015)

7. Russakovsky, O., Deng, J., Hao, S., Krause, J., Satheesh, S., Ma, S., Huang, Z., Karpathy, A., Khosla, A., Bernstein, M., Berg, A.C., Fei-Fei, L.: ImageNet large scale visual recognition challenge. IJCV **115**, 1–42 (2015)
8. Samek, W., Binder, A., Montavon, G., Bach, S., Müller, K.-R.: Evaluating the visualization of what a deep neural network has learned. CoRR, abs/1509.06321 (2015)
9. Simonyan, K., Vedaldi, A., Zisserman, A.: Deep inside convolutional networks: visualising image classification models and saliency maps. CoRR, abs/1312.6034 (2013)
10. van de Sande, K.E.A., Gevers, T., Snoek, C.G.M.: Evaluating color descriptors for object and scene recognition. IEEE Trans. Pattern Anal. Mach. Intell. **32**(9), 1582–1596 (2010)
11. Zeiler, M.D., Fergus, R.: Visualizing and understanding convolutional networks. In: Fleet, D., Pajdla, T., Schiele, B., Tuytelaars, T. (eds.) ECCV 2014, Part I. LNCS, vol. 8689, pp. 818–833. Springer, Heidelberg (2014)
12. Zhou, B., Lapedriza, A., Xiao, J., Torralba, A., Oliva, A.: Learning deep features for scene recognition using places database. In: Advances in NIPS, pp. 487–495 (2014)

Analysis of Dropout Learning Regarded as Ensemble Learning

Kazuyuki Hara[1]($\boxtimes$), Daisuke Saitoh[2], and Hayaru Shouno[3]

[1] College of Industrial Technology, Nihon University, 1-2-1 Izumi-cho,
Narashino-shi, Chiba 275-8575, Japan
hara.kazuyuki@nihon-u.ac.jp
[2] Graduate School of Industrial Technology, Nihon University, Chiba, Japan
[3] Graduate School of Informatics and Engineering, The University
of Electro-Communications, 1-5-1 Chofugaoka, Chofu-shi, Tokyo 182-8585, Japan

Abstract. Deep learning is the state-of-the-art in fields such as visual object recognition and speech recognition. This learning uses a large number of layers, huge number of units, and connections. Therefore, overfitting is a serious problem. To avoid this problem, dropout learning is proposed. Dropout learning neglects some inputs and hidden units in the learning process with a probability, p, and then, the neglected inputs and hidden units are combined with the learned network to express the final output. We find that the process of combining the neglected hidden units with the learned network can be regarded as ensemble learning, so we analyze dropout learning from this point of view.

Keywords: Dropout learning · Overfitting · Regularization · Ensemble learning · Soft-committee machine · Teacher-student formulation

1 Introduction

Deep learning [1,2] is attracting much attention in the field of visual object recognition, speech recognition, object detection, and many other domains. It provides automatic feature extraction and has the ability to achieve outstanding performance [3,4].

Deep learning uses a very deep layered network and a huge number of data, so overfitting is a serious problem. To avoid overfitting, regularization is used. Hinton et al. proposed a regularization method called "dropout learning" [5] for this purpose. Dropout learning follows two processes. At learning time, some hidden units are neglected with a probability p, and this process reduces the network size. At test time, learned hidden units and those not learned are summed up and multiplied by p to calculate the network output. We find that summing up the learned and not learned units multiplied by p can be regarded as ensemble learning.

In this paper, we analyze dropout learning regarded as ensemble learning [6]. On-line learning [7,8] is used to learn a network. We analyze dropout learning regarded as ensemble learning, except for using different sets of hidden units in dropout learning. We also analyze dropout learning regarded as an L2 normalizer [9].

© Springer International Publishing Switzerland 2016
A.E.P. Villa et al. (Eds.): ICANN 2016, Part II, LNCS 9887, pp. 72–79, 2016.
DOI: 10.1007/978-3-319-44781-0_9

2 Model

In this paper, we use a teacher-student formulation and assume the existence of a teacher network (teacher) that produces the desired output for the student network (student). By introducing the teacher, we can directly measure the similarity of the student weight vector to that of the teacher. First, we formulate a teacher and a student, and then introduce the gradient descent algorithm.

The teacher and student are a soft committee machine with N input units, hidden units, and an output, as shown in Fig. 1. The teacher consists of K hidden units, and the student consists of K' hidden units. Each hidden unit is a perceptron. The kth hidden weight vector of the teacher is $\boldsymbol{B}_k = (B_{k1}, \ldots, B_{kN})$, and the k'th hidden weight vector of student is $\boldsymbol{J}_{k'}^{(m)} = (J_{k'1}^{(m)}, \ldots, J_{k'N}^{(m)})$, where m denotes learning iterations. In the soft committee machine, all hidden-to-output weights are fixed to be $+1$ [8]. This network calculates the majority vote of hidden outputs.

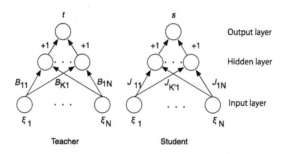

Fig. 1. Network structures of teacher and student

We assume that both the teacher and the student receive N-dimensional input $\boldsymbol{\xi}^{(m)} = (\xi_1^m, \ldots, \xi_N^{(m)})$, that the teacher outputs $t^{(m)} = \sum_{k=1}^{K} t_k^{(m)} = \sum_{k=1}^{K} g(d_k^{(m)})$, and that the student outputs $s^{(m)} = \sum_{k'=1}^{K'} s_{k'}^{(m)} = \sum_{k'=1}^{K'} g(y_{k'}^{(m)})$. Here, $g(\cdot)$ is the output function of a hidden unit, $d_k^{(m)}$ is the inner potential of the kth hidden unit of the teacher calculated using $d_k^{(m)} = \sum_{i=1}^{N} B_{ki}\xi_i^{(m)}$, and $y_{k'}^{(m)}$ is the inner potential of the k'th hidden unit of the student calculated using $y_{k'}^{(m)} = \sum_{i=1}^{N} J_{k'i}^{(m)}\xi_i^{(m)}$.

We assume that the ith elements $\xi_i^{(m)}$ of the independently drawn input $\boldsymbol{\xi}^{(m)}$ are uncorrelated random variables with zero mean and unit variance; that is, that the ith element of the input is drawn from a probability distribution $P(\xi_i)$. The thermodynamic limit of $N \to \infty$ is also assumed. The statistics of the inputs in the thermodynamic limit are $\left\langle \xi_i^{(m)} \right\rangle = 0$, $\left\langle (\xi_i^{(m)})^2 \right\rangle \equiv \sigma_\xi^2 = 1$, and $\langle \|\boldsymbol{\xi}^{(m)}\| \rangle = \sqrt{N}$, where $\langle \cdots \rangle$ denotes the average and $\| \cdot \|$ denotes the norm of a vector. Each element B_{ki}, $k = 1 \sim K$ is drawn from a probability distribution with zero mean and $1/N$ variance. With the assumption of the thermodynamic limit, the statistics of the teacher weight vector are $\langle B_{ki} \rangle = 0, \langle (B_{ki})^2 \rangle \equiv \sigma_B^2 = 1/N$, and $\langle \| \boldsymbol{B_k} \| \rangle = 1$. This means that any combination of $\boldsymbol{B}_l \cdot \boldsymbol{B}_{l'} = 0$. The distribution of inner potential $d_k^{(m)}$ follows a Gaussian distribution with zero mean and unit variance in the thermodynamic limit.

For the sake of analysis, we assume that each element of $J_{k'i}^{(0)}$, which is the initial value of the student vector $\boldsymbol{J}_{k'}^{(0)}$, is drawn from a probability distribution with zero mean and $1/N$ variance. The statistics of the k'th hidden weight vector of the student are $\left\langle J_{k'i}^{(0)} \right\rangle = 0, \left\langle (J_{k'i}^{(0)})^2 \right\rangle \equiv \sigma_J^2 = 1/N$, and $\left\langle \| \boldsymbol{J}_{k'}^{(0)} \| \right\rangle = 1$ in the thermodynamic limit. This means that any combination of $\boldsymbol{J}_l^{(0)} \cdot \boldsymbol{J}_{l'}^{(0)} = 0$. The output function of the hidden units of the student $g(\cdot)$ is the same as that of the teacher. The statistics of the student weight vector at the mth iteration are $\left\langle J_{k'i}^{(m)} \right\rangle = 0, \left\langle (J_{k'i}^{(m)})^2 \right\rangle = (Q_{k'k'}^{(m)})^2/N$, and $\left\langle \| \boldsymbol{J}_{k'}^{(m)} \| \right\rangle = Q_{k'k'}^{(m)}$. Here, $(Q_{k'k'}^{(m)})^2 = \boldsymbol{J}_{k'}^{(m)} \cdot \boldsymbol{J}_{k'}^{(m)}$. The distribution of the inner potential $y_{k'}^{(m)}$ follows a Gaussian distribution with zero mean and $(Q_{k'k'}^{(m)})^2$ variance in the thermodynamic limit.

Next, we introduce the stochastic gradient descent (SGD) algorithm for the soft committee machine. The generalization error is defined as the squared error ε averaged over possible inputs:

$$\varepsilon_g^{(m)} = \left\langle \varepsilon^{(m)} \right\rangle = \frac{1}{2} \left\langle (t^{(m)} - s^{(m)})^2 \right\rangle = \frac{1}{2} \left\langle \left(\sum_{k=1}^{K} g(d_k^{(m)}) - \sum_{k'=1}^{K'} g(y_{k'}^{(m)}) \right)^2 \right\rangle, \tag{1}$$

At each learning step m, a new uncorrelated input, $\boldsymbol{\xi}^{(m)}$, is presented, and the current hidden weight vector of the student $\boldsymbol{J}_{k'}^{(m)}$ is updated using

$$\boldsymbol{J}_{k'}^{(m+1)} = \boldsymbol{J}_{k'}^{(m)} + \frac{\eta}{N} \left(\sum_{l=1}^{K} g(d_l^{(m)}) - \sum_{l'=1}^{K'} g(y_{l'}^{(m)}) \right) g'(y_{k'}^{(m)}) \boldsymbol{\xi}^{(m)}, \tag{2}$$

where η is the learning step size and $g'(x)$ is the derivative of the output function of the hidden unit $g(x)$.

On-line learning uses a new input at once, therefore, overfitting does not occur. To evaluate the dropout learning in on-line learning, pre-selected whole inputs frequently use in a on-line manner. From our experiences, when the input dimension is N, then overfitting occurs for pre-selected whole $10 \times N$ inputs.

3   Dropout Learning and Ensemble Learning

In this section, we compare dropout learning and ensemble learning regarded as a way of calculating network output.

3.1   Ensemble Learning

Eensemble learning is performed by using many learners (referred to as students) to achieve better performance [6]. In ensemble learning, each student learns the teacher independently, and each output is averaged to calculate the ensemble output s_{en}.

$$s_{en} = \sum_{k'_{en}=1}^{K_{en}} C_{k'_{en}} s_{k'_{en}} = \sum_{k'_{en}=1}^{K_{en}} C_{k'_{en}} \sum_{k'=1}^{K'} g(y_{k'}) \tag{3}$$

Here, $C_{k'_{en}}$ is a weight for averaging. K_{en} is the number of students.

Figure 2 shows computer simulation results. The teacher and student include two hidden units. The output function $g(x)$ is the error function $\mathrm{erf}(x/\sqrt{2}) = \int_{-x}^{x} dt \exp(-t^2/s)/\sqrt{2\pi}$. In the figure, the horizontal axis is time $t = m/N$. Here, m is the iteration number, and N is the dimension of input units. Input dimension is $N = 10000$, and $10 \times N$ inputs are frequently used. The vertical axis is the mean squared error (MSE) for N input data. Each elements $\xi_i^{(m)}$ of the independently drawn input $\boldsymbol{\xi}^{(m)}$ are uncorrelated random variables with zero mean and unit variance. Target for $\boldsymbol{\xi}^{(m)}$ is the teacher output. The teacher and the initial student weight vectors are set as described in Sect. 2. In the figure, "Single" is the result of using a single student. "m2" is the result of using an ensemble of two students, "m3" is that of an ensemble of three students, and "m4" is that of ensemble of four students. As shown, the ensemble of four students outperformed the other two cases.

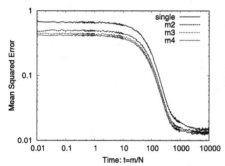

Fig. 2. Effect of ensemble learning

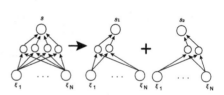

Fig. 3. Network divided into two networks to apply ensemble learning

Next, we modify the ensemble learning. We divide the student (with K' hidden units) into K_{en} networks (See Fig. 3. Here, $K' = 4$ and $K_{en} = 2$). These divided networks learn the teacher independently, and then we calculate the ensemble output s_{en} by averaging the outputs $s_{k'_{en}}$ as:

$$s_{en} = \frac{1}{K_{en}} \sum_{k'_{en}=1}^{K_{en}} s_{k'_{en}} = \frac{1}{K_{en}} \sum_{k'_{en}=1}^{K_{en}} \sum_{l'=1}^{M/K_{en}} g(y_{k'_{en}l'}). \tag{4}$$

Here, $s_{k'_{en}}$ is the output of a divided network with M/K_{en} hidden units, and $g(y_{k'_{en}l'})$ is the l'th hidden output in the k'_{en}th divided network. Equation (4) corresponds to Eq. (3) when $C_{k'_{en}} = \frac{1}{K_{en}}$ and $K' = \frac{M}{K_{en}}$.

3.2 Dropout Learning

In this subsection, we introduce dropout learning [5]. Dropout learning is used in deep learning to prevent overfitting. A small number of data compared with the size of a network may cause overfitting [10]. In the state of overfitting, the learning error (the error for learning data) and the test error (the error by cross-validation) become different. Figure 4 shows the result of the SGD and that of dropout learning. The soft committee machine was used for both the teacher and student. erf$(x/\sqrt{2})$ was used as the output function $g(x)$. Input dimension is $N = 1000$, and the teacher had two hidden units, and the student had 100 hidden units. The input and its target are generated as those of Fig. 2. The learning step size η was set to 0.01, and 1000 pieces of inputs were used iteratively for learning. In Fig. 4(a) shows the learning curve of the SGD. In this setting, overfitting occurred. Figure 4(b) shows the learning curve of the SGD with dropout learning. The learning error was small compared with the test error; however, the difference between the learning error and the test error was not as significant as that of the SGD. Therefore, these results shows that dropout learning prevent overfitting.

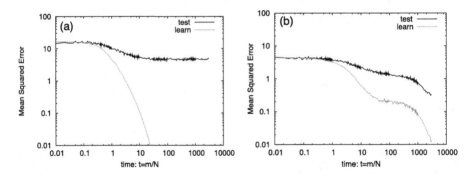

Fig. 4. Effect of dropout. (a) is learning curve of SGD, and (b) is that of dropout learning.

The learning equation of dropout learning for the soft committee machine can be written as the next equation.

$$\boldsymbol{J}_{k'}^{(m+1)} = \boldsymbol{J}_{k'}^{(m)} + \frac{\eta}{N} \left(\sum_{l=1}^{K} g(d_l^{(m)}) - \sum_{l' \notin D^{(m)}}^{(1-p)K'} g(y_{l'}^{(m)}) \right) g'(y_{k'}^{(m)}) \boldsymbol{\xi}^{(m)}, \quad (5)$$

Here, $D^{(m)}$ shows a set of hidden units that is randomly selected with respect to the probability p from all the hidden units at the mth iteration. The hidden units in $D^{(m)}$ are not subject to learning. After the learning, the student's output $s^{(m)}$ is calculated by the sum of learned hidden outputs and those not learned multiplied by p.

$$s^{(m)} = p * \left\{ \sum_{l' \notin D^{(m)}}^{(1-p)K'} g(y_{l'}^{(m)}) + \sum_{l' \in D^{(m)}}^{pK'} g(y_{l'}^{(m-1)}) \right\} \qquad (6)$$

This equation is regarded as the ensemble of a learned network (the first term) and that of a not learned network (the second term) when the probability is $p = 0.5$. Equation 6 is correspond to Eq. (4) when $p = 1/K_{en}$ and $K_{en} = 2$. However, a set of hidden units in $D^{(m)}$ is selected at random in every iteration. So, dropout learning is regarded as ensemble learning performed by using a different set of hidden units in every iteration. Instead, the original ensemble learning is the average of the fixed set of hidden units throughout the learning. This difference may cause the difference in performances between dropout learning and ensemble learning.

4   Results

4.1   Comparison Between Dropout Learning and Ensemble Learning

In this section, the error function $\mathrm{erf}(x/\sqrt{2})$ is used as the output function $g(x)$. We compared dropout learning and ensemble learning. We used two soft committee machines with 50 hidden units for ensemble learning. For dropout learning, we used one soft committee machine with 100 hidden units. We set $p = 0.5$; then, dropout learning selected 50 hidden units in $D^{(m)}$ with 50 unselected hidden units remaining. Therefore, dropout learning and ensemble learning had the same architectures. Input dimension is $N = 1000$, and the learning step size was set to $\eta = 0.01$. The input and its target are generated as those of Fig. 2. N inputs were used iteratively for learning. Figure 5 shows the results. The horizontal axes is time $t = m/N$, and the vertical axis is the MSE calculated for N input data. In Fig. 5(a), "single" shows the soft-committee machines with 50 hidden units. "ensemble" shows the results given by ensemble learning. Test errors are used in these figures. In Fig. 5(b), "test" shows the MSE given by the test data. "learn" shows the MSE given by the learning data. Results are obtained by average of 10 trials. As shown in Fig. 5(a), the ensemble learning achieved an MSE smaller than that of the single network. However, dropout learning achieved an MSE smaller than that of ensemble learning. Therefore, ensemble learning using a different set of hidden units in every iteration (this is the dropout) performs better than when using the same set of hidden units throughout the learning. Note that even with dropout learning using more hidden units than ensemble learning, overfitting did not occur. Therefore, in the next subsection, we will compare dropout learning with the SGD with L2 regularization.

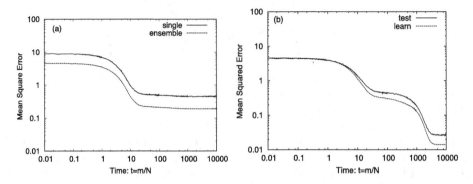

Fig. 5. Results of comparison between dropout learning and ensemble learning. (a) is ensemble learning of two networks, and (b) is dropout learning with respect to $p = 0.5$.

4.2 Comparison Between Dropout Learning and SGD with L2 Regularization

The next learning equation shows the SGD with L2 regularization.

$$J_{k'}^{(m+1)} = J_{k'}^{(m)} + \frac{\eta}{N} \left(\sum_{l=1}^{K} g(d_l^{(m)}) - \sum_{l'=1}^{K'} g(y_{l'}^{(m)}) \right) g'(y_{k'}^{(m)}) \boldsymbol{\xi}^{(m)} - \alpha \| J_{k'}^{(m)} \|^2. \quad (7)$$

Here, α is a coefficient of the L2 penalty.

In Fig. 6, we show the learning results of the SGD with L2 regularization with $\alpha = 1e - 6$. Results are obtained by average of 10 trials. The conditions were the same as those of Fig. 5.

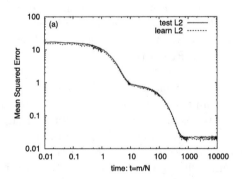

Fig. 6. Learning curve of SGD with L2 normalization

From comparison between Figs. 5(b) and 6, the residual error of dropout learning was almost the same as that of the SGD with L2 regularization.

Therefore, the regularization effort of dropout learning is the same as the L2 regularization. Note that for the SGD with L2 regularization, we must choose α in trials; however, dropout learning has no tuning parameter.

5 Conclusion

In this paper, we analyzed dropout learning regarded as ensemble learning. In ensemble learning, we divide the network into several sub-networks, and then we learn each sub-network independently. After the learning, the ensemble output is calculated by using the average of the sub-network outputs. We showed that dropout learning can be regarded as ensemble learning except for using a different set of hidden units in every learning iteration. Using a different set of hidden unit outperforms ensemble learning. We also showed that dropout learning achieves the same performance as the L2 regularizer. Our future work is the theoretical analysis of dropout learning with ReLU activation function.

Acknowledgments. The authors thank Dr. Masato Okada and Dr. Hideitsu Hino for insightful discussions.

References

1. Hinton, G.E., Osindero, S., Teh, Y.: A fast learning algorithm for deep belief nets. Neural Comput. **18**, 1527–1554 (2006)
2. LeCun, Y., Bengio, Y., Hinton, G.: Deep learning. Nature **521**, 436–444 (2015)
3. Krizhevsky, A., Sutskever, I., Hinton, G.E.: ImageNet classification with deep convolutional neural networks. Adv. Neural Inf. Process. Syst. **25**, 1097–1105 (2012)
4. Deng, L., Li, J., et al.: Recent advances in deep learning for speech research at Microsoft. In: ICASSP (2013)
5. Hinton, G.E., Srivastava, N., Krizhevsky, A., Sutskever, I., Salakhutdinov, R.R.: Improving neural networks by preventing co-adaptation of feature detectors. The Computing Research Repository CoRR, abs/ 1207.0580 (2012)
6. Hara, K., Okada, M.: Ensemble learning of linear perceptrons: on-line learning theory. J. Phys. Soc. Jpn. **74**(11), 2966–2972 (2005)
7. Biehl, M., Schwarze, H.: Learning by on-line gradient descent. J. Phys. A Math. General Phys. **28**, 643–656 (1995)
8. Saad, D., Solla, S.A.: On-line learning in soft-committee machines. Phys. Rev. E **52**, 4225–4243 (1995)
9. Wager, S., Wang, S., Liang, P.: Dropout training as adaptive regularization. Adv. Neural Inf. Process. Syst. **26**, 351–359 (2013)
10. Bishop, C.M.: Pattern Recognition and Machine Learning. Springer, New York (2006)

The Effects of Regularization on Learning Facial Expressions with Convolutional Neural Networks

Tobias Hinz[✉], Pablo Barros, and Stefan Wermter

Department of Computer Science, University of Hamburg,
Vogt-Koelln-Strasse 30, 22527 Hamburg, Germany
{4hinz,barros,wermter}@informatik.uni-hamburg.de
http://www.informatik.uni-hamburg.de/WTM

Abstract. Convolutional neural networks (CNNs) have become effective instruments in facial expression recognition. Very good results can be achieved with deep CNNs possessing many layers and providing a good internal representation of the learned data. Due to the potentially high complexity of CNNs on the other hand they are prone to overfitting and as a result, regularization techniques are needed to improve the performance and minimize overfitting. However, it is not yet clear how these regularization techniques affect the learned representation of faces. In this paper we examine the effects of novel regularization techniques on the training and performance of CNNs and their learned features. We train a CNN using dropout, max pooling dropout, batch normalization and different combinations of these three. We show that a combination of these methods can have a big impact on the performance of a CNN, almost halving its validation error. A visualization technique is applied to the CNNs to highlight their activations for different inputs, illustrating a significant difference between a standard CNN and a regularized CNN.

Keywords: Convolutional neural network · Facial expression recognition · Regularization · Batch normalization · Dropout · Max pooling dropout

1 Introduction

The increasing size and complexity of neural networks in the recent past give more freedom to developers and provide solutions for more complex problems, but also make them more prone to overfit the given input data. This is especially the case in supervised settings when there is only a very limited amount of training data.

To deal with this problem various regularization methods have been developed to reduce overfitting. These techniques include established techniques such as early stopping, where training is stopped as soon as the validation error stops to improve and L2 regularization, the neural network equivalent of the Ridge regression. More recently new methods for regularization were introduced, such as dropout [2], drop-connect [13], max pooling dropout [3], stochastic pooling [4] and to some degree batch normalization [5].

© Springer International Publishing Switzerland 2016
A.E.P. Villa et al. (Eds.): ICANN 2016, Part II, LNCS 9887, pp. 80–87, 2016.
DOI: 10.1007/978-3-319-44781-0_10

Dropout, max pooling dropout and batch normalization have been introduced in the previous four years. While they have been used and examined individually, the authors know of no work in which all three methods are tested and evaluated in conjunction with each other.

This research applies some of the most recently developed regularization methods to a CNN trained on images from the Cohn-Kanade dataset [7]. The Cohn-Kanade dataset contains human faces expressing different emotions, such as happiness, anger or surprise. We train a CNN on this dataset, using dropout, max pooling dropout and batch normalization. The effect of different combinations of these three techniques on the training of the CNN is examined by monitoring the development of the validation error over time, as well as by visualizing CNNs' activations for different input images.

2   Background

In this chapter we will first give a brief overview over the tested regularization methods, i.e. dropout [2], max pooling dropout [3] and batch normalization [5].

2.1   Dropout

In 2012 Hinton et al. [2] introduced the dropout method to prevent artificial neural networks from overfitting. Dropout prevents co-adaptation of the network's weights to the training data. To achieve this each hidden unit of the network is omitted with a given probability - usually 0.5 - for any training sample.

This means that for each training sample a selected subset of units, including their incoming and outgoing connections, are temporarily removed from the network. If a dropout probability p of 0.5 is used, roughly half of the activations in each layer are deleted for every training sample, thus preventing hidden units from relying on other hidden units being present.

For testing the network on independent test data, the "mean network" is used. It contains all the hidden units, but has to compensate for the fact that during testing roughly twice as many hidden units are active, compared to the training phase. Due to this the weights are rescaled proportional to the dropout probability, for example for a dropout probability of 0.5 all weights are divided by two [2].

2.2   Max Pooling Dropout

Max pooling dropout is a dropout variant especially designed for CNNs, introduced by Wu and Gu [3]. In a standard CNN we have alternating convolutional and pooling layers. Common pooling mechanisms include for example max or average pooling. Wu and Gu suggested using dropout within the pooling layers to introduce stochasticity into the training process. Instead of deterministically choosing the strongest activation in the pooling region, max pooling dropout allows smaller activations to be chosen instead.

To achieve this, dropout is applied to each pooling regions, before max pooling is performed. Using max pooling dropout is therefore sampling from a multinomial distribution to select an index i to choose the pooled activation a_i. As such max pooling dropout can be seen as a special variant of stochastic pooling [4], with the difference that activations are used with a probability proportional to their rank, instead of the strength of their activation.

2.3   Batch Normalization

During training the distribution of inputs to a given layer changes as parameters in the previous layer are updated. Therefore, parameter initialization and the learning rate can have a high impact on the progress of the training. This phenomenon, also called internal covariate shift, is addressed by the technique called batch normalization [5]. Batch normalization works by normalizing each layer's input for each mini batch during training. This allows much higher learning rates, more freedom regarding parameter initialization and also acts as a regularizer.

To that end each layer's input is normalized. To preserve what each layer can represent for each activation $x^{(k)}$, a pair of parameters $< \gamma^{(k)}, \beta^{(k)} >$ is introduced, which scales and shifts the normalized values. These additional parameters are learned along with the original model parameters and make sure the representational capability of the network is not changed.

Batch normalization can work as a form of regularization, since a training example is seen in conjunction with other examples in a mini batch. Due to shuffling, the composition of mini batches changes during training, so the network no longer produces deterministic values for a given training example.

3   Methodology

To test the previously described regularization methods we examined a CNN and trained it to classify images from the Cohn-Kanade dataset [7]. The Cohn-Kanade dataset consists of images depicting human faces in seven emotions: anger, contempt, disgust, fear, happiness, sadness and surprise. In line with other research [8] we only used six classes, neglecting contempt for our training and testing. Each example of emotion contains a sequence of up to 60 frames, that starts with a neutral expression and continues to the peak of the expression. Our training and testing set comprised the last three images of each sequence. These images were rescaled to 128×128 pixels, converted to gray scale and whitened.

3.1   Experiments

The CNN used for the experiments consists of six layers. The first three layers are convolutional layers, followed by two fully connected layers and one softmax layer for classification on top. Max pooling is performed after each convolutional layer

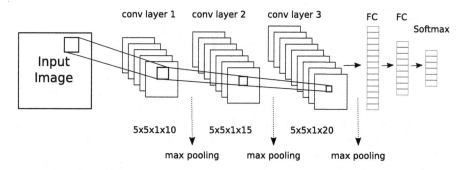

Fig. 1. CNN architecture: our CNN consists of three convolutional layers with 10, 15 and 20 filters, each with a filter size of 5×5. 2×2 max pooling is performed after each convolutional layer. The convolutional layers are followed by two fully connected layers with 500 and 200 units and one classification layer with 6 units.

and the number of filters per convolutional layer are 10, 15 and 20 respectively. A filter size of 5×5 is used on each convolutional layer. The two fully connected layers consist of 500 and 200 units and the logistic regression layer has 6 units for classification, see Fig. 1.

As activation function ReLU was used on all layers and weight initialization was performed according to current guidelines [6]. The initial learning rate is 0.001, which is linearly reduced by 1% per epoch. A momentum of 0.9 was used and L2 regularization with a small penalty of 0.0001 was introduced since it improved stability during training.

With this fixed architecture we then proceeded to test the effects of the different methods on the set classification task. The following eight settings were tested:

1. no regularization,
2. standard dropout after each layer,
3. max pooling dropout after each convolutional layer,
4. batch normalization (BN) after each layer,
5. max pooling dropout after each convolutional layer and standard dropout after each fully connected layer,
6. max pooling dropout after each convolutional layer and BN after each layer,
7. standard dropout after each layer and BN after each layer,
8. max pooling dropout after each convolutional layer and standard dropout after each fully connected layer and BN after each layer.

For each individual setting training was performed using stochastic gradient descent for a total of 150 epochs. We split our dataset into ten independent subsets of equal size and performed 10-fold cross-validation in the manner presented by Liu et al. [9]. After training was completed we applied a visualization technique [10] to our CNN, to demonstrate the potential impact of regularization methods on the learned features. For this we deconvolve our CNN and then visualize the activations of the third convolutional layer for various input images.

3.2   Results

The most important evaluation criterion for the proposed methods is whether they are able to decrease the validation error, i.e. improve the system's generalization capability. Figure 2 depicts plots of the development of the validation error over time for each regularization method. The plots show the average validation error of all runs for a given regularization method and the combination of that method with batch normalization. Table 1 gives the average best validation error and the standard deviation of the best validation errors for each tested regularization method.

Except for batch normalization each combination of regularization methods outperformed no regularization. The improvements from all combinations from max dropout and batch normalization onward are statistically significant when compared to no regularization. The results also indicate that the combination of several regularization methods, as opposed to using one single method, further improves regularization. Each combination of at least two regularization methods performed better than using only one single method.

Table 1. Average accuracy and standard deviations for 10-fold cross-validation for the combinations of different methods. Sorted in order of increasing accuracy.

Method	Accuracy	Std
Batch Normalization (BN)	86.9 %	4.4
No Regularization	89.6 %	4.5
Dropout	92,4 %	3.3
Max Dropout	92,8 %	3.4
Max Dropout + BN	93.3 %	4.0
Dropout + BN	93,9 %	4.1
Max Dropout + Dropout + BN	94.3 %	4.2
Max Dropout + Dropout	94.3 %	2.5

The addition of batch normalization to any regularization methods did not improve the final accuracy. However Fig. 2 shows quite clearly that the addition of batch normalization had the advantage of converging quicker to better results. Since the differences in the results between any regularization method and that regularization method in combination with batch normalization are not statistically significant, it seems that the addition of batch normalization helps the training process.

Figure 3 shows a visualization [10] of each filter on the third convolutional layer for the input image depicted in the respective leftmost column. The images on the left of the second and third column depict the activations of a standard CNN trained without regularization and the images on the right a regularized CNN trained with the combination of max dropout and dropout. It can be seen that the activations of the regularized CNN are much more focused on certain parts of the face, while the standard CNN is activated for much bigger regions. This can explain the higher accuracy of the regularized CNN, as the regularization methods seem to force it to focus on certain aspects of the face. The filters of the standard CNN on the other hand are often quite blurry and indistinct, explaining its lower accuracy.'

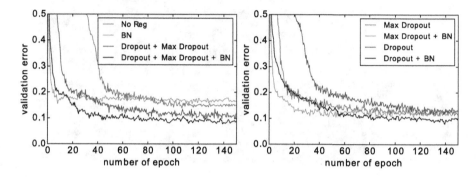

Fig. 2. Development of validation errors during training time.

3.3   Discussion

The differences in the filters' activations shown in Fig. 3 for the third convolutional layer between the standard and the regularized CNN are notable. Many of the standard CNN's filters do not focus on specific parts of the face, but are instead spread over the whole input. As a result we have many activations in areas of the input that are not relevant to the classification, such as the corners of the image.

In all images of the Cohn-Kanade dataset the faces are quite centered in the image and as a result the corners of the inputs do not provide relevant information for the classification task. This is reflected by the activations of the regularized CNN, which are mostly focused on the facial features themselves. Here the filters are much more selective and mostly focus on the center part of the image. This focus is likely to improve the overall accuracy of the CNN compared to one without applied regularization.

Indeed, Khorrami et al. [8] showed in their work that the most important features are centered around the eyes, the nose and the mouth. The visualizations show that the regularized CNN mainly focuses on these areas. It is also noteworthy that our accuracy is comparable to previous results [8,11,12]. While we do not achieve state-of-the art accuracy it has to be noted that we do not perform data augmentation and only use roughly a tenth of the number of filters as e.g. Khorrami et al. [8]. It can be expected that the accuracy of our network can be further improved by utilizing data augmentation techniques even without increasing the number of used filters.

gray scale input   standard   regularized   standard   regularized

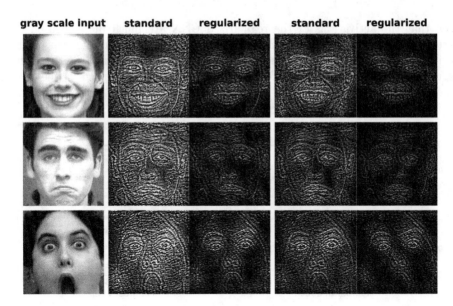

Fig. 3. Visualization of third convolutional layer's activations for the input image on the left of each row. The left image of the second and third column depicts the activations of a standard CNN, while the right image of the respective column shows the activations of the same filter in a CNN regularized with a combination of max pooling dropout and common dropout.

4   Conclusion

In this work we showed that for the training of a CNN the combination of max dropout and standard dropout can achieve very high accuracy on the Cohn-Kanade dataset, even without applying data augmentation and with a comparatively small number of used filters. A visualization of the trained networks shows a big difference between a regularized and a standard CNN, exemplifying the effects of regularization firsthand. While the standard CNN's filters are often blurry and indistinct, the regularized CNN's filters exhibit a much higher selectivity and are more focused on important features.

In our experiments batch normalization had no effect on the generalization capability of a trained CNN. However, it did not affect the accuracy of a CNN in a negative way, while simultaneously reducing the training time until good results are achieved. It therefore seems that the addition of batch normalization to the training procedure is advantageous.

Finally, we have shown that with the right combination of applied regularization techniques it is possible to achieve good results with small networks and without data augmentation. In the future, these regularization techniques can be applied together with data augmentation and more complex CNNs, either with more filters or more layers, to potentially achieve an even higher accuracy on challenging datasets.

Acknowledgments. This work was partially supported by the CAPES Brazilian Federal Agency for the Support and Evaluation of Graduate Education (p.n.5951–13–5), the German Research Foundation DFG under project CML (TRR 169), and the Hamburg Landesforschungsförderungsprojekt.

References

1. Krizhevsky, A., Sutskever, I., Hinton, G.E.: Imagenet classification with deep convolutional neural networks. In: Advances in Neural Information Processing Systems, pp. 1097–1105 (2012)
2. Srivastava, N., Hinton, G., Krizhevsky, A., Sutskever, I., Salakhutdinov, R.: Dropout: A simple way to prevent neural networks from overfitting. J. Mach. Learn. Res. **15**(1), 1929–1958 (2014)
3. Wu, H., Gu, X.: Towards dropout training for convolutional neural networks. Neural Netw. **71**, 1–10 (2015)
4. Zeiler, M.D., Fergus, R.: Stochastic pooling for regularization of deep convolutional neural networks. arXiv preprint 1301.3557 (2013)
5. Ioffe, S., Szegedy, C.: Batch normalization: Accelerating deep network training by reducing internal covariate shift. arXiv preprint 1502.03167 (2015)
6. He, K., Zhang, X., Ren, S., Sun, J.: Delving deep into rectifiers: surpassing human-level performance on imagenet classification. In: Proceedings of the IEEE International Conference on Computer Vision, pp. 1026–1034 (2015)
7. Lucey, P., Cohn, J.F., Kanade, T., Saragih, J., Ambadar, Z., Matthews, I.: The extended cohn-kanade dataset (ck+): a complete dataset for action unit and emotion-specified expression. In: Proceedings of the Third International Workshop on CVPR for Human Communicative Behavior Analysis, pp. 94–101 (2010)
8. Khorrami, P., Paine, T., Huang, T.: Do deep neural networks learn facial action units when doing expression recognition? In: Proceedings of the IEEE International Conference on Computer Vision Workshops, pp. 19–27 (2015)
9. Liu, M., Li, S., Shan, S., Chen, X.: Au-aware deep networks for facial expression recognition. In: 10th IEEE International Conference and Workshops on Automatic Face and Gesture Recognition (FG), pp. 1–6 (2013)
10. Zeiler, M.D., Fergus, R.: Visualizing and understanding convolutional networks. In: Fleet, D., Pajdla, T., Schiele, B., Tuytelaars, T. (eds.) ECCV 2014, Part I. LNCS, vol. 8689, pp. 818–833. Springer, Heidelberg (2014)
11. Barros, P., Weber, C., Wermter, S.: Emotional expression recognition with a cross-channel convolutional neural network for human-robot interaction. In: IEEE-RAS 15th International Conference on Humanoid Robots, pp. 582–587 (2015)
12. Liu, P., Han, S., Meng, Z., Tong, Y.: Facial expression recognition via a boosted deep belief network. In: Proceedings of the IEEE Conference on Computer Vision and Pattern Recognition, pp. 1805–1812 (2014)
13. Wan, L., Zeiler, M., Zhang, S., Cun, Y.L., Fergus, R.: Regularization of neural networks using dropconnect. In: Proceedings of the 30th International Conference on Machine Learning (ICML 2013), pp. 1058–1066 (2013)

DeepChess: End-to-End Deep Neural Network for Automatic Learning in Chess

Omid E. David[1,2]([✉]), Nathan S. Netanyahu[2,3], and Lior Wolf[1]

[1] The Blavatnik School of Computer Science, Tel Aviv University, Tel Aviv, Israel
mail@omiddavid.com, wolf@cs.tau.ac.il
[2] Department of Computer Science, Bar-Ilan University, Ramat-gan, Israel
nathan@cs.biu.ac.il
[3] Center for Automation Research, University of Maryland, College Park, MD, USA
nathan@cfar.umd.edu

Abstract. We present an end-to-end learning method for chess, relying on deep neural networks. Without any a priori knowledge, in particular without any knowledge regarding the rules of chess, a deep neural network is trained using a combination of unsupervised pretraining and supervised training. The unsupervised training extracts high level features from a given position, and the supervised training learns to compare two chess positions and select the more favorable one. The training relies entirely on datasets of several million chess games, and no further domain specific knowledge is incorporated.

The experiments show that the resulting neural network (referred to as DeepChess) is on a par with state-of-the-art chess playing programs, which have been developed through many years of manual feature selection and tuning. DeepChess is the first end-to-end machine learning-based method that results in a grandmaster-level chess playing performance.

1 Introduction

Top computer chess programs are based typically on manual feature selection and tuning of their evaluation function, usually through years of trial and error. While computer chess is one of the most researched fields within AI, machine learning has not been successful yet at producing grandmaster level players.

In this paper, we employ deep neural networks to learn an evaluation function *from scratch*, without incorporating the rules of the game and using no manually extracted features at all. Instead, the system is trained from end to end on a large dataset of chess positions.

Training is done in multiple phases. First, we use deep unsupervised neural networks for pretraining. We then train a supervised network to select a preferable position out of two input positions. This second network is incorporated into a new form of alpha-beta search. A third training phase is used to compress the network in order to allow rapid computation.

Our method obtains a grandmaster-level chess playing performance, on a par with top state-of-the-art chess programs. To the best of our knowledge, this is

© Springer International Publishing Switzerland 2016
A.E.P. Villa et al. (Eds.): ICANN 2016, Part II, LNCS 9887, pp. 88–96, 2016.
DOI: 10.1007/978-3-319-44781-0_11

the first machine learning-based method that is capable of learning from scratch and obtains a grandmaster-level performance.

2   Previous Work

Chess-playing programs have been improved significantly over the past several decades. While the first chess programs could not pose a challenge to even a novice player, the current advanced chess programs have been outperforming the strongest human players, as the recent man vs. machine matches clearly indicate. Despite these achievements, a glaring deficiency of today's top chess programs is their severe lack of a learning capability (except in most negligible ways, e.g., "learning" not to play an opening that resulted in a loss, etc.).

During more than fifty years of research in the area of computer games, many learning methods have been employed in several games. *Reinforcement learning* has been successfully applied in backgammon [16] and checkers [13]. Although reinforcement learning has also been applied to chess [1,10], the resulting programs exhibit a playing strength at a human master level at best, which is substantially lower than the grandmaster-level state-of-the-art chess programs. These experimental results confirm Wiering's [17] formal arguments for the failure of reinforcement learning in rather complex games such as chess. Very recently, a combination of a *Monte-Carlo search* and deep learning resulted in a huge improvement in the game of Go [15]. However, Monte-Carlo search is not applicable to chess, since it is much more tactical than Go, e.g., in a certain position, all but one of the moves by the opponent may result in a favorable result, but one refutation is sufficient to render the position unfavorable.

In our previous works, we demonstrated how genetic algorithms (GA's) could be applied successfully to the problem of automatic evaluation function tuning when the features are initialized randomly [3–6]. Although to the best of our knowledge, these works are the only successful automatic learning methods to have resulted in grandmaster-level performance in computer chess, they do not involve learning the features themselves from scratch. Rather, they rely on the existence of a manually created evaluation function, which consists already of all the required features (e.g., queen value, rook value, king safety, pawn structure evaluation, and many other hand crafted features). Thus, GAs are used in this context for *optimization* of the weights of existing features, rather than for *feature learning* from scratch.

3   Learning to Compare Positions

The evaluation function is the most important component of a chess program. It receives a chess position as an input, and provides a score as an output. This score represents how good the given position is (typically from White's perspective). For example, a drawish position would have a score close to 0, a position in which white has two pawns more than black would have a score of +2, and a position in which black has a rook more than white, would be scored around −5. A good evaluation function considers typically a large number (i.e., on the order of hundreds and even thousands) of properties in addition to various piece-related parameters, such as king safety, passed pawns, doubled pawns, piece centrality, etc. The resulting score is a linear combination of all the selected features. The more accurately these features and their associated values capture the inherent properties of the position, the stronger the corresponding chess program becomes.

In this paper, we are interested in developing such an evaluation function from scratch, i.e., with absolutely no a priori knowledge. As a result, we do not provide our evaluation function with any features, including any knowledge about the rules of chess. Thus, for our training purposes, we are limited to observing databases of chess games with access only to the results of the games (i.e., either a win for White or Black, or a draw).

Since the real objective of an evaluation function is to perform relative comparisons between positions, we propose a novel training method around this concept. The model receives two positions as input and learns to predict which position is better. During training, the input pair is selected as follows: One position is selected at random from a game which White eventually won and the other from a game which Black eventually won. This relies on the safe assumption that, on average, positions taken from games that White won are preferable (from White's perspective) to those taken from games that White lost. Additionally, the proposed approach allows for the creation of a considerably larger training dataset. For example, if we have a million positions from games that White had won, and a million positions from games that White had lost, we can

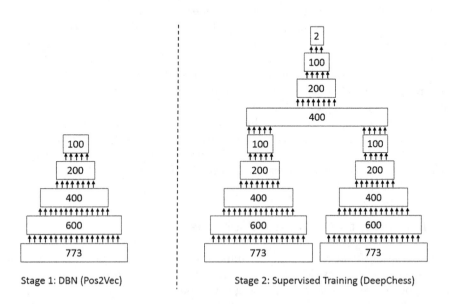

Fig. 1. Architecture illustration of DeepChess.

create 2×10^{12} training pairs (multiplied by 2 because each pair can be used twice, as [win, loss] and [loss, win]).

Our approach consists of multiple stages. First, we train a deep autoencoder on a dataset of several million chess positions. This deep autoencoder functions as a nonlinear feature extractor. We refer to this component as *Pos2Vec*, since it converts a given chess position into a vector of values which represent the high level features. In the second phase, we use two copies of this pretrained Pos2Vec side by side, and add fully connected layers on top of them, with a 2-value softmax output layer. We refer to this structure as *DeepChess*. It is trained to predict which of the two positions results in a win. Note that similar to the most successful object detection methods [11], we found a 2-value output to outperform one binary output. Figure 1 illustrates the neural network architecture.

Dataset: We employed the games dataset of CCRL (www.computerchess.org. uk/ccrl), which contains 640,000 chess games, out of which White won 221,695 games and Black won 164,387 games, the remaining games ended in a draw. Our experiments show that the inclusion of games that ended in a draw is not beneficial, so we only use games which ended in a win.

From each game we randomly extracted ten positions, with the restriction that the selected position cannot be from one of the first five moves in the game, and that the actual move played in the selected position is not a capture. Capture moves are misleading as they mostly result in a transient advantage since the other side is likely to capture back rightaway. The dataset thus contains 2,216,950 positions from games which White won (W positions), and 1,643,870 positions from games which White lost (L positions), for a total of 3,860,820 positions.

Each position is converted to a binary bit-string of size 773. There are two sides (White and Black), 6 piece types (pawn, knight, bishop, rook, queen, and king), and 64 squares. Therefore, in order to represent a position as a binary bit-string, we would require $2 \times 6 \times 64 = 768$ bits (this is known as *bitboard* representation). There are an additional five bits that represent the side to move (1 for White and 0 for Black) and castling rights (White can castle kingside, White can castle queenside, Black can castle kingside, and Black can castle queenside).

Training Pos2Vec: We first trained a deep belief network (DBN) [2], which would later serve as the initial weights for supervised training. The DBN is based on stacked autoencoders which are trained using layer-wise unsupervised training. The network consists of five fully connected layers of sizes: 773–600–400–200–100. We initially trained the first layer (i.e., a 3-layer (773–600–773) autoencoder), before fixing its weights and training the weights of a new (600–400–600) autoencoder, and so on.

We used a random subset of 2,000,000 chess positions for training the DBN, of which 1,000,000 were White win (W) positions and 1,000,000 were Black win (L) positions. The DBN uses a rectified linear unit (ReLU), i.e., $f(x) = max(0, x)$, and a learning rate that starts from 0.005 and is multiplied by 0.98 at the end of each epoch. No regularization is used. The DBN is trained for 200 epochs.

Training DeepChess: As described earlier, this Siamese network is the core component of our method. We used the previously trained Pos2Vec DBN as the initial weights for the supervised network. Placing two disjoint copies of Pos2Vec side by side, we added on top of them four fully connected layers of size 400, 200, 100, and 2, which are connected to both Pos2Vec components. The first five layers of Pos2Vec thus serve as high level feature extractors, and the last four layers compare the features of the positions to determine which one is better.

During the supervised training phase, the entire network including the Pos2Vec parts is modified. We tie the weights of the two Pos2Vec-based feature extraction components, i.e., we use shared weights.

We trained this network for 1000 epochs. In each epoch, we created 1,000,000 random input pairs, where each pair consists of one position selected at random from the 2,116,950 W positions, and one position selected at random from the 1,543,870 L positions. (we set aside 100,000 W positions and 100,000 L positions for validation). The pair is then randomly ordered as either (W, L) or (L, W). Since the number of potential training pairs is 6.5×10^{12}, virtually all training samples in each epoch are new, thus guaranteeing that no overfitting would take place. For this reason, we do not use any regularization term. The activation used in all layers is the ReLU function. The learning rate starts from 0.01, and is multiplied by 0.99 after each epoch. The cross entropy loss is used. The training and validation accuracies obtained were 98.2 % and 98.0 %, respectively. This is remarkable, considering that no a priori knowledge of chess, including the very rules of the games are provided.

Improving Inference Speed by Network Distillation: Before incorporating the trained network into a chess program and evaluating its performance, we first had to address the problem that the network is too computationally expensive in prediction (inference) mode, running markedly slower than a typical evaluation function in a chess program. Several previous works have demonstrated how a considerably smaller neural network could be trained to mimic the behavior of a much more complex neural network [8,12]. These network compression or distilling approaches train the smaller network to produce the same output as the larger network (learning from soft targets).

We first trained a smaller four-layer network of 773–100–100–100 neurons to mimic the feature extraction part of DeepChess, which consists of the five layers 773–600–400–200–100. We then added three layers of 100–100–2 neurons (originally 400–200–100–2) and trained the entire network to mimic the entire DeepChess network.

Further optimization was achieved by realizing that while most of the weights are concentrated in the first layer of the two Pos2Vec components (733–100 layer), there are at most 32 chess pieces in a given position and less than 5 % of the weights in the input layer would be activated. Thus the amount of floating point operations required to be performed during inference is much reduced.

Table 1 summarizes the validation results post compression. The distilled network is comparable to the full original network. When training from scratch using the smaller network size (with pretraining but without first training the larger network and then distilling it), the performance is much reduced.

4   A Comparison-Based Alpha-Beta Search

Chess engines typically use the alpha-beta search algorithm [9]. Alpha-beta is a depth-first search method that prunes unpromising branches of the search tree earlier, improving the search efficiency. A given position is the root of the search tree, and the legal moves for each side create the next layer nodes. The more time available, the deeper this search tree can be processed, which would result in a better overall playing strength. At leaf nodes, an evaluation function is applied.

In an alpha-beta search, two values are stored; α which represents the value of the current best option for the side to move, and β which is the negative α of the other side. For each new position encountered if $value > \alpha$, this value would become the new α, but if $value > \beta$, the search is stopped and the search tree is pruned, because $value > \beta$ means that the opponent would not have allowed the current position to be reached (better options are available, since $value > \beta$ is equivalent to $-value < \alpha$ for the other side). Given a branching factor of B and search depth D, alpha-beta reduces the search complexity from B^D for basic DFS, to $B^{D/2}$.

In order to incorporate DeepChess, we use a novel version of an alpha-beta algorithm that does not require any position scores for performing the search. Instead of α and β values, we store positions α_{pos} and β_{pos}. For each new position, we compare it with the existing α_{pos} and β_{pos} positions using DeepChess, and if the comparison shows that the new position is better than α_{pos}, it would become the new α_{pos}, and if the new position is better than β_{pos}, the current node is pruned. Note that since DeepChess always compares the positions from White's perspective, when using it from Black's perspective, the predictions should be reversed.

Position hashing: When searching a tree of possible moves and positions, many of the positions appear repeatedly in different parts of the search tree, since the same position can arise in different move orders. To reduce the required computation, we store a large hash table for positions and their corresponding feature extraction values. For each new position, we first query the hash table, and if the position has already been processed, we reuse the cached values. Since we use a symmetric feature extraction scheme, where the weights are shared, each position needs only be stored once.

5   Experiments

We provide both quantitative and qualitative results.

5.1   Static Understanding of Chess Positions

In order to measure the chess understanding of DeepChess, we ran it on a manually generated dataset consisting of carefully designed inputs. Each input pair in this dataset contains two nearly identical positions, where one contains a certain feature and the other one does not. Starting from simple piece values (e.g., two identical positions where a piece is missing from one), to more complex imbalances (e.g., rook vs. knight and a bishop), the predictions of DeepChess show that it has easily learned all of the basic concepts regarding piece values. We then measured more subtle positional features, e.g., king safety, bishop pair, piece mobility, passed pawns, isolated pawns, doubled pawns, castling rights, etc. All of these features are also well understood by DeepChess.

More interestingly, DeepChess has learned to prefer positions with dynamic attacking opportunities even when it has less material. In many cases, it prefers a position with one or two fewer pawns, but one that offers non-material positional advantages. This property has been associated with human grandmasters, and has always been considered an area in which computer chess programs were lacking. While the scores of current evaluation functions in state-of-the-art chess programs are based on a linear combination of all the features present, DeepChess is a non-linear evaluator, and thus has a far higher potential for profound understanding of chess positions (also similar to human grandmaster analysis of positions). Figure 2 shows a few examples where this preference of DeepChess for non-materialistic advantages leads to favoring positional sacrifices, as played by human grandmasters.

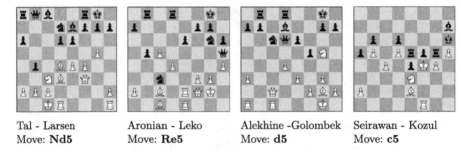

Tal - Larsen   Aronian - Leko   Alekhine -Golombek   Seirawan - Kozul
Move: **Nd5**   Move: **Re5**   Move: **d5**   Move: **c5**

Fig. 2. Examples where DeepChess prefers to play the same positional sacrifices that were played by grandmasters. It is White's turn to move in all the above positions.

5.2 Playing Strength Vs. State-of-the-Art Competitors

We used the FALCON chess engine as a baseline for our experiments. FALCON is a grandmaster-level chess program, which has successfully participated in several World Computer Chess Championships (WCCCs); in particular, it won second place at the World Computer Speed Chess Championship in 2008. FALCON's extensive evaluation function consists of more than 100 parameters, and its implementation contains several thousands of lines of code.

Despite all the computational improvements mentioned earlier for DeepChess, and numerous other implementation improvements which result in substantial additional computational speedup, DeepChess is still four times slower than FALCON's own evaluation function. Nevertheless, we incorporate

Table 1. Validation accuracy of the Uncompressed and compressed networks, and a small network trained from scratch.

Method	Accuracy
Uncompressed	98.0 %
Compressed	97.1 %
Small	95.4 %

Table 2. DeepChess vs. FALCON and CRAFTY (RD is the Elo rating difference). Time control: 30 min per game for FALCON and CRAFTY. 30 min or two hours for DeepChess.

Match	Result	RD
DeepChess 30 min - CRAFTY	59.0–41.0	+63.2
DeepChess 30 min - FALCON	51.5–48.5	+10.4
DeepChess 120 min - FALCON	63.5–36.5	+96.2

DeepChess into FALCON, completely replacing the evaluation function of the program.

To measure the performance of DeepChess, we conducted a series of matches against FALCON, and also against the chess program CRAFTY. CRAFTY has successfully participated in numerous WCCCs, and is a direct descendant of Cray Blitz, the WCCC winner of 1983 and 1986. It has been frequently used in the literature as a standard reference.

Each of the matches of DeepChess vs. FALCON and CRAFTY consisted of 100 games under a time control of 30 min per game for each side. Table 2 provides the results. As can be seen, DeepChess is on a par with FALCON. FALCON uses a manually tuned evaluation function developed over nearly ten years, containing more than a hundred parameters which grasp many subtle chess features. And yet, without any chess knowledge whatsoever (not even basic knowledge as the rules of chess), our DeepChess method managed to reach a level which is on a par with the manually tuned evaluation function of FALCON. The results also show that DeepChess is over 60 Elo [7] stronger than CRAFTY, a program which has won two WCCCs and has been manually tuned for thirty years.

DeepChess performs on a par with FALCON despite the fact that it is four times slower. We ran a separate experiment where we allowed DeepChess to use four times more time than FALCON (2 h vs 30 min). Running 100 such matches, DeepChess resoundingly defeated FALCON with a result of 63.5–36.5, corresponding to a 96 Elo performance difference. This shows that DeepChess is actually not on par with FALCON's evaluation function, but is considerably superior to it. In order to utilize the full potential of this enhanced chess understanding, it is critical to decrease the runtime of the neural network in the inference mode.

6   Concluding Remarks

We presented the first successful end-to-end application of machine learning in computer chess. Similarly to human chess masters, DeepChess does not assign numeral evaluation values to different positions, but rather, *compares* different positions that may arise, and opts for the most promising continuation.

Having observed the playing style of DeepChess, we note that it plays very aggressively, often sacrificing pieces for long term positional gains (i.e., non-tactical gains). This playing style resembles very much the playing style of human grandmasters. While computer chess programs have long been criticized for being materialistic, DeepChess demonstrates the very opposite by exhibiting an adventurous playing style with frequent positional sacrifices.

References

1. Baxter, J., Tridgell, A., Weaver, L.: Learning to play chess using temporal-differences. Mach. Learn. **40**(3), 243–263 (2000)
2. Bengio, Y., Lamblin, P., Popovici, D., Larochelle, H.: Greedy layer-wise training of deep networks. In: NIPS (2007)
3. David, O.E., Koppel, M., Netanyahu, N.S.: Genetic algorithms for mentor-assisted evaluation function optimization. In: GECCO (2008)
4. David, O.E., van den Herik, H.J., Koppel, M., Netanyahu, N.S.: Simulating human grandmasters: evolution and coevolution of evaluation functions. In: GECCO (2009)
5. David, O.E., Koppel, M., Netanyahu, N.S.: Expert-driven genetic algorithms for simulating evaluation functions. Genet. Program. Evolvable Mach. **12**(1), 5–22 (2011)
6. David, O.E., van den Herik, H.J., Koppel, M., Netanyahu, N.S.: Genetic algorithms for evolving computer chess programs. IEEE Trans. Evol. Comput. **18**(5), 779–789 (2014)
7. Elo, A.E.: The Rating of Chessplayers, Past and Present. Batsford, London (1978)
8. Hinton, G., Vinyals, O., Dean, J.: Distilling knowledge in a neural network. In: Deep Learning and Representation Learning Workshop, NIPS (2014)
9. Knuth, D.E., Moore, R.W.: An analysis of alpha-beta pruning. Artif. Intell. **6**(4), 293–326 (1975)
10. Lai, M.: Giraffe: Using deep reinforcement learning to play chess. Master's Thesis, Imperial College London (2015)
11. Ren, S., He, K., Girshick, R., Sun, J.: Faster R-CNN: towards real-time object detection with region proposal networks. In: NIPS (2015)
12. Romero, A., Ballas, N., Ebrahimi Kahou, S., Chassang, A., Gatta, C., Bengio, Y.: FitNets: hints for thin deep nets. In: ICLR (2015)
13. Schaeffer, J., Hlynka, M., Jussila, V.: Temporal difference learning applied to a high-performance game-playing program. In: Joint Conference on Artificial Intelligence (2001)
14. Schaeffer, J., Burch, N., Björnsson, Y., Kishimoto, A., Müller, M., Lake, R.: Checkers is solved. Science **317**, 1518–1522 (2007)
15. Silver, D., et al.: Mastering the game of Go with deep neural networks and tree search. Nature **529**, 484–489 (2016)
16. Tesauro, G.: Practical issues in temporal difference learning. Mach. Learn. **8**(3–4), 257–277 (1992)
17. Wiering, M.A.: TD learning of game evaluation functions with hierarchical neural architectures. Master's Thesis, University of Amsterdam (1995)

A Convolutional Network Model of the Primate Middle Temporal Area

Bryan P. Tripp[(✉)]

University of Waterloo, Waterloo, Canada
bptripp@uwaterloo.ca

Abstract. Convolutional neural networks have many parallels with the primate visual cortex, including deep structures with sparse retinotopic connections, and feature maps with increasing specificity and invariance along feedforward paths. The present study explores the possibility of specifically training convolutional networks to resemble the primate cortex more closely. In particular, in addition to supervised learning to minimize an output error function, a deep layer is directly trained to approximate primate electrophysiology data. This method is used to develop a model of the macaque monkey dorsal stream that estimates heading and speed from visual input.

Keywords: Middle temporal area · Dorsal stream · Convolutional network · Visual odometry · Motion · Disparity · Speed tuning

1 Introduction

The visual cortex makes up a large fraction of the primate brain. It contains dozens of regions with distinct activity patterns, which are organized in a rough hierarchy [1]. Most visual areas contain retinotopic maps of multiple visual features [2,3]. The visual cortex is largely segregated into dorsal and ventral streams [4]. The former extracts complex features that are relevant to object identity and category [5,6], and has rich connections with areas involved in long-term memory and recognition [7]. The latter is specialized for motion and three-dimensional form, and has rich connections with parts of the brain that control movement (e.g. [8]).

There is enduring interest in imitating the visual cortex within artificial neural networks, leading to convolutional networks [9] and related approaches [10,11]. Modern computer hardware has particularly exposed the potential of convolutional networks for difficult vision tasks such as object recognition in natural scenes [12]. Notably, activity in various layers of convolutional networks that are optimized for object recognition is highly predictive of activity in corresponding parts of the primate ventral stream [13]. Nonetheless, the primate visual system outperforms convolutional networks on most practical vision tasks, suggesting that more intensive imitation of the cortex may be fruitful.

Much information has been amassed in the literature about the responses of neurons at all stages of the visual hierarchy to a wide variety of stimuli.

© Springer International Publishing Switzerland 2016
A.E.P. Villa et al. (Eds.): ICANN 2016, Part II, LNCS 9887, pp. 97–104, 2016.
DOI: 10.1007/978-3-319-44781-0_12

This paper explores the possibility of using the statistics of these responses to directly train deep layers of convolutional networks, both to simplify training and to create convolutional networks that are somewhat more brain-like.

For simplicity, this study is restricted to training a single deep layer to emulate certain response properties of the primate middle temporal area (MT), specifically direction tuning, speed tuning [14], and disparity tuning [15]. It is hoped that this relatively simple model will shed light on how to train additional features of MT activity, e.g. [16], as well as properties of other visual areas. There is a rich literature spanning half a century [17] on responses throughout the visual cortex to a wide range of stimuli [3], as well as increasingly comprehensive information about network structure [18]. Recording density is also steadily increasing [19]. These circumstances suggest a promising path forward from the present prototype.

2   Methods

2.1   Network Structure

The network structure is shown in Table 1. Input consisted of ten stereo video frames with 100×100-pixel resolution. There were four convolutional layers. The first two were meant to correspond roughly to the primary visual area (V1), the third to the middle temporal area (MT), and the fourth to the middle superior temporal area (MST). Sizes of the convolution kernels, and of the pools for max-pooling operations (Table 1) were chosen to correspond qualitatively with these areas. For example, outputs from the second V1 layer were pooled to provide phase invariance (after complex cells), and receptive field sizes were much larger in the MT layer than the V1 layers. Following the convolutional layers were two fully-connected layers. The two units of the output layer were trained to estimate anteroposterior and mediolateral components of self-motion velocity from the video input. The model was implemented in Keras [20] using Theano [21] as a backend, and trained on a NVIDIA GeForce GTX 680 GPU.

The first convolutional layer lacked a nonlinearity, because it was used to introduce a certain linear basis as a starting point for training. The approach was a slight generalization of that in Adelson &Bergen's model of motion selectivity in V1 [22]. In their model, various linear combinations of separable spatiotemporal kernels produce non-separable direction-selective kernels. The present approach was similar, in that the kernels of the first layer were initialized to spatial gabors of various frequencies and phases, multiplied by the same (physiologically inspired) functions of time [22]. However, Adelson & Bergen's hand-engineered linear combinations of kernels were replaced by optimized linear combinations via the learned kernels of the next layer.

2.2   Training

The network was trained at different times to minimize two different costs. One of these was,

$$E_f = (y_0 - v_{ml})^2 + (y_1 - v_{ap})^2, \tag{1}$$

Table 1. Network parameters. ReLU stands for "rectified linear unit" [12].

Layer	# Kernels	Kernel size	Pool	# Hidden units	Nonlinearity
1	640	7×7	None		None
2	320	1×1	3×3		ReLU
3	240	5×5	2×2		ReLU
4	60	9×9	3×3		ReLU
5				256	ReLU
6				2	None

where v_{ml} and v_{ap} are mediolateral and anteroposterior components of self-motion velocity, and y_0 and y_1 are the network's outputs. E_f is called the "functional" cost, because it relates to the network's overt function.

The network was also separately trained to minimize the "physiology cost",

$$E_p = \sum_i (y_i - r_i)^2,\qquad(2)$$

where y_i are activities of the 3rd convolutional layer, and r_i are neuron responses from a statistical model of MT activity (based on electrophysiology literature). The index i is over feature maps of the 3rd convolutional layer, and over an equal number of target responses from the statistical model. Since kernel weights are shared across pixels, the cost was only calculated at the central pixel of each feature map in the MT layer.

Labelled datasets for both types of training were generated using the Unity game engine (unity3d.com). A simulated stereo camera was made to move through a scene with random speed and direction, for sequences of ten frames. Every 30 sequences, the camera was relocated to a different part of the scene at random (data were shuffled during training; multiple sequences were taken from each location to save time, because changing location required dropping the camera over uneven terrain and waiting for it to fall to the ground).

Example frames are shown in Fig. 1. Target self-motion velocities v_{ml} and v_{ap} were taken from movement commands. The camera followed the contour of the ground, so on slopes the motion also had a vertical component that was not reflected in these target values. In some sequences, the actual horizontal movement differed from the movement command due to an obstacle. 75,000 labeled movement sequences were generated in this way.

Target values for physiological training were based on a simple statistical model of direction, speed, and disparity tuning in MT. The model population had speed tuning and disparity tuning based on [14,15], respectively. Features of the tuning curves included gaussian tuning for log-speed, and gabor disparity tuning.

To generate examples for physiological training, frames were taken at random from the self-motion sequences, and processed to create new image sequences of spatially uniform disparity and motion velocity. Specifically, for each new

Fig. 1. Four example stereo frames from the training data.

sequence, motion velocities and disparities were drawn at random, then a sequence of subimages was taken from a random frame in order to produce a stereo sequence with the corresponding disparity and velocity. The subimage size corresponded to the receptive field size of units in the third convolutional layer ("MT"). MT responses have been studied much more extensively with simple artificial stimuli than naturalistic stimuli (e.g. [23,24]), but responses to these different kinds of stimuli are closely related [25].

The Adam algorithm [26] was used throughout for weight and bias updates. The network was trained with 50 % dropout [12] in the final hidden layer. The network was trained in stages. First, the kernels of the first layer were held fixed, and the network up to the MT layer was trained to minimize (2). All parameters were then trained with a lower step size. Similarly, to minimize (1), the parameters up to the MT layer were fixed for an initial stage of training, then the step size was reduced and the full network was trained further.

3   Results

Figure 2 shows results of physiological training. Mean-squared error on validation data averaged .009 in the last ten epochs of training. Speed and direction tuning were similar to their targets (which were based on MT electrophysiology literature). Disparity tuning was much less accurate.

Figure 3 shows visual odometry predictions of the full network for novel inputs. The correlation between self-motion commands and the network's image-based estimates was $r = .92$.

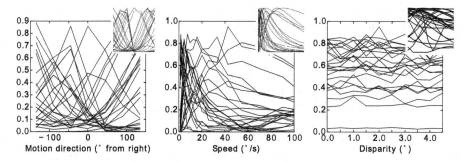

Fig. 2. Tuning curves of randomly selected neurons for motion direction (left), speed (centre), and disparity (right). Each point corresponds to a neuron's normalized output, averaged over ten *novel* naturalistic stimuli (i.e. stimuli not seen in training). Each curve shows variation in normalized rate, with preferred values of other stimulus parameters. The insets show corresponding target values. Variations in image texture contribute to the differences. The mean-squared error over validation examples was .009. The network's direction and speed tuning distributions were fairly realistic, but its disparity tuning was not.

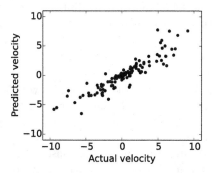

Fig. 3. Self-motion velocities estimated from visual input vs. targets, on examples not seen in training. The points include both medio-lateral and antero-posterior velocities.

4   Discussion

This study explored direct training of a deep convolutional layer to approximate statistics of primate neuron responses. A deep layer of the network approximated specified MT-like activity. Furthermore, the output of the full network was strongly correlated with self-motion velocity labels, despite some inconsistency between the actual and labelled velocity due to obstacles. Interestingly, direction and speed tuning were approximated much more closely than disparity tuning, perhaps due to unaccounted-for correlations between disparity preferences and other tuning features. Disparity tuning was slightly improved in a larger network (not shown). Direction and speed tuning were also surprisingly MT-like in networks trained only to minimize (1). The fit to neural data might be improved by incorporating additional physiologically-inspired mechanisms into the network, such as divisive normalization [27].

Despite recent successes, training deep networks remains difficult and computationally intensive, and requires a great deal of training data. The present approach may simplify deep learning in a way that is complementary to unsupervised learning. In particular, it suggests another way to organize deep layers into good initial representations for supervised learning.

Others have previously trained neural networks to approximate electrophysiological data [13], and even combined the training of a hidden layer to match electrophysiology data with output training for a task [28], as was done here.

Notably, despite increasing recording density, available data in the near future will be sparse relative to the large number of neurons in the primate visual cortex and the large variety of visual stimuli that animals encounter in life. The present approach suggests a principled way to extrapolate from the available electrophysiology data, by further constraining models to perform appropriate functions. This approach, which draws from brain structure, activity, and function, may make better use of available data than models with only brain-related structure and activity (but not function, e.g. [25]), or even models with brain-related structure and function, which also exhibit brain-related deep activity but are not specifically optimized to do so [13].

4.1 Future Work

Three major directions for future work are training with additional physiology data, using richer simulations for functional training on a wider range of tasks (e.g. grasping), and incorporating computational mechanisms that more closely resemble those of the brain.

There is an extensive literature on the responses of neurons in many visual areas to a wide range of stimuli. It is a labour-intensive process to organize this information (which appears as tuning curves, histograms of tuning preferences, percentages of neurons with different kinds of responses, etc.) into a statistical response model. However, on the basis of ongoing experience, it appears that a fairly rich statistical model of responses in a given area can be produced with about one-two person-years of effort, and there are only about thirty visual areas in the macaque monkey [1]. Furthermore, there is a trend toward more comprehensive physiological data sets (e.g. [29,30]).

There are, of course, large differences between convolutional networks and the visual cortex. One is the predominance of lateral and feedback connections in the cortex. Some potential approaches to modeling feedback connections include accounting for more subtle receptive field properties [31], modeling response dynamics [32], recurrent neural networks [33], and Markov random fields with convolutional layers as input [34]. For example, loopy belief propagation on a Markov random field may have parallels with gradual emergence of pattern selectivity in MT [16].

Acknowledgments. This work was supported by a Discovery Grant from the Natural Sciences and Engineering Reseach Council of Canada.

References

1. Felleman, D.J., Van Essen, D.C.: Distributed hierarchical processing in the primate cerebral cortex. Cereb. Cortex **1**, 1–47 (1991)
2. Wandell, B.A., Winawer, J.: Imaging retinotopic maps in the human brain. Vis. Res. **51**(7), 718–737 (2011)
3. Krüger, N., Janssen, P., Kalkan, S., Lappe, M., Leonardis, A., Piater, J., Rodríguez-Sánchez, A.J., Wiskott, L.: Deep hierarchies in the primate visual cortex: what can we learn for computer vision? IEEE Trans. Pattern Anal. Mach. Intell. **35**(8), 1847–1871 (2013)
4. Goodale, M.A., Milner, A.D.: Separate visual pathways for perception and action. Trends Neurosci. **15**(1), 20–25 (1992)
5. Tanaka, K.: Inferotemporal cortex and object vision. Ann. Rev. Neurosci. **19**, 109–139 (1996)
6. Ungerleider, L.G., Bell, A.H.: Uncovering the visual "alphabet": advances in our understanding of object perception. Vis. Res. **51**(7), 782–799 (2011)
7. O'Neil, E.B., Protzner, A.B., McCormick, C., McLean, D.A., Poppenk, J., Cate, A.D., Köhler, S.: Distinct patterns of functional and effective connectivity between perirhinal cortex and other cortical regions in recognition memory and perceptual discrimination. Cereb. Cortex **22**(1), 74–85 (2012)
8. Borra, E., Belmalih, A., Calzavara, R., Gerbella, M., Murata, A., Rozzi, S., Luppino, G.: Cortical connections of the macaque anterior intraparietal (AIP) area. Cereb. Cortex **18**(5), 1094–1111 (2008)
9. LeCun, Y., Boser, B., Denker, J.S., Henderson, D., Howard, R.E., Hubbard, W., Jackel, L.D.: Handwritten digit recognition with a back-propagation network. In: NIPS 1989, pp. 396–404 (1990)
10. Fukushima, K.: Neocognitron: a self-organizing neural network model for a mechanism of pattern recognition unaffected by shift in position. Biol. Cybern. **36**(4), 193–202 (1980)
11. Serre, T., Wolf, L., Bileschi, S., Riesenhuber, M., Poggio, T.: Robust object recognition with cortex-like mechanisms. IEEE Trans. Pattern Anal. Mach. Intell. **29**(3), 411–426 (2007)
12. Krizhevsky, A., Sutskever, I., Hinton, G.E.: ImageNet classification with deep convolutional neural networks. In: NIPS 2012, pp. 1–9 (2012)
13. Yamins, D.L.K., Hong, H., Cadieu, C.F., Solomon, E.A., Seibert, D., Dicarlo, J.J.: Performance-optimized hierarchical models predict neural responses in higher visual cortex. PNAS **111**(23), 8619–8624 (2014)
14. Nover, H., Anderson, C.H., DeAngelis, G.C.: A logarithmic, scale-invariant representation of speed in macaque middle temporal area accounts for speed discrimination performance. J. Neurosci. **25**(43), 10049–10060 (2005)
15. DeAngelis, G.C., Uka, T.: Coding of horizontal disparity and velocity by MT neurons in the alert macaque. J. Neurophysiol. **89**(2), 1094–1111 (2003)
16. Pack, C.C., Born, R.T.: Temporal dynamics of a neural solution to the aperture problem in visual area MT of macaque brain. Nature **409**(6823), 1040–1042 (2001)
17. Hubel, D.H., Wiesel, T.N.: Receptive fields of single neurones in the cat's striate cortex. J. Physiol. **148**, 574–591 (1959)

18. Markov, N.T., Ercsey-Ravasz, M.M., Ribeiro Gomes, A.R., Lamy, C., Magrou, L., Vezoli, J., Misery, P., Falchier, A., Quilodran, R., Gariel, M.A., Sallet, J., Gamanut, R., Huissoud, C., Clavagnier, S., Giroud, P., Sappey-Marinier, D., Barone, P., Dehay, C., Toroczkai, Z., Knoblauch, K., Van Essen, D.C., Kennedy, H.: A weighted and directed interareal connectivity matrix for macaque cerebral cortex. Cereb. Cortex **24**(1), 17–36 (2014)

19. Stevenson, I.H., Kording, K.P.: How advances in neural recording affect data analysis. Nat. Neurosci. **14**(2), 139–142 (2011)

20. Chollet, F.: Keras (2015). https://github.com/fchollet/keras

21. Bergstra, J., Bastien, F., Breuleux, O., Lamblin, P., Pascanu, R., Delalleau, O., Desjardins, G., Warde-Farley, D., Goodfellow, I., Bergeron, A., Bengio, Y.: Theano: deep learning on GPUs with Python. In: NIPS 2011 BigLearning Workshop, pp. 1–4 (2011)

22. Adelson, E.H., Bergen, J.R.: Spatiotemporal energy models for the perception of motion. J. Opt. Soci. Am. A, Opt. Image Sci. **2**(2), 284–299 (1985)

23. Britten, K.H., Shadlen, M.N., Newsome, W.T., Movshon, J.A.: The analysis of visual motion: a comparison of neuronal and psychophysical performance. J. Neurosci. **12**(12), 4745–4765 (1992)

24. Cook, E.P., Maunsell, J.H.R.: Dynamics of neuronal responses in macaque MT and VIP during motion detection. Nat. Neurosci. **5**(10), 985–994 (2002)

25. Nishimoto, S., Gallant, L.: A three-dimensional spatiotemporal receptive field model explains responses of area MT neurons to naturalistic movies. J. Neurosci. **31**(41), 14551–14564 (2011)

26. Kingma, D., Ba, J.: Adam: A Method for Stochastic Optimization. arxiv:1412.6980 [cs], pp. 1–15 (2014)

27. Carandini, M., Heeger, D.J.: Normalization as a canonical neural computation. Nat. Rev. Neurosci. **13**, 51–62 (2011)

28. Arai, K., Keller, E.L., Edelman, J.A.: Two-dimensional neural network model of the primate saccadic system. Neural Netw. **7**(6–7), 1115–1135 (1994)

29. Lehky, S.R., Kiani, R., Esteky, H., Tanaka, K.: Statistics of visual responses in primate inferotemporal cortex to object stimuli. J. Neurophysiol. **106**(3), 1097–1117 (2011)

30. Schaffelhofer, S., Scherberger, H.: From vision to action: a comparative population study of hand grasping areas AIP, F5, and M1. In: Bernstein Conference 2014 (2014)

31. Rubin, D.B., Van Hooser, S.D., Miller, K.D.: The stabilized supralinear network: a unifying circuit motif underlying multi-input integration in sensory cortex. Neuron **85**(1), 1–51 (2015)

32. Eliasmith, C.: A unified approach to building and controlling spiking attractor networks. Neural Comput. **17**(6), 1276–1314 (2005)

33. Pinheiro, P.H.O., Collobert, R.: Recurrent Convolutional Neural Networks for Scene Parsing, June 2013

34. Liu, F., Lin, G., Shen, C.: CRF learning with CNN features for image segmentation. Pattern Recogn. **48**(10), 2983–2992 (2015)

Pseudo Boosted Deep Belief Network

Tiehang Duan$^{(\boxtimes)}$ and Sargur N. Srihari

Department of Computer Science and Engineering,
The State University of New York at Buffalo, Buffalo, NY 14260, USA
tiehangd@buffalo.edu, srihari@cedar.buffalo.edu

Abstract. A computationally efficient method to improve classification performance of a Deep Belief Network (DBN) is introduced. In the Pseudo Boost Deep Belief Network (PB-DBN), top layers are boosted while lower layers of the base classifiers share weights for feature extraction. PB-DBN maintains the same time complexity as a DBN with fast convergence to optimality by introducing the mechanism of pseudo boost. Experiments in classification show that after only a few iterations, the PB-DBN has higher accuracy than a classic DBN.

1 Introduction

A Deep Belief Network (DBN) is a layered network formed with undirected connections between its top two layers and downward directed connections between all its lower layers (Fig. 1(a)) [13]. They are used to infer posterior probabilities and make generative predictions. Restricted Boltzmann Machines (RBM) formed by adjacent layers in DBN are pre-trained from bottom-up layer by layer, then the whole network is fine tuned with back propagation to serve discriminative purposes or up down algorithms for generative purposes [7]. Many approaches to improve the performance and time efficiency of DBNs have been published since G. Hinton et al. proposed the method in 2006 [7]. The improvements include new training methods such as re-weighted wake sleep algorithm [4], exponential loss function gradient method [11]; new architectures of the network such as convolutional architectures [9], sparse architectures [8], hierarchical architectures [15], sequential architectures [1]; and there are also works combining the power of other learning methods [16].

Boosting is an ensemble learning method that is used to improve the performance of base classifiers. Ping Liu et al. combined DBN with boosting for facial expression recognition [10], and revealed the potential to integrate boosting mechanism into DBN (Fig. 1(b)). In this paper, we integrate the power of boosting into DBN with the boosting mechanism re-weighting each data vector for each iteration and DBN re-represent the data on each layer. As the time complexity of boosting is polynomial to weak classifier's time complexity (the number of classifiers determine the order of polynomial), it is impractical to directly apply DBN to be the base classifier– since a single DBN is already computationally expensive. We address this issue with a computationally efficient weight sharing boost mechanism, with the resulting time complexity being of the same order as that of a single DBN.

© Springer International Publishing Switzerland 2016
A.E.P. Villa et al. (Eds.): ICANN 2016, Part II, LNCS 9887, pp. 105–112, 2016.
DOI: 10.1007/978-3-319-44781-0_13

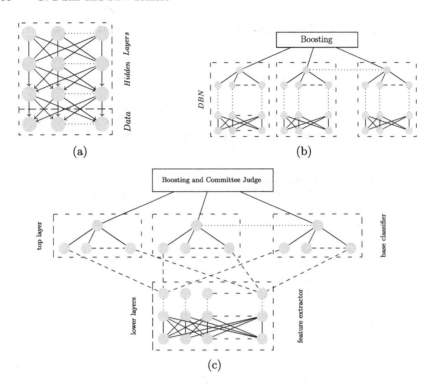

Fig. 1. Structure of (a) Deep Belief Network (DBN), (b) Boosted Deep Belief Network (BDBN) and (c) Pseudo Boosted Deep Belief Network (PB-DBN).

2   Pseudo Boosted Deep Belief Network

2.1   Initialization of the Network

Initialization of the proposed Pseudo-Boosted Deep Belief Network (PB-DBN) (Fig. 1(c)) is analogous to that of a DBN. RBMs formed by adjacent layers are trained in turn from bottom up by minimizing the *contrastive divergence*:

$$KL(P^0\|P_\theta^\infty) - KL(P_\theta^n\|P_\theta^\infty) \tag{1}$$

The first term in (1) is the Kullback Leibler divergence between the distribution of the data P^0 and the equilibrium distribution of the model P_θ^∞. The second term is the KL divergence between the posterior distribution P_θ^n and P_θ^∞ [2]. To make the probabilistic model computationally tractable and also easy to fine tune, we assume direct probabilistic dependence only exists between the adjacent layers, and the probability of activation for each hidden layer is the generalized linear sigmoid model of the adjacent hidden layer:

$$P(s_j = 1) = \frac{1}{1 + exp(-b_j - \sum_i s_i w_{ij})} \tag{2}$$

where s_i is the node in adjacent layer, s_j is the node in current layer, w_{ij} is the corresponding edge weight and b_j is the bias term. The adjustment of weights during the pre-training phase follows the gradient of log probability of training data:

$$\frac{\partial log(p(v^0))}{\partial w_{ij}} = < v_i^0 h_j^0 > - < v_i^\infty h_j^\infty > \tag{3}$$

where v_i^0 is the node in the visible layer under initialization, v_i^∞ is the node in the visible layer after reaching equilibrium, h_j^0 is the node in the hidden layer after initialization, h_j^∞ is the node in the hidden layer after reaching equilibrium, $< v_i^0 h_j^0 >$ is the correlation between v_i^0 and h_j^0, and $< v_i^\infty h_j^\infty >$ is the correlation between v_i^∞ and h_j^∞ [5]. After the training of each RBM, the value in hidden layer is stored and used as data for the next layer's training.

When all RBMs finish training, the change of weights in the higher layers make the lower layers no longer optimal for the whole network [2]. Two fine-tuning methods can be used to further adjust weights. Error back propagation can be used for discriminative tuning and up down algorithms can be used for generative purposes. A detailed description can be found in [7].

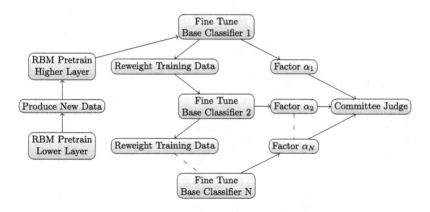

Fig. 2. Illustration of PB-DBN mechanism.

2.2 Mechanism of Pseudo Boost

The boosting mechanism assigns different weights to data points based on the importance of each data [3]. The data weights are iteratively adjusted based on classification result in previous iteration:

$$w_n^{(m+1)} = w_n^{(m)} exp\left(\alpha_m I(y_m(\mathbf{x}_n) \neq t_n) \right) \tag{4}$$

where $\mathbf{x}_n$ is the n th data, $y_m(\mathbf{x_n})$ is the classification decision made by the m th base classifier, t_n is the label of training data $\mathbf{x_n}$, $w_n^{(m)}$ is the weight of

n th data in the m th iteration, and α_m is defined as the log odd of the weighted error rate ε_m:

$$\varepsilon_m = \frac{\sum_{n=1}^{N} w_n^{(m)} I(y_m(\mathbf{x}_n) \neq t_n)}{\sum_{n=1}^{N} w_n^{(m)}} \tag{5}$$

$$\alpha_m = \frac{1}{2} log \left(\frac{1 - \varepsilon_m}{\varepsilon_m} \right) \tag{6}$$

Then the updated data is used to train the next base classifier so the next base classifier can learn something new [6,14]. And when the training phase is over, the final classification is made based on decision of the committee formed by the base classifiers:

$$Y_M(\mathbf{x}_n) = sign \left(\sum_{m=1}^{M} \alpha_m y_m(\mathbf{x}_n) \right) \tag{7}$$

where $y_m(\mathbf{x}_n)$ is as defined in (4) and α_m as defined in (6).

The model can be easily implemented with simple base classifiers such as Stumps, SVMs or simple decision trees [12]. However, it is met with computational complexity issues when a DBN is the base classifier. Since time complexity of boosting is polynomial to time complexity of each base classifier with the order of the polynomial being the number of classifiers. For most instances, it is impractical to directly adopt the classic boosting mechanism. Pseudo boosting can be viewed as a partial boost that operates only on the top layers of the network (Fig. 1(c)).

In the proposed method, lower layers of the individual deep belief network serve as feature extractors and as they share great similarity to one another [7], it would be a waste of computational resource if we repeatedly train the lower layers every time we initialize a new base classifier, so every time when we start training the new classifier in PB-DBN, the lower layers of previous base classifier is directly used. In the fine tuning phase, different classifiers get different emphasis on the difficult training data(which is done by changing the data sampling distribution). Then the mechanism of boosting allows these classifiers to be unified together to minimize the total exponential error function:

$$E = \sum_{n=1}^{N} exp \left(- t_n y_m(\mathbf{x_n}) \right) \tag{8}$$

where $y_m(\mathbf{x_n})$ and t_n are the same as defined in (4). Detailed illustration of the PB-DBN mechanism is shown in Fig. 2.

2.3   Time Complexity Analysis

We denote the training time needed for each RBM as t_{rbm}, the fine tuning time for the whole network as t_{tune}, and the time for classifier committee to make the judgment as t_c, then the training time of the PB-DBN model is:

$$T_{PB-DBN} = t_{rbm} + k \times t_{tune} + t_c \tag{9}$$

Table 1. Experiment result on different network settings

Hidden layers	Iterations	Train error rate		Test error rate	
(Lower -> Upper)	(Pretrain – Fine Tune)	DBN	PB-DBN	DBN	PB-DBN
784 -> 256	6 – 6	2.58 %	0.42 %	3.66 %	1.83 %
784 -> 256	10 – 10	0.62 %	0.12 %	2.10 %	1.76 %
784 -> 256	20 – 20	0.02 %	0.02 %	1.78 %	1.70 %
784 -> 256	50 – 50	0.00 %	0.00 %	1.68 %	1.60 %
784 -> 784 -> 256	6 – 6	3.44 %	0.36 %	3.99 %	1.86 %
784 -> 784 -> 256	10 – 10	0.91 %	0.20 %	2.40 %	1.72 %
784 -> 784 -> 256	20 – 20	0.09 %	0.07 %	1.82 %	1.65 %
784 -> 784 -> 256	50 – 50	0.00 %	0.00 %	1.71 %	1.64 %

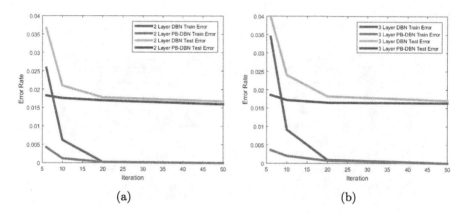

(a)   (b)

Fig. 3. Comparison of performance between DBN and PB-DBN. (a) Train error and test error of 2 layer networks. (b) Train error and test error of 3 layer networks.

where k is the number of classifiers in the model. And if we adopt the normal boosting procedure, the training time would be:

$$T_{Boost-DBN} = k \times t_{rbm} + k \times t_{tune} + t_c \qquad (10)$$

Comparing (9) and (10), the PB-DBN model reduces time complexity by avoiding repetitive training in the RBMs.

3   Experimental Results

As the performance of DBN is superior to boosting with normal base classifiers such as stumps, decision trees or single-hidden layer neural networks, here we compare the performance of PB-DBN with DBN.

We performed batch training with each batch containing 100 data and a total of 600 batches. Conjugate gradient descent is used in the fine tuning phase

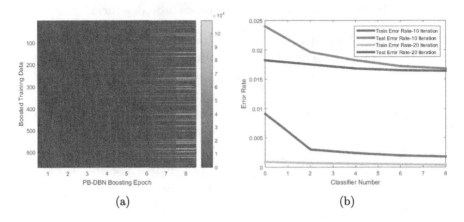

Fig. 4. (a) Evolution of boosted weights in PB-DBN. (b) Performance of PB-DBN with different number of base classifiers.

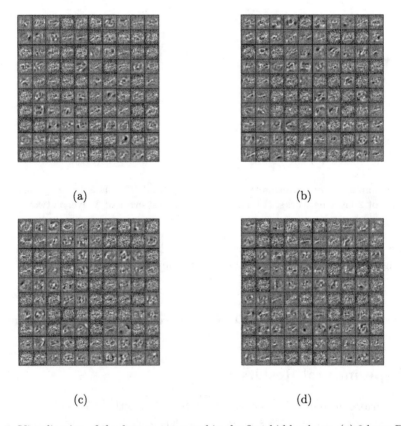

Fig. 5. Visualization of the feature extracted in the first hidden layer. (a) 2 layer DBN, 20 iterations training; (b) 3 layer DBN, 50 iterations training; (c) 2 layer PB-DBN, 20 iterations training; (d) 3 layer PB-DBN, 50 iterations training.

Table 2. Performance with different number of classifiers (10 iterations)

Classfier number	Hidden layers	Train error rate	Test error rate
1	784 -> 784 -> 256	0.91 %	2.40 %
2	784 -> 784 -> 256	0.30 %	1.96 %
4	784 -> 784 -> 256	0.24 %	1.88 %
6	784 -> 784 -> 256	0.20 %	1.72 %
8	784 -> 784 -> 256	0.18 %	1.68 %

and we test our method with base classifier DBN of both 2 hidden layers and 3 hidden layers (Table 1). We see PB-DBN outperforms DBN on all sets of comparative experiments. The unique strength of PB-DBN method as revealed in Fig. 3 is its fast convergence to optimality, as the boosting mechanism is making the difficult data to be more significant and makes the training phase more efficient. The parameters including learning rate(0.1), momentum(0.2), weight initialization(0.1) and weight-decay(0.0002) are chosen by training the network several times and observing its performance on the separate validation dataset. Figure 5 shows most of the features extracted in the lower layers of the base classifiers are similar to one another, confirms the rationality of the mechanism. From Fig. 4(a), we see the weight increase of the difficult digits is rapid under boosting, which is the major reason that PB-DBN is achieving superior performance. And with more base classifiers involved in the committee judgement, the performance of PB-DBN improves (Table 2 and Fig. 4(b)).

4   Conclusion

In this paper, we described the Pseudo Boost Deep Belief Network (PB-DBN). Its unique strength is fast convergence to optimality while maintaining the same time complexity as DBN. In the model, top layers of DBNs are boosted based on different weighted data which helps the base classifiers (DBNs) to focus on more difficult data points, while the lower layers of the belief networks share weights for feature extraction. The method is computationally efficient and can be readily used for practical applications.

References

1. Andrew, G., Bilmes, J.: Sequential deep belief networks. In: IEEE International Conference Acoustics, Speech Signal Proceedings (ICASSP), pp. 4265–4268 (2012)
2. Bengio, Y., Lamblin, P., Popovici, D., Larochelle, H., et al.: Greedy layer-wise training of deep networks. Adv. Neural Inf. Process. Syst. **19**, 153 (2007)
3. Bishop, C.M.: Pattern Recognition and Machine Learning (Information Science and Statistics). Springer-Verlag New York Inc., Secaucus (2006)
4. Bornschein, J., Bengio, Y.: Reweighted wake-sleep. CoRR abs/1406.2751 (2014)

5. Fischer, A., Igel, C.: An introduction to restricted Boltzmann machines. In: Alvarez, L., Mejail, M., Gomez, L., Jacobo, J. (eds.) CIARP 2012. LNCS, vol. 7441, pp. 14–36. Springer, Heidelberg (2012)

6. Friedman, J., Hastie, T., Tibshirani, R.: Additive logistic regression: a statistical view of boosting (with discussion and a rejoinder by the authors). Ann. Statist. **28**(2), 337–407 (2000)

7. Hinton, G.E., Osindero, S., Teh, Y.W.: A fast learning algorithm for deep belief nets. Neural Comput. **18**(7), 1527–1554 (2006)

8. Lee, H., Ekanadham, C., Ng, A.Y.: Sparse deep belief net model for visual area v2. In: Platt, J.C., Koller, D., Singer, Y., Roweis, S.T. (eds.) Advances in Neural Information Processing Systems, vol. 20, pp. 873–880. Curran Associates (2008)

9. Lee, H., Grosse, R., Ranganath, R., Ng, A.Y.: Convolutional deep belief networks for scalable unsupervised learning of hierarchical representations. In: Proceedings of the 26th Annual International Conference on Machine Learning, ICML 2009, pp. 609–616. ACM, New York (2009)

10. Liu, P., Han, S., Meng, Z., Tong, Y.: Facial expression recognition via a boosted deep belief network. In: IEEE Conference on Computer Vision and Pattern Recognition (CVPR) (2014)

11. Liu, Y., Zhou, S., Chen, Q.: Discriminative deep belief networks for visual data classification. Pattern Recogn. **44**(10–11), 2287–2296 (2011)

12. Pham, T.V., Smeulders, A.W.M.: Quadratic boosting. Pattern Recogn. **41**(1), 331–341 (2008)

13. Salakhutdinov, R., Hinton, G.E.: Deep boltzmann machines. In: Proceedings of the International Conference on Artificial Intelligence and Statistics, vol. 5, pp. 448–455 (2009)

14. Sun, Y., Todorovic, S., Li, J.: Increasing the robustness of boosting algorithms within the linear-programming framework. J. VLSI Signal Process. Syst. Signal Image Video Technol. **48**(1), 5–20 (2007)

15. Wang, Y., Yang, J.A., Lu, J., Liu, H., Wang, L.W.: Hierarchical deep belief networks based point process model for keywords spotting in continuous speech. Int. J. Commun. Syst. **28**(3), 483–496 (2015)

16. Zhiqiang, C., Chuan, L., Sánchez, R.V.: Multi-layer neural network with deep belief network for gearbox fault diagnosis. J. Vibroengineering **17**(5), 2379–2392 (2015)

Keyword Spotting with Convolutional Deep Belief Networks and Dynamic Time Warping

Baptiste Wicht[1,2]([⊠]), Andreas Fischer[1,2], and Jean Hennebert[1,2]

[1] University of Applied Science of Western Switerzland, Delémont, Switzerland
[2] University of Fribourg, Fribourg, Switzerland
baptiste.wicht@hefr.ch

Abstract. To spot keywords on handwritten documents, we present a hybrid keyword spotting system, based on features extracted with Convolutional Deep Belief Networks and using Dynamic Time Warping for word scoring. Features are learned from word images, in an unsupervised manner, using a sliding window to extract horizontal patches. For two single writer historical data sets, it is shown that the proposed learned feature extractor outperforms two standard sets of features.

1 Introduction

Although it has been the subject of research for decades, handwriting recognition remains a widely unsolved problem [23]. For large vocabularies, different writing styles and degraded documents, the accuracy of automatic transcription is not perfect. Under these conditions, keyword spotting solutions have been suggested instead of a complete transcription for spotting words in document images [13].

Keyword spotting solutions fall in two categories. *Template-based* methods match a query word image with labeled keyword template images. This approach has the advantage that it is rather easy to gather template images and it is not necessary to know the underlying language or its alphabet. However, for each keyword that is to be spotted, at least one template image is necessary. Furthermore, such systems typically do not generalize well to unknown writing styles. Such systems have been applied to speech [16,21], poorly printed documents [1,10] and handwritten text [14]. Many features have been proposed for keyword spotting with Dynamic Time Warping (DTW) and a sliding window [18], such as word profiles [19] and local gradients features [20].

On the other hand, *learning-based* systems are using statistical learning to train a model to score query images. Hidden Markov Model (HMM) were first used for keyword spotting at character level with template images [5]. Similar solutions were developed at word level using local gradient features [2]. Although trained word models are expected to exhibit better generalization than template-based methods, they still need a large amount of training templates. Moreover, such systems are not able to spot out-of-vocabulary keywords. Recently, a lexicon-free approach using character HMMs has been proposed [3], as well as character models based on Recurrent Neural Networks [6].

© Springer International Publishing Switzerland 2016
A.E.P. Villa et al. (Eds.): ICANN 2016, Part II, LNCS 9887, pp. 113–120, 2016.
DOI: 10.1007/978-3-319-44781-0_14

Both categories are relying on features extracted from the images. Such features are generally handcrafted and optimizing them is often non-trivial. In recent years, the emergence of *Deep Learning* has shown that it was possible to learn features directly from pixels. While Restricted Boltzmann Machines (RBM) have originally been used to initialize the weights of a neural network in an unsupervised manner [8], they also have been extensively used to extract features from a dataset [9]. RBMs can also be stacked into Deep Belief Networks (DBN) to extract multi-layer features [12,24]. Convolutional RBMs have proved especially successful to extract features from images [12,25].

In the present paper, we propose a hybrid word spotting system for handwritten text, based on Convolutional Deep Belief Networks and Dynamic Time Warping. While this system is essentially *template-based*, it has the advantage that features are automatically extracted from the images using unsupervised learning, making use of unlabeled handwriting images which are abundantly available. When compared with learning-based approaches, the proposed method has the advantage that no labeled images are needed. However, it requires a segmentation of images into words, which can be prone to errors.

The proposed system has been tested on two well-known benchmark data sets for keyword spotting, namely the George Washington and Parzival data sets. Our features are compared with two benchmark feature sets [15,20].

2   Keyword Spotting System

Keyword spotting is the task of retrieving keywords from document images. The present research focuses on handwritten documents. The input of the system is a word image and a keyword. For each input, the system must decide whether the image contains the requested keyword or not. The decision for the image X and keyword K is decided by a threshold over a dissimilarity measure: $ds(X, K) < T$. T can be selected based on a trade-off between system precision and recall.

In this work, we focus on perfectly segmented text word images. The images are first binarized and then normalized to remove the skew and slant of the text. The complete normalization process is described in details in [15]. From each input image, patches are extracted using a horizontal sliding window. The patch height is always equal to the height of the image. Each patch is W pixels wide. The window is moved two pixels at a time from left to right.

2.1   Convolutional Restricted Boltzmann Machine

A Restricted Boltzmann Machine (RBM) is a generative stochastic Artificial Neural Network (ANN). It is designed to learn a probability distribution over the inputs. The training of an RBM tries to maximize the Log-Likelihood of the learned input distribution. RBMs only rose to a large audience, after the Contrastive Divergence (CD) algorithm was introduced [7]. CD is a fast learning algorithm to train an RBM, very similar to the gradient descent of a neural network. CD approximates the Log-Likelihood gradients of the input distribution by minimizing the reconstruction error, thus training the RBM into an autoen-coder. An RBM has two layers, a visible layer and an hidden layer. There are no connection between units of the same layer (bipartite graph).

The RBM model was extended to the Convolutional RBM (CRBM) model [12]. Taking advantage of convolution, a CRBM learns feature detectors shared among all locations in an image. This allows the feature representations to be invariant to local translations in the input and allows learning to scale to realistically sized images. The model is outlined in Fig. 1. It is the build-ing block of the proposed feature extraction system. The visible layer is made of $N_V \times N_V$ binary units. The hidden layer is made of K groups of $N_H \times N_H$ binary units. The layers are connected by K convolutional filters of shape $N_W \times N_W$ $(N_W \triangleq N_V - N_H + 1)$.

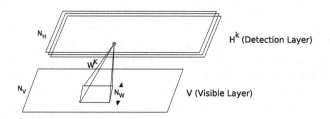

Fig. 1. A Convolutional Restricted Boltzmann Machine.

2.2   Feature Extraction

Features are extracted from one patch using a Convolutional Deep Belief Network (CDBN) [12]. This network is composed of two CRBM. The network is only trained in an unsupervised manner, i.e. labels are not used to train the network. Once the first layer is trained, its weights are frozen and its features are passed to the next layer. The network used for feature extraction is presented in Fig. 2.

Generally, higher levels of an ANN encode information about progressively larger input regions. Typical Convolutional Neural Networks use pooling lay-ers to shrink the representation by a small factor. Probabilistic Max Pooling was introduced for generative models to support both top-down and bottom-up inference [12]. This operator shrinks the representation by a factor C. Each layer of the proposed CDBN model uses this operator in order to improve translation-invariance, reduce the computational cost and reduce the number of features.

One patch is passed to the first layer. Then, the activation probabilities of the pooling layer are computed. These probabilities are passed to the second layer, which computes the final features for the patch from its pooling layer. From the network, we define $F(X)$ as a sequence of feature vectors (one for each patch):

$$F(X) = [CDBN(x_1), CDBN(x_2), ..., CDBN(x_N)] \tag{1}$$

The features are normalized so that each feature vector has zero-mean and unit variance.

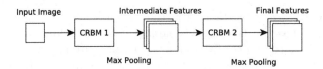

Fig. 2. Convolutional Deep Belief Network used for feature extraction

2.3 Dynamic Time Warping

Dynamic Time Warping (DTW) is a technique used to find an optimal alignment between two sequences of different length. Sequences are warped non-linearly so that they match each other. It is well established in the field of keyword spotting [19]. The cost of an alignment is the sum of the $d(x, y)$ distances of each aligned pair. This system uses the squared Euclidean distance.

The DTW distance $D(F(X), F(Y))$ of two feature vector sequences $F(X)$ and $F(Y)$ is given by the minimum alignment cost. For speeding up the process and improving the results, a Sakoe-Chiba band [22] is used. When several occurrences of the keyword are available in the training set, the example that minimizes the distance for the currently tested image is selected. The DTW distance over the features is used as the final dissimilarity measure $ds(X, K)$.

3   Experimental Evaluation

We compare the features extracted by the proposed system with two other feature sets known to work well with DTW. Marti2001 [15] is a well-established heuristic set of features and has been used repeatedly for keyword spotting. It is made of nine geometrical features per column of the image. Rodriguez2008 [20] uses local gradient histogram features with overlapping windows.

The proposed system was evaluated using two benchmark data sets. The George Washington data set (GW) [11] is composed of 20 pages of letters written by George Washington and his associates. Due to the small amount of samples, a four-fold cross validation is used for experimental evaluation. It is made of 4894 word images. The Parzival data set (PAR) [4] contains 45 pages of a medieval manuscript, written in the 13th century. The set contains 23485 word images. Although the data sets have several writers, the styles being very similar, they are considered as *single-writer*. The system uses the normalized word images, ground truth, keywords, training sets, validation sets and test sets made available by [3].

For evaluation, a set of keywords is spotted on the test set of both data sets. The performance is measured for two different scenarios. The *global* scenario measures the Average Precision (AP) of the system, using a single *global threshold*. The *local* scenario measures the Mean Average Precision (MAP), using a *local threshold* for each keyword. These values are considered to assess the system performance. The `trec_eval`[1] software is used to compute these values [3].

---

[1] http://trec.nist.gov/trec_eval.

Since the DTW algorithm requires an example in order to compute a distance, the keywords considered for performance evaluation are constrained to those that appear at least once in the training set and once in the test set.

3.1 System Setup

The parameters for training the model and the architecture parameters were optimized for the task. For each data set, these parameters have been optimized individually with respect to the MAP and AP performance on the validation set. The performance of the system is measured on the independent test set.

Both networks have 2 layers of CRBM with Probabilistic Max Pooling. Each patch is 20 pixels wide (W). The GW network first layer is made of 8 9×9 filters followed by 8 3×3 filters. The PAR network has 12 9×9 filters followed by 10 3×3 filters. The pooling ratio (C) for each layer has been set to 2. The networks have been trained for 50 epochs of Contrastive Divergence, using mini-batch training. To improve generalization, L2 weight decay has been applied to all weights. The filters have been initialized using a zero-mean normal distribution with a variance of 0.01, the hidden biases to -0.1 and the visible biases to 0.

4 Results and Discussion

The experimental results are presented in Table 1. In both scenarios and for both data sets, the proposed system outperformed both reference feature sets. In the following discussion, the relative improvements are reported with respect to the Rodriguez2008 system which always outperforms Marti2001.

Table 1. Mean Average Precision (MAP) and Average Precision (AP) for the different features. The relative improvement over the best baseline is also mentioned. For the GW data set, the results have been averaged over the four cross validation runs.

System	GW		PAR	
	AP	MAP	AP	MAP
Marti2001	33.24	45.26	50.67	46.78
Rodriguez2008	41.20	63.39	55.82	47.52
Proposed	**55.65**	**67.43**	**58.82**	**62.42**
Improvement	35.07 %	6.37 %	5.37 %	31.35 %

For the GW data set, in the global scenario, the proposed system clearly outperformed both reference systems, by 35.07 %. In the local scenario, our system is also able to outperform the local gradient features by 6.37 %. For the PAR data set, the proposed system performs much better than the benchmark in the local scenario, outperforming it by 31.35 %. In the global scenario, our system also outperforms the baseline by 5.37 %.

Overall, the proposed system exhibits more stable performance than the two baselines. While both datasets are quite different, the performance are quite similar, showing the utility of the unsupervised feature learning system over handcrafted features that are harder to generalize over different datasets. This can be observed with the local histogram features that are clearly outperforming the local geometrical features on GW, but are almost on par on the PAR dataset.

In spite of the significant improvements, optimization of our model proved quite challenging. The model has many parameters and their parametrization is very important. Moreover, the model needs to be tuned in order to provide features that can be used with DTW. The number of outputs revealed very important to tune with respect to the system performance on the independent validation set. Due to the simple Euclidean Distance used in the DTW distance, having too many output features can decrease the performance. Therefore, we focused on networks yielding reasonable number of features. Models with only one layer proved to learn only low-level features and produced too many features. On the contrary, the inputs were not complex enough for a three layer network, which failed to generalize. For these reasons, a two-layer model was selected. The number of filters (K) has different effects. Increasing it improves the learning capacity of the model. Thus, it is typically large in convolutional networks, ranging from 50 to 400 per layer. However, increasing the number of filters of the final layer also increases the number of features used by the DTW. Experiments have shown that large number of filters strongly decreased the performance.

The patch width proved an important factor. This parameter was limited by the size of the convolutional filters (the patch must be at least as wide as the filter), so they had to be optimized together. Experimentally, for both data sets, the optimal patch width was found to be 20 pixels. Interestingly, this is slightly larger than the average width of a character in the data sets. Narrower patches proved rather unsuccessful and wider patches only increased the computational burden of the system without increasing its performance.

While binary hidden units proved to work well for both data sets, Rectified Linear Units (ReLU) [17] proved more effective on the PAR data set. They improved the AP by 20 % and the MAP by 24 %. While producing good results on the GW data set, they did not prove as effective as binary hidden units, being around 5 % to 8 % less effective. It seems that they were not able to learn generic features with the small number of available samples, while the large number of images in the PAR data set helped them generalize more effectively. This may indicate that there were too many ReLUs for the small number of samples.

For the network with binary units, enforcing sparsity of the hidden units improved the performance by 21 % in the global scenario and 13 % in the local one, on the validation set. This helped learning generic features, better for discrimination. While the network was able to learn reconstruction without sparsity, the features were not generic enough. We followed Lee et al. regularization method [9] where updates are made to the visible biases to reach a certain sparsity with some learning rate. The sparsity parameters have been chosen so that the sparsity was reached while still allowing the network to learn.

5   Conclusion and Future Work

A keyword spotting system extracting features using Convolutional Deep Belief Networks and scoring word with Dynamic Time Warping was presented for handwritten keyword spotting. The proposed system was experimentally compared with two other sets of features on two different benchmark data sets. On both data sets, the proposed system outperformed the two baselines. The best improvements were observed in the scenario where a single threshold is used for the whole data set when deciding whether or not a word is spotted and very few templates per keyword were available. Moreover, the proposed system proved similarly effective on two very different data sets.

Future work could go in several directions. The discriminative power of the learned features could be improved by training the network for classification, using the word labels after pretraining. This could lead to more discriminative features. Augmenting the data set with geometrical distortions may also lead to a more generic feature extractor. Better normalization of the extracted features is also likely to improve the results. Testing the system on a multiple writer data set would prove useful in evaluating the genericity of the extracted features.

The C++ implementations of the proposed system[2] and our CDBN library[3] are freely available on-line.

References

1. Chen, F.R., Wilcox, L.U., Bloomberg, D.S.: Word spotting in scanned images using Hidden Markov Models. In: Proceedings of the IEEE International Conference on Acoustics Speech and Signal Processing, vol. 5, pp. 1–4. IEEE (1993)
2. Choisy, C.: Dynamic handwritten keyword spotting based on the NSHP-HMM. In: Proceedings of the IEEE International Conference on Document Analysis and Recognition, vol. 1, pp. 242–246. IEEE (2007)
3. Fischer, A., Keller, A., Frinken, V., Bunke, H.: Lexicon-free handwritten word spotting using character HMMs. Pattern Recogn. Lett. **33**, 934–942 (2012)
4. Fischer, A., Wüthrich, M., Liwicki, M., Frinken, V., Bunke, H., Viehhauser, G., Stolz, M.: Automatic transcription of handwritten medieval documents. In: Proceedings of the International Conference on Virtual Systems and Multimedia, pp. 137–142. IEEE (2009)
5. Forsyth, D., Jaety, E., Teh, Y.W., Maire, M., Bock, R.B., Vesom, G.: Making latin manuscripts searchable using gHMMs. In: Proceedings of the Advances in Neural Information Processing Systems, vol. 17, p. 385. MIT Press (2005)
6. Frinken, V., Fischer, A., Manmatha, R., Bunke, H.: A novel word spotting method based on recurrent neural networks. IEEE Trans. Pattern Anal. Mach. Intell. **34**, 211–224 (2012)
7. Hinton, G.E.: Training products of experts by minimizing contrastive divergence. Neural Comput. **14**, 1771–1800 (2002)
8. Hinton, G.E., Salakhutdinov, R.R.: Reducing the dimensionality of data with neural networks. Science **313**(5786), 504–507 (2006)

---

[2] https://github.com/wichtounet/word_spotting/tree/paper_v2.
[3] https://github.com/wichtounet/dll.

9. Honglak, L., Chaitanya, E., Ng, A.Y.: Sparse deep belief net model for visual area V2. In: Proceedings of the Advances in Neural Information Processing Systems, pp. 873–880 (2008)
10. Kuo, S.S., Agazzi, O.E.: Keyword spotting in poorly printed documents using pseudo 2-D Hidden Markov Models. IEEE Trans. Pattern Anal. Mach. Intell. **16**, 842–848 (1994)
11. Lavrenko, V., Rath, T.M., Manmatha, R.: Holistic word recognition for handwritten historical documents. In: Proceedings of the International Workshop on Document Image Analysis for Libraries, pp. 278–287. IEEE (2004)
12. Lee, H., Grosse, R., Ranganath, R., Ng, A.Y.: Convolutional deep belief networks for scalable unsupervised learning of hierarchical representations. In: Proceedings of the International Conference on Machine Learning, pp. 609–616. ACM (2009)
13. Manmatha, R., Croft, W.: Word spotting: indexing handwritten archives. In: Intelligent Multimedia Information Retrieval Collection, pp. 43–64 (1997)
14. Manmatha, R., Han, C., Riseman, E.M.: Word spotting: a new approach to indexing handwriting. In: Proceedings of the IEEE Conference on Computer Vision and Pattern Recognition, pp. 631–637. IEEE (1996)
15. Marti, U.V., Bunke, H.: Using a statistical language model to improve the performance of an HMM-based cursive handwriting recognition system. Int. J. Pattern Recogn. Artif. Intell. **15**, 65–90 (2001)
16. Myers, C., Rabiner, L., Rosenberg, A.: An investigation of the use of dynamic time warping for word spotting and connected speech recognition. In: Proceedings of the IEEE International Conference on Acoustics Speech and Signal Processing, vol. 5, pp. 173–177. IEEE (1980)
17. Nair, V., Hinton, G.E.: Rectified linear units improve restricted Boltzmann machines. In: Proceedings of the International Conference on Machine Learning, pp. 807–814 (2010)
18. Rath, T.M., Manmatha, R.: Word image matching using dynamic time warping. In: Proceedings of the IEEE Conference on Computer Vision and Pattern Recognition, vol. 2, pp. 521–527. IEEE (2003)
19. Rath, T.M., Manmatha, R.: Word spotting for historical documents. Int. J. Doc. Anal. Recogn. (IJDAR) **9**, 139–152 (2007)
20. Rodrıguez, J.A., Perronnin, F.: Local gradient histogram features for word spotting in unconstrained handwritten documents. In: Proceedings of the International Conference on Frontiers in Handwriting Recognition, pp. 7–12 (2008)
21. Rose, R.C., Paul, D.B.: A Hidden Markov Model based keyword recognition system. In: Proceedings of the International Conference on Acoustics Speech, and Signal Processing, pp. 129–132. IEEE (1990)
22. Sakoe, H., Chiba, S.: Dynamic programming algorithm optimization for spoken word recognition. IEEE Trans. Acoust. Speech Signal Process. **26**, 43–49 (1978)
23. Vinciarelli, A.: A survey on off-line cursive word recognition. Pattern Recogn. **35**, 1433–1446 (2002)
24. Wicht, B., Hennebert, J.: Camera-based Sudoku recognition with deep belief network. In: Proceedings the of IEEE International Conference of Soft Computing and Pattern Recognition, pp. 83–88. IEEE (2014)
25. Wicht, B., Hennebert, J.: Mixed handwritten and printed digit recognition in Sudoku with convolutional deep belief network. In: Proceedings of the IEEE International Conference on Document Analysis and Recognition. IEEE (2015)

Computational Advantages
of Deep Prototype-Based Learning

Thomas Hecht and Alexander Gepperth[✉]

U2IS, Flowers Team, Inria, Université Paris-Saclay,
828 Blvd des Maréchaux, 91762 Palaiseau Cedex, France
`alexander.gepperth@ensta.fr`

Abstract. We present a deep prototype-based learning architecture which achieves a performance that is competitive to a conventional, shallow prototype-based model but at a fraction of the computational cost, especially w.r.t. memory requirements. As prototype-based classification and regression methods are typically plagued by the exploding number of prototypes necessary to solve complex problems, this is an important step towards efficient prototype-based classification and regression. We demonstrate these claims by benchmarking our deep prototype-based model on the well-known MNIST dataset.

Keywords: Prototype-based learning · Pattern recognition · Deep learning · Incremental learning

1 Introduction

This study is conducted in the field of *prototype-based machine learning*, and especially regarding the question how to render such machine learning approaches more efficient w.r.t. memory consumption. In prototype-based learning, the probability distribution in data space is not expressed in parametric form but by a learned set of samples, the so-called *prototypes*. Prototype-based machine learning methods were originally motivated by prototype theory from cognitive psychology (see, e.g., [1]) which claims that semantic categories in the human mind are represented by a set of "most typical" examples (or prototypes) for these categories. Well-known prototype-based approaches are the learning vector quantization (LVQ) model [2], the RBF model [3] or the self-organizing map (SOM) model [4]. A very popular prototype-based method in computer vision in is particle filtering [5], where a continuous, evolving probability density function is described and updated as a set of prototypes (here denoted *particles*) whose local density represents local probability density. Prototype-based methods are well suited for incremental learning [6,7] since prototypes have a very obvious interpretation, and can thus be manipulated easily, e.g., by adding,

---

A. Gepperth—Thomas Hecht gratefully acknowledges funding support by the "Direction Générale de l'Armement" (DGA) and Ecole Polytechnique.

A.E.P. Villa et al. (Eds.): ICANN 2016, Part II, LNCS 9887, pp. 121–127, 2016.
DOI: 10.1007/978-3-319-44781-0_15

adapting or removing prototypes (see [8] for a precise definition of incremental learning).

Prototype-based learning usually has a "flat" architecture (such as the RBF or the LVQ models) with one hidden layer between input and output, where hidden layer weights (the prototypes) describe the input distribution. An obvious problem of such flat architectures is the curse of dimensionality: complex probability distributions in high-dimensional spaces may conceivably require a great number of prototypes to be well approximated, so the memory requirements of flat prototype-based learning can become excessive depending on the problem at hand [9].

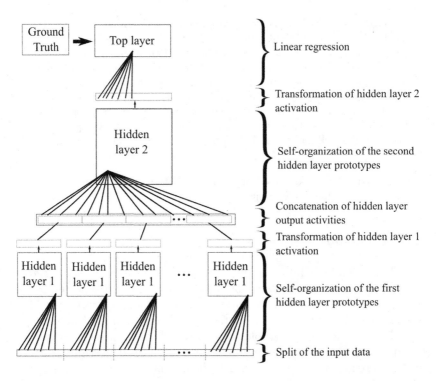

Fig. 1. Hierarchical system used in this study, composed of one input layer, two hidden layers and one top layer.

This study generalizes "flat" prototype-based learning as presented in [7] to a deep architecture (see Fig. 1), with localized receptive fields in the lower layers, just as it is the case in convolutional neural networks (CNNs, see [10]). This makes use of the probabilistic structure of images whose distant parts (receptive fields) are often approximately independent. In this case, it is far more efficient to model their distributions independently as well. If this is done by prototypes, the curse of dimensionality is reversed: as the required number of prototypes can *increase* exponentially with dimensionality, it can also *decrease* exponentially since the dimension of receptive fields is small. In its simplest form, this comes down to a deep four-layer architecture (see Fig. 1), where the first hidden layer now contains prototype activities related to local descriptions of the input, which are subsequently integrated into a global representation in the second hidden layer.

What is presented here adds an entirely new quality to [7] by passing from a "flat" architecture to a deep one. In doing so, we show that all desirable properties, notably incremental learning capacity, can be retained while offering considerable added value. In fact, the principal goal of this study is to show that such a deep prototype-based classifier can achieve a performance that is comparable to its flat counterpart but at a dramatically reduced number of connection weights, which reduces memory consumption and training time. For this purpose, we use the well-known MNIST dataset [11] which is an accepted benchmark in the field of machine learning, and offers the advantage of comparing both flat and deep prototype-based architectures to other machine learning methods. We therefore feel that the results reported here are truly novel, w.r.t. the state of the art but also w.r.t. our previous work on incremental learning [7].

2   Methods

For representing both first and second hidden layers inputs of the architecture shown in Fig. 1, we use a prototype-based learning algorithm which is loosely based on the self-organizing map model, see [7]. Inputs are represented by graded neural activities arranged in *maps* organized on a two-dimensional grid lattice. Each unit (i, j) of the map X is associated with a weight vector $w_{ij}^X \in \mathbf{W^X}$ which is called *prototype*.

Each map of the M^{h1} first hidden-layer maps has the same size $N_1 = n^{h1} \times n^{h1}$ units and receives a crop from the system input data of size $n^{crop} \times n^{crop}$. M^{h1} is determined by the size of non-overlapping receptive fields in the input layer: the smaller the receptive fields (each associated with a map in $h1$) is, the greater is M^{h1}. The single map in the second hidden-layer $h2$, of size $n^{h2} \times n^{h2}$, receives a concatenation of activities in the M^{h1} maps of $h1$. The top-layer (output) consists of a linear regression module that computes the prediction $\mathbf{W^{top}}(t)^T \cdot \mathbf{Z^{h2}}(t)$ of the system concerning its current input with $\mathbf{W^{top}}$ the linear regression factors and $\mathbf{Z^{h2}}(t)$ the output activities of the second hidden-layer $h2$.

Because we wish to work in an on-line fashion, weights vectors of all layer are updated at the same time (in contrast to conventional deep architectures which require layer-wise training). Prototypes of the two hidden layers are updated following the Kohonen rule. Each unit's associated weight vector (its *prototype*) is updated using the learning rule and good practices proposed by [4] which decreases learning rate $\epsilon(t)$ and Gaussian neighborhood radius $\sigma(t)$ from initially large values to their asymptotic values $\epsilon_\infty, \sigma_\infty$. For each iteration step $t <= T$, prototypes of maps ($\mathbf{W^X}$) are updated depending on the current input $\mathbf{x}$ with the following rule:

$$\mathbf{W^X}(t+1) \leftarrow \mathbf{W^X}(t) + \epsilon(t) \cdot \mathbf{\Phi}(t) \cdot (\mathbf{x}(t) - w^{X^\star}(t)) \tag{1}$$

where ϵ is the learning rate and $\mathbf{\Phi}(t) = \phi(w^{X^\star}(t), \sigma(t))$ is a discretized Gaussian kernel with σ variance, centered on the current best-matching $w^{X^\star}$ unit and representing the neighborhood influence of the weights adaptation (Fig. 2).

For any map X, the *map activity* $z_{ij}^X \in \mathbf{Z^X}$ at position (i, j) is then derived from the Euclidean distance between the unit prototype w_{ij}^X and the current input $\mathbf{x}$:

$$z_{ij}^X(t) = \mathbf{f}\left(g_\kappa\left(\|w_{ij}^X(t) - \mathbf{x}(t)\|\right)\right) \tag{2}$$

where, as described in [7], $g_\kappa(\cdot)$ is a Gaussian function with an adaptive para-meter κ that converts distances into the $[0, 1]$ interval, and $\mathbf{f}(\cdot)$ is a monotonous non-linear *transfer function*, defined as:

$$m_0 = \max_{\boldsymbol{y}} \bar{z}^P(\boldsymbol{y}, t)$$

$$m_1 = \max_{\boldsymbol{y}} \left(z^P(\boldsymbol{y}, t)\right)^{20}$$

$$\mathbf{f}\left((z^P(\boldsymbol{y}))\right) = m_0 \frac{\left(z^P(\boldsymbol{y})\right)^{20}}{m_1} \tag{3}$$

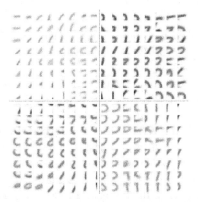

Fig. 2. An overview of prototypes in 4 maps of the first hidden layer $h1$ corresponding to 2×2 receptive fields of 14×14 pixels over MNIST inputs.

The top-layer weights vector is updated following an on-line stochastic gra-dient descent mechanism with a fixed learning rate η over time by comparison of its own prediction and the current ground truth label of the current input data. Because we apply our system to classification tasks, labels $\mathbf{y}$ and predictions $\mathbf{p}$ are not scalars but vectors of c values where the position of the maximum indicates respectively the target class label and the system decision (population coding).

$$\mathbf{W^{top}}(t+1) \leftarrow \mathbf{W^{top}}(t) - \eta \cdot (\mathbf{y}(t) - \mathbf{p}(t)) \cdot \mathbf{Z^{h2}}(t) \tag{4}$$

We use two indicators to assess performance: mean classification errors and total number of connection weights.

Mean Classification Error. This indicator is a commonly used measure for comparing performances of a classification system. During the testing phase, when all the learning processes (i.e. weights updates) are stopped, classification errors are logged on the MNIST test set following the simple rule: $\gamma = 0$. if $\operatorname{argmax}(\mathbf{y}(t))$ equals $\operatorname{argmax}(\mathbf{p}(t))$ and $\gamma = 1$. otherwise. Then, we just compute the mean for all these errors $\mu = \frac{1}{T^{test}} \cdot \sum_{t=1}^{T^{test}} \gamma$.

Total Number of Weighted Connexions. This indicator is a simple means to compare our hierarchical architecture and a "flat" architecture, only composed of a huge map and a linear regression module, in terms of number of connexions. Let M^{h1} be the number of maps in the first hidden layer each composed of $N_1 = n^{h1} * n^{h1}$ units and $M^{h2} = 1$ the number of maps in the second hidden layer, composed of $N_2 = n^{h2} * n^{h2}$ units. Because connexions between the second hidden layer and the top layer are negligible in the two architectures, we do not take them into account. The total number of weighted connexions is then computed as: $K = N_1 * (d + N_2 * M^{h1})$ for a hierarchical architecture and $\tilde{K} = d * N_2$ for a "flat" one. By example, an architecture with 4 hidden maps of 4×4 units receiving crops extracted from 784 pixels images (such as MNIST images), followed by a hidden map of 10×10 units followed by the linear regression module gives $K = (4 \times 4) * (784 + (10 \times 10) * 4) = 18'944$. For a comparable "flat" system without the first hidden layer, we would need $\tilde{K} = 784 * (10 \times 10) = 78'400$ connexions.

3 Experiments

3.1 Protocol

Each experiment run consists of $T^{train} = 1'000'000$ training iterations followed by $T^{test} = 50'000$ testing iterations. For all self-organizing maps, we use exponentially decreased values of learning rate and neighbourhood radius and a fixed linear regression learning rate: $\epsilon_0 = 0.25$, $\epsilon_\infty = 0.001$, $\sigma_0 = 0.5 * n^X$, $\sigma_\infty = 0.085$ and $\eta = 0.009$. Both self-organizing maps and linear regression weight vectors are initialized to random uniform values between -0.001 and 0.001. Samples are always randomly and uniformly picked and are provided to the system as input data $\mathbf{x}$ and ground truth y. Results presented below are averaged measures over 10 runs. Datasets targets are split into c different classes and each input data is d dimensional.

We use the publicly available MNIST classification benchmark as described in [11]. It contains $c = 10$ classes, corresponding to the 10 handwritten digits from "0" to "9" and comes separated into a well-defined train set and a smaller test set. Each sample has a dimensionality of $d = 28 \times 28 = 784$.

3.2 Results

As shown in Table 1, our hierarchical system with 4 hidden layer maps can achieve comparable performances with less connexions involved. When comparing mean classification errors in the hierarchical case (μ) and in the "flat" one

($\tilde{\mu}$), it seems that, with respect to the same parameters set, there is no need to add hidden layers. But when looking at the total number of weighted connexions, K is always smaller than $\tilde{K}$: by example, with $M^{h1} = 4$ maps of $N_1 = 6 \times 6$ units in the first hidden layer and one map of $N_2 = 20 \times 20$ unit in the second hidden layer, after T^{train} on-line iterations the hierarchical system can achieve, in average, equivalent classification performances than a system only composed of a single 20×20 self-organizing map but with three times less connexions.

If we try with another number of hidden layer maps - by instance with $M^{h1} = 16$ and $n^{crop} = 7$ - it seems that performances drop down and that the ratio $K/\tilde{K}$ is no longer a real advantage. Because we are dealing with raw pixels and no extracted features on this dataset, the system is extremely sensible to the size of the receptive fields. It seems to us that there is an interesting research question about the well suited n^{crop}: "what is the link with the dataset distribution?", "are overlapping receptive fields a good idea or can the system adapt itself this parameter during the incremental learning paradigm?"

Table 1. MNIST mean classification errors

$n^{crop} = 14, M^{h1} = 2 \times 2$					
n^{h1}	n^{h2}	μ	$\tilde{\mu}$	K	$\tilde{K}$
4	10	10.8 ($\pm$0.7)	9.1 ($\pm$0.5)	18'944	78'400
6	10	9.4 ($\pm$0.8)	9.1 ($\pm$0.5)	42'624	78'400
8	10	11.2 ($\pm$0.6)	9.1 ($\pm$0.5)	75'776	78'400
4	20	6.7 ($\pm$0.4)	6.3 ($\pm$0.6)	38'144	313'600
6	20	**5.9 ($\pm$0.3)**	6.3 ($\pm$0.6)	85'824	313'600
8	20	6.4 ($\pm$0.6)	6.3 ($\pm$0.6)	152'576	313'600
$n^{crop} = 7, M^{h1} = 4 \times 4$					
n^{h1}	n^{h2}	μ	$\tilde{\mu}$	K	$\tilde{K}$
4	10	12.9 ($\pm$0.9)	9.1 ($\pm$0.5)	38'144	78'400
6	10	11.1 ($\pm$0.8)	9.1 ($\pm$0.5)	85'824	78'400
8	10	11.0 ($\pm$0.9)	9.1 ($\pm$0.5)	152'576	78'400
4	20	10.5 ($\pm$0.6)	6.3 ($\pm$0.6)	114'944	313'600
6	20	10.1 ($\pm$0.5)	6.3 ($\pm$0.6)	258'624	313'600
8	20	10.8 ($\pm$0.5)	6.3 ($\pm$0.6)	459'776	313'600

4   Discussion, Conclusion, Perspectives

This article has shown that a deep prototype-based architecture is capable of achieving performances comparable to those of a flat architecture of the same type, while drastically reducing the number of connection weights, and therefore memory usage and processing time. We believe that this effect may be observed for any prototype-based method (notably LVQ) if approximate independence relations hold between separate parts of the input. As stated in Sect. 1, this is almost always the case if inputs are visual images, although of course the right parameters have to be found in the form of receptive field sizes and overlaps. However to be fair, this parameter search would also have to be performed for convolutional neural network (CNN) and is a property of all deep architectures based on local receptive fields.

Given that prototype-based methods in machine learning have a number of highly desirable properties, such as online and incremental learning capacity [6,7], a simple probabilistic interpretation [12] and a natural way of processing multi-class problems, the reduction of resource requirements even when treating complex visual problems seems an important step towards wide-spread use of prototype-based machine learning methods.

References

1. Rosch, E.: Cognitive reference points. Cogn. Psychol. **7**, 532–547 (1975)
2. Biehl, M., Ghosh, A., Hammer, B.: Dynamics and generalization ability of LVQ algorithms. J. Mach. Learn. Res. **8**, 323–360 (2007)
3. Moody, J., Darken, C.J.: Fast learning in networks of locally tuned processing units. Neural Comput. **1**, 281–294 (1989)
4. Kohonen, T.: Self-organized formation of topologically correct feature maps. Biol. Cybern. **43**, 59–69 (1982)
5. Arulampalam, M.S., Maskell, S., Gordon, N., Clapp, T.: A tutorial on particle filters for online nonlinear, non-Gaussian Bayesian tracking. IEEE Trans. Sig. Process. **50**(2), 174–188 (2002)
6. Losing, V., Hammer, B., Wersing, H.: Interactive online learning for obstacle classification on a mobile robot. In: IEEE (2015)
7. Gepperth, A., Karaoguz, C.: A bio-inspired incremental learning architecture for applied perceptual problems. Cogn. Comput. (2015, accepted)
8. Gepperth, A., Hammer, B.: Incremental learning algorithms and applications. In: European Sympoisum on Artificial Neural Networks (ESANN) (2016)
9. Carse, B., Fogarty, T.C.: Tackling the "curse of dimensionality" of radial basis functional neural networks using a genetic algorithm. In: Voigt, H.-M., Ebeling, W., Rechenberg, I., Schwefei, H.-P. (eds.) Parallel Problem Solving from Nature – PPSN IV. LNCS, pp. 707–719. Springer, Heidelberg (1996)
10. Sermanet, P., Kavukcuoglu, K., Chintala, S., LeCun, Y.: Pedestrian detection with unsupervised multi-stage feature learning. In: Proceedings of the IEEE Conference on Computer Vision and Pattern Recognition, pp. 3626–3633 (2013)
11. LeCun, Y., Bottou, L., Bengio, Y., Haffner, P.: Gradient-based learning applied to document recognition. Proc. IEEE **86**(11), 2278–2324 (1998)
12. Schneider, P., Biehl, M., Hammer, B.: Hyperparameter learning in probabilistic prototype-based models. Neurocomputing **73**(7–9), 1117–1124 (2010). Advances in Computational Intelligence and Learning 17th European Symposium on Artificial Neural Networks 2009

Deep Convolutional Neural Networks for Classifying Body Constitution

Haiteng Li[1,2(✉)], Bin Xu[1,2(✉)], Nanyue Wang[1,2(✉)], and Jia Liu[1,2(✉)]

[1] Department of Computer Science and Technology,
Tsinghua University, Beijing, China
liht14@mails.tsinghua.edu.cn, xubin@tsinghua.edu.cn
[2] China Academy of Chinese Medical Sciences, Beijing, China
wangnanyue1981@hotmail.com, 15101068956@163.com

Abstract. Body constitution is a classification of individuals into different types of physical condition in order to prevent disease and promote health. The problem of standardizing constitutional classification has become a constraint on the development of Chinese medical constitution. Traditional recognition methods, such as questionnaire and medical examination have the shortcoming of inefficiency and low accuracy. We present an advanced deep convolutional neural network (CNN) to simulate the function of pulse diagnosis, which is able to classify an individuals constitution based only his or her pulse. The CNN model employed the latest activation unit, rectified linear unit and stochastic optimization. This model takes the lead in trying to classify individual constitution using CNN. During the experiment, the CNN model attained a recognition accuracy 95 % on classifying 9 constitutional types.

Keywords: Convolutional neural network · Body constitution · Health · Medical science

1 Introduction

Medical science has long been focusing on researching on disease while ignoring research the human body itself. However, Chinese medicine constitution discipline is committed to research on the physiological and pathological characteristics of each constitution, analyze the state of the disease and the development of the disease based on different constitutions in order to guide disease prevention and medical treatment. An individual's constitution exhibits morphological structure, physiological function, psychological status and other relatively stable characteristics of an individual. The future of medicine will focus on preventive medicine, and therefore classifying individual constitution is essential action to protect health. The classification of body constitution cannot only accurately reflect the physical difference between individuals but also lay a solid foundation for the future standardization of Chinese Medicine constitution.

Nowadays, there is a controversial issue about the method to accurately identify constitution. Since 2009, Wang Qi's research of nine body constitutions has

A.E.P. Villa et al. (Eds.): ICANN 2016, Part II, LNCS 9887, pp. 128–135, 2016.
DOI: 10.1007/978-3-319-44781-0_16

been the standard for Chinese medical diagnosis and treatment. Nine body constitutions are classified as Gentleness, Qi-deficiency, Qi-depression, Dampness-heat, Phlegm-dampness, Blood-stasis, Special diathesis, Yang-deficiency and Yin-deficiency [1]. To classify an individual's constitution, he or she can complete a paper constitution test or conduct a medical examination. These two methods either produce high error rate or require medical devices, time and manpower. On the other hand, pulse diagnosis can accurately identify constitution, but it requires a physician who has long-term accumulated experience. There are a lot of researches on using modern science and technology to classify Traditional Chinese Medicine (TCM) pulse. Traditional identification methods such as MLP, SVM ignore the complexity and deep hidden features of TCM pulse. As a result, these methods often have low accuracy rate on TCM pulse multi-classification.

This paper introduces a deep CNN model to achieve an applicable multi-classification accuracy rate on TCM pulse. The architecture of the CNN model is carefully designed in order to extract deep hidden feature and model small training dataset, which suits well for TCM pulse. The pulse dataset collected by the China Academy of Traditional Chinese Medicine (CACMS) is used to evaluate the performance of the CNN model. As far as we know, this dataset contains the largest number of samples of different constitutions pulse signals in the world. The experiment result shows that the CNN model has an adaptive accuracy rate on classification of nine constitutions.

The major contributions of this paper is summarized as follow:

- The method uses CNN to classify 9 body constitution types and achieves an accuracy of 95 %.
- The CNN model uses a large number of convolution layers, compound regularization layer, advanced activation layer and high efficiency optimizer to be adaptive to TCM pulse dataset.

This paper has five sections. The second section will present related work. The third section will describe the details of applying CNN model to body constitution classification. The fourth section will show the experiment result. The final section will draw a conclusion of this paper.

2 Related Work

Classification of TCM pulse has drawn a lot of attention in the past few years. The approaches focus primarily on two directions of TCM pulse, namely classification of TCM pulse conditions and the classification of certain diseases. Traditional methods, such as support vector machine (SVM), random forest (RF) used to predict recognize a certain disease. After the arising of neural network, researchers began to classify TCM pulse conditions using back propagation (BP) neural network and probabilistic neural networks (PNN).

However, most traditional methods perform poorly on pulse signal multi-classification. The core problem of previous models is that most researchers use pulse signal only from one single diagnosis point which is insufficient to cover the entire information of pulse diagnosis. Another important cause of low accuracy is that these neural networks are incapable of extreme deep neural network structure, which makes it unable to extract deep hidden features.

3   Body Constitution CNN Model

The following section will describe the preprocessing of pulse signal, major improvements and the overall architecture of the CNN model.

3.1   Signal Preprocessing

Signal Cropping. Since pulse signal is a weak physiological signal, hand movement or interference from other devices can cause irrational fluctuations in the process of acquisition. Manual signal cropping is applied to pulse signal that has distorted wave.

Signal Smoothing. Signal smoothing is used to retain the original signal while eliminating the noise from the signal. A 10th-order Butterworth band-pass filter of 0.00001 Hz–48 Hz is applied to the signal to dispel noise.

Detrending. Irregular breathing can cause an intrinsic overall pattern in pulse signal. A 10th-order polynomial curve fitting is applied to the signal, and then the outcome polynomial function is subtracted to remove the trending noise from the signal.

Decimation. Decimation reduces the original pulse signal sampling rate of 1000 Hz to 500 Hz. Due to the graphic memory limitation of our experiment, this process optimizes the learning efficiency of the neural network and provides more flexibility for the architecture of the neural network.

Segmentation. Each samples signal is separated into four parts. The original pulse data contains too many data points, so these points may be thrown away during the training process. Therefore, separating the dataset would save as many features as possible and at the same time increase recognition accuracy.

Synthetic Sampling. To handle the unbalance distribution of the dataset, an adaptive oversampling method, called adaptive synthetic (ADASYS) is implemented [2]. K-nearest-neighbors, imbalance ratio threshold and growth percentage are set to 7, 0.6 and 0.75.

3.2 Leaky Rectified Linear Unit

The traditional way to train a neural network is by using a saturated counterpart, such as tanh or sigmoid function. Non-saturated activation function, such as ReLU is far more superior to these saturated functions, in terms of addressing vanishing gradient and enhancing convergence efficiency. Following Maass neural network acoustic model, the CNN model trains neurons with leaky rectified linear unit (LReL) [3]. LReL allows saturated and inactive gradients to approach very low and non-zero value. LReL is proven to have better performance and higher learning rate in deep neural network comparing to tanh and ReLU [3].

3.3 Initialization

Initialization determines the probability distribution function for the initial weights. The model uses uniform initialization scaled by fan in, He weight initialization [4]. This initialization method effectually solves the bottleneck of training extremely deep neural network. Initialized with a fixed standard deviation, CNN models that have more than 8 convolutional layers often have difficulty with converging. Therefore, He initializes weights with a standard deviation,

$$\sigma = gain\sqrt{\frac{1}{fan_{in}}} \tag{1}$$

This derivation takes the rectifier nonlinearities of rectified linear unit into consideration. He initialization ensures the weights to be adaptive through multi layers in extremely deep rectified network models.

3.4 Optimization

A stochastic optimization method, Adam is applied to the CNN model to update the network parameter in order to optimize the objective function. Adam is well suited for a neural network that has large number of parameters [5]. The method combines the strength of both AdaGrad and RMSProp. The CNN model uses $\beta_1 = 0.9, \beta_2 = 0.999, \varepsilon = 10^{-8}$ as optimizers parameters.

3.5 Overfitting Prevention

Overfitting occurs when the CNN model has a large number of parameters due to its complex structure and numerous filters in each convolutional layer. It is a major shortcoming that the model must overcome. In order to prevent overfitting, two techniques were implemented, in terms of dropout and regularization.

Dropout. Dropout is the most immediate way to prevent overfitting. The idea of dropout is to drop a given fraction of units at each epoch during the training process, which prevent units from co-adapting [6]. This technique enhances the robustness of each unit by forcing them to conjunct with other randomly chosen units in order to learn new features by themselves. The experiment shows strong overfitting when the model does not use dropout.

Regularization. Regularization adds regularization penalties to parameters or activities of a neural network layer to reduce regression coefficient overfitting. Weight regularization penalty, known as Ridge and L2 activity regularization are applied in fully connected layer. Ridge regularization decreases the approximated regression coefficients towards zero in order to prevent overfitting that is caused by high dimensionality [7]. The penalty parameter is set to 0.01.

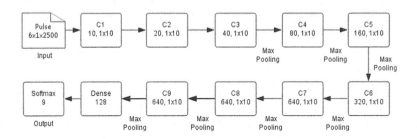

Fig. 1. The visualization of the CNN model

3.6 Overall Architecture

The basic architecture of the CNN model is presented in Fig. 1. The input dimension of the 1st convolutional layer is $6 \times 1 \times 2500$. The 1st, 2nd, 3rd convolutional layers convolute the input from the previous layer with 10 convolutional kernels of size 1×10. The 4th, 5th, 6th, 7th, 8th, 9th convolutional layers follow this structure with an identical size of kernels and a following max-pooling layer subsamples the output which furthers reduces the output size with a factor of 2. The numbers of kernels of the 2rd, 3rd, 4th, 5th, 6th convolutional layers are 20, 40, 80, 160, 320. The 7th, 8th, 9th convolutional layers have the exact same number of convolutional kernels, 640. The final input feature map is a size of $6 \times 1 \times 6$. A small size of the final input feature map enhances the model to completely see and learn the sample. A dropout layer is applied to the output with a probability of 0.25 on the 3rd, 4th, 5th convolutional layers and more dropout layers with a probability of 0.5 on 6th, 7th, 8th, 9th convolutional layers and fully connected layer. The final layer of the CNN model is the 9-way softmax which classifies the output into 9 class labels.

4   Experiment

This section introduces the dataset, experiment environment and the overall performance of the CNN model.

4.1 The Dataset

The dataset collecting process and the details of the dataset will be described in this section.

Data Acquisition. Pulse signal acquisition system obtains the pulse signal from 6 pulse locations simultaneously on the participant's hands, in terms of left hands Cun, Guan, Chi and right hand's Cun, Guan, Chi. Traditional Chinese medicine defines Cun, Guan, Chi as pulse diagnosis locations that infer the change of a disease and identify an individual's health condition. The sampling rate is 1000 Hz. Each acquisition takes 40 s.

Constitution Classification. TCM researchers will record participants blood biochemical determination, symptoms, result of pulse diagnosis and result of body constitution scale sheet. TCM researchers will analyses the overall scale result to identify each participant's constitutional types.

Details of Dataset. The pulse dataset contains a total of 1661 participants'pulse signals that are unevenly distributed into nine constitutional types. The numbers of gentleness, dampness-heat, qi-depression, qi-deficiency, yang-deficiency, yin-deficiency, blood-stasis, special diathesis and phlegm-dampness constitutions in the dataset are 867, 79, 83, 205, 234, 76, 43, 33, 43 accordingly. Each pulse data is sampled at 1000 Hz with a length of 40 s, which produces a sequence of length of 40000 data points. Each person has 6 pulse locations to acquire signal, and therefore the dimension of one sample is 6 × 40000. After signal preprocessing, the total number of samples is 12046, and the length of each sample is 2500. All samples are shuffled in the dataset before input to the CNN model. 80 % of the samples are randomly selected as training set while the remaining 20 % are used as validation set.

4.2   Experiment Settings

The experiment is built based on Keras and Scikit-learn [8]. We evaluate the classification performance using GTX TITAN with 12 GB of memory.

4.3   Result

We perform classification experiment of nine constitutional types on seven different classifiers to compare the effects of various methods. The results of each method are shown in Table 1. Accuracy defined as to the number of correctly identified samples divided by the total number of test samples. The task is to classify pulse signals into 9 constitutional types. SVM and RF models achieve relatively close results, 54.66 % and 54.34 %. The initial CNN model achieves an higher accuracy rate of 62.49 %. With dropout, the accuracy rate significantly increases by 29.09 %. Applying L2 regularization slightly increases the rate to 92.31 %. With the ADASYS method, the rate decreases by 3.24 %. The final CNN model with He initialization produces the best performance of 95.33 %.

In addition to the global accuracy, we perform classification testing on each individual constitutional type by randomly selecting 100 samples from each type. According to Table 2, Gentleness (0), Qi-deficiency (1), Qi-depression (2),

Table 1. Comparison of results on the pulse dataset

Method	Accuracy (%)
SVM	54.66
RF	54.34
CNN with LReL	62.49
CNN with LReL, dropout	91.58
CNN with LReL, dropout, L2	92.31
CNN with LReL, dropout, L2, ADASYS	89.07
CNN with LReL, dropout, L2, He	**95.33**

Table 2. Prediction on every body constitutions

Constituion type	0	1	2	3	4	5	6	7	8
Accuracy (%)	100	94	94	97	97	96	95	91	95

Table 3. Results of different classification tasks

Classification Task	Accuracy (%)
Gender (Male/Female)	94.42
Age (16–44/45–59/60+)	99.38
Acquisition Time (Spring/Summer/Autumn/Winter)	95.76

Dampness-heat (3), Phlegm-dampness (4), Blood-stasis (5), Special diathesis (6), Yang-deficiency (7), Yin-deficiency (8) types achieve accuracy rates of 100 %, 94 %, 94 %, 97 %, 97 %, 96 %, 95 %, 91 %, 95 %.

To verify the CNN model can be applied to a wide range of pulse diagnosis tasks, we preform the classification on gender, age and acquisition time within 748 gentleness type participants. The ratio between male female is 1.6 to 1, while the numbers for the three age groups (14–44, 45–59 and 60+) are 647, 77 and 24. Another set of data is acquisition time data where the numbers corresponding to spring, summer autumn and winter is 230, 117, 181 and 220. According to Table 3, the classifications on gender, age and acquisition time achieve accuracies of 94.42 %, 99.38 % and 95.76 %.

4.4 Discussion

Comparing to other classifier, the CNN model has demonstrated its superiority base on very complex and multidimensional pulse input and limited samples. However, the CNN model requires a much longer training time, approximately 6 h because of the implementation of the dropout.

5 Conclusion

Convolutional neural network avoids the shortcomings of traditional recognition methods and improves the multi-classification accuracy rate on compound pulse signals. The experiment shows that the CNN model is capable of achieving adaptive accuracy rate on an extremely complex pulse dataset. Ultimately, we want to implement the CNN model on multi-classification of diseases to enhance public health and provide help for clinical treatment.

Acknowledgments. This study was supported by the key project of MOST basic work 2013 (No. 2013FY114400), National Natural Science Foundation of China (No. 81403325), Ministry of Education-China Mobile Research Fund under grant MCM20130381 and Tsinghua University Initiative Scientific Research Program (No. 20131089190). Beijing Key Lab of Networked Multimedia also supports our research work.

References

1. Wang, Q.: Classification and diagnosis basis of nine basic constitutions in Chinese medicine. J. Beijing Univ. Tradit. Chin. Med. **28**(4), 1 (2005)
2. He, H., Bai, Y., Garcia, E.A., Li, S.: Adasyn: adaptive synthetic sampling approach for imbalanced learning. In: IJCNN, pp. 1322–1328. IEEE (2008)
3. Xu, B., Wang, N., Chen, T., Li, M.: Empirical evaluation of rectified activations in convolutional network. CoRR, abs/1505.00853 (2015)
4. He, K., Zhang, X., Ren, S., Sun, J.: Delving deep into rectifiers: surpassing human-level performance on imagenet classification. CoRR, abs/1502.01852 (2015)
5. Kingma, D.P., Ba, J.: Adam: a method for stochastic optimization. CoRR, abs/1412.6980 (2014)
6. Srivastava, N., Hinton, G., Krizhevsky, A., Sutskever, I., Salakhutdinov, R.: Dropout: a simple way to prevent neural networks from overfitting. J. Mach. Learn. Res. **15**, 1929–1958 (2014)
7. Hoerl, A.E., Kennard, R.W.: Ridge regression: biased estimation for nonorthogonal problems. Technometrics **12**, 55–67 (1970)
8. Chollet, F.: Keras (2015). https://github.com/fchollet/keras

Feature Extractor Based Deep Method to Enhance Online Arabic Handwritten Recognition System

Mohamed Elleuch[1(✉)], Ramzi Zouari[2], and Monji Kherallah[3]

[1] National School of Computer Science (ENSI), University of Manouba, Manouba, Tunisia
elleuch.mohameds@gmail.com
[2] National School of Engineers (ENIS), University of Sfax, Sfax, Tunisia
ramzi.zouari@gmail.com
[3] Faculty of Sciences, University of Sfax, Sfax, Tunisia
monji.kherallah@gmail.com

Abstract. To enhance Arabic handwritten recognition (AHR) performance, a combination between online and offline features is investigated. In this paper we exploit handcrafted features based on beta-elliptic model and automatic features using deep classifier called Convolutional Deep Belief Network (CDBN). The experiments are conducted on two different Arabic databases: LMCA and ADAB databases which including respectively isolated characters and Tunisian names towns handwritten by several different writers. The advantage of the both databases was the offline images had built at the same time as the online trajectory. The test results show a significant improvement in recognition rate.

Keywords: Handcrafted · CDBN · Arabic handwritten recognition · LMCA · ADAB

1 Introduction and Related Work

With his two sections offline and online, the handwriting recognition field has gained huge consideration during the four last decades. Arabic handwritten script recognition is a challenging problem that has been intensely studied for many years.

Multiple approaches were developed, such as Support Vector Machine (SVM), Neural Networks (NN), Bidirectional Long Short-Term Memory (BLSTM) and Hidden Model Markov (HMM). They have been found extremely efficient in many fields as pattern recognition task [1, 2] and Automatic Speech Recognition (ASR) [3]. Indeed, a fast review of the literature shows that the effectiveness of these approaches strongly depends on the extracted features.

For the recognition of offline and online Arabic handwriting many researchers have insisted more on recognition aspects. Tagougui et al. [4] for example, suggested a hybrid model reliant on Hidden Markov Models and Multi-Layer Perceptron NN for Online Arabic handwriting recognition. This model was assessed on the ADAB database [5] and realized perfect work compared with state-of-the-art recognition systems. In offline handwriting recognition, Elleuch et al. [6] profoundly inquired into a deep architecture named Convolutional DBN practiced on high-level dimension in textual images with

© Springer International Publishing Switzerland 2016
A.E.P. Villa et al. (Eds.): ICANN 2016, Part II, LNCS 9887, pp. 136–144, 2016.
DOI: 10.1007/978-3-319-44781-0_17

Offline IFN/ENIT database [7]. The experimental research has shown promising outcomes comparable to the state-of-the-art Arabic OCR.

A few researches and studies have been conducted with combining on/off-line feature extraction technique for Arabic handwritten recognition problem. The combination of features can give more general description of the text. Stating as an example, Houcine et al. [8] who introduced an experimental investigation demonstrated the fruitful result of the integration of offline parameters in the features vector of an online handwriting modeling system focused on grapheme segmentation. As for, Hamdani et al. [9], they suggested an offline handwriting recognition system reliant on the combination of multiple HMMs. The different HMMs are reliant on online and offline handcrafted features. They showed that the combination of an online system with offline ones works better than the combination of multiple offline recognizers.

In our studies, model based on Deep learning and Beta-elliptic approach is investigated to the handwritten Arabic field. To further better the efficiency rate, the combination of hierarchical representations building from raw data using CDBN with handcrafted features is a must. We practiced the system in the first trial on the LMCA database and in the second one on the ADAB database exploiting a classifier module based on Support Vector Machines.

The remaining of this paper is set as follows: In the second Section, we describe feature extraction based methods and we introduce our architecture of the proposed system. Our experimental study and results using this system are presented in the Sect. 3. As for Sect. 4, we present some concluding remarks.

2   Our Proposed Model

In this section we briefly introduce our proposed model for Arabic handwriting recognition using on/off-line feature extraction techniques.

2.1   Feature Extraction Based Methods

For the feature extraction methods, the Beta-Elliptic strategy and the Deep Architectures are investigated. The first was applied an online Arabic word database ADAB [5] and the second approach deal textual images from the same database. Again the same strategy was applied with LMCA database.

Beta-Elliptic approach: The Beta-elliptic approach comprises the modeling of the trajectory by an association of kinematic and geometric features. These features are able to be divided into two classes. The first class comprises the dynamic features considering the velocity profile as for the second class, it takes static features depicting handwriting trajectory. The resulting feature vector is made up of 10 parameters: 6 dynamic features and 4 static features. Refer to work in [10] for deeper analysis.

Deep approach: In this work, we utilized Convolutional Deep Belief Network (CDBN) for feature extraction. Taking advantages of the power of this deep network that can manage large dimensions input allowing the use of raw data inputs was our objective.

2.2   Architecture of the Proposed System

Having the online and the offline feature extraction methods described in [6, 10] for AHR, it may be beneficial to combine both methods. As shown in Fig. 1, our proposed system was designed by combining two techniques for feature extraction. The first technique aims to build hierarchical structures of features using the Convolutional DBN feature extractor. Then, online features are added to improve the aptitude of generalization of the system. The latter are obtained using Beta–Elliptical model feature. Finally, SVM takes on/offline features as input and proceed to do classification.

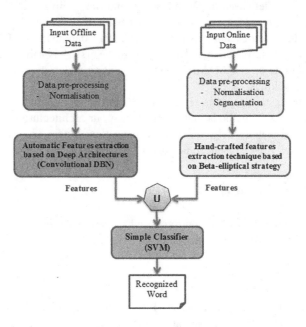

Fig. 1. Proposed system

2.3   Convolutional Deep Belief Network

In recent years, Deep learning methods have been effectively used for handwritten recognition and applied to digits and handwritten Arabic/Latin text databases. For examples: Deep Belief Networks [11] and Convolutional DBN [6, 12].

Convolutional DBN is a hierarchical generative model, consists of several layers of max-pooling convolutional Restricted Boltzmann Machines (CRBMs) stacked on top of one another (See Fig. 2). Building convolutional deep belief network, the algorithm learns high-level features, like groups of the strokes and object-part.

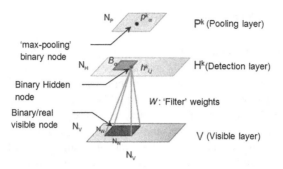

Fig. 2. Illustration of a probabilistic max-pooling CRBM [12]. N_V and N_H refer to the size of visible and hidden layer, and N_W to the size of convolution filter.

The input layer is made of $N_V \times N_V$ real/binary units. There are K groups (or maps) in the hidden layer and each group is an array of $N_H \times N_H$ binary units and is associated with a $N_W \times N_W$ convolutional filter (where $N_W \triangleq N_V - N_H + 1$). All hidden units of a group share the filter weights. A shared bias b_k for each group and a shared bias c for the visible units exists as well. The pooling layer has K groups of binary units, each group of size $N_P \times N_P$. Pooling, also called probabilistic max-pooling operation, shrinks the representation of the detection layers by a C, usually small with $N_P \triangleq N_H/C$. For more details on the above you can refer to [6, 12].

The training of the max-pooling CRBM network was achieved by utilizing contrastive divergence (CD) algorithm allowing us to estimate an approximate gradient effectively.

2.4 Support Vector Machines (SVM)

Support Vector Machine is powerful discriminative classifier invented by Vapnik [13] and Cortes [14], and has been extensively utilized successfully for many pattern classification/recognition tasks [15]. The algorithm detects the optimal separating hyperplane (H_0), bearing the maximum distance to the training points that are near to the hyper-plane.

In this study we select the radial basis function (RBF) kernel as a non-linear similarity function in the SVM classifier. The RBF kernel calculates the following similarity value between two input vectors:

$$K\left(x_i, x_j\right) = \exp\left(-\gamma \left\| x_i - x_j \right\|^2\right) \tag{1}$$

With $\gamma = 1/\sigma^2$, is a kernel parameter of the RBF kernel that will be define empirically. 5-fold cross-validation is utilized to search the perfect parameters by assessing the work of the classifiers in the one-vs-all classification tasks. We mentioned that in our experiments LIBSVM [16] package is utilized to construct multi-class SVM with RBF kernel.

3   Experimental Setup and Results

We conducted our experimental studies using proposed system for recognizing Arabic handwritten characters and words. This architecture was tested on two different on/offline databases. The first one is an Arabic character database LMCA [17] and the second is an Arabic word database which is ADAB [5]. These databases provide us with the option of recovering the online signal and offline textual image of the same handwriting. Unlike the online method which is reliant on collecting coordinate (x, y) of the handwritten trajectory, the offline method is reliant on collecting images of the handwritten trajectory. Advancement is detailed and discussed in the next subsections.

3.1   LMCA Database

LMCA (Lettres Mots Chiffres Arabes) database [17] contains 30.000 shapes for ten digits, 100.000 shapes for 56 Arabic letters (See Fig. 3) and 500 Arabic words. 55 respondents were hosted to participate in the development of the handwritten LMCA. The data is divided into a training set of 70 % images/signals and a test set of 30 %. In this work, we used only characters forms.

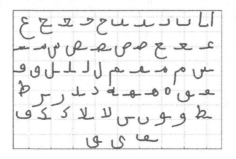

Fig. 3. 56 shapes of Arabic letters [17]

3.2   ADAB Database

In our experiments, we exploited sample data from ADAB (Arabic DAtaBase) database [5] which includes 946 different labels of Tunisian town's names. The data processing consists of online and offline handwritten Arabic words. It contains 33164 sub words written by 166 persons. We have selected only 24 shapes of Tunisian cities from Dataset 1, 2 and 3 for training phase whereas the fourth is used as a test set with the same selection of shapes. To effectively train our proposed model on more data so as to perfectly handle the variability of handwriting, the size of the training set is extended five times by the elastic deformation technique.

3.3 Experiments Setting

The CDBN Network is used to extract higher level features from the characters and words. The description of the automatic features extractor used in experiments applied to LMCA and ADAB database is given as follows: CDBN architecture is made up of two layers of Convolutional Restricted Boltzmann Machines (CRBM), each layer holds n_i maps and the pooling ratio C for each layer was 2. Every map in the hidden layer is related to one pooling unit (See Fig. 4). The first layer takes real-valued visible units and binary hidden units whereas the second layer takes binary visible and hidden units.

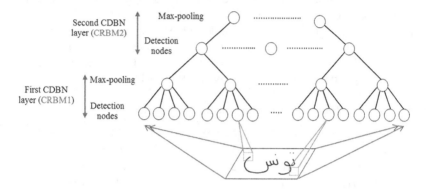

Fig. 4. Illustration of the proposed CDBN architecture [6]

We give the description of the CDBN architecture used in experiments applied to LMCA database as follows: The input of the CDBN is a 28 × 28 grayscale image $(N_V = 28)$. The first and the second layer have 40 maps of 11 × 11 pixels filters. Both CRBM have been trained using Contrastive Divergence (CD) of 150 epochs.

On the other hand, for the ADAB datasets we train following CDBN: the size of the input image is a 300 × 100, the first layer includes 24 groups of 12 × 12 pixel filters ($K = 24$, $N_H = 12$). The second layer includes 40 maps, each 10 × 10 pixels ($K = 40$, $N_H = 10$).

In the second phase, online feature extraction used Beta-Elliptical strategy. Decomposing the signal into segments is our objective. Each segment is defined as a continuous handwriting stroke between two extremities points representing pen-up or pen-down moments. Each segment trajectory is modeled by arcs of ellipse. Therefore, each stroke is modeled by a feature vector of 10 parameters [4, 10].

In order to evaluate the effectiveness of the new features vectors obtained by two different approaches, we investigated its performance using SVM for recognizing characters and words applying on LMCA and ADAB database respectively.

The choice of parameters, kernel parameter σ and penalty parameter C, was proved to be experimentally effective by applying a grid-search with the 5-fold stratified cross validation method. We synthesized the most favorable usefulness of principal parameters obtained after the tests on the training on/off-line Arabic handwritten databases, LMCA and ADAB, as follows (Table 1):

Table 1. The best training parameter values for the SVM with RBF kernel

Parameters	Databases	
	LMCA	ADAB
Sigma σ	0.05	0.004
C	30	100

3.4 Results and Discussion

The proposed system founded on combination of two extractor methods already described, has reached a character recognition rate (RR) of 97.51 % when applied to the LMCA database on the testing dataset with 56 classes while with ADAB database we attained a word recognition rate of 86.3 % (without distortion) and 91.8 % (with distortion) on the testing dataset with 24 classes (See Table 2). Therefore, our present work yields a satisfactory performance compared with the previous reported RR in the literature.

Table 2. Recognition rate for our proposed system

Database	Number of classes	RR
LMCA	56	**97.51 %**
ADAB (without distortion)	24	**86.3 % (set4)**
ADAB (with distortion)		**91.8 % (set4)**

The recognition rate obtained with our system on the both databases, LMCA and ADAB (with distortion), is efficient compared to previous results reported in the literature (see Table 3). Unlike the recognition rate reported on the ADAB database without distortion which can be explained by the small number of samples of each shape. To solve this problem we have extended data by the elastic deformation technique. A comparative study of our system with other techniques utilizing on/off-line Arabic handwritten databases (see Table 3) was also realized. Our proposed system still performs better than hand-crafted features-based approach like MLP [17], HMM [18] and hybrid NN/HMM [4] methods. Finally, we can see from the results that the achieved accuracy is due to the discriminatory power of features which extracted automatically from raw data using deep architecture and the regression capabilities of SVM classifiers.

Table 3. Performance comparisons with Arabic database

Database	Approach / Database	RR
Present work	SVM / LMCA	**97.51 %**
	SVM / ADAB (with distortion)	**91.8 %**
Boubaker et al. [17]	MLP / LMCA	94.14 %
Ahmed and Abdel Azeem [18]	HMM / ADAB	89.7 %
Tagougui et al. [4]	Hybrid NN-HMM /ADAB	91.23 %

4   Conclusion

In this paper we presented our system for Arabic handwritten character/word recognition. The system used two methods for feature extraction based on deep learning and Beta-elliptic approach. The new extracted offline features are introduced with the beta-elliptical features vector to improve its discriminative power. Hence, our proposed system can be considered promising in the handwriting recognition domain. As perspective, we have to test HMM and BLSTM classifier to be able to deal with dynamic features for enhance recognition rate.

References

1. Elarian, Y., Ahmad, I., Awaida, S., Al-Khatib, W.G., Zidouri, A.: An Arabic handwriting synthesis system. Pattern Recogn. **48**, 849–861 (2015)
2. Huang, G.-B., Zhou, H., Ding, X., Zhang, R.: Extreme learning machine for regression and multiclass classification. IEEE Trans. Syst. Man Cybern. Part B Cybern. **42**(2), 513–529 (2012)
3. Lee, H., Pham, P.T., Largman, Y., Ng, A.Y.: Unsupervised feature learning for audio classification using convolutional deep belief networks. In: Advances in Neural Information Processing Systems (NIPS), pp. 1096–1104 (2009)
4. Tagougui, N., Boubaker, H., Kherallah, M., Alimi, M.A.: A hybrid NN/HMM modeling technique for online Arabic handwriting recognition. Int. J. Comput. Linguist. Res. **4**(3), 107–118 (2013)
5. El Abed, H., Kherallah, M., Märgner, V., Alimi, A.M.: On-line Arabic handwriting recognition competition - ADAB database and participating systems. IJDAR **14**(1), 15–23 (2011)
6. Elleuch, M., Tagougui, N., Kherallah, M.: Deep learning for feature extraction of Arabic handwritten script. In: Azzopardi, G., Petkov, N., Effenberg, A.O. (eds.) CAIP 2015, Part II. LNCS, vol. 9257, pp. 371–382. Springer, Heidelberg (2015). doi:10.1007/978-3-319-23117-4_32
7. Pechwitz, M., Maddouri, S.S., Märgner, V., Ellouze, N., Amiri, H.: IFN/ENIT database of handwritten Arabic words. In: Colloque International Francophone sur l'Ecrit et le Document (CIFED), pp. 127–136 (2002)
8. Boubaker, H., Chaabouni, A., Tagougui, N., Kherallah, M., Elabed, H., Alimi, A.M.: Off-line features integration for on-line handwriting graphemes modeling improvement. In: The 13th International Conference on Frontiers of Handwriting Recognition ICFHR 2012, Bari, Italy, pp. 69–74, 18–21 September, 2012
9. Hamdani, M., El Abed, H., Kherallah, M., Alimi, A.M.: Combining multiple HMMs using on-line and off-line features for offline Arabic handwriting recognition. In: Proceedings of the 10th International Conference on Document Analysis and Recognition (ICDAR), vol. 1, pp. 201–205, July 2009
10. Boubaker, H., Kherallah, M., Alimi, A.M.: New strategy for the on-line handwriting modeling. In: Proceedings of the Ninth International Conference on Document Analysis and Recognition (ICDAR), vol. 2, pp. 1233–1247 (2007)
11. Hinton, G.E.: A practical guide to training restricted Boltzmann machines. In: Montavon, G., Orr, G.B., Müller, K.-R. (eds.) Neural Networks: Tricks of the Trade, 2nd edn. LNCS, vol. 7700, pp. 599–619. Springer, Heidelberg (2012)

12. Lee, H., Grosse, R., Ranganath, R., Ng, A.Y.: Unsupervised learning of hierarchical representations with convolutional deep belief networks. Commun. ACM **54**(10), 95–103 (2011)
13. Vapnik, V.: Statistical Learn Theory. John Wiley, New York (1998)
14. Cortes, C., Vapnik, V.: Support vector networks. Mach. Learn. **20**, 273–297 (1995)
15. Burges, C.: A tutorial on support vector machines for pattern recognition. Data Min. Knowl. Discov. **2**(2), 121–167 (1998)
16. Chang, C.C., Lin, C.J.: LIBSVM: a library for support vector machines (2001). http://www.csie.ntu.edu.tw/~cjlin/libsvm
17. Boubaker, H., Tagougui, N., Elbaati, A., Kherallah, M., Elabed, H., Alimi, A.M.: Online arabic databases and applications. In: Märgner, V., El Abed, H. (eds.) Guide to OCR for Arabic Scripts, Part IV: Applications, pp. 541–557. Springer, London (2012)
18. Ahmed, H., Abdel Azeem, S.: On-line Arabic handwriting recognition system based on HMM. In: Proceedings of International Conference on Document Analysis and Recognition (ICDAR), pp. 1324–1328 (2011)

On Higher Order Computations and Synaptic Meta-Plasticity in the Human Brain

Stanisław Ambroszkiewicz[1,2(✉)]

[1] Siedlce University of Natural Sciences and Humanities, Siedlce, Poland
[2] Institute of Computer Science, Polish Academy of Sciences, Warszawa, Poland
sambrosz@gmail.com

Abstract. Glia modify neuronal connectivity by creating structural changes in the neuronal connectome. Glia also influence the functional connectome by modifying the flow of information through neural networks (Fields et al. 2015 [6]). There are strong experimental evidences that glia are responsible for synaptic meta-plasticity. Synaptic plasticity is the modification of the strength of connections between neurons. Meta-plasticity, i.e. plasticity of synaptic plasticity, may be viewed as mechanisms for dynamic reconfiguration of neural circuits. Since synapse creation corresponds to the mathematical notion of function composition, the mechanisms may serve as a grounding for functionals, i.e. higher order functions that take functions as their arguments.

1 Introduction

Gedankenexperiment: a backward time travel of a computer. *A contemporary computer was moved into the XIX-th century so that scientists could make experimental research. Actually, the idea underlining the functioning of a computer is extremely simple; it is the von Neumann computer architecture. Would it be possible for the scientists of nineteenth century to discover the idea by examining the electric circuits and their complex functioning of the working computer system consisting of monitor, a motherboard, a CPU, a RAM, graphic cards, expansion cards, a power supply, an optical disc drive, a hard disk drive, a keyboard and a mouse? What about BIOS and operating system as well as many applications installed?*

Perhaps the Gedankenexperiment may serve as a metaphor of the research on (the human) brain functioning. Although great achievements have been made in the brain research, the basic mechanisms (idea) underling the human brain functioning are still a great mystery.

A short review of the current research on higher order computations in the brain is presented below. Astrocytes are a kind of glial cells (simply glia). Let us cite the recent views of the role of glia and metaplasticity in the brain.

Fields et al. 2015 [6]: *"Astrocytes have anatomical and physiological properties that can impose a higher order organization on information processing and integration in the neuronal connectome. Neurons compute via membrane voltage, but how do astrocytes compute? What do glia contribute to information*

A.E.P. Villa et al. (Eds.): ICANN 2016, Part II, LNCS 9887, pp. 145–152, 2016.
DOI: 10.1007/978-3-319-44781-0_18

processing that neurons cannot accomplish? ... In comparison to neurons, glia communicate slowly and over broader spatial scales. This may make glia particularly well suited for involvement in integration, in homeostatic regulation, and alterations in structural or functional connectivity of neural networks taking place over periods of weeks or months".

Min et al. 2015 [11]: *"Many studies have shown that astrocytes can dynamically modulate neuronal excitability and synaptic plasticity, and might participate in higher brain functions like learning and memory. ... mathematical modeling will prove crucial for testing predictions on the possible functions of astrocytes in neuronal networks, and to generate novel ideas as to how astrocytes can contribute to the complexity of the brain. ..."*

Gilson et al. 2015 [7]: *"Experiments have revealed a plethora of synaptic and cellular plasticity mechanisms acting simultaneously in neural circuits. How such diverse forms of plasticity collectively give rise to neural computation remains poorly understood. ... To learn how neuronal circuits self-organize and how computation emerges in the brain it is therefore vital to focus on interacting forms of plasticity".*

The research on computational models of neural circuits is well established starting from McCulloch-Pitts networks [10] via the Hopfield model [8] to recurrent neural networks (RNNs). It seems that RNNs represent adequately the computations done in the human brain by the real neural networks. From the Computer Science point of view, RNNs are Turing complete (Siegelmann and Sontag [12]), i.e., every computable function may be represented as a RNN. However, Turing machine is a flat model of computation. There are also higher order computations (see the review Longley and Norman 2015 [9]), i.e. computable functionals where arguments (input) as well as values (output) are functions.

The Virtual Brain (TVB www.thevirtualbrain.org) project aims at building a large-scale simulation model of the human brain. It is supposed that brain function may emerge from the interaction of large numbers of neurons, so that, the research on TVB may contribute essentially to our understanding of the spatiotemporal dynamics of the brain's electrical activity. However, it is unclear how this activity may contribute to the comprehension of the principles of the human mind functioning.

Adolphs 2015 [1]: *"Some argue that we can only understand the brain once we know how it could be built. Both evolution and development describe temporally sequenced processes whose final expression looks very complex indeed, but the underlying generative rules may be relatively simple ..."*

Another interesting approach is due to Juergen Schmidhuber: *"The human brain is a recurrent neural network (RNN): a network of neurons with feedback connections"*; see http://people.idsia.ch/~juergen/rnn.html. Indeed, real neural circuits can be modeled as (continuous time) RNNs. Despite the enormous complexity of a hypothetical RNN modeling the human brain, there is a paradox here because (continuous time) RNNs are nonlinear dynamic systems. It means that RNNs are high level mathematical abstractions (of human mind) involving the notion of space-time Continuum that comprises actual infinity. These very abstractions are created in the human brain (consisting of a finite number of cells), i.e. the notions related to space-time continuum are represented (in the brain) in a finitray way as finite structures.

The foundations of the mind functioning might be ingenious in its simplicity although the underlying biological mechanism are extremely complex and sophisticated. Hence, in order to model neural circuits and the mechanisms responsible for structural changes in the neuronal connectome, let us use much more simple (than RNN) primitive notions from Mathematics and Computer Science, i.e. the computable functions and computable functionals. Since Mathematics is a creation of the human mind, the Foundations of Mathematics may shed some light on the principles of the brain functioning.

2   Neural Circuits, Computable Functions and Functionals

Several assumptions are to be made. The first one is that elementary neural circuits (corresponding to functional units in the brain) can be distinguished. The second assumption is that any such circuits (at least temporary) has clearly identified input (dendrite spines of some postsynaptic neurons) and output (axons of some presynaptic neurons). It means that the output is exactly determined by the input. The third assumption is that such circuits can be composed by linking the output of one circuit to the input of another circuit; it may be done by creating a synapse connecting an axon (of the output of one circuits) to a dendrite spine of the input of the other circuit. Actually, the assumptions have been already verified experimentally. Hence, a neural circuit can be represented as a first order function defined on natural numbers. That is, spike sequences (bursts), generated by a neuron, may be interpreted as natural numbers in the unary code, input of the circuit as arguments whereas output as values of the function.

Simple operations on functions may have their counterparts as operations on circuits. Given two functions f and g (defined on natural numbers), the new function h defined as $h(x, y) = f(x) + g(y)$ may serve as an example. If f^c, g^c and $+^c$ denote corresponding neural circuits, then the circuit corresponding to function h may be created by establishing (activating) some synapses between input neurons of $+^c$, and the output neuron of f^c and the output neuron of g^c. This may correspond roughly to the synaptic meta-plasticity. It is interesting (however, not surprising) that this very synapse creation corresponds to a basic notion of Mathematics, i.e. function composition.

Sockets and plugs are the crucial notions. A function consists of input, body and output, see Fig. 1. Input may consists of multiple sockets, whereas output may consists of multiple plugs. A plug-socket directed link may correspond to synapse as connection of axon and dendrite.

There are also higher order functions (called functionals) where arguments as well as values may be functions. It is also not surprising that these higher level functionals can be constructed by establishing links in the circuits of plugs and sockets.

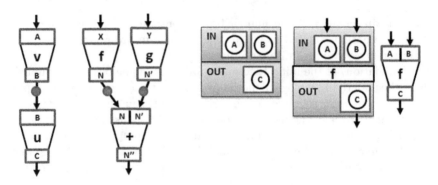

Fig. 1. Function as input (socket,) body, and output (plug). Simple composition of f, g, and $+$. Function type, and functions

Each function is of some type. Since the natural numbers (finite sequences (bursts) of spikes) are assumed as the basic type (denoted by N), the type of first order functions is of the form $(N^{s_1};\ N^{s_2};...; N^{s_k}) \rightarrow (N^{p_1};\ N^{p_2};...; N^{p_m})$, where $(N^{s_1};\ N^{s_2};...; N^{s_k})$ denotes different sockets of the input, whereas $(N^{p_1};\ N^{p_2};...; N^{p_m})$ denotes different plugs of the output. This type may be realized as a board consisting of sockets and plugs, see Fig. 1.

It seems that second (and higher) order computations in the brain are done by dynamic (re)configurations of links (synapses) between the neural circuits. Although the links are established between concrete neurons, these neurons belong to fixed circuits, so that (from functional point of view) the links are between circuits, and correspond to the circuit composition.

Let us take as granted that glia are responsible for creating synapses and managing their activity. Then, there must be a generic meta-composition process for doing so (corresponding to a functional), where the parameters are: two circuits (to be composed), presynaptic neurons of one circuit, and postsynaptic neurons of the second one.

Hence, such generic process may be represented as a second order function (functional) that takes (as input) two first order functions, a plug of one function and a socket of the second function; then it returns (as the output) a first order function as a composition of these two functions. The problem is how such generic process is realized in the brain. First of all, the circuits to be composed must be discriminated, and then passed, as parameters, to the composition process.

Glia are responsible for higher order computations, i.e. for dynamic creating, composing, and reconfiguring neural circuits. At the bottom level it is realized by creating new synapses; this corresponds to function composition. Since the function composition is the basis for construction of the higher order functions (functionals), the processes of dynamic synapse creation correspond to functionals.

Hypothesis. The primitive rules for construction of the computable functionals may have their counterparts in the human brain.

2.1   A Sketch of Formal Framework for Constructing Higher Order Computation Based on Functionals

Turing machines and partial recursive functions are not concrete constructions. Their definitions involve actual infinity, i.e. infinite type for Turing machines, and minimization operator μ for partial recursive functions. This results in possibility of *non terminating computations* that are abstract notions and have no grounding in the human brain. The proposed approach is fully constructive, and if restricted only to first order computable functions, it corresponds to the general recursive function according to the Herbrand-Gödel definition.

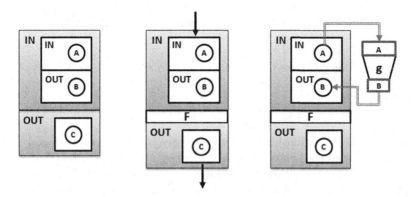

Fig. 2. More complex function type, and higher order application of functional F to a function $g : A \to B$. The result $F(g)$ is an object of type C

At the basic level it consists of some primitive types, primitive functions and type constructors, i.e. the type of natural numbers, the successor function, constant functions, projections, constructors for product and function type. However, the key primitive functionals correspond to application, composition, copy and iteration. It is crucial that these functionals can be constructed by (dynamic, in the case of iteration) establishing links between plugs (corresponding to output types) and sockets (corresponding to input types).

At the higher level of the approach, types are considered as objects, i.e. constructed as **boards of plugs and sockets**. This gives rise to introduce relations (according to the propositions-as-types correspondence of Curry-Howard), and polymorphism.

Hence, it is important to grasp the constructions of the boards as higher order types. The type of functions from natural numbers into natural numbers (denoted by $N^s \to N^p$) may be realized as a simple board consisting of a socket and a plug, see Fig. 1. Types of higher order are presented in Figs. 1 and 2. Note that for the type $(A \to B) \to C$, the input $A \to B$ becomes the socket. For the type $(A \to B) \to (C \to D)$, the output $C \to D$ becomes the plug.

Application of a functional $F : (A \to B) \to C$ to a function $g : A \to B$ is realized as follows. $A \to B$ is the socket of the functional F. The application is

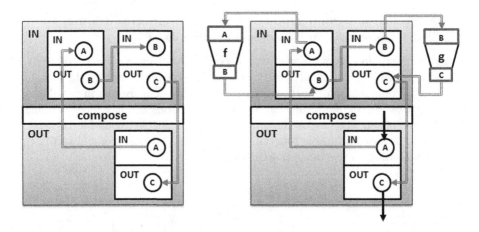

Fig. 3. The functional $Comp$ of type $((A \to B); (B \to C)) \to (A \to C)$. Input objects are: f of type $A \to B$ and g of type $B \to C$. When applied to $Comp$, the output object is a function of type $A \to C$

done (see Fig. 2) by establishing appropriate directed connections (links). That is, the link between the socket A of the socket of F and the socket A of g, and the link between the plug B of g and the plug of the socket of F.

Composition functional (denoted by $compose_{A,B,C}$) for simple composition of two functions (the first function f of type $A \to B$, and the second one g of type $B \to C$) is realized as two boards with appropriate links shown in Fig. 3. It is easy to check (by following the links) that applying $compose_{A,B,C}$ to two functions (see Fig. 3) results in their composition.

Note that a higher order application (i.e. application of a functional to a function), and a functional for composition are constructed just by providing some links between sockets and plugs. Since link corresponds to synapse, it might be interesting whether these functionals have counterparts in the brain.

Each construction, like $F(g)$ and $compose_{A,B,C}(f; g)$, can be distinguished as an individual object (notion). Perhaps, in the brain, they correspond to concrete regions.

Generally, discrimination of new notions by the human mind is crucial for reasoning. Once a notion is distinguished, it may be used in more sophisticated reasoning. This evidently corresponds to the *reflective abstraction* introduced by Piaget, especially if the notions emerge as the results of constructions. Note that here *constructions* mean dynamic (re)configuration of links between sockets and plugs.

A functional of special interest is $Copy$. Once an object a is constructed, repeat the construction once again. So that $Copy(a)$ returns two object: the original a, and its copy a'. Although the meaning of $Copy$ seems to be simple, its realization in the brain may be quite complex especially if the object a is of a higher order type.

If it is supposed that the construction of object a occupies some well defined region in the brain, then *Copy* may be realized by copying this region into a new "free region". Since in Biology (living organisms) copying (procreation) is ubiquitous, let us take the implementation of the functional *Copy* as granted.

Iteration as generalization of composition. That is, compose n-times a function $f : A \to A$ with itself. Note that n, as a natural number, is a parameter. The iteration is denoted by $Iter_A$ and it is a functional of type $(N; (A \to A)) \to (A \to A)$. So that $Iter_A(n; f)$ is the function being n-time composition of f. The realization of $Iter_A$ requires *Copy* for making copies of f, and $(n-1)$ copies of the composition functional. Since natural numbers are involved in the functional, it seems that, a hypothetical realization of $Iter$, in the brain, requires neurons.

Note that there are next higher orders of constructions of functionals. Functionals operate on functionals (second order functions) are third order functions that operate on the second order functions by re(configuring) links in the boards of sockets and plugs. And so on.

Higher order primitive recursion schema (also known as Grzegorczyk's iterator) can be constructed as a functional. For arbitrary type A, the iterator, denoted by R^A, of type $A \to ((N \to (A \to A)) \to (N \to A))$, is defined by the following equations.

for any $a : A$, $c : N \to (A \to A)$, and $k : N$
$$((R^A(a))(c))(1) = a \quad \text{and} \quad ((R^A(a))(c))(k+1) = (c(k))(((R^A(a))(c))(k))$$

However, a construction of R^A does not follow from the definition. Actually, it is based on the iteration functional and consists on dynamic formation of links in boards of plugs and sockets. Higher order primitive recursion allows to define a large subclass of general recursive functions, e.g. the famous Ackerman function. This can be done on the basic level of the proposed approach to computable functionals. At higher levels of the approach (where functionals are used) all general recursive functions can be constructed. It seems that higher order computation involving the functionals is useful, especially as efficient and smart organizations of complex and sophisticated first order computations.

Coming back to the neural circuits, the circuits may be represented as first order functions. Functionals operate on first order functions (circuits) by re(configuring) links inside and between the circuits. In this way, the functionals may be viewed as higher order computations on neural circuits.

3   Conclusion

Primitive types resulted from the most simple (primitive) and obvious data transfer methods: spike bursts (as natural numbers), and bundles of adjacent spike bursts as objects of Continuum (see the full version of the paper at google arXiv Ambroszkiewicz). The first order computable functions (as a static interpretation of the neural circuits) seems to be justified. This may give rise to expect that higher order computable functions (functionals) have counterparts in the human brain.

Composition (as link creation) is the basic operation for function construction as well as for construction of higher order functions (functionals). This very composition corresponds to synapse creation in the brain.

The two functionals (*Copy* and *Iter*) together with the higher order application, composition, and the primitive types constitute the cornerstone for building a constructive (intuitionistic) part of Arithmetics and Analysis, see [3,4]. According to the original meaning of L.E.J. Brouwer, intuitionism is the constructive mental activity of the human mind.

Since the architecture of human brain is definitely different than von Neumann computer architecture, the mechanisms of the meta-plasticity may give rise to develop a non-von Neumann computer architecture and a corresponding function-level programming language postulated by John Backus 1977 [5]; for more on this subject see [2].

For the full version of the paper and a mathematical approach to computable and constructive functionals see [3,4] (google arXiv Ambroszkiewicz).

References

1. Adolphs, R.: The unsolved problems of neuroscience. Trends Cogn. Sci. **19**(4), 173–175 (2015)
2. Ambroszkiewicz, S.: On the notion of "von Neumann vicious circle" coined by John Backus (2016). arXiv:http://arxiv.org/abs/1602.02715
3. Ambroszkiewicz, S.: Types and operations (2015). arXiv:http://arxiv.org/abs/1501.03043
4. Ambroszkiewicz, S.: Continuum as a primitive type (2015). arXiv:http://arxiv.org/abs/1510.02787
5. Backus, J.: Can programming be liberated from the von Neumann style? A functional style and its algebra of programs. Commun. ACM **21**(8), 613–641 (1979)
6. Fields, R.D., Woo, D.H., Basser, P.J.: Glial regulation of the neuronal connectome through local and long-distant communication. Neuron **86**(2), 374–386 (2015)
7. Gilson, M., Savin, C., Zenke, F.: Editorial: emergent neural computation from the interaction of different forms of plasticity. Front. Comput. Neurosci. **9**(145) (2015). http://doi.org/10.3389/fncom.2015.00145
8. Hopfield, J.J., Tank, D.W., et al.: Computing with neural circuits - a model. Science **233**(4764), 625–633 (1986)
9. Longley, J., Dag Normann, D.: Higher-Order Computability. Theory and Applications of Computability. Springer, Heidelberg (2015)
10. McCulloch, W.S., Pitts, W.: A logical calculus of the ideas immanent in nervous activity. Bull. Math. Biophys. **5**(4), 115–133 (1943)
11. Min, R., Santello, M., Nevian, T.: The computational power of astrocyte mediated synaptic plasticity. Front. Comput. Neurosci. **6** (2014). http://dx.doi.org/10.3389/fncom.2012.00093
12. Siegelmann, H.T., Sontag, E.D.: On the computational power of neural nets. J. Comput. Syst. Sci. **50**(1), 132–150 (1995)

Compression of Deep Neural Networks on the Fly

Guillaume Soulié, Vincent Gripon$^{(\boxtimes)}$, and Maëlys Robert

Télécom Bretagne, Brest, France
vincent.gripon@telecombretagne.eu

Abstract. Thanks to their state-of-the-art performance, deep neural networks are increasingly used for object recognition. To achieve the best results, they use millions of parameters to be trained. However, when targetting embedded applications the size of these models becomes problematic. As a consequence, their usage on smartphones or other resource limited devices is prohibited. In this paper we introduce a novel compression method for deep neural networks that is performed during the learning phase. It consists in adding an extra regularization term to the cost function of fully-connected layers. We combine this method with Product Quantization (PQ) of the trained weights for higher savings in storage consumption. We evaluate our method on two data sets (MNIST and CIFAR10), on which we achieve significantly larger compression rates than state-of-the-art methods.

1 Motivation

Deep Convolutional Neural Networks (CNNs) [1–4] have become the state-of-the-art for object recognition and image classification. As a matter of fact, most recently proposed systems are using this architecture [4–9]. With this global trend arise questions on how to to import CNNs on embedded platforms [10], including smartphones, where data storage and bandwidth are limited. Today the size of a typical CNN is often too large (typically hundred of megabytes for vision applications) for most smartphone users. The purpose of this paper is to propose new techniques for compressing deep neural networks without sacrificing performance.

In this work we focus on compressing CNNs used for vision, although our methodology is not taking any advantage of this particular application field and we expect it to perform similarly on other types of learning tasks. A typical state-of-the-art CNN [5,7,8] for visual recognition contains several convolutional layers followed by several fully connected layers. For the most challenging datasets, these layers may require hundred of millions of parameters to be trained in order to be efficient.

These parameters are overparameterized [11] and we aim at compressing them. Note that our motivation is mainly to reduce the model size rather than speeding up the computation time [12]. Compressing deep neural networks has

© Springer International Publishing Switzerland 2016
A.E.P. Villa et al. (Eds.): ICANN 2016, Part II, LNCS 9887, pp. 153–160, 2016.
DOI: 10.1007/978-3-319-44781-0_19

been the subject of several recent works. In [12,13] the authors use compression methods for speeding up CNN testing time.

More recently, some works focus on compressing neural network specially to reduce storage of the network. These works can generally be put into two different categories: some of them focus on compressing the fully connected layers and others on compressing the convolutional layers. In [14] the authors focus on compressing densely connected layers. In their work, they use signal processing vector quantization methods [15,16] such as k-means or Product Quantization (PQ). In [17] the authors focus on compressing the fully connected layers of a Multi-Layer Perceptron (MLP) using Hashing Trick, a low cost hash function to randomly group connection weights into hash buckets, and set the same value to all the parameters in the same bucket. In [18] the authors propose compressing convolutional layers using a Discrete Cosinus Transform applied on the convolutional filters, followed by Hashing Trick, as for the fully connected layers.

An interesting point showed by [14] is that in a typical sate-of-the-art CNN, more than 90 % of the storage is taken up by the densely connected layers, whereas about 90 % of the running time is taken by the convolutional layers. This is why, in order to compress the size of a CNN, we mainly focus on compressing the densely connected layers.

Instead of using a post-learning method to compress the network, our approach consists in modifying the regularization function used during the learning phase in order to favor quantized weights in some layers – especially the output ones. To achieve this, we use an idea that was originally proposed in [19]. In order to compress furthermore our obtained networks, we also use PQ as described in [14] afterwards. We perform some experiments both on Multi-Layer Perceptrons (MLP) and Convolutionnal Neural Networks.

In this paper, we introduce a novel strategy to quantize weights in deep learning systems. More precisely:

- We introduce a regularization term that forces weights to converge to either 0 or 1, before using the product quantization on the trained weights.
- We show how this extra term impacts performance depending on the depth of the layer it is used onto.
- We experiment our proposed method on celebrated benchmarks and compare with state-of-the-art techniques.

The outline of the paper is as follows. In Sect. 2 we discuss related work. Section 3 introduced our methodology for compressing layers in deep neural networks. In Sect. 4 we run experiments on celebrated databases. Section 5 is a conclusion.

2   Related Work

Throughout this paper, we term *compression rate* associated with a compression method the ratio of the memory used after the method is processed to that before it is used. As already mentioned in the introduction, the densely connnected layers of a state-of-the-art CNN usually involve hundreds of millions of parameters, thus requiring an important storage that may be hard to obtain in practice. Several works have been published on speeding up CNN prediction speed. In [20] the authors use tricks of CPUs to speed up the execution of CNN. In [21], the authors show that carrying the convolutional operations in the Fourier domain may lead to a speed-up of 200 %. Two very recent works, [12, 13], use linear matrix factorization methods for speeding up convolutions and obtain a 200 % speed-up gain with almost no loss in classification accuracy.

The previously mentionned works mainly focus on speeding up the CNN feedforward operations. Recently, several works have been devoted to compressing the CNN size. In [11], the authors demonstrate the overparametrization in neural network parameters. Indeed, they show that only 5 % of parameters are enough to accurately predict the 95 % remaining ones. These results motivate [9] to apply vector quantization methods to benefit from redundancy and compress the network parameters. This compression allows them to obtain results similar to those of [11]: they are able to achieve a compression rate of about 20 without sacrificing accuracy. In their paper, they tackle the model size issue by applying PQ on the trained weights. They are able to achieve a good balance between storage and test accuracy. For the ImageNet challenge ILSVRC2012, they achieve a 16–24 compression rate for the whole network with only 1 % loss on accuracy, using a state-of-the-art CNN.

In [17], for the first time a learn-based method is proposed to compress neural networks. This method, based on Hashing Trick, allows efficient compression rates. In particular, they show that compressing a large neural network may be more efficient than directly training a smaller one: in their example they are able to divide the loss by two using a eight times larger neural network compressed eight times. The same authors also propose in [18] to compress filters in convolutional layers, arguing that the size of the convolutional layers in state-of-the-art's CNN is increasing year after year.

3   Methodology

In this section, we present two methods for compressing the parameters in CNN layers. First we introduce the PQ method from [14], and then we introduce our proposed learn-based method.

3.1   Product Quantization (PQ)

This method has been extensively studied in [14]. The idea is to exploit the inner redundancy of trained weights. In order to do that, the authors propose to use PQ. PQ consists of partitioning the parameters space into disjoint sub-spaces, and performing quantization in each of them. The term "product" refers to the fact that the quantized points in the original parameter space are the cartesian product of the quantized points in each sub-space. PQ performs increasingly better as the redundancy in each subspace grows.

Specifically, given a layer L, let us denote by W the matrix of the corresponding weights and by (m, n) the dimensions of W. Assuming n is divisible by s, we can partition W column-wise into s sub-matrices:

$$W = [W^1, W^2, ..., W^s], \tag{1}$$

where $W^i \in \mathbb{R}^{m(n/s)}$. In [14], the authors point out that applying PQ on the x-axis or the y-axis of W does not leads to major difference in experiments. We can then perform k-means for each sub-matrix W^i, i.e. minimize:

$$\sum_{z=1}^{m} \sum_{j=1}^{k} \|w_z^i - c_j^i\|_2^2, \tag{2}$$

where w_z^i denotes the z-th row of sub-matrix W^i, and c_j^i denotes the j-th row of sub-codebook $C^i \in \mathbb{R}^{k(n/s)}$. The c^i which minimize this expression are named centroids.

Thus, the reconstructed matrix is:

$$\hat{W} = [\hat{W}^1, \hat{W}^2, ..., \hat{W}^s], \tag{3}$$

where

$$\hat{w}_j^i = c_j^i, j \text{ being a minimizer of } \min_j \|w_z^i - c_j^i\|_2^2.$$

We replace w_j^i by $\hat{w}_j^i$: the nearest centroid of w_j^i. We need to store the nearest centroid indexes for each w_j^i and codebooks of all the $\hat{w}_j^i$ for each sub-vector. The codebook is not negligible, therefore the compression rate is $(32mn)/(\log_2(k)ms + 32kn)$. With a fixed segment size, increasing k will lead to decreasing the compression rate.

3.2   Proposed Method

Our proposed method is twofold: first, we use a specific added regularization term in order to attract network weights to binary values, then we coarsely quantize the output layers.

Let us recall that training a neural network is generally performed thanks to the minimization of a cost function using a derivative of a gradient descent algorithm. In order to attract network weights to binary values, we add a binarization cost (regularizer) during the learning phase. This added cost pushes weights to binary values. As a result, solutions of the minimization problem are expected to be binary or almost binary, depending on the scaling parameter of the added cost with respect to the initial one. This idea is not new, although we did not find any work applying it to deep learning in the literature. Our choice for the regularization term has been greatly inspired by [19].

More precisely, let us denote by W the weights of the neural network, $f(W)$ the cost associated with W, $h_W(X)$ and $y(X)$ respectively the output and the label for a given input X, we obtain:

$$f(W) = \sum_X \|h_W(X) - y(X)\|_2 + \alpha \sum_{w \in W} \|w - 1\|_2 \|w + 1\|_2, \qquad (4)$$

where α is a scaling parameter representing the importance of the binarization cost with respect to the initial cost. Note that possible values for binary weights have been empirically explored and those centered on 0 (here $\{-1, +1\}$) led to the best results.

Finding a good value for α may be tricky, as a too small value results in a failure of the binarization process and a too large value results in the creation of local minima that will prevent the network from successfully training. To facilitate this selection of α, we use a barrier method [19] that consists in starting with small values of α and incrementing it regularly to help the quantization process. In our experiments, at each iteration, we multiply α by a constant $c = 1.001$ (this value has been empirically found to work best).

We observed that some layers are typically very well quantized at the end of this learning phase, whereas others are still far from binary. For that reason we then binarize some of the layers but not all. Again, this selection is made by exploring empirically the possibilities, for example using the results depicted in Fig. 1.

In order to improve further our compression rate, we then use the PQ method presented in the previous subsection.

The compression rate for our method is $(32mn)/(kn + \log_2(k)ms)$ (instead of $(32mn)/(32kn + \log_2(k)ms)$ for single Product Quantization). With a fixed segment size, increasing k will lead to decreasing the compression rate.

4   Experiments

We evaluate these different methods on two image classification datasets : MNIST and CIFAR10. The parameters used for Product Quantizer are a segment size m varying in $\{2, 4, 5, 8\}$ and a number of cluster k varying in $\{4, 8, 16\}$.

4.1   Experimental Settings

MNIST. The MNIST database of handwritten digits has a training set of 60,000 examples, and a test set of 10,000 examples. It is a subset of a larger set available from NIST. The digits have been size-normalized and centered in a fixed-size image. The neural network we use with MNIST is LeNet5. LeNet5 is a convolutional neural network introduced in [22].

CIFAR10. The CIFAR10 database has a training set of 50,000 examples, and a test set of 10,000 examples. It is a subset of a larger set available from the 80 million tiny images dataset. It consists of 32×32 colour images partitioned into ten classes. With the CIFAR10 database, we use a convolutional neural network made of four convolutional layers followed by two fully connected layers. This network has been introduced in [23].

4.2 Layers to Quantify

Our first experiments (with the MNIST database) depicted in Fig. 1 shows the influence of quantified layers on performance. We observe that performance strongly depends on which layers are quantized. More precisely, this experiment shows that one should quantize layers from the output to the input rather than the contrary. This result is not surprising to us as input layers have often been described as similar to wavelet transforms, which are intrinsically analog operators, whereas output layers are often compared to high level patterns which detection in an image is often enough for good classification results.

Layer 0	Layer 1	Layer 2	Layer 3	Test error
-	-	-	-	0,90%
binarised	-	-	-	23,19%
binarised	binarised	-	-	81,26 %
binarised	binarised	binarised	-	90,26%
binarised	binarised	binarised	binarised	90,1 %
-	binarised	binarised	binarised	7,54%
-	-	binarised	binarised	1,13%
-	-	-	binarised	0,88%

Fig. 1. Performance of the classification task depending on which layers of the network are quantized, on the MNIST database. Layer 0 is the input layer, whereas layer 3 is the output one.

4.3 Performance Comparison

Our second experiment shows a comparison with previous work. The results are depicted in Fig. 2. Note that in both cases compared networks have the exact same architecture.

As far as our proposed method is concerned, we choose to compress only the two outputs layers, which are fully connected. Since their sizes are distinct, we are not able to use the same PQ coefficients k and m twice. Note that layer 2 contains almost all weights and is therefore the one we chose to investigate the role of each parameters.

We observe that our added regularization cost allows to significantly improve performance. For example for the MNIST database, if we want to respect a loss of 2 %, we have a compression rate of 33 with single PQ, whereas our learn-based method leads to a compression rate of 107.

This compression rate concern only the two output layers. However, as the output layers contains almost all weights, we still have a significant compression: on this specific example, using our proposed method the memory used to store the network weights fall down from 26 MB to 550 kb.

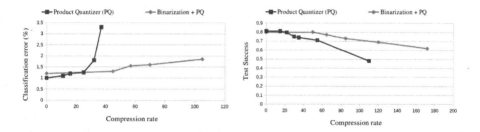

Fig. 2. Comparison of our proposed method with previous work on the MNIST dataset.

5   Conclusion and Perspectives

In this paper we introduced a new method to compress convolutional neural networks. This method consists in adding an extra term to the cost function that forces weights to become almost binary. In order to compress even more the network, we then apply Product Quantization and the combination of both allows us to reach performance above state-of-the-art methods.

We also demonstrate the influence of the depth of the binarized layer on performance. These findings are of particular interest to us, and a motivation to further explore the connections between actual biological data and deep neural systems.

In future work, we consider applying this method to larger datasets (e.g. ImageNet). Such datasets typically require larger networks, leading to an increased interest in obtaining good compression factors. In addition, these network are expected to be deeper, and thus allow studying thoroughly the impact of binarization depending on the deepness of layers. We also consider exploring more complex regularization functions, in particular in order to extend our work to q-ary values, q being layer-dependent and determined on the fly.

Finally, the next step consists in making activities of neurons also binary. With both connections and activities binary, one could propose optimized digital implementations of these networks leading to higher throughput, lesser energy consumption and lesser memory usage than conventional implementations.

Acknowledgments. This work was founded in part by the European Research Council under the European Union's Seventh Framework Program (FP7 / 2007 - 2013) / ERC grant agreement number 290901.

References

1. Krizhevsky, A., Sutskever, I., Hinton, G.E.: Imagenet classification with deep convolutional neural networks. In: Advances in Neural Information Processing Systems, pp. 1097–1105 (2012)
2. LeCun, B.B., Denker, J.S., Henderson, D., Howard, R.E., Hubbard, W., Jackel, L.D.: Handwritten digit recognition with a back-propagation network. In: Advances in Neural Information Processing Systems. Citeseer (1990)

3. Szegedy, C., Liu, W., Jia, Y., Sermanet, P., Reed, S., Anguelov, D., Erhan, D., Vanhoucke, V., Rabinovich, A.: Going deeper with convolutions, arXiv preprint arXiv:1409.4842 (2014)
4. Simonyan, K., Zisserman, A.: Very deep convolutional networks forlarge-scale image recognition, arXiv preprint arXiv:1409.1556 (2014)
5. Jia, Y.: Caffe: an open source convolutional architecture for fast feature embedding, arXiv preprint arXiv:1310.1531 (2013)
6. Donahue, J., Jia, Y., Vinyals, O., Hoffman, J., Zhang, N., Tzeng, E., Darrell, T.: Decaf: a deep convolutional activation feature for generic visualrecognition, arXiv preprint arXiv:1310.1531 (2013)
7. Sermanet, P., Eigen, D., Zhang, X., Mathieu, M., Fergus, R., LeCun, Y.: Overfeat: integrated recognition, localization and detection usingconvolutional networks, arXiv preprint arXiv:1312.6229 (2013)
8. Zeiler, M.D., Fergus, R.: Stochastic pooling for regularization of deepconvolutional neural networks, arXiv preprint arXiv:1301.3557 (2013)
9. Gong, Y., Wang, L., Guo, R., Lazebnik, S.: Multi-scale orderless pooling of deep convolutional activation features. In: Fleet, D., Pajdla, T., Schiele, B., Tuytelaars, T. (eds.) ECCV 2014, Part VII. LNCS, vol. 8695, pp. 392–407. Springer, Heidelberg (2014)
10. Gokhale, V., Jin, J., Dundar, A., Martini, B., Culurciello, E.: A 240 G-ops/s mobile coprocessor for deep neural networks. In: 2014 IEEE Conference on Computer Vision and Pattern Recognition Workshops (CVPRW), pp. 696–701. IEEE (2014)
11. Denil, M., Shakibi, B., Dinh, L., de Freitas, N., et al.: Predicting parameters in deep learning. In: Advances in Neural Information Processing Systems, pp. 2148–2156 (2013)
12. Denton, E.L., Zaremba, W., Bruna, J., LeCun, Y., Fergus, R.: Exploiting linear structure within convolutional networks for efficient evaluation. In: Advances in Neural Information Processing Systems, pp. 1269–1277 (2014)
13. Jaderberg, M., Vedaldi, A., Zisserman, A.: Speeding up convolutional neuralnetworks with low rank expansions, arXiv preprint arXiv:1405.3866 (2014)
14. Gong, Y., Liu, L., Yang, M., Bourdev, L.: Compressing deep convolutional networks using vector quantization, arXiv preprint arXiv:1412.6115 (2014)
15. Jegou, H., Douze, M., Schmid, C.: Product quantization for nearest neighbor search. IEEE Trans. Pattern Anal. Mach. Intell. 33(1), 117–128 (2011)
16. Chen, Y., Guan, T., Wang, C.: Approximate nearest neighbor search by residual vector quantization. Sensors 10(12), 11259–11273 (2010)
17. Chen, W., Wilson, J.T., Tyree, S., Weinberger, K.Q., Chen, Y.: Compressingneural networks with the hashing trick, arXiv preprint arXiv:1504.04788 (2015)
18. Chen, W., Wilson, J.T., Tyree, S., Weinberger, K.Q., Chen, Y.: Compressing convolutional neural networks, arXiv preprint arXiv:1506.04449 (2015)
19. Murray, W., Ng, K.-M.: An algorithm for nonlinear optimization problems with binary variables. Comput. Optim. Appl. 47(2), 257–288 (2010)
20. Vanhoucke, V., Senior, A., Mao, M.Z.: Improving the speed of neural networks on CPUs. In: Proceedings of Deep Learning and Unsupervised Feature Learning NIPS Workshop, vol. 1 (2011)
21. Mathieu, M., Henaff, M., LeCun, Y.: Fast training of convolutional networks through FFTS, arXiv preprint arXiv:1312.5851 (2013)
22. LeCun, Y., Bottou, L., Bengio, Y., Haffner, P.: Gradient-based learning applied to document recognition. Proc. IEEE 86(11), 2278–2324 (1998)
23. Chollet, F.: Keras: Theano-based deep learning library (2015). http://keras.io/

Blind Super-Resolution with Deep Convolutional Neural Networks

Clément Peyrard[1,2]([✉]), Moez Baccouche[1], and Christophe Garcia[2]

[1] Orange Labs, 4 rue du Clos Courtel, 35510 Cesson-Sévigné, France
{clement.peyrard,moez.baccouche}@orange.com
[2] University of Lyon, INSA Lyon, LIRIS, UMR5205 CNRS,
69621 Villeurbanne, France
christophe.garcia@liris.cnrs.fr

Abstract. Example-based methods have demonstrated their ability to perform well for Single Image Super-Resolution (SR). While very efficient when a single image formation model (non-blind) is assumed for the low-resolution (LR) observations, they fail when a LR image is not compliant with this model, producing noticeable artifacts on the final SR image. In this paper, we address blind SR (*i.e.* without explicit knowledge of the blurring kernel) using Convolutional Neural Networks and show that such models can handle different level of blur without any a priori knowledge of the actual kernel used to produce LR images. The reported results demonstrate that our approach outperforms state-of-the-art methods for the blind set-up, and is comparable with the non-blind approaches proposed in previous work.

Keywords: Single Image Super-Resolution · Blind Super-Resolution · Convolutional Neural Networks

1 Introduction

Single Image Super-Resolution (SISR) aims at reconstructing high-resolution images from low-resolution ones. During the last decade, many methods have been proposed to address this ill-posed problem. Among them, example-based SISR has known good progress in the past ten years, notably due to the use of bigger amount of data and new capabilities to handle it. During the training phase, these systems receive pairs of low and high resolution patches, and model this relationship to generalize to unseen pairs. However, low-resolution (LR) images used for training such systems are often synthetically created from high-resolution (HR) ones, with a fixed downsampling procedure that involves a single low-pass filter and a decimation operator. Several works [3,11] have been outlining that learning on such synthetic data can lead to a bad prediction or regularization of the SR image, yielding over-smooth or over-ringing artifacts. This happens when the given low-resolution image acquisition model does not comply with the learned one. In [3,11], authors show that example-based methods have

© Springer International Publishing Switzerland 2016
A.E.P. Villa et al. (Eds.): ICANN 2016, Part II, LNCS 9887, pp. 161–169, 2016.
DOI: 10.1007/978-3-319-44781-0_20

their performance bounded to the type of data they have seen during the learning phase. They rely on a strong a priori on the blur that has been applied before decimation during the LR image creation process, and are therefore *non-blind*. Regarding those considerations, one might want to produce SR images independently from a precise decimation model, in a *blind* fashion. Some learning-based methods do incorporate slightly different version of the LR images. The main contribution of this paper is to show that deeper convolutional neural networks can handle SR for LR images generated with different blurs levels as an input while targeting the same ideal HR examples.

We start with a review of the existing neural example-based approaches in super-resolution and the approaches for blind set-up in Sect. 2. In Sect. 3, we recall the super-resolution problem formulation and give details on the used CNN model. In Sect. 4, we present extensive experiments and report the obtained performances on studied models. Finally, conclusions and discussions regarding future works are summarized in Sect. 5.

2   Related Work

Image Super-Resolution has been an active research area since the 70's. Many example-based state-of-the-art methods including dictionary learning, neighbor embedding or deep learning via neural networks, report good results as long as the inverse problem is non-blind *i.e.* precisely bounded to one decimation model (LR images generation model from HR images).

2.1   Neural Based SISR

Many recent SISR methods rely on Convolutional Neural Networks (CNN) that learn to perform SR from high and low-resolution examples. The proposition of a CNN-based SR method in [2] marked the first high impact study on such methods. The authors proposed an elegant end-to-end framework to produce SR images from single upscaled LR ones. Since then, several works based on CNN have reported good results for example-based SR. In [6], the authors also used CNN to perform text image SR, but taking the original LR image instead of the upscaled one. In [9], a convolutional autoencoder scheme allows to perform SR, and exhibit good results by using data augmentation and fine-tuning for image-specific SR. Authors in [4] train a 5 to 20 layer CNN to perform SR using large data and gradient clipping at backpropagation to speed-up the learning process. Learned on different scales, they show that the variety of artefacts can be corrected by a single model trained on augmented data. In [13], the authors address face SR using a bichannel CNN. The used data contain several degradation (Gaussian blur, motion blur) and resolutions. The method is constrained by the presence of face and learns a 2,000 element dictionary to produce HR face. Recently, the authors of [1] have proposed an interesting hallucination scheme that samples SR images from a distribution of features of a deep CNN. Being learned on recognition tasks and using a certain degree of abstraction via convolutions and pooling layers, those features present the interesting property of carrying knowledge about textures, long-term spatial consistency and semantics that often miss in reconstruction-only example-based SR methods. A second CNN allows to predict those features from a LR image at test time. Although [4, 9] include variations in the addressed resolutions, Neural networks, along with other example-based SR are essentially being used for non-blind SR.

2.2   Blind Approaches in Example-Based SR

Blind SR refers to methods that have no a priori on the used image formation model, especially the blurring kernel. Practically, most of the blind methods estimate the most probable blurring kernel and/or use statistics about the desired SR images. Therefore, iterative and MAP approaches are preferred, while direct example-based methods are not the most popular approaches. Recent works [3, 11] show the importance of knowing a precise blurring kernel in the learned prior by example-based approaches. When evaluating such methods without retraining the models with the right kernel, results exhibit over-smoothed or over-sharpened images: evaluating on non-blind models gives much better results. In [3], the authors study the influence of a gaussian blur kernel with variable variance applied before an antialisaed bicubic downsampling. They show that a simple prior on the SR image may already produce good results as long as the exact image formation process is known. In [11] an extended study compares recent learning-based approaches. Both studies show that retraining example-based approaches with the right kernel give better results. In [5], a joint estimation of the blurring kernel and the SR image is performed. Later in [8], authors address both SR and deblurring, using the output of a learning-based SR method as a constraint on the final image. A global MAP optimization scheme is then applied along with other deblurring constraints on SR and LR images. This unified approach is very interesting as blur is one noticeable artifact in interpolated images, along with jagged edges and other kinds of noise. In [12], the authors combine blur kernel estimation and per-image dictionary learning, which is more precise but also slower. In [7], the authors proposed a richer collection of blurring kernels using oriented bivariate gaussian ones. Although the main purpose is to propose adaptive scheme in a non-blind fashion, they conduct the so-called blind experiments with several example-based algorithms. Another problem we can relate to blind SR is the unknown scale problem, where the scale factor is not known in advance. Cascading approaches have been proposed, like in [10] where the same model can be used for ×2 and ×4 SR. In [4, 9], different scales are used for data augmentation that enhance the performance of neural network by learning more robust convolution kernels in [9] or being blind across the scales for [4]. In [13], the learned hallucinating CNN is also blind and robust to several blur kernel and resolution. However, it is likely constrained to aligned faces, which allows a strong prior on the type of output data.

From the literature, we can see that in order to benefit from the potential of learning-based approaches, we may non exhaustively consider three strategies:

(i) projecting the LR images into the known LR space – or alternatively predicting the right model to use from a collection – to fit the distribution of image seen during training (ii) online retuning a pre-trained model (iii) designing a learning machine able to implicitly model the projections into an end-to-end framework, the latter being a more relaxed problem for constrained image category such as faces or text. In this paper, we investigate the third strategy by using deeper CNN to try to absorb the different blurring kernels. Experiments from [7] indicate that using a blind CNN already brings a gain over a simple bicubic interpolation.

3   Problem Formulation and Proposed Model

In this section, we first recall the SR problem formulation for the blind set-up, and describe the proposed approach to address it.

3.1   Blind SR

In most of the example-based SR works, a LR image is considered sampled from a HR one with the following formula:

$$y = D\bar{B}x \tag{1}$$

where y is the LR image, x is the HR image, $\bar{B}$ is a blurring operator and D a decimation operator that discard every other S pixel for a given scaling factor S. Generally, the image digitalization process from continuous scene to digital image is not taken into account and x is considered to exhibit statistical properties of desired HR images, being rather free of artifacts although some may appear due to digital compression or varying quality. Note the bar on the blurring kernel as it is subject to variability in the blind set-up. In most of the non-blind configurations addressed by example-based SR methods, the blurring kernel is an anti-aliased bicubic kernel that partially removes high-frequencies and avoids ending up with aliased LR images. In this work, we use gaussian blur kernels with variable variance and orientation as proposed in [7]. Figure 1 shows the generation of different LR images from a single HR sample.

3.2   Proposed Approach

We propose to use a single CNN to recover a SR image as close as possible to the HR image x. This means we expect it to absorb the different levels of blur and be able to project different visual structure into a HR feature space decorrelated from the applied blur. Figure 1 shows an example of such visually different structures that should produce the same HR content. As an input, although other approaches generally use upscaled LR patches, our network takes a LR patch, and performs upsampling at the output layer by using S^2 maps instead of one, rearranged to produce the correct output size. This allows to have

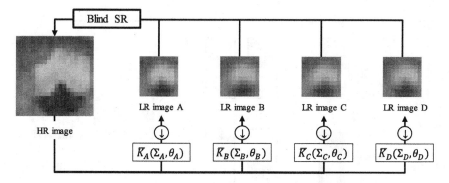

Fig. 1. Generation of several LR images using various blurring kernels from a single HR image and scale factor of 2. Each blurring kernel has different variances and orientations, leading to different LR images. LR examples have been rescaled to the same size for visualization.

a bigger input retina with less 3×3 layers, but requires several output maps. The model can either target the HR patch in graylevel or the high frequencies obtained by difference between the HR patch and upsampled LR patch. Aside from the upsampling approach, the proposed network architecture (Fig. 2) is very similar to [4]. It has L layers of 3×3 convolutions, each of which is fully connected to the previous one; *i.e.* each convolutional kernel has $M \times 3 \times 3 + 1$ parameters including bias, except for the first layer which is directly connected to the input image and the last one that holds $S^2 \times 3 \times 3 + 1$. We use rectified linear units (ReLU) activations after each convolution map. For simplicity, we use zero-padding on borders to keep the feature maps of the same size from the first to the last layer. Using large training patches diminishes the importance of this side effect.

We train a CNN with parameters θ and input y to output a full size image $\tilde{x}_i = \Psi(y_i, \theta)$, minimizing MSE between the output maps and the target sample.

In the next section, we provide more details about the experimental architectures and the data used for training.

4   Experimental Results

We experiment different configuration for the described approach, using the data from [7].

4.1   Data Generation

The data is generated according to [7] for scale $S = 2$. The LR patches are used as an input *i.e.* without bicubic upsampling. We sample $29,026$ pairs of patches from 91 images for each gaussian blurring kernel. These kernels vary in variance and orientation. A total of 58 kernels are used: variances go from 0.75 to 3.0

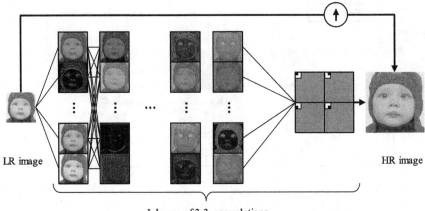

Fig. 2. Proposed CNN for blind SR. At each layer, the convolutions and ReLU activation functions produce maps that are processed by the next layer. The last layer is composed of $S^2 = 4$ maps, rearranged on the HR grid to produce the details missing in the interpolated LR image. Maps dynamic has been modified for visualization.

with a 0.75 step in both dimensions while orientation lies in $[0, \pi]$ with a $\frac{\pi}{8}$ step. This gives a total amount of $K = 1,683,508$ example pairs. Input LR patch dimension is 18×18 pixels and 36×36 pixels for output size. For testing, we use the same procedure on 19 images from "Set5" and "Set14". Comparative results are presented in Subsect. 4.3.

4.2 Experiments

Using the Caffe framework[1], we train each network from scratch, with a random initialization. We set the global learning rate to 10^{-4}. Although different batch sizes have been tested (4, 16, 128, 256), the reported results were obtained with a pure stochastic gradient descent, which converges faster than using mini-batch and lead to the same order of performances. Note that a "mini-batch" effects already takes place as each sample brings a 36×36 error map in which each pixel contributes to the parameter update. Using higher learning rates as in [4] might compensate for the apparent slow convergence. We target the high frequencies components instead of the direct graylevel as in previous works [4,6]. In Table 1, we present the experiments with variations in the number of kernels M and number of layers L. The reported test loss allows to monitor the learning process and select the best models. Test samples are extracted from "Set5". We can see that increasing the number of parameters of the proposed model allows to decrease the global MSE. We choose model 7 with 7 layers (comparable to 8) to evaluate on the full test images.

---

[1] http://caffe.berkeleyvision.org/.

Table 1. 8 configurations with the number of layers L (including the 4-map output layer), the number of kernels per layer M, the total number of parameters and the best obtained test MSE.

Configuration	L	M	#parameters	Loss
1	4	16	5,380	0.816
2	4	32	19,970	0.766
3	4	64	76,804	0.756
4	4	128	301,060	0.751
5	5	64	113,734	0.739
6	6	64	150,660	0.737
7	7	64	187,588	0.731
8	8	64	224,516	0.730

4.3   Comparison with State-of-the-Art Example-Based SR

We have computed the PSNR for "Set5" and "Set14" for the best obtained model and compared our results to those reported in [7], using the same protocol, especially cropping 7 pixels at test time to avoid border effects. Results are reported in Table 2. We can observe that our approach outperforms the others for the blind set-up. It is also competitive with the non-blind approaches as the mean PSNR is higher than the non-blind A+ and SRCNN methods on "set5" and the highest for "set14", while our approach cannot take advantage of the a priori knowledge of the blurring kernel.

Table 2. PSNR scores (dB) on Set5 and Set14. We report the blind and non-blind results of three experiments of [7] as a comparison.

	Blind (AB)			Non-blind (CAB)		
	Ours	A+	SRCNN	SRF	A+	SRCNN	SRF
PSNR on Set5	34.24	33.21	33.58	33.50	33.76	33.92	**34.43**
PSNR on Set14	**30.82**	30.00	30.27	30.11	30.35	30.50	30.73

5   Conclusion and Future Work

We have presented a blind approach to Super-Resolution using a Convolutional Neural Network architecture. The network is trained with LR and HR image pairs where LR images are produced with different blurring kernels. Although shallow networks perform well for the non-blind set-up [2], the experiments show that by using more parameters and deeper neural models than in previous work, we can improve the robustness of CNN-based models for blind SR.

The proposed network has a larger number of weights than those used in [2,7]. For the training, the authors of [4] propose to speed up the process with higher learning rates and gradient clipping to avoid exploding gradients that occur in deep networks. In a similar way, example selection and discarding near-zero values for details could avoid many useless backpropagation steps. This is not straightforward for large training patches where a binary map should indicate whether or not an error should be backpropagated. Moreover, great care should be given on such operation to conserve parallel computation efficient.

Another track of investigation is to force the abstraction in the CNN, to make it less dependent on the input image and its potential artifacts. Even if more robust, the proposed model is composed of fine grain 3×3 convolutions that allow to carry localized errors through the different layers until the output one. Motivated by [1], we believe that blind SR may profit from spatial abstraction via pooling layers. It may constrain the encoding process of the CNN to extract meaningful internal representation independently from the spatial inconvenience of the different blurring effects.

References

1. Bruna, J., Sprechmann, P., LeCun, Y.: Super-resolution with deep convolutional sufficient statistics. In: International Conference on Learning Representations (2016)
2. Dong, C., Loy, C.C., He, K., Tang, X.: Learning a deep convolutional network for image super-resolution. In: Fleet, D., Pajdla, T., Schiele, B., Tuytelaars, T. (eds.) ECCV 2014, Part IV. LNCS, vol. 8692, pp. 184–199. Springer, Heidelberg (2014)
3. Efrat, N., Glasner, D., Apartsin, A., Nadler, B., Levin, A.: Accurate blur models vs. image priors in single image super-resolution. In: International Conference on Computer Vision (2013)
4. Kim, J., Lee, J.K., Lee, K.M.: Accurate image super-resolution using very deep convolutional networks. In: Computer Vision and Pattern Recognition (2016)
5. Michaeli, T., Irani, M.: Nonparametric blind super-resolution. In: International Conference on Computer Vision (2013)
6. Peyrard, C., Mamalet, F., Garcia, C.: A comparison between multi-layer perceptrons and convolutional neural networks for text image super-resolution. In: International Conference on Computer Vision Theory and Applications (2015)
7. Riegler, G., Schulter, S., Rather, M., Bischof, H.: Conditioned regression models for non-blind single image super-resolution. In: International Conference on Computer Vision (2015)
8. Shao, W.-Z., Elad, M.: Simple, accurate, and robust nonparametric blind super-resolution. In: Zhang, Y.-J. (ed.) ICIG 2015. LNCS, vol. 9219, pp. 333–348. Springer, Heidelberg (2015)
9. Wang, Z., Yang, Y., Wang, Z., Chang, S., Han, W., Yang, J., Huang, T.: Self-tuned deep super resolution. In: Computer Vision and Pattern Recognition Workshops (2015)
10. Wang, Z., Liu, D., Yang, J., Han, W., Huang, T.S.: Deeply improved sparse coding for image super-resolution. In: International Conference on Computer Vision (2015)

11. Yang, C.-Y., Ma, C., Yang, M.-H.: Single-image super-resolution: a benchmark. In: Fleet, D., Pajdla, T., Schiele, B., Tuytelaars, T. (eds.) ECCV 2014, Part IV. LNCS, vol. 8692, pp. 372–386. Springer, Heidelberg (2014)
12. Zhao, X., Wu, Y., Tian, J., Zhang, H.: Single image super-resolution via blind blurring estimation and anchored space mapping. Comput. Vis. Media **2**(1), 71–85 (2016)
13. Zhou, E., Fan, H., Cao, Z., Jiang, Y., Yin, Q.: Learning face hallucination in the wild. In: AAAI Conference on Artificial Intelligence (2015)

DNN-Buddies: A Deep Neural Network-Based Estimation Metric for the Jigsaw Puzzle Problem

Dror Sholomon[1], Omid E. David[1($\boxtimes$)], and Nathan S. Netanyahu[1,2]

[1] Department of Computer Science, Bar-Ilan University, 52900 Ramat-Gan, Israel
dror.sholomon@gmail.com, mail@omiddavid.com, nathan@cs.biu.ac.il
[2] Center for Automation Research, University of Maryland,
College Park, MD 20742, USA
nathan@cfar.umd.edu

Abstract. This paper introduces the first deep neural network-based estimation metric for the jigsaw puzzle problem. Given two puzzle piece edges, the neural network predicts whether or not they should be adjacent in the correct assembly of the puzzle, using nothing but the pixels of each piece. The proposed metric exhibits an extremely high precision even though no manual feature extraction is performed. When incorporated into an existing puzzle solver, the solution's accuracy increases significantly, achieving thereby a new state-of-the-art standard.

1 Introduction

Jigsaw puzzles are a popular form of entertainment, available in different variation of difficulty to challenge children, adults and even professional players. Given $n \times m$ different non-overlapping tiles of an image, the objective is to reconstruct the original image, taking advantage of both the shape and chromatic information of each piece. Despite the popularity and vast distribution of jigsaw puzzles, their assembly is not trivial computationally, as this problem was proven to be NP-hard [1,8]. Nevertheless, a computational jigsaw solver may have applications in many real-world applications, such as biology [16], chemistry [25], literature [18], speech descrambling [27], archeology [2,15], image editing [5], and the recovery of shredded documents or photographs [3,7,14,17]. Regardless, as noted in [11], research of the topic may be justified solely due to its intriguing nature.

Recent years have witnessed a vast improvement in the research and development of automatic jigsaw puzzle solvers, manifested in both puzzle size, solution accuracy, and amount of manual human intervention required. In its most basic form, every puzzle solver requires some function to evaluate the compatibility of adjacent pieces and a strategy for placing the pieces as accurately as possible. Most strategies are greedy and rely heavily on some "trick" to estimate whether two pieces are truly adjacent (e.g. two pieces that are each the most compatible piece from all pieces to one another, four pieces that form a loop

© Springer International Publishing Switzerland 2016
A.E.P. Villa et al. (Eds.): ICANN 2016, Part II, LNCS 9887, pp. 170–178, 2016.
DOI: 10.1007/978-3-319-44781-0_21

(a)   (b)

Fig. 1. Jigsaw puzzle before and after reassembly using our DNN-Buddies scheme in an enhanced solver.

where each pair's compatibility is above a threshold, etc.). Such heuristics were dubbed an "estimation metric" in [20], as they allow estimating the adjacency correctness of two pieces without knowing the correct solution. The majority of recent works focused on devising elaborate, hand-crafted compatibility functions and high-precision estimation metrics.

Despite the proven effectiveness of neural networks in the field of computer vision, no attempt has been made to automatically devise a high-precision estimation metric for the jigsaw puzzle problem. This might be due to the highly imbalanced nature of the puzzle problem, as in each $n \times m$ puzzle, there are $\mathcal{O}(n \times m)$ matching piece-pairs and $\mathcal{O}(n^2 \times m^2)$ possible mismatching ones. In this paper we propose a novel estimation metric relying on neural networks. The proposed metric achieves extremely high precision despite the lack of any manually extracted features.

The proposed metric proves to be highly effective in real-world scenarios. We incorporated the metric in our GA-based solver, using no hand-crafted sophisticated compatibility measure and experimented with the currently known challenging benchmarks of the hardest variant of the jigsaw puzzle problem: non-overlapping, (28×28) square pieces (i.e. only chromatic information is available to the solver) where both piece orientation and puzzle dimensions are unknown. The enhanced solver proposed sets a new state-of-the-art in terms of the accuracy of the solutions obtained and the number of perfectly reconstructed puzzles.

2   Previous Work

Jigsaw puzzles were first introduced around 1760 by John Spilsbury, a Londonian engraver and mapmaker. Nevertheless, the first attempt by the scientific community to computationally solve the problem is attributed to Freeman and Garder [9] who in 1964 presented a solver which could handle up to nine-piece problems. Ever since then, the research focus regarding the problem has shifted from shape-based to merely color-based solvers of square-tile puzzles. In 2010 Cho et al. [4] presented a probabilistic puzzle solver that could handle up to 432 pieces, given some a priori knowledge of the puzzle. Their results were improved a year later by Yang et al. [26] who presented a particle filter-based solver. Furthermore, Pomeranz et al. [20] introduced that year, for the first time, a fully automated square jigsaw puzzle solver that could handle puzzles of up to 3,000 pieces. Gallagher [10] has further advanced this by considering a more general variant of the problem, where neither piece orientation nor puzzle dimensions are known. Son et al. [24] improved the accuracy of the latter variant using so-called "loop-constraints". Palkin and Tal [19] further improved the accuracy and handled puzzles with missing pieces. Sholomon et al. [21] presented a genetic algorithm (GA)-based solver for puzzles of known orientation which was later generalized to other variants [22, 23].

2.1 Compatibility Measures and Estimation Metrics

As stated earlier, most works focus on the compatibility measure and an estimation metric. A compatibility measure is a function that given two puzzle piece edges (e.g. the right edge of piece 7 versus the upper edge of piece 12) predicts the likelihood that these two edges are indeed placed as neighbors in the correct solution. This measure applies to each possible pair of piece edges. The estimation metric, on the other hand, predict whether two piece edges are adjacent but may not apply to many possible pairs. Following is a more detailed review of the efforts made so far in the field.

Cho et al. [4] surveyed four compatibility measures among which they found dissimilarity the most accurate. Dissimilarity is the sum (over all neighboring pixels) of squared color differences (over all color bands). Assuming pieces x_i, x_j are represented in some three-dimensional color space (like RGB or YUV) by a $K \times K \times 3$ matrix, where K is the height/width of a piece (in pixels), their dissimilarity, where x_j is to the right of x_i, for example, is

$$D(x_i, x_j, r) = \sqrt{\sum_{k=1}^{K} \sum_{cb=1}^{3} (x_i(k, K, cb) - x_j(k, 1, cb))^2}, \qquad (1)$$

where cb denotes the color band.

Pomeranz et al. [20] also used the dissimilarity measure but found empirically that using the $(L_p)^q$ norm works better than the usual L_2 norm. Moreover, they presented the high-precision *best-buddy* metric. Pieces x_i and x_j are said to best-buddies if

$$\forall x_k \in Pieces, \ C(x_i, x_j, R_1) \geq C(x_i, x_k, R_1)$$

$$\text{and} \qquad (2)$$

$$\forall x_p \in Pieces, \ C(x_j, x_i, R_2) \geq C(x_j, x_p, R_2)$$

where *Pieces* is the set of all given image pieces and R_1 and R_2 are "complementary" spatial relations (e.g. if R_1 = right, then R_2 = left and vice versa).

Gallagher [10] proposed yet another compatibility measure, called the *Mahalanobis gradient compatibility* (MGC) as a preferable compatibility measure to those used by Pomeranz *et al.* [20]. The MGC penalizes changes in intensity gradients, rather than changes in intensity, and learns the covariance of the color channels, using the Mahalanobis distance. Also, Gallagher suggested using *dissimilarity ratios*. Absolute distances between potential piece edge matches are sometimes not indicative (for example in smooth surfaces like sea and sky), so considering the absolute score, divided by the second-best score available seems more indicative.

Son *et al.* [24] suggested "loop-constraints", four or more puzzle piece edges where the compatibility ratio between each pair is in the top ten among all possible pairs of piece edges in the given puzzle. Palkin and Tal [19] proposed a greedy solver based on an L_1-norm asymmetric dissimilarity and the best-buddies estimation metric.

3 DNN-Buddies

3.1 Motivation

We propose a novel estimation metric called "DNN-Buddies". Our goal is to obtain a classifier which predicts the adjacency likelihood of two puzzle piece edges in the correct puzzle configuration.

Note that despite the exponential nature of the problem (as there are $\mathcal{O}((nm)!)$ possible arrangements of the pieces, taking into account rotations), the problem can be solved theoretically by assigning correctly, in a consecutive manner, $n \times m - 1$ piece-edge pairs. (This is reminiscent of finding a minimal spanning tree, as noted by [10].) Hence, the classifier's precision is of far greater importance than its recall. A classifier with perfect precision and a recall of

$$\frac{n \times m - 1}{\text{all possible matches}} = \frac{n \times m - 1}{4 \times (n \times (m-1) + (n-1) \times m)} < \frac{1}{8} \qquad (3)$$

might achieve a perfect solution by itself.

3.2 Challenges

A straight-forward solution might have been to train a neural network against matching-pairs vs. non-matching ones. However, the issue of a jigsaw puzzle piece matching is of an imbalanced nature. In each $n \times m$ puzzle, there are $\mathcal{O}(n \times m)$ matching pairs of piece edges and $\mathcal{O}(n^2 \times m^2)$ possible nonmatching ones. A thorough review on the challenges and tactics to avoid them can be found in [13].

The trivial approach of random or uninformed undersampling, i.e. randomly choosing the required number of nonmatching pairs leads to a low-precision and high-recall metric, the very opposite of the goal set beforehand. We believe that the reason for this shortcoming is that there exist many "easy-to-spot" mismatches but only a handful of "hard-to-spot" ones. Thus, we resort to informed undersampling, choosing a subset of "good" mismatching pairs according to some criterion. Nevertheless, we avoid using any manual feature selection or other sophisticated image-related means.

In the jigsaw puzzle domain, similarly to many other problem domains, the solver does not actually try to reassemble the original image (as this problem is not mathematically defined), but rather tries solving a "proxy problem" which is to achieve an image whose global overall score between abutting-edges is minimal. Thus, we choose using the compatibility measure as the undersampling criterion.

3.3   Neural Network Training

For training and cross-validation, we use the 2,755 images of size 360×480 pixels from the IAPR TC-12 Benchmark [12]. Each image is first converted to YUV space followed by the normalization of each channel separately (via z-score normalization). Next, each (puzzle) image is divided to 12×17 tiles, where each tile is of size 28×28 pixels (as in all previous works); finally, we create a balanced set of positive and negative samples of puzzle-piece pairs, using informed undersampling as will be described below. In the end, we obtain a balanced set of 970,224 pairs overall.

To balance our dataset, we use the most basic compatibility score which is the dissimilarity between two piece-edges in the YUV color-space, as described in Eq. 1, as an undersampling criterion. For each puzzle piece edge $x_{i,j}(i = 1..n \times m, j = 1..4)$, we find its most compatible piece edge $x_{k1,l1}$ and its second most compatible piece edge $x_{k2,l2}$. If the pair of edges $x_{i,j} - x_{k1,l1}$ is indeed adjacent in the original image, we add this pair to the pool of positively-labeled samples and toss the pair $x_{i,j} - x_{k2,l2}$ to the pool of negatively-labeled samples. Otherwise, $x_{i,j} - x_{k1,l1}$ is added to the negatively-labeled samples and the other pair is discarded. The latter is done to avoid training the network on adjacent pieces which happen to be vastly different due to a significant change of the image scenery in the corresponding region. In other words, we restrict our interest to highly compatible piece edges that are indeed adjacent. Since this method leads to more negative samples than positive ones, we eventually randomly throw some negative samples to balance out the set.

From each image pair we extract the two columns near the edge, i.e. the column of abutting pixels in each edge and the one next to it. This results is an input of size $(28 \times 4 \times 3 =)$ 336 pixels. We use a feed-forward neural network (FFNN) of five fully connected layers of size 336, 100, 100, 100, and 2. The output is a softmax layer containing two neurons. We expect (0, 1) for matching pairs and (1, 0) otherwise. The activation used in all layers is the rectified linear unit (ReLU) function, i.e. $f(x) = max(0, x)$. Figure 2 depicts the network's structure.

We trained the network in a supervised manner using *Stochastic Gradient Descent* that minimizes the negative log likelihood of the error for 100 iterations.

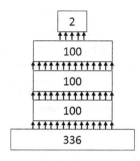

Fig. 2. Architecture of our DNN-Buddies scheme.

The resulting network reaches 95.04 % accuracy on the training set and 94.62 % on a held-out test set.

All dataset preparation and network training was performed using Torch7 [6].

4   Experimental Results

For each piece edge $x_{i,j}(i = 1..n \times m, j = 1..4)$, if its most compatible piece edge $x_{k,l}$ is classified positively using the DNN-Buddies network, we define $x_{k,l}$ to be $x_{i,j}$'s *DNN-buddy* piece edge. Note that each piece edge can have only a single DNN-buddy; also, some pieces might not have a DNN-buddy at all (if the most compatible piece is not classified as one by the DNN-Buddies network).

First, we evaluate the precision of the proposed metric, i.e. how many DNN-buddies are indeed adjacent in the original image. Using the well known dataset presented by Cho *et al.* [4] of 20 432-piece puzzles, we obtained a precision of 94.83 %.

Next, we incorporated the estimation metric (due to the proposed DNN-Buddies scheme) into the GA-based solver proposed by us previously [23]. Unfortunately, due to lack of space, no self-contained review of genetic algorithms and the proposed method can be included in this paper. Nevertheless, the modification required with respect to the existing GA framework is rather simple; if a DNN-buddy pair appears in one of the parents, assign this pair in the child. Figure 3 describes the modified crossover operator in the GA framework according to the above (see Step 2, which includes the new DNN-buddy phase).

We ran the augmented solver on the 432-piece puzzle set and on the two additional datasets proposed by Pomeranz *et al.* [20] of 540- and 805- piece puzzles. We evaluated our results according to the *neighbor comparison* which measures the fraction of correct neighbors and the number of puzzles perfectly reconstructed for each set.

Table 1 presents the accuracy results of the same solver with and without the DNN-Buddies metric. For each dataset we achieve a considerable improvement in the overall accuracy of the solution, as well as the number of perfectly reconstructed puzzles. Moreover, our enhanced deep neural network-based scheme

Until $(n - 1)$ relative relations are assigned **do**

1. Try assigning all *common* relative relations in the parents.
2. Try assigning all *DNN-buddy* relative relations in the parents.
3. Try assigning all *best-buddy* relative relations in the parents.
4. Try assigning all existing *most-compatible* relative relations.
5. Try assigning *random* relative relations.

Fig. 3. Crossover overview ·

Table 1. Comparison of our accuracy results with and without the new DNN-Buddies estimation metric.

	GA		Our (GA + DNN-Buddies)	
# of Pieces	Neighbor	Perfect	Neighbor	perfect
432	94.88 %	11	95.65 %	12
540	94.08 %	8	96.37 %	11
805	94.12 %	6	95.86 %	8

appears to outperform the current state-of-the-art results, as it yields accuracy levels of 95.65 %, 96.37 % and 95.86 %, which surpass, respectively, the best results known of 95.4 % [19], 94.08 % and 94.12 % [23].

5   Conclusions

In this paper we presented the first neural network-based estimation metric for the jigsaw puzzle problem. Unlike previous methods, no manual feature crafting was employed. The novel method exhibits high precision and when combined with a real-world puzzle solver, it significantly improves the solution's accuracy to set a new state-of-the art standard.

References

1. Altman, T.: Solving the jigsaw puzzle problem in linear time. Appl. Artif. Intell. Int. J. **3**(4), 453–462 (1989)
2. Brown, B., Toler-Franklin, C., Nehab, D., Burns, M., Dobkin, D., Vlachopoulos, A., Doumas, C., Rusinkiewicz, S., Weyrich, T.: A system for high-volume acquisition and matching of fresco fragments: Reassembling Theran wall paintings. ACM Trans. Graph. **27**(3), 84 (2008)
3. Cao, S., Liu, H., Yan, S.: Automated assembly of shredded pieces from multiple photos. In: IEEE International Conference on Multimedia and Expo, pp. 358–363 (2010)

4. Cho, T., Avidan, S., Freeman, W.: A probabilistic image jigsaw puzzle solver. In: IEEE Conference on Computer Vision and Pattern Recognition, pp. 183–190 (2010)

5. Cho, T., Butman, M., Avidan, S., Freeman, W.: The patch transform and its applications to image editing. In: IEEE Conference on Computer Vision and Pattern Recognition, pp. 1–8 (2008)

6. Collobert, R., Kavukcuoglu, K., Farabet, C.: Torch7: a matlab-like environment for machine learning. In: BigLearn, NIPS Workshop. No. EPFL-CONF-192376 (2011)

7. Deever, A., Gallagher, A.: Semi-automatic assembly of real cross-cut shredded documents. In: ICIP, pp. 233–236 (2012)

8. Demaine, E., Demaine, M.: Jigsaw puzzles, edge matching, and polyomino packing: Connections and complexity. Graphs Comb. **23**, 195–208 (2007)

9. Freeman, H., Garder, L.: Apictorial jigsaw puzzles: The computer solution of a problem in pattern recognition. IEEE Trans. Electron. Comput. **EC-13**(2), 118–127 (1964)

10. Gallagher, A.: Jigsaw puzzles with pieces of unknown orientation. In: IEEE Conference on Computer Vision and Pattern Recognition, pp. 382–389 (2012)

11. Goldberg, D., Malon, C., Bern, M.: A global approach to automatic solution of jigsaw puzzles. Comput. Geom.: Theory Appl. **28**(2–3), 165–174 (2004)

12. Grubinger, M., Clough, P., Müller, H., Deselaers, T.: The IAPR TC-12 benchmark: a new evaluation resource for visual information systems. In: International Workshop OntoImage, vol. 5, p. 10 (2006)

13. He, H., Garcia, E.A.: Learning from imbalanced data. IEEE Trans. Knowl. Data Eng. **21**(9), 1263–1284 (2009)

14. Justino, E., Oliveira, L., Freitas, C.: Reconstructing shredded documents through feature matching. Forensic Sci. Int. **160**(2), 140–147 (2006)

15. Koller, D., Levoy, M.: Computer-aided reconstruction and new matches in the forma urbis romae. Bullettino Della Commissione Archeologica Comunale di Roma, 103–125 (2006)

16. Marande, W., Burger, G.: Mitochondrial DNA as a genomic jigsaw puzzle. Science **318**(5849), 415–415 (2007)

17. Marques, M., Freitas, C.: Reconstructing strip-shredded documents using color as feature matching. In: ACM Symposium on Applied Computing, pp. 893–894 (2009)

18. Morton, A.Q., Levison, M.: The computer in literary studies. In: IFIP Congress, pp. 1072–1081 (1968)

19. Paikin, G., Tal, A.: Solving multiple square jigsaw puzzles with missing pieces. In: 2015 IEEE Conference on Computer Vision and Pattern Recognition, pp. 4832–4839. IEEE (2015)

20. Pomeranz, D., Shemesh, M., Ben-Shahar, O.: A fully automated greedy square jigsaw puzzle solver. In: IEEE Conference on Computer Vision and Pattern Recognition, pp. 9–16 (2011)

21. Sholomon, D., David, O.E., Netanyahu, N.S.: A genetic algorithm-based solver for very large jigsaw puzzles. In: IEEE Conference on Computer Vision and Pattern Recognition, pp. 1767–1774 (2013)

22. Sholomon, D., David, O.E., Netanyahu, N.S.: A generalized genetic algorithm-based solver for very large jigsaw puzzles of complex types. In: AAAI Conference on Artificial Intelligence, pp. 2839–2845 (2014)

23. Sholomon, D., David, O.E., Netanyahu, N.S.: Genetic algorithm-based solver for very large multiple jigsaw puzzles of unknown dimensions and piece orientation. In: ACM Conference on Genetic and Evolutionary Computation, pp. 1191–1198 (2014)

24. Son, K., Hays, J., Cooper, D.B.: Solving square jigsaw puzzles with loop constraints. In: Fleet, D., Pajdla, T., Schiele, B., Tuytelaars, T. (eds.) ECCV 2014, Part VI. LNCS, vol. 8694, pp. 32–46. Springer, Heidelberg (2014)
25. Wang, C.S.E.: Determining molecular conformation from distance or density data. Ph.D. Thesis, Massachusetts Institute of Technology (2000)
26. Yang, X., Adluru, N., Latecki, L.J.: Particle filter with state permutations for solving image jigsaw puzzles. In: IEEE Conference on Computer Vision and Pattern Recognition, pp. 2873–2880 (2011)
27. Zhao, Y., Su, M., Chou, Z., Lee, J.: A puzzle solver and its application in speech descrambling. In: WSEAS International Conference on Computer Engineering and Applications, pp. 171–176 (2007)

A Deep Learning Approach for Hand Posture Recognition from Depth Data

Thomas Kopinski[1,2]($\boxtimes$), Fabian Sachara[1,2], Alexander Gepperth[1,2],
and Uwe Handmann[1,2]

[1] Hochschule Ruhr West, Computer Science Institute, Lützowstrasse 5,
46236 Bottrop, Germany
{fabian.sachara,uwe.handmann}@hs-rw.de
[2] UIIS Lab and FLOWERS Team, Inria, Université Paris-Saclay,
858 Blvd des Maréchaux, 91762 Palaiseau, France
{thomas.kopinski,alexander.gepperth}@ensta-paristech.fr

Abstract. Given the success of convolutional neural networks (CNNs) during recent years in numerous object recognition tasks, it seems logical to further extend their applicability to the treatment of three-dimensional data such as point clouds provided by depth sensors. To this end, we present an approach exploiting the CNN's ability of automated feature generation and combine it with a novel 3D feature computation technique, preserving local information contained in the data. Experiments are conducted on a large data set of 600.000 samples of hand postures obtained via ToF (time-of-flight) sensors from 20 different persons, after an extensive parameter search in order to optimize network structure. Generalization performance, measured by a leave-one-person-out scheme, exceeds that of any other method presented for this specific task, bringing the error for some persons down to 1.5 %.

Keywords: Deep learning · Hand posture recognition · 3D data

1 Introduction, Context and Related Work

Making freehand gestures an efficient means of Human-Computer Interaction (HMI) is an important and simultaneously complex task, as the steadily increasing number of research studies demonstrates over the course of the last decade. The number of potential applications is growing due to the advent of low-cost off-the-shelf depth sensors. However, due to various reasons such as active illumination interference or noise in the process of data acquisition, robust learning methods are still an important requirement. The main advantages of ToF sensors are their high frame rate and robustness w.r.t. illumination conditions, hence their fields of application covers outdoor scenarios as well. However, recognizing hand gestures solely from 3D data is a non-trivial task which raises the question whether CNNs, which excel in object recognition tasks from RGB data, can perform just as well for this task.

© Springer International Publishing Switzerland 2016
A.E.P. Villa et al. (Eds.): ICANN 2016, Part II, LNCS 9887, pp. 179–186, 2016.
DOI: 10.1007/978-3-319-44781-0_22

When positioning this contribution in the broader field of object recognition from 3D data with CNNs, occupancy grids have been successfully applied, e.g. in the field of mobile robotics, in order to create maps from potentially highly noisy data samples [1]. The basic idea is to have a representation of an evenly divided environment with the possibility of telling whether there is an object at a certain location. Maturana et al. [2] make use of this algorithm in order to create various kinds of occupancy grids, serving as input for their 3D-CNN implementation by either taking into account the amount of free space within the grid or not. 3D input is presented by Wu et al. [3] to a 3D-CNN in the form of a stacked 3D cube consisting of multiple frames acquired over time, which is convolved with a 3D kernel and applied to the problem of hand gesture recognition. Glatt [6] has shown how Deep Learning can be successfully applied to achieve HGR from Kinect data with the help of Deep Belief Networks. The best recognition results oscillate between 75 % to 85 % and are partially comparable scores achieved in this contribution although similar accuracy scores as high as >98 % are never reached. Barros et al. [7] show how CNNs can effectively be applied to recognize Italian sign gestures from Kinect data achieving error scores of 8.3 % for the best model with their system also working in real-time. Tang et al. [8] show how Deep Neural Networks can be utilized to discriminate between 20 different hand poses using a Kinect sensor achieving high accuracy ratings.

In this contribution, we demonstrate how a data transformation step allows for fast and robust hand gesture recognition from depth data by CNNs. As these are primarily intended to process 2D data e.g., images), their application to 3D data is not straightforward at all: either one needs to create a feature computation method that transforms 3D data into 1d or 2D feature vectors, or the convolution structure of the network itself needs to be modified to handle 3D data directly (e.g., by 3D convolutions). Both approaches being feasible, we opt for the first possibility since 3D convolutions are very inefficient operations and real-time capability is important for our targeted HMI scenario. Given a complex hand gesture recognition problem of 10 different gestures obtained from a large number of individuals, we propose a particular feature transform of depth data to make them treatable by CNNs.

The following sections give a description of our approach as well as the resulting network structure (Sect. 2). Experiments are conducted in two phases (cf. Sect. 3), determining the optimal parameter setting in an initial step and evaluating the optimal performance of the CNN in a second step. Section 4 concludes with a summary and an outlook on future work.

2 Network Architecture and Training

In order to be able to deal with three-dimensional input, this contribution presents an approach which transforms the raw 3D data into a format readable by CNNs. The need for a fixed-size input requires a specific partitioning of the 3D input. Given a set of 3D data points (voxels) of arbitrary extension (also referred to as point cloud), we propose the subdivision of the entire cloud into a fixed number of cubes, all having the same size. To this end, the maximal extension of the data points has to be calculated for the entire problem. This approach is explained in the following sections.

2.1 3D Subdivision of Point Cloud Input

In order to be able to work on 3D input data we employ a modified LeNet 5 implementation of the Theano library [4] with two convolutional layers. The input space is subdivided into n^3 hypercubes of fixed size. Each hypercube then contains a subset of data points from the original object. Depending on the density of the cloud, a certain number of cubes remains empty. In order to avoid too many empty hypercubes, which form the input for the CNN, we stretch the data to fit into the raster. To this end, the input cloud is normalized to the range (0,1) on each axis. This guarantees the data to be evenly distributed over all hypercubes. The value contained within a hypercube is determined by the number of data points it contains.

Each slice of the input vector, which will be described here on basis of an $8 \times 8 \times 8$ sized example, has to be reshaped to fit a designated pattern: The vector is reshaped in a way that each row fed into the convolutional layer represents one (x-y) slice of depth data in the original, resulting in an input matrix of 8×64 (cf. Fig. 1 showing this for the case of 4^3). This way, a convolutional kernel of size 8×1 can be used to initially convolve the depth-axis, resulting in an 1×64 output of the first kernel. No max-pooling is used in this layer. The second layer reshapes this 1×64 output to 8×8, so that a 3×3 kernel can subsequently be utilized. This layer also implements 2×2 max-pooling, resulting in an output of 3×3. This output is then fed into the multilayer perceptron (MLP) layer of the convolutional net, which determines the output class.

2.2 Training Setup

Training is performed on a single GeForce GTX 780 Ti graphics card. The main limit here is the device's memory capacity as our training/testing data set exceeds it's memory capability.

We evaluate our approach on the REHAP [5] data set consisting of 600.000 data samples obtained from 20 different persons, each posing for 10 different hand gestures (cf. Fig. 2). Each of the gestures is represented by 3.000 snapshots summing up to 30.000 data samples per person. This would result in the transformation and storage of 570.000 data samples by the Theano library during training for 19-on-1 cross-validation (based on persons not on individual samples), including weights as well as the subsequent image transformation steps, which is more than the device can store during the training phase. The amount of data samples during training is therefore reduced to about 2.000 samples per gesture, each randomly taken from the whole sample set. This still yields a training set of 380.000 hand poses - more than enough to validate our approach.

Two different experimental runs are performed: an initial parameter search is started in order to determine the optimal setup for the CNN architecture.

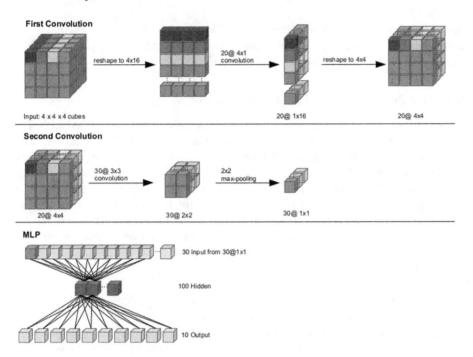

Fig. 1. Setup of the CNN structure with two convolutional layers. Top row: First convolution step and reshaping. Center: Second convolution step and max-pooling. Bottom: MLP structure and input.

To this end, the whole data set is subsampled by randomly retrieving 100 data samples per person and pose, yielding 1000 samples per person for 10 randomly selected individuals. The number of test runs therefore amounts to:

$$\sum_{i=0}^{n} k_i^1 \sum_{j=0}^{m} k_j^2 \sum_{s=0}^{o} k_s^1 \sum_{s=0}^{o} k_s^2 \sum_{l=0}^{p} k_{mp}^2$$

Here, k_i^1 and k_j^2 denote the number of kernels within their respective layers. k_s^1 denotes a specific combination for the first layer, since we first transform the input as described in Sect. 2.1 (cf. Fig. 1). If $k_s^1 = 0$ this conforms to an 8×1 kernel with no max-pooling. If $k_s^1 = 1$ this corresponds to a 7×1 kernel with 2×1 max-pooling etc. k_s^2 defines the size of the second kernel while k_2^{mp} consequently corresponds to the kernel size in the max-pooling layer. The resulting kernels from the first convolution layer are depicted in Fig. 3.

3   Experiments and Results

The experiments are subdivided into two phases: In the first phase, the optimal parameters are determined by an extensive grid-search. This is followed by the

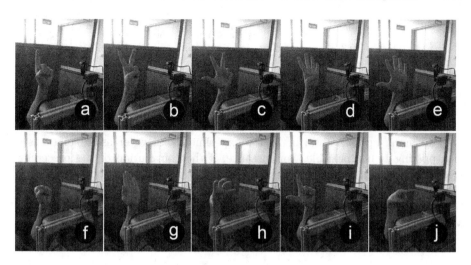

Fig. 2. The ten different hand postures from the REHAP data set.

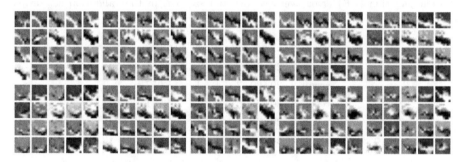

Fig. 3. The resulting kernels from the first filter grouped together for each posture from the REHAP data set (compare with Fig. 2). The first layer of the CNN produces 20 different kernels. All 20 kernels produced per gesture are grouped and presented in analogous order from left to right, top to bottom.

second phase, namely the training and subsequent leave-one-person-out cross-validation test of the CNN on the REHAP dataset of 20 different persons.

3.1   Parameter Grid Search

For efficient grid search in order to determine optimal parameters, 70 % of the data samples are randomly subsampled for training and the remaining 30 % are retained for validation during each iteration. Each data sample is transformed by the scheme described in the preceding section and subsequently presented to the CNN for training. Parameters are exhaustively varied within the following ranges:

$$k_i^1 \in \{5, 10, 15, 20\}$$
$$k_j^2 \in \{5, 10, 15, 20, 25, 30, 35, 40, 45, 50\}$$
$$k_s^1 \in [0, 7]$$
$$k_s^2 \in [0, 7]$$
$$k_{mp}^2 \in [1, 8]$$

This sums up to a total of 20.480 experiments, however as in some cases max-pooling is not possible. For instance, if the convolution of the preceding layer of 8×8 with a 3×3 kernel results in a 6×6 layer, max-pooling can only be performed with either a 6×6, 3×3, 2×2 or 1×1 kernel. Therefore, ignoring those invalid cases results in ca. 5400 experiments to be conducted (training time was approx. 1 week).

Table 1. The top 5 results taken from all 5400 iterations of our parameter grid-search. The classification (CE) error averaged over all samples in the validation set drops to 5,5 %.

	k_i^1	k_j^2	k_s^1	k_s^2	k_2^{mp}	CE
result 1	20	30	3	6	1	5,557
result 2	20	20	3	4	1	5,957
result 3	20	25	3	6	1	5,971
result 4	20	35	3	6	1	5,971
result 5	20	35	3	7	1	5,985

The most significant insight of these experiments is the correlation of increase or decrease of the classification error (CE) values depending on the number of chosen kernels, the kernel size or kernel size for max-pooling. Unsurprisingly, CE drops if the number of kernels per layer is increased. However, increasing the k_s^1 parameter leads to an increase in CE. This means that we achieve optimal results for small values of k_s^1, with a small max-pooling value of $k_2^{mp} = 1$ or $k_2^{mp} = 2$. Best CE scores achieved in this grid-search are 5.6 % averaged across all samples in the test set with the aforementioned parameters (cf. Table 1). Moreover, to achieve best results, the number of kernels usually should be chosen around 20 for the first convolution layer and around 25–35 for the second layer. Setting the parameters to the optimal values, a generalization test is conducted which is described in the subsequent section.

3.2   Leave-one-person-out Cross-Validation

Choosing the best parameter setup from the grid-search in the preceding section yields improved results compared to approaches on the same data set achieved so far. With respect to the parameters presented in Table 1, we set $k_i^1 = 20$, $k_j^2 = 30$, $k_s^1 = 3$, $k_s^2 = 6$, $k_2^{mp} = 1$. The results of our leave-one-person-out generalization (train on samples from all persons but one, test on all samples from the omitted person) tests are presented in Table 2. For each column n, the entry shows the CE obtained when testing the CNN architecture on all data samples coming from person n and trained on all data samples except those from person n.

Table 2. The top row indicates the validation run performed for all samples from person n in the data set. The rounded CE scores (in %)for the respective person are indicated in the bottom row per table entry. Training is performed on all persons but the one indicated in respective column while testing is the performed on the person indicated by the same column.

Person	p1	p2	p3	p4	p5	p6	p7	p8	p9	p10
CE	22,3	51,3	22,1	32,5	11,6	17,4	40,0	27,1	13,6	15,3
Person	p11	p12	p13	p14	p15	p16	p17	p18	p19	p20
CE	13,2	12,4	1,3	4,0	5,5	15,1	4,2	17,5	30,7	21,4

Hence this table shows the performance of the CNN on hand gestures performed by persons previously unknown to the net. Best results are obtained on persons 13, 14 and 17 with errors of 1,7 %, 4,0 % and 4,2 % respectively. These are strong results given the aforementioned fact we are dealing with unseen data. Moreover, CEs are below the 20 % mark for 12 persons and only increase significantly for 4 individuals, namely persons 2, 4, 7 and 19 with worst results achieved on person 2. This is highly respectable for a large and complex data set of 400.000 hand postures obtained from a highly noisy sensor.

4 Conclusion and Outlook

In this contribution a novel approach to training CNNs for the problem of hand gesture recognition from depth data is presented. Depth input from ToF sensors in normalized, stretched and subdivided into hypercubes and subsequently convolved in a specifically tailored intermediate step as to be presentable to a CNN. An extensive parameter search is performed to yield the optimal setup for our deep network architecture. Around 5400 test runs conducted during this search over the course of one week show that the CNN peaks in performance for a large number of kernels in the initial layers and small max-pooling kernels. Given these settings, a leave-one-person-out cross-validation run is performed over the course of approx. 14h demonstrating strong recognition results on previously unseen data. The main benefit of this contribution lies in its efficient subdivision and transformation of input data. Given the fact that we outperform previously achieved results on this large-scale data set, achieving error rates of 1,5 %–4 %

for some persons and averaging around 15 %–20 % over all persons, this proves the validity of this approach. Future work will focus on the transferability of this approach onto problems of object recognition in the three-dimensional domain, in order to prove its general applicability. We strongly believe it can easily be extended to other, similar tasks allowing for improved performance of CNNs under difficult circumstances.

References

1. Thrun, S.: Learning occupancy grid maps with forward sensor models. Auton. Robot. **15**(2), 111–127 (2003). ISO 690
2. Maturana, D., Scherer, S.: VoxNet: a 3D convolutional neural network for real-time object recognition. In: IEEE/RSJ International Conference on Intelligent Robots and Systems (IROS), pp. 922–928. IEEE, September 2015
3. Wu, D., Shao, L.: Deep dynamic neural networks for gesture segmentation and recognition. In: Agapito, L., Bronstein, M.M., Rother, C. (eds.) ECCV 2014 Workshops. LNCS, vol. 8925, pp. 552–571. Springer, Heidelberg (2015)
4. Bastien, F., Lamblin, P., Pascanu, R., Bergstra, J., Goodfellow, I., Bergeron, A., Bengio, Y.: Theano: new features and speed improvements. arXiv preprint arXiv:1211.5590 (2012)
5. REHAP, Large-scale data set for Recognition of Hand Postures. http://www.gepperth.net/alexander/postures.php
6. Glatt, R.: Deep learning architecture for gesture recognition (2014)
7. Barros, P., Parisi, G. I., Jirak, D., Wermter, S.: Real-time gesture recognition using a humanoid robot with a deep neural architecture. In: 2014 IEEE-RAS International Conference on Humanoid Robots, pp. 646–651. IEEE, November 2014
8. Tang, A., Lu, K., Wang, Y., Huang, J., Li, H.: A real-time hand posture recognition system using deep neural networks. ACM Trans. Intell. Syst. Technol. (TIST) **6**(2), 21 (2015)

Action Recognition in Surveillance Video Using ConvNets and Motion History Image

Sheng Luo[✉], Haojin Yang, Cheng Wang, Xiaoyin Che, and Christoph Meinel

Hasso Plattner Institute, University of Potsdam,
Prof.-Dr.-Helmert-Str. 2-3, 14482 Potsdam, Germany
{Sheng.Luo,Haojin.Yang,Cheng.Wang,Xiaoyin.Che,Meinel}@hpi.de

Abstract. With significant increasing of surveillance cameras, the amount of surveillance videos is growing rapidly. Thereby how to automatically and efficiently recognize semantic actions and events in surveillance videos becomes an important problem to be addressed. In this paper, we investigate the state-of-the-art Deep Learning (DL) approaches for human action recognition, and propose an improved two-stream ConvNets architecture for this task. In particular, we propose to use Motion History Image (MHI) as motion expression for training the temporal ConvNet, which achieved impressive results in both accuracy and recognition speed. In our experiment, we conducted an in-depth study to investigate important network options and compared to the latest deep network for action recognition. The detailed evaluation results show the superior ability of our proposed approach, which achieves state-of-the-art in surveillance video context.

Keywords: Convolutional neural network · Surveillance videos · Optical flow · Motion History Image

1 Introduction

Due to the rapid development of semiconductor industries, ITS forecasts that the global market for video surveillance equipment will grow by over 10 % in 2015 and the majority of surveillance cameras are running 24/7 [8]. Those increment and uninterrupted recording bring impressive growth for surveillance video. Therefore how to automatically and efficiently recognize semantic actions from them is eager to be solved. Recently, deep convolutional neural networks (ConvNets or CNNs) has been recognized as the state-of-the-art for image classification [11], and has been further successfully applied to action recognition for video data [10,15]. In [15], Simonyan et al. first introduced the two-stream CNNs architecture for video action recognition, in which spatial (RGB-frames) and temporal (optical flow) representations of video have been proposed. Since then many related studies [13,16–19] and derived architectures have been reported. Compared with other video types, surveillance video is normally recorded by still camera. The background is thus mostly stationary but the actor insider is relative small, and the camera may often capture more actors or other noises in one

© Springer International Publishing Switzerland 2016
A.E.P. Villa et al. (Eds.): ICANN 2016, Part II, LNCS 9887, pp. 187–195, 2016.
DOI: 10.1007/978-3-319-44781-0_23

frame. Therefore the classification difficulty increased. In this paper, we propose an improved two-stream CNNs architecture for action recognition in surveillance video. For the spatial stream we apply human detector to crop human area from its background for the subsequent spatial CNNs training, while to train the temporal CNNs, we propose to apply Motion History Image (MHI) [5] (cf. Fig. 1(b)(a)). In our experiment MHI shows impressive performance in both accuracy and processing speed comparing to the commonly used optical flow. The core benefit of MHI is that it records object motion changes from a certain video scene, and can explicitly describe them in a single image. It contains less background noise and further decreases the training difficulty. All of those features make MHI more suitable for CNNs. The performance of proposed approach has been evaluated on UCF-ARG and UT-interaction dataset. The experimental results show that our proposed model achieves state-of-the-art in classification accuracy with much higher processing speed.

The rest of this paper is organized as follows: Sect. 2 gives a brief introduction of existing deep learning method and different trials for action recognition. In Sect. 3, we introduce our approach, in particular the MHI method in temporal stream. Evaluation method, implementation details and performance are given in Sect. 4. Section 5 concludes the paper and our future work.

2   Related Work

After CNNs showed its excellent performance in image classification, it attracted huge attention among the research community, and has been further successfully applied to many other application areas. The authors of [3,9] firstly extended image CNN to video domains by treating space and time as equivalent dimensions of the input, and performing convolutions in both time and space. After that, Karpathy et al. studied these extensions and adapted the CNN model by using stacked video frames as input to the network [10]. Unfortunately, this method didn't made significant performance improvement on action recognition task in video (on UCF101 dataset). After that, Simonyan et al. proposed a two-stream CNNs architecture, which incorporates spatial and temporal networks [15]. This work proved that CNNs trained on multi-frame dense optical flow is able to capture object motion in an explicit way (by stacking sequential flow images in one input frame), which achieved impressive result in spite of limited training data. Since then, this method became a commonly used architecture for action recognition in video data. In [13], Nina et al. applied this method for action recognition in the Chalearn 2014 competition, and achieved promising result. Based on [15] the authors of [7,19] proposed a recurrent convolutional architecture (Recurrent-CNNs), which further improves the classification accuracy, however it also increases the model complexity and processing time in a certain manner. In [17] the authors proposed a regularized feature fusion network, which is based on the outputs of two-stream Recurrent-CNNs. The final classification result is obtained by combining the output of spatial Recurrent-CNNs, flow Recurrent-CNNs and their fused network. Obviously, this method brings much higher complexity with limited improvement on certain datasets. In contrast to increasing the network complexity, the authors of [16, 18] intended to investigate important implementation options of deep networks on video classification, which provide more useful practices for two-stream CNNs.

3   Methodology

Video is made up of spatial (objects) and temporal (motion changes) components. Thereby the two-stream architecture is naturally constructed for representing video content by taking advantages of two modalities. According to the fact above, we also applied this architecture in our work. By considering several characteristics of surveillance video such as stationary but complicated background, still camera, much smaller actor view etc., we rebuilt the design of each stream. Since smaller actor view of the original video frame not only brings difficulty to actor localization, but also leads to poor spatial CNN models. Therefore for the spatial stream we first extract actor from background by using human detection algorithm, which is help to filter out some useless information as e.g., scene objects and background. Under this circumstances, it is worth to note that the motion information turns into a more important role for action recognition in surveillance video. Regarding the temporal part, almost all the related work are based on optical flow images. Optical flow represents the direction of image motion by calculating the motion between two consecutive frames. However, an entire action normally consists of a set of sequential motion steps. Thus CNNs have to estimate the motion implicitly for a better understanding about the action. In order to make the learning process easier, researchers manually stack sequential optical flow images into a multi-channel input image. In this way, a consecutive motion scene has been explicitly stored in every newly created input image and is further used to train the CNNs (cf. Fig. 1(a,b)).

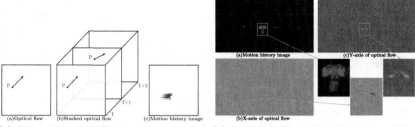

(a) Principle of different motion templates

(b) Motion information based on different templates

Fig. 1. Motion templates comparison

On the other hand, MHI can capture and express the short-term motion changes in a more compact way. To create a MHI H_r, binary image difference frames are firstly generated with a defined buffer length. Then consecutive temporal motion information is collapsed into H_r according to their temporal appearances, i.e. the pixel intensity in H_r is a function of the temporal history of motion at that point. Hence, H_r can be presented by utilizing a replacement and a decay operator D [5]:

$$H_r(x,y,t) = \begin{cases} \tau, & D(x,y,t) = 1 \\ max(0, H_r(x,y,t-1) - 1) & otherwise \end{cases} \tag{1}$$

The essence of MHI is to record where the motion is happening and how the motion is occurring in one image, as depicted in Fig. 1(a) (c). More clearly, we created MHI and optical flow representations example which is a waving action and shown in Fig. 1(b). It is obvious that MHI contains more complete motion information, the action is thus easier to be recognized. In addition, MHI is generally more capable to reject background noise. This can also be realized by Fig. 1(b), where Y-axle optical flow comprises much more noises. Moreover, MHI shows strong computational advantage comparing to dense optical flow. The detailed processing speed comparison is given in Sect. 4.

Figure 2 depicts our tow-stream architecture. For each clip, we convert it into spatial and temporal part. For spatial part, we apply extracted actor images, while regarding temporal part, we generate MHI directly from the video. After data preparation, we train spatial and temporal CNNs respectively, which is followed by the data fusion part. For data fusion we adopt late-prediction-fusion metric to get the final prediction result. The category label of a clip is obtained by selecting the class with the highest average-probabilities. In particular, our architecture accepts single image as the input to CNNs in both two streams, which decreases the training difficulty.

4   Evaluation

4.1   Datasets and Data Preparation

We conduct experiments on UCF-ARG [2] and UT-Interaction dataset [14]. UCF-ARG dataset consists of 10 actions performed by 12 actors recorded from a ground camera, a rooftop camera, and an aerial camera. In this work we only adopted the video data taken by the ground camera. We put the first 3/4 clips into train set and the rest 1/4 into test set.

Same background and small actor in surveillance videos make it hard for the classifier to distinguish tiny differences of actors. Therefore extracting the actor view image for the further processing is necessary. After trying several method, we adopted ACF method [6] for the actor image extraction. The original output of ACF is quite closed to actor, to enable better data augmentation (e.g. cropping), we triple the width and 1.4x the height. Concerning the temporal stream, we train our model based on three different data sets—single frame optical flow (SFOF) set, stacked optical flow (SOF) set and MHI set. We adopted the off-the-shelf GPU implementation of [1] from the OpenCV[1] library for flow image

---

[1] http://opencv.org/.

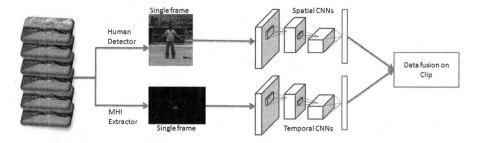

Fig. 2. Proposed architecture for action recognition

creation, where horizontal and vertical flow vector field are stored separately. We created stacked flow images with a duration length $L = 10$, i.e. each stacked flow image has 20 channels. The evaluation of L can be found in [15]. For MHI creation we also applied the implementation of OpenCV library. We set the buffer size to 2 and the threshold parameter to 15.

The UT-Interaction dataset contains 6 classes of human-human interactions: shake-hands, point, hug, push, kick and punch. We adopted set 1 to further verify our method. The first 8 clips of each action are put into training set whereas the rest 2 clips are used for test. Actor images are cropped based on ground truth from dataset in case of data overlapping across different actions. SFOF and SOF images are generated from actor-images in the same manner as above. We also cropped MHI based on ground truth to avoid giving one image repeatedly. Unlike UCF-ARG, the duration of action is longer and the actor is bigger in UT-Interaction. Therefore, we use buffer size 5 (MHI-5) & 10 (MHI-10)and set threshold parameter to 30 for MHIs extraction.

In particular, we reject the first 30 MHIs in UCF-ARG to avoid background noise. Because action in UT-Interaction is only performed once, images of some clips are not enough for generating stack optical flow sample, we use all images from ground truth.

4.2   Implementation Details

In general, pre-training is an effective method to initialize deep CNNs when the training dataset is quite limited. Regarding UCF-ARG and UT-Interaction dataset, they only have around 100 k and 4 k images for training respectively. Therefore, fine-tuning from robust models is obviously more appropriate rather than training from scratch. Our spatial model is fine-tuned based on VGG_CNN_S model for both datasets. This reference model is also applied for fine-tuning on MHIs and SFOF images. Here for the SOF, it is not able to fine-tune on any VGG model immediately which is trained on RGB images, since the SOF image has 20 channels. However, inspired by [16] we further modified the original structure of the reference model, in which we average the filter-weights of the first layer across its 3 RGB channels, and extend the first layer to 20 channels by using averaged weights. This way we can use the modified

VGG_CNN_S model for fine-tuning on SOF images. In addition, we also applied the Fudan SOF model from [18] in the UCF-ARG evaluation, which is based on VGG_CNN_M structure. We set the learning rate to 10^{-3} , which was decreased to its 1/10 every 10 k iterations and stopped at 40 k iterations.

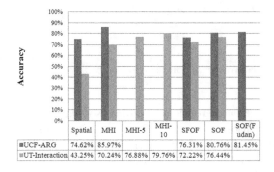

	Spatial	MHI	MHI-5	MHI-10	SFOF	SOF	SOF(Fudan)
■UCF-ARG	74.62%	85.97%			76.31%	80.76%	81.45%
■UT-Interaction	43.25%	70.24%	76.88%	79.76%	72.22%	76.44%	

Fig. 3. Finetune result on UCF-ARG and UT-interaction

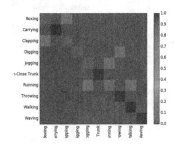

Fig. 4. Confusion matrix of ten actions in UCF-ARG

4.3   Performance

Based on Image: In Fig. 3, SOF means the model finetuned from modified VGG_CNN_S model, while SOF(Fudan) means the model from Fudan SOF model. It is obvious that temporal model based on MHI acquires outstanding performance among all the others on UCF-ARG and UT-Interaction. Overall, we can draw following conclusions base on UCF-ARG:

1. Motion information is significant for action recognition in surveillance video.
2. SOF can better describe the temporal clue than SFOF.
3. Well-trained model has more optimized network parameters than modified model. (Comparison between Fudan and Modified VGG model).
4. MHI significantly outperformed the other settings, which proves that this temporal representation can be well learned by CNNs.

The evaluation result on UT-Interaction dataset shows the similar trend as well. Particularly, it further demonstrates that for relative longer actions, using larger buffer size of MHI can further improve the performance.

Based on Clip: The clip-level evaluation can be described as follows:

1. For every clip, we use ACF detector, MHI extractor, optical flow extractor to generate spatial images, MHIs, SFOF and SOF images.
2. We create the probability prediction result for every input image in the sequential manner.
3. We further generate the fused result using several combinations including spatial & MHI, spatial & SFOF, and spatial & SOF.

Table 1. Clip-level classification result on UCF-ARG

Method	Accuracy
Spatial & MHI	**94.87 %**
Spatial & SFOF	92.31 %
Spatial & SOF	93.16 %
Spatial & SOF (Fudan)	94.02 %
Piotr Bilinski [4]	82.05 %
Laptev et al. [12]	80.98 %

Table 2. Computation performance of MHI and optical flow

Method	Frame per second	Processor
MHI	~60	CPU (Intel i5-4670)
Optical flow	~1/8	CPU (Intel i5-4670)
Optical flow	1-2	GPU (Nvidia GTX780)

4. The final prediction (clip label) is obtained by averaging the output of each input image taken from two models.

As shown in Table 1, the proposed spatial & MHI two-stream networks achieved the best classification accuracy. It improves on the best shallow method [4] by almost **14 %**. Figure 4 depicts the confusion matrix based on the proposed two-stream model. Two issues may lead to the confusion between jogging and running. The first one is undetermined speed boundary between them, and the other is the starting and ending process in these clips. The angle of action should take responsibility for the confusion between boxing and clapping, digging and throwing.

Table 2 shows the computation cost of creating MHI and dense optical flow image. In this experiment, we adopted a test video from UCF-ARG dataset with the frame rate of 30 fps. In the CPU mode, MHI method can process 60 fps, while the optical flow algorithm needs 8 s for one frame. We also evaluated the GPU implementation of the optical flow algorithm, but it can only process 1-2 fps. Obviously, MHI algorithm needs much less computation resources, even fulfill the real-time requirement.

5 Conclusion

In this paper, we investigate the state-of-the-art approach for action recognition in video using CNNs. Based on the analysis of characteristics of surveillance video, we propose an improved two-stream CNNs architecture. In which, we proposed to apply MHI as a more efficient temporal representation for training the network, where it shows excellent performance in both accuracy and processing speed. The following two conclusions have been proven by our evaluation:

1. Our proposed approach acquires state-of-the-art performance on UCF-ARG dataset, while it significantly decreases the complexity for training and recognition using CNNs.
2. High classification accuracy and real-time MHI extraction enable the action recognition on live surveillance recordings.

As the future work, we plan to further improve the MHI quality by filter out camera movement and shaking effect, and how to apply MHI to first-view videos is still need to be studied. In addition, a more efficient actor detection algorithm can further improve the overall recognition performance.

References

1. Brox, T., Bruhn, A., Papenberg, N., Weickert, J.: High accuracy optical flow estimation based on a theory for warping. In: Pajdla, T., Matas, J.G. (eds.) ECCV 2004. LNCS, vol. 3024, pp. 25–36. Springer, Heidelberg (2004)
2. UCF-ARG Data Set. http://crcv.ucf.edu/data/UCF-ARG.php. Accessed 10 Nov 2015
3. Baccouche, M., Mamalet, F., Wolf, C., Garcia, C., Baskurt, A.: Sequential deep learning for human action recognition. In: Salah, A.A., Lepri, B. (eds.) HBU 2011. LNCS, vol. 7065, pp. 29–39. Springer, Heidelberg (2011)
4. Bilinski, P., Bremond, F.: Statistics of pairwise co-occurring local spatio-temporal features for human action recognition. In: Fusiello, A., Murino, V., Cucchiara, R. (eds.) ECCV 2012 Ws/Demos, Part I. LNCS, vol. 7583, pp. 311–320. Springer, Heidelberg (2012)
5. Davis, J.W., Bobick, A.E.: The representation and recognition of human movement using temporal templates. In: 1997 IEEE Computer Society Conference on CVPR, pp. 928–934. IEEE (1997)
6. Dollár, P., Belongie, S., Perona, P.: The fastest pedestrian detector in the west. In: BMVC, vol. 2, p. 7. Citeseer (2010)
7. Donahue, J., Anne Hendricks, L., Guadarrama, S., Rohrbach, M., Venugopalan, S., Saenko, K., Darrell, T.: Long-term recurrent convolutional networks for visual recognition and description. In: 2015 IEEE Conference on CVPR, pp. 2625–2634 (2015)
8. Gropley, J.: Top Video Surveillance Trends for 2015. IHS Technology, 1 edn. (2015). https://technology.ihs.com/api/binary/520143
9. Ji, S., Xu, W., Yang, M., Yu, K.: 3D convolutional neural networks for human action recognition. IEEE Trans. Pattern Anal. Mach. Intell. **35**(1), 221–231 (2013)
10. Karpathy, A., Toderici, G., Shetty, S., Leung, T., Sukthankar, R., Fei-Fei, L.: Large-scale video classification with convolutional neural networks. In: 2014 IEEE Conference on CVPR, pp. 1725–1732. IEEE (2014)
11. Krizhevsky, A., Sutskever, I., Hinton, G.E.: Imagenet classification with deep convolutional neural networks. In: NIPS, pp. 1097–1105 (2012)
12. Laptev, I., Marszałek, M., Schmid, C., Rozenfeld, B.: Learning realistic human actions from movies. In: 2008 IEEE Conference on CVPR, pp. 1–8. IEEE (2008)
13. Nina, O., Rubiano, C., Shah, M.: Action recognition using ensemble of deep convolutional neural networks (2014)
14. Ryoo, M.S., Chen, C.-C., Aggarwal, J.K., Roy-Chowdhury, A.: An overview of contest on semantic description of human activities (SDHA) 2010. In: Ünay, D., Çataltepe, Z., Aksoy, S. (eds.) ICPR 2010. LNCS, vol. 6388, pp. 270–285. Springer, Heidelberg (2010)
15. Simonyan, K., Zisserman, A.: Two-stream convolutional networks for action recognition in videos. In: NIPS, pp. 568–576 (2014)
16. Wang, L., Xiong, Y., Wang, Z., Qiao, Y.: Towards good practices for very deep two-stream convnets. CoRR abs/1507.02159 (2015)

17. Wu, Z., Wang, X., Jiang, Y.G., Ye, H., Xue, X.: Modeling spatial-temporal clues in a hybrid deep learning framework for video classification. In: Proceedings of the 23rd ACM MM, pp. 461–470. ACM (2015)
18. Ye, H., Wu, Z., Zhao, R.W., Wang, X., Jiang, Y.G., Xue, X.: Evaluating two-stream CNN for video classification. In: ICMR 2015, pp. 435–442. ACM (2015)
19. Ng, J.Y-H., Hausknecht, M., Vijayanarasimhan, S., Vinyals, O., Monga, R., Toderici, G.: Beyond short snippets: Deep networks for video classification. In: 2015 IEEE Conference on CVPR, pp. 4694–4702 (2015)

Classification and Forecasting

Bi-Modal Deep Boltzmann Machine Based Musical Emotion Classification

Moyuan Huang[1], Wenge Rong[1(✉)], Tom Arjannikov[2], Nan Jiang[1],
and Zhang Xiong[1]

[1] School of Computer Science and Engineering, Beihang University, Beijing, China
{moyuanhuang,w.rong,nanjiang,xiongz}@buaa.edu.cn
[2] Department of Computer Science, University of Victoria, Victoria, Canada
tom.arjannikov@gmail.com

Abstract. Music plays an important role in many people's lives. When listening to music, we usually choose those music pieces that best suit our current moods. However attractive, automating this task remains a challenge. To this end the approaches in the literature exploit different kinds of information (audio, visual, social, etc.) about individual music pieces. In this work, we study the task of classifying music into different mood categories by integrating information from two domains: audio and semantic. We combine information extracted directly from audio with information about the corresponding tracks' lyrics using a bi-modal Deep Boltzmann Machine architecture and show the effectiveness of this approach through empirical experiments using the largest music dataset publicly available for research and benchmark purposes.

Keywords: Music · Emotion · Deep Boltzmann Machine · Audio · Lyrics

1 Introduction

Music plays an important and influential role in most of our lives; for instance, we often listen to specific kinds of music to help enhance or alter our mood, particularly during special occasions (e.g. a romantic dinner, a national sports event, etc.). Hence, it is essential that we use information about emotions and mood in music retrieval tasks, such as classification and recommendation [11].

To this end, many approaches based on audio analysis were proposed and proved applicable, but they quickly reached a so called "glass ceiling" performance barrier [13]. As it became evident that using features based on audio alone is not enough, many researchers started combining features from different domains [9]. One such domain, music lyrics, has become a popular source of features for music emotion and mood classification among other music retrieval tasks. Mayer et al. [14] show that, in some emotion categories, when features derived from lyrics are included, the classifier performance improves over using the leading audio features alone. However, Hu et al. [6] reveal that this is not

© Springer International Publishing Switzerland 2016
A.E.P. Villa et al. (Eds.): ICANN 2016, Part II, LNCS 9887, pp. 199–207, 2016.
DOI: 10.1007/978-3-319-44781-0_24

true for all of the mood categories. To further improve the classification performance, some researchers integrate audio features with lyrics together and form hybrid features that could carry information from two different modalities (domains) simultaneously [6]. Accordingly different integration strategies (e.g., early fusion [5], late fusion [10] and model fusion [20]) are proposed in the literature.

In this work, we follow the feature fusion model and use a hybrid model based on Multimodal Deep Boltzmann Machine; in addition to fusing different modalities, it is also able make use of unlabelled data to further improve performance [19]. Additionally, we adopt the commonly used Russell's 2-dimensional Valence-Arousal (V-A) model of affect [15] to capture the emotional content of music lyrics. To show the effectiveness of our approach, we conduct an experimental study on the largest dataset that is publicly available for music retrieval research, the Million Song Dataset [1], from which we are able to use over 230,000 music tracks that contain both lyric and audio features.

2   Related Work

Among the first to tackle the task of automatically classifying music into emotion-based categories, Li and Ogihara used Support Vector Machines (SVM) with audio-based features (related to timbre, pitch and rhythm) and reported 45 % accuracy on a dataset of consisting of 499 music clips and 13 mood categories [12].

Starting in 2007, the Audio Music Mood Classification task appeared regularly in the literature to encourage the development of improved music-IR systems. Since then, datasets comprised of hundreds of music tracks were collected and made available to the research community and more than two hundred systems have been evaluated. Despite other supervised methods like Gaussian Mixture Model [13], Random Forest and K-Nearest Neighbor, many studies found that SVM combined with spectral features often yield the best results [21].

Due to the limiting factors of features based solely on audio [13] and because of the semantically rich nature of music lyrics, lyric-based features found their way into emotion-based music classification. Among others, Hu et al. [6] investigate the usefulness of low-level text features such as the Bag-of-Words (BoW) representation of lyrics, also parts of speech and function words. They also combine lyric and audio features and report accuracy as high as 72 % on a private dataset consisting of 5,585 music tracks and 18 mood categories [7]. He et al. [3] report that higher-order BoW features such as tf-idf weighted unigram, bigram and trigram, can capture more semantic relations in lyrics for mood classification. Similarly, other lyric features derived from the Affective Norm of English Words also obtain encouraging results [8].

There are several ways to combine information from different domains, such as audio and text. The *early fusion* methods simply concatenate audio and lyric features to create feature vectors in a new space [5]; in the *late fusion normally* separate classifiers are trained on the features from their own separate domains [10]. While Xue et al. [20] fused audio and ltext domains through a model fusion scheme. In this work, we follow the idea to use Deep Boltzmann Machines for multimodal learning [19] and demonstrate its effectiveness on the largest publicly available music dataset.

3   Bi-Modal Deep Boltzmann Machine Model

Deep Boltzmann Machine (DBM) [16] is a deep neural network architecture based on Restricted Boltzmann Machine [18]. It contains a set of visible units $\mathbf{v} \in \{0,1\}^D$ and a sequence of layers comprised of hidden units $\mathbf{h}^{(1)} \in \{0,1\}^{F_1}, \mathbf{h}^{(2)} \in \{0,1\}^{F_2}, ..., \mathbf{h}^{(n)} \in \{0,1\}^{F_n}$. The connections are available only between units in adjacent layers, i.e. no connection is allowed between any two units within the same layer or between any two units in non-adjacent layers. The energy of the joint configuration $\{\mathbf{v}, \mathbf{h}\}$ is defined according to $\mathbf{h} = \{\mathbf{h}^{(1)}, \mathbf{h}^{(2)}, ..., \mathbf{h}^{(n)}\}$ and parameters $\theta = \{\mathbf{W}^{(1)}, \mathbf{W}^{(2)}, ..., \mathbf{W}^{(n)}, \mathbf{b}, \mathbf{b}^{(1)}, \mathbf{b}^{(2)}, ..., \mathbf{b}^{(n)}\}$. The DBM assigns probability to a set of visible units according to the Boltzmann distribution:

$$P(\mathbf{v}; \theta) = \frac{1}{Z(\theta)} \sum_{\mathbf{h}} exp(-E(\mathbf{v}, \mathbf{h}^{(1)}, \mathbf{h}^{(2)}; \theta)) \tag{1}$$

where $Z(\theta)$ is the normalising constant.

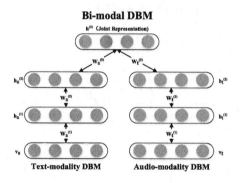

Fig. 1. Bi-modal Deep Boltzmann Machine

Multimodal DBM is a generative model for that can create fused representations by combining features from different modalities in a model fusion scheme [19]. Figure 1 illustrates the proposed audio-text aware bi-modal DBM architecture; it consists of two 2-layer DBM networks, with an additional layer of hidden units added on top to join the two DBMs and form a single model.

Let $\mathbf{v}_a \in \mathbb{R}^D$ denote the audio input and $\mathbf{v}_t \in \mathbb{R}^K$ denote the text input, where $K, D \in \mathbb{R}$ is the dimension of audio and text features. Then, the joint distribution of bi-modal input can be then written as:

$$P(\mathbf{v}_a, \mathbf{v}_t; \theta) = \sum_{\mathbf{h_a^{(2)}}, \mathbf{h_t^{(2)}}, \mathbf{h}^{(3)}} P(\mathbf{h_a^{(2)}}, \mathbf{h_t^{(2)}}, \mathbf{h}^{(3)}) \left(\sum_{\mathbf{h_a^{(1)}}} P(\mathbf{v}_a, \mathbf{h_a^{(1)}} \mid \mathbf{h_a^{(2)}}) \right)$$

$$\left(\sum_{\mathbf{h_t^{(1)}}} P(\mathbf{v}_t, \mathbf{h_t^{(1)}} \mid \mathbf{h_t^{(2)}}) \right)$$

(2)

The second term in Eq. 2 denotes the probability distribution of the audio modality, which assigns probability to $\mathbf{v}_a$ in a Gaussian RBM scheme:

$$P(\mathbf{v_a}; \theta_a) = \sum_{\mathbf{h_a^{(1)}}, \mathbf{h_a^{(2)}}} P(\mathbf{v_a}, \mathbf{h_a^{(2)}}, \mathbf{h_a^{(1)}}; \theta_a)$$

$$= \frac{1}{Z(\theta_a)} \sum_{\mathbf{h_a^{(1)}}, \mathbf{h_a^{(2)}}} exp \left(-\sum_i \frac{(v_{ai} - b_{ai})^2}{2\sigma_i^2} + \sum_{ij} \frac{v_{ai}}{\sigma_i} W_{aij}^{(1)} h_{aj}^{(1)} + \right.$$

(3)

$$\left. \sum_{jl} W_{ajl}^{(1)} h_{aj}^{(1)} h_{al}^{(2)} + \sum_j b_{aj}^{(1)} h_{aj}^{(1)} + \sum_l b_{al}^{(2)} h_{al}^{(2)} \right)$$

The third term in Eq. 2 denotes the probability distribution of the text modality, where $\mathbf{v} \in \mathbb{N}^k$ denotes a vector of visible units and each v_k is the number of times word k occurs in the lyrics with the dictionary size M. The model assigns probability to $\mathbf{v}_t$ in a Replicated Softmax RBM scheme:

$$P(\mathbf{v_t}; \theta_t) = \sum_{\mathbf{h_t^{(1)}}, \mathbf{h_t^{(2)}}} P(\mathbf{v_t}, \mathbf{h_t^{(2)}}, \mathbf{h_t^{(1)}}; \theta_t)$$

$$= \frac{1}{Z_M(\theta_t)} \sum_{\mathbf{h_t^{(1)}}, \mathbf{h_t^{(2)}}} exp \left(\sum_{jk} W_{tk,j}^{(1)} h_{tj}^{(1)} v_{tk} + \sum_{jl} W_{tjl}^{(2)} h_{tj}^{(1)} h_{tl}^{(2)} + \right.$$

(4)

$$\left. \sum_k b_{tk} v_{tk} + M \sum_j b_{tj}^{(1)} h_{tj}^{(1)} + \sum_l b_{tl}^{(2)} h_{tl}^{(2)} \right)$$

The parameters of DBM can be initialised randomly. However, here we use a greedy layer-wise pre-training strategy [16,19].

4   Experimental Study

In our experiments, we use the largest publicly available music dataset, the Million Song Dataset (MSD) [1]. It is a conglomeration of several datasets containing different information about the tracks; we use two of its subsets. First, MusiXmatch, contains information about the lyrics, each song is described as a set of words from the recorded top 5,000 frequent words across all lyrics. Second, Last.fm, contains annotations obtained from music listeners in a form of tags, like "happy" and "upbeat"; from it, we select tracks that are described by emotion related tags. Additionally, we obtain already pre-extracted audio-based features from the MSD Benchmarking dataset, which is an extension of MSD and was created for the purposes of comparing different approaches while maintaining invariability in various experimental parameters [17]. To capture both modalities, in our experiments, each music track is represented by both lyrics (found in MusiXmatch dataset) and audio-based features (from MSDB dataset), there are 236,486 tracks that satisfy these conditions.

Initially, to test the validity of our approach, we select only the tracks that contain "happy" and "sad" tags. After removing ambiguous tracks that contain both tags, we obtain 7,945 "happy" songs and 5,840 "sad" tracks. To avoid classifier bias due to class imbalance, we perform random subsampling and then conduct a binary emotion classification experiment.

In a multi-class scenario, some songs may cover a variety of emotions, rendering the representation by independent dimensions inadequate. For this reason, we employ Russell's Valence-Arousal model [15] and follow Corona's and O'Mahony's scheme of selecting social tags that clearly indicate the song's emotional trend [2]. We group the tags according to their quadrants in the Valence-Arousal model and report the final number of tracks tagged by each emotion group in Table 1. We use the tracks that have the emotion-related tags as labelled data for training the classifier, and the remainder as unlabelled data for unsupervised pre-training. Our final dataset contains 41,727 labelled and 194,759 unlabelled tracks.

Table 1. Mood quadrants and their corresponding number of songs

Quadrant	Group	Tag	Songs
v^-a^+	G29	aggressive,aggression	28,168
	G28	anger,angry,choleric,etc	
v^+a^+	G6	cheerful,jolly,festive,etc	16,315
	G5	happy,happiness,etc	
v^-a^-	G15	sad,sadness,unhappy,etc	10,154
	G16	depressed,blue,dark,gloom,etc	
	G17	heartbreak,grief,sorrow,etc	
v^+a^-	G8	brooding,contemplative,etc	2,629
	G12	calm,comfort,quiet,etc	

The deep learning architecture is configured as following. The audio pathway is modeled by an RBM with 194 visible units, each taking as input acoustic content descriptors, such as MFCC and SSD features. The visible layer is followed by two layers of hidden units, 100 and 50 each. The text modality is formed by RBM consisting of 5,000-unit visible layer followed by hidden layers of 2,048 and 1,024 units each. A joint layer combines the two modalities and consists of 1,074 hidden units. Its output can be considered as a complex probability estimate of the mood classes. We use the output from our Mulimodal RBM as input to either Softmax or SVM for the final classification decision. Additionally, to test the robustness of our chosen audio features, we expand the audio modality from 194 to 3,456 dimensions by including additional audio-based features. The hidden layers are also expanded to 2,048 and 1,024 respectively; and the joint layer to 2,048 units.

Because the SVM classifier performs slightly better on average, we omit the Softmax results. In our experiments, we perform k-fold repeated random subsampling validation with $k = 5$. In each fold, 60 % (6,984) tracks are selected for training and 40 % (4,656) for testing. We compute Mean Average Precision (MAP) and Accuracy as metrics to comprehensively evaluate the models. The initial experimental results are shown in Fig. 2, where we also illustrated the baseline SVM performance (no DBM) using early concatenation method to join the two modalities into a single input vector.

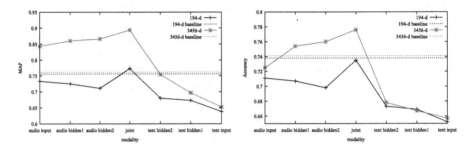

Fig. 2. MAP and Accuracy achieved by the Bi-modal Boltzmann Machine in the "happy"/"sad" binary classification task

As can be seen from Fig. 2, audio-based features indeed outperform the lyric-based features to some extent. We conjecture that this may be because the audio modality is represented by features that were hand-crafted and improved over the years. Meanwhile, the text modality is represented by a shallow BoW statistical measure with large vocabulary, which results in a sparse input vector. This again urges the study on higher level lyric features, which may yield interesting results. We also noticed that the classification performance declined through the audio pathway, which indicates that some valuable information are lost through the extracting process in the audio modality. After expanding the audio modality with additional features, this phenomenon disappears. This indicates the necessity of feature selection. Among all results, the best performance is achieved at the joint layer, which shows the effectiveness of the fusing ability of the proposed approach. After expanding the audio features from 194 to 3,456, the baseline SVM performance did not improve much.

In addition to using the lyric- and audio-based features with our approach, we also compare the model fusion, early fusion and late fusion methods.

In late fusion, we first trained two SVM classifiers to represent the two modalities separately, denoting as p_a and p_t. Then the output mood class is assigned by

$$p = \alpha p_a + (1 - \alpha)p_t \tag{5}$$

where α indicates the relevant importance between audio and lyric features. We set $\alpha = 0.6$, as per Hu et al. [4]. As before, in order to avoid classifier bias towards majority class, we attempt to maintain class balance by ensuring that both training and testing instances are equally distributed across mood classes. Results are shown in Table 2.

Table 2. Comparison of accuracy achieved by the different fusion models

	audio_only	text_only	early_fusion	late_fusion	Bi-modal DBM
$v^- a^+$	0.645	0.600	0.689	0.666	**0.706**
$v^+ a^+$	0.625	0.607	0.653	0.639	**0.692**
$v^- a^-$	0.634	0.620	0.661	0.642	**0.704**
$v^+ a^-$	0.730	0.702	0.745	0.729	**0.785**

Our model outperformed other baseline models in every mood category. The moods in $v^+ a^-$ quadrant obtain the highest accuracy. This is interesting given that the $v^+ a^-$ quadrant has the least number of songs. The reason may be that music pieces in this mood group has many unique lyric terms. Between other mood categories, however, there is no significant differences in the classification accuracy. Moreover, the fusion methods' accuracy all outperformed the accuracy of classification on single modality, affirming the effectiveness of multi-modal mood classification in the same way as many prior studies show.

5   Conclusion

In this work, we used a deep learning architecture, inspired by the work of Srivastava and Salakhutdinov [19], to effectively fuse the audio and text modalities for music mood classification. Results show that fusing modalities is indeed advantageous in the music mood classification task. In addition to including information from other domains/modalities, it would be interesting to see how other lyric derived features perform with this and other multimodal approaches in the music-IR literature, we leave this to our future work.

Acknowledgements. This work was partially supported by the National Natural Science Foundation of China (No. 61332018), the National Department Public Benefit Research Foundation (No. 201510209), and the Fundamental Research Funds for the Central Universities.

References

1. Bertin-Mahieux, T., Ellis, D.P.W., Whitman, B., Lamere, P.: The million song dataset. In: Proceedings of 12th International Society for Music Information Retrieval Conference, pp. 591–596 (2011)
2. Corona, H., O'Mahony, M.P.: An exploration of mood classification in the million songs dataset. In: Proceedings of 12th Sound and Music Computing Conference (2015)
3. He, H., Jin, J., Xiong, Y., Chen, B., Sun, W., Zhao, L.: Language feature mining for music emotion classification via supervised learning from lyrics. In: Kang, L., Cai, Z., Yan, X., Liu, Y. (eds.) ISICA 2008. LNCS, vol. 5370, pp. 426–435. Springer, Heidelberg (2008)
4. Hu, X., Choi, K., Downie, J.S.: A framework for evaluating multimodal music mood classification. J. Assoc. Inf. Sci. Technol. (2016) (In press)
5. Hu, X., Downie, J.S.: When lyrics outperform audio for music mood classification: a feature analysis. In: Proceedings of 11th International Society for Music Information Retrieval Conference, pp. 619–624 (2010)
6. Hu, X., Downie, J.S., Ehmann, A.F.: Lyric text mining in music mood classification. In: Proceedings of 10th International Society for Music Information Retrieval Conference, pp. 411–416 (2009)
7. Hu, X., Downie, J.S., Laurier, C., Bay, M., Ehmann, A.F.: The 2007 MIREX audio mood classification task: lessons learned. In: Proceedings of 9th International Conference on Music Information Retrieval, pp. 462–467 (2008)
8. Hu, Y., Chen, X., Yang, D.: Lyric-based song emotion detection with affective lexicon and fuzzy clustering method. In: Proceedings of 10th International Society for Music Information Retrieval Conference, pp. 123–128 (2009)
9. Kim, Y.E., Schmidt, E.M., Migneco, R., Morton, B.G., Richardson, P., Scott, J.J., Speck, J.A., Turnbull, D.: State of the art report: music emotion recognition: a state of the art review. In: Proceedings of 11th International Society for Music Information Retrieval Conference, pp. 255–266 (2010)
10. Laurier, C., Grivolla, J., Herrera, P.: Multimodal music mood classification using audio and lyrics. In: Proceedings of 7th International Conference on Machine Learning and Applications, pp. 688–693 (2008)
11. Li, T., Mitsunori, O., Tzanetakis, G. (eds.): Music Data Mining. CRC Press, Boca Raton (2012)
12. Li, T., Ogihara, M.: Detecting emotion in music. In: Proceedings of 4th International Society for Music Information Retrieval Conference (2003)
13. Lu, L., Liu, D., Zhang, H.: Automatic mood detection and tracking of music audio signals. IEEE Trans. Audio Speech Lang. Process. $14(1)$, 5–18 (2006)
14. Mayer, R., Neumayer, R., Rauber, A.: Combination of audio and lyrics features for genre classification in digital audio collections. In: Proceedings of 16th International Conference on Multimedia, pp. 159–168 (2008)
15. Russell, J.A.: A circumplex model of affect. J. Pers. Soc. Psychol. $39(6)$, 1161–1178 (1980)
16. Salakhutdinov, R., Hinton, G.E.: Deep boltzmann machines. In: Proceedings of 12th International Conference on Artificial Intelligence and Statistics, pp. 448–455 (2009)
17. Schindler, A., Mayer, R., Rauber, A.: Facilitating comprehensive benchmarking experiments on the million song dataset. In: Proceedings of 2012 International Society for Music Information Retrieval Conference, pp. 469–474 (2012)

18. Smolensky, P.: Information processing in dynamical systems: foundations of harmony theory. Technical report, DTIC Document (1986)
19. Srivastava, N., Salakhutdinov, R.: Multimodal learning with deep boltzmann machines. J. Mach. Learn. Res. **15**(1), 2949–2980 (2014)
20. Xue, H., Xue, L., Su, F.: Multimodal music mood classification by fusion of audio and lyrics. In: He, X., Luo, S., Tao, D., Xu, C., Yang, J., Hasan, M.A. (eds.) MMM 2015, Part II. LNCS, vol. 8936, pp. 26–37. Springer, Heidelberg (2015)
21. Yang, Y.H., Chen, H.H.: Machine recognition of music emotion: a review. ACM Trans. Intell. Syst. Technol. **3**(3), 338–343 (2012)

StreamLeader: A New Stream Clustering Algorithm not Based in Conventional Clustering

Jaime Andrés-Merino and Lluís A. Belanche$^{(\boxtimes)}$

Computer Science Department, Technical University of Catalonia,
Jordi Girona, 1-3, 08034 Barcelona, Spain
jaime.andres@est.fib.upc.edu, belanche@cs.upc.edu

Abstract. Stream clustering algorithms normally require two phases: an *online* first step that statistically summarizes the stream while forming special structures – such as *micro-clusters*– and a second, *offline* phase, that uses a conventional clustering algorithm taking the micro-clusters as pseudo-points to deliver the final clustering. This procedure tends to produce oversized or overlapping clusters in medium-to-high dimensional spaces, and typically degrades seriously in noisy data environments. In this paper we introduce STREAMLEADER, a novel stream clustering algorithm suitable to massive data that does not resort to a conventional clustering phase, being based on the notion of *Leader Cluster* and on an aggressive noise reduction process. We report an extensive systematic testing in which the new algorithm is shown to consistently outperform its contenders both in terms of quality and scalability.

Keywords: Stream algorithms · Clustering · Big Data

1 Introduction

There is undoubtedly a growing need for clustering algorithms able to cope with Big Data environments (especially the *velocity* and *volume* components). New solutions must handle several challenges, such as potentially unbounded volumes, unrestricted dimensionality, unknown – and possibly significant – amounts of noise, and concept drift (non-stationary distributions). Besides, the clustering should preferably be performed in one single pass (data is *not* reused), while computing very fast and scaling well.

Most existing stream clustering algorithms comprise two phases: first an online phase *summarizes* the stream by using higher-level structures called *micro-clusters*. These usually take the form of *Cluster Feature Vectors* or CFVs – as in BIRCH [1], Clustream [2] and Denstream [3]. Other representations include *Coresets/Coreset Trees* (as in StreamKM++ [4]) or *Grids* – as in D-Stream [6]. A second, offline phase uses conventional clustering algorithms – Gaussian, like k-means or arbitrarily-shaped, as in DBScan [3] – using the previously formed micro-clusters to deliver a final clustering. This situation is less than ideal. First, it relies on clustering algorithms which were not designed to cope with the challenges posed by Big Data; second, CFVs tend to grow in size in high-dimensional

© Springer International Publishing Switzerland 2016
A.E.P. Villa et al. (Eds.): ICANN 2016, Part II, LNCS 9887, pp. 208–215, 2016.
DOI: 10.1007/978-3-319-44781-0_25

spaces, and their clustering tends to produce oversized or overlapping clusters; and third, CFVs absorb noise that the conventional clustering inherits, thus rendering it highly inefficient in noisy environments. In this paper we propose STREAMLEADER, a new stream clustering algorithm designed to operate in these data scenarios by using a novel approach that does not resort to a posteriori conventional clustering in a separate offline phase. Instead, it is based on the notion of *Leader Cluster* (explained below) and on an aggressive noise reduction phase based on staged distributional cuts. The MOA platform was created to gather stream mining techniques and foster research, enabling to test and compare several such algorithms within an integrated framework [5]. We test the algorithm systematically against other solutions within MOA – thus equalling computational conditions – and report experimental results in which the new algorithm consistently outperforms its contenders both in terms of quality (measured by several stream clustering metrics) and scalability.

2 The StreamLeader Stream Clustering Algorithm

2.1 Online Phase: Statistical Absorption of the Stream

Consider a stream of instances $x^{(1)}, x^{(2)}, \ldots, x^{(n)}, \ldots$ of $\mathbb{R}^d$, each described by a feature vector $x^{(n)} = (x_j^{(n)})_{j=1}^d$. The time stamps of arriving instances are denoted $T^{(1)}, T^{(2)}, \ldots, T^{(n)}, \ldots$. In the context of anytime stream mining, microclusters are structures intended to compress the incoming data stream and then – every now and then – deliver them to conventional clustering algorithms [7]. In Big Data environments, this process may become highly inadequate and inefficient. Our algorithm follows a single-pass strategy that aims at capturing the essential statistical information describing the stream. Call *leader* any potential cluster centroid in $\mathbb{R}^d$. Each cluster is captured by constructing a *Leader Cluster* – an extension of the CFV concept – around a leader, as described next.

Definition. A **Leader Cluster** is a structure:
$$LC = (N, LS, SS, LST, SST, LSD, \delta_{\mathrm{MAX}}, T_{cr}, \text{is-expanded?}, R_{exp}), \text{ with:}$$

- `scalar` N: number of own instances so far
- `vector` $LS = \sum_n x^{(n)}$, sum of own instances so far
- `vector` SS, where $SS_j = \sum_n (x_j^{(n)})^2$, the square sum of own instances so far
- `scalar` $LST = \sum_n T^{(n)}$, sum of time stamps of own instances so far
- `scalar` $SST = \sum_n (T^{(n)})^2$, square sum of time stamps of own instances so far
- `scalar` $LSD = \sum_n D^{(n)}$, sum of distances to own leader of own instances so far
- `scalar` $\delta_{\mathrm{MAX}} \in [0, 1/2)$: radius of influence, taking own leader as origin
- `scalar` T_{cr}: creation time stamp (when the structure was created)
- `boolean` is-expanded?: indicates expansion of the structure
- `scalar` R_{exp}: if is-expanded?, radius of the expanded structure.

We use the dot notation (.) to access the components of the structure.

Definition 2 (Leader). The **leader** l of a *Leader Cluster* LC is its statistical representative and can be computed as $l = \frac{LC.LS}{LC.N}$.

The algorithm – shown in pseudocode in **Algorithm 1** – works in the normalized metric space $(\mathbb{R}^d, \delta)$. In the present case, choosing $d(\boldsymbol{x}, \boldsymbol{y}) = \|\boldsymbol{x} - \boldsymbol{y}\|$ to be the standard Euclidean distance, we take $\delta(\boldsymbol{x}, \boldsymbol{y}) = \|\boldsymbol{x} - \boldsymbol{y}\| / (\|\boldsymbol{x} - \boldsymbol{y}\| + 1)$, which is a metric in the range $[0, 1)$. This metric is used to measure $D^{(n)} = \delta(\boldsymbol{x}^{(n)}, l)$, how *close* an incoming stream instance $\boldsymbol{x}^{(n)}$ is from an arbitrary leader l (line **5**). Every *Leader Cluster* has a volume of influence (a ball) around it given by the current radius $LC.\delta_{\text{MAX}}$, which is the only parameter used by the STREAMLEADER algorithm. Operations to add an instance to an existing *Leader Cluster* and to merge two existing *Leader Clusters* are quite straightforward and omitted.

In order to allow *Leader Clusters* to handle concept drift, removal capabilities must be implemented. In data streaming scenarios, where only one-pass over the data is allowed, the concepts of "recent" or "old" data apply. All algorithms in MOA use a *Horizon H* to create a moving time window to evaluate clustering quality. Given a *Leader Cluster* LC, the *mean* $\mu = \frac{LC.LST}{LC.N}$ and the *standard deviation* $\sigma = \sqrt{\frac{LC.SST}{LC.N} - (\frac{LC.LST}{LC.N})^2}$ of its timestamps are used to define its *temporal relevance* as $\mu + \sigma$. All *Leader Clusters* whose temporal relevance is smaller than the current time stamp minus H are eliminated (line **10**). In contrast, existing algorithms would use H simply to switch from the online to the offline phase. It is important to emphasize that H is not a clustering parameter in itself; rather, it is used in MOA to indicate *when* to produce a clustering.

2.2 Offline Phase: Avoiding Conventional Clustering Algorithms

The offline phase is composed of two main processes: first, noise (understood to mean random data not belonging to the true clustering) is aggressively detected and eliminated; second, *Leader Clusters* are allowed to expand or contract – if need be – to adapt to current true clusters.

Noise Reduction. The existing *Leader Clusters* are sorted according to their size in descending order, obtaining a positive distribution. Noise will then appear in the right (lower) tail (line **13**). We first eliminate this tail by performing a 45th percentile cut. When the tail is gone, many *Leader Clusters* representing scattered noise could still exist in the elbow. We assume this noise to be roughly one order of magnitude less than the *Leader Cluster* capturing the largest amount of instances. Therefore, the leftout distribution is cut at one logarithm of the size of the largest *Leader Cluster* at that moment in time (line14) – see Fig. 1.

Dynamic Radiuses. The next step allows expansions/contractions of particular *Leader Clusters* to a new radius larger/smaller than the initially set δ_{MAX}. There is a need to dynamically adapt the clustering to the changing reality of a data stream, allowing it to match as much as possible the current size of the true

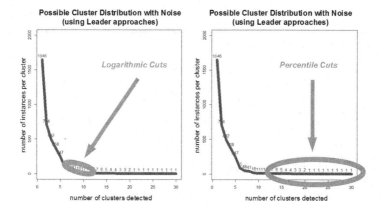

Fig. 1. Distributional cuts of *Leader Cluster* sizes: (left) elbow; (right) lower tail.

clusters. First, when two *Leader Clusters* of radius δ_{MAX} overlap, they will merge into one with radius $\delta_{\text{MAX}} + 60\,\%$. Second, if a *Leader Cluster* of radius δ_{MAX} is isolated, but likely to be contained in a bigger true cluster, it will expand to radius $\delta_{\text{MAX}} + 30\,\%$. Third, overlapping *Leader Clusters* of radius $\delta_{\text{MAX}} + 30\,\%$ will merge into one with radius $\delta_{\text{MAX}} + 60\,\%$. Finally, letting $\delta = \frac{LC.LSD}{LC.N}$, a *Leader Cluster* will contract to radius 2δ when $\delta < 0.4 \cdot \delta_{\text{MAX}}$ (line **15**).

3   Evaluation of Clustering Performance

In this section, we empiricallly evaluate the clustering performance of the proposed algorithm. Seven stream clustering quality metrics are averaged to form a normalized unique score $Q \in [0, 1]$: CMM (*Cluster Mapping Measure*), RS (*Rand Statistic*), SC (*Silhouette Coefficient*), HOM (*Homogeneity*), COM (*Completeness*), F1-P (*F1-Precision*), and F1-R (*F1-Recall*), all of which are available in MOA. We perform a thorough comparison against three state-of-the-art stream algorithms: Clustream [1], Clustree [2] and Denstream (with DBScan) [3].

Clustering Quality Comparison on Synthetic Data. We first perform a extensive comparison using MOA-generated synthetic datasets, especially desgined for clustering streaming data. Demonstrating improvement on synthetic data sets can be more convincing that doing so in scenarios where the true solution is completely unknown. The power inherent in fully controlled experimental environments basically relies on systematically varying chosen experimental conditions – thus facilitating the derivation of meaningful conclusions.

We simulate 10 kinds of synthetic streams (*scenarios*), by playing with the number and size of the clusters – see top boxes in Table 2. For each scenario, we also change dimensionality ($d \in \{2, 5, 10, 50\}$), noise level ($10\,\%$, $33\,\%$), and study two algorithm parametrizations (default, optimal). The former refers to the parametrization that MOA gives by default to each algorithm; for the

---

Algorithm 1. STREAMLEADER (δ_{MAX})

---

1 CREATE new *Leader Cluster* with instance $x^{(1)}$
2 $n \leftarrow 2$
3 **while** *DATA-STREAM-ACTIVE* **do**
       // Online Phase
4      $x^{(n)} \leftarrow$ GET-NEXT-INSTANCE
5   **if** *the closest Leader Cluster LC to* $x^{(n)}$ *has* $\delta(x^{(n)}, LC.l) < LC.\delta_{\text{MAX}}$ **then**
6   ADD-INSTANCE $x^{(n)}$ to *Leader Cluster* LC
7   **else**
8   CREATE new *Leader Cluster* with instance $x^{(n)}$
9   **end**
10   REMOVE all *Leader Clusters* older than the horizon H
11     $n \leftarrow n + 1$
       // Offline Phase
12   **if** *CURRENT-TIME-WINDOW-COMPLETED (H)* **then**
13   SORT all *Leader Clusters* according to size N in descending order
14   ELIMINATE-NOISE based on tail and elbow procedures
15   MERGE, EXPAND and CONTRACT *Leader Clusters*
16   **end**
17 **end**

STREAMLEADER, based on the fact that it works on a normalized distance space, this is set as $\delta_{\text{MAX}} = 0.11$ because it represents a trade-off between capturing bigger clusters (using expansion) and small ones using a single *Leader Cluster* (using contraction). The latter ("optimal") is obtained adjusting the parameters to the general knowledge of the scenario, according to the author's guidelines in the corresponding papers. In all, a total of 240 tests are developed, with half-a-million random instances generated anew for each test. Although quality criteria can be monitored continuously, for space reasons we show the results averaged throughout the entire streams. A detailed view is presented in Table 2; a graphical summary in Fig. 2. The results clearly show the ability of STREAMLEADER to consistently outperform Clustream, Denstream and Clustree – the latter degrading specially with larger dimensionalities and noise levels.

Scalability Comparison on Synthetic Data. We also independently test the *scalability* of the new algorithm, both with respect to the number of clusters and data dimensionality. We test the same four algorithms against 2, 5, 20, 40 and 50 clusters, in spaces of dimensionality 2, 5, 20 and 50. This results in 20 tests per algorithm; each of which is executed 10 times to get average results, totaling 800 tests, producing the results shown in Fig. 3. It is seen that STREAMLEADER behaves very well (as Clustree does), supporting our intuition that the proposed algorithm seems also well suited for intensive high-throughput clustering tasks, although this issue should be verified further.

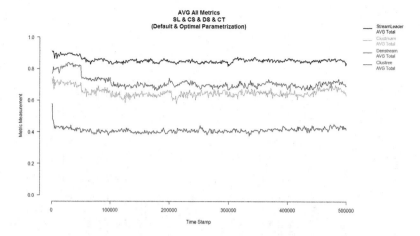

Fig. 2. Average of Q across all scenarios as a function of instance number n. Top to bottom: STREAMLEADER, Clustream, Denstream and Clustree.

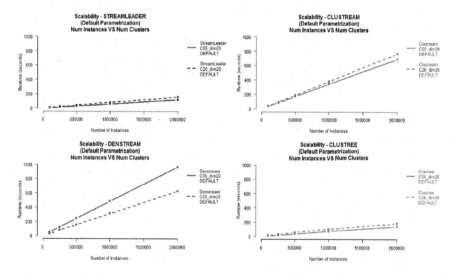

Fig. 3. Scalability tests: running time as a function of number of instances (in seconds).

Table 1. *Network Intrusion*: quality test results.

		SLeader	CluSTR	DenSTR	CTree
dim.	Default	0.71	0.79	0.80	0.65
$d = 33$	Optimal	0.90	0.79	0.82	0.65

Comparison on Real Data. Additionally, the new algorithm is tested in the KDD-CUP99 Network Intrusion data set; this problem is often used in stream

Table 2. Synthetic quality testing average results for each scenario: the bottom row shows averages across similar scenarios; the rightmost columns show averages across same dimensionalities. Best averaged quality scores are shown boldfaced; D = default, O = optimal; 'NA' indicates MOA limitations; 'crash' refers to out of RAM issues.

Scenarios 1–5 (10% NOISE) — each cell group: SLeader | ClusTR | DenSTR | CTree

	Scenario 1 FEW BIG CLUSTERS				Scenario 2 FEW SMALL CLUSTERS				Scenario 3 MANY SMALL CLUSTERS				Scenario 4 MEDIUM AMOUNT SMALL/BIG CLUSTERS				Scenario 5 MANY SMALL/BIG CLUSTERS				Average Q Scenarios 1-5			
	SL	Cl	Dn	CT	SL	Cl	Dn	CT	SL	Cl	Dn	CT	SL	Cl	Dn	CT	SL	Cl	Dn	CT	SL	Cl	Dn	CT
dim. d=2 D	0.62	0.65	0.25	0.65	0.83	0.77	0.73	0.75	0.71	0.79	0.63	0.77	0.71		0.53	0.74	0.57		0.32	0.67	0.69	0.72	0.49	0.71
d=2 O	0.62	0.65	0.48	0.67	0.83	0.77	0.51	0.77	0.91	0.84	0.23	0.82	0.76	0.71	0.34	0.74	0.67	0.68	0.33	0.71	0.75	0.73	0.38	0.74
dim. d=5 D	0.80	0.83	0.23	0.80	0.87	0.81	0.70	0.81	0.90	0.84	0.32	0.85	0.92	0.83	0.54	0.83	0.91	0.86	0.31	0.84	0.88	0.83	0.42	0.83
d=5 O	0.82	0.83	0.5	0.84	0.87	0.81	0.69	0.82	0.92	0.93	0.28	0.90	0.92	0.83	0.55	0.87	0.92	0.90	0.28	0.90	0.89	0.86	0.46	0.87
dim. d=20 D	NA	NA	NA	NA	0.90	0.74	0.71	0.80	0.95	0.69	0.37	0.57	0.93	0.81	0.70	0.85	0.95	0.92	0.64	0.32	0.93	0.72	0.52	0.68
d=20 O	NA	NA	NA	NA	0.91	0.74	0.72	0.80	0.96	0.91	0.37	0.72	0.93	0.81	0.72	0.87	0.95	0.92	0.35	0.75	0.94	0.84	0.54	0.78
dim. d=50 D	NA	NA	NA	NA	0.91	0.55	0.66	0.63	0.95	0.24	0.32	crash	0.93	0.55	0.55	0.77	0.95	0.42	0.36	0.69	0.93	0.44	0.47	0.64
d=50 O	NA	NA	NA	NA	0.91	0.55	0.67	0.66	0.96	0.67	0.32	0.42	0.93	0.73	0.58	0.70	0.95	0.73	0.36	0.64	0.93	0.67	0.48	0.60

Scenarios 6–10 (33% NOISE) — each cell group: SLeader | ClusTR | DenSTR | CTree

	Scenario 6 FEW BIG CLUSTERS				Scenario 7 FEW SMALL CLUSTERS				Scenario 8 MANY SMALL CLUSTERS				Scenario 9 MEDIUM AMOUNT SMALL/BIG CLUSTERS				Scenario 10 MANY SMALL/BIG CLUSTERS				Average Q Scenarios 6-10			
	SL	Cl	Dn	CT	SL	Cl	Dn	CT	SL	Cl	Dn	CT	SL	Cl	Dn	CT	SL	Cl	Dn	CT	SL	Cl	Dn	CT
dim. d=2 D	0.57		0.21	0.57	0.86	0.59	0.54	0.60	0.68	0.64	0.51	0.64	0.73	0.61	0.49	0.62	0.57	0.59	0.29	0.60	0.68	0.60	0.40	0.60
d=2 O	0.57		0.46	0.58	0.88	0.59	0.39	0.61	0.89	0.63	0.28	0.68	0.8	0.61	0.34	0.67	0.67	0.60	0.35	0.63	0.76	0.60	0.36	0.63
dim. d=5 D	0.69		0.28	0.61	0.80	0.70	0.44	0.69	0.93	0.80	0.35	0.85	0.89	0.81	0.36	0.84	0.87	0.74	0.33	0.82	0.84	0.73	0.35	0.76
d=5 O	0.69		0.36	0.63	0.83	0.70	0.59	0.71	0.95	0.85	0.48	0.89	0.89	0.81	0.52	0.85	0.87	0.83	0.34	0.91	0.85	0.76	0.46	0.80
dim. d=20 D	NA	NA	NA	NA	0.88	0.51	0.43	0.78	0.95	0.34	0.34	0.85	0.89	0.51	0.49	0.77	0.93	0.33	0.33	0.80	0.90	0.42	0.40	0.80
d=20 O	NA	NA	NA	NA	0.91	0.51	0.45	0.78	0.96	0.66	0.35	0.86	0.89	0.51	0.57	0.76	0.94	0.84	0.35	0.84	0.92	0.63	0.43	0.81
dim. d=50 D	NA	NA	NA	NA	0.87	0.47	0.35	0.59	0.90	0.12	0.31	crash	0.92	0.39	0.38	crash	0.92	0.12	0.32	crash	0.90	0.27	0.34	0.52
d=50 O	NA	NA	NA	NA	0.90	0.47	0.40	0.54	0.94	0.34	0.32	0.40	0.92	0.42	0.37	0.69	0.93	0.43	0.32	0.40	0.92	0.41	0.35	0.51

Bottom average row (averages across similar scenarios):

0.67 0.66 0.35 0.67 | 0.87 0.64 0.56 0.71 | 0.90 0.64 0.36 0.70 | 0.87 0.50 0.75 | 0.85 0.64 | 0.64 0.33 0.70

clustering algorithm benchmarking[1]. The data describes 4.8 million computer connections (sequences of TCP packets) of about 100 bytes, totalling 42 features (33 of which are continuous and used for the clustering). It is known (though not used) that each connection is either normal, or an intrusion or attack. The results are displayed in Table 1, again showing average performance of the four compared algorithms, under default and optimal parametrizations. STREAMLEADER compares again fairly well against `Clustream`, `Denstream` and `Clustree`.

4   Conclusions

In this work we have introduced STREAMLEADER, a novel stream clustering algorithm based on a simple structure gathering basic data statistics, fast enough and sufficiently rich to perform effective stream clustering when combined with operations for noise elimination, cluster merging, removal and expansion. The algorithm has been extensively tested against state-of-the-art methods within the MOA platform, consistently outperforming them in cluster quality, and scaling remarkably well due to its avoidance of off-line conventional clustering algorithms. As the next step, we plan to introduce dynamic distribution cuts and horizons – dependent on the current summarization of the stream – by using adaptive windowing techniques [8] and integrating the new algorithm in MOA. In the medium term, the goal is to migrate to the Apache SAMOA (Scalable Advanced Massive Online Analysis)[2] distributed streaming machine learning framework.

References

1. Aggarwal, C., Han, J., Wang, J., Yu, P.: A framework for clustering evolving data streams. In: Proceedings of the Conference on Very Large Data Bases, pp. 81–92 (2003)
2. Cao, F., Ester, M., Qian, W., Zhou, A.: Density-based clustering over an evolving data stream with noise. In: Proceedings of ICDM, pp. 328–339 (2006)
3. Kranen, P., Assent, I., Baldauf, C., Seidl, T.: The ClusTree: indexing micro-clusters for anytime stream mining. Knowl. Inf. Syst. **29**(2), 249–272 (2011)
4. Ackermann, M.R., Martens, M., Raupach, C., et al.: StreamKM++: a clustering algorithm for data streams. ACM J. Exp. Algorithmics **17**(1), 2–4 (2012)
5. Bifet, A., Holmes, G., Pfahringer, B., et al.: MOA: massive online analysis, a framework for stream classification and clustering. J. Mach. Learn. Res. **22**, 44–50 (2010)
6. Chen, Y., Tu, L.: Density-based clustering for real-time stream data. In: Proceedings of KDD, pp. 133–142 (2007)
7. Kremer, H., Kranen, P., Jansen, T., et al.: An effective evaluation measure for clustering on evolving data streams. In: Proceedings of SIGKDD, pp. 868–876 (2011)
8. Bifet, A., Gavaldà, R.: Learning from time-changing data with adaptive windowing. In: Proceedings of SIAM International Conference on Data Mining, pp. 443–448 (2007)

---

[1] The data was used for the 3rd International Knowledge Discovery & Data Mining Tools Competition, held as part of the Knowledge Discovery & Data Mining conference (KDD-99) – see kdd.ics.uci.edu/databases/kddcup99/kddcup99.html.

[2] http://samoa.incubator.apache.org/.

Comparison of Methods for Community Detection in Networks

Hassan Mahmoud[1], Francesco Masulli[1,2](✉), Stefano Rovetta[1], and Amr Abdullatif[1]

[1] DIBRIS - Department of Informatics, Bioengineering, Robotics and Systems Engineering, University of Genoa, Via Dodecaneso 35, 16146 Genoa, Italy
{hassan.mahmoud,francesco.masulli,stefano.rovetta, amr.abdullatif}@unige.it
[2] Sbarro Institute for Cancer Research and Molecular Medicine, College of Science and Technology, Temple University, Philadelphia, PA, USA

Abstract. Community detection refers to extracting dense interacting nodes or subgraphs that form relevant aggregation (aka, communities) within networks. We present nine community detection methods based on different approaches, and we compare them on the Girvan-Newman community detection benchmark network. Two methods proposed by our group using spectral graph theory and fuzzy clustering obtain the best experimental results evaluated using the Omega Index.

1 Introduction

Networks are widely used to model various kinds of complex systems such as the World Wide Web, Internet, gene regulatory networks, metabolic networks, social networks, pathway networks, epistemological networks, gene regulatory networks, protein interaction networks, metabolic networks, etc [1,20]. The art of inferring the modular structures in networks is called community detection [7], which refers to finding large subgraphs with high internal connection strengths within nodes belonging to them, and sparse interaction between entities residing in other subgraphs or communities. It is worth to note that a community can provide a scalable way to identify functionally important or closely related classes of nodes rather than analyzing data independently.

Many community detection methods have been proposed, but even if few papers propose comparatives studies of their performances, the choice of the more suited method is still an open problem. Most community detection methods can be classified as *"crisp"* as they are able to detect not-overlapping communities only, while few of them can be categorized as *"fuzzy"* ass they are able to detect overlapping communities. The ability of a community detection method to detect overlapping communities let us identify nodes (e.g., proteins) participating with different strengths to different significant processes (e.g., pathways).

Work partially funded by a grant of the University of Genoa.

In this paper, we shall present the main characteristics of some state of art community detection methods and of some proposed by our group and we will compare their performances on a popular benchmark proposed by Girvan and Newman [7].

2   Community Detection Methods in Networks

In this section we give a quick survey of the state of the art approaches for community detection in graphs that employ betweenness, modularity and spectral clustering and two proposed by our group. We will denote the number of edge as m, and the number of nodes (or vertices) as n; moreover, we will set in italic the shortnames that we will use in the following sections to refer to the methods listed here.

2.1   Betweenness Based Methods

Those methods are based on shortest path analysis, by exploiting the concept of betweenness $C_B(e)$ of an edge e that is measured as the ratio between the shortest path $\sigma_{st}(e)$ linking each vertex pair (s, t) that pass through e and the shortest path between these pairs σ_{st} [4]:

$$C_B(e) = \sum_{s,t \in V, s \neq t} \frac{\sigma_{st}(e)}{\sigma_{st}}, \tag{1}$$

Betweenness can be computed for all vertices in time $O(mn)$ and requires $O(n+m)$ space for a network with m edges and n vertices [4].

Girvan and Newman [14] proposed a crisp divisive method for community detection based on progressive removal of edges. Edges to be eliminated are chosen on the basis of the updated evaluation of *betweenness* scores after each edge removal. This approach presents a main con as its complexity makes it unfeasible in application to large networks.

2.2   Blondel's Method

The Network Modularity Q [15] is defined as:

$$Q = \frac{1}{2m} \sum_{i,j} \left[A_{ij} - \frac{k_i k_j}{2m} \right] \delta(c_i, c_j) \tag{2}$$

where A_{ij} is the weight of edge linking vertices i and j, $k_i = \sum_j A_{ij}$ is the degree of vertex i, c_i is the community to which node i is assigned, $m = \frac{1}{2} \sum_{ij} A_{ij}$, and $\delta(c_i, c_j)$ is 1 if c_i is the same as c_j and 0 otherwise.

Network modularity Q is a scalar value ranging in the interval $[-1, 1]$. It gives a measure of the strength of community structure in a network: High modularity implies the existence of dense connections within communities and of sparse links between them. Although modularity suffers a resolution limit specially in case of detecting small communities, it does not require prior knowledge about the number or sizes of communities, and it is capable of discovering network partitions composed of communities having different sizes.

Blondel et al. proposed in [3] a crisp greedy method that often is considered as the "reference" method. It implements an iterative optimization process aimed to maximize the modularity Q in a small local community scale. After a partition is identified, communities are replaced by their super-nodes. This approach leads to hierarchical decomposition of the network. The computational time is $O(m)$, which makes it more scalable than other greedy approaches, but it may get stuck in a local minima and then may not find a good optimum.

2.3   Eigenvector Based Method

An adjacency matrix of a graph is a square $n \times n$ matrix A describing the graph (network) topology, such that $A[i,j]$ is one when there is an edge from vertex i to vertex j, and zero when there is no edge.

The *leading eigenvector method*, proposed by Newman et al. [17], is a crisp method aimed to maximize the network modularity Q using eigenvalues and eigenvectors derived from the adjacency matrix of the original graph. This method obtains good results in case of graph bisection, while it is less accurate with more than two communities. The algorithm converges in $O(n^2 log(n))$ time.

2.4   Cluster Overlap Newman-Girvan's Algorithm

The Cluster Overlap Newman-Girvan's Algorithm (*CONGA*) [9] is a fuzzy divisive method that develops the Newman algorithm [17] that is able to detect overlapping communities. It splits the vertices linkages among clusters when their betweenness exceeds the an assigned maximum edge betweenness threshold. The complexity of this approach is $O(m^3)$ or $O(n^3)$ in case of sparse graphs.

2.5   Simulated Annealing Based Method

In [16] *Nepusz* proposed a fuzzy version of Newman's approach that optimizes the network modularity Q using the simulated annealing procedure. Nepusz introduces the concept of node bridgeness b that quantifies the degree to which a given vertex (or node) is shared among different clusters:

$$b(s) = 1 - \sqrt{k\sigma^2(U_{1...k}(s))}, \tag{3}$$

where σ refers to the variance between node memberships U in k communities. If a vertex s belongs to all the communities in the graph with equal probabilities, then the variance evaluates to zero, which in turn gives a bridgeness score of one. Then, the ideal bridges in the network will belong to multiple communities with equal probabilities. Moreover, vertices with low degree and high bridgeness usually correspond to outliers (nodes that do not have a dominant community).

2.6   Spectral Clustering Based Methods

The degree matrix of a graph is a diagonal matrix which contains information about the degree of each vertex that is the number of edges of each vertex.

Starting from the adjacency and the degree matrices, several matrices characterizing the network properties are derived from them, such as the Laplacian matrix, the normalized Laplacian matrix, the correlation matrix and others.

Spectral clustering based methods for community detection in networks apply a central clustering technique (such as the K-Means) to data in a subspace spanned by the first k eigenvectors of one of those derived matrices.

The direct application of central clustering techniques for communities detection in networks is biased to dense spherical clusters and then performs poorly due to the complexity of most real-world networks. Instead, the spectral clustering approach smartly exploits the Laplacian or related matrices to infer complex network community structures. Moreover, an hypothesis behind spectral approaches is that the eigenvector components corresponding to nodes in the same community should be similar [6].

Another community detection method that we will evaluate in this paper is a crisp spectral clustering method using the Shi and Malik spectral clustering approach [19] based on the un-normalized Laplacian (*Spectral-Shi*).

Zhang [22] proposed a fuzzy approach for community detection that assumes to know the number of communities in advance then use it to calculate the eigenvectors.

In the following parts of this subsection we shall sketch some methods for community detection in networks, proposed by our group, that exploit:

– The maximization of modularity procedure by Neuman and Girvan in [15];
– The spectral theory for data clustering (in particular we used the approach by Ng et al. [18] based on the normalized Laplacian);
– Central clustering techniques, both fuzzy and possibilistic [2,12].

The Fuzzy c-means Spectral clustering Modularity (or *FSM*) is a fuzzy community detection method introduced in [13] that applies the following three improvements to the original Ng et al. [18] spectral clustering algorithm, when used to detect communities in networks:

1. First of all, the estimation of the number of clusters say k is performed using the maximization of modularity procedure depicted by Neuman and Girvan in [15]; the estimated number of clusters is applied both for selecting the top eigenvectors of the Laplacian matrix, and for setting the number of clusters for the central clustering algorithm.
2. Then, the clustering in the affine subspace spanned by the first k eigenvectors is performed with the application of the Fuzzy C-Means (FCM) clustering algorithm [2] instead of K-Means (used in [18]).
3. After FCM, we apply an α-cut to remove nodes with low membership and to discover communities below an assigned threshold α that can be evaluated as:

$$\alpha = \frac{\eta}{l} , \tag{4}$$

where l is the number of expected clusters. The parameter η (with $0 < \eta \leq 1$) is a tuning term controlling the number of simultaneous communities to which a single node can be attributed. When $\eta = 1$, each node can belong to one community only, whereas for $\eta \to 0$ each node will be attributed to all communities.

We also proposed also the Possibilistic c-means Spectral clustering Modularity (*PSM*) [13] that is a fuzzy community detection method that is variation of the FSM, employing the Possibilistic C-Means (PCM) [12] as the clustering algorithm. This approach allows us to overcome the problem of sensibility to outlier.

3   Experimental Comparison

3.1   Girvan-Newman's Benchmark

Various versions of the planted ℓ-partition model [8] are used in the literature as reference benchmarks in network research. In this model one "plants" a partition, consisting of a certain number of groups of nodes. Each node has a probability p_{in} of being connected to nodes of its group and a probability p_{out} of being connected to nodes of different groups. As long as $p_{in} > p_{out}$ the groups are communities, whereas when $p_{in} \leq p_{out}$ the network is essentially a random graph, without community structure.

In [7,8] Girvan and Newman proposed a version of ℓ-partition model (*GN* benchmark). This model consists of 128 nodes, each of them with expected degree 16, which are divided into four groups of 32 nodes each. The *GN* benchmark is often used to test algorithms for community detection, even if it shows two drawbacks: (1) All nodes have the same expected degree; (2) All communities have equal size. These features are unrealistic as complex networks are known to be characterized by heterogeneous distributions of degree and community sizes. This implies that $p_{in} + 3p_{out} \simeq \frac{1}{2}$, so the probabilities p_{in} and p_{out} are not independent parameters. Hence the internal degree is given by $k_{in} = p_{in}(g-1) = 31p_{in}$ and the external degree k_{out} is given by: $k_{out} = p_{out}g(\ell - 1) = 96p_{out}$. For evaluating a community detection method one can increase k_{out} (reduce the strength of community structure), then regenerate the benchmark and check the method accuracy compared to the generated ground truth.

The literature reports that most of the methods degrade when k_{out} approaches 6 and may fail at $k_{out} = 8$ [7] due to the weakness of community structure.

3.2   Omega Index

The Omega Index [5] is an extension of the Adjusted Rand Index (ARI) [10]. We say that a pair of nodes is considered to be in agreement if they are clustered in exactly the same number of communities. Let K_1 and K_2 be the number of communities in partitions C_1 and C_2, respectively, the Unadjusted Omega Index ω_u is defined as:

$$\omega_u(C_1, C_2) = \frac{2}{n(n-1)} \sum_{j=0}^{max(K_1,K_2)} |t_j(C_1) \cap t_j(C_2)|, \tag{5}$$

and the Expected Omega Index ω_e is:

$$\omega_e(C_1, C_2) = \left(\frac{2}{n(n-1)}\right)^2 \sum_{j=0}^{max(K_1,K_2)} |t_j(C_1)| \cdot |t_j(C_2)|, \tag{6}$$

where $n(n-1)/2$ is the number of node pairs and $t_j(C)$ is the set pairs that appear exactly j times in a partition c. The Omega Index is then defined as:

$$\omega(C_1, C_2) = \frac{\omega_u(C_1, C_2) - \omega_e(C_1, C_2)}{1 - \omega_e(C_1, C_2)}. \tag{7}$$

Note that the subtraction of the expected value takes into account agreements resulting from chance alone. The Omega Index ranges in the interval $[0, 1]$. The best matching between the two partitions happens for $\omega = 1$. When there is no overlap among communities, the Omega Index reduces to the ARI.

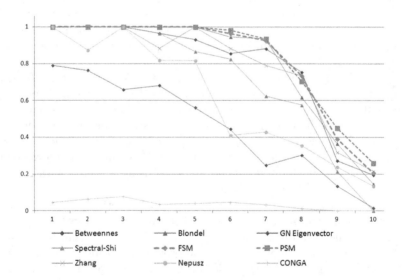

Fig. 1. Comparison of 9 community detection methods on the *GN* benchmark. The graph reports the value of the fuzzy Omega Index versus the value of k_{out}.

3.3   Results and Discussion

In the experiments reported in this section we varied k_{out} from 1 to 10. Figure 1 reports the comparison of the community detection methods presented in Sect. 2 on the *GN* benchmark with k_{out} varying from 1 to 10. The graph reports the value of the fuzzy Omega Index versus the value of k_{out} [7,9,21].

The proposed *PSM* as well as *FSM* methods show high partition similarity values (generally approaching 1 when $k_{out} < 6$) compared to the other methods. Note that most community detection methods give reasonable communities and as a consequence obtain a high partition similarity in GN benchmark when k_{out} is less than 6. This is a well known characteristic of *GN* benchmark in the literature [7] because the community structure becomes vague for values of k_{out} larger than this value. As long as k_{out} increases the community structure becomes weaker and only a few methods can infer the communities in this settings: among them *PSM* and *FSM* that reported high values compared to other methods even when increasing k_{out}.

We note that, while many community detection methods obtained noisy results varying from the *GN* benchmark, the proposed methods inferred node assignment similar to the *GN* benchmark. Moreover, we highlight that the Newman's edge betweenness community detection method [14] is not meaningful on large subgraphs because the random null model underlying modularity becomes unreasonable. We remark also that the proposed methods *FSM* and *PSM* are more accurate than *Nepusz* [16] that may miss some nodes and fail to assign them to their correct community (it considers them outliers), and the proposed methods get a reasonable number of communities by using modularity maximization in spectral space, unlike the divisive approaches like *Newman leading eigenvector*.

We extended our study on more complex networks using the **LFR** benchmark illustrated in [7]. We tested the community detection methods on graphs of size 5000 and even 10000 nodes. We found that some methods halted specially the fuzzy methods such as *CONGA*. Moreover, the crisp methods like *Nepusz* [16], *Zhang* [22], and *Blondel* et al. [3] could not detect the fuzziness in the network, while *FSM*, and *PSM* obtained fuzzy communities in a reasonable time (in average 4 min for 10000 nodes network using a laptop with 2.00 GHz dual-core processor and 2 GB of Ram).

We conclude that the proposed *FSM* and *PSM* methods have the following characteristics compared to the other methods discussed in this paper: (1) Unlike *Nepsuz* method for instance, due to employing spectral clustering that is capable characterizing complex graphs, the proposed methods could infer communities efficiently in complex networks, (2) Unlike many spectral based community detection methods such as the *Spectral-Shi* method, the proposed methods does not require assigning number of clusters (k) and we infer k automatically using the modularity maximization procedure, (3) Unlike the crisp methods like *Nepusz* [16], *Zhang* [22], and *Blondel*, the proposed methods could infer overlapping communities efficiently due to employing Fuzzy C-Means in *FSM* method, and Possiblistic C-Means in *PSM* method. We note that *PSM* overcomes the limitation *FSM* in case of outliers detection, (4) Unlike some fuzzy methods such as *CONGA*, the proposed *FSM*, and *PSM* infered the fuzzy communities efficiently in reasonable time. Moreover, the proposed methods regardless of many overlapping approaches exist in the literature [7,9,21] infers the significance of each node in the detected fuzzy communizes.

4   Conclusions

In this paper we presented nine community detection methods following different approaches, and compared them on the Girvan-Newman community detection benchmark network. The Fuzzy c-means Spectral clustering Modularity *FSM* and the Possibilistic c-means Spectral clustering Modularity *PSM* proposed by our group using spectral graph theory and fuzzy clustering obtained the best results evaluated using the Omega Index.

The *PSM* and *FSM* methods by our group inferred the fuzzy communities efficiently using the *LFR* overlapping benchmark regardless of the crisp methods. Moreover, they characterized complex networks in a reasonable time (in average 4 minutes for 10000 nodes network) regardless of many methods such as *COGNA* that halted on such large networks. Unlike many community detection methods, the proposed methods do not require apriori information about the number of communities in advance and they support characterizing the significance of the detected communities.

References

1. Albert, R., Barabási, A.-L.: Statistical mechanics of complex networks. Rev. Mod. Phys. **74**(1), 47 (2002)
2. Bezdek, J.C.: Pattern Recognition with Fuzzy Objective Function Algorithms. Kluwer Academic Publishers, Norwell (1981)
3. Blondel, V.D., Guillaume, J.-L., Lambiotte, R., Lefebvre, E.: Fast unfolding of communities in large networks. J. Stat. Mech. Theor. Exp. **2008**(10), P10008 (2008)
4. Brandes, U.: A faster algorithm for betweenness centrality. J. Math. Sociol. **25**(2), 163–177 (2001)
5. Collins, L.M., Dent, C.W.: Omega: a general formulation of the rand index of cluster recovery suitable for non-disjoint solutions. Multivar. Behav. Res. **23**(2), 231–242 (1988)
6. Donetti, L., Munoz, M.A.: Detecting network communities: a new systematic and efficient algorithm. J. Stat. Mech. Theor. Exp. **2004**(10), P10012 (2004)
7. Fortunato, S.: Community detection in graphs. Phys. Rep. **486**(3), 75–174 (2010)
8. Girvan, M., Newman, M.E.: Community structure in social and biological networks. Proc. Natl. Acad. Sci. **99**(12), 7821–7826 (2002)
9. Gregory, S.: An algorithm to find overlapping community structure in networks. In: Kok, J.N., Koronacki, J., Lopez de Mantaras, R., Matwin, S., Mladenič, D., Skowron, A. (eds.) PKDD 2007. LNCS (LNAI), vol. 4702, pp. 91–102. Springer, Heidelberg (2007)
10. Hubert, L., Arabie, P.: Comparing partitions. J. Classif. **2**, 193–218 (1985)

11. Jonsson, P.F., Cavanna, T., Zicha, D., Bates, P.A.: Cluster analysis of networks generated through homology: automatic identification of important protein communities involved in cancer metastasis. BMC Bioinform. **7**(1), 1 (2006)
12. Krishnapuram, R., Keller, J.M.: The possibilistic c-means algorithm: insights and recommendations. IEEE Trans. Fuzzy Sys. **4**(3), 385–393 (1996)
13. Mahmoud, H., Masulli, F., Rovetta, S., Russo, G.: Community detection in protein-protein interaction networks using spectral and graph approaches. In: Formenti, E., Tagliaferri, R., Wit, E. (eds.) CIBB 2013. LNCS, vol. 8452, pp. 62–75. Springer, Heidelberg (2014)
14. Newman, M.E.: Detecting community structure in networks. Eur. Phys. J. B-Condens. Matter Complex Sys. **38**(2), 321–330 (2004)
15. Newman, M.E., Girvan, M.: Finding and evaluating community structure in networks. Phys. Rev. E **69**(2), 026113 (2004)
16. Nepusz, T., Petróczi, A., Négyessy, L., Bazsó, F.: Fuzzy communities and the concept of bridgeness in complex networks. Phys. Rev. E **77**(1), 016107 (2008)
17. Newman, M.E.: Modularity and community structure in networks. Proce. Natl. Acad. Sci. **103**(23), 8577–8582 (2006)
18. Ng, A.Y., Jordan, M.I., Weiss, Y., et al.: On spectral clustering: analysis and an algorithm. Adv. Neural Inf. Proc. Syst. **2**, 849–856 (2002)
19. Shi, J., Malik, J.: Normalized cuts and image segmentation. IEEE Trans. Pattern Anal. Mach. Intell. **22**(8), 888–905 (2000)
20. Watts, D.J., Strogatz, S.H.: Collective dynamics of "small-world" networks. Nature **393**(6684), 440–442 (1998)
21. Xie, J., Kelley, S., Szymanski, B.K.: Overlapping community detection in networks: the state-of-the-art and comparative study. ACM Comput. Surv. **45**(4), 43 (2013)
22. Zhang, S., Wang, R.-S., Zhang, X.-S.: Identification of overlapping community structure in complex networks using fuzzy c-means clustering. Phys. A Stat. Mech. Appl. **374**(1), 483–490 (2007)

A Robust Evolutionary Optimisation Approach for Parameterising a Neural Mass Model

Elham Zareian$^{(\boxtimes)}$, Jun Chen, and Basabdatta Sen Bhattacharya

School of Engineering, University of Lincoln, Lincoln, UK
ezareian@lincoln.ac.uk

Abstract. In this paper, a robust optimisation approach is introduced for parameterising a thalamic neural mass model that simulates brain oscillations such as observed in electroencephalogram and local field potentials. In a previous work, the model was informed by physiological attributes of the Lateral Geniculate Nucleus in mammals and rodents; the synaptic connectivity parameters in the model were set manually by trial and error to oscillate within the alpha band (8–13 Hz). However, such manual techniques constrain modelling approaches involving a larger parameter space, for example towards exploring alternative parameter sets that may underlie similar brain states under different environmental conditions and owing to inter-individual differences. In this work, we implement a robust optimisation technique that is based on single-objective Genetic Algorithms, and incorporate newly devised objective and penalty functions for tackling the stochastic nature of the model input. Furthermore, a clustering algorithm is employed to identify robust and distinct parameter regions that will mimic spontaneous changes in thalamic circuit parameters under similar brain states due to environmental and inter-individual differences. The results from our study suggest that multiple robust and distinct parameter regions indeed exist, and the model shows consistent dominant frequency of oscillation within the alpha band corresponding to all of these identified parameter sets.

Keywords: Neural mass models · Parameterisation · Robust optimization · Clustering

1 Introduction

Neural mass computational models of the thalamocortical brain circuitry are often used in current times to mimic the meso-scale neuronal population behaviour such as observed in electroencephalogram (EEG) and local field potentials (LFP) [1, 2]. The approach is based on physiological evidence of the fundamental role of feed-forward and – back connections between the thalamus and the cortex in generating and sustaining brain oscillations, also referred to as 'brain rhythms'. However, the main constraint in current times is the huge parameter space of these models; most of the model-based studies tune parameters by trial-and-error method [3, 4], that produce a huge computational constraint in terms of time and efficiency. At the same time,

© Springer International Publishing Switzerland 2016
A.E.P. Villa et al. (Eds.): ICANN 2016, Part II, LNCS 9887, pp. 225–234, 2016.
DOI: 10.1007/978-3-319-44781-0_27

biological plausibility of the parameter space is desirable to correlate model-based findings with physiological attributes, thus adding to model validation [5] as well as to the translational value of the research.

The inherent nature of thalamocortical oscillations is highly non-linear and stochastic. Thus, it will not be too far removed to hypothesise that the neuronal and synaptic parameters and attributes are in a constant state of change that may be major in the case of brain state changes such as from wakefulness to sleep; while local fluctuations within an 'acceptable upper and lower bounds' may underlie similar brain states under different environmental conditions. In fact, it may be hypothesised that minor variations in parameter values corresponding to similar brain states may underlie the well-known inter-individual differences observed in EEG. Towards this, our aim in this work is to use a biologically inspired optimisation algorithm for parameterising a neural mass model so that it oscillates with a dominant frequency within the EEG alpha band (8–13 Hz).

Alpha rhythms are a prominent feature of the EEG occipital scalp electrode (the seat of the visual cortex) when a subject is in a relaxed but awake state with eyes closed. Furthermore, these oscillations are believed to be crucial for both conditions of visual attention and perception as well as for diminished cognition [6]. More importantly, alpha band alterations often serve as EEG biomarkers in several disease conditions; for example longitudinal EEG studies show a shift of peak frequency within the alpha band (commonly known as 'slowing') as a definitive marker of Alzheimer's disease (AD) [3]. For the research presented here, we study the neural mass computational model of the thalamo-cortico-thalamic (TCT) circuitry in [3, 4], originally used to simulate alpha rhythm slowing in AD. The visual pathway is by far the most widely studied thalamocortical pathway in experimental research [7]. Thus, the parameterisation of the thalamic module in the TCT model has been based on physiological data on the synaptic structure and connectivities in the Lateral Geniculate Nucleus (LGN) of mammalian and rodent brains [8]. It may be noted that most computational models of the thalamocortical circuitry ignore the feedforward inhibition to the thalamocortical relay cells from the thalamic interneurons. This in spite the interneurons of the LGN receiving around 47 % of their inputs from the retinal spiking neurons [3]. Furthermore, research suggest that the interneurons play a dominant role in efficient information transmission from the retina to the cortex [9]. To the best of our knowledge, the thalamic module in [4] looks into integrating thalamic inhibitory interneurons for the first time in neural mass models of the thalamocortical circuitry. For brevity in this work, we ignore the cortical module of the TCT model and focus on optimising the parameter space of the thalamic module in the model. Hereafter in this work, we refer to the de-corticated thalamic module as the 'thalamic model'.

Several optimisation approaches has been adopted for parameterising neural mass models [11–15], among which Genetic Algorithms (GAs) represent a promising technique for parameterising neural mass models [13–15]. Compared to the manual fitting or least squares mean method [11], and methods based on Kalman filters [12], GAs offer the capability to capture different features of the observed EEG recordings in both frequency and time domains [13]. Owing to GAs' flexible framework and population-based search strategy, multi-objective GAs has been adopted to simultaneously capture different fitting requirements [15] rather than aggregating various features into a single objective [14].

The parameterisation approach proposed in this work is based on single-objective GAs [16] incorporating more recent concepts in robust optimisation [17, 18], and a clustering algorithm [19]. The novelty of this paper lies in a set of newly devised objective and penalty functions in order to tackle the stochastic nature of the extrinsic inputs. The clustering algorithm is used to identify several potential regions that are responsible for generating alpha rhythms. This systematic approach facilitates a more rigorous search of the wider parameter space under conditions of uncertainties introduced by stochastic extrinsic model inputs, as well as by minor variations in parameter values (that simulate environmental and inter-individual differences in the model); which cannot otherwise be explored in a trial-and-error or standard optimisation approach.

In Sect. 2, we present an overview of the thalamic neural mass model and the proposed robust optimisation algorithm that is used for the model parameter search. Results are presented in Sect. 3. We conclude with a brief discussion in Sect. 4.

2 Materials and Methods

2.1 The Thalamicl Neural Mass Model

The thalamic model is defined in (1) – (5), and consists of three cell populations: Thalamocortical Relay cells (TCR), Interneurons (IN) and Thalamic Reticular Nucleus (TRN).

$$\textbf{TRN} : \ddot{y}_1 = a_1 H_e S\left(C_{tre}y_r + C_{tpe}y_4 - C_{tii}y_2 - C_{tmi}y_3\right) - 2a_1\dot{y}_1 - a_1^2 y_1 \tag{1}$$

$$\textbf{IN} : \ddot{y}_2 = b_1 H_i S\left(C_{ire}y_r + C_{ipe}y_4 - C_{isi}y_2\right) - 2b_1\dot{y}_2 - b_1^2 y_2 \tag{2}$$

$$\textbf{TRN} : \ddot{y}_3 = b_1 H_i S\left(C_{nte}y_1 + C_{npe}y_4 - C_{nsi}y_3\right) - 2b_1\dot{y}_3 - b_1^2 y_3 \tag{3}$$

$$\textbf{Retinal} : \ddot{y}_r = a_1 H_e P_1(t) - 2a_1\dot{y}_r - a_1^2 y_r \tag{4}$$

$$\textbf{Sigmoid Function} : S(w) = \frac{2e_0}{1 + e^{v(s_0 - w)}} \tag{5}$$

$H_{e/i}$ is the strength of the excitatory (e) or inhibitory (i) post-synaptic-potential (PSP); a_1 (b_1) is the inverse of the time constant of the excitatory (inhibitory) PSP; $P_1(t)$ is simulated by a Gaussian white noise and represents the background firing activity of the retinal ganglion cells in the condition of eyes-closed, i.e. no sensory input; and $S(w)$ is a sigmoid function, where e_0 is the maximum firing rate of a neuronal population, s_0 is the resting membrane potential and v is the sigmoid steepness parameter; C_{xyz} are synaptic connectivity parameters with x representing the afferent population, y representing the efferent population and z representing either an excitatory or inhibitory synapse, and are defined in Table 1. (The reader may please refer to [10] for the other parameter values used in the Equations).

Table 1. Basal values for the synaptic connectivity parameters used in (1)–(3). The Thalamo-Cortical connectivity parameter is a constant and is sourced from [8] as in prior [3, 4].

Module	Afferent (to)	Efferent (from)	Connectivity parameter	Value
	TCR	Retinal	C_{tre}	7.1
		IN	C_{tii}	15.45
		TRN	C_{tni}	15.45
Thalamic	IN	Retina	C_{ire}	47.4
		IN	C_{isi}	23.6
	TRN	TCR	C_{nte}	35
		TRN	C_{nsi}	15

2.2   Simulation and Signal Processing Methods

Model simulation is implemented using the 4th order Runge-Kutta ODE solver within the Simulink® environment in Matlab®. The total simulation time is 30 s at a sampling rate of 250 Hz. Each output vector thus obtained is bandpass filtered with a Butterworth filter of order 10 with a lower and upper cut-off frequencies of 3 and 50 Hz respectively. The power spectral density analysis (PSDA) defined in (6) is performed in Matlab® using a Welch periodogram, with a Hamming window of segment length consisting of 125 data points and overlap of 50 %. For computational purpose, the output of the thalamic module generated in Simulink® (simmodel) is passed through the PSDA (see (6)). The outputs of the PSDA are two vectors: (a) the power density p, and (b) its corresponding frequencies frq. The relative power RP is the normalised value of p with respect to the mean power and is computed using (7).

$$(p, frq) = PSDA(simmodel(C_{xyz})) \quad (6)$$

$$RP = p./mean(p) \quad (7)$$

2.3   Problem Description

Our objective in this work is to perform a rigorous search for the suitable values of C_{xyz} such that the model output dominant frequency lies within the alpha band (8 – 13 Hz). We expect that such an approach will provide us with a set of basal values for the connectivity parameter set C_{xyz} in the model. Towards this, we apply a standard search strategy using a single-objective GA.

In this case, C_{xyz} are encoded as real values. The search space of C_{xyz} is created using ± 30 % across the basal values. The only exception is made for C_{tre}, which is varied ± 15 % due to its relatively smaller value. In order to have the overall power content within the alpha band, the standard GA searches for the maximum power $|mx|$ such that its corresponding frequency frq_{mx} lies within the alpha band. $|mx|$ and frq_{mx} are computed using (8). As the standard GA minimises the objective function, a minus sign is included in (8) for maximising $|mx|$.

$$(mx, frq_{mx}) = (-\max(RP)) \tag{8}$$

The objective function *FP1* defined in (9) penalises the situation when $|mx|$ is outside of the alpha band.

$$FP1 = \begin{cases} mx & \text{if } 8 \leq frq_{mx} \leq 13 \\ \frac{mx}{1.5 + |8 - frq_{mx}|} & \text{if } frq_{mx} < 8 \\ \frac{mx}{1.5 + |13 - frq_{mx}|} & \text{if } frq_{mx} > 13 \end{cases} \tag{9}$$

As shown in Fig. 1, the search process stagnates as variations in the extrinsic input is changing the objective landscape of *FP1,* leading to an entirely new search process for every generation of the GA. Thus, we observe that the standard optimisation algorithm fails, which may be attributed to the stochastic nature of the extrinsic input to the model.

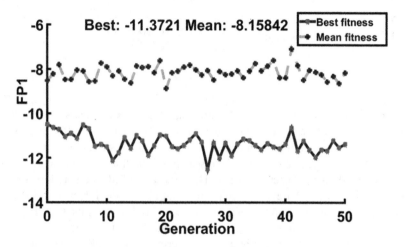

Fig. 1. The evolutionary curve of the GA using *FP1.*

In light of this and drawn upon more recent concepts in robust optimisation, an improved robust parameterising approach is proposed in Sect. 2.4 to address the stochastic issue due to the extrinsic input, and to identify reliable regions to account for small variation in C_{xyz} (e.g. due to environmental/inter-individual differences).

2.4   A Robust Evolutionary Optimisation Approach for Parameterising C_{xyz}

Here, 'robustness' is defined as the likelihood of $|mx|$ within the alpha band given a certain set of C_{xyz}. To enhance the robustness of the chosen C_{xyz}, two revised objective functions based on (9) are introduced, followed by a clustering algorithm and finally the overall parameterising framework.

Revised Objective Functions Considering External Uncertainty. *FP2* is defined in (10) as the averaged power spectra peak calculated over n randomly generated extrinsic inputs to take into account the stochastic nature of the extrinsic inputs. Here, $n = 35$ and is an empirical number derived from the experiment.

$$FP2 = \sum_{i=1}^{n} FP1_i/n \qquad (10)$$

Compared with (9) which maximises the peak with respect to only one fixed Gaussian white noise, the effect of (10) is to maximise the robustness indirectly. To directly maximise robustness, a counter which calculates how many times $|mx|$ is located outside of the alpha band is defined in (11). *FP3* is further developed in (12) to take into account robustness and *FP2* so that the constraint devised as the penalty function in (9) is also incorporated.

$$cr = \sum_{i=1}^{n} counter(i) \qquad (11)$$

$$counter(i) = \begin{cases} 0 & if\ 8 \leq frq_{mx}(i) \leq 13 \\ 1 & otherwise \end{cases}$$

$$FP3 = cr + 1/|FP2| \qquad (12)$$

Clustering and Robust Regions Considering Minor Variations in Parameter Values. As discussed in Sect. 1, instead of a fixed set of C_{xyz}, it often makes more sense to have robust regions which can accommodate small variations in C_{xyz}. To this aim, solutions from each generation of the search will be filtered through a predefined threshold based on their objective values. The collection of filtered solutions represent the solution set to C_{xyz}. An evolutionary clustering algorithm-G3Kmeans [19] is then applied to group these solutions. G3Kmeans is the hybridisation of the GA [19] and the K-means algorithm, resulting in a less sensitive clustering to the initial settings. To identify the number of clusters, subtractive clustering in Matlab® is first applied with the cluster radii set to the default value of 0.5.

The obtained clusters after G3Kmeans provide the upper and lower bounds for each region. To further investigate whether these regions are robust for all possible C_{xyz} within them, m random C_{xyz} within the identified bounds are sampled. The robustness RG of each region is then computed using (13), where, cr is defined in (11).

$$RG = \frac{\sum_{j=1}^{m} cr_j}{m} \qquad (13)$$

The Overall Robust Parameterising Framework. The overall robust parameterising framework is outlined in Fig. 2. In Line 1, C_{xyz} are encoded as real values. In Line 3, the GA calls one of the objective functions defined in (10) and (12). The collected c_{xyz} solutions from the GA will then be passed to the clustering algorithms (Lines 6–8). RG will then be calculated for each of these regions to evaluate their robustness (Lines 9–10).

1:	Set the decision variables (C_{xyz}) in the GA
2:	**For** *gen* = 1 **to** *gen_max* **do**:
3:	**GA calls** the objective function
4:	**Save** C_{xyz}
5:	**End**
6:	**Collect** all the good C_{xyz} with a threshold
7:	**Subclust** to give the number of candidate regions
8:	**G3Kmeans** to obtain the potential robust regions
9:	**Randomly generate** other C_{xyz} within the robust regions
10:	**Investigate robustness** of the identified regions

Fig. 2. The overall robust parameterising framework.

3 Results

3.1 Performances of the Robust Optimisation Approach

The experiments for the proposed robust optimisation approach are implemented using the GA toolbox in MATLAB®. To derive statistically reliable results, the experiments were carried out 10 times respectively for *FP2* and *FP3*, with 25 generations and the population size of 10. Other parameters are set as default. The evolutionary curves of the robust optimisation approach using *FP2* and *FP3* are illustrated in Fig. 3 (a) and (b) respectively. A significant improvement and better convergence in terms of the mean fitness were achieved compared to the one using *FP1*. Furthermore, Fig. 3 (b) shows that *FP3* leads to better convergence than *FP2* due to the direct optimisation of the robustness. Therefore, the results reported in the following text are based on *FP3*. It is worth noting that the negative signs in Figs. 1 and 3 (a) are due to the reason mentioned in Sect. 2.3.

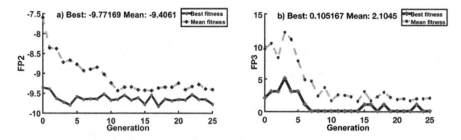

Fig. 3. The evolutionary curves of the GA using (a) *FP2* and (b) *FP3*.

3.2 The Identified Regions Using Clustering

Following Line 6 in Fig. 2, 260 solutions (C_{xyz}) obtained from the robust optimisation approach are collected. Subtractive clustering indicates there are 3 clusters representing three potential regions (R1–R3). Figure 4 (a) shows these regions and their centres after G3Kmeans clustering using the dimensions C_{nsi}, C_{tre} and C_{nte}.

3.3   Robustness of the Identified Regions

To further investigate robustness of the regions identified in Sect. 3.2, their corresponding RG is calculated using (13) following Lines 9–10 in Fig. 2, with $m = 50$. For comparison purpose, $m = 40$ are used for the basal values. Table 2 summarises the comparison results based on the basal values (BV) and the identified regions using $FP3$. Results indicate that the identified regions are robust not only at solutions obtained using $FP3$ (e.g. R1 via $FP3$), but also at randomly generated solutions within these regions (e.g. Random R1). Results also reveal that multiple robust regions may exist, which are more robust than the region around the basal values.

Table 2. Comparison of robustness of the synaptic connectivity parameter sets C_{xyz}.

Methods	Synaptic Connectivity Parameters [$C_{tre}, C_{isi}, C_{tre}, C_{tii}, C_{tni}, C_{nte}, C_{nsi}$]		Robustness (Mean RG)
Basal values (BV)	[47.4,23.6,7.1,15.45,15.45,35,15]		13.00
C_{xyz} out of the identified R	[53,28.15,9,17.8,20,45,18]		14.00
	Lower Band	**Upper Band**	
R around BV	[42.66,21.24,7.09,13.90,13.90,31.5,13.5]	[42.66,21.24,7.09,13.90,13.90,31.5,13.5]	9.50
R1 via $FP3$	[33.18,16.52,6.04,10.87,10.87,24.5,10.5]	[35.18,25.66,7.53,15.12,19.83,40.2,13.13]	0.57
R2 via $FP3$	[33.18,16.52,6.31,10.87,10.87.24.5,11]	[40.32,27.24,8.04,16.46,19.83,36.73,19.13]	0.32
R3 via $FP3$	[33.18,16.52,7.53,10.87,10.87,40.2,10.5]	[33.68,17.52,8.09,12.87,19.44,44.75,14.35]	0.24
Random R1	[33.18,16.52,6.04,10.87,10.87,24.5,10.5]	[35.18,25.66,7.53,15.12,19.83,40.20,13.13]	4 .26
Random R2	[33.18, 16.52,6.31,10.87,10.87.24.5,11]	[40.32,27.24,8.04,16.46,19.83,36.73,19.13]	6.08
Random R3	[33.18,16.52,7.53,10.87,10.87,40.2,10.5]	[33.68,17.52,8.09,12.87,19.44,44.75,14.35]	2.10

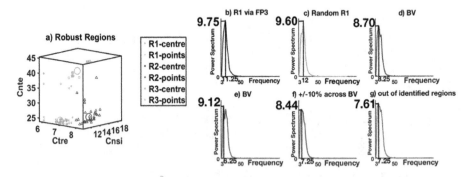

Fig. 4. (a) Three potential regions identified using the revised objective function $FP3$; (b)-(g) The power spectrum corresponding to different C_{xyz} within different regions

In Fig. 4 (b)-(g), C_{xyz} are randomly generated from R1 via $FP3$, Random R1, BV, $\pm 10\%$ across BV and those outside of any identified regions, and their corresponding power spectrum are plotted. Figure 4 (b)-(c) show that the aim of maximising the likelihood of |mx| towards the alpha band is achieved. Indeed, the resulted dominant frequency is consistently within the upper-alpha band which is in line with the EEG of a young healthy adult. This conclusion holds true for R2 and R3 although they are not included here for brevity. Figure 4 (d)-(e) and (g) show that the maximum power content is frequently (up to 40 %) below the alpha band. For C_{xyz} outside of any identified regions, the chance of below the alpha band (as shown in Fig. 4 (f)) is up to 30 %.

4 Conclusion

In this paper, a robust parameterising approach is proposed to obtain robust sets of synaptic connectivity parameters of a thalamic neural mass model. The approach combines a single-objective GA and a clustering algorithm with a set of newly devised objective and penalty functions. The proposed method is able to address issues due to extrinsic uncertainty, as well as minor variations in parameters due to environmental or inter-individual differences. Preliminary results suggested that multiple robust regions exist, which are distinct from the suggested basal values.

This preliminary work opens several directions worth further investigation: (a) investigation of the biological meanings associated with the identified robust regions through fitting the thalamic model to the EEG recordings; (b) currently, the identified robust regions are for alpha rhythms; the same robust optimisation procedure can be carried out for the adjacent rhythms, such as beta rhythms to investigate if there is any transitional behaviour in the synaptic connectivity parameters; and (c) extending the work to the TCT model [3, 4] and include more parameters, such as the variance of the extrinsic input.

References

1. Liljenström, H.: Mesoscopic brain dynamics. Scholarpedia. **7**, 4601 (2012)
2. Woldman, W., Terry, J.R.: Multilevel computational modelling in epilepsy: classical studies and recent advances. In: Bhattacharya, B.S., Chowdhury, F.N. (eds.) Validating Neuro-Computational Models of Neurological and Psychiatric Disorders. Springer Series in Computational Neuroscience, pp. 161–188. Springer, Switzerland (2015)
3. Coyle, D., Bhattacharya, B.S., Zou, X., Wong-Lin, K., Abuhassan, K., Maguire, L.: Neural Circuit Models and Neuropathological Oscillations. In: Kasbov, N.K. (ed.) Springer Handbook of Bio-/Neuroinformatics, pp. 673–702. Springer, Heidelberg (2014)
4. Bhattacharya, B.S., et al.: A thalamo-cortico-thalamic neural mass model to study alpha rhythms in Alzheimer's disease. Neural Network **24**, 631–645 (2011)
5. Moran, R.: Introduction. In: Bhattacharya, B.S., Chowdhury, F.N. (eds.) Validating Neuro-Computational Models of Neurological and Psychiatric Disorders. Springer Series in Computational Neuroscience, pp. 1–14. Springer, Heidelberg (2015)
6. Lorincz, M.L., et al.: Temporal framing of thalamic relay-mode firing by phasic inhibition during the alpha rhythm. Neuron **63**(5), 683–696 (2009)
7. Sherman, S.: Thalamus. Scholarpedia **1**, 1583 (2006)
8. Van Horn, S.C., et al.: Relative distribution of synapses in the A-laminae of the lateral geniculate nucleus of the cat. J. Comp. Neurol. **416**, 509–520 (2000)

9. Wang, X., Sommer, F.T., Hirsch, J.A.: Inhibitory circuits for visual processing in thalamus. Curr. Opin. Neurobiol. **21**, 726–733 (2011)
10. Lopes da Silva, F.H., et al.: Model of brain rhythmic activity. Kybernetik **15**, 27–37 (1974)
11. Zavaglia, M., et al.: The effect of connectivity on EEG rhythms, power spectral density and coherence among coupled neural populations: analysis with a neural mass model. IEEE Trans. Biomed. Eng. **55**, 69–77 (2008)
12. Liu, X., Gao, Q.: Parameter estimation and control for a neural mass model based on the unscented Kalman filter. Phys. Rev. E. Stat. Nonlin. Soft Matter Phys. **88**, 042905 (2013)
13. Cona, F., et al.: Changes in EEG power spectral density and cortical connectivity in healthy and tetraplegic patients during a motor imagery task. Comput. Intell. Neurosci. **2009**, 3 (2009)
14. Nevado-Holgado, A.J., et al.: Characterising the dynamics of EEG waveforms as the path through parameter space of a neural mass model: application to epilepsy seizure evolution. Neuroimage **59**, 2374–2392 (2012)
15. Nevado-Holgado, A.J., et al.: Effective connectivity of the subthalamic nucleus-globus pallidus network during Parkinsonian oscillations. J. Physiol. **592**, 1429–1455 (2014)
16. Goldberg, D.E.: Genetic Algorithms in Search, Optimization, and Machine Learning. Addison-Wesley, Boston (1989)
17. Salomon, S., et al.: Active robust optimization: enhancing robustness to uncertain environments. IEEE Trans. Cybern. **44**, 2221–2231 (2014)
18. Paenke, I., Branke, J.: Efficient search for robust solutions by means of evolutionary algorithms and fitness approximation. IEEE Trans. Evol. Comput. **10**, 405–420 (2006)
19. Chen, J., et al.: Intelligent data compression, diagnostics and prognostics using an evolutionary-based clustering algorithm for industrial machines (2014)

Kernel Depth Measures for Functional Data with Application to Outlier Detection

Nicolás Hernández$^{(\boxtimes)}$ and Alberto Muñoz$^{(\boxtimes)}$

Department of Statistics, University Carlos III, Madrid, Spain
{nicolas.hernandez,alberto.munoz}@uc3m.es

Abstract. In the last years the concept of data depth has been increasingly used in Statistics as a center-outward ordering of sample points in multivariate data sets. Data depth has been recently extended to functional data. In this paper we propose a new intrinsic functional data depth based on the representation of functional data on Reproducing Kernel Hilbert Spaces, and test its performance against a number of well known alternatives in the problem of functional outlier detection.

Keywords: Kernel depth · Functional data analysis · Reproducing Kernel Hilbert Spaces · Outlier detection

1 Introduction and Review of Depth Measures for Functional Data

The concept of data depth in the multivariate framework constitutes an extension of the univariate concept of order and introduces a center-outward ordering of a multivariate data set. According to [6] a depth function defines a measure of the degree of 'centrality' or 'outlyingness' of a point in a multivariate data set given an underlying distribution. In [2,4,5,7] the authors define functional data depths measures from the original plain representation $\{(\mathbf{x}_i, y_i)\}$ of the data points (i.e. curves):

Consider a data set $\mathbf{X} = \{x_1, \ldots, x_n\} \subset \mathbb{R}^d$. When $d = 1$ the degree of centrality of a given point x_i with respect to a probability distribution can be defined by ranking all the values from the smallest to the largest and compute the Euclidean distance to the median. In the multivariate case $(d \geq 2)$, we first define the deepest (central) point of the distribution/data set and the degree of centrality is given by ranking the distances of the data points to the deepest point (depth functions). Thus, depth measures compute how deep is a point with respect to a distribution/data set [6,13].

Depth can be extended to functional data in several ways. For a sample of n curves, the modified band depth (MBD) method [7] considers 'bands' defined for combinations of $2, 3, \ldots$ up to n curves, and accounts for the proportion of 'x' axis coordinate that a curve c_l is contained in the band (depth index). Hence, the depth of c_l is defined as the average of the depth index for all the possible bands.

© Springer International Publishing Switzerland 2016
A.E.P. Villa et al. (Eds.): ICANN 2016, Part II, LNCS 9887, pp. 235–242, 2016.
DOI: 10.1007/978-3-319-44781-0_28

The deepest curve is the curve with the maximum depth. Figure 1 illustrates the idea for a band defined by three curves.

The Fraiman and Muniz depth (FMD) measures the conditional quantile on all points. In particular when working with curves it measures how long a curve remains in the middle of a sample of curves (in the distributional sense described in [5]). The random Tukey depth (RTD) [4], is a random approximation of the Tukey depth or halfspace depth. It considers all possible one-dimensional projections of the curves using the halfspace depth. The functional spatial depth (FSD) [2] is the extension of the spatial depth from $\mathbb{R}^d$ into infinite-dimensional spaces, and computes the spatial median based on the notion of spatial quantile.

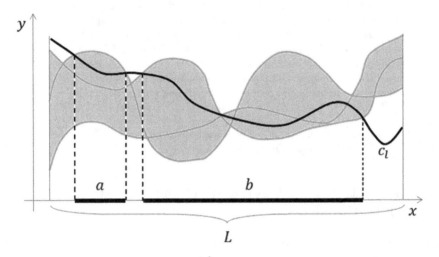

Fig. 1. Depth index for $c_l = \dfrac{a+b}{L}$ and a band defined by three curves.

Nevertheless, the core idea of functional data analysis (FDA) is to consider functional data as points in a function space, as a previous step to the projection of such functions onto a finite dimensional Euclidean space. This process necessarily involves obtaining new representations for functional data, which can be achieved by using basis of functions [11] or kernel methods, as we will describe in Sect. 2.

In this paper we want to test if the performance of statistical functional measures (such as depth) is preserved or enhanced when we work with nontrivial functional representations of functional data (as opposed to the measures defined on the plain representation of data). Thus we propose a kernel depth measure that will use the FDA coordinates instead of the plain curve representations. Because depth induces a center-outward ordering of multivariate data sets/curves, a natural problem to test the utility of different depth definitions is outlier detection.

The rest of the paper is organized as follows: We present a kernel depth measure for functional data in Sect. 2. In Sect. 3 we show the performance of the proposed depth measure applied to the outlier detection task considering three experiments. The conclusions and future research ideas are presented in Sect. 4.

2   K-depth Measures for Functional Data

We start from an available set of sample curves $\{\hat{c}_1, \ldots, \hat{c}_m\}$, where $\hat{c}_l \equiv \{(\mathbf{x}_{il}, \mathbf{y}_{il}) \in X \times Y\}_{i=1}^n$, where X is a compact subset of $\mathbb{R}^n$ and, in most cases, $Y = \mathbb{R}$. We can assume that the $\mathbf{x}_i's$ are common for all the curves, and that for each $\hat{c}_l$, exists a continuous function $c_l : X \longrightarrow Y$ such that $E[y_l|\mathbf{x}] = c_l(\mathbf{x})$ (with respect to a given probability measure).

These functions are the functional data curves and can be considered as points in some functional space. We will project these points onto some finite-dimensional function subspace, in our case, a Reproducing Kernel Hilbert Space (RKHS), H_K, generated by a Mercer kernel K. Consider the integral operator T_K defined by $T_K(f) = \int_X K(\cdot, s)f(s)ds$. T_K has a countable sequence of eigenvalues $\{\lambda_j\}$ and (orthonormal) eigenfunctions $\{\phi_j\}$ and K can be expressed as $K(x, y) = \sum_j \lambda_j \phi_j(x) \phi_j(y)$ where the convergence is absolute and uniform (Mercer theorem).

Given a function f in a function space containing H_K, it will be projected onto H_K using the operator T_K. By the Spectral Theorem, the projection $f^* = T_K(f) \in H_K$ takes the form $f^* = T_K(f) = \sum_j \lambda_j \langle f, \phi_j \rangle \phi_j$. To determine the $\langle f, \phi_j \rangle$ coefficients, we solve the Support Vector Machine (SVM) regularization problem:

$$\arg \min_{c \in H_K} \frac{1}{n} \sum_{i=1}^n L(y_i, c(\mathbf{x}_i)) + \gamma \|c\|_K^2,$$

where $\gamma > 0$, $\|c\|_K$ is the norm of the function c in H_K, $y_i = \hat{c}_i$ and $L(y_i, c(\mathbf{x}_i)) = (|c(\mathbf{x}_i) - y_i| - \varepsilon)_+, \varepsilon \geq 0$.

The Representer theorem (see [3]) states that the solution to this optimization problem is given by $c_l^*(x) = \sum_{i=1}^n \alpha_{il} K(\mathbf{x}_i, \mathbf{x}), \forall \mathbf{x} \in X$, where $\alpha_{il} \in \mathbb{R}$ are the Lagrange multipliers associated to the support vectors.

Let c_l be a curve, whose sample version is $\hat{c}_l \equiv \{(\mathbf{x}_{il}, y_{il}) \in X \times Y\}_{i=1}^n$. Consider the functional representation for c_l given by $\lambda_l^* = (\lambda_{1l}^*, \ldots, \lambda_{dl}^*)$, where

$$\lambda_{jl}^* = \sum_{i=1}^n \hat{\lambda}_j \alpha_{il} \hat{\phi}_{ji}, \tag{1}$$

α_{il} are given by the solution of the SVM (see [9]), $\hat{\lambda}_j$ is the eigenvalue corresponding to the eigenvector $\hat{\phi}_j$ of the matrix $K_S = (K(\mathbf{x}_i, \mathbf{x}_j))_{i,j}$, and $d = \min(n, r(K_S))$.

Now $f^* = T_K(f) = \sum_j \lambda_j \langle f, \phi_j \rangle \phi_j = \sum_j \lambda_j^* \phi_j \simeq \sum_j \left(\hat{\lambda}_j \sum_{i=1}^n \alpha_i \hat{\phi}_{ji} \right) \phi_j$ and $\sum_{i=1}^n \alpha_i \hat{\phi}_{ji} \simeq \langle f, \phi_j \rangle$, (see [10] for details).

Definition 1. K-deepest point. *Given a set of sample functional data* $\{\hat{c}_1, \ldots, \hat{c}_m\}$ *and the corresponding* H_K-*representations* $\lambda_l^* \equiv (\lambda_{1l}^*, \ldots, \lambda_{dl}^*)$, *we* *define the K-deepest functional data point as the multivariate median of the d-dimensional functional data points, computed as the vector of the coordinate-wise medians in $\mathbb{R}^d$: $\mathbf{P}^* = (p_1^*, \ldots, p_d^*)$, where $p_i^* = median\{\lambda_{il}^*\}$.*

Definition 2. Kernel Depth. *Given the d-dimensional K-deepest point $\mathbf{P}^*$, the Kernel depth from a functional data point $\hat{c}_l$ to $\mathbf{P}^*$ is defined as the Mahalanobis distance between the H_K-representation of $\hat{c}_l$ and $\mathbf{P}^*$:*

$$D_K(\hat{c}_l, \mathbf{P}^*) = 1/[(\lambda_l^* - \mathbf{P}^*)^T \Sigma_{\lambda^*}^{-1} (\lambda_l^* - \mathbf{P}^*)]^{-1/2} \tag{2}$$

where $\Sigma_{\lambda^*}^{-1}$ is the inverse of covariance matrix of the functional data set (computed from its H_K-representation).

3   Experimental Work

In this section we will test the performance of the proposed kernel depth on the task of functional outlier detection, for a set of simulated curves, and for two real functional data sets. Unlike the case of multivariate data, now we can also have shape outliers, that is, curves which are not far away from the bulk of data, but they present a different shape [8]. To empirically test the independence of the measure with respect to the kernel we choose three different and typical kernel functions, namely: (i) Gaussian kernel $K_G(x_i, x_j) = e^{-\sigma\|x_i - x_j\|^2}$; (ii) polynomial kernel $K_p(x_i, x_j) = (a\langle x_i, x_j \rangle + b)^d$; (iii) spline kernel $K_s(x_i, x_j) = \prod_{d=1}^{D} 1 + x_i x_j + x_i x_j min(x_i, x_j) - \frac{x_i + x_j}{2} min(x_i, x_j)^2 + \frac{x_i + x_j}{3} min(x_i, x_j)^3$. All the parameters, including the penalization coefficient γ of the SVM regularization problem (to obtain the H_K representations) were defined through cross-validation.

Artificial data set. We simulate 100 curves, 95 drawn from the same population given by the distribution of the coefficients a_i plus 5 curves with a different parametrization in the role of outlying curves. The shape of the two types of curves are different as can be appreciated in Fig. 2:

$$f_i(x_t) = a_i + 0.05t + sin(\pi x_t^2), \; i = 1, \ldots 95,$$

$$f_i^o(x_t) = b_i + 0.05t + cos(20\pi x_t), \; i = 96, \ldots 100, \; \text{(outlying curves)}$$

where $x_t = \dfrac{t}{500} \in [0, 1]$, $t = 1, \ldots, 500$, $a_i \sim N(\mu_a = 5, \sigma_a = 4)$, $b_i \sim N(\mu_b = 5, \sigma_b = 3)$.

The kernel parameters used are $\sigma = 500$ for the the Gaussian kernel and $a = 1$, $b = 1$, $d = 10$ for the polynomial kernel. The penalization coefficient of the SVM regularization problem is $\gamma = 10^{-7}$, and the trimmed mean for the depth measures (MBD, FMD, RTD, FSD) is $\alpha = 0.5$. The results are summarized in Table 1. The kernel depth is able to detect exactly the five outlying curves. The 'non kernel' techniques fail to capture any of the true outliers. Moreover in Fig. 3 are illustrated the two first projections of the curves onto a functional space. Throughout this representation the data can be perfectly discriminated (down-red points).

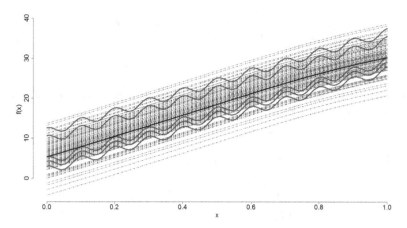

Fig. 2. Artificial data set. The five waved curves are the outliers, and the black line is the deepest curve.

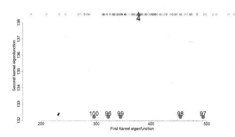

Fig. 3. RKHS projections. Main population (up-black dots), the outlying curves (down-red dots) and the deepest curve (up-blue triangle). (Color figure online)

Table 1. Number of outliers, false-positive and false-negative identifications.

Measure	True different outliers	False-positive	False-negative
MBD	0	5	5
FMD	0	5	5
RTD	0	5	5
FSD	0	5	5
K_G	5	0	0
K_p	5	0	0
K_s	5	0	0

3.1 Real Data Experiment

Berkeley Growth Study data. We consider the Berkeley Growth Study data, that contain the heights of 39 boys and 54 girls from age 1 to 18 and the ages at which they were collected, (see [11]). First we consider all the boys (main data) and contaminate them with 5 randomly selected girls (the 'outlying' curves). This procedure was repeated 100 times so we obtain 100 random samples contaminated with outliers. Next we consider the opposite case, taking the girls as the main data contaminate them with groups of 5 randomly selected boys as 'outlying' data.

The kernel parameters used are $\sigma = 70$ for the the Gaussian kernel and $a = 1$, $b = 1$, $d = 2$ for the polynomial kernel. The penalization coefficient of the SVM regularization problem is $\gamma = 10^{-6}$, and the trimmed mean for the

240   N. Hernández and A. Muñoz

depth measures (MBD, FMD, RTD, FSD) is $\alpha = 0.5$. The results are presented in Table 2. Again the kernel depth obtains the best results in detecting the outliers in both cases.

Table 2. Mean and standard deviation (in parentheses) of the proportion of correctly identified outliers, for n = 100.

Measures	K_G	K_s	K_p	MBD	FMD	RTD	FSD
Main data:	**0,262**	**0,262**	**0,654**	0,178	0,148	0,204	0,212
Boys	**(0,1698)**	**(0,1698)**	**(0,1553)**	(0,1630)	(0,1466)	(0,1582)	(0,1677)
Main data:	**0,308**	**0,308**	**0,514**	0,11	0,158	0,180	0,164
Girls	**(0,122)**	**(0,122)**	**(0,1456)**	(0,1077)	(0,1342)	(0,1645)	(0,1114)

Australia mortality rates. Here we consider age-specific mortality rates for Australian males for 1901–2003, in logarithmic scale, which is publicly available in the R package 'fds' [12]. In this experiment we do not know a priori if there is an outlying curve, so we define as outlier the curve that satisfies that $Pr(D_K < C) = 0.01$, where C is the inverse of the empirical distribution function of D_K evaluated at $x = 0.01$, $C = F_{D_K}^{-1}(x = 0.01)$.

In a previous work [1], the authors identified a 'shape' outlier, corresponding to the mortality rate of the year 1919. The aim of this experiment is to demonstrate that kernel depths are also able to detect this type of outliers. The kernel parameters used are $\sigma = 0.01$ for the the Gaussian kernel and $a = 1$, $b = 1$, $d = 2$ for the polynomial kernel. The penalization coefficient of the SVM regularization problem is $\gamma = 0.015$ (except for the case of polynomial kernel where the γ considered was 1).

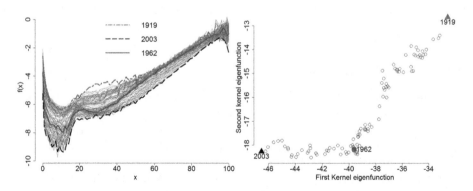

Fig. 4. Observed curves and outliers detected. K-depth outliers: year 1919 in red (dash-dotted line), year 2003 in black (dashed line) and the deepest curve year 1962 (left panel). RKHS projections and outliers detected year 1919 (red triangle), year 2003 (black triangle) and the deepest point year 1962 (right panel). (Color figure online)

The results presented in Fig. 4 show that the kernel depth is also able to identify shape outliers. The dash-dotted curve highlighted in red that correspond to the year 1919, is the shallowest curve. The dashed curve in black, that correspond to the year 2003, is the second most outlying curve. These outliers were identified using the three kernel functions $(K_G,\ K_s,\ K_p)$ described. The deepest curve in blue correspond to the year 1962. If we apply the competitor depth measures MBD, FMD, RTD and FSD we find that the outliers detected are the mortality rate for the year 2003 and 2002. Both curves can be considered as extreme observations, but that share the same pattern with the rest of the curves of the sample (excepting the year 1919).

4   Conclusions and Future Research

In this paper we present a new definition of deepest point for functional data that induces a center-outward ordering for functional data sets. We introduce kernel depths as Mahalanobis distances between the RKHS representations of functional data points and the deepest curve. These kernel depths perform better than the traditional depth functions for the task of functional outlier detection in a number of artificial and real functional data sets.

The experiments seem to indicate that kernel depth is independent of the kernel choice. Our next goal is to prove this assessment or to characterize families of Mercer kernels with this property.

'Traditional' depth measures are based on plain representations of the curves which implies that the deepest curve is not necessarily invariant to affine transformations. In an upcoming work we will investigate the robustness of kernel and non-kernel depths to data transformations.

Acknowledgments. This work was supported by project ECO2015-66593-P.

References

1. Arribas-Gil, A., Romo, J.: Shape outlier detection and visualization for functional data: the outliergram. Biostatistics **15**(4), 603–619 (2014)
2. Chakraborty, A., Chaudhuri, P.: On data depth in infinite dimensional spaces. Ann. Inst. Stat. Math. **66**(2), 303–324 (2014)
3. Cucker, F., Smale, S.: On the mathematical foundations of learning. Bull. Am. Math. Soc. **39**(1), 1–49 (2001)
4. Cuesta-Albertos, J.A., Nieto-Reyes, A.: The random Tukey depth. Comput. Stat. Data Anal. **52**(11), 4979–4988 (2008)
5. Fraiman, R., Muniz, G.: Trimmed means for functional data. Test **10**(2), 419–440 (2001)
6. Liu, R.Y., Parelius, J.M., Singh, K.: Multivariate analysis by data depth: descriptive statistics, graphics and inference, (with discussion and a rejoinder by Liu and Singh). Ann. Stat. **27**(3), 783–858 (1999)
7. López-Pintado, S., Romo, J.: On the concept of depth for functional data. J. Am. Stat. Assoc. **104**(486), 718–734 (2009)

8. Moguerza, J.M., Muñoz, A., Psarakis, S.: Monitoring nonlinear profiles using support vector machines. In: Rueda, L., Mery, D., Kittler, J. (eds.) CIARP 2007. LNCS, vol. 4756, pp. 574–583. Springer, Heidelberg (2007)
9. Moguerza, J.M., Muñoz, A.: Support vector machines with applications. Stat. Sci. **21**(3), 322–336 (2006)
10. Muñoz, A., González, J.: Representing functional data using support vector machines. Pattern Recogn. Lett. **31**(4), 511–516 (2010)
11. Ramsay, J.O., Silverman, B.W.: Functional Data Analysis. Wiley, New York (2006)
12. Shang, H.L., Hyndman, R.J.: FDS: functional data sets. R package version 1.7 (2013)
13. Zuo, Y., Serfling, R.: General notions of statistical depth function. Ann. Stat. **28**(2), 1–20 (2000)

Nesterov Acceleration for the SMO Algorithm

Alberto Torres-Barrán[(⊠)] and José R. Dorronsoro

Department of Computer Science and Instituto de Ingeniería del Conocimiento,
Universidad Autónoma de Madrid, 28049 Madrid, Spain
alberto.torres@uam.es

Abstract. We revise Nesterov's Accelerated Gradient (NAG) procedure for the SVM dual problem and propose a strictly monotone version of NAG that is capable of accelerating the second order version of the SMO algorithm. The higher computational cost of the resulting Nesterov Accelerated SMO (NA–SMO) is twice as high as that of SMO so the reduction in the number of iterations is not likely to translate in time savings for most problems. However, understanding NAG is presently an area of strong research and some of the resulting ideas may offer venues for even faster versions of NA–SMO.

Keywords: Nesterov Accelerated Gradient · SMO · SVM

1 Introduction

Big data and its need for simple optimization procedures have caused a renewed interest in ways to accelerate gradient descent (often the only viable method in big problems). In turn, this has led to a recent strong research effort to understand Nesterov's Accelerated gradient (NAG) descent, either from a theoretical point of view [1,5,12,14] or from an applied one [11,13]. If we want to minimize a smooth convex function $f(\alpha)$ over $\mathbb{R}^N$, in Nesterov's Accelerated Gradient (NAG) we generate a sequence α^t by a two step update at each iteration. First we compute an intermediate point x^t using a momentum–like update $x^t = \alpha^t + \mu_t(\alpha^{t-1} - \alpha^t)$ and then we arrive by gradient descent to the new $\alpha^{t+1} = x^t - \epsilon_t \nabla f(x^t)$. In theoretical work and when applied to a L smooth convex f (i.e., ∇f is L Lipschitz), we take $\epsilon_t = \frac{1}{L}$; when L is not known, ϵ_t can be thought as a learning rate [13]. There have been several proposals for the above μ_t, some as simple as $\mu_t = 1 - \frac{3}{t+2}$ [12] or more generally $\mu_t = 1 - \frac{1+a}{t+a}$ with $a \geq 2$ [6]. Here we will use Nesterov's own proposal [10], namely

$$\lambda_t = \frac{1 + \sqrt{1 + 4\lambda_{t-1}^2}}{2}, \quad \mu_t = \frac{\lambda_t - 1}{\lambda_{t+1}}.$$

NAG has been applied to improve the speed of plain gradient descent in various problems, such as sparse regression [4] or deep network training [13]. For a general, L–smooth f the convergence speed of gradient descent with a rate $1/L$ is

© Springer International Publishing Switzerland 2016
A.E.P. Villa et al. (Eds.): ICANN 2016, Part II, LNCS 9887, pp. 243–250, 2016.
DOI: 10.1007/978-3-319-44781-0_29

$O\left(\frac{1}{t}\right)$ and NAG improves it to $O\left(\frac{1}{t^2}\right)$. Some of the most recent work on NAG deals with quadratic functions [2,9] as a particularly simple proving ground. We shall consider it here for solving SVM's dual problem where we are given a sample $\{(x^p, y^p = \pm 1) : 1 \leq p \leq N\}$ and want to minimize $f(\alpha)$ defined as

$$f(\alpha) = \frac{1}{2}\sum_i \sum_j \alpha_i \alpha_j Q_{ij} - \sum_i \alpha_i p_i = \frac{1}{2}\alpha \cdot Q\alpha - \alpha \cdot p, \tag{1}$$

subject to $0 \leq \alpha_i \leq C, 1 \leq i \leq N$, $\sum_i \alpha_i y_i = 0$ and where $Q_{ij} = y^i y^j K(x^i, x^j)$ is the kernel matrix. Thus, we have a constrained problem with a quadratic objective function. If one uses the Gaussian kernel and there is no pattern x that appears in the sample with both $y = 1, -1$, the kernel matrix is positive definite [8], i.e., we have $\ell I \preceq Q \preceq L I$, $0 \leq \ell \leq L$, and the SMO algorithm (see Sect. 2), that performs a kind of approximated gradient descent, achieves a linear convergence rate, i.e., $f(\alpha^t) - f(\alpha^*) \leq C\lambda^t$ for some $\lambda < 1$ at iteration t.

For such a Q, $f(\alpha)$ is not only L smooth but also ℓ strongly convex, although both ℓ, L are unknown. Then, gradient descent with a fixed rate $1/L$ achieves an $O(\gamma^{2t})$ linear convergence, where $\gamma = \frac{\kappa-1}{\kappa+1}$ and $\kappa = L/\ell$ is the condition number of f [10], Theorem 2.1.14. In addition, using a modified λ_t sequence that includes κ in its definition, NAG achieves a $O(\Gamma^{2t})$ convergence rate, with $\Gamma = \frac{\sqrt{\kappa}-1}{\sqrt{\kappa}+1}$ ([10], Theorem 2.2.2). Since L and ℓ are usually not known, this NAG version cannot be used in practice. However, the previous results lead naturally to consider the potential effectiveness of NAG when applied to the SMO algorithm in SVM's dual problem, first as a testing ground and also perhaps as a faster SMO. Recall that SVM's dual problem is a constrained one and, also, that SMO is only an approximation to gradient descent that, nevertheless, achieves a linear convergence rate with a rather low cost of $3N$ floating point products per iteration.

With these considerations in mind, the goal of the present work is to explore how to define and apply a version of NAG suitable to the SMO algorithm and to check whether it reduces the number of iterations. The simplest approach would be the straight application of Nesterov's procedure, but this would result in an algorithm much worse than SMO, as NAG is not monotone whereas SMO ensures $f(\alpha^{t+1}) < f(\alpha^t)$ at each iteration. A solution for this is to use a **monotone** versions of NAG [3] where writing $\alpha' = x^t - \epsilon_t \nabla f(x^t)$, one checks whether $f(\alpha') < f(\alpha^t)$. If this is the case, α' becomes the new α^{t+1}, but when $f(\alpha') \geq f(\alpha^t)$, α^t is retained (i.e., we take $\alpha^{t+1} = \alpha^t$) and we try with a new x^{t+1} defined as $x^{t+1} = \rho_t x^t + (1 - \rho_t)\alpha^t$, where $\rho_t = \frac{\lambda_t}{\lambda_{t+1}}$. Observe that since $0 \leq \rho_t \leq 1$, x^{t+1} can be seen as a convex combination of x^t and α^t that seeks to reduce the overshooting influence of x^t. However, note that this doesn't guarantee that $f(\alpha') > f(\alpha^{t+1}) = f(\alpha^t)$ and we may end up with a possibly long sequence of α values with the same f value. Besides, this has the extra drawback of requiring the computation of the value $f(x^t)$ of the SVM dual function, with a cost of N products if done using gradient information. We will alleviate both drawbacks by taking advantage of the quadratic structure of f to directly compute the exact

ρ_t and x^{t+1} that minimize f and will call this approach the **monotone** Nesterov acceleration (NA) of SMO, or monotone NA–SMO.

A second way to try to squeeze at each iteration some extra gain in f could be to split this gain $f(\alpha^t) - f(\alpha^{t+1})$ as

$$f(\alpha^t) - f(\alpha^{t+1}) = f(\alpha^t) - f(x^t) + f(x^t) - f(\alpha^{t+1}) = \Delta_1^t + \Delta_2^t$$

and maximize each gain separatedly. This is what SMO does for Δ_2^t and, in principle, an optimal μ_t for Δ_1^t can be computed analytically. However, and as we will briefly discuss, this is very likely to result in small $\mu_t \simeq 0$ and $x^t \simeq \alpha^t$, i.e., to revert to standard SMO negating somehow the advantage of the momentum step in NAG and we will not consider it in the experiments. In other words, we would risk ending up with SMO's iterations but with the extra overhead of computing x^t. In summary, our main contributions are

– To present a basic set up for the application of NAG to the SMO algorithm.
– To propose a strictly monotone version of NAG for SMO.
– To numerically study both approaches and to show that they do indeed reduce the number of iterations of standard SMO.

The paper is organized as follows. In Sect. 2 we will briefly SMO's choice of descent directions, its updates and its computational cost. We discuss monotone NA–SMO in Sect. 3, where we analyze its computational complexity and relate it to that of SMO. We will numerically compare SMO and monotone NA–SMO in Sect. 4, where we will show it to require less iterations than SMO to converge to a given tolerance. We finish the paper with a short discussion and conclusions in Sect. 5.

2 Second Order SMO

We give a brief review focused on SMO's computational costs; see [7] for more details. The initial versions of SMO selected a descent direction of the form $d = y^L e_{L^t} - y^U e_{U^t}$ with e_j the canonical 0–1 basis vectors and where L^t, U^t correspond to a sample pair x^{L^t}, x^{U^t} most violating the SVM's KKT conditions at iteration t. This guarantees that $d^t \cdot \nabla f(\alpha^t) < 0$ and that it is the most negative among all feasible choices of L and U. The resulting unconstrained gain will be

$$f^t - f^{t+1} = \frac{(d^t \cdot \nabla f(\alpha^t))^2}{2\|x^{L^t} - x^{U^t}\|^2}. \qquad (2)$$

This turns out to be maximal on the numerator but perhaps not so in the denominator, which suggests to improve on this using the same L^t as before but taking now U^t so as to maximize (2). This results in the WSS1 method or second order SMO of [8]; we will refer to it simply as SMO from now on. The unconstrained α updates would then be

$$\alpha_{L^t}^{t+1} = \alpha_{L^t}^t + y_{L^t}\rho_t', \quad \alpha_{U^t}^{t+1} = \alpha_{U^t}^t - y_{U^t}\rho_t',$$

for an appropriate ρ'_t which we may have to clip if necessary so that they verify the box constraints. Note that $\sum_p y^p d_p^t = 0$ and, hence, $\sum_p y^p \alpha_p^{t+1} = 0$, provided it does so for α^t. The SMO iterates continue until a stopping condition $M(\alpha_t) - m(\alpha_t) < \epsilon_{KKT}$ is met for a pre-selected KKT tolerance ϵ_{KKT}, where

$$m(\alpha) = \min_{p \in \mathcal{I}_{up}} y^p \nabla f(\alpha_p), \quad M(\alpha) = \max_{q \in \mathcal{I}_{low}} y^q \nabla f(\alpha_q),$$

for appropriate index sets $\mathcal{I}_{up}, \mathcal{I}_{low}$ (see [7], Sect. 4.1.2). The floating point cost per iteration of SMO is determined by the second order choice of U_t and the update of the gradient $g_t = \nabla f(\alpha_t)$. Selecting U_t requires $2N$ products and for the gradient update we have

$$g^{t+1} = Q\alpha^{t+1} - p = Q\alpha^t - p + \rho_t Q d^t = g^t + \rho_t(y^{L_t} Q^{L_t} - y^{U_t} Q^{U_t}),$$

where Q^j denotes Q's j-th column. This requires N products and, hence, $3N$ floating point operations are needed in total for each SMO update.

3   Monotone Nesterov Accelerated SMO

Recall that standard NAG includes two steps: to compute an intermediate point $x^t = \alpha^t + \mu_t(\alpha^{t-1} - \alpha^t)$ with a fixed μ_t and then to perform gradient descent to arrive at the new $\alpha^{t+1} = x^t - \epsilon_t \nabla f(x^t)$ where ϵ_t is a step parameter. When applied to SVM's dual problem this last step can obviously be replaced by an SMO step from x^t choosing L, U according to the gradient $G^t = \nabla f(x^t)$ of f at x^t. Moreover, we must also ensure the feasibility of x^t. This requires first that $\sum y^p x_p^t = 0$, which will clearly hold if both α^t and α^{t-1} are feasible. We must also have $0 \le x_p^t \le C$, which can be easily achieved by clipping it if needed on the coordinates p where $m_p^t \ne 0$, with $m^t = \alpha^t - \alpha^{t-1}$.

In any case, while SMO guarantees a strictly monotone decrease of the dual function f, standard NAG is not monotone and, as already mentioned, a monotone variant has been proposed [3] in which $f(\alpha^t)$ and $f(x^t)$ are compared at each iteration and if $f(\alpha^t) < f(x^t)$, we compute x^{t+1} as $x^{t+1} = \rho_t x^t + (1-\rho_t)\alpha^t$, with $\rho_t = \frac{\lambda_t}{\lambda_{t+1}}$. Notice that x^{t+1} is automatically feasible, being a convex combination of x^t and α^t. However, there is no guarantee that even after using x^{t+1} to estimate the new α', we arrive at $f(\alpha') < f(\alpha^t)$, and a series of steps may follow in which f remains constant. Nevertheless, we can compute here an optimal ρ that ensures $f(x^{t+1}) < f(\alpha^t)$. In fact, let $x_\rho = \rho x^t + (1-\rho)\alpha^t$; $f(x_\rho)$ is then a function $\phi(\rho)$ for which is easy to see that its minimum is reached at

$$\rho^* = \frac{(x^t - \alpha^t) \cdot \mathbf{1} + \|\alpha^t\|_Q^2}{\|\alpha^t\|_Q^2 + \|x^t\|_Q^2}.$$

To compute $\|\alpha^t\|_Q^2 = \alpha^t \cdot Q\alpha^t$ and $\|x^t\|_Q^2$, observe that $f(\alpha^t) = \frac{1}{2}\|\alpha^t\|_Q^2 - \alpha^t \cdot \mathbf{1}$, i.e., writing $s_\alpha = \alpha \cdot \mathbf{1} = \sum \alpha_p$, we have $\|\alpha^t\|_Q^2 = 2(f(\alpha^t) + s_{\alpha^t})$ and, therefore,

$$\rho^* = \frac{s_{x^t} - s_{\alpha^t} + 2(f(\alpha^t) + s_{\alpha^t})}{2(f(\alpha^t) + s_{\alpha^t}) + 2(f(x^t) + s_{x^t})} = \frac{2f(\alpha^t) + s_{\alpha^t} + s_{x^t}}{2(f(\alpha^t) + f(x^t) + s_{\alpha^t} + s_{x^t})}.$$

To estimate the complexity of the previous steps, note that $2N$ products will be needed to compute $x^{t+1} = \alpha^t + \rho(x^t - \alpha^t)$ and $G^{t+1} = g^t + \rho G^t$ if we perform either a standard momentum or an exact monotone Nesterov step. To this we must add N products to compute $f(x_t)$ as $f(x^t) = \frac{1}{2}(x^t \cdot G^t - s_{x^t})$ (we can retain $f(\alpha^t)$ from the previous iteration) plus another N products to update g_t from G^t. Summing things up, monotone NA–SMO adds $3N$ products to the $3N$ ones of standard SMO, with a total complexity of $6N$ products per iteration, i.e., twice that of standard SMO.

As mentioned, we could try to replace NAG's μ_t by an "exact" value that minimizes $f(\alpha^t) - f(x^t)$. Writing $m^t = \alpha^t - \alpha^{t-1}$ and $\phi(\mu) = f(\alpha^t + \mu m^t) = f(\alpha^t) + \mu m^t \cdot g^t + \frac{\mu^2}{2}\|m^t\|_Q^2$, it is easy to see that its minimum μ_t^e is given by $\mu_t^e = -\frac{m^t \cdot g^t}{\|m^t\|_Q^2}$. However, if we have $\mu_{t-1} = 0$ (by, say, clipping), then $x^{t-1} = \alpha^{t-1}$ and we would arrive at α^t by a standard SMO step $\alpha^t = \alpha^{t-1} + \epsilon_{t-1}d^{t-1}$. But if this step is not clipped, it would follow that $0 = g^t \cdot d^{t-1} = g^t \cdot m^t$. As a consequence, we would also have $\mu_t = 0$, i.e., perform a new standard SMO iteration instead of a NAG one but with an extra cost of at least N products.

Thus, we have the risk of making supposedly better "exact" choices of μ_t that, in fact, reduce to SMO updates, i.e., we will get no acceleration but with much costlier iterations. We have numerically observed this to happen very often and, as a consequence, we will not use exact NAG iterations in our experiments.

4 Numerical Experiments

In this section we will compare the behavior of second order SMO and monotone Nesterov Accelerated SMO working with 8 two class datasets, namely, the australian, diabetes, german (in its numeric version), heart, adult4, adult8, web7 and web8, that are all available in the LIBSVM page. While the first datasets are small, adult8 and web8 have 22,696 and 49,749 patterns respectively; it is important to note that these are the dimensions of the dual problem. We will work with a Gaussian kernel $k(x, x') = e^{\frac{\|x - x'\|^2}{d}}$, with d the sample dimension; that is, we use LIBSVM's default Gaussian kernel width. For the first 4 problems we use the dataset version where their features are scaled to $[-1, 1]$; the adult and web problems have binary features to begin with.

We shall consider three different C values, $C = 10, 100, 1000$ and two KKT tolerances $\epsilon_{KKT} = 0.1, 0.001$. Table 1 gives for each dataset and these C and ϵ values the number of iterations of plain SMO, monotone Nesterov (NA-SMO) and the corresponding ratio. We have separately checked that both methods yield essentially the same final SVM in the sense that they arrive basically at the same value $f(\alpha^T)$ of the SVC objective function at the final α^T, and have very similar number of support vectors (SVs). Figure 1 shows the evolution of the SVM objective function in the adult4 dataset for the standard updates and the Nesterov accelerated ones, with $\epsilon = 0.001$.

As it can be seen, all the SMO to NA-SMO ratios are bigger than 1 except for the web7 and web8 problems, where the number of iterations is considerably

Table 1. Number of iterations for SMO and monotone Nesterov Accelerated SMO (NAS), together with the ratio SMO/NAS.

Dataset	C	Eps	SMO	NAS	Ratio	Dataset	C	Eps	SMO	NAS	Ratio
			Iters.						Iters.		
heart	10^1	10^{-1}	217	210	1.03	adult4	10^1	10^{-1}	3523	2592	1.36
		10^{-3}	551	444	1.24			10^{-3}	8961	4734	1.89
	10^2	10^{-1}	612	530	1.15		10^2	10^{-1}	16738	9294	1.80
		10^{-3}	1590	1281	1.24			10^{-3}	47286	21689	2.18
	10^3	10^{-1}	1097	739	1.48		10^3	10^{-1}	58429	32566	1.79
		10^{-3}	2568	1513	1.70			10^{-3}	157741	80872	1.95
diabetes	10^1	10^{-1}	435	369	1.18	adult8	10^1	10^{-1}	15419	11328	1.36
		10^{-3}	923	620	1.49			10^{-3}	44309	25088	1.77
	10^2	10^{-1}	2295	1533	1.50		10^2	10^{-1}	85822	49770	1.72
		10^{-3}	7697	3830	2.01			10^{-3}	289351	146941	1.97
	10^3	10^{-1}	14366	9320	1.54		10^3	10^{-1}	433268	241796	1.79
		10^{-3}	52343	36492	1.43			10^{-3}	1407541	750967	1.87
australian	10^1	10^{-1}	427	407	1.05	web7	10^1	10^{-1}	2191	2321	0.94
		10^{-3}	1441	865	1.67			10^{-3}	8141	8004	1.02
	10^2	10^{-1}	1574	1358	1.16		10^2	10^{-1}	5529	6222	0.89
		10^{-3}	5772	3217	1.79			10^{-3}	22708	24808	0.92
	10^3	10^{-1}	5687	4363	1.30		10^3	10^{-1}	10874	12277	0.89
		10^{-3}	13099	9641	1.36			10^{-3}	38348	41745	0.92
german	10^1	10^{-1}	1257	1037	1.21	web8	10^1	10^{-1}	3490	3712	0.94
		10^{-3}	3139	2037	1.54			10^{-3}	14457	15265	0.95
	10^2	10^{-1}	4491	2974	1.51		10^2	10^{-1}	9628	9782	0.98
		10^{-3}	12559	6681	1.88			10^{-3}	41530	43585	0.95
	10^3	10^{-1}	10269	7283	1.41		10^3	10^{-1}	20919	20251	1.03
		10^{-3}	26335	18395	1.43			10^{-3}	71297	67910	1.05

worse for NA-SMO. These ratios generally grow with both C (a more difficult problem) and ϵ (a more precise solution). This effect is also shown in Fig. 1, where the convergence of the objective function starts improving much earlier for C = 100 in the `adult4` problem.

These results have been obtained using our own Python implementation of monotone NA-SMO and this is the reason we do not provide time values, as they may be affected by the particular way Python code is executed. Our current implementation of NA-SMO is based on NumPy and, while its kernel is well known for its very efficient C implementation, other parts of our code may rely on other less efficient Python components. The SMO values are obtained using the LIBSVM wrapper in sklearn. In order to provide a fair time comparison our code would have to be implemented in C, for instance as a modification of the LIBSVM library. In any case, the above ratios for the number of iterations make it clear that, at this point, the time reduction they would imply would not compensate the higher cost per iteration of monotone Nesterov acceleration.

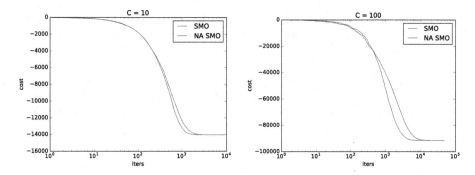

Fig. 1. Evolution of the objective function for the `adult4` dataset with eps = 0.001, C = 10 (left) and C = 100 (right).

5   Discussion and Conclusions

In this work we have presented monotone NA-SMO, a first approach to apply Nesterov Acceleration to SVM's dual problem that ensures monotonicity at each iteration and that achieves a clear reduction of the number of iterations needed by SMO to converge, particularly in problems with higher C or smaller ϵ_{KKT} values. From a practical point of view, and as we have made clear, the smaller number of iterations of NA-SMO are not likely to result in training times smaller than those of standard SMO, for the iteration complexity of monotone NA–SMO is twice as large as that of SMO (although gains could be larger for kernel matrices with high condition numbers). On the other hand, this extra cost won't have an impact in the initial iterations, as their cost is dominated by that of building a cache for the kernel matrix. Thus, SMO acceleration may be worthwhile if it initially achieves a substantial reduction of the cost function while the kernel matrix cache is built, even if one reverts to standard SMO afterwards. This should be more pronounced in large sample problems and also in higher C penalty ones.

In any case, understanding NAG behavior can be still considered as an open problem but in the past couple of years there has been a flurry of activity on the subject [1,5,12,14], particularly for the unconstrained, strongly convex case. As mentioned, most of this is theoretical work based on the knowledge of the condition number κ of f which makes very difficult to render it into practical algorithms; for instance, notice that while aiming at a strongly convex f, we have just been using NAG's version for the L smooth case. Moreover, it is likely that this large research may result in better versions of SMO. Of particular interest is here the work in [11] that while using the μ_t coefficients of smooth NAG when dealing with a strongly convex f, suggests to restart NAG's μ_t when it yields a non–monotone step so as to control the over– or under–damping effect of a possibly too large momentum term leading to x^k. While very simple, in the experiments of [11] this results in a convergence for strongly convex f much faster than the one achieved working with the standard NAG μ_t schedule.

In turn, if properly applied, this may help to improve the gains in the number of SMO iterations reported here. We are currently working on these and other related issues.

Acknowledgments. With partial support from Spain's grants TIN2013-42351-P and S2013/ICE-2845 CASI-CAM-CM, and also of the Cátedra UAM–ADIC in Data Science and Machine Learning. The first author is also supported by the FPU–MEC grant AP-2012-5163. The authors also gratefully acknowledge the use of the facilities of Centro de Computación Científica (CCC) at UAM.

References

1. Allen-Zhu, Z., Orecchia, L.: Linear coupling: an ultimate unification of gradient and mirror descent. arXiv:1407.1537 (2014)
2. Arjevani, Y., Shalev-Shwartz, S., Shamir, O.: On lower and upper bounds for smooth and strongly convex optimization problems. CoRR abs/1503.06833 (2015)
3. Beck, A., Teboulle, M.: Fast gradient-based algorithms for constrained total variation image denoising and deblurring problems. IEEE Trans. Image Process. **18**(11), 2419–2434 (2009)
4. Beck, A., Teboulle, M.: A fast iterative shrinkage-thresholding algorithm for linear inverse problems. SIAM J. Imaging Sci. **2**(1), 183–202 (2009)
5. Bubeck, S., Lee, Y.T., Singh, M.: A geometric alternative to Nesterov's accelerated gradient descent. arXiv:1506.08187 (2015)
6. Chambolle, A., Dossal, C.: How to make sure the iterates of FISTA converge. https://hal.inria.fr/hal-01060130
7. Chang, C.C., Lin, C.J.: LIBSVM: a library for support vector machines. ACM Trans. Intell. Syst. Technol. **2**(3), 27:1–27:27 (2011)
8. Chen, P.H., Fan, R.E., Lin, C.J.: A study on SMO-type decomposition methods for support vector machines. IEEE Trans. Neural Networks **17**, 893–908 (2006)
9. Flammarion, N., Bach, F.R.: From averaging to acceleration, there is only a step-size. In: Proceedings of the 28th Conference on Learning Theory, COLT 2015, Paris, France, 3–6 July 2015, pp. 658–695 (2015)
10. Nesterov, Y.: Introductory Lectures on Convex Optimization: A Basic Course. Applied Optimization. Kluwer Academic Publishers, Boston (2004)
11. O'Donoghue, B., Candès, E.J.: Adaptive restart for accelerated gradient schemes. Found. Comput. Math. **15**(3), 715–732 (2015)
12. Su, W., Boyd, S., Candes, E.: A differential equation for modeling nesterovs accelerated gradient method: theory and insights. In: Ghahramani, Z., Welling, M., Cortes, C., Lawrence, N.D., Weinberger, K.Q. (eds.) Advances in Neural Information Processing Systems, vol. 27, pp. 2510–2518 (2014)
13. Sutskever, I., Martens, J., Dahl, G.E., Hinton, G.E.: On the importance of initialization and momentum in deep learning. In: Dasgupta, S., Mcallester, D. (eds.) Proceedings of the 30th International Conference on Machine Learning (ICML 2013), vol. 28, pp. 1139–1147 (2013)
14. Wibisono, A., Wilson, A., Jordan, M.: A variational perspective on accelerated methods in optimization. arXiv:1603.04245 (2016)

Local Reject Option for Deterministic Multi-class SVM

Johannes Kummert, Benjamin Paassen, Joris Jensen, Christina Göpfert,
and Barbara Hammer$^{(\boxtimes)}$

CITEC Centre of Excellence, Bielefeld University, 33615 Bielefeld, Germany
bhammer@techfak.uni-bielefeld.de

Abstract. Classification with reject option allows classifiers to abstain
from the classification of unclear cases. While it has been shown that
global reject options are optimal for probabilistic classifiers, local reject
schemes can enhance the performance of deterministic classifiers which
do not provide faithful probability estimates [6,10]. A first efficient
scheme how to optimise local threshold parameters has recently been
introduced [8]. In this contribution, we improve and simplify this scheme
by restricting to a fewer number of possible candidates, and we demonstrate its performance for a one-versus-rest SVM classifier. Further, we
have a glimpse at accompanying generalisation bounds.

Keywords: Reject option · Multi-class SVM classification · Local
thresholds · Generalisation ability

1 Introduction

Noisy sensor data, missing information, or overlapping classes necessarily cause
errors for any deterministic classifier. For this reason, many classification techniques provide additional information besides the mere class label such as a
judgment of the classification certainty. In particular in safety critical applications or in the context of interactive systems, it is often advisable to abstain
from a classification in case of a low classification certainty, i.e. output 'reject',
rather than an erroneous (and possibly harmful) misclassification. This is relevant e.g. for iterative schemes such a medical diagnosis based on first, cheap but
not very sensitive tests and a more detailed analysis for unclear cases. Further,
explicit reject options can efficiently trigger online models capable of lifelong
learning [7]. It has recently been shown, that rejects can enable the consistency
of simple surrogate loss functions which are not consistent if a classification is
enforced for the full data set [18].

Starting with the pioneering work of Chow [4], researchers have addressed
the question how to enhance classifiers by efficient and effective reject strategies.
Provided the underlying conditional distributions are known, a simple optimum
reject strategy based on a global reject threshold exists [4,11]. If the underlying
distribution is not known, plugin rules which estimate the underlying probability
distribution can be used, and consistency has been shown provided a reject
margin is present [12]; however, these results are based on suitable estimates of
the underlying probabilities, which causes quite some effort in the context of

© Springer International Publishing Switzerland 2016
A.E.P. Villa et al. (Eds.): ICANN 2016, Part II, LNCS 9887, pp. 251–258, 2016.
DOI: 10.1007/978-3-319-44781-0_30

deterministic classifiers such as SVM. Typically, such classifiers do not aim for a representation of class probabilities, but focus on the decision boundaries [3].

If costs for a reject are priorly given, popular classifiers can be modified to simultaneously optimise the decision boundary as well as a reject threshold [2,19]. These methods, however, restrict to a global threshold, and they crucially rely on priorly fixed costs for a reject. Hence retraining is required for such methods whenever reject costs change. We will deal with the question whether local reject thresholds can be determined posterior to training given reject costs. This setting, on the one hand, bases on the observation that local reject options can severely enhance the performance of deterministic classifiers [8–10]; further, in many applications, reject costs are not necessarily known prior to training, and they can easily change depending on the given circumstances (such as the required security level of a classifier).

In this contribution, we will investigate possibilities to efficiently enhance a multi-class classifier by local reject thresholds posterior to training for the full range of possible reject costs. Inspired by the work [8], we propose an exact optimisation scheme as well as an efficient greedy approximation, which constitutes a simplification and improvement of the method as proposed in [8]; we evaluate its performance for the one-versus-rest SVM in comparison to a state-of-the-art extension of SVM to a probabilistic classifier and plugin reject rules. Further, we have a short glimpse on generalisation error bounds.

2   Optimum Reject Thresholds for Trained Multi-class Classifiers

Assume data $x \in \mathbb{R}^N$ and class labels $y \in \{1, \ldots, C\}$. Assume trained functions $f_c : \mathbb{R}^N \to \mathbb{R}$ provide a classification signal for class c. In addition, we assume that a certainty measure is available $g_c : \mathbb{R}^N \to \mathbb{R}$ with high values $g_c(x)$ corresponding to a high degree of certainty for class c; for the moment, we choose $g_c = f_c$, and both will be given as a linear decision function in kernel space as provided by a one-versus-rest SVM. A one-versus-rest classifier results in the prescription

$$f : x \mapsto \mathrm{argmax}_c f_c(x). \tag{1}$$

A *local reject scheme* is characterised by a threshold vector $\theta = (\theta_1, \ldots, \theta_C)$; it modifies the classifier via

$$f_R : x \mapsto \begin{cases} \mathrm{argmax}_c f_c(x) & \text{if } g_{\mathrm{argmax}_c f_c(x)}(x) \geq \theta_{\mathrm{argmax}_c f_c(x)} \\ \circledR & \text{otherwise} \end{cases} \tag{2}$$

where $\circledR$ indicates a reject. For given training data $\mathcal{P} := \{(x_i, y_i) | i = 1, \ldots, M\}$, and given costs of a reject D, the empirical loss is given as

$$\hat{E}_M := \frac{1}{M} \cdot \sum_{i=1}^{M} \mathcal{L}_D(f_R(x_i), y_i) \tag{3}$$

where $\mathcal{L}_D$ equals 0 for correct classification, D for reject, and 1 for misclassification. Unlike local reject, a *global reject* would enforce equal thresholds for all classes $\theta_1 = \ldots = \theta_C$, i.e. assuming a universal scaling of the certainty measures g_c. Since this is the case whenever $g_c(\boldsymbol{x})$ equals the probability $p(c|\boldsymbol{x})$, a global threshold selection strategy is optimum for probabilistic classifiers [4,11], but local threshold choices offer more freedom whenever the local scaling of the certainties $g_c(\boldsymbol{x})$ is not clear.

Pareto Front: Note that threshold selection corresponds to a Pareto-optimisation problem: we can decompose the training data $\mathcal{P} = E \cup L$ into errors $E := \{(\boldsymbol{x}_i, y_i) \mid f(\boldsymbol{x}_i) \neq y_i\}$, and correctly classified data $L := \{(\boldsymbol{x}_i, y_i) \mid f(\boldsymbol{x}_i) = y_i\}$. These sets decompose into $\mathcal{P}^c := \{(\boldsymbol{x}_i, y_i) \mid f(\boldsymbol{x}) = c\}$, $E^c := \mathcal{P}^c \cap E$ and $L^c := \mathcal{P}^c \cap L$ according to the classes. For every class label c, a threshold θ_c singles out a set of rejected points $R_{\theta_c} := \{(\boldsymbol{x}_i, y_i) \in \mathcal{P}^c \mid g_c(\boldsymbol{x}_i) < \theta_c\}$ whereby $T_{\theta_c}^c := R_{\theta_c} \cap E^c$ are correctly rejected points (these are errors of f), and $F_{\theta_c}^c := R_{\theta_c} \cap L^c$ are wrongly rejected points (f maps those correctly). Minimising the empirical error corresponds to thresholds with a maximum number of correctly rejected points and a minimum number of wrong rejects, i.e. $T_{\boldsymbol{\theta}} := \cup_c T_{\theta_c}^c$ should be large while $F_{\boldsymbol{\theta}} := \cup_c F_{\theta_c}^c$ should be small. Such extremal pairs of true and false rejects form a Pareto front, and it is straightforward to select an optimum pair from this front for given costs D. Hence we focus on algorithms to determine this Pareto front given trained classifiers.

Optimum Thresholds for One Class c: In the following, we propose two algorithms to determine the Pareto front $(T_{\boldsymbol{\theta}}, F_{\boldsymbol{\theta}})$ and corresponding thresholds $\boldsymbol{\theta}$, thereby improving [8] by a simpler formulation which is due to the restriction to a smaller number of possible threshold vectors. The algorithms rely on one essential observation: We consider one class c, and sort the certainty values $g_c(\boldsymbol{x}_i)$ for $\boldsymbol{x}_i \in \mathcal{P}^c$. An optimum threshold θ_c for class c necessarily lies between two consecutive values $g_c(\boldsymbol{x}_i) < g_c(\boldsymbol{x}_j)$ where $\boldsymbol{x}_i \in E^c$ and $\boldsymbol{x}_j \in L^c$; otherwise, the resulting pair $T_{\theta_c}^c$ and $F_{\theta_c}^c$ would not be Pareto-optimal, since we could remove one wrong reject or add one true reject by shifting the threshold. Hence an optimum threshold θ_c for class c comes from a finite and usually small number of possible thresholds $\theta_c(0) < \ldots < \theta_c(I_c)$, induced by such consecutive values $g_c(\boldsymbol{x}_i)$. These candidates can be determined in time $\mathcal{O}(M \log M)$ by sorting. We denote by $I := I_1 + \ldots + I_c$ the overall number of thresholds; this is limited by M, but it is usually much smaller. In contrast, the approaches [8] consider all $\boldsymbol{x}_i \in L^c$ as possible thresholds $g_c(\boldsymbol{x}_i)$, resulting in more complex optimisation schemes.

Greedy Optimisation: We are interested in optimum combinations of such thresholds θ_c into threshold vectors $\boldsymbol{\theta}$ for all classes c. One problem consists in the fact that, while every optimum threshold vector $\boldsymbol{\theta}$ contains only optimum thresholds θ_c for every c, the converse is not true; optimum θ_c for the classes c can be combined to threshold vectors $\boldsymbol{\theta}$ which do not induce a pair of the Pareto front. Hence we have to search the space of possible threshold vectors, which is finite, but exponential w.r.t the number of classes C. As first approach, we propose an efficient but possibly suboptimal greedy optimisation strategy: starting from the smallest possible threshold $\theta_c(0)$ for every class c, we iteratively increase the threshold which yields maximum gain; thereby, the gain is measured as the

number of true rejects minus the number of false rejects which are caused by the
increasing of the threshold: the quantity

$$G_c(i+1) := \left(|T^c_{\theta_c(i+1)}| - |T^c_{\theta_c(i)}| \right) - \left(|F^c_{\theta_c(i+1)}| - |F^c_{\theta_c(i)}| \right) \tag{4}$$

quantifies this gain for the class c, provided its threshold is increased from number i to $i+1$. The following greedy algorithm results:

> $\boldsymbol{\theta} \leftarrow (\theta_1(0), \dots, \theta_L(0))$;
> **while** *at least one threshold* $\theta_c(i)$ *can be increased* **do**
> $\theta_c(i) \leftarrow \theta_c(i+1)$ for $(c, i) = \text{argmax}_{(c', i')} G_{c'}(i'+1)$
> **end**

We return all threshold vectors obtained this way. This greedy algorithm has
memory complexity $\mathcal{O}(C)$ and time complexity $\mathcal{O}(I)$.

Dynamic Programming: Threshold optimisation is an instance of the so-called
multiple-choice knapsack problem – for every class label c, we have to select a
threshold from a finite set of possibilities such that the overall costs (given by the
sum of false rejects) are minimised and the overall value (given by the sum of true
rejects) is maximised [5]. This problem is polynomial in our case, since costs and
values are limited by M, and the multiple-choice knapsack problem is pseudo-
polynomial. Additionally, we face the specific situation that the thresholds are
linearly ordered for every class c, such that the problem can be solved by a
simple dynamic programming scheme as follows: For $n \le |L|$, $j \le C$, and $i \le I_c$
we define

$$\text{opt}(n, j, i) := \max\{|T_{\boldsymbol{\theta}}| \mid |F_{\boldsymbol{\theta}}| \le n, \theta_l \in \{\theta_c(0), \dots, \theta_c(I_c)\} \ \forall c < j, \tag{5}$$
$$\theta_j \in \{\theta_j(0), \dots, \theta_j(i)\}, \theta_c = \theta_c(0) \ \forall c > j\}.$$

This refers to the optimum number of true rejects which can be achieved provided
at most n false rejects are present, arbitrary thresholds can be chosen for classes
1 to $j-1$, the threshold for class j equals one of the thresholds with number 0
to i, and thresholds are restricted to the first possible ones for all classes $c > j$.
For these values, the following Bellman inequality holds:

$$\text{opt}(n, j, i) = \begin{cases} \sum_{c=1}^{C} |T^c_{\theta_c(0)}| & \text{if } n = 0 \text{ or } j = 0, \\ \text{opt}(n, j-1, I_{j-1}) & \text{if } n > 0, j > 0, i = 0, \\ \text{opt}(n, j, i-1) & \text{if } n > 0, j > 0, i > 0, n < |F^j_{\theta_j(i)}|, \\ \max\{\text{opt}(n, j, i-1), \\ \text{opt}(n - |F^j_{\theta_j(i)}|, j-1, I_{j-1}) + |T^j_{\theta_j(i)}| - |T^j_{\theta_j(0)}| & \text{otherwise.} \end{cases}$$
$$\tag{6}$$

The first three cases correspond to instantiations or trivial settings: the first
setting corresponds to the selection of the first possible threshold for every class
corresponding to the choice $n = 0$, i.e. no false rejects are present, and the
value $|T^c_{\theta_c(0)}|$ accumulates the true rejects. Setting two realises the equivalence
of threshold 0 for class j and the decrease of the class number j by one. Setting
three realises a decrease of the threshold i for class j until the threshold becomes
feasible in the sense that the number of allowed false rejects caused by this

threshold is limited by n. The last equality captures the important optimality-preserving problem-decomposition: we can either pick a threshold smaller than the threshold number i for class j, or we can pick threshold i, the latter results in a gain of $|T^j_{\theta_j(i)}| - |T^j_{\theta_j(0)}|$ true rejects as compared to the default (threshold 0 yields $|T^j_{\theta_j(0)}|$ true rejects), at the costs of $|F^j_{\theta_j(i)}|$ false rejects.

This recursion is well founded since the sum $n + j + i$ is decreased in all cases. Its optimality can easily be proved by induction over $n + j + i$. Since a polynomial number of values $\mathrm{opt}(n, j, i)$ exists, this scheme can be implemented efficiently via dynamic programming. The resulting space complexity is $\mathcal{O}(|L| \cdot C)$ (it is sufficient to store array elements $\mathrm{opt}(n, j)$ for the most recent i) and time complexity $\mathcal{O}(|L| \cdot I)$ (computation can be arranged as loop over n and all thresholds). Optimum threshold vectors can efficiently be retrieved from the value matrix $\mathrm{opt}(n, j)$ by back-tracing in time $\mathcal{O}(|L| \cdot I)$.

Table 1. Results of different reject strategies for two data sets as evaluated on a test set, the area under the accuracy-reject curve is reported, its standard deviation is in parenthesis.

Data	DP	Greedy	Global	Probabilistic
Sat (linear kernel)	0.963 (0.0018)	0.962 (0.0028)	0.958 (0.0028)	0.971 (0.0032)
Glass (linear kernel)	0.734 (0.0593)	0.734 (0.0630)	0.707 (0.0657)	0.729 (0.0844)
Glass (RBF kernel)	0.827 (0.0645)	0.829 (0.0645)	0.757 (0.0600)	0.821 (0.0367)

3   Experiments

We compare the performance of the proposed model for a multi-class SVM classifier. The one-versus-rest SVM induces a function $f_c = g_c$ for every class c given by the linear activation in kernel space. This is correlated to the distance to the decision boundary, and we will base local rejects and certainty estimation on this measurement. We compare the performance of local rejects, where the thresholds are either optimised by dynamic programming or the greedy heuristic, to two alternatives: (1) reject based on the same functions $f_c = g_c$ and one global threshold, i.e. $\theta_c = \theta$ for all classes $c \leq C$; (2) reject based on a probabilistic plugin rule which estimates the conditional class probabilities and a global reject option. For both cases, optimum reject thresholds can be determined by linear search, since they are global. For setting (2), we use the state-of-the-art transformation technique of SVM outputs to probabilities as provided in LibSVM [3]; this relies on a logistic rescaling of one-versus -one SVMs and a suitable coordination of the resulting probabilities [17,20]; thereby the rescaling relies on a costly cross-validation, hence the method is computationally demanding.

We evaluate the performance for two data sets, glass (214 training points, 6 classes, 13 attributes) and sat-image (6435 training points, 6 classes, 36 attributes), using the same parameter values (linear or RBF kernel, 10-fold cross-validation) as presented in [13]. Note that reject options do not improve a classification with high accuracy where rejection is not necessary, such that we restrict the evaluation to these simple cases. The resulting accuracy is evaluated in the form of an accuracy-reject curve, which displays the accuracy achieved for the points which are not rejected as compared to the percentage of points which are rejected. We report the resulting area under the curve for the test set averaged within a 10-fold cross-validation and the standard deviation in Table 1. One typical accuracy-reject curve is displayed in Fig. 1. For all settings, the efficient but approximate greedy strategy reaches the performance of an optimum threshold choice based on dynamic programming. For the glass data, local reject options significantly improve the accuracy as compared to a global reject threshold for the one-versus-rest setting. Interestingly, for all settings, a local reject option reaches the accuracy of the (more demanding) probabilistic modelling on top of a one-versus-one SVM.

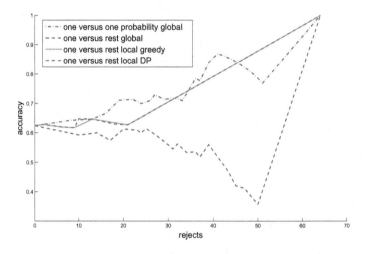

Fig. 1. Accuracy-reject curve on the test set for the glass data and RBF kernel in one typical fold of a cross-validation. Rejects are given in percentage, accuracy as the ratio in between 0 and 1.

4   Generalization Ability

Some research addresses the consistency of classification with a reject option in particular for two-class classifiers, see e.g. [2,21]. Here we have a first glimpse at the question whether empirical risk minimisation allows valid generalization bounds for local reject thresholds which are attached to the classes. Thereby, we restrict to simple multi-class models such as discussed in [1,14], and we disregard recent tighter bounds such as offered in [15,16].

Inspired by the multi-class margin of SVMs as introduced in [16], for example, we consider the following certainty

$$g_c(\boldsymbol{x}) := \frac{1}{\theta_c}\left(h_c(\boldsymbol{x}) - \max_{c'\neq c} h_{c'}(\boldsymbol{x})\right) \tag{7}$$

which already integrates the adaptive scaling term θ_c such that $g_c(\boldsymbol{x})$ is rejected for the interval $[0, 1]$, and which is based on the relative margin $h_c(\boldsymbol{x}) - \max_{c' \neq c} h_{c'}(\boldsymbol{x})$ rather than the value $h_c(\boldsymbol{x})$. We consider the following upper bound function Φ_D^ρ for the resulting 0-1-loss given by $\mathcal{L}_D$:

$$\Phi_D^\rho(\boldsymbol{g}_1(\boldsymbol{x}), \ldots, g_C(\boldsymbol{x}), y)$$

$$= \begin{cases} 0 & \text{if } g_y(\boldsymbol{x}) \geq 1 + \rho \\ D \cdot (1 + \rho - g_y(\boldsymbol{x}))/\rho & \text{if } 1 \leq g_y(\boldsymbol{x}) \leq 1 + \rho \\ D & \text{if } \rho \leq g_y(\boldsymbol{x}) \leq 1 \\ (\rho - g_y(\boldsymbol{x}))/\rho + D \cdot g_y(\boldsymbol{x})/\rho & \text{if } 0 \leq g_y(\boldsymbol{x}) \leq \rho \\ 1 & \text{if } g_y(\boldsymbol{x}) \leq 0 \end{cases} \quad (8)$$

for a fixed margin $\rho > 0$. Here we have made the dependencies on the certainty values $g_c(\boldsymbol{x})$ explicit. Φ_D^ρ is Lipschitz continuous w.r.t. the first C arguments with constant $1/\rho$.

It is a direct consequence of Corollary 15 in [1] that the following inequality holds for M i.i.d. data $(\boldsymbol{x}_i, y_i)$ and probability at least $1 - \delta$

$$\mathbf{E}\left(\mathcal{L}_D(f_R(\boldsymbol{x}), y)\right) \leq \frac{1}{M} \sum_{i=1}^{M} \Phi_D^\rho(\boldsymbol{g}_1(\boldsymbol{x}_i), \ldots, g_C(\boldsymbol{x}_i), y_i) + \frac{2C}{\rho} G_M(\mathcal{F}) + \sqrt{\frac{8 \ln(2/\delta)}{M}} \quad (9)$$

where $\mathbf{E}$ denotes expectation w.r.t. $(\boldsymbol{x}, y)$ and the loss $\mathcal{L}_D$ is determined with respect to the certainty g_y as above. $G_M(\mathcal{G})$ is the Rademacher complexity of the function class of functions of the form $g_c(\boldsymbol{x})$ as given in (7). Due to the structural results as derived in [1], Theorems 12 and 14 and the Lipschitz continuity of max with constant 1, this Rademacher complexity can be upper bounded by $C \cdot G_M(\mathcal{H})$ with $\mathcal{H}$ containing functions of the form $h_c(\boldsymbol{x})/\theta_c$. For $h_c(\boldsymbol{x})$ given by SVM with kernel k, this is limited by the term $\frac{2B}{M}\sqrt{\frac{\mathbf{E}(k(\boldsymbol{x},\boldsymbol{x}))}{M}}$, provided the weight vector is restricted by $\|\boldsymbol{w}\|/\theta_C \leq B$ (see [1], Lemma 22). Hence the generalisation ability of multi-class-classification with local reject can be guaranteed provided the local reject thresholds θ_C are limited from below by a constant.

5 Discussion

We have discussed local reject options for deterministic multi-class classification, deriving efficient a posteriori threshold optimisation algorithms which run in linear time related to the number of classes. We have demonstrated its performance in the context of one-versus-rest SVM, and we had a first glimpse at its generalisation ability for SVM. For the latter, we relied on a slightly modified certainty measure as compared to our experiments, inspired by a notion of margin for multi-class SVM as provided in the literature. It will be a matter of future research to also experimentally test this certainty measure as well as alternative proposals for the margin in multi-class settings. Note that the proposed optimisation scheme is independent of the exact choice of the certainty measure. For future research, we will built on the time and memory efficiency of the particularly efficient greedy realisation, and we will investigate how this scheme can be integrated into online settings where data arrive in a stream.

Acknowledgement. Funding by the CITEC centre of excellence is gratefully acknowledged.

References

1. Bartlett, P.L., Mendelson, S.: Rademacher and gaussian complexities: risk bounds and structural results. J. Mach. Learn. Res. **3**, 463–482 (2002)
2. Bartlett, P.L., Wegkamp, M.H.: Classification with a reject option using a hinge loss. J. Mach. Learn. Res. **9**, 1823–1840 (2008)
3. Chang, C.-C., Lin, C.-J.: Libsvm: a library for support vector machines. ACM Trans. Intell. Syst. Technol. **2**(3), 27:1–27:27 (2011)
4. Chow, C.: On optimum recognition error and reject tradeoff. IEEE Trans. Inf. Theor. **16**(1), 41–46 (2006)
5. Dudzinski, K., Walukiewicz, S.: Exact methods for the knapsack problem and its generalizations. Eur. J. Oper. Res. **28**(1), 3–21 (1987)
6. Fischer, L., Hammer, B., Wersing, H.: Local rejection strategies for learning vector quantization. In: Wermter, S., Weber, C., Duch, W., Honkela, T., Koprinkova-Hristova, P., Magg, S., Palm, G., Villa, A.E.P. (eds.) ICANN 2014. LNCS, vol. 8681, pp. 563–570. Springer, Heidelberg (2014)
7. Fischer, L., Hammer, B., Wersing, H.: Combining offline and online classifiers for life-long learning. In: IJCNN (2015)
8. Fischer, L., Hammer, B., Wersing, H.: Optimum local rejection for classifiers. Neurocomputing (accepted 2016)
9. Fischer, L., Nebel, D., Villmann, T., Hammer, B., Wersing, H.: Rejection strategies for learning vector quantization – a comparison of probabilistic and deterministic approaches. In: Villmann, T., Schleif, F.-M., Kaden, M., Lange, M. (eds.) Advances in Self-Organizing Maps and Learning. AISC, vol. 295, pp. 109–118. Springer, Heidelberg (2014)
10. Fumera, G., Roli, F., Giacinto, G.: Reject option with multiple thresholds. Pattern Recogn. **33**, 2099–2101 (2000)
11. Hansen, L.K., Liisberg, C., Salamon, P.: The error-reject tradeoff. Open Syst. Inf. Dynamics **4**(2), 159–184 (1997)
12. Herbei, R., Wegkamp, M.H.: Classification with reject option. Can. J. Stat. **34**(4), 709–721 (2006)
13. Hsu, C.-W., Lin, C.-J.: A comparison of methods for multiclass support vector machines. Trans. Neur. Netw. **13**(2), 415–425 (2002)
14. Koltchinskii, V., Panchenko, D., Lozano, F.: Some new bounds on the generalization error of combined classifiers. In: Advances in Neural Information Processing Systems 13, Papers from Neural Information Processing Systems (NIPS) 2000, Denver, CO, USA, pp. 245–251 (2000)
15. Lei, Y., Dogan, Ü., Binder, A., Kloft, M.: Multi-class SVMs: from tighter data-dependent generalization bounds to novel algorithms. CoRR, abs/1506.04359 (2015)
16. Maximov, Y., Reshetova, D.: Tight risk bounds for multi-class margin classifiers. CoRR, abs/1507.03040 (2015)
17. Platt, J.C.: Probabilistic outputs for support vector machines and comparisons to regularized likelihood methods. In: Advances in Large Margin Classifiers, pp. 61–74. MIT Press (1999)
18. Ramaswamy, H.G., Tewari, A., Agarwal, S.: Consistent algorithms for multiclass classification with a reject option. CoRR, abs/1505.04137 (2015)
19. Villmann, T., Kaden, M., Bohnsack, A., Villmann, J.-M., Drogies, T., Saralajew, S., Hammer, B.: Self-adjusting reject options in prototype based classification. In: Workshop on Self-Organizing Maps (2015)
20. Wu, T.-F., Lin, C.-J., Weng, R.C.: Probability estimates for multi-class classification by pairwise coupling. J. Mach. Learn. Res. **5**, 975–1005 (2004)
21. Yuan, M., Wegkamp, M.H.: Classification methods with reject option based on convex risk minimization. J. Mach. Learn. Res. **11**, 111–130 (2010)

Palmprint Biometric System Modeling by DBC and DLA Methods and Classifying by KNN and SVM Classifiers

Raouia Mokni[1]([⊠]) and Monji Kherallah[2]([⊠])

[1] Faculty of Economics and Management of Sfax, University of Sfax,
Road Aeroport Km 4, 3018 Sfax, Tunisia
`raouia.mokni@gmail.com`
[2] Faculty of Sciences of Sfax, University of Sfax,
Road Soukra Km 3, 3038 Sfax, Tunisia
`Monji.kherallah@enis.rnu.tn`

Abstract. Biometric technology is an automatic personal identification method based on physical or behavioral characteristics of the individuals. Among of the physical characteristics, palmprint is useful in various applications such as forensic science access control, thus resulting in an increasing of research interest. In this paper, we explore a new methodology focused on integrating the fractal and Multi-fractal techniques for human identification based on extracting the texture pattern features. Therefore, we extract the palmprint texture information based on the calculation of the fractal dimensions using the Differential Box Counting (DBC) and the Diffusion Limited Aggregates (DLA) methods corresponding to the Fractal and Multi-Fractal techniques respectively. These methods have been broadly applied in image processing fields to estimate the fractal dimensions of an image as important parameters for analyzing the irregular shapes of the texture image. The proposed method produces encouraging recognition rates by 94.02 % and 93.44 % when tested on benchmark databases "CASIA-Palmprint" and "IITD-Palmprint" respectively. The performance of our method is compared with palmprint recognition accuracy gained from well-known state-of-the-art palmprint recognition, producing favorable results.

Keywords: Palmprint · Fractal technique · Multi-fractal technique · DBC · DLA · Texture analyses · SVM

1 Introduction and Related Works

In order to identify the person with a great effectiveness as related to physiological or behavioral characteristics, biometrics techniques have been often used among which is palmprint recognition. Thanks to its pros mainly the increasing motivation of security, usability, low cost of equipment, and high recognition accuracy, easy availability, etc., palmprint recognition has drawn the attention of many researchers. In order to be recognized, one can acquire the palmprint in a low-resolution and high-resolution mode. For civilian applications, one uses the low resolution imaging where the contact manner captured the palmprint images. At a low resolution palmprint image, i.e., about

© Springer International Publishing Switzerland 2016
A.E.P. Villa et al. (Eds.): ICANN 2016, Part II, LNCS 9887, pp. 259–266, 2016.
DOI: 10.1007/978-3-319-44781-0_31

75 dpi, palmprint including principal lines, wrinkles, texture. Until recently, a lot of focus has been given to high resolution palmprint recognition. At a high resolution palmprint image, i.e., about 400–500 or greater dpi, ridges, minutiae and pores could be detected. Up to present time, palmprint recognition at high resolution is restricted to forensic applications. Thanks to the great value of civilian applications, in this paper, our work has also given importance to low resolution palmprint recognition. Up to now, many researchers have proposed many approaches for low resolution palmprint recognition. The current approaches can be roughly categorized as line based methods and texture based methods. The first are the structural approaches based on the principal lines [1], wrinkles [2] and ridge [3]. However, regrettably only these mentioned features are unable to give enough information for effective recognition. The texture based methods, which are the global approaches being based on the texture image, are very important in palmprint recognition field. On the one hand, it is noticeable that many approaches have been developed in this second category such as Local Binary Pattern [4], SIFT [5], Gabor filter [6, 7], Eigenpalms [8], Fisherpalms [9], Wavelets [10] and Co-occurrence Matrix [11]. On the other hand, it is clear that the fractal and multi-fractal methods [12, 13] have not been deeply exploited yet for the analysis of the texture of palmprint recognition. Therefore, an application of these methods for analyzing the texture pattern of palmprint was proposed.

In this research paper, we suggest a new approach in order to analyze the texture patterns of palmprint by using the fractal technique consisting in acquiring and calculating the fractal dimension by the Differential Box Counting (DBC) method and the multi-fractal technique founded on the calculation of the generalized fractal dimension using the Diffusion Limited Aggregates (DLA) method.

The organization of the rest of the paper is the following. In Sect. 2, the details of system overview were presented and the basic concepts behind Fractal and Multi-Fractal techniques were introduced. We presented and analyzed the experimental study and results in Sect. 3. As for Sect. 4, it is devoted to presenting some concluding remarks.

2 System Overview

The proposed system includes the following four steps listed in their order of application: (1) Hand-Pre-processing (2) Feature Extraction based on Fractal and multi-Fractal analysis (3) Classification and (4) Final Decision.

2.1 Hand Pre-processing

The pre-processing step is devoted to extract the region of interest (ROI) of the palmprint by various following phases:

- Using the Otsu's method, we convert the original image into binary image.
- To eliminate the noise and remove the holes curve, we detect the edge image and apply the smoothing filter by a low pass filter.

- In order to stabilize the coordinate system able to successfully locate the ROI, we extract the finger-webs (i.e. the key points between the fingers).
- We rotate the extracted ROI to a vertical position and fixe its size to T × T with T = 150 pixels.
- In order to improve the quality of this ROI, we apply a low pass filter for reducing the noise.

The full details of the hand pre-processing step have been described in our previous works [11, 14]. Figure 1 shows the original image and the extracted ROI of the palmprint.

2.2   Feature Extraction Based on Fractal and Multi-Fractal Analysis

To achieve the task of feature extraction, we are based on the texture pattern information, and more specifically on the fractal and Multi-fractal techniques [15].

Fractal Analysis. Developed by Mandelbrot [15] so that to design the objects having a very irregular, interrupted or fragmented (geometrically complicated) shape, the fractal method is considered as an efficient technique. It is a mathematical object coming from an iterative process and possessing a self-similarity character, i.e. its shape is repeated at different scales. Each object is then characterized by the Fractal Dimension that often denoted FD which was obtained by several methods. Generally, FD is described by the following equation:

$$FD = \lim_{\varepsilon \to 0} \frac{\log(N(\varepsilon))}{\log\left(\frac{1}{\varepsilon}\right)} \tag{1}$$

Where, $N(\varepsilon)$ and $1/\varepsilon$ are the numbers of specimen of the initial object and the scale factor, respectively. The FD is obtained by a least squares regression method.

The Box Counting (BC) method which is one of these many methods of fractal technique is deeply exploited for the image processing field due to its usefulness to designate and to measure the complexity and irregularity of the image texture surface. This method gives a great importance to divide the image space into a number of boxes (fixed-grid of square boxes) for different scale ε and in calculating the number of the boxes containing the information $N(\varepsilon)$ for each scale.

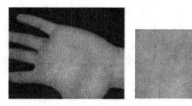

Fig. 1. The ROI extraction

262 R. Mokni and M. Kherallah

In the BC method, a big limit in term of the computation of box counting is present. Consequently, along with the application of the counting process of non-empty boxes, it is vital to use binary images rather than gray scale images. In accordance to the BC method, Sarkar et al. [16] proposed an extension of the standard method to the gray scale image which is named the Differential Box Counting (DBC).

Differential Box Counting method (DBC). The DBC is one of the most effective methods to analyze the gray scale image texture. It is an efficient method to precisely estimate the fractal dimension of a gray level image. A description of this method is presented as follows: Given that an image of size $M \times M$ pixels is partitioned into $s \times s$ non-overlapping grids, where $1 < s \leq M/2$ and s is the current scale of the image. Consider the image as a 3-Dimensional space (x,y,z), (x,y) represents a point in the plane of the coordinate system and z corresponds to the gray values at position (x,y). The grid is filled by the use of $s \times s \times s'$ sized boxes. If the minimum and the maximum gay levels of the image in the $(i, j)'$ th grid downfall in the box numbers k and l, respectively i.e. the minimum and the maximum gray levels of each grid are located in the k-*th* box and l-*th* box, the number of boxes in the grid is:

$$n_\varepsilon(i, j) = 1 - k + 1 \tag{2}$$

Where $\varepsilon = s/M$, the number of boxes in the all grids (image) can be computed by:

$$N_\varepsilon = \sum_i \sum_j n_\varepsilon(i,j) \tag{3}$$

$N\varepsilon$ is counted for different values of s i.e. different value of ε. Hence, the Fractal Dimension (FD) is given by:

$$FD = slope\left(\frac{\log(N(\varepsilon))}{\log\left(\frac{1}{\varepsilon}\right)}\right) \tag{4}$$

According to Eq. (1), the Fractal Dimension is estimated as the slope of the least squares linear fit of *log (N(ε))* along *log (1/ε)*. Therefore, for each ROI image, 1feature are obtained.

Multi-Fractal analysis. Mathematically, fractal objects have an infinite number of scales. For these objects, the fractal dimension is the same on all scales. Indeed, the properties of self-similarity of a set of points can be characterized by the fractal dimension. This characterization is complete only for simple cases. In fact, most fractals are not homogeneous. There is rarely an identical pattern repeated on all scales, and self-similarity properties can change from point to point. In this case, the object may have different dimensions at different scales. Thus, fractal analysis can be generalized by introducing the Multi-Fractal concept as the Diffusion Limited Aggregates (DLA) Method [13].

Diffusion Limited Aggregates. Given the palmprint texture image with the number of Pixel is M_0 of the size L, covered by grid boxes of size l, the Multi-Fractal dimensions or the generalized fractal dimension Dq for this image is defined as follows:

$$\sum_i \left(\frac{M_i}{M_0}\right)^q \approx \left(\frac{1}{L}\right)^{(q-1)D_q} \tag{5}$$

Where M_i and q are the number of pixels in the *ith* box and a variable which allows distinguish fractals properties at different scales, respectively.

The DLA methods consists in randomly choosing N pixels belonging to the structure, and counting for every pixel *i* the number of pixels M_i, inside boxes of linear dimension R, centered on the selected pixel. In the left of the Eq. 5 can be interpreted as the average of the quantity $\left(\frac{M_i}{M_0}\right)^{(q-1)}$ according to the probability distribution $\left(\frac{M_i}{M_0}\right)$, when the centers of the boxes are chosen randomly, the averaging is made during this distribution, and consequently, Eq. 5 becomes:

$$\left\{\left(\frac{M(R)}{M_0}\right)^{q-1}\right\} \approx \left(\frac{R}{L}\right)^{(q-1)D_q} ; \quad D_q = \frac{1}{q-1} \frac{\log\left[\left(\frac{M(R)}{M_0}\right)^{q-1}\right]}{\log\left[\frac{R}{L}\right]} \tag{6}$$

Where the {…} denotes the average over the centers.

In our experiment, we split the palmprint ROI in s*s sub-regions, where s = 10. Then, we calculate the multi-fractal dimensions using the DLA method based on the calculation of generalized fractal dimensions which is made for $(-10 \leq q \leq 10)$ to obtain 21 features for each sub-regions. Therefore, for each ROI image, 210 features are obtained. For the case where q = 1, the Eq. (6) is non-analytical, hence the choice of $q \pm \varepsilon$, with $\varepsilon = 0.001$. The equation becomes: $D_q \cong (D_{q+\varepsilon} + D_{q-\varepsilon})/2$.

2.3   Feature Classification

In this section, the K-Nearest Neighbor (KNN) and the Support Vector Machine (SVM) classifiers were briefly summarized. In fact, The K-Nearest Neighbor (KNN) classification algorithm [17] is widely applied in pattern recognition for classification, which is famous for its simplicity and high correct rate. In our experiment, The KNN is considered as a supervised classifier insisting on calculating the Euclidean Distance (ED) between the features vector of the test palmprint (input image) and all the feature vectors of the training set so that to classify this test palmprint. It is imminent that the parameter K be determined by the user: $k \in N$, where N = {1,3,5,7,9,…}.

Being developed by Vapnik [18], Support Vector Machine (SVM) is regarded as a strong discriminative classifier. It is noticeable that it has been deeply used with advantageous results for a variety of pattern classification/recognition tasks [7, 11]. SVM is both basically exploited to identify an optimal separating hyper-plane or decision surface by assuming a novel technique reliant on mapping the sample points into a high-dimensional feature space and categorized by using a nonlinear transformation, even when the data are linearly inseparable. By working out a quadratic programming problem which is reliant on regularization parameters, the optimal hyper-plane is obtained. This transformation was realized by kernel functions like Linear kernel (LK), radial basis function (RBF), Polynomial kernel (PK) types being exploited in this work.

3 Experiments, Results and Discussion

3.1 CASIA and IITD Datasets

Chinese Academy of Sciences Institute of Automation (CASIA) dataset [19] and Indian Institute of Technology Delhi (IITD) dataset [20] are used for assessing the performance of the proposed approach. The CASIA-Palmprint database contains 5502 palmprint images corresponding to 312 subjects. For each subject, 8 palmprint images have been collected from both left and right palms. The IITD-Palmprint database contains 2300 palmprints images captured from 230 individuals aged from 14 to 56 years. For each subject, 5 palmprint images have been collected from both left and right palms. So, 1150 left palmprints and 1150 right palmprints.

3.2 Experimental Results and Discussion

The execution of the suggested palmprint identification system is assessed exploiting two databases. So, we indiscriminately singled out 5 samples of each person from CASIA database as the gallery data and we exploited 3 samples or the probe data. For IIDT database, we arbitrarily chose 3 samples of each person as the gallery data and the rest of samples as the probe data. In our experiments and in order to classify the extracted features in this system, we exploited the K-Nearest Neighbor classifier (KNN) with deferent values of K and the SVM classifier with a variety of kernel functions. Table 1 highpoints the different recognition rates (RRs) of our suggested systems with various values of K and a lot of kernel functions.

Likewise, our suggested system was applied with different values of K. Remarkably from the referred results in Table 1, k = 3 provides the finest recognition rates for both databases. Moreover, it is obviously remarked that the SVM with the RBF produces the foremost Recognition rates for both databases in comparison to other functions of SVM. It is clear that the performance of our experiments with the SVM method provides higher recognition rates than the KNN approach. Besides, it is evident that the

Table 1. The various recognition rates of our suggested system

RRs (%)	KNN			SVM		
	1	3	5	LK	RBF	PK
CASIA-Database	92.20	93.87	91.50	93.00	94.02	91.03
IIDT-Database	92.00	93.00	91.00	92.25	93.44	90.85

Table 2. Comparing the performance of our proposed method with the state-of-the-art methods.

Approaches		Palmprint database	RR %
Method in [5]	SIFT + KNN	IIDT (1150 left hands images)	94,05 %
Method in [6]	Gabor filter, PCA, LDA + ED	CASIA	90,00 %
		IIDT (All images)	91,00 %
Method in [4]	LBP, LLDP + Manhattan distance	IIDT (All images)	92,00 %
The proposed method	DBC, DLA + SVM	CASIA	94.02 %
		IIDT (All images)	93,44 %

recognition rate for the CASIA database attains 94.02 % being a higher RR than the IIDT database. More importantly, it is necessary note that many ROI images in this database possess a black area being imminent to minimize recognition performance.

Exploiting the same palmprint datasets, a comparative study of the performance of our methodology was also carried out with other methods. The experimental outcomes prove that the suggested palmprint recognition system provides a higher performance in comparison to most well–known systems in the state-of-the-art [4, 6]. We presented the outcomes of this comparison in Table 2. The experimental outcomes of the image texture gained from the CASIA and IITD databases prove that our suggested method provides recognition rates of about 94.02 % and 93,44 % being impressively surpasses the ones presented in [4, 6]. These outcomes prove the certainty of our work.

4   Conclusions and Perspectives

In this paper, the applicability of fractal and Multi-fractal techniques have been explored in order to analyze the complexity of the palmprint texture by calculating the fractal dimensions based on Differential Box Counting (DBC) and Diffusion Limited Aggregates (DLA) methods. The effectiveness of these methods for palmprint identification applied on CASIA and IITD datasets was demonstrated. As a result, the experimental outcomes prove that the Recognition Rates reached 94.02 % and 93.44 %, respectively. Overall, we deduce that our approach provides the state-of-the-art comparable and favorable results. In future works, we will insist on fusing the different palmprint characteristics like the texture and the principal lines to come up with a significant palmprint recognition of individuals.

References

1. Wu, X., Zhang, D., Wang, K., Huang, B.: Palmprint classification using principal lines. Pattern Recogn. **37**, 1987–1998 (2004)
2. Chen, J., Zhang, C., Rong, G.: Palmprint recognition using crease. In: Proceedings of the 2001 International Conference on Image Processing, pp. 234–237. IEEE (2001)

3. Duta, N., Jain, A.K., Mardia, K.V.: Matching of palmprints. Pattern Recogn. Lett. **23**, 477–485 (2002)
4. Luo, Y.-T., Zhao, L.-Y., Zhang, B., Jia, W., Xue, F., Lu, J.-T., Zhu, Y.-H., Xu, B.-Q.: Local line directional pattern for palmprint recognition. Pattern Recogn. **50**, 26–44 (2016)
5. Charfi, N., Trichili, H., Alimi, A.M., Solaiman, B.: Bimodal biometric system based on SIFT descriptors of hand images. In: 2014 IEEE International Conference on Systems, Man and Cybernetics (SMC), pp. 4141–4145. IEEE (2014)
6. Jaswal, G., Nath, R., Kaul, A.: Texture based palm Print recognition using 2-D Gabor filter and sub space approaches. In: 2015 International Conference on Signal Processing, Computing and Control (ISPCC), pp. 344–349. IEEE (2015)
7. Mokni, R., Kherallah, M.: Biometric palmprint identification via efficient texture features fusion. In: 2016 International Joint Conference on Neural Networks (IJCNN). IEEE (2016)
8. Lu, G., Zhang, D., Wang, K.: Palmprint recognition using Eigenpalms features. Pattern Recogn. Lett. **24**, 1463–1467 (2003)
9. Wu, X., Zhang, D., Wang, K.: Fisherpalms based palmprint recognition. Pattern Recogn. Lett. **24**, 2829–2838 (2003)
10. Masood, H., Mumtaz, M., Butt, M., Mansoor, A. Bin, Khan, S.A.: Wavelet based palmprint authentication system. In: International Symposium on Biometrics and Security Technologies, ISBAST 2008, pp. 1–7. IEEE (2008)
11. Mokni, R., Kherallah, M.: Palmprint identification using GLCM texture features extraction and SVM classifier. J. Inf. Assur. Secur. **11**, 77–86 (2016)
12. Zouari, R., Mokni, R., Kherallah, M.: Identification and verification system of offline handwritten signature using fractal approach. In: 2014 First International Image Processing, Applications and Systems Conference (IPAS), pp. 1–4. IEEE (2014)
13. Chaabouni, A., Boubaker, H., Kherallah, M., Alimi, A.M., El Abed, H.: Fractal and multifractal for arabic offline writer identification. In: 2010 20th International Conference on Pattern Recognition (ICPR), pp. 3793−3796. IEEE (2010)
14. Mokni, R., Zouari, R., Kherallah, M.: Pre-processing and extraction of the ROIs steps for palmprints recognition system. In: International Conference on 15th Intelligent Systems Design and Applications (ISDA 2015), pp. 380−385. IEEE (2015)
15. Mandelbrot, B.B.: Les Objets Fractals: Forme, Hasard et Dimension. Flammarion, Paris (1975)
16. Sarkar, N., Chaudhuri, B.B.: An efficient differential box-counting approach to compute fractal dimension of image. IEEE Trans. Syst. Man Cybern. **24**, 115–120 (1994)
17. Lowe, D.G.: Similarity metric learning for a variable-kernel classifier. Neural Comput. **7**, 72–85 (1995)
18. Vapnik, V.: The nature of statistical learning theory. Springer, New York (1995)
19. Biometrics Ideal Test. http://biometrics.idealtest.org/dbDetailForUser.do?id=5
20. IIT Delhi, Indian Institute of Technology Delhi: IIT Delhi Touchless Palmprint Database (Version 1.0), http://web.iitd.ac.in/∼ajaykr/Database_Palm.htm

Ensemble Models of Learning Vector Quantization Based on Bootstrap Resampling

Fumiaki Saitoh[(⊠)]

Department of Industrial and Systems Engineering, Aoyama Gakuin University,
5-10-1, Fuchinobe, Chuo-ku, Sagamihara, Kanagawa, Japan
saitoh@ise.aoyama.ac.jp

Abstract. The purpose of this study is to improve the classification accuracy and stability of learning vector quantization using ensemble learning. We focused on an ensemble learning algorithm based on bootstrap resampling; this algorithm has been widely used in recent years. LVQs were extended to the ensemble model using three similar approaches: bagging, random forest, and double bagging. Through computational experiments using benchmark data, we investigated the compatibility between each approach and LVQ. The results showed that the double bagging approach was superior in ensemble LVQ.

Keywords: Learning Vector Quantization (LVQ) · Ensemble learning · Bootstrap · Double bagging · Random forest

1 Introduction

In the construction of a learning system, it is important to design a model with high generalization performance. Ensemble learning is widely used as a means to improve the generalization performance of a learning model [1]. Ensemble learning models are composed of a plurality of weak learners; that is, the model has a shallow fit to the data. By integrating the components based on majority voting or averaging, it is possible to improve the accuracy of the overall output system. In general, because the risk of overfitting is reduced by using a plurality of weak learners as components, ensemble learning models are widely used in data processing tasks such as prediction and identification. In recent years, bootstrap [2] sampling-based ensemble learning models represented by random forests [3] have been successfully applied to various tasks.

Vector quantization neural network models have been expanded to the ensemble learning model. For example, unsupervised vector quantization models represented by self-organizing maps (SOMs) and neural gas networks (NGNs) have been applied to ensemble learning algorithms [4] such as AdaBoost and bagging [5]. To expand learning vector quantization (LVQ) [6] to the ensemble learning model, Bermejo et al. [7] proposed a supervised learning model using local averaging. However, it is insufficient to discuss the compatibility between the bootstrap-based ensemble approach and LVQ, as these previous studies

© Springer International Publishing Switzerland 2016
A.E.P. Villa et al. (Eds.): ICANN 2016, Part II, LNCS 9887, pp. 267–274, 2016.
DOI: 10.1007/978-3-319-44781-0_32

have done. In particular, because they have worked effectively in many tasks such as bagging and random forest, various neural networks have been extended to bootstrap-based ensemble learning in recent works [8–10]; we believe that they should be considered for LVQ as well.

Therefore, this study applies a bootstrap-based ensemble learning framework to LVQ, and verifies this approach through experiments. We expect to eliminate various LVQ problems by applying ensemble learning. LVQ's identification performance is dependent on the data's input order and the initial value of the weight vectors; thus, its learning results are frequently stuck in shallow local minima. These problems are likely to be resolved by smoothing the identification boundary using ensemble learning, without overfitting.

In experiments using benchmark data sets, our approach and normal LVQ were compared in terms of identification performance. Through computational experiments, the performance of these models is evaluated and discussed.

2   Preparation

2.1   Learning Vector Quantization

LVQ is one of the nearest neighbor classifier models proposed by Kohonen [6], and is classified as a supervised neural network. LVQ is composed of an input layer and a competitive layer. Competitive layers have a set of prototype vectors to which labels are assigned for class information identification. LVQ discrimination boundaries are associated with Voronoi regions constructed by a set of prototype vectors, and inputted data are classified into the class label with the winner node. There are several LVQ learning algorithms, including LVQ1, LVQ2, LVQ3, and optimized-learning-rate LVQ1 (OLVQ1).

In this study, we adopt LVQ1 because it is the most popular and simple LVQ algorithm. Here, we present the definition of LVQ1 and its updating equations. Let n be a natural number, and let $(\boldsymbol{x}_i, y_i), i \in (1, 2, ..., n)$ be the training data, where $(\boldsymbol{x}_i, y_i)$ denotes a pair consisting of attribute data $\boldsymbol{x}_i$ and a class label y_i. Let k be a natural number, and let $(\boldsymbol{m}_j, l_j), j \in (1, 2, ..., k)$ be the training data, where $(\boldsymbol{m}_j, l_j)$ denotes a pair consisting of prototype LVQ1 vectors $\boldsymbol{m}_j$ and its class label l_j.

The updating equations of LVQ1 are described as follows. At time step t, all weight vectors $(\boldsymbol{m}_1, \boldsymbol{m}_2, ..., \boldsymbol{m}_k)$ are updated to the data $\boldsymbol{x}(t)$ using the following equation:

$$\boldsymbol{m}_c(t+1) = \begin{cases} \boldsymbol{m}_c(t) + \alpha(t)(\boldsymbol{x}(t) - \boldsymbol{m}_c(t)), \ y(t) = l_c(t) \\ \boldsymbol{m}_c(t) - \alpha(t)(\boldsymbol{x}(t) - \boldsymbol{m}_c(t)), \ y(t) \neq l_c(t) \end{cases} \tag{1}$$

$$\boldsymbol{m}_i(t+1) = \boldsymbol{m}_i(t), i \neq c \tag{2}$$

where $\alpha(t)$ is learning rate. Index c of winner node $\boldsymbol{m}_c$ of input data $\boldsymbol{x}$ is determined using the following formula: $c = \arg\min_i \|\boldsymbol{x} - \boldsymbol{m}_i\|$.

2.2   Bootstrap Based Ensemble Learning

In the bootstrap-based ensemble learning algorithm that is analyzed in this study, weak learners are components of the model learning the bootstrap samples. Because each weak learner learns with different data, it is possible to provide diversity to the process of learning the results of the components. Bagging and random forest can be cited as typical bootstrap-based ensemble learning algorithms. In particular, random forest is widely known as a high-performance method, and has recently been applied in various fields.

The benefits and advantages of these models are as follows:

(1) By shallow fitting of components to the data, these models avoid overfitting and provide enhanced generalization performance;
(2) They are relatively robust to noise such as outliers;
(3) Because each weak learner is processed independently, it is possible to apply parallel computing.

3   Applying Bootstrap Aggregating Algorithm for LVQ

3.1   Training Phase

Ensemble learning is composed of a training phase and a classification phase. We describe applying each phase to LVQ in this chapter.

The diversity of component learning results is one of the most important factors for improving the performance of the ensemble learning model. Even when applying the LVQ ensemble, we considered it important to give diversity to LVQs, which are components of the ensemble. By changing the input order of the data and the initial value of the weight vector of LVQs, which learn in parallel, it is possible to perturb the weak diversity output of components, because the LVQ has an initial value dependency.

However, only employing the collateral of diversity caused by the initial value dependency is insufficient. To increase the diversity of LVQ, the bootstrap-based ensemble learning algorithm is promising. In the training phase, by resampling using bootstraps from target data, components diversity is "squeezed through," which increases the variation of LVQ learning data. Here, we adopt three types of algorithms: bagging, random forest, and double bagging [11]; these algorithms are widely used in decision tree ensemble learning.

First, we describe bagging. Typically, the only processing performed in this phase involves resampling of training data for each LVQ. In this algorithm, LVQ learns independently resampled data in parallel. Second, we outline the process employed by random forest. The random forest, in addition to the resampling in bagging, gives diversity to classifiers by performing randomly selected features. Because the component of the model is not a tree, this paper will refer to this process as bagging with random feature selection. The random forest improves the overall model performance by increasing the variation of the conditional branch in the decision tree by random feature selection. The number of features selected by this algorithm was determined as the square root of the total number of features, which is generally recommended when using random forest.

Finally, a description of double bagging will be provided. This is an ensemble learning algorithm designed specifically for learning classification models; it aims to improve the classification accuracy through supervised dimensional reduction. In this model, a canonical variate in linear discriminant analysis has been used as a dimensional reduction tool; bagging uses this canonical variate as an attribute, which may improve classification performance. Here, by calculating the canonical variate in linear discriminant analysis on the basis of out-of-bag samples, the generalization of weak learners is considered.

The learning phase is intended to improve the performance of the entire ensemble model by applying these respective processes to ensemble model. In particular, bagging with random feature selection and double bagging have been used successfully in the ensemble of the decision tree; thus, higher performance can be expected.

3.2   Classification Phase

Because LVQ is a nearest neighbor classifier, the output value of the classification result of the ensemble model is determined based on a majority vote by the classifiers, which are components. This phase processes the processing results of all the previous training phases. Let $y_m(\boldsymbol{x}_i) \in \{C_1, C_2, ..., C_k\}$ be the classification result of classifier V_m for i-th data $\boldsymbol{x}_i$. The output of an LVQ ensemble model $\{V_m\}_{m=1}^{M}$ is obtained using the following equation:

$$C_i = \arg\max_j |C_j| \qquad (3)$$

where $|C_j|$ is the number of LVQ classifiers that classify data $\boldsymbol{x}_i$ to class C_j.

4   Experimental

4.1   Experimental Settings

The validity of our approach was confirmed through a computational simulation, which is described in the following section.

For our experiment, we used the "Iris," "Seeds," "Wholesaler Customer," "Abalone," "Connectionist Bench," and "Wine," data sets published in the UCI Machine Learning Repository, because they are widely used as benchmark data for classification tasks. We compared the proposed method against a normal LVQ model, as well as LVQ ensemble models that follow other approaches. The other ensemble LVQ models utilize the following three approaches: randomizing the initial value, applied bagging, bagging with variable selection (as random forest), and double bagging. In addition, in order to evaluate the computational complexity of ensemble learning, we confirmed the runtime with different numbers of ensembles at each algorithm.

We applied 5-fold cross validation for each data set, and compared the average accuracy rate of the experiment 50 times for each model. Here, the classification accuracies of each method were compared for each benchmark data set. Further, to investigate the relationship between the classification accuracy and the number of ensembles (while increasing the number of weak learners by one for each test), a similar experiment was performed. The parameters used in the experiment are as follows. Number of LVQ nodes are 2 times the number of classes, Bootstrap sample sizes are one-third of in-sample size, Learning rate $\gamma = 0.03$, Number of ensembles $E = 20$.

4.2   Experimental Results

This section describes the experimental results. Figure 1 shows the experimental results for each data set. Subfigures (a), (b), (c), (d), (e), and (f) correspond to "Iris," "Seeds," "Wholesaler customer," "Abalone," "Connectionist Bench," and "Wine," respectively. These figures are box plots of classification accuracy; the vertical axis shows classification accuracy, and the horizontal axis corresponds to each approach. Box plots in each figure represent results of normal LVQ1, ensemble LVQ without bootstrap, bagging of LVQ, LVQ bagging with random feature selection, and LVQ double bagging, from left to right. Mean values of classification accuracy for each method obtained as a result of cross-validation are listed in Table 1; the standard deviations of the classification accuracy are shown in parentheses. In this table, the maximum average value and the minimum standard deviation value for each data set are shown in bold.

Figures 2 and 3 show line charts that represent the relationship between the classification accuracy and the number of ensembles in each data set. The horizontal axis represents the number of ensembles and the vertical axis represents the classification accuracy. Figures 2 and 3 are corresponding to average value and standard deviation respectively. Table 2 shows the computational cost for seeds data set. It can be confirmed the relationship between the computational cost and the number of ensemble.

Table 1. Mean value and standard deviation of classification accuracy

	LVQ1	Randomized initial weights	Normal bagging	Bagging (rand feat slct)	Double bagging
Connectionist	68.15(6.80)	71.98(5.35)	71.45(5.47)	71.43(5.41)	**72.90(4.82)**
Wine	95.61(2.55)	96.93(1.94)	96.85(1.95)	96.07(2.26)	**97.73(1.81)**
Iris	90.59(4.73)	92.19(4.15)	91.26(4.07)	92.03(4.40)	**97.27(1.90)**
Wholesale	63.83(5.20)	71.30(2.73)	71.52(**2.58**)	**71.55(2.60)**	70.88(2.65)
Seeds	90.49(2.82)	91.92(2.43)	91.72(2.53)	91.30(2.71)	**95.83(1.88)**
Abalone	54.63(4.70)	**62.97(4.42)**	57.45(4.54)	57.48(4.61)	62.70(**4.23**)

4.3 Discussion

As shown in Fig. 1 and Table 1, double bagging provides the highest accuracy in four of the six data sets. Among the algorithms covered in this study, double bagging appears to provide the highest accuracy in the ensemble of LVQ. In addition, it can be confirmed that the standard deviation of the identification accuracy for this algorithm is lowest in five of the six data sets. Based on these findings, double bagging should be considered the most effective technique for practical applications, because the learning results can be stable and highly accurate.

In ensemble learning based on general decision trees, it is well known that random forests have higher prediction accuracy than bagging. However, in the framework of this study, namely ensemble learning of LVQ, the experimental results produced using the same variables as random forest do not indicate clear differences from the experimental results of bagging. The number of variables available to conditional branching within the decision tree is limited. On the other hand, LVQ constructs a decision boundary based on the Voronoi tessellation, using the full attributes provided. Because of this, it is more difficult to create diversity in LVQ ensembles than in decision tree-based ensemble models. We concluded that random feature selection is less effective in the performance improvement of ensemble learning of LVQ.

On the other hand, when comparing the normal LVQ and ensemble model, it is evident that all algorithms are better than the normal LVQ in terms of accuracy and stability. Furthermore, based on the results shown in Figs. 2 and 3, it can be confirmed that classification accuracy improves when the number of ensembles is increased. From the above, it was confirmed that applying ensemble learning in LVQ contributes to improving the performance of the model.

Ensemble size haves influence on the increase of the computational cost (See Table 2). Especially, it is larger than the others computational cost of double bagging. It can be considered that double bagging algorithm requires a large amount of calculation to supervised dimension reduction and learning of OOB data. However, we believe that computational cost of double bagging for LVQ is viable. Furthermore, since each of the bootstrap-based ensemble learning algorithms are capable of extension to parallel computing, improving the efficiency of computing is possible.

Table 2. Runtime with different numbers of ensembles at each algorithm

The number of ensembles	10	20	50	100	200	500
Randomized initial weights	0.03 s	0.04 s	0.12 s	0.27 s	0.59 s	1.86 s
Normal bagging	0.05 s	0.10 s	0.27 s	0.58 s	1.14 s	3.53 s
Bagging (rand feat slct)	0.01 s	0.05 s	0.15 s	0.28 s	0.64 s	2.06 s
Double bagging	0.14 s	0.26 s	0.61 s	1.23 s	2.56 s	6.83 s

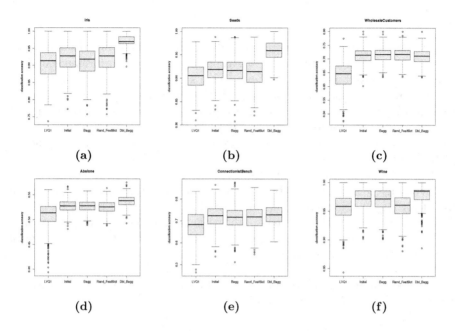

Fig. 1. Boxplots of experimental results for each model

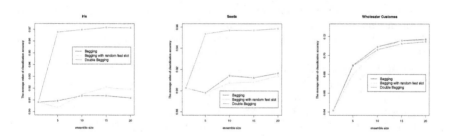

Fig. 2. Relationship between the average of the classification accuracy and the number of ensembles

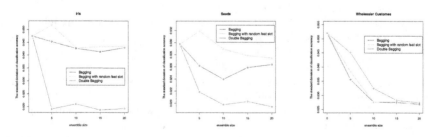

Fig. 3. Relationship between the standard deviation of the classification accuracy average and the number of ensembles

5   Conclusion

In this study, we applied a bootstrap-based ensemble learning algorithm to LVQ. The effectiveness of this technique was confirmed through performance evaluations that employed computational experiments using benchmark data sets. The result shows that bootstrap-based ensemble learning contributes to an improvement in LVQ's classification performance, particularly in the ensemble learning general neural nets and decision trees. Because these extensions to the LVQ are relatively straightforward, they can be expected to improve the performance of real-world tasks.

The following is a list of future issues to be addressed by this study: 1. Discussing the use of ensemble algorithms other than those already adopted in this study [12], 2. Discussing other versions of LVQ, including LVQ2, LVQ3 and OLVQ1, 3. Evaluating the relevance of the parameter settings on the performance of these models, and 4. Evaluating performance based on a theoretical point of view, such as information value.

Acknowledgments. This work was supported by JSPS KAKENHI Grant-in-Aig for Young Scientists (B) Numbers 15K1625.

References

1. Seni, G., Elder, J.: Ensemble Methods in Data Mining - Improving Accuracy Through Combining Predictons. Morgan and Claypool, San Rafael (2010)
2. Efron, B., Tibshirani, R.J.: An Introduction to the Bootstrap. Springer, New York (1993)
3. Breiman, L.: Random Forest. Mach. Learn. **45**, 5–32 (2001)
4. Shigei, N., Miyajima, H., Maeda, M., Ma, L.: Bagging and AdaBoost algorithms for vector quantization. Neurocomputing **73**, 106–114 (2009)
5. Breiman, L.: Bagging predictors. Mach. Learn. **24**, 123–140 (1996)
6. Kohonen, T.: Self-Organizing Maps. Springer, Heidelberg (1995)
7. Bermejo, S., Cabestany, J.: Local averaging of ensembles of LVQ-based nearrest neighbor classifiers. Appl. Intell. **20**, 47–58 (2004)
8. Pulido, M., Melin, P., Castillo, O.: Particle swarm optimization of ensemble neural networks with fuzzy aggregation for time series prediction of the Mexican Stock Exchange. Inf. Sci. **280**, 188–204 (2014)
9. Alhamdoosh, M., Dianhui, W.: Fast decorrelated neural network ensembles with random weights. Inf. Sci. **264**, 104–117 (2014)
10. Kourentzes, N., Barrow, D., Crone, S.: Neural network ensemble operators for time series forecasting. Expert Syst. Appl. **41**, 4235–4244 (2014)
11. Hothorn, T., Lausen, B.: Double-bagging: combining classifiers by bootstrap aggregation. Pattern Recogn. **36**, 1303–1309 (2003)
12. Rodrigez, J.J., Kuncheva, L.I.: Rotation forest: a new classifier ensemble method. IEEE Trans. Pattern Anal. Mach. Intell. **28**(10), 1619–1630 (2006)

Cluster Ensembles Optimization Using Coral Reefs Optimization Algorithm

Huliane M. Silva[1], Anne M.P. Canuto[1,2($\boxtimes$)], Inácio G. Medeiros[2], and João C. Xavier-Júnior[1,2]

[1] Department of Informatics and Applied Mathematics,
Federal University of Rio Grande do Norte, Natal, RN, Brazil
`huliane@ppgsc.ufrn.br`, `anne@dimap.ufrn.br`, `jcxavier@imd.ufrn`
[2] Digital Metropolis Institute, Federal University of Rio Grande do Norte,
Natal, RN, Brazil
`inacio.medeiros@ifrn.edu.br`

Abstract. The main aim of this paper is to combine multiple partitions generated by different clustering algorithms into a single clustering solution (consensus partition), using a new bio-inspired optimization technique to optimize the cluster ensembles. In this proposed technique, the cluster ensembles are heterogeneously created and the initial partitions are combined through a method which uses the Coral Reefs Optimization algorithm, resulting in a consensus partition.

Keywords: Machine learning · Clustering ensembles · Optimization

1 Introduction

There is a huge variety of clustering algorithms proposed in literature which have been successfully applied in different applications. However, in an attempt to overcome the limitations of the individual clustering algorithms, combining different methods can provide further information about the problem to be solved. Systems that combine several different clustering methods are called Cluster Ensembles. In this context, the goal is to find a consensus partition taken from various methods applied to a given dataset. Although the cluster ensembles are usually more accurate methods than individual clustering algorithms, such methods do not always perform well. One possibility to improve the efficiency of clustering ensembles is by using optimization techniques. The optimization of cluster ensembles is aimed at improving stability and robustness of the final partition of an ensemble.

Generally, optimization techniques can follow two different approaches: the first one is the generation of initial partition of the ensemble, in which various clustering algorithms are applied to a particular dataset; the second approach focuses on the combination of the initial partitions. This article will focus on the second approach, optimizing the consensus function in the context of cluster ensembles. In this sense, we aim to propose an approach towards the optimization

A.E.P. Villa et al. (Eds.): ICANN 2016, Part II, LNCS 9887, pp. 275–282, 2016.
DOI: 10.1007/978-3-319-44781-0_33

in creating an ensemble consensus function, through a bio-inspired optimization technique, more specifically, the Coral Reefs Optimization (CRO) algorithm. This optimization algorithm was recently proposed by [7] and applied on problems in the mobile network field [9] and sustainable energy [8,10], achieving a good performance. In a previous work of the authors, [6], the CRO algorithm was applied to data clustering problems using individual algorithms. As a consequence of the promising results obtained in [6], this paper applies CRO for cluster ensembles.

2   Cluster Ensembles

The combination of clustering algorithms, also called Cluster Ensembles consists of finding a final solution, i.e., a consensus partition, based on the combination of multiple partitions provided by one or more clustering algorithms. This consensus partition should be better than the initial partitions [11]. By using cluster ensembles, usually the goals are: robustness (obtaining a more robust consensus partition than the initial partitions), novelty (achieving an original consensus partition, which cannot be individually obtained from any algorithm) and stability (finding solutions of clusters with less sensitivity to noise, outliers, sampling variations or algorithm variance) [4].

In the context of clusters of ensembles it is necessary to consider two important aspects, which are: the generation of the initial partitions and the creation of consensus function to combine the initial partitions. In the first case, in order to have a final partition with good quality, it is important to have diversity in the generation of initial partitions; which means that initial partitions must be different from one another so that each of them may add relevant information to the final partition [3].

The consensus function is defined as combining the generated initial partitions in a single partition, or the final partition, also called consensus partition. The consensus partition must be better than the initial partitions, which is why the choice of a consensus function should be made carefully. Furthermore, it is important to note that the combination of initial partitions is a complex task taking into account the absence of labels on objects to be clustered, resulting in partitions not explicitly matching the initial partitions [11].

3   Coral Reefs Optimization – CRO

The Coral Reefs optimization algorithm is a meta-heuristic evolutionary algorithm based on coral reefs reproduction. Basically, the algorithm creates an N x M sized square grid, in which some cells are initially occupied at random by corals, while others empty cells will be occupied by new corals, when they establish themselves freely and grow in the future. Each position on the grid, i.e., each cell may contain a coral, which represents a possible solution for the optimization problem. Each coral is associated with a health function, which represents the function which is the objective of the problem. In this way, for a coral reef to progress, it will depend on the health degree of the corals. That is, the healthier the corals are (which represents the best solutions for the problem) more likely to survive they will be. In contrast, the less healthy corals are more likely to die [8]. After the algorithm is started, an iterative process takes place, in which each iteration corresponds to a generation of corals. In every iteration, the corals reproduce and new individuals, called larvae, are generated. The main operators used by CRO are [8]:

1. External Sexual Reproduction: This type of reproduction is composed of two stages: the first consists in selecting a fraction of corals on the reef to be diffuse reproductive. The rest of the corals will reproduce in litters at a later stage of the algorithm. The second step is to select pairs to reproduce, where each individual in the pair forms one or two larvae of coral by sexual breeding. Once the pair is selected to be parents of a larva, the individuals in the pair are no longer chosen to reproduce in the same iteration.
2. Internal Sexual Reproduction: in this type of reproduction, the fraction of coral that was not selected in the previous step reproduces in litters. The litter modelling consists in forming a coral larva through a random mutation of the coral. Thus, the larva produced is then released, along with larvae formed by spawning or transmission.
3. Definition of the Larvae: this is the main step of the algorithm. Since all larvae are formed, they will try to establish and grow on the reef. This process happens as follows: initially, the health function of each larva is calculated. Then each larva will randomly try to occupy a cell in the reef grid. So, if the cell is empty (free space on the reef), the coral larva grows on it, no matter despite the value of its health function. However, if the selected cell is already occupied by a coral, the new larva will establish only if its health function is better than the existing coral's. This larva makes a given number of attempts to define on the reef; in case several unsuccessful attempts occur, the larva will be preyed upon by animals on the reef.
4. Asexual Reproduction: in the asexual reproduction modelling (also called budding or fragmentation), the global set of existing coral on the reef are classified according to their level of health. Then a small fraction of the best corals is duplicated and then try to settle in a different part of the reef, following the configuration process described in step 3.
5. Preying: in this phase a part of the worst coral reef can be preyed upon, therewith clearing some space on the coral reef for the next generation. In each step, the prey operator is applied with a small probability and exclusively to fraction of the more poor and less healthy coral.

4 The Proposed Approach

As mentioned previously, CRO is a bio-inspired meta-heuristic algorithm which was recently proposed for optimization problems. Nevertheless, to the best of our knowledge, up to the present, no applications of CRO in the context of cluster ensembles has been found in literature. Therefore, this paper proposes the usage of CRO algorithm to provide optimization in cluster ensembles, specifically applied on the generation of the consensus function, as can be described in the following steps.

- The original dataset is divided into subsets, which can have the same size of the original dataset (samples with replacement, as in Bagging or Boosting) or not (feature and/or instance selection methods for ensembles);
- Once the subsets are created, the subsets are presented to the clustering algorithms to provide the initial partition.
- The following stage combines these partitions, in order to obtain a consensus cluster, which is obtained by the combination of the listed methods. The generation of this function is brought about by the CRO algorithm. In this sense, the best partition of each iteration of CRO is selected.
- Finally, the final partition will be assessed by evaluation indices.

5   Experimental Setting Up

In order to analyze the efficiency of the CRO algorithm on optimizing cluster ensembles, an experimental analysis was conducted. In this analysis, 12 datasets were exported from UCI Machine Learning Repository, described in Table 1.

Table 1. Dataset features

Dataset	Instances	Atrributes	Classes
Automobile	205	26	7
Balance scale	625	4	3
Breast cancer	286	9	2
Sonar	208	60	2
Dermatology	366	34	6
Ecoli	336	7	8
Glass	214	10	7
Hepatitis	155	19	2
Iris	150	4	3
Lung cancer	32	56	3
Diabete	768	8	2
Wine	178	13	3

The initial partitions of the ensemble are generated by three different clustering algorithms, which are: K-Means, Expectation-Maximization and agglomerative Hierarchical. The listed algorithms have been chosen based on their wide applicability on cluster ensembles in which they had worked success-fully. In addition, they are simple and easily applicable methods. In this work the implementations of the used algorithms were exported from the WEKA package [5].

Taking into consideration that the optimization techniques and cluster-ing algorithms used in this work (except the Hierarchical algorithm) are non-deterministic ones, 10 executions were performed. In addition, for each clustering algorithm, the number of groups varies from 2 to 10. Therefore, for each config-uration, there will be 90 values (10 executions × 9 number of groups) and they will be averaged to be presented in this paper.

In this work, three different fitness functions are used, both in the CRO algorithm and in the genetic algorithm (GA), which are:

- Corrected Rand (CR): it determines how similar two partitions are, in which one of the partitions must be a previously known data structure, while the other partition is the one being assessed;
- Davies-Bouldin (DB): It is a function which calculates the rate between the sum of dispersion inside the groups and the dispersion among the groups;
- MX, proposed in [6]: it evaluates how near a given partition and a new parti-tion are.

Therefore, for the generation of the ensemble consensus function, six different configurations will be analyzed, in which three of them use the proposed (CRO), varying the fitness function. The remaining three configurations will be used to provide a comparison with CRO algorithm. The comparative configurations were genetic algorithms (varying the fitness function). For comparison purposes, the GA-based configurations will use the same methodology of CRO to provide the consensus function, as explained in Sect. 4.

In order to assess the obtained consensus partition, two clustering validation indices were taken into consideration, namely: the Calinski-Harabasz index [2] and Jaccard [1].

6 Results

This section presents an overall evaluation of all of the six analysed approaches (GA-CR, GA-DB, GA-MX, CRO-CR, CRO-DB, CRO-MX). Keeping in mind that different datasets with different precision values are being evaluated in this analysis, the direct use of these values can lead to a mistaken analysis of the obtained results. In order to address this issue, the performance of these approaches is assessed taking into consideration the mean ranking of the obtained results. These rankings are based on their precision (CH or Jaccard), always assigning 1 to the best value, followed by 2, 3, 4, 5 and 6 in ascending order according to its performance. This ranking is calculated for each configuration (index value and objective functions), taking all 9 analysed number of groups (from 2 to 10). The average score for each approach is then calculated and the final classification is made according to their average score for each dataset.

Table 2 presents the results of the mean ranking for each of the six approaches and each dataset, considering, respectively, the CH and Jaccard indices. The shaded values represent the lowest value in the ranking for each dataset. The last row in each table is the overall average ranking of the compared approaches for all analyzed datasets.

Table 2. Ranking results for Calinski-Harabasz (CH) and Jaccard indices

Calinski Harabasz (CH)					
Dataset	GA-CR	GA-DB	GA-MX	CRO-CR	CRO-DB	CRO-MX
Dermatology	2.72±0.90	6.61±0.22	5.72±1.62	2.33±1.22	4.22±0.97	1.50±0.86
Iris	3.00±0.86	5.50±1.69	5.22±0.83	1.66±0.5	4.33±0.86	1.77±0.83
Automobile	3.00±1.73	5.94±1.95	4.72±1.76	2.55±1.23	3.88±1.90	2.55±1.23
Breast	3.33±1.00	6.61±0.22	5.94±1.48	2.88±0.92	3.77±0.83	1.22±0.44
Diabetes	3.11±0.6	6.11±0.22	5.66±0.70	1.88±0.33	3.88±0.60	1.22±0.66
Lung	4.00±1.32	5.61±1.69	5.88±1.05	2.66±1.22	5.22±0.97	1.55±0.52
Ecoli	4.22±0.44	6.72±0.26	5.61±1.11	2.27±0.66	5.44±0.52	1.88±0.92
Sonar	2.88±0.78	6.33±0.35	4.11±1.53	1.33±0.7	4.83±0.61	2.38±1.21
Wine	4.00±1.00	6.00±1.88	4.11±1.59	2.5±2.00	4.88±1.05	2.22±0.97
Hepatitis	3.55±0.72	6.27±0.26	5.22±1.46	2.00±0.50	4.44±0.52	1.11±0.33
Glass	3.55±0.88	5.88±0.78	4.22±1.20	1.55±0.52	4.44±0.88	1.55±0.72
Balance	4.00±0.70	5.44±0.52	4.11±0.92	2.00±0.00	3.88±0.92	1.00±0.00
Ave±ST	3.44±0.91	6.08±0.83	5.04±1.27	2.13±0.81	4.43±0.88	1.66±0.72
Jaccard					
Dermatology	5.88±0.82	2.55±0.88	5.22±0.97	3.22±0.83	6.44±0.72	2.44±1.13
Iris	5.33±0.86	1.00±0.00	5.00±1.22	3.44±0.88	6.66±0.70	2.55±0.72
Automobile	4.00±2.48	3.11±2.01	4.11±1.02	4.11±1.13	4.66±0.82	3.77±2.63
Breast	5.44±0.88	1.55±0.52	3.00±0.00	5.00±0.70	4.55±0.72	1.44±0.52
Diabetes	5.33±0.70	1.66±0.70	3.22±1.09	3.77±0.66	5.44±0.72	1.00±0.00
Lung	4.77±1.09	1.38±0.48	3.00±0.00	4.66±0.50	6.11±0.92	1.61±0.48
Ecoli	5.66±0.70	1.77±0.44	5.55±1.01	3.22±0.66	6.44±0.72	1.55±0.88
Sonar	4.88±0.78	1.00±0.00	2.66±0.70	3.88±0.60	6.27±0.66	3.44±2.12
Wine	5.55±0.52	1.11±0.33	3.33±1.11	3.55±1.13	6.00±1.22	4.88±2.61
Hepatitis	5.33±1.22	1.22±0.44	2.66±0.70	4.11±0.92	5.77±1.09	3.55±2.65
Glass	5.66±0.86	1.00±0.00	3.33±0.70	3.66±1.41	6.55±0.52	3.44±1.5
Balance	5.00±1.50	1.66±0.50	4.11±1.45	4.44±1.33	5.11±0.6	1.00±0.00
Ave±ST	5.23±1.03	1.58±0.52	3.76±0.83	3.92±0.89	5.83±0.78	2.55±1.27

By analyzing the mean ranking results, considering the overall average of the approaches for each dataset, using the CH index, it is possible to assert that the CRO-MX approach (CRO using MX as fitness function), achieved the lowest mean ranking (the best performance). While using the GA-DB approach (genetic algorithm using DB as fitness function) had the best performance; and when using the Jaccard index.

Of the different approaches used for the proposed method, the CRO-MX approach has achieved the best performance, for both evaluation indices. In fact, the CRO-MX approach achieved the best performance in 9 out of the 12 datasets, when the CH index was used for evaluation. When the Jaccard index was used, the best performance was achieved in 5, out of the 12 datasets. Therefore, we can state that the proposed approach (CRO-MX) had provided the best performance in majority of datasets, when using CH index. For the remaining datasets, the performance of CRO-MX was similar to the one provided by the genetic algorithms (GA-DB).

6.1   The Statistical Tests

In order to more significantly validate the performance of the approaches used in the empirical analysis we used the Friedmann and post-hoc Nemenyi test, since these non-parametric tests are suitable to compare performance of different learning algorithms, being applied on several datasets. Friedmann test is used to compare the performance of all of the six approaches. Therefore, it is applied directly on the index values, rather than on the ranking results.

As a result of the Friedman test, we observe that the index values provided by all six approaches proved to be statistically significant for all two evaluation indices (p-value $= 3.9347e - 11$ for CH and p-value $= 9.2012e - 07$ for Jaccard). We then applied the post-hoc Nemenyi test, for all two evaluation indices. The results of the post-hoc Nemenyi test are shown in Table 3 and its first column describes the comparison shown in this paper. In this case, all three CRO configurations, changing the fitness function (CR, DB and MX), are compared to the other approaches. It is important to highlight that each CRO configuration was compared only to the approach similar to the GA, such as, for instance, CRO-CR was compared to GA-CR.

Table 3. P-value results the Friedmann test

Friedman	CH	Jaccard
CRO-CR Vs GA-CR	0.11	0.006
CRO-DB Vs GA-DB	0.005	**0.96**
CRO-MX Vs GA-MX	0.00	0.036

In Table 3, the shaded cells represents the values in which the CRO approach has achieved better performance, from a statistical point of view. In contrast, the bold cells represents the cases in which the GA approach is better than the CRO approach. For the regular cells, the performance of both approaches are similar, from a statistical point of view. We can observe that the CRO approach had better performance (shaded cells) than the GA approach, from a statistical point of view, in 4 cases. In addition, the CRO approach had worse performance (bold numbers) in only 1 case and similar performance in 1 case. In general, the performance provided by CRO, for all three objective functions, was better than the corresponding GA approach. In the statistical analysis, the CRO approach either proved to be statistically better or similar. The only exceptions was when using the DB index as objective function. The results obtained in this paper are very promising since it shows that the use of the CRO algorithm for cluster ensembles can provide better or similar results than genetic algorithms, which is the most applied optimization algorithm for a cluster ensemble.

7   Final Remarks

This paper presented a new approach for defining the consensus partition for cluster ensembles. The proposed approach applied a recently proposed bio-inspired optimization technique, called the Coral Reefs Optimization (CRO) algorithm, to provide the consensus partition from a set of initial partitions. In order to assess the performance of the proposed approach, an empirical analysis was conducted. In this analysis, the proposed approach used three different objective functions (CR, DB and MX) and they were all applied to 12 different datasets. For comparison purposes, we also applied a genetic algorithm, using the same three objective functions.

Through this analysis, we can conclude that the performance provided by CRO, for all three objective functions, was better than the corresponding GA approach. In the statistical analysis, the CRO approach either proved to be statistically better or similar. The only exception was when using the DB index as objective function. The results obtained in this paper are very promising since it shows that the use of the CRO algorithm for cluster ensembles can provide better or similar results than genetic algorithms, which is the most applied optimization algorithm for a cluster ensemble.

References

1. Boutin, F., Hascoet, M.: Cluster validity indices for graph partitioning. In: Eighth International Conference on Information Visualisation (IV 2004), London, England, pp. 376–381 (2004)
2. Calinski, R., Harabasz, J.: A dendrite method for cluster analysis. Commun. Stat. **3**, 1–27 (1974)
3. Faceli, K.: A framewors for analysing the consensus partition provided by the multi-objective cluster ensembles (in portuguese). Ph.D. thesis, Universidade de São Paulo (2006)
4. Faceli, K., Lorena, A.C., Gama, J., de Carvalho, A.C.P.L.F: Artificial Intelligence: A Machine Learning Approach (in portuguese). LTC, Rio de Janeiro (2011)
5. Hall, M., Frank, E., Holmes, G., Pfahringer, B., Reutemann, P., Witten, I.H.: The weka data mining software: an update. SIGKDD Explor. **11**(1), 10–18 (2009)
6. Medeiros, I.G., ao C. Xavier-Júnior, J., Canuto, A.M.P.: Applying the coral reefs optimization algorithm to clustering problems. In: International Joint Conference on Neural Networks (IJCNN), Proceedings of International Joint Conference on Neural Networks (IJCNN), vol. 1, pp. 1–8 (2015)
7. Salcedo-Sanz, S., Casanova-Mateo, C., Pastor-Sanchez, A., Sanchez-Giron, M.: Daily global solar radiation prediction based on a hybrid coral reefs optimization - extreme learning machine approach. Sol. Energy **105**, 91–98 (2014)
8. Salcedo-Sanz, S., Gallo-Marazuela, D., Pastor-Sanchez, A., Carro-Calvo, L., Portilla-Figueras, A., Prieto, L.: Offshore wind farm design with the coral reefs optimization algorithm. Renew. Energy **63**, 109–115 (2014)
9. Salcedo-Sanz, S., García-Díaz, P., Portilla-Figueras, J.A., Ser, J.D., Gil-López, S.: A coral reefs optimization algorithm for mobile network optimal deployment with electromagnetic pollution control criterion. App. Soft. Comp. **24**, 239–248 (2014)
10. Salcedo-Sanz, S., Pastor-Sanchez, A., Ser, J.D., Prieto, L., Geem, Z.: A coral reefs optimization algorithm with harmony search operators for accurate wind speed prediction. Renew. Energy **75**, 93–101 (2015)
11. Topchy, A., Jain, A.K., Punch, W.: Combining multiple weak clusterings. In: Proceedings of the IEEE International Conference on Data Mining (ICDM 2003), Melbourne, Florida, USA, pp. 331–338 (2003)

Classification of Photo and Sketch Images Using Convolutional Neural Networks

Kazuma Sasaki$^{(\boxtimes)}$, Madoka Yamakawa, Kana Sekiguchi, and Tetsuya Ogata

Intermedia Art and Science, Waseda University, Shinjuku, Tokyo, Japan
ssk.sasaki@suou.waseda.jp

Abstract. Content-Based Image Retrieval (CBIR) system enables us to access images using only images as queries, instead of keywords. Photo-realistic images, and hand-drawn sketch image can be used as a queries as well. Recently, convolutional neural networks (CNNs) are used to discriminate images including sketches. However, the tasks are limited to classifying only one type of images, either photo or sketch images, due to the lack of a large dataset of sketch images and the large difference of their visual characteristics. In this paper, we introduce a simple way to prepare training datasets, which can enable the CNN model to classify both types of images by color transforming photo and illustration images. Through the training experiment, we show that the proposed method contributes to the improvement of classification accuracy.

Keywords: Content Based Image Retrieval · Hand-drawn sketch

1 Introduction

We can locate a variety of images in large datasets using searching systems with a set of keywords as the query. However, sometimes we want to find images with an unknown name. Content Based Image Retrieval (CBIR) is an effective way to search for such content, for which we have no discriminating metadata [1]. Hand-drawn sketch images were applied to CBIR system [2–4], because users do not have to take pictures or download images, but just draw some simple lines. In order to develop and improve the sketch-based CBIR systems, a well-designed image feature extraction method was utilized [5]. In addition, convolutional neural networks (CNNs) [6] recently became the major approach to recognizing images, due to its high accuracy in image classification tasks, which was achieved by training over one million images [7]. Due to this good scalability for discriminating a lot of images, the CNN classier can be used to recognize user's query in a CBIR system.

However the CNN's classification targets are unfortunately limited to photorealistic images (Fig. 1(a)) or sketch images (Fig. 1(b)), even though CBIR systems have various kinds of query images. Discriminating both photorealistic and sketch images through a CNN model is still a challenging task because there is no large scale database set of sketch images. Eitz et al. proposed using an open

© Springer International Publishing Switzerland 2016
A.E.P. Villa et al. (Eds.): ICANN 2016, Part II, LNCS 9887, pp. 283–290, 2016.
DOI: 10.1007/978-3-319-44781-0_34

image database set with 20,000 non-professional hand-sketch images [5], but the size of the dataset is small. In addition, training CNNs with both types of images is also difficult, because there are large differences between these two types of images, which prevent networks from extracting the general features required for classification. Yang et al. proposed the idea of a sketch-image retrieval system but they utilized two CNN models divided by type of image [8], due to the difficulty of integrating training of photo and sketch images. Sketch images do not have color or texture information, which is basic for the differentiation of the input images in the internal CNN process. In addition, the shapes in sketch images are not well-shared among the classes, because the shape is often altered during the drawing process. Yu et al. proposed a CNN based model for recognizing sketch images using stroke ordering of sketching. Their system marks 74.9 % of accuracy in classifying 250 categories of hand drawn sketch images [9]. This is better than human performance, but this system can recognize only sketch images with stroke ordering information. By contrast, CBIR systems may be input photo realistic images or sketch images without the information about stroke ordering.

(a) Photo   (b) Illlustration   (c) Sketch

Fig. 1. Examples of images. (a) Photo image. (b) Illustration image. (c) Sketch image.

In this paper, we introduce a simple way that enables one CNN model to classify photo and sketch images by training data argumentation. To overcome the problem of the sketch image dataset's size, we utilize color transformed illustration images (Fig. 1(b)). Illustration images are a type of non-photorealistic images, but they are more detailed than sketch images; they have coloring, and they can be easily found by crawling the web. For the training dataset, we enhanced the edged of the illustration images to imitate sketch images. Furthermore, we added gray-scaled versions of photo and illustration images to bridge the difference between the photo and the edge-emphasized illustration images.

This paper is organized as follows. In Sect. 2, we explain how to prepare training datasets of CNNs with the proposed method. After that, we describe a simple experiment for classifying 20 classes of animal images and confirm the ability of the proposed method in Sect. 3. The results of the experiment are described in Sect. 4. In the same section, we also visualize the acquired image features by the CNN. Finally we summarize our work in Sect. 4.

2   Method for Preparing Datasets

To prepare the training dataset for the CNN model to classify photo and sketch book, we utilize the mixed image dataset comprising of photo images, illustration images, and color-transformed versions of these images.

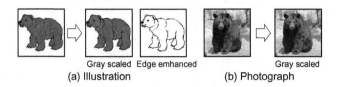

Gray scaled Edge emhanced   Gray scaled
(a) Illustration   (b) Photograph

Fig. 2. The method to prepare the training date set for CNN. The training data set consists of (a) illustration images and (b) photo images. Illustration images additionally have two types of varieties: grayscale ones and sketch-liked ones. Photo image are transformed into grayscale images.

Figure 2 presents the purposed method to prepare training datasets. Through the forward propagation process of CNNs, information about color, texture and shapes is converted through many layers of CNN to the probability of each class. This means that the classification accuracy of CNNs strongly depends on the color distribution on the input image. If CNNs are trained by only photo images, they cannot discriminate non-photorealistic images well, because they do not often share color information with the trained images. When we want to train CNN with both photo and sketch images, it is difficult to collect a lot of hand drawn sketch images. Therefore we utilize illustration images instead of sketch images. Illustration images are more detailed than sketch images and non-photorealistic images, and they are easily collected by image search engines. To imitate sketch images, we emphasize edges of illustration images by using a canny edge detector [10]. In addition, we include the grayscale versions of the photos and illustration images to bridge the gap between the two types of images. These grayscale images are aligned with the input value, and offer a compromise between sketch and photo images.

3   Experiments

To confirm the ability of the proposed method to prepare datasets, we conduct a preliminary experiment that pertains to assigning animal images into 20 classes. Four CNN models with different training datasets are compared with respect to classification accuracy based on the untrained datasets, which consist of photos and sketch images.

(a) Examples of photo images

(b) Examples of illustration images

(c) Examples of sketch images

Fig. 3. Examples of the images used to prepare the training datasets, which consists of 20 animal categories (classes). (a) Photo graph images. (b) Illustration images. (c) Hand-drawn sketch images.

3.1   Datasets

Figure 3 shows examples of images used in the training datasets. We collected 27,927 images of animals belonging to 20 classes. In order to collect these images, we searched the web with the names of animals. In the test dataset, 100 sketch images were drawn by five participants. The size of the images was 256×256 pixels, and all images were randomly cropped into 227×227 pixels when the images were inputted into the CNN.

Table 1. Details of the training datasets.

Dataset	Photo	Illust	Photo (Gray)	Illust (Gray)	Illust (Edge)	Number of images
(A) Illust	-	x	-	-	-	12,734
(B) Photo	x	-	-	-	-	38,468
(C) Illust and Photo	x	x	-	-	-	51,202
(D) Proposed method	x	x	x	x	x	115,138

To compare the dataset's classification effectiveness and accuracy, four types of training datasets were examined, as described in Table 1. First, we prepared two datasets with only one type of image, named (A) Illust and (B) Photo. In addition, we prepared the mixed training dataset, (C) Illust and Photo. Finally we tested the proposed method (D). All Images of the training datasets were duplicated by mirroring to avoid overfitting.

In order to check the classification accuracy of photo and sketch images, 200 images were used as the test dataset. This dataset comprised 100 sketch images and 100 untrained photo images.

3.2   Learning CNNs

As a learning model, we utilize a CNN model which with five convolutional layers, the corresponding pooling layers, and three fully connected layers. The network architecture was based on Alex-net [6] which is known as a standard CNN model for classifying images. Under all training conditions, we utilized common layer parameters and hyper training parameters. All CNNs were optimized over 1400 k iterations by stochastic gradient descent [11] with mini batches, which have 100 images each. The optimization process was calculated with a single GPU, and Caffe [12] as framework.

4   Results and Discussion

4.1   Classification Accuracy of Photo and Sketch Images

Table 2 summarizes the classification accuracy obtained after training four CNNs. Each accuracy value reflects the best classification performance on the mixed dataset of photo and sketch images, in the optimization process. The CNN model trained with the dataset (D) outperforms the others. When the CNN model is trained with the dataset (A), it can classify 33 % of the images, but classifies the sketch images with high accuracy. On the other hand, the CNN model trained with the dataset (D) can classify photo images well, but it cannot discriminate sketch images well. Training both types of images improves the classification by 20 %. Adding color transformed images of illustrations and photo images in dataset (C) further improves the process by over 10 %. Thus, the proposed method is successful in significantly improving the classification.

4.2   Image Activation Features in CNNs

Furthermore, we visualize activation features of the training images obtained by the trained CNNs with the proposed method. We perform principal component analysis (PCA) on the training image's features, which are extracted in the second fully connected layer (the second from the last layer). The contribution values of the three PCA's components are 1.84 %, 1.06 % and 0.97 %, respectively. As shown in Fig. 4, the features are separated by the labels of images.

Figure 5 depicts how the different types of images are organized in the CNNs by shifting the target layer in order to the extract the features. (a) pool5 is the

Table 2. Comparison results of classification accuracy by changing the training dataset. Each line presents the best classification accuracy of models trained with illustrations, photos, and the mixed dataset.

Dataset	Photo	Sketch	Mixed
(A) Illust	26 %	41 %	33 %
(B) Photo	99 %	11 %	55 %
(C) Illust and Photo	99 %	42 %	71 %
(D) **Proposed method**	99 %	76 %	**85 %**

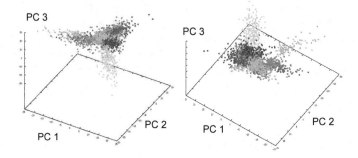

Fig. 4. Activation features of the training dataset obtained by the CNN trained using the proposed method. Two plots depict the same features projected by principal component analysis, but viewed from different angles. Each color indicates the class of the images, and PC1 to PC3 axes correspond to principal components 1–3, respectively.

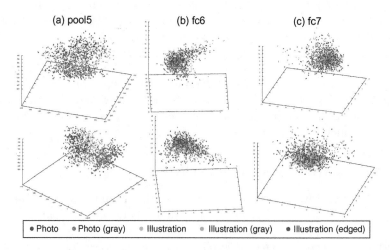

Fig. 5. Activation features of the images labeled "bear" projected in the same manner as Fig. 4. Each row (a), (b) and (c) corresponds to each CNN layer. The top and bottom rows depict the same features from different angles. All features are colored based on the type of images.

fourth layer from the last. From this layer, we visualize the features of the same images labeled "bear" by shifting the target layer. We then extract the features one by one toward the output, at which (a) pool5 is the fourth layer from the last and (c) fc7 is the second layer from the last, which outputs the probability of images activated by the softmax function. All the features are visualized using the PCA components, as in Fig. 4, but they are colored according to the types of images. At the (a) pool5 layer, the features are separated by the types of images. By shifting the target layer, these features are gradually gathered. We evaluate how these features are gathered by the ratio S between the between-class covariance s_b and the within-class covariance s_w calculated by

$$s_w = \frac{1}{N} \sum_{i \in class} \sum_{m_i \in m} (m - \overline{m_i})^{\mathrm{T}} (m - \overline{m_i}) \tag{1}$$

$$s_b = \frac{1}{N} \sum_{i \in class} (\overline{m_i} - \overline{m})^{\mathrm{T}} (\overline{m_i} - \overline{m}) \tag{2}$$

$$S = \frac{s_b}{s_w}, \tag{3}$$

where m is the feature, $\overline{m_i}$ is the average of the features labeled i, and $\overline{m}$ is the average of all the features. This ratio S is obtained as each set of features is projected by the three principal components: 0.53, 0.11, and 0.03 for (a) pool5, (b) fc6, (c) fc7, respectively. This suggests that the difference of the image type, especially between photos and illustrations is significant in shallow layers, and they are gradually united into a cluster, which can be considered as one class, shifting into deeper layers.

5   Conclusion

In this paper, we introduce a simple way to prepare a training dataset, which enables CNNs to classify photorealistic and non-photorealistic sketch images. In order to obtain a dataset that contains sketch-like images with an adequate size, we use illustration images with enhanced edges. In addition, photo and illustration images are transformed to grayscale and added to augment the training dataset. In order to test our proposed method, we train CNNs to classify animal images in 20 classes. This experiment confirms that the present method succeed in augmenting the training dataset and contributes to the classification accuracy of untrained photo and sketch images. In addition, we attempted to visualize the image features in the middle layers in order to analyze how the CNN trained by the proposed method processes training datasets. One possibility for future work is to apply CNNs for sketch interfaces, which can retrieve the images that the user wants to depict.

Acknowledgments. The work has been supported by MEXT Grant-in-Aid for Scientific Research (A) 15H01710.

References

1. Liu, Y., Zang, D., Lu, G., Ma, W.: A survey of content-based image retrieval with high-level semantics. Pattern Recogn. **40**, 262–282 (2007)
2. Eitz, M., Hildebrand, K., Boubekeur, T., Alexa, M.: Sketch-based image retrieval: benchmark and bag-of-features descriptors. IEEE Trans. Visual Comput. Graphics **17**, 1624–1636 (2011)
3. Cao, Y., Wang, H., Wang, C., Li, Z., Zhang, L., Zang, L.: MindFinder: interactive sketch-based image search. In: Proceedings of ACM Multimedia International Conference, pp. 1605–1608 (2010)
4. Cao, Y., Wang, C., Zhang, L., Zhang, L.: Edgel index for large-scale sketch-based image search. In: Proceedings of the IEEE Computer Society Conference on Computer Vision and Pattern Recognition, pp. 761–768 (2011)
5. Eitz, M., Hays, J., Alexa, M.: How do humans sketch objects? ACM Trans. Graph. **31**, 1–10 (2012)
6. Krizhevsky, A., Sutskever, I., Hinton, G.E.: Imagenet classification with deep convolutional neural networks. In: Advances in Neural Information Processing Systems, pp. 1106–1114 (2012)
7. He, K., Zhang, X., Ren, S., Sun, J.: Deep Residual Learning for Image Recognition. arXiv:1512.03385 (2015)
8. Yang, Y., Hospedales, T.M.: Deep Neural Networks for Sketch Recognition. arXiv:1501.07873 (2015)
9. Yu, Q., Yang, Y., Song, Y., Xiang, T., Hospedales, T.: Sketch-a-Net that beats humans. In: Proceedings of the British Machine Vision Conference, pp. 7.1–7.12 (2015)
10. Canny, J.: A computational approach to edge detection. IEEE Trans. Pattern Anal. Mach. Intell. **8**, 679–698 (1986)
11. Bottou, L.: Stochastic gradient descent tricks. In: Montavon, G., Orr, G.B., Müller, K.-R. (eds.) Neural Networks: Tricks of the Trade, 2nd edn. LNCS, vol. 7700, pp. 421–436. Springer, Heidelberg (2012)
12. Jia, Y., Shelhamer, E., Donahue, J., Karayev, S., Long, J., Girchick, R., Guadarrama, S., Darrell, T.: Caffe: Convolutional Architecture for Fast Feature Embedding. arXiv:1408.5093 (2014)

Day-ahead PV Power Forecast by Hybrid ANN Compared to the Five Parameters Model Estimated by Particle Filter Algorithm

Emanuele Ogliari[(✉)], Alberto Bolzoni, Sonia Leva, and Marco Mussetta

Department of Energy, Politecnico di Milano,
Via Lambruschini 4, 20156 Milano, Italy
{emanuelegiovanni.ogliari,alberto.bolzoni,sonia.leva,
marco.mussetta}@polimi.it
http://www.energia.polimi.it/english/index.php?

Abstract. A comparison between the hybrid method (PHANN – Physical Hybrid Artificial Neural Network) and the 5 parameter Physical model, which have been determined by the particle filter algorithm, is presented here. These methods have been employed to perform the day-ahead forecast of the output power of a photovoltaic plant. The aim of this work is to assess the forecast accuracy of the two methods.

Keywords: Day-ahead energy forecast · Artificial neural networks · Particle filter algorithm

1 Introduction

Photovoltaic (PV) systems and, more in general, Renewable Energy Sources (RES) are highly unpredictable due to the uncertainty of the weather forecast. The energy prediction has been often applied to the electric loads and is a typical application of time series analysis methods. In recent years several power forecasting models related to PV plants have been developed. Many methods have been employed to perform the day-ahead forecast of the hourly output power curve (given from 24 up to 48 h in advance) as reported in [1]. The existing methods can be mainly classified into three categories: physical, statistical and hybrid. A physical algorithm can be defined as a deterministic model which mathematically identifies the relationship between the input and the output of the system. An Artificial Neural Network, instead, stochastically describes the relationships between the input parameters and the output of the system with a weighted average sum of the input. A hybrid method is considered as any combination of the previous groups of forecasting models. Some of these models have been employed to forecast solar radiation [2,3], while other works present models specifically dedicated to the forecasting of the hourly power output from PV plants [4,5]. Nowadays the most applied techniques to model the stochastic nature of solar irradiance at the ground level, and thus the power output of

© Springer International Publishing Switzerland 2016
A.E.P. Villa et al. (Eds.): ICANN 2016, Part II, LNCS 9887, pp. 291–298, 2016.
DOI: 10.1007/978-3-319-44781-0_35

PV installations, are the statistical methods. In particular, regression methods are often employed to describe complex non-linear atmospheric phenomena for few-hours ahead forecast and specific soft-computing techniques based on artificial neural network (ANN) are used for few-hours power output forecast [6]. Some other authors using physical methods report the comparison of the results obtained with different models based on two or more forecasting techniques [7]. Only a few papers describe the forecasting models used to predict the daily irradiance or directly the energy production of the PV plant for all the daylight hours of the following day [7–9].

ANN needs to be trained with historical data, and sometimes these data are not available. Therefore, it is necessary to adopt a different forecasting algorithm combining weather forecast with the PV plant physical parameters [10] estimated by knowing the specific model of the PV system.

In this paper a comparison between two forecasting models, namely a physical and a hybrid one is provided. The first is the well known five parameters model of the PV module, which are estimated with the particle filter algorithm, and the second is the recently developed PHANN (Physic Hybrid Artificial Neural Network), presented in [11].

2   Physical Model of the PV Cell

One of the most complete physical model to describe the PV module power is based on five parameters. The equivalent circuit in Fig. 1 includes $R_{SH,c}$ called "cell shunt resistance", which is connected in parallel to the photo-current generator I_{PV} and second resistance ($R_{S,c}$), called "cell series resistance", which is connected in series to the cell terminals. Therefore the five-parameter model, can be defined by:

- I_{PV}, the light-generated current,
- I_D, the reverse saturation current of the PN junction,
- n, the diode ideality factor.

$$I = I_{PV} - I_0 \cdot \left(e^{\dfrac{V + R_{s,c} \cdot I}{n \cdot V_t}} - 1 \right) - \dfrac{V + Rs, c \cdot I}{R_{SH,c}} \tag{1}$$

The IV characteristic curve of the PV cell mainly depends on solar irradiance and PN junction temperature. The latter depends on several parameters such as: the actual irradiance G_{TOT} on the cell, the ambient temperature T_{amb}, the wind speed and the wind direction. The cell temperature can also be evaluated starting from the measurement of the ambient parameters by means of two different models: the nominal operating cell temperature (NOCT) [12], which is the cell operating temperature under certain conditions ($T_{amb} = 20°C$, $G_{NOCT} = 800$ W/m^2, wind speed = 1 m/s without thermal convection on the back of the PV module), and the SANDIA model [13].

The complete dissertation of this model, linking solar radiation, ambient temperature and PV power output of the module is described in [10,14].

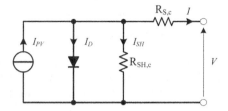

Fig. 1. Circuit of the five-parameter equivalent model.

3 Physical Hybrid Artificial Neural Network

In this work the recently developed [11] Physic Hybrid Artificial Neural Network (PHANN) is adopted to enhance the forecast by combining both the physical Clear Sky Solar Radiation Algorithm (CSRM) by Hottel [15] and the stochastic ANN method. The physical algorithm has been used to identify the maximum solar radiation exploitable in a given PV plant, the sunrise and the sunset hours, in order to exclude all the night time steps with null PV power output.

4 Particle Filter

In this section, an innovative algorithm for state and parameter estimation will be applied for the evaluation of characteristic quantities associated to a PV module. Then the results obtained with the following technique will be compared to those derived from the PHANN method reported in this paper.

Particle filters are a set of algorithms based on Monte Carlo technique for the estimation of the dynamic evolution of a system [16]. Let's consider a dynamical system in the continuous time, described by:

$$\dot{x} = f_1(x, u, \theta, w) \tag{2}$$

$$y = g_1(x, u, \theta, v) \tag{3}$$

where $x \in \mathbb{R}^n$ is the vector of state variables, $u \in \mathbb{R}^q$ is the vector of control quantities, $y \in \mathbb{R}^m$ is the set of output measured variables and $\theta \in \mathbb{R}^p$ is the space of unknown parameters; w and v represent the random variables used to express the uncertainty associated to the model and to the measurement procedure.

In order to implement the technique, it is necessary to first discretize the model of both the system evolution and of the measurement procedure.

$$x_k = f_2(x_{k-1}, u_{k-1}, \theta_{k-1}, w_{k-1}) \tag{4}$$

$$y_k = g_2(x_k, u_k, \theta_k, v_k) \tag{5}$$

In this context, the model has been applied mainly for parameter estimation; thus it is convenient to add a fictitious dynamic of the unknown parameters in order to take into account the incremental estimation process:

$$\theta_k = \mathbb{H}(\theta_{k-1}, \epsilon_{k-1}) \tag{6}$$

$$y_k = \mathbb{G}(\theta_k, \eta_k) \tag{7}$$

In (6) and (7) the fictitious model associated to the parameter evolution and the actual measurement process description are shown, respectively. In general, both $\mathbb{H}$ and $\mathbb{G}$ are non-linear functions subjected to white noise.

4.1 Particle Filter Implementation

The particle filter algorithm based on Sequential Monte Carlo simulation [16] has been implemented for the parameter estimation. This technique is based on the Bayesian approach and it aims at identifying, among a group of N independently simulated dynamical evolutions of the system called *particles*, the ones that are most likely to match the actual condition of the equipment, according to the comparison with measured data. At each time step, the filter evaluates the probability distribution a posteriori of each unknown state or parameter, starting from a given state supposed a prior. Each particle is then weighted according to its likelihood function.

One of the problems associated with the Bayesian approach is that it needs to deal with probabilistic functional analysis, as all the terms involved are probability distribution functions. In general it is not so easy to analytically derive the product of these functions, especially in non-linear systems having non-Gaussian distributions. Therefore a Monte Carlo scheme may be adopted to numerically retrieve the result. A certain number N of independent dynamics of the systems (*particles*) are simulated and each of them is weighted by the likelihood function, in order to assess its coherence with the measurements performed on the system.

First of all it is necessary to guess a state a priori for the Bayesian scheme. In order to keep track of the previous values of the parameter and improve the convergence rate of the estimation process, this state is evaluated starting from the estimation at the previous step, according to the fictitious dynamical process introduced in (6). In the following, a linear model is adopted.

$$\tilde{\theta}_{k,i} = \theta_{k-1,i} + \epsilon_{k-1,i} \qquad i = 1..N \tag{8}$$

Once the prior state is determined, the weight of each particle is evaluated considering a Gaussian distribution for the likelihood as in (9) and the normalized weights are obtained (10).

$$\mathcal{L}_{k,i}(y_k|\theta_{k,i}) = \frac{1}{\sqrt{(2\pi)^m |R_k|}} e^{-0.5(y_k - \mathbb{G}(\tilde{\theta}_{k,i}))^T R_k^{-1}(y_k - \mathbb{G}(\tilde{\theta}_{k,i}))} \tag{9}$$

$$w_{k,i} = \frac{\mathcal{L}_{k,i}}{\sum_{i=1}^{N} \mathcal{L}_{k,i}} \tag{10}$$

Once the weights of all the particles in all the independent N cases are known, it is possible to calculate the mean and standard deviation as compact indexes of the discrete probability distribution function, according to (11) and (12):

$$\theta_k = \sum_{i=1}^{N} w_{k,i}\tilde{\theta}_{k,i} \tag{11}$$

$$\sigma_{\theta_k}^2 = \sum_{i=1}^{N} w_{k,i}(\tilde{\theta}_{k,i} - \theta_k)^2 \tag{12}$$

The whole process is then carried out iteratively for all the time steps.

5   Case Study and Data Analysis

In the considered application, the particle filter has been implemented for estimation of characteristic input of the five parameter model, described in Sect. 2. Indeed these quantities are peculiar for each PV module, are time-varying and they strongly depend on the actual operating conditions of the system. Thus a model-based algorithm able to track them in real time starting from the model equations and the measurements during operation may allow an effective estimation of such parameters.

The particle filter has been used, in particular to track the values of the series resistance R_s and the photo-generated current I_{PV}. The diode ideality factor n and the reverse leakage current I_0 have been taken from literature. The fictitious dynamical model explained in (8) by considering the *ClearSky* algorithm [15] which has been calculated in two successive samples of time $k-1$ and k, has been implemented as follows:

$$I_{PV}(k) = I_{PV}(k-1) \cdot \frac{ClearSky(k)}{ClearSky(k-1)} \cdot \epsilon \tag{13}$$

$$R_s(k) = R_s(k-1) + K \cdot Rs(k-1) \cdot \epsilon \tag{14}$$

where ϵ is a number randomly drawn by a Gaussian distribution. The filter is disabled when the *ClearSky* algorithm predicts a null power production and the current is randomly initialized after the filter is reactivated.

As regards the measurement, the following equations can be derived from the equivalent model of the photovoltaic cell.

$$I_{out} = (I_{PV}(k) - I_D) \cdot \frac{R_p(k)}{Rs(k,i) + Rp(k,i)} - \frac{V_{DC}}{Rs(k,i) + Rp(k,i)} \tag{15}$$

$$P_{out} = (I_{PV}(k) - I_D) \cdot (V_{DC} + R_s(k)) - R_s(k) \cdot I_{out}^2 - \frac{(V_{DC} + R_s(k) \cdot I_{out})}{R_p} \tag{16}$$

In Fig. 2(a) a comparison between the particle estimator and the analytic solution of the model has been carried out. The last values have been derived considering the exact solution of the model, obtained assuming the values of the equivalent circuit parameters measured on the plant. These data have been assumed as reference values and are used in order to test the algorithm effectiveness. The error associated to the estimation process is reported in Fig. 2(b) with respect to the photo-generated current; here it is possible to see that the maximum difference is located in the first and last hours of each day, where the approximation introduced by the filter is higher; however it is possible to see an asymptotic decrease of the error thanks to the filter convergence.

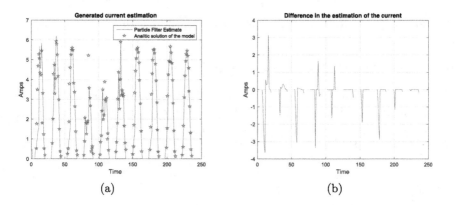

(a)   (b)

Fig. 2. Estimated photo-generated current and its error

5.1   Numerical Results and Discussion

The parameters of the physical model have been estimated by means of the particle filter, as already explained in the previous section. These parameters have been employed to forecast the PV power output and to make a comparison with the actual ones provided by a PV module. These experimental data are collected at the SolarTechLab, Politecnico di Milano (Italy), whose geographical coordinates are: latitude 45.502941N, longitude 9.156577E. One 245 Wp rated power crystalline silicon PV module facing South, 30 deg tilted is considered. The weather forecasts for this site are provided 24 h in advance by a meteorological service (at 11PM of the day before the forecast one). A full list of the parameters employed for the training of the PHANN is reporter here below:

- Day of the year and hour of the day
- Global Horizontal Clear Sky Solar Radiation
- Wind Direction and speed
- Pressure
- Humidity Relative
- Rain
- Ambient temperature
- Global Horizontal Solar Radiation
- PV module DC Power Output

According to preliminary setup, PHANN is composed by two layers with 100 neurons in the first hidden layer and 50 neurons in the second. The activation

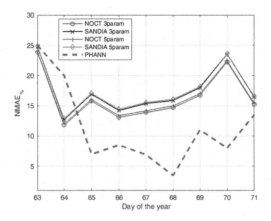

Fig. 3. Daily Normalised Mean Absolute Error calculated by different methods

function in the neurons is the sigmoidal function. These settings have been chosen after preliminary results which are exposed in a previous work [11]. PHANN is trained with the hourly parameters of the 11 days before of the forecast ones. The results shown in Fig. 3 are referred to 9 days between February and March 2014. This period is considered meaningful in terms of continuous succession of sunny and cloudy days and all the data are consistent without interruptions in the recordings. In this Figure these results are compared with those obtained considering different physical models, namely the combinations of thermal models (SANDIA and NOCT) of the considered PV cell power output with 3 and 5 parameter models described in Sect. 2.

Figure 3 shows the daily Normalised Mean Absolute Error NMAE. By observing this figure, the day-ahead forecast performed by the PHANN method is outperforming in several days the physical forecasting methods.

6 Conclusions

In this paper the comparison between the day-ahead forecast performed by the PHANN (Physical Hybrid Artificial Neural Network) and the 5 parameter Physical model (determined by the particle filter algorithm) has been assessed. The reported results show that the PHANN method generally provides better results and a more accurate forecast, with lower daily errors.

References

1. Yadav, H.K., Pal, Y., Tripathi, M.M.: Photovoltaic power forecasting methods in smart power grid. In: 2015 Annual IEEE India Conference (INDICON), pp. 1–6, December 2015

2. Mellit, A., Pavan, A.M.: A 24-h forecast of solar irradiance using artificial neural network: application for performance prediction of a grid-connected PV plant at trieste, Italy. Solar Energ. **84**(5), 807–821 (2010). http://www.sciencedirect.com/science/article/pii/S0038092X10000782

3. Reikard, G.: Predicting solar radiation at high resolutions: a comparison of time series forecasts. Solar Energ. **83**(3), 342–349 (2009). http://www.sciencedirect.com/science/article/pii/S0038092X08002107

4. İzgi, E., Öztopal, A., Yerli, B., Kaymak, M.K., Şahin, A.D.: Short–mid-term solar power prediction by using artificial neural networks. Solar Energ. **86**(2), 725–733 (2012). http://www.sciencedirect.com/science/article/pii/S0038092X11004245

5. Shi, J., Lee, W.-J., Liu, Y., Yang, Y., Wang, P.: Forecasting power output of photovoltaic system based on weather classification and support vector machine. In: 2011 IEEE Industry Applications Society Annual Meeting (IAS), pp. 1–6, October 2011

6. Pedro, H.T., Coimbra, C.F.: Assessment of forecasting techniques for solar power production with no exogenous inputs. Solar Energ. **86**(7), 2017–2028 (2012). http://www.sciencedirect.com/science/article/pii/S0038092X12001429

7. Monteiro, C., Fernandez-Jimenez, L.A., Ramirez-Rosado, I.J., Muñoz-Jimenez, A., Lara-Santillan, P.M.: Short-term forecasting models for photovoltaic plants: analytical versus soft-computing techniques. Math. Probl. Eng. **2013**, 1–9 (2013)

8. Wang, F., Mi, Z., Su, S., Zhao, H.: Short-term solar irradiance forecasting model based on artificial neural network using statistical feature parameters. Energies **5**(5), 1355 (2012). http://www.mdpi.com/1996-1073/5/5/1355

9. Yang, H.T., Huang, C.M., Huang, Y.C., Pai, Y.S.: A weather-based hybrid method for 1-day ahead hourly forecasting of PV power output. IEEE Trans. Sustain. Energ. **5**(3), 917–926 (2014)

10. Dolara, A., Leva, S., Manzolini, G.: Comparison of different physical models for PV power output prediction. Solar Energ. **119**, 83–99 (2015)

11. Dolara, A., Grimaccia, F., Leva, S., Mussetta, M., Ogliari, E.: A physical hybrid artificial neural network for short term forecasting of PV plant power output. Energies **8**(2), 1138–1153 (2015)

12. IEC, Procedures for Temperature and Irradiance Corrections to Measured IV Characteristics (2010)

13. Nelson, J.: The Physics of Solar Cells, vol. 1. World Scientific, Singapore (2003)

14. De Soto, W., Klein, S., Beckman, W.: Improvement and validation of a model for photovoltaic array performance. Solar Energ. **80**(1), 78–88 (2006)

15. Hottel, H.C.: A simple model for estimating the transmittance of direct solar radiation through clear atmospheres. Solar Energ. **18**(2), 129–134 (1976)

16. Doucet, A., De Freitas, N., Gordon, N.: An introduction to sequential monte carlo methods. In: Doucet, A., et al. (eds.) Sequential Monte Carlo Methods in Practice. Statistics for Engineering and Information Science, pp. 3–14. Springer, New York (2001)

Extended Weighted Nearest Neighbor
for Electricity Load Forecasting

Mashud Rana[1](✉), Irena Koprinska[2](✉), Alicia Troncoso[3],
and Vassilios G. Agelidis[1]

[1] Australian Energy Research Institute, University of New South Wales,
Sydney, Australia
{md.rana,vassilios.agelidis}@unsw.edu.au
[2] School of Information Technologies, University of Sydney, Sydney, Australia
irena.koprinska@sydney.edu.au
[3] School of Engineering, University Pablo de Olavide, Seville, Spain
atrolor@upo.es

Abstract. We present EWNN, a new approach for forecasting the hourly
electricity load profile for the next day, from a time series of previous electricity
loads. EWNN extends the well-known and successful weighted nearest neighbor
method WNN by operating at an hourly level and by incorporating feature
selection. We evaluate EWNN using two years of electricity load data for
Australia, Spain and Portugal. The results show that EWNN provides accurate
predictions outperforming WNN on all datasets, and also outperforming two
other advanced methods (pattern sequence similarity and iterative neural network) and three baselines used for comparison.

Keywords: Electricity load forecasting · Weighted nearest neighbor · Neural
networks · Feature selection

1 Introduction

We consider the task of forecasting the hourly electricity load profile for the next day,
from a time series of previous hourly electricity loads. Specifically, given a time series
of hourly electricity loads up to day d, the goal is to forecast the 24 hourly loads for day
$d + 1$. This task is classified as short-term load forecasting. Accurate short-term load
forecasting is important for the planning and operation of power systems, e.g. for
scheduling of generation units, dispatch of generated electricity and supporting the
electricity market participants in their bidding and spot acquisition of electricity.

The electricity load time series is complex. It has daily, weekly and seasonal cycles,
and is also influenced by weather variables, fluctuations in the electricity usage of large
industrial units, and random effects due to unusual days (e.g. special events, holidays
and unexpected weather changes). Various forecasting approaches based on statistical
and machine learning methods have been proposed, with different complexity, flexibility and data requirements. The most prominent approaches use statistical methods
such as exponential smoothing and linear regression [1–3], and machine learning
methods such as neural networks [4–6].

© Springer International Publishing Switzerland 2016
A.E.P. Villa et al. (Eds.): ICANN 2016, Part II, LNCS 9887, pp. 299–307, 2016.
DOI: 10.1007/978-3-319-44781-0_36

One of the most promising recent forecasting approaches using machine learning techniques is the Weighted Nearest Neighbor (WNN) [7]. WNN stores all training examples; to make a prediction for the load profile for the new day $d + 1$, it finds the k nearest neighbors of the load profile for the previous day, by considering sequences of previous days. The prediction for the new day is the weighted linear combination of the load for the days following the nearest neighbors, where the weights are determined by the distance of the previous days to the neighbors. WNN was applied for predicting both electricity loads and electricity prices and was shown to outperform a number of approaches including neural networks and GARCH autoregressive models.

In this study, we present an extension of WNN, called EWNN (Extended WNN). EWNN extends WNN: (1) by working at an hourly level instead of a daily level, and (2) by applying a feature selection algorithm. While WNN uses all lag variables from the previous days without feature selection, EWNN applies a two-stage feature selection to choose a subset of informative lag variables. Another distinct difference between WNN and EWNN is that EWNN builds a separate prediction model for each hour of the day while WNN builds a single model. We investigate if the extensions lead to an improved performance, in particular higher accuracy. Our evaluation is conducted using three large datasets of electricity load data for three different countries; Australia, Spain and Portugal. We also compare the performance of EWNN with two other advanced methods for load forecasting: Pattern Sequence-based Forecasting (PSF) [8] and Iterative Neural Network (INN) [9]), and three naive baselines.

2 Data

We use electricity load data for three countries – Australia, Spain, and Portugal. Each dataset is for two years (from 1 January 2010 to 31 December 2011) and is measured at hourly intervals, and thus contains $365 \times 24 \times 2 = 17,520$ samples. The Australian dataset is provided by the Australian Energy Market Operator (AEMO) [10] and the Spanish and Portuguese datasets are provided by the Spanish Electricity Price Market Operator (OMEL) [11].

3 EWNN

Our proposed approach EWNN is an extension of WNN. It extends WNN in two ways: (1) by operating at an hourly level instead of a daily level and (2) by incorporating feature selection. Another notable difference between EWNN and WNN is that EWNN builds a separate prediction model for each hour of the day while WNN builds a single model.

As Fig. 1 shows, EWNN divides that task of predicting the daily load profile for the next day into 24 subtasks, one for each hour. It conducts a separate feature selection for each hour and then builds a separate prediction model using an adapted WNN prediction model as shown in Fig. 2. The two main phases of EWNN, feature selection and building prediction models, are discussed in more details below.

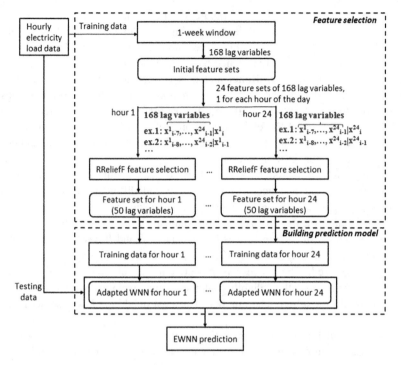

Fig. 1. EWNN

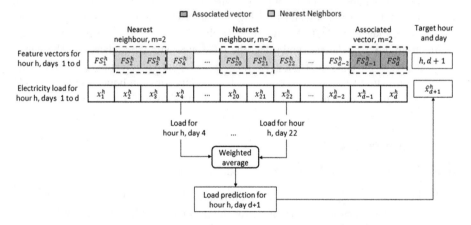

Fig. 2. Adapted WNN to an hourly level

3.1 Feature Selection

Feature selection is the process of removing irrelevant and redundant features and selecting a small set of informative features that are necessary and sufficient for good prediction [12]. Appropriate feature selection improves the accuracy and reduces the training time. It also typically leads to prediction models that are easier to understand, which increases the customer confidence in using these models for decision making.

To select informative lag variables, we applied the RReliefF feature selection algorithm [13]. RReliefF is an instance-based method that evaluates and ranks all features. The core algorithm is Relief and it is applicable to two-class classification problems; its main idea is that high quality features should have similar values for instances from the same class and different values for instances from different classes. RReliefF is an extension of Relief for regression problems; it models the probability of two instances to belong to the same or different class as the relative distance between the predicted values for these instances.

Specifically, RReliefF assigns a weight w_f to each feature f based on how well f distinguishes between instances from the same and different classes. It works by randomly selecting an instance R from the training data and finding its nearest neighbor from the same class (nearest hit H) and the opposite class (nearest miss M). It then updates the weight w_f of each feature as follows: (1) if R and H have different values of f (not desirable), w_f is decreased and (2) if R and M have different values of f (desirable), w_f is increased. The process is repeated for a subset of randomly selected examples R. To increase the reliability of the feature weights, we used all training examples instead of a subset. The number of nearest neighbors k was set to 10 in our experiments.

RReliefF is suitable for load forecasting as it works well on noisy and correlated features - it can capture both feature-to-feature and feature-to-output variable correlations, and can detect both linear and non-linear relationships. It is also an efficient algorithm due to its linear time complexity.

To conduct feature selection using RReliefF, as shown in Fig. 1, we firstly form a candidate features set that includes all lag variables from a 1-week sliding window ($7 \times 24 = 168$ lag variables). We then use RReliefF to compute the weight w_f for all features from the candidate set and select the n features with the highest w_f. The value of n was set to 50 since after that w_f does not change significantly and gradually flattens. The feature selection was conducted separately for each hour of the day, each time considering a different hour as a target value, as shown in Fig. 1.

3.2 Building Prediction Model

We firstly describe the WNN prediction model and then its extension, EWNN.

WNN. Let $X_i = \left[x_i^1, x_i^2, \ldots, x_i^{24}\right]$ be a 24-dimensional vector consisting of the hourly load for a day i. To predict the load X_{d+1} for the new day $d + 1$, WNN firstly finds the k nearest neighbors of X_d. This is done by matching the sequence of m previous days ending with X_d and finding the most similar sequences of days. The prediction for the new day is the weighted average of the load for the days following the nearest neighbors, where the weights are determined by the distance of the neighbors to X_d.

EWNN. Let $FS_d^h = [f_1, f_2, \ldots, f_n]$ be a feature vector that represents the n selected features for predicting the electricity load x_d^h at hour h of day d. Following WNN, we define an associated vector of FS_d^h. In EWNN it is defined at an hourly level not at a daily level as in WNN, and will include the m input vectors for the same hour h, for m consecutive days from day d backwards: $Y_{d,m}^h = \left[FS_{d-m+1}^h, \ldots, FS_{d-1}^h, FS_d^h \right]$.

The following steps are similar to WNN but are applied at an hourly level not a daily level as in WNN. As shown in Fig. 2, to predict the load x_{d+1}^h for hour h of day $d + 1$, EWNN firstly identifies the k nearest neighbors of the associated vector $Y_{d,m}^h$ using a distance measure and finds the set of neighbors $NS = \left\{ q_1, \ldots, q_k, \right\}$, where $q_1, \ldots, q_k$ are the k closest days to day d for hour h, in order of closeness. EWNN then computes the forecast for x_{d+1}^h as a weighted linear combination of the loads for hour h for the days following the nearest neighbors:

$$ \hat{x}_{d+1}^h = \frac{1}{\sum_{s \in NS} \alpha_s} \cdot \sum_{s \in NS} \alpha_s . x_{s+1}^h $$

The weights α_s are computed as: $\alpha_s = \frac{dist\left(Y_{q_k,m}^h, Y_{d,m}^h \right) - dist\left(Y_{s,m}^h, Y_{d,m}^h \right)}{dist\left(Y_{q_k,m}^h, Y_{d,m}^h \right) - dist\left(Y_{q_1,m}^h, Y_{d,m}^h \right)}$, where $dist$ is the chosen distance measure (we used Euclidian distance), m is the number of feature vectors included in $Y_{d,m}^h$ and k is the number of neighbors. The values of m and k are determined as in WNN by resolving the false nearest neighbors and minimizing the prediction error on the training data, respectively.

4   Experimental Setup

4.1   Evaluation Procedure and Performance Measures

The data for each country is divided into three non-overlapping subsets – training, validation and testing. The training set contains 70% of the data for 2010 (6,132 samples) and is used for feature selection and model training. The validation set contains the remaining 30% of the data for 2010 (2,628 samples) and is used for parameter tuning (e.g. to selecting the best NN architecture). The testing set contains all data for 2011 (8,760 samples) and is used to evaluate the performance of the prediction models.

We assess the accuracy of the prediction models using two standard performance measures: Mean Absolute Error (MAE) and Mean Absolute Percentage Error (MAPE):

$$ MAE = \frac{1}{D}\frac{1}{H} \sum_{d=1}^{D} \sum_{h=1}^{H} \left| x_d^h - \hat{x}_d^h \right|, \quad MAPE = \frac{1}{D}\frac{1}{H} \sum_{d=1}^{D} \sum_{h=1}^{H} \left| \frac{x_d^h - \hat{x}_d^h}{x_d^h} \right| . 100\% $$

where x_d^h and $\hat{x}_d^h$ are the actual and predicted load for day d at hour h, respectively, D is the number of days in the test data and H is the number of predicted hours, $H = 24$.

4.2   Methods Used for Comparison

In addition to WNN, we compare the performance of our approach with two other state-of-the-art methods (INN and PSF) and three baselines (B_{pday}, B_{pweek} and B_{mean}).

PSF [8] combines clustering with sequence matching. It firstly groups all vectors X_i from the training data into k clusters and labels them with the cluster number. It then extracts a sequence of consecutive days, from day d backwards, and matches the cluster labels of this sequence against the training data to find a set of sequences that are the same, ES_d. It then follows a nearest neighbor approach similar to WNN - finds the following day for each element of ES_d and averages the 24 hourly loads of these following days, to produce the final 24 hourly predictions for day $d + 1$. PSF was evaluated on electricity load and electricity prices time series and shown to be more accurate than ARIMA, support vector regression and neural network based methods.

INN [9] is an iterative approach that combines an efficient mutual information feature selection method with a neural network forecasting algorithm. It builds a single prediction model that is trained to predict one step ahead. This model is used iteratively to predict the load for all 24 h from the forecasting horizon, i.e. the prediction for $h + 1$ is considered as an actual value and used to predict the value for $h + 2$, and this continues for all points from the forecasting horizon. INN was shown to be more accurate than a number of methods, including a non-iterative counterpart, where a separate neural network is built for each hour of the forecasting horizon.

We also implemented three naive prediction methods (baselines): (1) B_{pday} (load from the previous day at the same time) - the prediction for x_i^h is x_{i-1}^h; (2) B_{pweek} (load from the previous week at the same time) - the prediction for x_i^h is x_{i-7}^h; (3) B_{mean} (mean load value in the training data for hour h) - the prediction for x_i^h is $mean(x_j^h)$ over all days j in the training data.

5   Results and Discussion

Table 1 presents the accuracy results (MAE and MAPE) of EWNN and the methods used for comparison. Table 2 shows the pair-wise comparison of these accuracies for statistically significant differences using the Wilcoxon rank sum test. The MAPE results from the Table 1 are also plotted in Fig. 3 for visual comparison.

The results show that EWNN is more accurate than the method it extends, WNN, for all three datasets and that the differences in accuracy are statistically significant. Specifically, EWNN achieved an improvement of 7.64–9.36% in MAPE and 7.73–8.94% in MAE, compared to WNN. This shows that predicting the load for each hour separately, applying WNN at an hourly level and using feature selection (with the RReliefF algorithm) was beneficial.

EWNN outperforms not only WNN but also the other methods used for comparison – it is the most accurate prediction method for the Australian and Spanish datasets, and the second most accurate method for the Portuguese dataset, after INN. All pair-wise differences between EWNN and the other methods are statistically significant. Specifically, EWNN achieved an improvement in MAPE of 16.25–37.43% compared to PSF on the three datasets and 4.15–6.55% compared to INN on the Australian and Spanish datasets.

Table 1. Predictive accuracy of EWNN and the methods used for comparison

Pred. method	Australian data		Spanish data		Portuguese data	
	MAE [MW]	MAPE [%]	MAE [MW]	MAPE [%]	MAE [MW]	MAPE [%]
EWNN	283.68	3.14	1083.03	5.55	496.96	13.55
INN	304.89	3.36	1134.63	5.79	426.43	11.70
WNN	307.46	3.40	1179.89	6.03	538.87	14.95
PSF	352.03	3.96	1711.38	8.87	589.77	16.18
B_{pday}	420.46	4.82	1888.02	9.47	579.61	16.06
B_{pweek}	471.20	5.20	1460.07	7.45	695.38	19.12
B_{mean}	719.44	8.08	2671.69	14.32	653.55	18.11

Table 2. Pair-wise statistical significance comparison for MAE and MAPE (Wilcoxon rank sum test): $\sqrt{\ }$ difference is statistically significant at $p \leq 0.05$, ×- difference is not statistically significant; the order of the results is: Australian, Spanish and Portuguese data

	EWNN	INN	WNN	PSF	B_{pday}	B_{pweek}	B_{mean}
EWNN		√√√	√√√	√√√	√√√	√√√	√√√
INN			√√√	√√√	√√√	√√√	√√√
WNN				√√√	√√√	√√√	√√√
PSF					√√×	√√√	√√√
B_{pday}						√√√	√√√
B_{pweek}							√√√
B_{mean}							

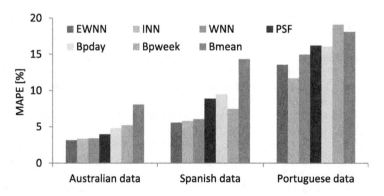

Fig. 3. Comparison of accuracy results (MAPE) for all prediction methods

By comparing EWNN with the three baselines, we can see that it considerably outperformed them achieving an improvement of 34–61% for the Australian data, 41–61% for the Spanish data and 15–29% for Portuguese data.

Overall the best method is EWNN, followed by INN and WNN, then PSF and the three baselines.

Among the three baselines, B_{pday} is the most accurate for the Australian and Portuguese data, and B_{pweek} is the most accurate for the Spanish data. This indicates a stronger daily pattern for the Australian and Portuguese data, and a stronger weekly pattern for the Spanish data. $B_{mean,}$ is the least accurate baseline for all three datasets, with substantially lower accuracy.

6   Conclusion

We considered the task of forecasting the daily electricity profile for the next day at hourly intervals, from previous electricity load data. We presented EWNN, a new approach for time series forecasting, an extension of the successful weighted nearest neighbor method WNN. The extension includes working at an hourly level instead of a daily level and incorporating feature selection. EWNN also builds a separate prediction model for each hour of the day while WNN builds a single model. We evaluated the performance of EWNN using data for two years for three countries – Australia, Spain and Portugal. Our results showed that EWNN was more accurate than WNN for all three datasets achieving a statistically significant improvement of 7.64–9.36% in MAPE 7.73–8.94% in MAE. In addition to WNN, we compared EWNN with two advanced methods (PSF and INN) and three baselines. EWNN was the most accurate method in all cases except on the Portuguese data where it came second after INN. Hence, we conclude that EWNN is a promising approach for forecasting the hourly electricity load profile.

References

1. Taylor, J.W.: Short-term load forecasting with exponentially weighted methods. IEEE Trans. Power Syst. **27**, 458–464 (2012)
2. Taylor, J.W.: Triple seasonal methods for short-term electricity demand forecasting. Eur. J. Oper. Res. **204**, 139–152 (2010)
3. Fan, S., Hyndman, R.J.: Short-term load forecasting based on a semi-parametric additive model. IEEE Trans. Power Syst. **27**, 134–141 (2012)
4. Chen, Y., Luh, P.B., Guan, C., Zhao, Y., Michel, L.D., Coolbeth, M.A., Friedland, P.B., Rourke, S.J.: Short-term load forecasting: similar day-based wavelet neural network. IEEE Trans. Power Syst. **25**, 322–330 (2010)
5. Rana, M., Koprinska, I.: Forecasting electricity load with advanced wavelet neural networks. Neurocomputing **182**, 118–132 (2016)
6. Koprinska, I., Rana, M., Troncoso, A., Martínez-Álvarez, F.: Combining pattern sequence similarity with neural networks for forecasting electricity demand time series. In: International Joint Conference on Neural Networks (IJCNN) (2013)
7. Troncoso, A., Riquelme, J.M., Riquelme, J.C., Martinez, J.L., Gomez, A.: Electricity market price forecasting based on weighted nearest neighbor techniques. IEEE Trans. Power Syst. **22**, 1294–1301 (2007)

8. Martínez-Álvarez, F., Troncoso, A., Riquelme, J.C., Aguilar-Ruiz, J.S.: Energy time series forecasting based on pattern sequence similarity. IEEE Trans. Knowl. Data Eng. **23**, 1230–1243 (2011)
9. Rana, M., Koprinska, I., Troncoso, A.: Forecasting hourly electricity load profile using neural networks. In: International Joint Conference on Neural Networks (IJCNN) (2014)
10. Australian Electricity Market Operator (AEMO). www.aemo.com.au
11. Spanish Electricity Price Market Operator (OMEL). http://www.omelholding.es
12. Koprinska, I., Rana, M., Agelidis, V.G.: Correlation and instance based feature selection for electricity load forecasting. Knowl. Based Syst. **81**, 29–40 (2015)
13. Sikonja, M.R., Kononenko, I.: Theoretical and empirical analysis of ReliefF and RReliefF. Mach. Learn. **53**, 23–69 (2003)

Using Reservoir Computing and Trend Information for Short-Term Streamflow Forecasting

Sabrina G.T.A. Bezerra$^{(\boxtimes)}$, Camila B. de Andrade, and Mêuser J.S. Valença

Polytechnic School, University of Pernambuco, Recife, Brazil
{sgtab,cba2,meuser}@ecomp.poli.br

Abstract. Streamflow forecasting is a fundamental tool in water resource studies. If information on the nature of the inflow is determinable in advance, then a given reservoir can be operated by some decision rule to minimize downstream flood damage and maximize the generated power with low costs. However, traditional methods such as linear time series models do not model the series properly, ignoring its dynamical behavior. This paper provides a method based on the Reservoir Computing (RC) technique combined with trend information extracted from the series for short-term streamflow forecasting. The model was tested in five hydroelectric plants located in different river basins in Brazil. Experimental results show that the proposed method is able to achieve better generalization performance than the traditional methods.

Keywords: Time series · Streamflow forecasting · Artificial Neural Networks · Trend information

1 Introduction

Accurate streamflow forecasts are an important component of watershed planning and sustainable water resource management [1]. With such information, it is possible to minimize any damage that can be caused by floods and maximize the energy generated by the power plant. Conceptual models for simulation, such as ARMA (Auto-Regressive Moving Average) models [2], and the linear time-series models are some of the traditional techniques used for streamflow forecasting.

Several companies in the Brazilian Electrical Sector use the linear time-series models. Even though they have been found to provide satisfactory predictions in many applications, they are unable to manage the nonlinear informations contained in the streamflow series. Hence, Artificial Neural Networks [3] are an attractive technology for inflow forecasting. With the ability to process massive information and deal with high nonlinearity, ANNs have been widely studied and successfully applied to various fields, *e.g.*, hydrology and water resources, in recent years [4–6].

However, networks as the Multi-Layer Perceptron (MLP) have the inability of properly modeling dynamic behaviors. Considering this, for this work the

© Springer International Publishing Switzerland 2016
A.E.P. Villa et al. (Eds.): ICANN 2016, Part II, LNCS 9887, pp. 308–316, 2016.
DOI: 10.1007/978-3-319-44781-0_37

Reservoir Computing (RC) [7] neural network was used. The RC works with a set of interconnected artificial neurons, which allows the network to present a dynamic behavior, becoming more adequate to the task [8].

The use of ANNs can increase the accuracy of the prediction, but the network inputs are usually composed of only past information. The use of only past information has downsides, including the underestimation of the series values. For this reason, detection of trends in streamflow forecasting has an expressive importance to an adequate management of water resources [9]. Since artificial neural networks are not able to capture seasonal or trend variations effectively [10], past inflows combined with a numerical trend information of the given time series could provide a more complete data, thus allowing better generalization.

In this paper, a model based on the Reservoir Computing method combined with trend information for short-term streamflow forecasting is proposed. The model was tested with the time series of five Brazilian power plants, each located in different river basins with different characteristics, and experimental results show that the proposed model achieved better generalization rates than the current used methods.

This paper is organized as follows: Sect. 2 explains the Reservoir Computing and details about the trend information; Sect. 3 describes the methodology adopted; Sect. 4 presents the experiments and the results; and finally, Sect. 5 presents the conclusions.

2   Concepts and Definitions

This study proposes a model based on the Reservoir Computing recurrent network and the use of a variable that can be extracted from the series, called trend information, for short-term streamflow forecasting. This section presents the main definitions and concepts which represent the necessary background to comprehend the work.

2.1   Reservoir Computing

Recurrent neural networks (RNNs) have been used for short-term streamflow forecasting and presented better accuracy for multi-step ahead [11], but they are difficult to train. Independent researches on new methods of design and training of RNNs originated two different neural networks with very similar properties: the Echo State Network (ESN) [12] and the Liquid State Machine (LSM) [13]. Later, these networks were unified under the generic name of Reservoir Computing (RC) [7].

The Reservoir Computing is composed of three main parts: the input layer, the reservoir itself and a readout function. The reservoir is a nonlinear dynamic system with recurrent processing nodes where the connections between the nodes are generated randomly and are globally reescalated to achieve a stable state.

An interesting property of the reservoir is the echo state property. This property defines that the effects of a previous state $x(n)$ and the input value of a future state $x(n + 1)$ should fade gradually. Because of these recurrent nodes the network maintain a rich set of nonlinear transformations and a mix of input signals of past and present moments (called echoes).

Since this is a recurrent network and RC stores its states (M_{est}) in a matrix, it is necessary that the final values found by the network are not so influenced by the initialization. Therefore, the literature suggests that before starting the training process, a set of cycles called warm up is executed in order to perform updates in the states of the neurons in the reservoir and overlook the influence of the initial value [7]. The states are updated according to (1).

$$x[k + 1] = f(W_{res}x[k] + W_{in}u[k]) \tag{1}$$

where $W_{in}u[k]$ represents the matrix containing the resulting product of the values derived from the input layer by the weights connecting the input to the reservoir at a time k; and $W_{res}x[k]$ is the matrix containing the states of the neurons from the reservoir at the same time k. The result will be assigned to $x[k + 1]$, $i.e.$, the state of the neuron RC in an instant forward will be the result of calculating the activation function of the neuron from the sum of the two parcels described above.

Among the existing training methods for the Reservoir Computing, the one used in this work was the Moore-Penrose (MP) Pseudoinverse. Since the input weights and the biases are randomly generated, the nonlinear system was converted to a linear system according to (2).

$$\mathbf{H}\beta = \mathbf{T} \tag{2}$$

where H is the reservoir layer output matrix; T is the matrix of desired outputs. Thus, the determination of the output weights (linking the reservoir to the output layer) is the least-square solution to the given linear system. The minimum norm least-square (LS) solution to the linear system is presented by (3).

$$\hat{\beta} = \mathbf{H}^+\mathbf{T} \tag{3}$$

where $\mathbf{H}^+$ is the MP generalized inverse of matrix $\mathbf{H}$. The minimum norm LS solution is unique and has the smallest norm among all the LS solutions. MP inverse method tends to obtain good generalization performance with increased in learning speed.

2.2   Trend Information

Trend detection in streamflow series has an expressive importance to an adequate management of water resources. According to Joseph et $al.$ [9], the identification of seasonal trends in precipitation and inflow series allows a better comprehension of the climatic variability, which is essential for the development of hydrologic models, hydrologic forecasting and management of hydrologic resources [9,14,15]. Trend information as an input to the neural network can contribute to determine the hydrogram behavior of a given power plant. Moreover, the use of only past inflows generates a delayed prediction and underestimates the series peaks; and data related to other hydrological variables may not be available, making the trend information an option to increase accuracy since it only needs the original streamflow series.

In this study, a two-step process to extract the trend is used: first, we use a moving average to smooth the time series; then, we differentiate this new series generating first and second derivatives [16]. This intends to extract trend information of the time series in a numerical form, allowing it to be used as an input for the forecasting model.

Initially, a window of size N needs to be defined to calculate the arithmetic mean for the moving average. The result of this operation is a smoother time series with highlighted trends [17]. Consider M as the already softened time series. The second step is to calculate f first derivatives and s second derivatives. The first derivative is represented by (4).

$$d_{1f} = m_{n+1} - m_n \qquad (4)$$

where m_{n+1} and m_n are values from the moving average time series. Consider this new time series as F. The second derivative is represented by (5).

$$d_{2s} = f_{n+1} - f_n \qquad (5)$$

where f_{n+1} and f_n are values from the first derivative time series.

The signal of the derivative indentify the nature of the trend, if it is rising or falling, while the number indicates the amount this series is rising or falling. These f first derivatives and s second derivatives are inputs for the forecasting model.

3 Methodology

This section presents information about the datasets and the methodology for this work. The methodology is divided into four steps: acquisition of the trend information, data pre-processing, training and validation of models results and statistical tests.

3.1 Databases

Five datasets of Brazilian power plants were used to test the proposed method. These five datasets belongs to the power plants of: Governador Bento Munhoz, Três Marias, Tucuruí, Furnas and Itaipu. These series have information of the power plants' daily inflows. Each of these power plants is located in different river basins in Brazil, this means that the time series have different characteristics, e.g., some of them are seasonal, others have a more slow inflow.

3.2   Extracting the Trend Information

In this work, two window sizes were used: 3 days and 7 days with the intent of softening the daily time series. The window of 7 days was considered to analyze the sensibility of the series. With the moving average window size defined, the first and second derivatives were considered as the trend information. Then, it is necessary to define the f first derivatives and s second derivatives. Several values for f and s were selected and after tests, the value for f was considered as 3, and s as 2, representing 5 inputs to the model.

3.3   Pre-processing

To properly execute the training of a neural network, it is necessary that the data is normalized. The normalization process is performed according to (6).

$$y = \frac{(b - a)(x_i - x_{min})}{(x_{max} - x_{min})} + a \qquad (6)$$

This is a simple linear transformation where y is the normalized value; a is the lower limit and b the upper limit; x_i is the original value; x_{max} is the highest value this variable can achieve and x_{min} the lowest. The trend information is also normalized using the same rule described in (6).

The second step is to select the input variables. To accomplish this task, an auto-correlation function was used. A number of auto-regressive values (lags) was defined as possible inputs and the ones with auto-correlation above or equal to 0.5 were considered as inputs to the model. For the datasets used, up to thirty past values can influence the forecasting and were considered as possible inputs for each series. Also, lags with auto-correlation below 0.5 did not increase the accuracy of the forecasting.

After analyzing the auto-correlation, only 14 past values were selected. For each time series with trend information, 19 input values were considered: 14 of them representing the past inflows and the other 5 representing the trend information. The number of outputs was considered as 12, according to the Brazilian standard for short-term forecasting.

3.4   Training

Several RC parameters should be determined prior to the training process. Being a recent methodology, there are no studies that defines how many neurons are necessary in the reservoir to the neural network achieve its best performance, or the rate of connectivity between the reservoir neurons. Therefore, for this work, these parameters values were defined based on empirical tests.

To perform the simulation of both models, the database is divided into three sets: training, used to perform the update of the states of the neurons, cross-validation, used to stop the training of the neural network, and test set, used to calculate the error rate. The configuration for each model remained the same to all datasets used and can be found in Table 1.

Table 1. Representation of the parameters used for the simulations with the RC and MLP

Parameters	MLP value	RC value
RC Connectivity	N/A	30%
Number of neurons in the input layer	14	Depends on the trend information
Number of neurons in the reservoir	N/A	75
Number of neurons in the hidden layer	30	N/A
Number of neurons in the output layer	12	12
Number of warm up cycles	N/A	10
Activation function of the reservoir or hidden layer	Hyperbolic Tangent	Hyperbolic Tangent
Learning rate	0.8	N/A
Momentum	0.2	N/A

3.5 Statistical Tests

In order to scientifically validate the results, it was necessary to perform a sequence of statistical tests after all the simulations were completed. Before using a parametric test on a data set it is necessary to check whether the samples are normally distributed and if they have statistically equal variances. If these two assumptions are valid, it is possible to apply a parametric test, otherwise it must be used a non-parametric test. The Shapiro-Wilk test was applied to verify the first assumption. After that, it is necessary to validate the second assumption. For this, the F Test was applied.

If these two assumptions are true, then a parametric test can be applied. In this work, the Student's T-test was used. If these assumptions are not valid, then it's necessary to apply a non-parametric test which doesn't make any assumptions about the probability distribution of the samples. For this work, the Wilcoxon Rank-Sum Test was chosen. The significance level adopted was 0.05.

4 Results

For each data set, the comparison was made between: a MLP with past inflows, which acts as a benchmark, a RC with past inflows, and a RC with past inflows and trend information. The RC with past inflows and trend information have two variations of the window size. The 3-day window is refered as RC3 and the 7-day window, as RC7.

After all simulations were performed, the arithmetic mean and the standard deviation for each set of simulations were calculated. The error rate used was the Mean Absolute Percentual Error (MAPE) since it's a standard in the analysis of streamflow forecasting in Brazil. The experiments results can be found in Table 2.

Table 2. Experiments results for the five Brazilian datasets

	MLP		RC		RC3		RC7	
	Error mean	Std. deviation	Error mean	Std. deviation	Error mean	Std. deviation	Error mean	Std. deviation
Furnas	23.14 %	5.95	20.13 %	0.04	11.63 %	0.03	11.13 %	0.03
Itaipu	14.36 %	2.33	13.49 %	0.02	7.44 %	0.01	4.95 %	0.01
Gov. Bento Munhoz	41.52 %	12.60	35.89 %	0.13	19.22 %	0.11	18.09 %	0.11
Tucuruí	12.33 %	3.92	9 %	0.08	5.23 %	0.06	3.69 %	0.04
Trés Marias	32.56 %	9.21	28.11 %	0.11	16.80 %	0.16	15.44 %	0.09

Since all results of the RC3 and RC7 are much smaller than the ones found by the RC and MLP, there was no need to perform the statistical tests to compare the results of the predictions. The statistical tests were performed when comparing the results of the RC3 and the RC7 and when comparing the RC with the MLP. In all cases, the RC7 presented a statistically better performance than the RC3, and the RC with only past inflows presented a better generalization capacity when compared to the MLP.

It is also interesting to notice that the use of the Reservoir Computing provides more stable results when compared to the Multi-Layer Perceptron. And is clear that the incorporation of the trend information as an input can increase the accuracy of the prediction.

5   Conclusions

This study aimed to verify the performance of the Reservoir Computing technique combined with the trend information for short-term streamflow forecasting. Even though the RC is a dynamic network, thus more suitable to the task, and achieved better results in comparison to the MLP, it cannot identify the trend patterns existing in the streamflow data, requiring other variables to increase its accuracy. The trend information can be extracted from the series itself, providing an option when other hydrological variables are not available.

It also reduced the delay in the prediction and the underestimation of the series peaks.

From the statistical tests and simulations, it can be concluded that the RC with trend information presented a superior performance in all cases and more stable results when compared to the MLP and the RC without additional inputs. This method was not tested with time series that are not composed of daily observations. As future work, it is intended to use other neural network topologies with and without the trend information to make a comparison with those already used in this study and to test this method with other types of time series and for long-term streamflow forecasting.

References

1. Brooks, K., Ffolliott, P., Gregersen, H., DeBani, L.: Hydrology and the Management of Watersheds (2003)
2. Box, G., Jenkins, G.: Time Series Analysis - Forecasting and Control (1976)
3. Haykin, S.: Neural Networks: A Comprehensive Foundation (1998)
4. Kişi, O.: Evolutionary neural networks for monthly pan evaporation modeling. J. Hydrol. **498**, 36–45 (2013)
5. Chang, F.J., Chen, P.A., Lu, Y.-R., Huang, E., Chang, K.Y.: Real-time multi-step-ahead water level forecasting by recurrent neural networks for urban flood control. J. Hydrol. **517**, 836–846 (2014)
6. He, X., Guan, H., Qin, J.: A hybrid wavelet neural network model with mutual information and particle swarm optimization for forecasting monthly rainfall. J. Hydrol. **527**, 88–100 (2015)
7. Verstraeten, D.: Reservoir Computing: computation with dynamical systems. Ph.D. Dissertation (2009)
8. Lukoševičius, M., Jaeger, H.: Reservoir computing approaches to recurrent neural network training. Comput. Sci. Rev. **3**(3), 127–149 (2009)
9. Joseph, J.F., Falcon, H.E., Sharif, H.O.: Hydrologic trends and correlations in south texas river basins: 1950–2009. J. Hydrol. Eng. **18**(2), 1653–1662 (2013)
10. Zhang, G., Qi, M.: Neural network forecasting for seasonal and trend time series. European Journal of Operational Research **160**(2), 501–514 (2005)
11. Chang, F.J., Lo, Y.C., Chen, P.A., Chang, L.C., Shieh, M.C.: Multi-step-ahead reservoir inflow forecasting by artificial intelligence techniques. In: Tweedale, J., Jain, L.C., Watada, J., Howlett, R.J. (eds.) Knowledge-Based Information Systems in Practice. SIST, vol. 30, pp. 229–242. Springer, Heidelberg (2015)
12. Jaeger, H.: The "echo state" approach to analysing and training recurrent neural networks. Technical report, German National Research Center for Information Technology (2001)
13. Maass, W., Natschläger, T., Markram, H.: Real-time computing without stable states: a new framework for neural computation based on perturbations. Neural Comput. **14**(11), 2531–2560 (2002)
14. Marengo, J.A., Tomasella, J.: Trends in streamflow and rainfall in tropical South America: Amazonia, eastern Brazil, and northwestern Peru. J. Geophys. Res. **103**(2), 1775–1783 (1998)
15. Moura, L.Z.: Evaluation of monotonic trends for streamflow in austral Amazon, Brazil: a case study for the Xingu and Tapajós rivers. In: Proceedings of the International Association of Hydrological Sciences, vol. 371, pp. 125–130, June 2015

16. Baldwin, J.F., Martin, T.P., Rossiter, J.: Time series modelling and prediction using fuzzy trend information. In: Proceedings of the 5th International Conference on Soft Computing and Information Intelligent Systems, pp. 499–502 (1998)
17. Brockwell, P.J., Davis, R.A.: Introduction to Time Series and Forecasting, 2nd edn. Springer, New York (2002)

Effect of Simultaneous Time Series Prediction with Various Horizons on Prediction Quality at the Example of Electron Flux in the Outer Radiation Belt of the Earth

Irina Myagkova[(⊠)], Vladimir Shiroky, and Sergey Dolenko[(⊠)]

D.V. Skobeltsyn Institute of Nuclear Physics,
M.V. Lomonosov Moscow State University, Leninskie Gory, GSP-1,
Moscow 119991, Russian Federation
{irina,dolenko}@srd.sinp.msu.ru

Abstract. Prediction of the time series of relativistic electrons flux in the outer radiation belt of the Earth is a complicated task, due to complexity and nonlinearity of the system "solar wind - the Earth's magnetosphere". However, using artificial neural networks it is possible to predict the value of the electron flux several hours ahead, based on the hourly time series of electron flux, parameters of solar wind and interplanetary magnetic field. The purpose of this study was to check, which approach provided higher precision of prediction with various horizons from one to twelve hours: autonomous prediction for each of the 12 prediction horizons, or simultaneous prediction for several horizons. An explanation of the obtained results is suggested.

Keywords: Time series prediction · Prediction horizon · Simultaneous prediction · Earth's magnetosphere · Relativistic electrons of the outer radiation belt of the Earth · Multi-layer perceptron

1 Introduction

It is known that energetic charged particle radiation is detrimental to spacecraft operations (e.g. [1,2] and references there). The Earth's Radiation Belts (ERB) are inner zones of the Earth's magnetosphere, in which energetic charged particles - electrons and protons - are held by the geomagnetic field, which is close to dipolar. The radiation environment at geosynchronous orbit (GEO - about 35 thousands km altitude - the outer boundary of the radiation belts) is of particular interest due to the large number of satellites populating this region. Relativistic electrons of the outer ERB are sometimes called "killer electrons" since the electronic components of spacecraft can be damaged, resulting in temporary or even complete loss of spacecraft [3].

This study was supported by RFBR grant no. 14-01-00293-a.

© Springer International Publishing Switzerland 2016
A.E.P. Villa et al. (Eds.): ICANN 2016, Part II, LNCS 9887, pp. 317–325, 2016.
DOI: 10.1007/978-3-319-44781-0_38

The outer ERB is very unstable: its relativistic electrons (RE) flux may change for an order of magnitude and more within several hours. As a rule, RE flux falls sharply during the main phase of a magnetic storm. During the recovery phase of magnetic storm, approximately in half of the cases there is an increase of RE flux to a level significantly exceeding that before storm. Reasons of these variations are not understood yet. It is clear only that processes of both acceleration and losses are responsible for formation of ERB (e.g. [4]). High correlation among RE fluxes at geosynchronous orbit, SW speed and other parameters of SW and IMF was measured in space experiments and described back in 1979 [5].

A lot of attempts have therefore been made to predict high-energy electron flux at GEO using different methods: probabilistic [6], statistical data models and linear prediction filters [7–9], physical models based on experimental data [10,11], and also artificial neural networks (ANN) models [12–14].

While the success of data-based physical models depends strongly on correctly identifying and understanding physical processes, the statistical methods are usually less dependent on the selected physical models. It is useful to have effective forecasting based on statistical models that can help identify which quantities are important to include as input to any model. With this in mind, an effort was begun in the late 1990s to develop an improved ANN model. One of these, the neural network model of Koons and Gorney [12], served as both the starting point and the motivation for developing an improved neural network model for the prediction of RE fluxes in the outer ERB.

In most of the mentioned papers, the prediction is carried out for the daily flux a day or more ahead. However, taking into account the fact that the increase of electron flux on GEO may occur during a few hours, hourly forecast of RE flux in the outer ERB is also of much interest. In the paper [15], the electron flux is predicted using hourly values of time series, with prediction horizon of 1 to 12 h. The input data for the ANN are historical values of geomagnetic indices AL and Dst.

The authors of this study have already also created an ANN prediction model for hourly average values of the relativistic (>2 MeV) electrons of outer ERB at GEO with prediction horizon of 1 to 12 h [16,17]. Using historical values of the parameters of solar wind (SW) and interplanetary magnetic field (IMF) (in addition to the geomagnetic indices and electron flux of the outer ERB), it provides a significantly better prediction of hourly average of electron flux. Note that ANN prediction outperforms the best possible linear model provided by Partial Least Squares (PLS) method and the best autoregression modle provided by the Group Method of Data Handling (GMDH) [17].

It should be noted that use of such an approach became possible only in the latest several years, when a long enough time series of satellite measurements of parameters of SW and IMF has been accumulated. For the same reason - the need for a long and consistent time series measurements of RE fluxes by the spacecraft with nearly the same orbits - the RE flux prediction is performed for GEO orbit, where there are long-term data available from the GOES series spacecraft [18]. However, the available time series with high enough quality of SW data, which is about 18 years long, spans only about 1.5 solar cycles; it is highly non-stationary and it is driven by different physical laws at various phases of the cycle. This makes many well-known methods of time series analysis nearly useless; somewhat better results may be expected in such case from adaptive data-driven methods like ANN.

Thus, the purpose of the considered modeling is an hourly ANN prediction for the horizon from 1 to 12 h ahead from the same point in time, i.e. having the same input values for the ANN. Usually this problem is solved by building 12 separate single-output ANNs, each with its own prediction horizon (autonomous prediction). However, as all the inputs are common, it is also possible to build a single ANN with 12 outputs, one for each prediction horizon (simultaneous prediction). Finally, it is possible to perform group prediction by training networks with several outputs corresponding to several adjacent values of the prediction horizon.

In their preceding studies, the authors have investigated a similar problem solving a multi-parameter inverse problem with ANN [19]. It has been demonstrated that, at certain conditions, group determination of parameters provides improvement in the quality of the inverse problem solution in comparison with autonomous determination of parameters.

The purpose of this study was to find out, whether it is possible to improve prediction quality by group prediction in comparison with autonomous prediction, and at what conditions.

2   Data Sources and Preparation

Time series (TS) of hourly values of the following physical quantities were used as input for ANN prediction:

(a) SW parameters in Lagrange point L1 between the Earth and the Sun: SW speed v (measured in km/s), SW protons density n_P (measured in cm^{-3}), SW protons temperature T (measured in K).
(b) IMF vector parameters in the same Lagrange point L1 (measured in nT): Bx, By, Bz (IMF components in GSM system) and B amplitude (IMF modulus).
(c) Geomagnetic indexes: equatorial geomagnetic index Dst (measured in nT) and global geomagnetic index Kp (dimensionless).
(d) Flux of relativistic electrons with energies >2 MeV at geostationary orbit (measured in $(cm^2 \cdot s \cdot sr)^{-1}$).

Besides that, to account for daily and yearly variations of the predicted quantity, TS of sine and cosine values with daily and yearly period were also used as input data. The specific sources of data are listed elsewhere [16].

Relativistic electrons flux as a TS has a wide dynamical range of its values, covering more than 6 orders of magnitude. So its value was transferred to logarithmic scale, to level out relative prediction errors in different orders of magnitude. Comparison of statistical indexes of error and data interpolation were also carried out in logarithmic scale. Our preceding studies showed that in this case the prediction errors were lower than in the case when no transfer to the logarithmic scale was performed. To account for the previous history of input features, delay embedding of all TS for 24 h depth was used. Thus, the total number of input features was 254.

Delay embedding significantly increases the negative influence of data gaps on data volume and representativity. Based on the fact that rapid changes are not typical for virtually all kinds of data used, in this study we used filling of gaps 12 or less hours long by linear interpolation (for time moments when the gap is already over) or by extrapolation of the latest known value. Also, there is no reason for use of more sophisticated estimates. Unfortunately, presence of gaps and such a way of their filling make inefficient possible use of various types of recurrent neural networks with SW parameters as their inputs. At the same time, the values of SW parameters influence the electrons flux to a great extent.

As the learning sample, the data from October 22, 1997 till December 31, 2006, was used. After delay embedding, the learning sample was divided by random selection of patterns in the ratio of 75/25 into training set (59124 patterns) and validation set (19707 patterns). As out-of-sample data, two test sets were used to evaluate the obtained predictors: "long" (from January 1, 2007 till March 31, 2015) and "short" (from January 1, 2010 till March 31, 2015). The "short" examination set (45938 patterns) contained only data from the phases of the solar cycle whose data were present in the learning sample. The "long" set (72241 patterns) also contained data for the end of the solar cycle (2007–2009), with no similar data present in the learning sample. So it was expected that the results for the "long" set would be somewhat worse than for the "short" one.

3 Architecture and Parameters of Neural Networks

The ANN architecture used in the present study was the multi-layer perceptron (MLP). A special investigation has been performed to determine the optimal number of hidden layers (HL) of the MLP, and the optimal number of neurons in the HL. A MLP with a single HL performed much better than a simple perceptron without HL. However, MLPs with 2 and 3 HL failed to provide any substantial improvement in the performance as compared to the single HL MLP. It should be noted that the performance of the MLP remained practically unchanged in a wide range of the number of neurons in the HL, due to the stop training criterion used (500 epochs since minimum error on the validation set of data).

The finally selected ANN architecture was MLP with 32 neurons in the single hidden layer, tanh activation function in the hidden layer, linear activation function in the output layer, trained by standard error backpropagation with learning rate 0.01 and moment 0.5, with random presentation of patterns.

In each experiment, 3 MLPs were trained, differing only by weights initialization and by the seed of random presentation of the patterns. The statistical indexes used to assess prediction quality and presented below are in each case averaged over the 3 values provided by the corresponding MLPs. The standard deviation of the averaging was small in all cases, thus confirming weak dependence of the result on initial conditions of ANN training.

4   Results and Discussion

Autonomous prediction was performed by 12 separate MLPs with a single output each (whose results are denoted with values of the solid lines at the figures below). Simultaneous prediction was performed by a special MLP with 12 outputs (dashed lines). For group prediction, the prediction window (group) size - the number of simultaneously predicted values - was set to 2, 3, 4, 6, and 9. Each prediction window included adjacent values of prediction horizon, and all possible positions were tested. For example, for prediction window size 3, the groups of simultaneously predicted horizons were (1,2,3), (2,3,4), (3,4,5), ..., (8,9,10), (9,10,11), and (10,11,12); for prediction window size 9 - (1,2,3,...,7,8,9), (2,3,4,...,8,9,10), (3,4,5,...,9,10,11), and (4,5,6,...,10,11,12).

Figure 1 displays the values of multiple determination coefficient R^2 and the root mean squared error (RMSE), measured in orders of magnitude of RE flux, as functions of prediction horizon (from 1 to 12 h) for the average of predictions of 3 identical ANN with different sets of initial weights. The solid lines correspond to autonomous prediction (each horizon separately). The dashed lines present the results of simultaneous prediction (all horizons at once). All the markers display the results of group prediction, for all tested sizes and all possible positions of prediction window.

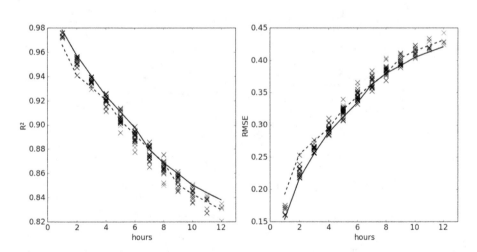

Fig. 1. Coefficient of multiple determination (R^2, left) and root mean squared error (RMSE, right) vs prediction horizon in hours, on the "long" test set. Solid line - autonomous prediction, dashed line - simultaneous prediction, markers - group prediction for various sizes and positions of prediction window.

Except the obvious degradation of the prediction quality with increasing prediction horizon, from Fig. 1 it can easily be seen that for small horizons any attempts of obtaining several predictions with various horizons with the same MLP fail to make the results of prediction better. However, starting from 3 h, we can observe positive effect of group prediction - for each prediction horizon, there are several combinations of prediction window size and position that provide better results than autonomous prediction. At the same time, Fig. 1 does not demonstrate the dependence of the effect neither on the size, nor on the position of the prediction window.

Figure 2 displays the dependence of RMSE on prediction window (group) size, separately for each of the 12 values of the prediction horizon. Upper two diagrams represent values averaged over all possible positions of the prediction window; lower two diagrams present the same results for the position of each window giving the best prediction among other positions of the window of the

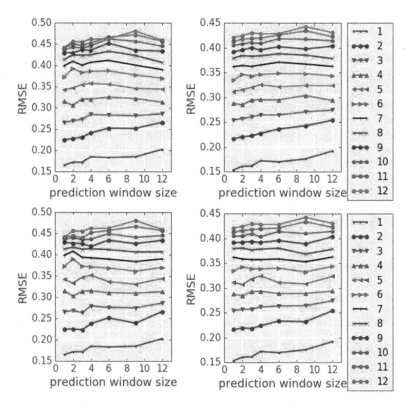

Fig. 2. Root mean squared error (RMSE) vs prediction window size on the "long" test set (left) and on the "short" test set (right). Top, values averaged over all window positions; bottom, values best among all window positions. Curves 1–12 (from bottom to top) correspond to various values of the prediction horizon.

same size. Note that the results are slightly better for the "short" test set (right), as it was expected.

A number of conclusions can be made from analysis of Figs. 1 and 2, and from comparison of the results of the present study with those of the study of parameter grouping in ANN solution of a multi-parameter inverse problem [19].

(1) The key value has the precision of prediction in autonomous prediction mode. The hypothesis is that, in general, positive effect for some horizon may be achieved if the prediction for this horizon is made by one ANN simultaneously with another horizon which is predicted better in autonomous mode. That is why the effect is not observed or less pronounced for small horizon values well predictable autonomously.

(2) For each horizon, there is an optimal size of grouping window, and it is in general increased with increasing horizon. Among windows of the same size, the one expected to bring the best prediction for a given horizon is the window most shifted towards smaller horizons. The main reason of this effect is monotonous decrease in the prediction quality with horizon.

(3) One more possible reason for the positive effect of grouping is averaging of noise in the outputs when training a several-output ANN. This effect may increase with increasing number of outputs (i.e. size of the prediction window).

(4) The key condition for the positive effect of group prediction is that all predictions should use the same (as in this study) or nearly the same set of input features. In this case, minimization of the error functional results in extraction of such features in the hidden layer that are produced from the same input features, and that are more or less useful for all the simultaneously predicted outputs.

(5) Summing up, it can be claimed that the observed effect is determined by the properties of a multi-layer perceptron as a data processing algorithm rather than by the properties of a specific problem. In particular, this is proved by similar effects observed in group prediction in this study and in group determination of parameters when solving a multi-parameter inverse problem [19].

5 Conclusions

This study considers the effect of simultaneous prediction of time series with different prediction horizons on the precision of the prediction, at the example of a complicated task from the domain of space physics - prediction of the flux of relativistic electrons at the geosynchronous orbit of the Earth. It is demonstrated that at certain conditions group prediction (simultaneous prediction with several adjacent horizon values) may improve prediction quality; the necessary conditions are discussed. The key conclusion made is that the observed effect is caused by the properties of a multi-layer perceptron as a data processing algorithm. Future studies should include testing of the effect on other problems solved by multi-layer perceptrons with several outputs.

References

1. Shea, M.A., Smart, D.F.: Space weather: the effects on operations in space. Adv. Space Res. **22**(1), 29–37 (1998)
2. Iucci, N., Levitin, A.E., Belov, A.V., et al.: Space weather conditions and spacecraft anomalies in different orbits. Space Weather **3**(1), S01001 (2005)
3. Pilipenko, V., Yagova, N., Romanova, N., et al.: Statistical relationships between the satellite anomalies at geostationary orbits and high-energy particles. Adv. Space Res. **37**(6), 1192–1205 (2006)
4. Friedel, R.H., Reeves, W.G.P., Obara, T.: Relativistic electron dynamics in the inner magnetosphere - a review. J. Atmos. Solar Terr. Phys. **64**, 265–283 (2002)
5. Paulikas, G.A., Blake, J.B.: Effects of the solar wind on magnetospheric dynamics: energetic electrons at the synchronous orbit. In: Olson, W.P., et al. (eds.) Quantitative Modeling of Magnetospheric Processes. Geophys. Monogr. Ser., vol. 21, pp. 180–202. AGU, Washington D.C. (1979)
6. Miyoshi, Y., Kataoka, R.: Probabilistic space weather forecast of the relativistic electron flux enhancement at geosynchronous orbit. J. Atmos. Solar Terr. Phys. **70**, 475–481 (2008)
7. Nagai, T.: "Space weather forecast": prediction of relativistic electron intensity at synchronous orbit. Geophys. Res. Lett. **15**, 425–428 (1988)
8. Baker, D.N., McPherron, R.L., et al.: Linear prediction filter analysis of relativistic electron properties at 6.6 R_E. J. Geophys. Res. **95**(A9), 15133–15140 (1990)
9. Wei, H.-L., Billings, S.F.A., Surjala, A., et al.: Forecasting relativistic electron flux using dynamic multiple regression models. Ann. Geophys. **29**, 415420 (2011)
10. Ukhorskiy, A.Y., Sitnov, M.I., Sharma, A.S., et al.: Data-derived forecasting model for relativistic electron intensity at geosynchronous orbit. Geophys. Res. Lett. **31**, L09806 (2004). doi:10.1029/2004GL019616
11. Degtyarev, V.I., Chudnenko, S.E., Kharchenko, I.P., et al.: Prediction of maximal daily average values of relativistic electron fluxes in geostationary orbit during the magnetic storm recovery phase. Geomag. Aeron. **49**(8), 1208–1217 (2009). doi:10.1134/S0016793209080349
12. Koons, H.C., Gorney, D.J.: A neural network model of the relativistic electron flux at geosynchronous orbit. J. Geophys. Res. **96**, 5549–5556 (1990)
13. Stringer, G.A., Heuten, I., Salazar, C., et al.: Artificial neural network (ANN) forecasting of energetic electrons at geosynchronous orbit. In: Lemaire, J.F. (ed.) Radiation Belts: Models and Standards. Geophys. Monogr. Ser., vol. 97, pp. 291–295. AGU, Washington, D.C. (1996)
14. Ling, A.G., Ginet, G.P., Hilmer, R.V., et al.: A neural network-based geosynchronous relativistic electron flux forecasting model. Space Weather **8**(9), S09003 (2010)
15. Fukata, M., Taguchi, S., Okuzawa, T., et al.: Neural network prediction of relativistic electrons at geosynchronous orbit during the storm recovery phase: effects of recurring substorms. Ann. Geophys. **20**(7), 947–951 (2002)
16. Myagkova, I., Dolenko, S., Shiroky, V., et al.: Horizon of neural network prediction of relativistic electrons flux in the outer radiation belt of the earth. In: Proceedings of the 16th EANN Conference, pp. 9–14. ACM, New York (2015)
17. Efitorov, A., Myagkova, I., Sentemova, N., et al.: Prediction of relativistic electrons flux in the outer radiation belt of the earth using adaptive methods. Adv. Intell. Syst. Comput. **449**, 281–287 (2016)

18. Geostationary Operational Environmental Satellite Project. http://goes.gsfc.nasa.gov/
19. Dolenko, S., Isaev, I., Obornev, E., et al.: Study of influence of parameter grouping on the error of neural network solution of the inverse problem of electrical prospecting. Commun. Comput. Inf. Sci. **383**, 81–90 (2013)

A Time Series Forecasting Model Based on Deep Learning Integrated Algorithm with Stacked Autoencoders and SVR for FX Prediction

Hua Shen[✉] and Xun Liang

School of Information, RenMin University of China, Beijing 100872, China
shenhuaustb@163.com

Abstract. This paper proposes a Deep Learning integrated algorithm with Stacked Autoencoders (SAE) and Support Vector Regression (SVR), it is also for the first time that applies the SAE-SVR integrated algorithm to Foreign Exchange (FX) rate forecasting. We adopt 28 currency pairs pertaining to G7 currencies and RenMinBi, and collect the real daily FX data for simulation. To implement the empirical study, we develop the program of SAE-SVR integrated algorithm independently, and benchmark the results with ANN and SVR models, which are considered as the best performance in Artificial Intelligence. Ultimately, the simulation results indicate that the SAE-SVR integrated algorithm performs much better over other benchmarks.

Keywords: Deep learning · Stacked autoencoders · Time series forecasting · Foreign Exchange

1 Introduction

Since the collapse of Bretton Woods Agreement in 1973, the Foreign Exchange market has become the most influential market in financial world, with an average daily turnover of 5345 billion dollars[1] for global Foreign Exchange market. Increasingly, Foreign Exchange rate plays a significant roll not only in people who engaged in financial fields, but also in international-level macroeconomic issues. Therefore, it arises an ascending number of governments, economists and financial institutions interest in developing high accuracy techniques for forecasting Foreign Exchange (FX) time series [1].

Taking it by and large, the main approaches on this problem have proceeded on three fronts in literatures. First of all, a majority of research efforts adopt the time-dependent conditional heteroskedasticity into standard models and use volatility as a key parameter. These models belong to the ARCH and GARCH approaches initiated by Engle and Bollerslev. Secondly, there are fundamental

---

[1] Source: The latest statistics of BIS (Bank for International Settlements) Triennial Central Bank Survey in the size and structure of global foreign exchange and OTC derivatives markets (updated 13 September 2015).

© Springer International Publishing Switzerland 2016
A.E.P. Villa et al. (Eds.): ICANN 2016, Part II, LNCS 9887, pp. 326–335, 2016.
DOI: 10.1007/978-3-319-44781-0_39

models attempting to project the exchange rates based on rational expectations hypotheses involving major macro-economical figures. These models are established on the foundations of supply and demand of domestic currency compared with a foreign currency. Last but not least, there are an increasing number of studies recently begin to focus on artificial intelligent approaches to forecast Foreign Exchange rate. This category mostly uses time-series statistics to predict currency movements and is proven to be outperformed than the traditional approaches [2]. Optimized Algorithms of Artificial Neural Networks (ANN) are best performed and most common in Artificial Intelligence (AI) field for the moment, But ANN can still not go beyond one or two hidden layers for the problematic non-convex optimization, therefore the difficult problem of learning in deep networks for higher precision is left dormant.

However, in 2006, Geoffrey Hinton et al. rekindled interest in ANN by showing substantially better performance by a deep neural network that proved successful at learning their parameters [3,4]. Deep learning algorithms trained in this fashion have been shown empirically to avoid getting stuck in the kind of poor solutions one typically reaches with only random initialization [5,6]. While until now there are few people make empirical study of time series modeling with the typical deep neural network naming Stacked Autoencoder (SAE) [7,8], which consists of multiple layers of Sparse Autoencoders, and the outputs of each layer is wired to the inputs of the successive layer [9].

Under this circumstance, this paper takes a novel perspective on the problem of optimizing the forecasting precision by proposing a Deep Learning Integrated Algorithm with Stacked Atutoencoders (SAE) and Support Vector Regression (SVR) to overcome the drawbacks contained in statistic models and ANN. The innovative proposed methodology could be adapted to different currencies exchange rate.

2   The FX Time Series Forecasting Model

2.1   The Forecasting Model Structure of SAE-SVR Integrated Algorithm

In general, SAE performs remarkably in deeply extracting dataset features, while SVR shows superior predicting capacity for time series. However, the time series forecasting model we proposed based on Deep Learning integrated algorithm with SAE and SVR combines merits in both of them.

To be specific, considering a network structure of SAE-SVR integrated algorithm as shown in Fig. 1, it consists of one Input Layer, one Output Layer and K Hidden Layers. With this greedy layer-wise training method, each hidden layer can gradually learn part-whole features of the dataset. During the implementation process, we train the SAE-SVR integrated algorithm layer by layer, and each layer represents a Sparse Autoencoder, which is illustrated in Fig. 2 below.

For the first Sparse Autoencoder, we initiate the net-config as $(W, b) = (W^{(1)}, b^{(1)}, W^{(2)}, b^{(2)})$, for $W_{ij}^{(1)}$ connects the jth unit in layer L with the ith

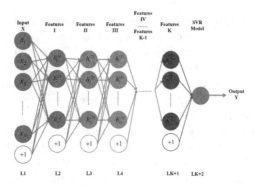

Fig. 1. The forecasting model structure of SAE-SVR integrated algorithm

unit in layer L+1, and $b_i^{(l)}$ represents the bias of ith unit in layer L+1. In addition, we define $a_i^{(l)}$ as the activation of ith unit in layer L, as well as the output of this neural unit, and $z_i^{(l)}$ as the input of this neural unit. Therefore, the functional relationship of the first Sparse Autoencoder for a single input loop is as below:

$$a_1^{(2)} = f(z_1^{(2)}) = f(\sum_{i=1}^{N} W_{1i}^{(1)} x_i + b_1^{(1)}) , ..., a_M^{(2)} = f(z_M^{(2)}) = f(\sum_{i=1}^{N} W_{Mi}^{(1)} x_i + b_M^{(1)});$$

$$a_1^{(3)} = \hat{x}_1 = f(z_1^{(3)}) = f(\sum_{i=1}^{M} W_{1i}^{(2)} a_i^{(2)} + b_1^{(2)})$$
$$,...., $$
$$a_N^{(3)} = \hat{x}_N = f(z_N^{(3)}) = f(\sum_{i=1}^{M} W_{Ni}^{(2)} a_i^{(2)} + b_N^{(2)});$$

Where $f(\cdot) : \Re \to \Re$, here we set it a Sigmoid Function as:

$$f(z) = \frac{1}{1 + \exp(-z)}$$

2.2 The Back-Propagation Fine-Tuning Process of the Forecasting Model Structure

As is known, the output of the first Sparse Autoencoder is $A^{(3)} = \{a_1^{(3)}, a_2^{(3)}, ..., a_N^{(3)}\} \in R$, while the real value of L3 equals to input $X = \{x_1, x_2..., x_N\} \in R$ according to attribute of Stacked Autoencoders. In the following, we conduct a Back-Propagation process to fine-tune the net-config during multi input loops for the first Sparse Autoencoder.

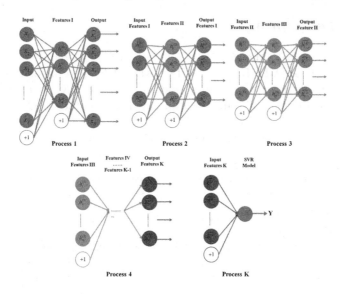

Fig. 2. The Feed-Forward Sub-Step Structure of SAE-SVR Integrated Algorithm

Firstly, we define a training set as $\{(x^{(1)}, \hat{x}^{(1)}), ..., (x^{(m)}, \hat{x}^{(m)})\}$, and a Square Error Cost Function $J(W, b)$ as

$$J(W, b) = \left[\frac{1}{m} \sum_{i=1}^{m} J(W, b; x^{(i)}, \hat{x}^{(i)})\right] + \frac{\lambda}{2} \sum_{l=1}^{2} \sum_{i=1}^{s_L} \sum_{j=1}^{s_{L+1}} \left(W_{ji}^{(l)}\right)^2 + \beta \sum_{j=1}^{s_2} KL(\rho||\hat{\rho}_j)$$

$$= \left[\frac{1}{m} \sum_{i=1}^{m} \left(\frac{1}{2}||\hat{x}^{(i)} - x^{(i)}||^2\right)\right] + \frac{\lambda}{2} \sum_{l=1}^{2} \sum_{i=1}^{s_L} \sum_{j=1}^{s_{L+1}} \left(W_{ji}^{(l)}\right)^2 + \beta \sum_{j=1}^{s_2} KL(\rho||\hat{\rho}_j)$$

Where $\frac{\lambda}{2} \sum_{l=1}^{2} \sum_{i=1}^{s_L} \sum_{j=1}^{s_{L+1}} \left(W_{ji}^{(l)}\right)^2$ is the Weight Decay Term to avoid over-fitting, s_L means the number of units of layer L, and ρ means SparsityParam, $\sum_{j=1}^{s_2} KL(\rho||\hat{\rho}_j)$ is Penalty Term based on Kullback-Leibler Divergence:

$$KL(\rho||\hat{\rho}_j) = \rho \log \frac{\rho}{\hat{\rho}_j} + (1 - \rho) \log \frac{1 - \rho}{1 - \hat{\rho}_j}$$

However, each Sparse Autoencoder learns itself with multi input loops during fine-tune procedure to obtain more precise forecasting results. And the activations outputs of each layer is wired to the inputs of the successive layer, until the Kth activations obtained from process K-1 will be directly conducted as input of a SVR model. After all the K processes are accomplished, there will be a further Back-Propagation fine-tune for the whole SAE-SVR integrated algorithm to descend the error of prediction outcomes.

3   Data Description

In this paper, we base the Foreign Exchange rate (FX) datasets on the G7 currencies (USD, GBP, EUR, JPY, AUD, CAD, CHF), and furthermore collect daily Foreign Exchange rate on MetaTrader4 platform of FXCM. In view of the ascending influences of RenMinBi, we additionally adopt daily CNY from SAFE (State Administration of Foreign Exchange) official website. Therefore, we use 28 currency pairs datasets in total illustrated in Table 1.

Table 1. The 28 currency pairs datasets in simulation test

-	USD	EUR	GBP	CAD	AUD	JPY	CHF	CNY
USD	-	-	-	5USDCAD	-	11USDJPY	16USDCHF	22USDCNY
EUR	1EURUSD	-	4EURGBP	6EURCAD	9EURAUD	12EURJPY	17EURCHF	23EURCNY
GBP	2GBPUSD	-	-	7GBPCAD	10GBPAUD	13GBPJPY	18GBPCHF	24GBPCNY
CAD	-	-	-	-	-	14CADJPY	19CADCHF	25CADCNY
AUD	3AUDUSD	-	-	8AUDCAD	-	15AUDJPY	20AUDCHF	26AUDCNY
JPY	-	-	-	-	-	-	-	27JPYCNY
CHF	-	-	-	-	-	21CHFJPY	-	28CHFCNY

As for the data frequency and time span, we extract the daily FX data in MetaTrader4 and SAFE from 21st Mar 2009 to 1st Feb 2016. Besides, we classify all the dataset into Training set and Testing set respectively for machine learning process, details are shown in Table 2.

Table 2. The details of 28 currency pair datasets

DataSet no.	Currency pair	Alldata	Start date	Expiry date	Trainingset	Testingset
1–21	Omit	2048*21	2009-03-20	2016-02-01	1548*21	500*21
22	USDCNY	1782	2008-10-06	2016-02-01	1282	500
23	EURCNY	1782	2008-10-06	2016-02-01	1282	500
24	GBPCNY	1782	2008-10-06	2016-02-01	1282	500
25	CADCNY	1014	2011-11-28	2016-02-01	514	500
26	AUDCNY	1014	2011-11-28	2016-02-01	514	500
27	JPYCNY	1782	2008-10-06	2016-02-01	1282	500
28	CHFCNY	59	2015-11-10	2016-02-01	39	20
Sum	-	52223	-	-	38703	13520

Before we conduct the simulation test, firstly, the data should be normalized between [0, 1] scale. For each currency pair time series data $S = (s_1, s_2, ..., s_T)$, the conversion formula is:

$$z_i = \frac{s_{max} - s_i}{s_{max} - s_{min}}$$

Then we get the normalized currency pair time series $Z = (z_1, z_2, ..., z_T)$, secondly, the normalized $Z = (z_1, z_2, ..., z_T)$ will be transformed into a L-lag-window multi-dimension time series vector $X = [X_1, ..., X_M] = (x_{ij})_{i,j=1}^{L,M}$, for $X_i = (z_i, ..., z_{i+L-1})' \in R^L$, $M = T - L + 1$, and the lag-window L is an integer meeting $2 \leq L \leq T/2$, So the new input vector is as below:

$$X = [X_1, ..., X_M] = (x_{ij})_{i,j=1}^{L,M} = \begin{bmatrix} z_1 & z_2 & z_3 & \cdots & z_M \\ z_2 & y_3 & z_4 & \cdots & z_{M+1} \\ \cdots & \cdots & \cdots & \ddots & \cdots \\ z_L & z_{L+1} & z_{L+2} & \cdots & z_T \end{bmatrix}$$

While the output vector is a one-dimensional time series vector:

$$Y = (y_1, ..., y_M) \in R$$

where $y_n = z_{n+L}$, and y_n indicates the forecasting value of $X_n = (z_n, ..., z_{n+L-1})' \in R^L$. Finally, we get the 28 time series input and output vectors after preprocessing.

4 Simulation and Results

In this paper, we estimate the error with MAE (Mean Absolute Error), MSE (Mean Square Error), RMSE (Root Mean Square Error) as criteria for assessing the validity of our integrated algorithm.

$$MAE = \sum_{i=1}^{n} \frac{|\hat{y}_i - y_i|}{n}; MSE = \sum_{i=1}^{n} \frac{(\hat{y}_i - y_i)^2}{n}; RMSE = \sqrt{\sum_{i=1}^{n} \frac{(\hat{y}_i - y_i)^2}{n}}$$

Where $\hat{y}_i$ is the predicted value of corresponding y_i.

The simulation environment is based on Matlab R2015a platform in 32-bit Windows7, as to the innovative SAE-SVR integrated algorithm, we refer to the UFLDL Tutorial of Deep Learning curriculum offered by Stanford University, and develop the codes independently. In addition, we benchmark our SAE-SVR integrated algorithm with ANN and SVR, the ANN model is conducted with Neural Network Time Series Toolbox in Matlab R2015a, while the SVR model is implemented with LIBSVM 3.12 Toolbox.

To be more concrete, the main program implement steps for the SAE-SVR integrated algorithm come down to:

Step1: Provide the relevant parameters, involving inputSize, hiddenSizeL1, hidenSizeLn, sparsityParam, lambda, beta, alpha, etc.
Step2: Load normalized vectors data, including Training Set and Testing Set.
Step3: Train the first sparse autoencoder with training set as input vector, and get the trained net-config sae1Theta, then optimize sae1Theta with SparseAE-Cost function to obtain sae1OptTheta, and further conduct feedForwardAutoencoder function to achieve the first feature vector sae1Features.

Step4: Train the second sparse autoencoder, set the sae1Features as input vector and obtain sae2Theta, sae2OptTheta, and sae2Features. Sae2Features is the input vector of the next step.

Step5: By that analogy, accomplish training N layer stacked autoencoders, until the Nth output vector saeNFeatures.

Step6: Set saeNFeatures as input vector to train the SVR model, and get the output svmoutput.

Step7: Fine-tune the whole SAE-SVR algorithm: make a comparison between the model output svmoutput with real forecasting value y, and fine-tune the model config with stackedAECost function, the updated parameters are saved in stack.

Step8: Predict the testing set with optimized SAE-SVR algorithm after fine-tuning, achieve the forecasting values with stackedAEPredict function, and evaluate MSE, RMSE, MAE results.

However, the SAE-SVR integrated algorithm flow chart is illustrated below in Fig. 3.

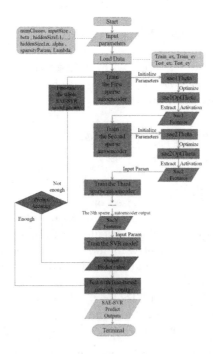

Fig. 3. the SAE-SVR integrated algorithm flow chart.

Eventually, the simulation outcomes of the SAE-SVR integrated algorithm are summarized in Table 3 below. Comparing with the ANN and SVR model, the 28datesets simulation results are aggregated in Table 3, from which we can tell, ANN model performs much better than SVR model in predicting Foreign Exchange rate, so we contrast SAE-SVR model directly to ANN model with calculation formula:

$$\text{Pr } omoted = \frac{|(SAESVR)MSE - (ANN)MSE|}{(ANN)MSE}$$

$$Sumup = \sum_{i=1}^{N=28} \text{Pr } omoted\_value(i)$$

The promoted column reveals that in 28 entire datesets, although the SAE-SVR model performs not better than ANN in 9 currency pairs involving 1EURUSD, 5USDCAD, 7GBPCAD, 10GBPAUD, 11USDJPY, 22USDCNY, 23EURCNY, 25CADCNY, 26AUDCNY, the other 21 currency pairs datasets all indicate a better performance than ANN and SVR model. Further we calculate

Table 3. The aggregated 28 datasets simulation results of ANN, SVR, SAE-SVR mdoels.

DataSeT Name	ANN MSE	SVR MSE	SAE-SVR MSE	Promoted	ANN MAE	SVR MAE	SAE-SVR MAE	Promoted
1EURUSD	2.7307e-04	0.0026098	2.88E-04	-5.60 %	0.0122	0.0399	0.02234	-83.11 %
2GBPUSD	6.8046e-04	0.0011528	6.09E-04	10.51 %	0.0193	0.0272	0.01169	39.43 %
3AUDUSD	2.3025e-04	0.0003145	1.95E-04	15.22 %	0.0113	0.0143	0.01012	10.44 %
4EURGBP	2.6657e-04	0.0015129	2.51E-04	5.72 %	0.0122	0.0307	0.01149	5.82 %
5USDCAD	1.3537e-04	0.0022363	1.82E-04	-34.15 %	0.0085	0.0332	0.00922	-8.47 %
6EURCAD	2.9867e-04	0.0005757	1.44E-04	51.94 %	0.0126	0.0189	0.00984	21.90 %
7GBPCAD	2.2838e-04	0.0007986	2.40E-04	-5.00 %	0.0167	0.0215	0.01808	-8.26 %
8AUDCAD	4.8400e-04	0.00068021	1.57E-04	67.65 %	0.0167	0.0198	0.01089	34.79 %
9EURAUD	1.3568e-04	0.00024962	4.12E-05	69.66 %	0.0084	0.0114	0.00513	38.93 %
10GBPAUD	2.1326e-04	0.00062255	2.77E-04	-29.73 %	0.0109	0.0191	0.01465	-34.40 %
11USDJPY	1.4181e-04	0.00465398	2.12E-04	-49.77 %	0.0088	0.0567	0.01577	-79.20 %
12EURJPY	2.7442e-04	0.00034466	7.06E-05	74.29 %	0.0120	0.0142	0.00655	45.42 %
13GBPJPY	1.9389e-04	0.00141236	9.14E-05	52.86 %	0.1299	0.0299	0.0082	93.69 %
14CADJPY	4.2757e-04	0.00055366	1.70E-04	60.21 %	0.0149	0.0177	0.00939	36.98 %
15AUDJPY	3.6397e-04	0.0002919	5.06E-05	86.11 %	0.0136	0.0129	0.0089	34.56 %
16USDCHF	2.8011e-04	0.0009669	3.42E-05	87.80 %	0.0101	0.0154	0.00788	21.98 %
17EURCHF	1.9228e-04	0.0022557	7.01E-05	63.56 %	0.0061	0.0304	0.0049	19.67 %
18GBPCHF	3.0714e-04	0.0010526	9.99E-05	67.46 %	0.0103	0.0155	0.00541	47.48 %
19CADCHF	2.9759e-04	0.00111476	4.82E-05	83.81 %	0.0107	0.0208	0.00978	8.60 %
20AUDCHF	4.1407e-04	0.0015979	9.80E-05	76.33 %	0.0129	0.0268	0.01181	8.45 %
21CHFJPY	2.2217e-04	0.0014423	4.14E-05	81.35 %	0.0086	0.0224	0.00835	2.91 %
22USDCNY	8.7996e-05	0.00103769	3.11E-04	-253.22 %	0.0061	0.0135	0.0099	-62.30 %
23EURCNY	2.2732e-04	0.0017301	2.94E-04	-29.22 %	0.0110	0.0318	0.01578	-43.45 %
24GBPCNY	4.5092e-04	0.00052641	1.68E-04	62.79 %	0.0149	0.0163	0.01114	25.23 %
25CADCNY	1.7722e-04	0.0045405	3.20E-04	-80.78 %	0.0097	0.0536	0.01675	-72.68 %
26AUDCNY	2.3929e-04	0.00255696	3.63E-04	-51.88 %	0.0118	0.0403	0.01772	-50.17 %
27JPYCNY	1.9699e-04	0.00179411	1.32E-04	33.10 %	0.0099	0.0349	0.00086	91.31 %
28CHFCNY	0.0187	0.0316333	1.92E-05	99.90 %	0.0886	0.1728	0.00438	95.06 %
Sum Up	-	-	-	**610.92 %**	-	-	-	**240.61 %**

the Sum Up of the SAE-SVRs proposed performance, it shows that the SAE-SVR is more than 6 times better than ANN model in MSE criteria, and more than 2 times better than ANN in MAE criteria, which comes to the conclusion that the SAE-SVR integrated algorithm we proposed is attained with distinction to some extent.

5   Conclusions

With the rapid variation in FX market, it brings an ascending number of attentions to make more precise forecasting for Foreign Exchange Rate. In this paper, we propose an innovative Integrated Algorithm based on Deep Learning with Stacked Autoencoders and SVR, we take a novel perspective to extract the high-dimensional abstract features from K layers Sparse Autoencoders and send the output activations into the SVR model for prediction. For the sake of verifying the integrated algorithm, we take advantage of FX real currency pairs pertaining to G7 and RenMinBi in MetaTrader4 and SAFE respectively, normalize and test the datasets before simulation. To implement the simulation, we develop the program independently referring to UFLDL Tutorial by Stanford University, and benchmark our SAE-SVR integrated algorithm with ANN and SVR model. Ultimately, the aggregated comparison indicates that the SAE-SVR integrated algorithm outperformed than ANN and SVR to some extent, which verifies the outperformance of our innovative algorithm. However, there is still a lot of room to improve for the SAE-SVR integrated algorithm. In the next, we will take more macroeconomic factors into account, and combine them with the SAE-SVR algorithm for a more outstanding performance.

References

1. Liao, G.C., Tsao, T.P.: Application of a fuzzy neural network combined with a chaos genetic algorithm and simulated annealing to short term load forecasting. IEEE Trans. Evol. Comput. **10**, 330–340 (2006)
2. Van Gestel, T., Suykens, K.J., Baestaens, D., Lambrechts, A., Lanckriet, G., Vandaele, B., De Moor, B., Vandewalle, J.: Financial time series prediction using least squares support vector machines within the evidence framework. IEEE Trans. Neural Netw. **12**, 809–821 (2001)
3. Bengio, Y., Lamblin, P., Popovici, D., Larochelle, H.: Greedy layer-wise training of deep networks. In: Scholkopf, B., Platt, J., Hoffman, T. (eds.) Advances in Neural Information Processing Systems 19 (NIPS06), pp. 153–160. MIT Press, Cambridge (2007)
4. Hinton, G.E., Osindero, S., Teh, Y.W.: A fast learning algorithm for deep belief nets. Neural Comput. **18**, 1527–1554 (2006)
5. Qiu, X., Zhang, L., Ren, Y., et al.: Ensemble deep learning for regression and time series forecasting. In: 2014 IEEE Symposium on Computational Intelligence in Ensemble Learning (CIEL), pp. 1–6. IEEE (2014)
6. Fakhr, M.W.: Online nonstationary time series prediction using sparse coding with dictionary update. In: 2015 International Conference on Information and Communication Technology Research (ICTRC), IEEE (2015)

7. Zhang, R., Shen, F., Zhao, J.: A model with fuzzy granulation and deep belief networks for exchange rate forecasting. In: International Joint Conference on Neural Networks, pp. 366-373. IEEE (2014)
8. Shen, F., Chao, J., Zhao, J.: Forecasting exchange rate using deep belief networks and conjugate gradient method. Neurocomputing **167**(C), 243–253 (2015)
9. Lee, H., Ekanadham, C., Ng, A.: Sparse deep belief net model for visual area V2. In: Platt, J.C., Koller, D., Singer, Y., Roweis, S. (eds.) Advances in Neural Information Processing Systems 20 (NIPS07), pp. 873–880. MIT Press, Cambridge (2008)

Multivariate Dynamic Kernels for Financial Time Series Forecasting

Mauricio Peña, Argimiro Arratia, and Lluís A. Belanche$^{(\boxtimes)}$

Department of Computer Science, Technical University of Catalonia,
Jordi Girona, 1-3, 08034 Barcelona, Spain
mpenagrass@gmail.com, {argimiro,belanche}@cs.upc.edu

Abstract. We propose a forecasting procedure based on multivariate dynamic kernels, with the capability of integrating information measured at different frequencies and at irregular time intervals in financial markets. A data compression process redefines the original financial time series into temporal data blocks, analyzing the temporal information of multiple time intervals. The analysis is done through multivariate dynamic kernels within support vector regression. We also propose two kernels for financial time series that are computationally efficient without a sacrifice on accuracy. The efficacy of the methodology is demonstrated by empirical experiments on forecasting the challenging S&P500 market.

Keywords: Support vector regression · Financial time series · Kernels

1 Introduction

The forecasting of financial markets is one of the most challenging tasks in predictive analytics. The non-stationarity and the noisy nature of financial time series have driven the debate about whether it is really possible to predict market movements with sufficient confidence. The "Efficient Market Hypothesis" provides theoretical grounds for the belief that the best strategy is the "buy-and-hold" passive investment strategy, since no excess return can be obtained consistently by predicting and timing the market [1].

Although many researchers in the statistical learning community –see e.g. [2–4]– have attempted to forecast the financial market using support vector machines (SVM) with standard kernels, the area still remains a challenge for practitioners. Therefore, there is a natural interest in applying kernels for financial forecasting by incorporating temporal information between misaligned time series or varying frequencies in the data patterns. In this article, we propose a forecasting methodology based on SVMs that permits the incorporation of granular temporal information of variable-length time series. The proposed forecasting methodology is a very flexible approach capable of analyzing market dynamics in

Supported by MINECO project APCOM (TIN2014-57226-P) and *Generalitat de Catalunya* 2014 SGR 890 (MACDA).

A.E.P. Villa et al. (Eds.): ICANN 2016, Part II, LNCS 9887, pp. 336–344, 2016.
DOI: 10.1007/978-3-319-44781-0_40

very short-term intervals, by integrating market micro-structure information in a compressed fashion. Standard kernels in the literature are replaced by *dynamic kernel functions* able to analyze multivariate temporal structures. We show how the use of these kernels leads to improvements in terms of both accuracy and forecasting performance. In addition, we propose some multivariate dynamic kernels that make it possible to reduce the complexity of kernel analytics to a manageable level without compromising on accuracy. The computational speed of these kernels makes them ideal candidates for intensive computational tasks. The approach can be extended to incorporate high-frequency information as well, aimed at market risk measurement.

2 Preliminaries

Support Vector Machines for Regression. We use Support Vector Regression (SVR) for predicting one-month ahead market performance by using its own history and a series of exogenous variables measured on a daily basis; thus, it is a mixed-frequency approach. More specifically, we choose the ν-SVR, a reformulation that involves the automatic adaptation of the ϵ parameter. The ν parameter is bounded in the interval $(0, 1]$, representing both an upper bound on the fraction of training samples which are errors and lower bound on the fraction of points which are support vectors [5]. The final dual expression for an SVR is

$$y_{\text{SVM}}(x) = \sum_{i=1}^{n} (\alpha_i - \alpha_i^*)k(x, x_i)$$

where α_i, α_i^* are the dual variables $(0 \leq \alpha_i, \alpha_i^* \leq C)$, $C > 0$ is the regularization parameter, the $\{x_i\}$ are the training points, and k is the kernel function.

Data Blocks for Temporal Information. Practitioners usually apply time series regression with SVR using standard static kernels such as the Gaussian, linear and polynomial. This means that, for one-month ahead predictions, there is only a single vector of prices for each input month. To extract additional information and incorporate more subtle patterns, we propose that daily quotes of financial assets be compressed into temporal time intervals on each month. Our compression process redefines the original dataset into new instances $\boldsymbol{X}_1, \ldots, \boldsymbol{X}_j, \ldots$ taking the form of *multivariate time series* (MVT), as described next. A univariate time series $x_i = \{x_i(1), x_i(2), \ldots, x_i(T_j)\} \in \mathbb{R}^{T_j}$ of length T_j is a set of observations from a random process measured at discrete intervals of time. The j-th MVT is then a P-by-T_j matrix $\boldsymbol{X}_j \in \mathbb{R}^{P \times T_j}$ of the form

$$\boldsymbol{X}_j = \left(\begin{bmatrix} x_1(1) \\ x_2(1) \\ \vdots \\ x_P(1) \end{bmatrix} \cdots \begin{bmatrix} x_1(t) \\ x_2(t) \\ \vdots \\ x_P(t) \end{bmatrix} \cdots \begin{bmatrix} x_1(T_j) \\ x_2(T_j) \\ \vdots \\ x_P(T_j) \end{bmatrix} \right) \tag{1}$$

where each row represents a univariate time series and each column is a vector of observations of the P variables in a time point. Letting $x(i)$ be the i-th column of $\boldsymbol{X}_j (i = 1, \ldots, T_j)$, the MVT $\boldsymbol{X}_j$ can be expressed as $\boldsymbol{X}_j = (x(1), \ldots, x(T_j))$.

Therefore, the original dataset is transformed into several intervals of different sizes where each instance is now expressed as in Eq. (1). This allows to model the temporal structure within months and, additionally, can be adapted to incorporate market dynamics in very small time intervals.

3 Multivariate Dynamic Kernels

The general goal is to define positive definite (p.d.) kernels between two time series (not necessarily of the same length), $\boldsymbol{X} = (x(1), \ldots, x(N))$ and $\boldsymbol{Y} = (y(1), \ldots, y(M))$, where the pairwise comparisons $(x(i), y(j))$ are reasonable. The main difficulty is that the commonly used Euclidean distance disregards the temporal dependency among the observations of time series. Moreover, the length of the different time series is variable since it is a function of the number of business days of each month, among other causes. In an attempt to overcome the aforementioned difficulties, Sakoe and Chiba proposed *dynamic time warping* (DTW), to find a good alignment between $\boldsymbol{X}$ and $\boldsymbol{Y}$ before computing any Euclidean distance [6]. An *alignment* (or *warping function*) π between two time series $\boldsymbol{X}$ and $\boldsymbol{Y}$ is a pair of increasing tuples (π_1, π_2) of length $P \leq N + M - 1$ such that $1 = \pi_1(1) \leq \ldots \leq \pi_1(P) = N$ and $1 = \pi_2(1) \leq \ldots \leq \pi_2(P) = M$, with unitary increments and no simultaneous repetitions. Intuitively, an alignment is a series of connecting lines that associate each time point of $\boldsymbol{X}$ to one or more time points in $\boldsymbol{Y}$, and vice versa, as:

$$D_\pi(\boldsymbol{X}, \boldsymbol{Y}) = \sum_{i=1}^{|\pi|} \|x_{\pi_1(i)} - y_{\pi_2(i)}\|^2$$

The *multivariate dynamic time warping* (MDTW) distance is the minimum distance for the set of all alignments $\mathrm{AL}(\boldsymbol{X}, \boldsymbol{Y})$:

$$\mathrm{MDTW}(\boldsymbol{X}, \boldsymbol{Y}) = \frac{1}{|\pi^*|} \min_{\pi \in \mathrm{AL}(\boldsymbol{X}, \boldsymbol{Y})} D_\pi(\boldsymbol{X}, \boldsymbol{Y}), \text{ with } \pi^* = \arg\min_{\pi \in \mathrm{AL}(\boldsymbol{X}, \boldsymbol{Y})} D_\pi(\boldsymbol{X}, \boldsymbol{Y}).$$

To convert a MDTW distance into a similarity we use the Gaussian function with parameter $\sigma > 0$ as $k_{\mathrm{MDTW}}(\boldsymbol{X}, \boldsymbol{Y}) = \exp(-\mathrm{MDTW}(\boldsymbol{X}, \boldsymbol{Y})/\sigma)$. The main drawback of the DTW measure is that it is not rigorously a metric (it does not satisfy the triangle inequality) and is also known *not* to be conditionally n.d.; hence its negative exponential is not a p.d. kernel in general. Moreover, since the DTW is based exclusively on the optimal alignment π^*, counter-intuitive behaviors can be obtained in some cases –see [7].

Global Alignment Kernel. In view of the limitations of the DTW, we consider an improvement given by the *global alignment* (GA) kernel [7], which instead of the minimum it considers the *soft-minimum* of $D_\pi(\boldsymbol{X}, \boldsymbol{Y})$ defined as

$$\text{Smin}(D_\pi(\boldsymbol{X}, \boldsymbol{Y})) = -\log \sum_{\pi \in \text{AL}(\boldsymbol{X}, \boldsymbol{Y})} e^{-D_\pi(\boldsymbol{X}, \boldsymbol{Y})}$$

To get a kernel, take $\exp(-\text{Smin}/\sigma)$ as $k_{\text{GA}}(\boldsymbol{X}, \boldsymbol{Y}) = \sum_{\pi \in \text{AL}(\boldsymbol{X}, \boldsymbol{Y})} e^{-D_\pi(\boldsymbol{X}, \boldsymbol{Y})/\sigma}$.

The GA kernel takes advantage of the distances spanned by all possible alignments: two time series are similar based on their *set* of efficient alignments. The σ parameter is taken from the adaptative grid:

$$\{0.2, 0.4, \ldots, 2\} \cdot \text{median}(\|x(t_1) - y(t_2)\|) \cdot \sqrt{\text{median}(|x(t_1)|)},$$

where $x(t_1)$ and $y(t_2)$ are time points for the days in which the target price reached its minimum variation during the month of each time series.

Vector Autoregressive Kernel. The previous kernels are shape-based similarities to compare two time series. In this work we also propose the extraction of higher-level dependencies across time series through a parametric statistical model. Our approach, a straightforward adaptation of the VAR kernel [8], is based on comparing the similarity of two time series using the transition matrices and intercepts of a *vector autoregressive model* VAR(L), such that $x(t) = \sum_{l=1}^{L} A_l x(t - l) + b + \varepsilon_t$, where $A_1, \ldots, A_L \in \mathbb{R}^{P \times P}$ are the transition matrices, $b \in \mathbb{R}^P$ is the intercept, and $\varepsilon \sim \mathcal{N}(0, \Sigma)$ is the noise. To implement the VAR kernel, we append the estimated parameters $\hat{A}$ and $\hat{b}$ into a single matrix $\hat{B} = (\hat{A}_1|\hat{A}_2|\ldots|\hat{A}_L|[\hat{b}])$. and then compute a distance between time series $\boldsymbol{X}$ and $\boldsymbol{Y}$ using the Frobenius norm over the difference of their $\hat{B}$ matrices

$$\text{FD}(\boldsymbol{X}, \boldsymbol{Y}) = \sqrt{\text{Trace}\left\{(\hat{B}_{\boldsymbol{X}} - \hat{B}_{\boldsymbol{Y}})(\hat{B}_{\boldsymbol{X}} - \hat{B}_{\boldsymbol{Y}})^T\right\}}$$

To convert the Frobenius distance to a similarity measure, we use a Gaussian function to get $k_{\text{VAR}}(\boldsymbol{X}, \boldsymbol{Y}) = \exp(-\text{FD}(\boldsymbol{X}, \boldsymbol{Y})/\sigma)$. For the experiments, we use a fixed lag of $L = 5$ as indicated in [8] and set σ as the median Frobenius distance.

Multivariate Dynamic Euclidean Distance Kernel. Finally we propose a simple but effective methodology to compare variable-length time series by constructing what we call the *multivariate dynamic euclidean distance* (MDED) kernel. Given that financial time series follow a filtration process, we propose an alignment that shortens the longer time series so to become equal in length to the shorter one. Formally, the MDED alignment between time series $\boldsymbol{X}$ and $\boldsymbol{Y}$ with respective lengths $N \geq M$ is $\pi_{\text{MDED}} = \{(N - (M - 1), 1), (N - (M - 2), 2), \ldots, (N - 1, M - 1), (N, M)\}$. We then define the multivariate dynamic

Euclidean distance as $\mathrm{MDED}(\boldsymbol{X}, \boldsymbol{Y}) = \frac{1}{M}\sum_{i=1}^{M}\|(x_{\pi_{\mathrm{MDED}}(i,1)} - y_{\pi_{\mathrm{MDED}}(i,2)}\|^2$. These distances can be fairly compared across variable-length time series in the compressed database. To convert the MDED distance to a similarity measure, we create again a RBF-like kernel as $k_{\mathrm{MDED}}(\boldsymbol{X}, \boldsymbol{Y}) = \exp(-\mathrm{MDED}(\boldsymbol{X}, \boldsymbol{Y})/\sigma)$, where the bandwidth parameter σ is set to the median of $\mathrm{MDED}(\boldsymbol{X}, \boldsymbol{Y})$.

4   Evaluation of Forecasting Performance

We evaluate the forecasting performance of the proposed methodology to capture the linear inter-dependencies among multiple time series. We base our experiments on SVR using different multivariate dynamic kernels, namely k_{GA}, k_{VAR} and k_{MDED}. We compare also against the VAR model, a standard in econometrics, although it does not allow to integrate mixed-frequency information from markets. The goal is to forecast the next month return of Standard and Poor's 500 Index (S&P500) by incorporating past information plus three *exogenous* predictors (hence $P = 4$): the volatility index (VIX), the yield of the U.S. 10-year treasury bond (US10Yr) and the price of cooper 3-month future contract (LME3m). All models were tested along three different time windows so as to evaluate the effect of distinct market regimes in prediction accuracy, based on compressed daily historical prices from January 2006 to December 2014.

The output variable of the model is the next month log-return of S&P500, R_{t+1}. We use the log-return because it has better statistical properties than price, as stationarity and ergodicity [9]. The inputs are constructed on a daily basis to capture temporal patterns of different scale on S&P500, VIX, US10yr and LME3m using the $\mathrm{ROC}_{t,n} = \ln(x_t) - \ln(x_{t-n})$ function for n days on day t.

For the i-th time series ($i = 1, \ldots, 4$), we derive a vector of several rates of changes on each day t, incorporating the time series at $n \in \{20, 40, 60, 100, 140\}$, allowing to capture temporal trend shifts of financial markets when analyzed on a monthly basis. Then the input features for day t take the form $x_t = [x_t^1, x_t^2, x_t^3, x_t^4]$, where $x_t^i = [\mathrm{ROC}_{t,20}^i, \mathrm{ROC}_{t,40}^i, \mathrm{ROC}_{t,60}^i, \mathrm{ROC}_{t,100}^i, \mathrm{ROC}_{t,140}^i]$.

Methodology and Parameter Selection. In the ν-SVR model, ν is constrained to the interval $(0, 1]$. We optimize it in the set $\{0.1, 0.2, \ldots, 1\}$. For the possible choices of C, we follow the analytic approach proposed by [10], which advocates parameter selection directly from the training data. Considering a standard SVR solution, a reasonable value for C can be roughly equal to the range of training output values. However, besides forecasting with a value $C = \mathrm{range}(R_{t+1})$, we also tried values in the set $\left\{ \mathrm{range}(R_{t+1}) \cdot \{0.8, 0.9, 1, 1.1, 1.2\} \right\}$.

To find the optimal parameters ν and C and the fitted models we use the methodology of [11], combining rolling windows with "training-validation-testing" blocks. Despite being a standard practice in financial applications, rolling windows are uncommon in the machine learning literature. An in-sample period of 6 months was decided to train the model to make predictions for the next month. The proposed methodology to predict the market performance is a multi-step procedure. First, we train the models on 6 months (the training set); second, we apply the resulting models on the next two months (the validation set) and select the values of parameters that achieve the minimum mean squared error; and third, we combine the last 4 months of the training set and the 2 months of the validation set into a new set, called "true training set", and train the final model using the selected values of ν and C. Finally, we apply the model on the next month (the test set) and record its performance. We then move one month forward, repeating the same procedure for the whole period.

Performance Metrics. A number of measures have been used in the literature to compare the forecasting accuracy of different models. Popular measures –such as the mean squared error– are not invariant to scaling. We use here the *mean absolute scaled error* (MASE), which scales the measured error using the mean absolute error of a naive forecast:

$$\text{MASE} = \text{mean} \left| \frac{e_t}{\frac{1}{n-1} \sum\limits_{t=2}^{n} |Y_t - Y_{t-1}|} \right|$$

where Y_t denotes the observation at time $t \in \{1, \ldots, n\}$, F_t is the model forecast and $e_t = Y_t - F_t$ is the forecast error. A MASE smaller than 1 indicates that forecasting performance is better than a naive forecast. In addition, we compute the accuracy or hit rate (HITS) –which should be maximized– as $\text{HITS} = \text{mean}|\{F_t \mid (Y_t - Y_{t-1}) \cdot (F_t - F_{t-1}) > 0, \ t = 1, \ldots, n\}|$.

Empirical Results. Table 1 shows the MASE and HITS results we obtain from using the multivariate dynamic kernels within the SVR framework; we also report the performance of the VAR model. All results are presented both for the whole database period and for balanced time windows, so as to capture the performance of kernels across different market regimes.

Table 1. MASE (left) and HITS (right) of the Multivariate Dynamic Kernels.

	MASE						HITS				
	Naive	k_{GA}	k_{VAR}	k_{MDED}	VAR		Naive	k_{GA}	k_{VAR}	k_{MDED}	VAR
2006–08	1.000	0.783	0.795	0.769	1.151	2006–08	0.657	0.778	0.750	0.722	0.639
2009–11	1.000	0.896	0.850	0.846	1.130	2009–11	0.500	0.583	0.528	0.556	0.611
2012–14	1.000	0.728	0.712	0.733	1.568	2012–14	0.583	0.722	0.722	0.722	0.417
Total	1.000	0.819	0.798	0.794	1.246	Total	0.579	0.694	0.667	0.667	0.556

The results clearly show the ability of SVR with multivariate dynamic kernels to forecast the financial market. The kernels are able to achieve overall mean absolute squared errors of about 80 %, accounting for an improvement of 20 % in performance with respect to the naive forecast. The most troublesome period for forecasting is between 2009 and 2011, when financial markets underwent profound trend shifts due to the world crisis. The VAR model is outperformed both by the naive forecast and the multivariate dynamic kernels in all periods. There are many possible explanations, the most important in our opinion is that it is based on strong assumptions (linearity, stationarity, etc.) that do not fit well to financial markets, particularly when working with small data sets.

In predicting market trends, the multivariate dynamic kernels reach a hit rate of up to 70 % over the whole period, compared to a hit rate of 58 % for the naive forecast. This is particularly remarkable because the hit rate is very used in algorithmic trading by signaling actions upon predicted market trend shifts.

As we demonstrate, the multivariate dynamic kernels lead to significant improvements in prediction accuracy and better performance than the naive forecast along different market regimes. They also outperform the VAR model in nearly all periods. The proposed MDED kernel and the modified version of the VAR kernel display a performance similar to that of the global alignment kernel, which is the state-of-the-art similarity measure in the literature for variable-length time series. In fact, when analyzed in each period, we can note there is no decisive winner among the kernels. The CPU times[1] (in seconds) are 156, 143, 33 and 0.7, respectively, for $k_{GA}, k_{VAR}, k_{MDED}$ and VAR, indicating the computational efficiency of the proposed MDED kernel. The VAR model is the fastest forecaster but it is not capable of performing better than the naive forecast.

An Experiment in Trading. We now apply the method to forecast the financial market and compare performance against the *buy-and-hold* strategy, widely used as a benchmark in financial research. We follow the approach of [11] defining a simple investing strategy: let $\hat{f}_{t+1}$ be the forecasted S&P500 next month log-return; if $\hat{f}_{t+1} \geq 0$, we buy at the closing price on month t; otherwise, we short it. Then the log-return $\hat{R}_{t+1}$, associated with our strategy, can be computed as:

$$\hat{R}_{t+1} = \begin{cases} |R_{t+1}| \text{ if } R_{t+1} \cdot \hat{f}_{t+1} \geq 0 \\ -|R_{t+1}| \text{ otherwise.} \end{cases}$$

The predicted performance of the financial market for the next month is thus used on a timing rotation strategy. A positive prediction turns into a "buy signal", in which an Exchange Traded Fund (ETF) tracking the S&P500 index is bought, whereas a negative one results in short-selling the ETF. We have included different levels of transaction costs that take off some basis points or bp (equal to a 0.01 %) of the capital for each trade. Table 2 shows a summary of the investment strategy performance with different kernels in the period between January 2006 and December 2014. What strikes at first sight, is that all kernels invariably yield better results than the buy-and-hold (B&H) strategy.

---

[1] Laptop with 4 GB of RAM and Intel Core i5 processor running at 2.5 GHz.

Table 2. Statistics for SVR timing rotation strategies with transactions costs.

	B&H	0 bp.	30 bp.	50 bp.		0 bp.	30 bp.	50 bp.
k_{GA}					k_{MDED}			
Total cum. (%)	50.04	145.64	133.62	125.59	Total cum. (%)	131.99	122.08	115.45
Mean (%)	5.56	16.18	14.85	13.96	Mean (%)	14.67	13.56	12.83
Stdev (%)	15.54	14.90	14.94	14.97	Stdev (%)	15.03	15.10	15.15
Sharpe ratio	0.36	1.09	0.99	0.93	Sharpe ratio	0.98	0.90	0.85
k_{VAR}					VAR			
Total cum. (%)	50.04	123.78	113.86	107.24	Total cum. (%)	67.19	45.86	31.60
Mean (%)	5.56	13.75	12.65	11.92	Mean (%)	7.47	5.10	3.51
Stdev (%)	15.54	15.11	15.16	15.21	Stdev (%)	15.47	15.57	15.65
Sharpe ratio	0.36	0.91	0.83	0.78	Sharpe ratio	0.48	0.33	0.22

Under the assumption of zero transaction cost, the average annual log-return of multivariate dynamic kernels ranges between 2.47 and 2.91 times the B&H strategy. Indeed, the GA kernel achieves an annual mean return of 16.18 %, the VAR kernel 13.75 % and the MDED kernel 14.67 %, compared to the buy-and-hold strategy of 5.56 %. Combining these results with the standard deviations yields improvements of more than 2.5 times in the Sharpe ratio. When adding conservative transaction costs of 30 bp. and 50 bp. the results remained superior to the buy-and-hold strategy. The VAR model modestly outperforms the passive strategy and only when transaction costs are smaller than 30 bp.

The MDED kernel might then be effectively applied when considering high-frequency time series for horizons of minutes or seconds. All the kernels can play a major role in market risk management by the approximation of quantiles for a certain distribution like, for example, in the value-at-risk (VaR) along with the incorporation of the latest intra-day market developments.

References

1. Fama, E.F.: Efficient capital markets: a review of theory and empirical work. J. Finance **25**(2), 383–417 (1970)
2. Duan, W., Stanley, H.: Cross-correlation and the predictability of financial return series. Phys. A: Stat. Mech. Appl. **390**(2), 290–296 (2011)
3. Kim, K.-J.: Financial time series forecasting using support vector machines. Neurocomputing **55**(1), 307–319 (2003)
4. Tay, F.E., Cao, L.: Application of support vector machines in financial time series forecasting. Omega **29**(4), 309–317 (2001)
5. Smola, A.J., Schölkopf, B.: A tutorial on support vector regression. Stat. Comput. **14**(3), 199–222 (2004)
6. Sakoe, H., Chiba, S.: A similarity evaluation of speech patterns by dynamic programming. In: Meeting of Institute of Electronic Communications, Engineers of Japan (1970)
7. Cuturi, M., Vert, J.-P., Birkenes, Ø., Matsui, T.: A kernel for time series based on global alignments. In: IEEE International Conference on ICASS 2007, p. II-413. IEEE (2007)

8. Cuturi, M., Doucet, A.: Autoregressive kernels for time series. Technical Report (2011). arXiv:1101.0673
9. Tsay, R.: Analysis of Financial Time Series. Wiley, Hoboken (2010)
10. Mattera, D., Haykin, S.: Support vector machines for dynamic reconstruction of a chaotic system. In: Advances in Kernel Methods: Support Vector Learning, pp. 211–241. MIT Press, Cambridge (1999)
11. Wang, L., Zhu, J.: Financial market forecasting using a two-step kernel method for the support vector regression. Ann. Oper. Res. **174**(1), 103–120 (2010)

Recognition and Navigation

Symbolic Association Using Parallel Multilayer Perceptron

Federico Raue[1,2]([✉]), Sebastian Palacio[2], Thomas M. Breuel[1],
Wonmin Byeon[1,2], Andreas Dengel[1,2], and Marcus Liwicki[1]

[1] University of Kaiserslautern, Kaiserslautern, Germany
{tmb,liwicki}@cs.uni-kl.de
[2] German Research Center for Artificial Intelligence (DFKI),
Kaiserslautern, Germany
{federico.raue,sebastian.palacio,wonmin.byeon,andreas.dengel}@dfki.de

Abstract. The goal of our paper is to learn the association and the semantic grounding of two sensory input signals that represent the same semantic concept. The input signals can be or cannot be the same modality. This task is inspired by infants learning. We propose a novel framework that has two *symbolic* Multilayer Perceptron (MLP) in parallel. Furthermore, both networks learn to ground semantic concepts and the same coding scheme for all semantic concepts in both networks. In addition, the training rule follows EM-approach. In contrast, the traditional setup of association task pre-defined the coding scheme before training. We have tested our model in two cases: mono- and multi-modal. Our model achieves similar *accuracy association* to MLPs with pre-defined coding schemes.

Keywords: Symbol grounding · Neural network · Cognitive model

1 Introduction

The relation between the real world via sensory input and abstract concepts helps humans to develop language. More formally, Harnad [5] investigated the process of coupling high level concepts and multimodal sensory signals. He called this process the *Symbol Grounding Problem*.

All modalities (visual, audio, and haptic) are important for language acquisition by infants. Cognitive researchers found that nouns are the first acquired words by infants [1]. In more detail, nouns correspond to visible elements, such as dog, cat, etc. In contrast, infants acquire vocabulary slower if one of their sensory input fails i.e. deafness, blindness [1,17]. Also, Neuroscience researchers discovered different patterns in infants' brain related to multimodal signals and abstract concepts [2]. The patterns showed different behavior depending on the existence or absence of a semantic relation between visual and audio signals. This finding shows a relation between both modalities.

Previous work has been inspired by the *Symbol Grounding Problem*. One of the first model was proposed by Plunket *et al.* [13]. The authors suggested a

© Springer International Publishing Switzerland 2016
A.E.P. Villa et al. (Eds.): ICANN 2016, Part II, LNCS 9887, pp. 347–354, 2016.
DOI: 10.1007/978-3-319-44781-0_41

feed-forward network for associating a visual stimuli and a label. Since then, more complex scenarios have been proposed. Yu and Hallard [18] presented a multimodal model for grounding spoken languages using Hidden Markov Models. Nakamura *et al.* [9] developed a model that ground the word meanings in a multimodal scenario based on Latent Dirichlet Allocation.

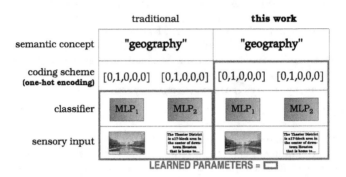

Fig. 1. Components of our learning problem. The coding scheme is unknown in this work and is learned during training.

In this paper, we are interested in a different setup of the *Symbol Grounding Problem* for two sensory input signals. Moreover, abstract concepts are represented by the sensory input, which can or cannot be of the same modality. Usually, each abstract concept is represented by a pre-defined coding scheme, which is used for training classifiers. Figure 1 shows an example to explain the difference between the traditional setup and this work for the association problem of two sensory input. This problem setup was introduced by Raue *et al.* [15], who only evaluated visual sequences, which was represented by text lines in an OCR case. Our contributions in this paper are

– We define a *symbolic* Multilayer Perceptron (MLP), which is trained without specifying a coding scheme. In this case, an EM-training algorithm is used for learning simultaneously the classification and the coding scheme during training. Hence, the abstract concepts are grounded to the input signals during training (Sect. 2).
– We propose (mono- and multi-modal) associations via symbol grounding, where two parallel symbolic MLPs learn to agree on the same coding scheme. As a result, the unknown agreements is learned using the information of one network as target of the other network. Moreover, the association is gradient based and can be extended to deeper architectures (Sect. 3).
– The *Association Accuracy* of the presented model reaches similar results to MLP training with a pre-defined coding scheme in two scenarios: mono-modal and multi-modal (Sects. 4 and 5).

2   Symbolic Multilayer Perceptron

In this paper, a new training rule for Multilayer Perceptron (MLP) is introduced. For explanation purposes, we define a MLP with one hidden layer, where x, y, and z are vectors that represent the input, hidden, and output layers, respectively. In addition, we define a set of *weighted concepts* γ_c where $c \in \{1, \ldots, C\}$. Each *weighted concept* learns the relation between the semantic concept and the output layer. In this case, the output layer is used as a symbolic feature at which the size of vectors z and γ_c is the same. The cost function matches the output vectors $z_1, \ldots, z_m$ in a mini-batch of size m with a uniform distribution. The proposed learning rule follows an *Expectation Maximization* approach [4].

2.1   Training

The *E-step* finds suitable candidates for the *coding scheme* given the network outputs and the *weighted concepts*. Initially, the *weighted concepts* are set to 1.0. First, we define an approximation vector $\hat{z}_c$ for each semantic concept c. It is defined as follows

$$\hat{z}_c = \frac{1}{m} \sum_{i=1}^{m} f(z_i, \gamma_c), \tag{1}$$

where z_i is the output vectors, γ_c is a weighted concept vector c, m is the size of the mini-batch, and the function f is the element-wise power operator between vectors z_i and γ_c. Equation 1 provides an approximation of all semantic concepts. Second, all approximation vectors $\hat{z}_c$ are concatenated in order to obtain the array $\boldsymbol{\Gamma}$

$$\boldsymbol{\Gamma} = g\bigg(\big[\hat{z}_1, \ldots, \hat{z}_C \big] \bigg), \tag{2}$$

where function g represents a row-column elimination procedure. In other words, all elements in the i-th row and j-th column of the input array are set to 0 (except at position (i,j), which are set to 1). This process is iteratively performed c times. As a result, $\boldsymbol{\Gamma}$ is a set of *one-hot vectors* and represents a one-to-one relation between semantic concepts and symbolic features. Consequently, $\boldsymbol{\Gamma}$ is an array where the columns encode the information about semantic concepts, while the rows represent the different symbolic features. To map any given symbolic feature to a semantic concept, it now suffices to look up $\boldsymbol{\Gamma}$.

The *M-Step* updates the *weighted concepts* given the current coding scheme. To that effect, we define the following loss function:

$$cost(\gamma_c) = \left(\hat{z}_c - \frac{1}{|C|} \boldsymbol{\Gamma}_c \right)^2, \tag{3}$$

where $\boldsymbol{\Gamma}_c$ denotes the c-th column vector of $\boldsymbol{\Gamma}$. Furthermore, we assume a uniform distribution among all elements in c. Thus, we normalize $\boldsymbol{\Gamma}_c$ by the number of semantic concepts c. Next, each weighted concept is updated using gradient descent

$$\gamma_c = \gamma_c - \alpha * \nabla cost(\gamma_c), \tag{4}$$

where $\nabla cost(\boldsymbol{\gamma}_c)$ is the derivative w.r.t. $\boldsymbol{\gamma}_c$ and α is the learning rate. In addition, this step not only learns the *coding scheme* but also provides information for updating the weights in the symbolic MLP. The current *coding scheme* provides the target vectors for propagating backward. In this case, the target vectors for the semantic concept c is the column vector $\boldsymbol{\Gamma_c}$.

2.2   Semantic Concept Prediction

After the symbolic MLP is trained, the semantic concept can be retrieved by a similar decision rule of the standard MLP. With this in mind, the decision rule is defined by

$$c^* = arg\ max_c\ f(z_{k^*}, \gamma_{c,k^*}),\quad where\ \ k^* = arg\ max_k\ z, \qquad (5)$$

z_{k^*} is the value from output vector $\boldsymbol{z}$ at index k^*, γ_{c,k^*} is the value from *weighed concept* vector $\boldsymbol{\gamma}_c$ at index k^*, and function f is the power operator.

3   Parallel Symbolic MLP

As we mentioned in Sect. 1, our problem is defined by the association of two different sensory input signals, which represent the same semantic concept with an *unknown* coding scheme. Note that, the sensory input signals may be or may not be the same modality. More formally, the input set is defined by $\mathcal{S} = \{(\boldsymbol{x}^{(1)}, \boldsymbol{x}^{(2)}, c)|\boldsymbol{x}^{(1)} \in \boldsymbol{X}^{(1)}, \boldsymbol{x}^{(2)} \in \boldsymbol{X}^{(2)}, c \in C\}$, where $\boldsymbol{X}^{(1)}$ and $\boldsymbol{X}^{(2)}$ are the set of elements for each input, and C is the set of all semantic concepts. We want to point out that our model does not have a pre-defined target vector via coding-scheme.

The proposed architecture combines two symbolic MLPs in parallel, where the information of one network is used as a target of the other network, and vice versa. Figure 2 shows an overview of the proposed model. The training follows a similar approach to the symbolic MLP (*cf.* Sect. 2).

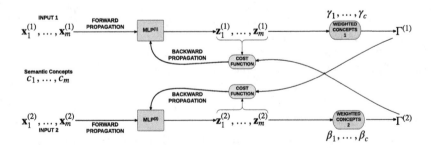

Fig. 2. Overview for the *parallel symbolic MLPs*. Parallel training sets are forwarded to each MLP. The EM-training rule learns to agree on the same coding scheme for both networks, where the coding schemes are unknown before training.

Initially, two symbolic MLPs propagates forward each sensory input ($x_i^{(1)}$ and $x_i^{(2)}$ where $i = 1, \ldots, m$) in the mini-batch of size m. Afterwards, the *weighted concepts* of both networks ($MLP^{(1)}$: $\gamma_1, \ldots, \gamma_c$ and $MLP^{(2)}$ $\beta_1, \ldots, \beta_c$) are applied to network outputs ($z_i^{(1)}$ and $z_i^{(2)}$) in order to obtain the candidates for the coding scheme for each network ($\Gamma^{(1)}$ and $\Gamma^{(2)}$). As a reminder, the coding scheme represents the relation between the semantic concepts and the symbolic features. Finally, the generated coding scheme from one network is used as a target for the other network in order to update the network weights, and vice versa. This step forces both networks to learn the same coding scheme. Figure 2 illustrates the presented architecture.

4 Experimental Design

4.1 Datasets

As we mentioned, our goal was to evaluate the symbolic association of two entities that represent the same semantic concept, where the coding scheme is not pre-defined before training. To that effect, we tested our model in two scenarios: mono-modal and multi-modal. Furthermore, we compared the presented model against the traditional classification problem, where the coding-scheme is already defined.

For the case of mono-modal input signals, two instances represented the same semantic concept, e.g., two images showing different instances of the same digit. With this in mind, we used MNIST [7] and COIL-20 [11] for generating the training and the testing set. We want to indicate that COIL-20 does not define a training and a testing set as MNIST does. However, we applied a common practice, which is to use the even view angles for training and the odd view angles for testing. For the multi-modal case, each input represents one modality of the same concept, e.g., image or text. We tested two multi-modal datasets: Wikipedia Articles [14] and TVGraz [6], where each multi-modal dataset represents the semantic concept using an image and a description of the image. All datasets were evaluated using training and testing sets of randomly sampled pairs with the constraint that all semantic concepts follow a uniform distribution. Table 1 gives an overview of such sampling.

Table 1. Sampling of datasets for training and testing. Each sample represents a pair of input signals.

DATASET	CONCEPT	TRAIN	TEST
MNIST	10	25000	4000
COIL-20	20	360	360
TVGraz	10	1942	652
Wikipedia	10	2146	720

4.2   Features and Network Setup

For each mono-modal dataset, we used the raw pixel values as input. For multi-modal datasets, we extracted *Latent Dirichlet Allocation* [3] features for text, based on a model with 100 topics and, *Bag-of-Visual-Words* [16] based on SIFT [8] using a codebook of size 1024 for the corresponding visual input. Moreover, we used NLTK[1] for extracting LDA features and VLFeat[2] for computing SIFT features. These are the same features used by Pereira and Vasconcelos [12] for the multi-modal datasets. Note that we rescaled the feature values to mean zero and standard deviation one, in the multi-modal datasets. These steps were not required for the mono-modal datasets.

The following parameters were used in MNIST and COIL-20 datasets for each symbolic MLP: hidden layer was set to 40 neurons, learning rate to 0.0001, momentum to 0.9, and learning rate for *weighted concepts* to 0.01. Moreover, the size of the mini-batch was set 1000 and 360 for MNIST and COIL-20, respectively. For multi-modal datasets, the following parameters were used: the size of the hidden layer was 150 neurons, the learning rate was 0.00001, momentum was 0.9, and the learning rate for *weighted concepts* was 0.01. The size of the mini-batch was 300 samples. In both cases, the same parameters were used for the standard MLP with a pre-defined coding scheme as upper bound.

5   Results and Discussion

In this paper, we compared the association accuracy of our model against an MLP with a pre-defined coding scheme. The association accuracy is defined by

$$Association\ Accuracy = \frac{1}{N} \sum_{i=1}^{N} h\big(z_i^{(1)}, z_i^{(2)}, gt_i\big) \qquad (6)$$

where $z_i^{(1)}$ and $z_i^{(2)}$ are the output classification from each network, gt_i is the ground-truth label, N is the total number of elements, and the function h is defined by 1 if $z_i^{(1)} == z_i^{(2)} == gt_i$, and 0 otherwise. We can see in Table 2 that the performance of our model was consistent with respect to the standard MLP. This suggests that the *symbolic* MLPs in our model were able to learn a unified coding scheme.

Figure 3 shows an example of several epochs and the components of our model during training for MNIST. Initially, the association matrix between $MLP^{(1)}$ and $MLP^{(2)}$ shows only one relation at position (0, 0). During training, the model starts learning the underlying *coding scheme* represented by both weighted concepts. The last row (epoch 50) shows the semantic prediction step. Here, the maximum value (dark blue) of the output vector is the index '3', which is associated with the semantic concept *four*. This behavior is consistent between both weighted concepts. Hence, the association matrix results in a diagonal matrix which indicates that both networks have agreed on the same symbolic structure.

---

[1] http://www.nltk.org/.
[2] http://www.vlfeat.org/.

Table 2. Association accuracy (%) of our model and the traditional approach using MLP.

Dataset	Our model	Standard MLP
MNIST	94.61 ± 0.24	95.02 ± 0.32
COIL-20	92.86 ± 1.65	92.94 ± 0.62
TVGraz	28.3 ± 1.45	31.5 ± 1.16
Wikipedia	11.82 ± 2.25	12.97 ± 1.11

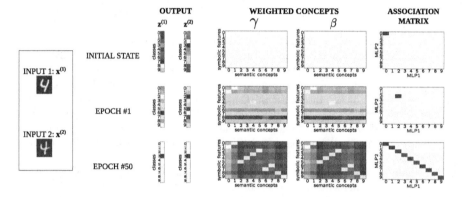

Fig. 3. Example of the learning behavior for the symbolic association model at different stages. (Color figure online)

6 Conclusions

The association between abstract concepts and parallel multimodal signals contributes to language development. In this work, we have shown a model that learns the association of two parallel sensory input signals, which both signals can or cannot be the same modality. Unlike the traditional approach where the coding scheme is pre-defined, we associate two parallel symbolic MLPs that learn a common coding scheme for each semantic concept. Hence, a new dimension is added to the association problem, which makes more sense because we are including the process that abstract concepts are grounded to their sensory representations. We have shown that our model achieved similar results to MLP with traditional training. This holds for both mono- and multi-modal association. *Symbol Grounding* is still an open problem, but reveals potential to understand more the development in this area [10]. One limitation of our work is to learn the association assuming a uniform distribution between the semantic concepts. We will extend our model with different statistical distributions. Another limitation is related to semantic concepts. The model requires more time to converge when the number of semantic concepts increases. Moreover, we are interested in exploiting robustness of deeper architectures and to learn the association when both networks have a different number of semantic concepts.

References

1. Andersen, E.S., Dunlea, A., Kekelis, L.: The impact of input: language acquisition in the visually impaired. First Lang. **13**(37), 23–49 (1993)
2. Asano, M., Imai, M., Kita, S., Kitajo, K., Okada, H., Thierry, G.: Sound symbolism scaffolds language development in preverbal infants. Cortex **63**, 196–205 (2015)
3. Blei, D.M., Ng, A.Y., Jordan, M.I.: Latent dirichlet allocation. J. Mach. Learn. Res. **3**, 993–1022 (2003)
4. Dempster, A., Laird, N., Rubin, D.: Maximum likelihood from incomplete data via the EM algorithm. J. Roy. Stat. Soc. **39**(1), 1–38 (1977)
5. Harnad, S.: The symbol grounding problem. Phys. D Nonlinear Phenom. **42**(1), 335–346 (1990)
6. Khan, I., Saffari, A., Bischof, H.: Tvgraz: multi-modal learning of object categories by combining textual and visual features. In: AAPR Workshop, pp. 213–224 (2009)
7. Lecun, Y., Cortes, C.: The MNIST database of handwritten digits
8. Lowe, D.: Object recognition from local scale-invariant features. In: Proceedings of the Seventh IEEE International Conference on Computer Vision, vol. 2, pp. 1150–1157 (1999)
9. Nakamura, T., Araki, T., Nagai, T., Iwahashi, N.: Grounding of word meanings in latent dirichlet allocation-based multimodal concepts. Adv. Robot. **25**(17), 2189–2206 (2011)
10. Needham, C.J., Santos, P.E., Magee, D.R., Devin, V., Hogg, D.C., Cohn, A.G.: Protocols from perceptual observations. Artif. Intell. **167**(1), 103–136 (2005)
11. Nene, S.A., Nayar, S.K., Murase, H.: Columbia Object Image Library (COIL-20). Technical report, February 1996
12. Pereira, J.C., Vasconcelos, N.: Cross-modal domain adaptation for text-based regularization of image semantics in image retrieval systems. Comput. Vis. Image Underst. **124**, 123–135 (2014)
13. Plunkett, K., Sinha, C., Møller, M.F., Strandsby, O.: Symbol grounding or the emergence of symbols? vocabulary growth in children and a connectionist net. connection Sci. **4**(3–4), 293–312 (1992)
14. Rasiwasia, N., Costa Pereira, J., Coviello, E., Doyle, G., Lanckriet, G., Levy, R., Vasconcelos, N.: A new approach to cross-modal multimedia retrieval. In: ACM International Conference on Multimedia, pp. 251–260 (2010)
15. Raue, F., Byeon, W., Breuel, T., Liwicki, M.: Parallel sequence classification using recurrent neural networks and alignment. In: 13th International Conference on Document Analysis and Recognition (ICDAR) (2015)
16. Sivic, J., Zisserman, A.: Video google: A text retrieval approach to object matching in videos. In: Proceedings of the Ninth IEEE International Conference on Computer Vision, ICCV 2003, vol. 2, p. 1470. IEEE Computer Society, Washington, DC (2003)
17. Spencer, P.E.: Looking without listening: is audition a prerequisite for normal development of visual attention during infancy? J. Deaf Stud. Deaf Educ. **5**(4), 291–302 (2000)
18. Yu, C., Ballard, D.H.: A multimodal learning interface for grounding spoken language in sensory perceptions. ACM Trans. Appl. Percept. (TAP) **1**(1), 57–80 (2004)

Solution of an Inverse Problem in Raman Spectroscopy of Multi-component Solutions of Inorganic Salts by Artificial Neural Networks

Alexander Efitorov[1]([✉]), Tatiana Dolenko[1,2], Sergey Burikov[1,2], Kirill Laptinskiy[1,2], and Sergey Dolenko[1]([✉])

[1] D.V. Skobeltsyn Institute of Nuclear Physics, M.V. Lomonosov Moscow State University, Moscow, Russia
sasha.efitorov@gmail.com, dolenko@srd.sinp.msu.ru
[2] Physical Department, M.V. Lomonosov Moscow State University, Moscow, Russia

Abstract. The paper presents a study of aspects of using single and multiple output artificial neural networks to determine concentrations of inorganic salts in multicomponent water solutions by processing their Raman spectra. The dependence of the results on complexity of the inverse problem has been demonstrated. The results are compared for two data arrays including spectra of solutions of: (1) 5 salts composed of 10 different ions, and (2) 10 salts composed of 10 different ions.

Keywords: Inverse problem · Artificial neural network · Multi-layer perceptron · Raman spectroscopy · Multi-component solutions · Inorganic salts

1 Introduction

There is a strong demand for operative control of the composition of water and water solutions in environmental monitoring, in industrial production and agricultural activity. Modern methods of chemical analysis provide determination of chemical composition with high accuracy, but they have serious drawbacks: they need laboratory processing of water samples with special reagents, and each test requires much time. More express are the methods based on measurement of the conductivity of solutions, but they provide only the value of total salinity of water; they are unable to detect presence of specific compounds in the solution and to determine their concentrations.

The authors of [1–4] proposed to determine the concentrations of salts dissolved in water by changes of the shape of Raman spectra of the solutions. Such an approach provides remote express determination of concentrations of individual salts. As it is known [2,5,6], Raman spectra are highly sensitive to

---

This study has been performed at the expense of the grant of Russian Science Foundation (project no. 14-11-00579).

A.E.P. Villa et al. (Eds.): ICANN 2016, Part II, LNCS 9887, pp. 355–362, 2016.
DOI: 10.1007/978-3-319-44781-0_42

types and concentrations of various dissolved ions. Complex ions (such as SO_4^{2-}, NO_3^-) have proper bands in the area around $1000\,\mathrm{cm}^{-1}$. The shape and position of water Raman valence band depends on concentrations of any ions present in the solution. If several components are present, there are nonlinear interactions affecting the shape of the spectrum. Thus, there is no simple analytic model to solve the described inverse problem (IP) of determination of concentrations of salts in a multi-component solution.

Unfortunately, physical and chemical interactions taking place in multi-component water solutions, primarily, due to the nature of hydrogen bonds, are the main reason of the fact that direct modeling of spectra of such solutions, including Raman spectra, is still beyond the capabilities of modern theory. Therefore, the only way out is use of data-driven methods, in particular, ANN. The main obstacle on this way is the need for a large enough and representative set of experimental data. The authors of the present study have available the experimental equipment which allowed them to obtain several unique arrays of experimental Raman spectra of multi-component solutions of inorganic salts, described below. At present, they are not aware of studies of other authors which could be directly compared to the studies presented here, if all the properties of the used method are taken into account - its express and remote character, the amount of components whose concentrations are determined simultaneously, and the obtained accuracy of determination of component concentrations. The main goal of the investigations at present is increasing the accuracy of the method.

Previously, the authors of this study suggested and developed the method to determine the concentrations of salts [7–9] and ions [10,11] in multi-component water solutions by Raman spectra using artificial neural networks (ANN). ANN are also used in solving other complicated multi-parameter problems, such as environmental monitoring of natural waters [12–14], determining the salinity of sea water [15] and metal ions in industrial waters [16,17], and others.

The subject of this study is comparison of two approaches: using single-output ANN (autonomous determination of parameters) or multiple-output ANN (simultaneous determination) [18] in respect to the accuracy of determination of concentrations of salts dissolved in water. Previously the authors have demonstrated some features of each approach at the example of solution of the inverse problem of electrical prospecting [18,19]. The present research is based on two similar inverse problems: determination of salts concentrations in water solutions of 5 and 10 inorganic salts.

2   Data Preparation

The first IP was solved for 5 inorganic salts: NaCl, NH_4Br, Li_2SO_4, KNO_3, CsI. The data array consisted of 9144 Raman spectra for known salts concentrations in water solutions. As all 10 ions were different, the concentrations on an anion and its corresponding cation always had the same ratio, making the task of determination of concentration of each dissolved salt easier.

Initially, each band of the Raman spectrum was recorded into the range 1024 spectral channels wide, in the frequency range 200–2300 cm^{-1} for the low frequency band, and 2300–4000 cm^{-1} for the valence band. For further processing, more narrow informative ranges were selected: 766 channels in the range 281–1831 cm^{-1} for the low frequency band, and 769 channels in the range 2700–3900 cm^{-1} for the valence band.

The second IP was solved for 10 inorganic salts: KF, $KHCO_3$, $LiCl$, $LiNO_3$, $MgSO_4$, $Mg(NO_3)_2$, $NaCl$, $NaHCO_3$, NH_4F, $(NH_4)_2SO_4$. The obtained data array consisted of 4445 Raman spectra for known salts concentrations. Every ion was contained in two salts: so the concentration of each anion was not bound to the concentration of any cation. Thus, the problem of determination of presence and concentration of each salt used to prepare the solutions was in this case much more complicated.

Every spectrum had 1824 channels in the frequency range 565–4000 cm^{-1}.

In both problems, salt concentrations did not exceed the limit of solubility for each specific combination of salts. The data array was randomly divided into training, validation (used to determine the moment to stop training), and test (out-of-sample) sets in the ratio of 70:20:10, respectively. 5 equal neural networks (multi-layer perceptron, MLP) were trained with different initial weight values, and the results of their application were averaged, to eliminate the influence of the initial MLP weights choice.

3   Results

The procedure of selection of the optimal architecture of ANN has been performed before [11, 20]. Briefly, it was the following. Several architectures of MLP with various numbers of hidden layers (HL) and neurons, were trained: 3 nets with 1 HL of 32, 64, or 80 neurons; 3 nets with 2 HL of 32 and 16 neurons (in the first and second HL, respectively), 64 and 32 neurons, 80 and 40 neurons; 2 nets with 3 HL of 40, 20, and 10 neurons (in the first, second and third layers, respectively), and with 64, 32, and 16 neurons. The best architecture was selected by the value of the multiple determination coefficient on the test set. For the 5-salts IP, it was the MLP with 2 HL containing 80 and 40 neurons; for the more complicated 10-ions IP, it was the MLP with 3 HL containing 64, 32, and 16 neurons [20]. These neural networks were used in all computational experiments described below.

The other parameters of all the networks were: logistic transfer function in the hidden layers and linear transfer function in the output layer (often performs better for regression-type tasks). Parameters used in the process of ANN training: error back-propagation with ordinary gradient descent [21], learning rate 0.01; momentum 0.5; stop training criterion - 1000 epochs after minimum of the error on validation dataset. In every experiment, 5 identical neural networks with various initial weight approximations were trained, and the results were averaged, to eliminate the influence of the initial MLP weights choice.

Also, some attempts were made to solve the even more complex IP of determination of concentrations of 10 ions (on the 10-salts data array) by alternative machine learning algorithms: the Group Method of Data Handling (GMDH) in the modes of polynomial neural network and combinatorial GMDH [22], and the Partial Least Squares (PLS) method [23]. As one of the methods of spectra preprocessing for use with PLS method, the exponential transformation 10^{-x}, where x is intensity in every spectrum channel, was used [9].

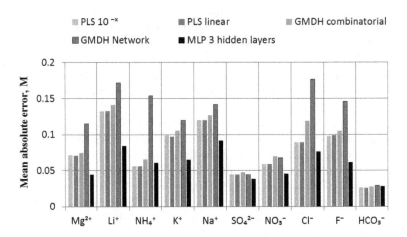

Fig. 1. The mean absolute error of determination of inorganic salts concentrations on the test set by various machine learning algorithms for the IP of 10 ions.

Figure 1 demonstrates comparison of the results of solution of the 10-ions IP. It can be seen that the best results are given by the MLP. Therefore, further comparisons (of the single-output and multiple-output approaches) were made for the 5-salts and 10-salts IPs, with the best MLP architectures described above.

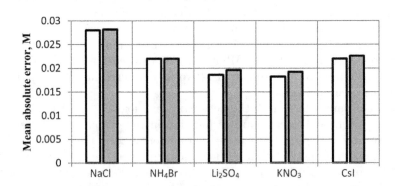

Fig. 2. The mean absolute error of determination of inorganic salts concentrations on the test set by separate single-output ANNs (white bars) and by single multiple output ANNs (grey bars) for the IP of 5 salts.

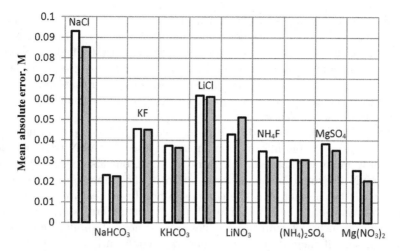

Fig. 3. The mean absolute error of determination of inorganic salts concentrations on the test set by separate single-output ANNs (white bars) and by single multiple output ANNs (grey bars) for the IP of 10 salts.

The results of solving the IPs of determination of concentrations of 5 and 10 salts by single-output and multiple-output MLPs are presented in Figs. 2 and 3.

It can be concluded that different approaches have given contradictory effect, depending on the complexity of the problem. Particularly, for the IP of 5 salts using single-output MLPs allowed decreasing the mean absolute error of determination of concentrations of Li_2SO_4 and KNO_3 by more than 5 %, and for CsI by 2.7 % compared with the results of simultaneous determination. Changes for the two other salts are of minor importance. On the other hand, for the IP of 10 salts, the opposite effect is observed. Autonomous determination demonstrated better result only for $LiNO_3$ (the mean absolute error was 16.3 % smaller, compared with simultaneous determination). At the same time, the mean absolute error of simultaneous determination was smaller for all salts by 4.2 % on the average (even together with the results for $LiNO_3$). In particular, for $Mg(NO_3)_2$, the error decreased by 23.3 %, for NaCl, NH_4F and $MgSO_4$, by more than 9 %.

4   Discussion

It can be seen that again we observe the effect, which we described earlier in [11] - reducing some significant amount of data used to train the neural network leads to degradation of accuracy of determining concentrations of salts for the IP of 10 components, but not for the IP of 5 components. However, in previous studies we investigated the possibility of reducing the dimensionality of the input data. Particularly, in [8], it has been demonstrated that the procedure of channel aggregation (averaging the intensities of adjacent spectral channels) provided improvement in the results of solution of 5 salts problem, and this positive effect persisted up to 32-fold aggregation. But in the case of 10 salts IP, this approach resulted in some small improvement only for 2-fold aggregation and only for a few components. Attempts to reduce the dimensionality by feature selection (significance of channels was estimated by standard deviation, cross-correlation, cross-entropy, amplitude of ANN weights) [10] demonstrated that no more than 15 % of spectra channels could be excluded resulting in only a small improvement of the results of the IP solution.

Summarizing, we can conclude that in the case of a high complexity nonlinear problem, all the available information should be used for ANN training. Note that not only input variables have high importance, but also output variables. Training ANN for simultaneous determination of the values of all the output variables leads to the fact that the composite non-linear features extracted in the hidden layers get to be suitable for all (or at least several) outputs at once. If the simultaneously determined variables have somewhat similar dependences on the inputs, or if they are in some other way significantly coupled, they pull the weight optimization procedure in nearly the same direction, thus improving the efficiency of MLP training and resulting in reduction of output error. Similar effects were observed by the authors before [18], in their studies of group determination of parameters of a multi-parameter inverse problem. So apparently the effects observed for the 10 salts IP are due to the high level of interaction of salts dissolved in water; the perceptron trained to solve this problem needs to take into account all the input components and output interactions to create the correct non-linear mapping.

Future studies should include investigation of group determination of parameters for the 10-salts problem, with search for optimal grouping based on similarity of influence of different salts on the shape of Raman spectrum.

5   Conclusion

Comparison of the results of applying autonomous and simultaneous determination approaches for the inverse problems of 5 salts and 10 salts shows that channel aggregation and focusing only on single output is efficient only for the simpler problem of 5 salts. The more complicated problem of 10 salts requires all the available information to be used as input and output variables. The paper presents detailed discussion of the reasons of the observed effects.

References

1. Baldwin, S.F., Brown, C.W.: Detection of ionic water pollutants by laser excited Raman spectroscopy. Water Res. **6**, 1601–1604 (1972)
2. Rudolph, W.W., Irmer, G.: Raman and infrared spectroscopic investigation on aqueous alkali metal phosphate solutions and density functional theory calculations of phosphate-water clusters. Appl. Spectrosc. **61**(12), 274A–292A (2007)
3. Furic, K., Ciglenecki, I., Cosovic, B.: Raman spectroscopic study of sodium chloride water solutions. J. Mol. Struct. **6**, 225–234 (2000)

4. Dolenko, T.A., Churina, I.V., Fadeev, V.V., Glushkov, S.M.: Valence band of liquid water Raman scattering: some peculiarities and applications in the diagnostics of water media. J. Raman Spectrosc. **31**(8–9), 863–870 (2000)
5. Terpstra, P., Combes, D., Zwick, A.: Effect of salts on dynamics of water: a Raman spectroscopy study. J. Chem. Phys. **92**(1), 65–70 (1989)
6. Gogolinskaia (Dolenko), T.A., Patsaeva, S.V., Fadeev, V.V.: The regularities of change of the 3100–3700 cm^{-1} band of water Raman scattering in salt aqueous solutions. Dokl. Akad. Nauk SSSR **290**(5), 1099–1103 (1986)
7. Gerdova, I.V., Dolenko, S.A., Dolenko, T.A., Churina, I.V., Fadeev, V.V.: New opportunity solutions to inverse problems in laser spectroscopy involving artificial neural networks. Izv. Akad. Nauk Ser. Fiz. **66**(8), 1116–1124 (2002)
8. Dolenko, S., Burikov, S., Dolenko, T., Efitorov, A., Gushchin, K., Persiantsev, I.: Neural network approaches to solution of the inverse problem of identification and determination of partial concentrations of salts in multi-component water solutions. In: Wermter, S., et al. (eds.) ICANN 2014. LNCS, vol. 8681, pp. 805–812. Springer, Switzerland (2014)
9. Efitorov, A.O., Burikov, S.A., Dolenko, T.A., Persiantsev, I.G., Dolenko, S.A.: Comparison of the quality of solving the inverse problems of spectroscopy of multi-component solutions with neural network methods and with the method of projection to latent structures. Opt. Mem. Neural Netw. (Inf. Opt.) **24**(2), 93–101 (2015)
10. Efitorov, A., Burikov, S., Dolenko, T., Laptinskiy, K., Dolenko, S.: Significant feature selection in neural network solution of an inverse problem in spectroscopy. Procedia Comput. Sci. **66**, 93–102 (2015)
11. Dolenko, S., Efitorov, A., Burikov, S., Dolenko, T., Laptinskiy, K., Persiantsev, I.: Neural network approaches to solution of the inverse problem of identification and determination of the ionic composition of multi-component water solutions. In: Iliadis, L., et al. (eds.) EANN 2015. CCIS, vol. 517, pp. 109–118. Springer, Heidelberg (2015). doi:10.1007/978-3-319-23983-5_11
12. Zhang, Y., Pulliainen, J., Koponen, S., Hallikainen, M.: Application of an empirical neural network to surface water quality estimation in the Gulf of Finland using combined optical data and microwave data. Remote Sens. Environ. **81**, 327–336 (2002)
13. Plaza, J., Martinez, P., Perez, R., Plaza, A., Cantero, C.: Nonlinear neural-network-based mixture model for estimating the concentration of nitrogen salts in turbid inland waters using hyperspectral imagery. In: Proceedings of the SPIE 5584, Chemical and Biological Standoff Detection II, p. 165 (2004). doi:10.1117/12.579805
14. Chen, L., Zhang, X.: Application of artificial neural networks to classify water quality of the yellow river. Fuzzy information and engineering. Adv. Soft Comput. **54**, 15–23 (2009)
15. Liu, M., Liu, X., Jiang, J., Xia, X.: Artificial neural network and random forest approaches for modeling of sea surface salinity. Int. J. Remote Sens. Appl. **3**(4), 229–234 (2013)
16. Hongwei, J.I., Yan, X.U., Shuang, L.I., Huizhen, X., Hengxia, C.: Simultaneous determination of calcium and magnesium in water using artificial neural network. Spectro-photometric method. J. Ocean Univ. Chin. **9**(3), 229–234 (2010)
17. Hongwei, J.I., Yan, X.U., Shuang, L.I., Huizhen, X., Hengxia, C.: Simultaneous determination of iron and manganese in water using artificial neural network. Catalytic spectrophotometric method. J. Ocean Univ. Chin. **11**(3), 323–330 (2012)

18. Dolenko, S., Isaev, I., Obornev, E., Persiantsev, I., Shimelevich, M.: Study of influ-
    ence of parameter grouping on the error of neural network solution of the inverse
    problem of electrical prospecting. In: Iliadis, L., Papadopoulos, H., Jayne, C. (eds.)
    EANN 2013, Part I. CCIS, vol. 383, pp. 81–90. Springer, Heidelberg (2013)
19. Dolenko, S.A., Isaev, I.V., Persiantsev, I.G., Obornev, I.E., Obornev, E.A.,
    Shimelevich, M.I.: Elaboration of a complex algorithm of neural network solu-
    tion of the inverse problem of electrical prospecting based on data classification.
    In: Proceedings of the 10th International Conference Problems of Geocosmos, St.
    Petersburgh, Russia, pp. 11–16, 6–10 October 2014. http://geo.phys.spbu.ru/
    materials_of_a_conference_2014/C2014/01_Dolenko.pdf
20. Efitorov, A., Dolenko, T., Burikov, S., Laptinskiy, K., Dolenko, S.: Neural network
    solution of an inverse problem in Raman spectroscopy of multi-component solu-
    tions of inorganic salts. In: Samsonovich, A.V., Klimov, V.V., Rybina, G.V. (eds.)
    Biologically Inspired Cognitive Architectures (BICA) for Young Scientists. AISC,
    vol. 449, pp. 273–279. Springer, Switzerland (2016)
21. Werbos, P.J.: Beyond regression: new tools for prediction and analysis in the behav-
    ioral sciences. Ph.D. thesis, Harvard University, Cambridge, MA (1974)
22. Madala, H.R., Ivakhnenko, A.G.: Inductive Learning Algorithms for Complex Sys-
    tems Modeling. CRC Press, Boca Raton (1994)
23. Wehrens, R.: Chemometrics with R, p. 286. Springer, Heidelberg (2011)

Sound Recognition System Using Spiking and MLP Neural Networks

Elena Cerezuela-Escudero[(✉)], Angel Jimenez-Fernandez, Rafael Paz-Vicente,
Juan P. Dominguez-Morales, Manuel J. Dominguez-Morales,
and Alejandro Linares-Barranco

Robotic and Technology of Computers Lab,
Department of Architecture and Technology of Computers,
University of Seville, Seville, Spain
ecerezuela@atc.us.es

Abstract. In this paper, we explore the capabilities of a sound classification system that combines a Neuromorphic Auditory System for feature extraction and an artificial neural network for classification. Two models of neural network have been used: Multilayer Perceptron Neural Network and Spiking Neural Network. To compare their accuracies, both networks have been developed and trained to recognize pure tones in presence of white noise. The spiking neural network has been implemented in a FPGA device. The neuromorphic auditory system that is used in this work produces a form of representation that is analogous to the spike outputs of the biological cochlea. Both systems are able to distinguish the different sounds even in the presence of white noise. The recognition system based in a spiking neural networks has better accuracy, above 91 %, even when the sound has white noise with the same power.

Keywords: Neuromorphic auditory hardware · Address-Event representation · Spiking neural networks · Sound recognition · Spike signal processing

1 Introduction

By the information provided from the hearing system, the human being can identify virtually any kind of sound (sound recognition) and where it comes from (sound localization) [1]. If this ability could be reproduced by artificial devices, many applications would emerge, from support devices for people with hearing loss to security devices.

Sound recognition is commonly treated as a two stages problem: filtering and classification [2–6]. Filtering is the stage where the signal is processed to extract acoustic features, so only relevant information will pass to the classification stage, where the sound will be identified. There are some factors that make sound recognition a hard task: the presence of electric noise in the signal, the environment's noise level and reverberation, the fact that the signal is a complex time series data and the wide dynamic range of sound. Biological cochlea has a huge dynamic range, is adapted to a wide variety of listening environments and it has high noise immunity [7]. In order to take advantage of these characteristics, in this work we use in the first recognition stage a Neuromorphic

© Springer International Publishing Switzerland 2016
A.E.P. Villa et al. (Eds.): ICANN 2016, Part II, LNCS 9887, pp. 363–371, 2016.
DOI: 10.1007/978-3-319-44781-0_43

Auditory System (NAS) that decomposes an audio signal into different frequency bands, which produces spikes, in the same way a biological cochlea processes and sends the audio information coded in spikes to the brain.

Artificial Neural Network is a generic classification method that can deal with several kinds of information and has found great success in the area of pattern recognition. However, standard artificial neuron models require input signals to be transformed into static vectors by windowing processes, as, for example, the Time Delay Neural Network [8]. Another approach for processing temporal data is the use of Spiking Neural Network (SNN) [9]. The neurons within this kind of network deal with input signals on the form of pulse (also called spike) trains, using a potential as a reference for generating pulses on its output. Spiking models can directly deal with temporal data and can be efficiently implemented in hardware, due to its simple structure. In this work, we present two classification systems based on two kinds of neural network: Multilayer Perceptron Neural Network (MLPNN) and SNN.

It is very common the use of techniques based in Fourier Transforms for filtering stage. In [2] the Fast Fourier Transform and the Harmonic Product Spectrum are proposed for the filtering stage and an MLPNN for the classification stage. The system achieved 97.5 % recognition accuracy for 12 musical notes using 20 neurons in the first hidden layer and 10 neurons in the second one. The sound classification model proposed in [3] extracts the pitch of the signal using the Harmonic Product Spectrum. Based on the pitch estimation, features are created and used in a probabilistic model. The accuracy of the model is 99.95 % for 3 classes of sounds.

Although techniques based in Fourier Transformations can have remarkably successful, their underpinnings are somewhat removed from the spiking, highly parallelized nature of the mammalian auditory perception systems. The work presented here is an attempt to work within a more biologically realistic framework, both for the formation of sound descriptors, and for the task of sound classification itself.

There are previous works that presents bio-inspired models of cochlea and neural coding scheme. Reference [10] presents a phenomenological model of the cochlea consists of a bank of nonlinear time-varying parallel filters and an active distributed feedback and reference [11] simulates a model of auditory nerve and cochlear nucleus neurons. Both models have several realistic properties. Reference [5] presents a sound recognition system using a bank of band-pass filters and pulsed generator implemented in software for extracting sound frequency characteristics and a hardware implementation of pulsed neural network to classify. The accuracy of the system is 98.7 % for 6 classes of sounds. In [6] the cochlea response is simulated with a gammatone filterbank and classification task is performed using a time-domain reservoir neural network known as the echo state network [12]. The accuracy of the system is 45 % for 5 classes. The system proposed in [13] uses an MLPNN to classify sounds between 5 vowel phonemes with percentage of success of 93.99 %. The characteristics extraction stage is not bio-inspired because it is based on electromyogram signals.

2   Neuromorphic Auditory System

Neuromorphic systems, because of their high level of parallelism, interconnectivity, and scalability, carry out complex processing in real time, with a good relation between quality, speed and resource consumption [7]. The signals in these systems are composed of short pulses in time, called spikes or events. The information can be coded in the polarity and spike frequency, often following a Pulse Frequency Modulation (PFM) scheme, or in the inter-spike-interval time (ISI) [14], or in the time-from-reset, where the most important (with the highest priority) events are sent first [15]. Address-Event Representation (AER), proposed by Mead lab in 1991 [16], faced the difficult problem of connecting silicon neurons along chips that implement different neuronal layers using a common asynchronous digital bus multiplexed in time, the AER bus. This representation gives a digital unique code (address) to each neuron, which is transmitted using a simple four-phase handshake protocol [17].

In the filtering stage of the audio recognition problem, we use a neuromorphic device which decomposes an audio signal into different frequency bands of spiking information, in the same way a biological cochlea sends the audio information to the brain. The biological cochlea performs the transduction between the pressure signal representing the acoustic input and the neural signals that carry information to the brain. Due to the physical characteristics of a part of cochlea, the basilar membrane, cochlea divides an input signal into its frequency components. Thousands of hair cells on the membrane generate action potentials, or spikes, that travel along nerve fibers to higher-order auditory brain areas [7]. The first silicon cochlea was proposed by Lyon and Mead [18]. In their design, the membrane basilar was modeled by a cascade of 480 second-order filter sections. There are several VLSI implementations of the cochlea based on Lyon's design (for example, [19–21]). Digital models of the cochlea process audio signals using classical Digital Signal Processing techniques [22–24].

The NAS is innovate respect previous systems because it processes information directly encoded as spikes with a Pulse Frequency Modulation (PFM), performing Spike Signal Processing techniques [25, 26], and using AER interfaces. The architecture of the NAS is shown in Fig. 1. The system's input is the digitalized audio streams, which represent the audio signals of a monaural system. A Synthetic Spike Generator [27] converts this digital audio source into a spike stream. Then, the cascade band pass filter bank splits the spike streams in 64 (64 is the number of channels of the NAS) frequency bands using 64 different spiking outputs that are combined by an AER monitor block into an AER output bus [28], which encodes each spike according to AER and transmits this information to the classification systems. All the elements required for designing the NAS components (Synthetic Spike Generators, cascade filter bank and the AER monitor) have been implemented in VHDL and designed as small spike-based building blocks [26]. Table 1 shows the NAS characteristics. The NAS has been used before in [29] to measure the speed of DC motor and in [30] that proposes a convolutional spiking neural network for audio sound classification. Although, for this work, the gain of the band pass filters have been modified looking for improving the recognition system accuracy.

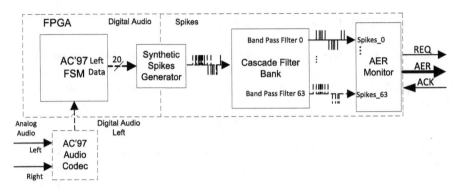

Fig. 1. NAS Architecture

Table 1. NAS characteristics

Number bands	Frequency range	Dynamic range	Max. Event rate	Clock frequency
64	9.6 Hz–14.06 kHz	75 dB	2.19 Mevents/s	27 MHz

3   Classification Systems

3.1   Multilayer Perceptron Neural Network

The topological structure of the MLPNN used consists of a two-layer feed-forward network, with a sigmoid transfer function in the hidden and output layer. The training algorithm used is the back-propagation. During this research, the optimal number of hidden units was found by running different performance tests, where a new MLPNN was created, trained and tested using a varying number of neurons in the hidden layer. This kind of neural network requires static vectors as input. The number of the network inputs is similar than the number of characteristics. The spiking signal has been transformed by windowing process and organized by characteristics like this: the spiking information of each NAS band has been integrated during 20 ms, generating a 64-element vector. We select 20 ms because the shortest audible sound ranges from 10 to 40 ms [31].

3.2   Spiking Neural Network

The SNN has been implemented by a two-layer neural network. The input layer consists of Integrate and Fire neurons [9]. The optimal number of input units was found by running different performance tests. The output layer has as many Winner-Take-All neurons as classes to classify. The SNN input are the 64 spiking streams from the NAS. This classification system was implemented in a FPGA, and the Integrate and Fire neuron hardware architecture is shown if Fig. 2, where W are the neuron weights and θ

is the neuron threshold. The SNN training is performed by a SNN simulation implemented in software.

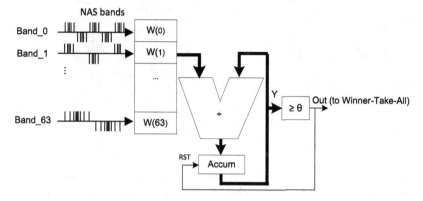

Fig. 2. Hardware architecture of Integrate and Fire Neuron of the SNN

4   Experimental Results

We have evaluated the capabilities of our sound recognition system using pure tone sounds in the presence of white noise. The fundamental frequencies of sounds are shown in Table 2. White noise was added to check the noise tolerance of the recognition system. The test set consisted of 50 20-millisecond samples of each tone. White noise was added to each sound with a SNR sweep from 46.05 to −21.97 dB (30 different values of SNR). Therefore, in total there are 1.500 samples of each tone.

Table 2. Fundamental frequency of sounds to recognize

Freq	130,81	174,61	261,62	349,22	523,25	698,45	1046,5	1396,91

The MLPNN was created, trained and tested using a varying number of neurons in the hidden layer. 70 % randomly-selected samples were used to training the MLPNN, including noisy samples. The results shows in Fig. 3 are obtained using 10 neurons in the hidden layer and 8 neuron in the output layer. The system achieves 98.95 % recognition accuracy for tones without white noise. Figure 3 (left) shows accuracy for each pure tone in the presence of different white noise powers as a color-map, being the X-axis the frequencies between 130.813 and 1.89 kHz, the Y-axis the SNR between 46.05 to −21.97 dB, and the color represents the percentage of successes.

The SNN, with 8 neurons in the input layer and 8 neuron in the output layer, training with 70 % noiseless samples, obtains the accuracy shown in Fig. 3 (right). The system achieves a mean success rate of 100 % for tones without white noise. Figure 3 shows that the hit rate decreases with the increase of white noise, and that there is a frequency less robust to white noise (698,45 Hz). Most of the pure tones have a hit rate over 90 % with a SNR over −8 dB.

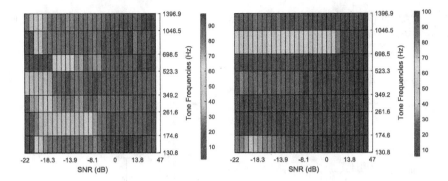

Fig. 3. Hit rate of sound recognition system using MLPNN (left) and using SNN (right)

The results shown in Fig. 3 (right), in general, are better than the results obtains with MLPNN. Furthermore, SNN uses 16 hardware implementation neurons and MLPNN uses 18 neurons.

5 Conclusions

In this study, we show that recognizing pure tones in presence of white noise can success using MLP neural network and SNN. The SNN achieves better accuracy with less neurons than MLPNN. In addition, SNN has been implemented in hardware. Audio information acquisition is carried out by a novel neuromorphic auditory system, which provided streams of spikes representing audio frequency components. As a future work, it would be valuable to evaluate the performance of the SNN with the models of the auditory system proposed in [10, 11], as well as performance of more complex sound recognition, like vowels [13].

In the audio context, traditional digital systems have to process several samples in a buffer, because sound makes sense along time, where Fast Fourier Transform (FFT) calculation prior to specific processing. However, NAS provide audio directly and continuously decomposed into its frequency components as a spike stream. This allows real time audio processing (without the need for buffering), using neuromorphic processing layers as SNN do.

The SNN-based system and MLPNN-based system have a percentage of success above 91 % even when the sound has white noise with the same power. When the SNR is −18.3 dB, the SNN-based system accuracy is kept on 85.3 %, but the MLPNN-based system accuracy is only 12.5 %. The SNN-based system achieves a mean success rate of 100 % for tones without white noise.

Most recognition systems exposed in the introduction cannot be implemented in dedicated hardware because of its high computational cost, however, we present a recognition system efficiently implemented in hardware, due to its simple structure. Furthermore, SNN architecture proposed is highly parallelizable. Regarding the classification stage, all the works presented in the introduction have more computational cost than SNN. For example, the method proposed in [2] achieved 97.5 % accuracy for 12 sounds using a MLPNN with 30 neurons. The bio-inspired recognition system proposed in [5] has a percentage of succeed of 98.7 % for 6 kinds of sounds, less than our recognition system and it is not fully implementable in hardware.

The system presented in this paper is being applied to animal behavior recognition, for example for horse behaviors, through a SNN-based sound recognition system associate to the animal movements.

Acknowledgements. This work is supported by the Spanish government grant BIOSENSE (TEC2012-37868-C04-02) and by the excellence project from Andalusian Council MINERVA (P12-TIC-1300), both with support from the European Regional Development Fund.

References

1. Pickles, J.O.: An Introduction to the Physiology of Hearing. Emerald, London (2012)
2. Guerrero-turrubiates, J.J., Gonzalez-reyna, S.E., Ledesma-orozco, S.E., Avina-cervantes, J.G.: Pitch estimation for musical note recognition using artificial neural networks. In: International Conference on Electronics, Communications and Computers (CONIELECOMP), pp. 53–58 (2014)
3. Nielsen, A.B., Hansen, L.K., Kjems, U.: Pitch based sound classification. In: 2006 Proceedings of International Conference on Acoustics, Speech and Signal Processing (ICASSP 2006), vol. 3, pp. 788–791 (2006)
4. Pishdadian, F., Nelson, J.K.: On the transcription of monophonic melodies in an instance-based pitch classification scenario. In: Proceedings of 2013 IEEE Digital Signal Processing and Signal Processing Education Meeting, DSP/SPE 2013, pp. 222–227 (2013)
5. Iwasa, K., Kugler, M., Kuroyanagi, S., Iwata, A.: A sound localization and recognition system using pulsed neural networks on FPGA. In: International Joint Conference on Neural Networks, IJCNN 2007, pp. 902–907. IEEE, August 2007
6. Newton, M.J., Smith, L.S.: Biologically-inspired neural coding of sound onset for a musical sound classification task. In: Proceedings of the International Joint Conference on Neural Networks, pp. 1386–1393 (2011)
7. Liu, S.C.: Event-Based Neuromorphic Systems. Wiley (2015)
8. Waibel, A., Hanazawa, T., Hinton, G., Shiano, K., Lang, K.J.: Phoneme recognition using time-delay neural networks. IEEE Trans. Acousti. Speech Sig. Process. **37**(3), 328–339 (1989)
9. Gerstner, W., Kistler, W.M.: Spiking Neuron Models: Single Neurons, Populations, Plasticity. Cambridge University Press, Cambridge (2002)
10. Robert, A., Eriksson, J.L.: A composite model of the auditory periphery for simulating responses to complex sounds. J. Acoust. Soc. Am. **106**(4), 1852–1864 (1999)
11. Eriksson, J.L., Robert, A.: The representation of pure tones and noise in a model of cochlear nucleus neurons. J. Acoust. Soc. Am. **106**(4), 1865–1879 (1999)
12. Jaeger, H.: Tutorial on training recurrent neural networks, covering BPPT, RTRL, EKF and the "echo state network" approach. GMD Report 159, German National Research Center for Information Technology (2002)
13. Mendes, J.A., Robson, R.R., Labidi S., Barros A.K.: Subvocal Speech recognition based on EMG signal using independent component analysis and neural network MLP. In: Congress on Image and Signal Processing, CISP 2008, vol. 1, pp. 221–224 (2008)

14. Indiveri, G., Chicca, E., Douglas, R.: A VLSI array of low-power spiking neurons and bistables synapses with spike-timig dependant plasticity. IEEE Trans. Neural Netw. **17**(1), 211–221 (2006)
15. Thorpe, S.J., Brilhault, A., Perez-Carrasco, J.A.: Suggestions for a biologically inspired spiking retina using order-based coding. In: 2010 IEEE International Symposium on Circuits and Systems Nano-Bio Circuit Fabrics and Systems, ISCAS 2010, pp. 265–268 (2010)
16. Mahowald, M.: VLSI analogs of neuronal visual processing: a synthesis of form and function, Ph.D. dissertation, California Institute of Technology, Pasadena (1992)
17. Boahen, K.A.: Communicating Neuronal Ensembles between Neuromorphic Chips. Neuromorphic Systems. Kluwer Academic Publishers, Boston (1998)
18. Lyon, R.F., Mead, C.: An analog electronic cochlea. IEEE Trans. Acoust. Speech Sig. Process. **36**, 1119–1134 (1988)
19. Wen, B.: Boahen, K.A silicon cochlea with active coupling. IEEE Trans. Biomed. Circ. Syst. **3**, 444–455 (2009)
20. Hamilton, T.J., Jin, C., van Schaik, A., Tapson, J.: An active 2-d silicon cochlea. IEEE Trans. Biomed. Circ. Syst. **2**, 30–43 (2008)
21. Liu, S-C., Van Schaik, A., Minch, B.A., Delbruck, T.: Event-based 64-channel binaural silicon cochlea with Q enhancement mechanisms. In: Proceedings of 2010 IEEE International Symposium on Circuits and Systems (ISCAS), 30 May–2 June 2010, pp. 2027–2030 (2010)
22. Leong, M.P., Jin, C., Leong, P.: An FPGA-based electronic cochlea. EURASIP J. Appl. Sig. Process. **2003**(7), 629–638 (2003)
23. Dundur, R., Latte, M.V., Kulkarni, S.Y., Venkatesha, M.K.: Digital filter for cochlear implant implemented on a field-programmable gate array. Int. J. Electr. Comput. Energ. Electron. Commun. Eng. **2**(7), 468–472 (2008)
24. Thakur, C.S., Hamilton, T.J., Tapson, J., van Schaik, A., Lyon, R.F.: FPGA Implementation of the CAR model of the Cochlea. In: IEEE International Symposium on Circuits and Systems (ISCAS), pp. 1853–1856 (2014)
25. Domínguez-Morales, M., Jimenez-Fernandez, A., Cerezuela-Escudero, E., Paz-Vicente, R., Linares-Barranco, A., Jimenez, G.: On the designing of spikes band-pass filters for FPGA. In: Honkela, T. (ed.) ICANN 2011, Part II. LNCS, vol. 6792, pp. 389–396. Springer, Heidelberg (2011)
26. Jimenez-Fernandez, A., Linares-Barranco, A., Paz-Vicente, R., Jiménez, G., Civit, A.: Building blocks for spike-based signal processing. In: International Joint Conference on Neural Networks, IJCNN, pp. 1–8 (2010)
27. Gomez-Rodriguez, F., Paz, R., Miro, L., Linares-Barranco, A., Jimenez, G., Civit, A.: Two hardware implementations of the exhaustive synthetic AER generation method. In: Cabestany, J., Prieto, A.G., Sandoval, F. (eds.) IWANN 2005. LNCS, vol. 3512, pp. 534–540. Springer, Heidelberg (2005)
28. Cerezuela-Escudero, E., Dominguez-Morales, M.J., Jiménez-Fernández, A., Paz-Vicente, R., Linares-Barranco, A., Jiménez-Moreno, G.: Spikes monitors for FPGAs, an experimental comparative study. In: Rojas, I., Joya, G., Gabestany, J. (eds.) IWANN 2013, Part I. LNCS, vol. 7902, pp. 179–188. Springer, Heidelberg (2013)
29. Rios-Navarro, A., Jimenez-Fernandez, A., Cerezuela-Escudero, E., Rivas, M., Jimenez, G., Linares-Barranco, A.: Live demostration: real-time motor rotation frequency detection by spike-based visual and auditory sensory fusion on AER and FPGA. In: Wermter, S., Weber, C., Duch, W., Honkela, T., Koprinkova-Hristova, P., Magg, S., Palm, G., Villa, A.E.P. (eds.) ICANN 2014. LNCS, vol. 8681, pp. 847–848. Springer, Switzerland (2014)

30. Cerezuela-Escudero, E., Jimenez-Fernandez, A., Paz-Vicente, R., Dominguez-Morales, M., Linares-Barranco, A., Jimenez-Moreno, G.: Musical notes classification with Neuromorphic Auditory System using FPGA and a Convolutional Spiking Network. In: Proceedings of the 2015 International Joint Conference on Neural Networks (IJCNN), pp. 1–7 (2015)
31. Lass, N.: Contemporary Issues in Experimental Phonetics. Elsevier (2012)

Using Machine Learning Techniques to Recover Prismatic Cirrus Ice Crystal Size from 2-Dimensional Light Scattering Patterns

Daniel Priori[1](✉), Giseli de Sousa[1,2], Mauro Roisenberg[1],
Christopher Stopford[2], Evelyn Hesse[2], Emmanuel Salawu[3],
Neil Davey[2], and Yi Sun[2]

[1] Connectionism and Cognitive Science Lab, Deparment of Informatic and Statistic,
Federal University of Santa Catarina, Florianopolis, SC, Brazil
`daniel.priori@posgrad.ufsc.br`, {`giseli,mauro`}`@inf.ufsc.br`
[2] Science and Technology Research Institute, University of Hertfordshire,
Hatfield, Herts, UK
{`c.stopford,e.hesse,n.davey,y.2.sun`}`@herts.ac.uk`
[3] TIGP Bioinformatics Program, Academia Sinica, Taipei 115, Taiwan

Abstract. In this paper, we present a prediction model developed to identify particles size of ice crystals in clouds. The proposed model combines a Feed Forward Multi-Layer Perceptron neural network with Bayesian regularization backpropagation and other machine learning techniques for feature reduction with Principal Component Analysis and rotation invariance with Fast Fourier Transform. The proposed solution is capable of predicting the particle sizes with normalized mean squared error around 0.007. However, the proposed network model is not able to predict the size of very small particles (between 3 and 10 μm size) with the same precision as for the larger particles. Therefore, in this work we also discuss some possible reasons for this problem and suggest future points that need to be analysed.

Keywords: 2d light scattering pattern · Atmospheric particle · Size prediction · Fast Fourier Transform · Neural network regression

1 Introduction

Clouds influence climate through radiative (scattering and absorbing solar and thermal radiation) and other physical processes that impact on the Earth's radiation budget and affect climate change. Such cloud feedbacks are a source of significant uncertainty in climate models [1]. This applies in particular to ice or mixed-phase cloud (the latter comprising both ice crystals and super-cooled droplets), since the radiative properties of such clouds are dependent upon the relative abundance of crystals and droplets, their size spectra and, in particular, the diverse crystal shapes present [2].

To be able to understand the radiative transfer properties of such particles, a detailed knowledge of their shapes and sizes is required. Imaging methods,

© Springer International Publishing Switzerland 2016
A.E.P. Villa et al. (Eds.): ICANN 2016, Part II, LNCS 9887, pp. 372–379, 2016.
DOI: 10.1007/978-3-319-44781-0_44

e.g. [12], are widely used to obtain in situ morphological data of atmospheric particles. However, for small particles, optical aberrations and constrained depth of field restrict the obtainable information. Such constraints do not apply to the detection of scattering patterns. Therefore, suitable detection instruments like the Small Ice Detector (SID) [11] have been developed. However, while conventional pattern recognition methods may be readily used to group recorded images of Two-Dimensional Light Scattering (2DLS) patterns into broad particle shape classes [11], the inversion of the patterns required to yield quantitative morphological data is much more involved. Therefore, the creation of databases of scattering patterns of known particle morphologies is extremely useful for particle characterization.

Here we use a database [19] of scattering patterns obtained from the Ray Tracing with Diffraction on Facets (RTDF) model [9] which is a hybrid model combining ray tracing with a physical optics approximation. While ice particles in clouds are known to cover a wide variety of shapes, such as columns, plates, rosettes, aggregates and variations thereof (e.g. hollow or rough and/or rounded crystals) [2], we focus on this initial study on pristine (i.e. undistorted) hexagonal prisms which vary in size and aspect ratio. The latter is defined as the ratio of crystal length to diameter, where the diameter is twice the edge length of a hexagonal facet. Therefore, aspect ratios are larger or smaller than one correspond to columns or plates, respectively. The characteristic crystal parameter we wish to determine from the 2DLS pattern is the crystal's projected size as seen by the incident light. This is an important parameter because, if averaged over ensembles of randomly oriented particles, it gives an indication of actual particle size, which is required as input parameter for radiative transfer computations which feed into climate models.

Therefore, to obtain the size information from the ice crystal particles that compose the analysed database, we present in this work a prediction model which uses as input the 2DLS patterns generated from the particles. The proposed model uses a Feed Forward Multi-Layer Perceptron neural network (NN) as a prediction technique, Fast Fourier Transform (FFT) [3,5] techniques to avoid problems with pattern rotation and Principal Component Analysis (PCA) [18] process for feature reduction.

2 Related Work

As the inverse light scattering problem occurs in various areas such as Geology, Biology, Astrophysics, and Engineering among others, there are some related works which use different neural networks models to extract information from light scattering for distinct purposes that we presented here.

In Ulanowski et al. [20], the approach used was a Radial Basis Function (RBF) neural network to predict the particle size from Multiangle Dynamic Light Scattering (MDLS) patterns. The results presented in [20] were satisfactory, however it focused on spherical particles. Therefore, the application of rotational invariance techniques was not necessary. Mie scattering patterns

[14] (which are based at Maxwell's equations [7] and are therefore numerically exact) were used as network training examples. Intercomparisons of inversion algorithms for particle-sizing using Mie scattering are given in [16]. Kaye et al. [10] investigated the applicability of a RBF neural network for classification of potentially hazardous airborne fibres based on their light scattering pattern. Other related works using MDLS measurements and NN differ from the current work as they predict particle size distribution in polymer latexes using General Regression Neural Network (GRNN), which is a particular case of a RBF network [8].

In the image processing area, El-Bakry and Mastorakis [5] used a normalized neural network for fast pattern detection for a given image. Like in the work described in this paper (see Sect. 3.2), they use a Multi-Layer Perceptron neural network for pattern recognition and a Fast Fourier Transform method for image preprocessing. However, they focused on improving speed of the pattern recognition process, by using images in the frequency domain and not in the space domain, as our present study does. In Beaudoin and Beauchemin [3], the authors discuss different methods for image processing using Fourier Transform. Their work showed that they could obtain the transformation results in frequency domain in a fast and accurate process, showing that the Fourier transform is a good method for image processing that can be applied in different fields of study.

Another image preprocessing method applied in this work is feature reduction. The most common approach which is also used in this work is the PCA. This preprocessing step is important to reduce the number of features analysed by neural network without losing precision [18].

In addition to using a NN for this work, other architectures are important to be investigated such as Radial Basis Function, Support Vector Machine [17], Incremental Gaussian Mixture Network [15] and the Deep Learning process [4] as alternative methods to improve preprocessing data and recognition of complex patterns. However, using a standard NN with Baeysian regularization backpropagation as done in this work has shown that this model solves the problem of predicting particle size for these 2DLS satisfactorily, since the data has been prepared by preprocessing routines properly, as we show in the Sect. 3.

3   Methodology

3.1   Analysed Particles

The particle dataset used in this work was generated by a simulator [19] obtained from the Ray Tracing with Diffraction on Facets (RTDF) model [9]. The dataset is composed of 162 particles and each particle has 133 orientations. For each orientation of the particle, a 2DLS pattern is produced. These are computed as intensity profile in spherical polar coordinates with one degree bins. The elevation angle is measured from the direction of incidence of the illuminating laser beam and is recorded between 6° and 25°; the full range of azimuth angles between 0° and 360° is considered. The combination of the elevation-azimuth angles generates pattern images with a resolution of 7,200 pixels.

3.2   The Network Model

The proposed NN model is a multi-layer feed-forward neural network with 50 nodes in the hidden layer, which uses a Bayesian regularization backpropagation as training function [13]. The number of nodes was chosen after analysing the network performance when considering the network model capacity of generalization and interpolation. However, as the training is based on a Bayesian regularization function, the number of nodes in the hidden layer is not an important factor, as this kind of training function minimises the problem of overfitting when a large number of nodes in the hidden layer is used [6].

For the NN training and testing we use a dataset of 21,546 patterns (162 particles × 133 orientations), which are split into two sets: 70 % of the patterns are used for the training process and 30 % for the testing process. In the testing process, we rotate the patterns randomly between 1° and 360°, trying to simulate the real conditions during particle observation in the atmosphere. The patterns analysed by the NN are intensity values of the diffraction images, which are then transformed and normalised by different computational techniques as described in this work. With this information, the NN analyses the size value of each orientation as training output value. Thus, the NN is capable of training and, after that, test with new patterns to predict particle sizes. In the diagram presented in Fig. 1, we summarize the prediction process performed by the NN.

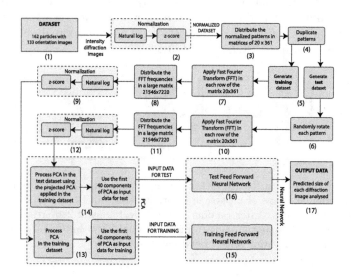

Fig. 1. Diagram of prediction process performed by the proposed neural network

As it is shown in Fig. 1, the prediction process proposed in this work begins by considering the particle dataset composed of 162 particles and 133 orientation images for each particle (step 1), which generates 21,546 diffraction pattern images. We then normalize the diffraction pattern images using natural log and z-score measurements (step 2). After that, we distribute each pattern in a matrix with 20×361 size (step 3), where the 20 rows of the matrix represent elevation angles (between $6°$ and $25°$) and 361 columns represent the azimuthal angles (between $0°$ and $360°$), thus generating a flat image of each orientation (this process is better explained in Sect. 3.3, where an example of a flat image can be seen on Fig. 2). Next, these images are duplicated into two different matrices (step 4) into the training dataset and the test dataset (step 5). The first matrix keeps the original images of all patterns and the second matrix uses all patterns randomly rotated (step 6. See an example on Fig. 2). After that, we apply the FFT method in each row of the generated matrices, both for the original images (steps 7 and 8) and for the rotated images (step 10 and 11), thus generating the pattern signal frequencies to achieve a rotation-invariant image (see Fig. 3). In the next steps, the frequency matrices are normalized (steps 9 and 12) and their dimensions are reduced by applying a PCA process (steps 13 and 14). From that, we generate the input data for training the proposed NN model (step 15). Finally, we use the rotated test patterns, which were rotated in step 6 and apply FFT process, normalization and PCA (step 14) for the NN test (step 16), where its output gives the predicted particle sizes (step 17).

3.3   Rotation Invariance

In order to make sure that patterns which only differ by a rotation around the axis corresponding to the direction of the laser beam are recognised as being identical, i.e., to generate only one pattern from the image analysis, regardless of its rotation, we use the FFT method [3,5].

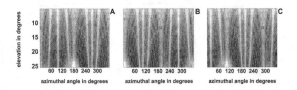

Fig. 2. Diffraction pattern images of the same particle with different rotations. Plot A shows the original image of a particle before its rotation. Plots B and C show two different diffraction images after random rotation by $189°$ and $286°$ respectively. The x-axis represents the azimuthal angle (ranges of values between $0°$ and $360°$) and the y-axis represents the elevation angle (between $6°$ and $25°$).

With the FFT method, we are able to convert the pattern from image values to frequency values [3,5], making the image rotation-invariant, and from that, can predict particle size. Without FFT, the rotation behavior shows different images to the NN (can be seen in Fig. 2), where plots B and C, each diffraction pattern image is a different image for the NN. These images are only displaced by different angles compared to the original image. That is, although it is the same image pattern, to the NN it appears as a completely different pattern.

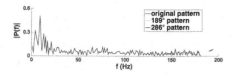

Fig. 3. Frequency values of the same 2DLS with different rotations, exemplifying the importance of using the FFT method. The blue line shows the frequency of a pattern before rotation. The green line and red line show the frequency of the same pattern at same elevation, after random rotation by 189° and 286°, respectively. The x-axis shows the pattern frequency (in hertz) and the y-axis represents the frequency amplitude. (Color figure online)

After transforming each pattern into a set of frequency patterns (one for each elevation angle) to solve the problem of rotation, the diffraction pattern images shown in Fig. 2 are converted into frequency patterns like those shown in Fig. 3. Each line in Fig. 3 represents a single elevation of each pattern shown in Fig. 2, transformed into frequency with FFT. Note that three lines are overlapped well, especially at the frequency range from the value of zero to the value of 100.

4 Results

In all performed tests using the proposed model, the NN could predict the projected size of the most analysed particles with a good precision. The results are plotted in Fig. 4, showing that using 30 % of the dataset for the test process, the results represent a normalized mean squared error around 0.007 and the value of Pearson's correlation coefficient was around 98 %. However, these results show that it is difficult for the NN to predict particles with small sizes, as shown in the highlighted box of Fig. 4 (plot A), where the predictions of particles between 3 and 10 μm size are plotted.

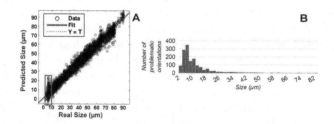

Fig. 4. Plot A is the plot with predicted against real pattern size. Each datapoint represents one pattern image at one particle orientation. The x-axis shows the projected size of each particle orientation and the y-axis shows the predicted size. The highlighted box (in red) shows that the proposed model has problems in predicting the projected size of these small particles. Plot B is the histogram with number of problematic orientations. Small size particles have most of the problematic orientations. (Color figure online)

In order to investigate the reasons that the model does not have a satisfactory performance for small size particles, we have carried out new experiments. During these experiments, we have found that the main problem in the proposed model is to distinguish particles with very different sizes but similar diffraction patterns.

We have also identified that this generalization problem happens when plotting the number of orientations for each particle in the dataset. The results have shown that the particles which have the largest number of problematic orientations are smaller, as shown in the histogram of Fig. 4 (plot B). The reason for this could be that smaller particles interact less with incident light than do larger ones, and that light scattered by small particles is more widely spread out. Ultimately, this means that there is less information recorded in the angular region covered by these investigations, which could explain the difficulty in recovering size information from smaller particles.

5   Final Discussion

The results presented in this paper have shown that the proposed NN model is capable of predicting the size of ice crystal particles with a good correlation between the predicted size and projected size using Pearson's coefficient with 98 % of correlation, as shown in Fig. 4. However, the results have also shown that some particle sizes, mainly the small particles, are more difficult to predict when compared with larger ones. These results were also found by other authors, as discussed in [20]. It is well known that NNs should be able to get small errors like this work presented with normalized mean squared error around 0.007. But with small particles, in this case in particular, the error increase substantially and for the purpose of particle size prediction inside the climatology field, it is important investigate why this is happen and test another techniques and computational processes to solve this kind of problem in particular. One point which we have investigated in this work is that particles with different sizes could have very similar diffraction patterns. Another investigated point was the number of orientations that are difficult for the network model to predict the particle size (results shown in Fig. 4B). We have found that most of the problematic orientations are found in the small particles. The reason for this could be that light scattered by small particles is more widely spread out than for larger particles and therefore 2DLS show less variation with particle orientation and aspect ratio.

To further analyse the problem related to the small particles prediction, we initiate tests with other machine learning approaches for prediction and classification problems such as Radial Basis Function (RBF), Support Vector Machine (SVM) [17], Incremental Gaussian Mixture Network (IGMN) [15], and deep learning process [4], which can help the model to have a better prediction.

References

1. Climate change 2013: The physical science basis. Contribution of Working Group I to the Fifth Assessment Report of the Intergovernmental Panel on Climate Change (2013)

2. Baran, A.J.: A review of the light scattering properties of cirrus. J. Quant. Spectrosc. Radiat. Transfer **110**(14–16), 1239–1260 (2009)
3. Beaudoin, N., Beauchemin, S.: An accurate discrete fourier transform for image processing. Object recognition supported by user interaction for service robots (2002)
4. Bengio, Y.: Learning deep architectures for AI. FNT Mach. Learn. **2**(1), 1–127 (2009)
5. El-Bakry, H.M., Mastorakis, N.: New fast normalized neural networks for pattern detection. Image Vis. Comput. **25**(11), 1767–1784 (2007)
6. Foresee, F.D., Hagan, M.T.: Gauss-newton approximation to bayesian learning. In: International Conference on Neural Networks, vol. 3, pp. 1930–1935 (1997)
7. Griffiths, D.: Introduction to Electrodynamics. Prentice Hall, Upper Saddle River (1999)
8. Gugliotta, L.M., Stegmayer, G.S., Clementi, L.A., Gonzalez, V.D.G., Minari, R.J., Leiza, J.R., Vega, J.R.: A neural network model for estimating the particle size distribution of dilute latex from multiangle dynamic light scattering measurements. Part. Part. Syst. Charact. **26**(1–2), 41–52 (2009)
9. Hesse, E., Call, D.M., Ulanowski, Z., Stopford, C., Kaye, P.: Application of RTDF to particles with curved surfaces. J. Quant. Spectrosc. Radiat. Transfer **110**(14–16), 1599–1603 (2009)
10. Kaye, P., Hirst, E., Wang-Thomas, Z.: Neural-network-based spatial light-scattering instrument for hazardous airborne fiber detection. Appl. Opt. **36**(24), 6149 (1997)
11. Kaye, P.H., Hirst, E., Greenaway, R.S., Ulanowski, Z., Hesse, E., DeMott, P.J., Saunders, C., Connolly, P.: Classifying atmospheric ice crystals by spatial light scattering. Opt. Lett. **33**(13), 1545–1547 (2008)
12. Lawson, R., Korolev, A., Cober, S., Huang, T., Strapp, J., Isaac, G.: Improved measurements of the drop size distribution of a freezing drizzle event. Atmos. Res. **47–48**, 181–191 (1998)
13. MacKay, D.J.: Bayesian interpolation. Neural Comput. **4**, 415–447 (1991)
14. Mie, G.: Beiträge zur optik trüber medien, speziell kolloidaler metallösungen. Annalen der Physik **330**(3), 377–445 (1908)
15. Pinto, R.C., Engel, P.M.: A fast incremental gaussian mixture model. PLOS ONE **10**(10), e0139931 (2015)
16. Riefler, N., Wriedt, T.: Intercomparison of inversion algorithms for particle-sizing using mie scattering. Part. Part. Syst. Charact. **25**(3), 216–230 (2008)
17. Sharma, A., Kumar, R., Varadwaj, P.K., Ahmad, A., Ashraf, G.M.: A comparative study of support vector machine, artificial neural network and bayesian classifier for mutagenicity prediction. Interdisc. Sci. Comput. Life Sci. **3**(3), 232–239 (2011)
18. Song, F., Guo, Z., Mei, D.: Feature selection using principal component analysis. In: 2010 International Conference on System Science, Engineering Design and Manufacturing Informatization (2010)
19. Stopford, C.: Ice crystal classification using two dimensional light scattering patterns. Ph.D. thesis, University of Hertfordshire, Hatfield, UK (2010)
20. Ulanowski, Z., Wang, Z., Kaye, P.H., Ludlow, I.K.: Application of neural networks to the inverse light scattering problem for spheres. Appl. Opt. **37**(18), 4027–4033 (1998)

25 Years of CNNs: Can We Compare to Human Abstraction Capabilities?

Sebastian Stabinger[(✉)], Antonio Rodríguez-Sánchez, and Justus Piater

University of Innsbruck, Technikerstrasse 21a, 6020 Innsbruck, Austria
{sebastian.stabinger,antonio.rodriguez-sanchez,justus.piater}@uibk.ac.at
http://iis.uibk.ac.at

Abstract. We try to determine the progress made by convolutional neural networks over the past 25 years in classifying images into abstract classes. For this purpose we compare the performance of LeNet to that of GoogLeNet at classifying randomly generated images which are differentiated by an abstract property (e.g., one class contains two objects of the same size, the other class two objects of different sizes). Our results show that there is still work to do in order to solve vision problems humans are able to solve without much difficulty.

Keywords: Convolutional neural networks · Abstract classes · Abstract reasoning

1 Introduction

Deep learning methods have gained interest from the machine learning and computer vision research communities over the past several years because these methods provide exceptional performance for a vast majority of classification tasks. An important example of deep learning methods are Convolutional Neural Networks (CNNs) — first introduced in 1989 by LeCun *et al.* [1] — which have become popular for object classification. CNNs were more widely used after the deep CNN from Krizhevsky *et al.* [2] outperformed state-of-the-art methods by a wide margin in the "ImageNet Large Scale Visual Recognition Competition" of 2012.

Convolutional neural networks consist of multiple layers of nodes, also called neurons. One important layer type is the convolutional layer, from which the networks obtain their name. In a convolutional layer, the responses of the nodes depend on the convolution of a region of the input image with a kernel. Additional layers introduce non-linearities, rectification, pooling, etc. The goal of training a CNN lies in optimizing the network weights (including the kernels used for convolution) using image-label pairs to best reconstruct the correct label, given an image. During testing, the network is confronted with novel images and expected to generate the correct label. The network is trained by gradient descent which is calculated by backpropagation of labeling errors. The general idea of CNNs is to automatically learn the features needed to distinguish classes

© Springer International Publishing Switzerland 2016
A.E.P. Villa et al. (Eds.): ICANN 2016, Part II, LNCS 9887, pp. 380–387, 2016.
DOI: 10.1007/978-3-319-44781-0_45

and generate increasingly abstract features as the information is transferred to higher layers.

Since CNNs are very popular at the moment and are being perceived — in parts of the computer vision community — as achieving human-like performance, we wanted to test their applicability on visual tasks slightly outside the mainstream which are still trivially solved by humans.

2 Materials and Methods

2.1 The Dataset

We use the framework presented by Fleuret *et al.* [3] to generate our dataset consisting of 23 different problems which are briefly summarized as follows: Each problem consists of two classes of images. Images of the first class exhibit some abstract property which is not present in images of the second class and vice versa. Figure 1 shows examples of the two classes for problem one. Both classes contain two random objects. In the first class the objects are different, while in the second they are identical. The goal is to assign the correct class to previously unseen images. These problems are reminiscent of the Bongard problems presented by Bongard [4] and further popularized by Hofstadter [5].

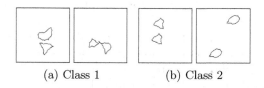

(a) Class 1   (b) Class 2

Fig. 1. Example images for Problem 1

For each class of each problem we generate 20000 training images. We also generate an additional 10000 images per class and problem as a testing set. The size of the generated images varies depending on the used CNN. We chose images of 64 × 64 pixels for LeNet, and 224 × 224 pixels for GoogLeNet.

2.2 Learning Framework

For training the CNNs, we used Caffe by Jia *et al.* [6]. More specifically, we used the implementations of LeNet and GoogLeNet provided with Caffe. Only slight adaptations were made to some hyperparameters. See the appendix for concrete values. In addition, we used ADAM by Kingma & Ba [7] as the solver method instead of stochastic gradient descent and changed the last fully connected layer to only contain two neurons representing our two classes.

3   Experimental Evaluation

Since we want to know how much progress has been made between the first CNNs and a state-of-the-art model, we compare the performance of LeNet by LeCun *et al.* [1] from 1989 to GoogLeNet by Szegedy *et al.* [8] from 2014. We chose GoogLeNet as the modern CNN since it is a very popular architecture and it performed best in a number of categories in ILSVRC14. LeNet was chosen since it is the oldest widely known CNN.

We train one instance of LeNet and GoogLeNet for each problem using 20000 training images per class. The trained networks are then evaluated on a testing set containing 10000 previously unseen images per class for the same problem. The reported accuracy of the network is the proportion of correctly classified images to the number of all tested images. For three problems (3, 11, 13) from Fleuret *et al.* [3] we could not generate images of the correct size. Since we do not think it will influence the overall conclusion, we excluded those problems from our evaluation.

4   Results

Table 1 gives an overview of the achieved accuracy of both tested network architectures, the method presented by Fleuret *et al.* [3], and human test subjects. In addition, the table gives a short description of the properties which are used to differentiate the two classes.

At first glance, CNNs do not seem to have made much progress over the last 25 years with the types of problems we tested, and even compare very unfavorably to the boosting method presented by Fleuret *et al.* [3]. The average accuracy of GoogLeNet even decreased slightly compared to LeNet.

Upon closer inspection, there seem to be two groups of problems: Ones which require the comparison of shapes and ones that do not. If we only consider problems which do not, the two CNNs perform very well. LeNet has an average accuracy of 0.95 and GoogLeNet achieves practically perfect accuracy. Both also compare very favorably to the method presented by Fleuret *et al.* [3] which achieves a mean accuracy of 0.86 on this subset of problems. We will discuss those two subsets of problems in the following sections in more detail.

4.1   Problems Not Involving Comparisons

Problems 2, 4, 9, 10, 12, 14, 18, and 23 can be differentiated by the relative positioning or grouping of the shapes. The shapes themselves are not relevant to the classification except for problems 9 and 12, where the size of some of the shapes play a roll in the classification. Apparently, those problems can be solved by detecting local and global features alone. Hence CNNs work well on those problems.

Table 1. Accuracy comparison of presented methods. The two groupings consist of problems which either need shape comparison to be solved or not. Accuracy of LeNet and GoogLeNet are experimentally determined in this paper. Fleuret are results from the best performing system proposed by Fleuret *et al.* [3] (Boosting with feature group 3). The human results are estimated accuracies of participants also tested by Fleuret *et al.* [3] and reinterpreted for this paper.

Problem	LeNet	GoogLeNet	Fleuret	Human	Difference between classes
1	0.57	0.50	0.98	0.98	Compare
5	0.54	0.50	0.87	0.90	Compare & grouping
6	0.76	0.86	0.76	0.70	Compare & grouping
7	0.53	0.50	0.76	0.90	Compare & grouping
8	0.94	0.91	0.90	1.00	Compare & relative position
15	0.52	0.50	1.00	0.95	Compare
16	0.98	0.50	1.00	0.78	Compare
17	0.75	0.95	0.67	0.78	Compare & relative position
19	0.51	0.50	0.61	0.98	Compare
20	0.55	0.50	0.70	0.98	Compare
21	0.51	0.51	0.50	0.83	Compare
22	0.59	0.50	0.97	1.00	Compare
2	1.00	1.00	0.98	1.00	Relative position
4	0.98	1.00	0.93	1.00	Relative position
9	0.93	1.00	0.68	0.93	Size & relative position
10	0.99	1.00	0.94	0.98	Relative position
12	0.97	1.00	0.84	0.95	Size & relative position
14	0.90	1.00	0.73	0.98	Alignment
18	0.99	0.99	0.99	0.93	Grouping
23	0.87	1.00	0.75	1.00	Relative position
Average	0.77	0.76	0.83	0.93	

4.2 Problems Involving Comparisons

Problems 1, 5, 6, 7, 8, 15, 17, 19, 20, 21, and 22 involve comparing shapes in one way or another. To solve these problems, an agent has to be able to decide whether two shapes are similar or not at one stage of the classification process; e.g., in problem 1 (Fig. 1) the two classes only differ by whether the two presented shapes are identical or not. Except for problems 6, 8, 16, and 17, LeNet as well as GoogLeNet do not achieve accuracies significantly above chance.

Problems 6, 8, and 17 seem to be solvable by the tested CNNs although they in theory also require the comparison of shapes. *Problem 6* (Fig. 2) presents two pairs of identical shapes and the two classes are separated by whether the distances between each pair is the same or not. *Problem 8* (Fig. 3) presents two

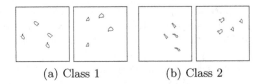

(a) Class 1   (b) Class 2

Fig. 2. Example images for Problem 6

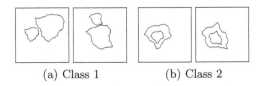

(a) Class 1   (b) Class 2

Fig. 3. Example images for Problem 8

shapes of differing size. One class always contains a small shape inside a bigger version of the same shape. The other class either has a smaller shape inside a different, bigger shape or two identical shapes which are not nested. *Problem 17* (Fig. 4) presents four shapes, of which three are identical. The two classes are separated by whether the distance between the identical shapes are all the same or not.

In theory, an agent has to be able to compare shapes to solve problems 6, 8, and 17; otherwise the additional information, like relative position, does not matter. We had the suspicion that the generation process for these problems imparts some unwanted pattern to the images which the CNNs can use to separate the classes thus avoiding the need to compare shapes. If this is the case, we can expect the same accuracy even if images of both classes contain identical shapes. Theoretically this should mean that those modified problems are not solvable. Training and testing the CNNs with those modified problems gives us similar results (Table 2) to the original problems, which indicates that the CNNs are exploiting some unintended pattern in the data and comparing the shapes does not contribute to the classification.

Problem 16 (Fig. 5) requires the agent to decide whether shapes on the right side are identical copies of the shapes on the left, or whether they are vertically mirrored. Surprisingly, LeNet solves this problem almost perfectly, with an

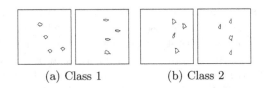

(a) Class 1   (b) Class 2

Fig. 4. Example images for Problem 17

Table 2. Results for problems 6, 8, and 17 when all images only contain identical shapes.

Problem	LeNet	GoogLeNet	Difference between classes
6	0.75	0.85	Compare and grouping
8	0.95	0.90	Compare and relative position
17	0.77	0.93	Compare and relative position

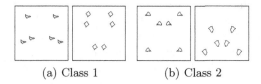

(a) Class 1   (b) Class 2

Fig. 5. Example images for Problem 16

accuracy of 0.98, while GoogLeNet cannot solve it at all, with an accuracy of 0.5. We suspected this to be an artifact and that generating the images with a relatively small size of 64×64 pixels for LeNet adds some unwanted pattern to the images which the network can exploit. Since GoogLeNet uses images with a size of 224×224 pixels it would not profit from this. To test this hypothesis, we trained LeNet using images with a size of 128×128 pixels, and, as expected, the accuracy dropped to 0.5.

4.3 Human Performance

Fleuret *et al.* [3] presented experiments to determine the performance of humans on the same dataset we use for our experiments. Each participant was tested on all problems. For each of the problems, an example which is randomly chosen from one of the two classes is presented and the participant has to indicate whether it is from class one or two. After choosing a class, the correct answer is revealed and the next example is shown. All previously seen images are kept on the screen with their correct class. What is recorded in the experiment is the number of examples the person has to see until he or she consistently chooses the correct class. It is also recorded if a test subject can not solve a problem at all.

Unfortunately, the mode of testing is sufficiently different from the way machine learning solutions are evaluated that a direct quantitative comparison is difficult. To get some accuracy values we can compare other methods to we define accuracy of humans as follows. We assume a person which was able to solve a problem to have an accuracy of 1.0 and one which was not of 0.5. We can then calculate an expected accuracy of the whole group of test subjects with

$$a = \frac{p_a + \frac{p_n}{2}}{n} \tag{1}$$

where a is the accuracy, p_a is the number of participants who were able to solve this problem, p_n being the number of participants who were not able to solve the problem and n being the number of all participants. The accuracies reported in Table 1 were calculated from the original data reported by Fleuret *et al.* [3] using Eq. 1.

5   Discussion

Looking at the results of our experiments one can come to very different conclusions. Simply looking at the overall performance looks very disappointing. The over 25 year old LeNet is better than the current GoogLeNet, although only marginally. A closer inspection reveals that there is a problem class which neither of the CNNs is capable of solving at all; namely problems which require the comparison of shapes. We showed that the few problems in this class which the CNNs can learn are actually learned because of some unexpected side effects of image generation. We conclude that CNNs have an inherent problem when it comes to comparative features. It should be noted that neither humans nor the boosting method employed by [3] show this big performance gap between the two subsets. The mean accuracy of the boosting method is 0.81 for problems with shape comparison versus 0.86 for problems without. The human test subjects show a mean accuracy of 0.90 and 0.97 for the two subsets respectively.

If we accept that CNNs are generally not capable of solving problems containing shape comparison, the results look a lot better. Not only do both networks perform very well on the other problems, but GoogLeNet achieves, for all intents and purposes, perfect accuracy. It even outperforms the human test subjects. Obviously, the CNNs need a much larger training set to achieve those accuracies. Where human subjects usually need below 20 images and often only require 2 images to correctly learn the class and achieve perfect accuracy, GoogLeNet generally needs about 4000 images to achieve an accuracy ≥ 0.99 (problem 2: 400 images, problem 4: 4000, 9: 4000, 10: 4000, 12: 40000, 14: 40000, 18: 4000, 23: 4000). Of course, humans have a lot of prior knowledge, so the results are hard to compare. An interesting difference between machine learning algorithms and humans is the fact that an algorithm can have an accuracy of e.g. 80 % on these abstract problems, but human subjects generally either understand what separates the two classes and achieve an accuracy of 100 %, or do not understand it and have an accuracy close to pure chance. This suggests that the underlying principles of classification are probably very different.

Further, our experiments show how difficult it can be to evaluate CNNs on abstract problems. One has to be extremely careful to guarantee that the network is actually solving the problem one wants to test and does not use some additional superficial pattern. In our case it would have appeared as if CNNs can in fact compare shapes because they were able to solve problems 6, 8, and 17 quite successfully. Only close scrutiny revealed that the networks were in fact exploiting patterns which were a side effect of the dataset generation.

We think it will be useful to further investigate the performance of deep learning methods on more abstract problems than are usually considered since it can reveal a lot about the shortcomings and strengths of specific methods and might inform further advances of the methods. We further hypothesize that if the shape comparison problem of CNNs can be solved they would presumably also perform better on more common tasks.

Acknowledgments. We want to thank nVidia for supporting this research with their "NVIDIA Hardware Grant". We also want to thank Franois Fleuret for providing us with the dataset used in this paper.

Appendix

- Parameters used for LeNet: iterations = 25000, base learning rate = 0.001, weight decay = 0.00005, solver = ADAM, $\beta_1 = 0.9$, $\beta_1 = 0.999$, $\epsilon = 10^{-8}$.
- Parameters used for GoogLeNet: iterations = 25000, base learning rate = 0.001, average loss = 100, weight decay = 0.002, solver = ADAM, $\beta_1 = 0.9$, $\beta_1 = 0.999$, $\epsilon = 10^{-8}$.

References

1. LeCun, Y., Boser, B., Denker, J.S., Henderson, D., Howard, R.E., Hubbard, W., Jackel, L.D.: Backpropagation applied to handwritten zip code recognition. Neural Comput. **1**(4), 541–551 (1989)
2. Krizhevsky, A., Sutskever, I., Hinton, G.E.: Imagenet classification with deep convolutional neural networks. In: Advances in Neural Information Processing Systems, pp. 1097–1105 (2012)
3. Fleuret, F., Li, T., Dubout, C., Wampler, E.K., Yantis, S., Geman, D.: Comparing machines and humans on a visual categorization test. Proc. Nat. Acad. Sci. **108**(43), 17621–17625 (2011)
4. Bongard, M.M.: Pattern Recognition. Spartan Books (1970)
5. Hofstadter, D.R.: Gödel, escher, bach: an eternal golden braid (1979)
6. Jia, Y., Shelhamer, E., Donahue, J., Karayev, S., Long, J., Girshick, R., Guadarrama, S., Darrell, T.: Caffe: Convolutional architecture for fast feature embedding (2014) arXiv preprint: arXiv:1408.5093
7. Kingma, D., Ba, J.: Adam: A method for stochastic optimization (2014). arXiv preprint: arXiv:1412.6980
8. Szegedy, C., Liu, W., Jia, Y., Sermanet, P., Reed, S., Anguelov, D., Erhan, D., Vanhoucke, V., Rabinovich, A.: Going deeper with convolutions (2014). arXiv preprint: arXiv:1409.4842

A Combination Method for Reducing Dimensionality in Large Datasets

Daniel Araújo[✉], Jhoseph Jesus, Adrião Dória Neto, and Allan Martins

Universidade Federal do Rio Grande do Norte, Natal, RN, Brazil
daniel@imd.ufrn.br, jhoseph.kelvin@gmail.com, adriao@dca.ufrn.br,
allan@dee.ufrn.br

Abstract. The amount of data in the world is growing exponentially due to the elevated number of applications in the most various contexts. This data needs to be analyzed in order to extract valuable underlying information from them. Machine learning is a useful tool to do this task, but the high complexity of the data forces to use other methods to reduce such complexity. Dimensionality reduction (feature selection) is one of the most used method to achieve this goal. As usual, many algorithms were proposed to reduce dimension of data, each one with its own advantages and drawbacks. The variety of algorithms usually makes researches to test several methods and choose the best solution. Based on that, this paper proposes a combination of feature selection algorithms in order to create a single and more stable solution. We tested this approach using real datasets and machine learning algorithms. Results showed we can use the combined solution with little or none loss in classification accuracy. So, our method can be used as a stable choice when there is few knowledge about the problem.

Keywords: Dimension reduction · Mutual information · Combination · Classification · Feature selection

1   Introduction

In the past years, the number of applications that generate data has grown in a tremendous way. Most of these applications are based on sensors that read some event and store a value corresponding to a state of what is been measured. This data need to be analyzed and machine learning is one of the most suitable option to discover underlying relations inside the data and extract valuable information.

However, real world scenarios tend to have high complexity and, in order to build more realistic models, a high number of variables (features) needs to be considered. Problems in the field of Bioinformatics, for instance, need to have thousands of gene expressions measures to describe just a few dozens of patients [3]. Image processing, like segmentation or pattern discovery, uses pixels as features of images, resulting in huge number of features to describe one single image [2].

A.E.P. Villa et al. (Eds.): ICANN 2016, Part II, LNCS 9887, pp. 388–397, 2016.
DOI: 10.1007/978-3-319-44781-0_46

With such amount of features, most machine learning algorithms suffers in find good solutions due to the curse of dimensionality and gathering more samples of the problem is often not possible. So, one viable solution is to reduce the number of features [6]. In this context, several methods to reduce the number of features that describes a problem were proposed. The general idea of reducing the dimensionality (number of features) of a dataset is to find a set of features that can represent the entire data in a way that the problem can be treated. This set can be composed of just a subset of the original data (feature selection) or can be a transformation of the initial features (feature extraction).

Most algorithms uses distinct heuristics to find a solution and each one has its own domains, advantages and drawbacks. For example, Principal Component Analysis (PCA) [7], one of the most popular technique, is based on linear projection of the largest eigenvectors of the correlation matrix to the original features, which means that it is very sensitive to the magnitude of values and, by consequence, to simple rotations and/or translation in data [6].

Recently, Information Theory descriptors, initially used to measure the efficiency of data transmission [10], are been used to quantify information in a variety of real world problems. The Dimension Reduction (DR) problem is one of them. For instance, [1] started a series of Mutual Information based techniques to select the most relevant features of a dataset regarding to the given classes of the problem. Methods based on Mutual Information have the advantage over traditional linear methods because it can actually measure the dependency of two variables, including non-linear correlation, which are very common in real world situations.

Based on that, this paper aims to define a simple way to combine features selected by several algorithms in order to join different perspectives in one more robust and stable single solution.

2   Proposed Combination Method

Instead of using one algorithm that could not be suitable for a particular data or several methods for reducing dimensionality of a dataset and choose the best one, it is possible to combine the outputs of multiple algorithms in one single solution. Some papers, like [11], successfully used this kind of approach.

This paper proposes a much simpler way of combining features selected by several methods. The general idea is to use a voting scheme to select the more relevant features according to the algorithms. The voting is based on the frequency that features appears in the outputs of each algorithm weighted by their relevance to that algorithm.

Let $X_{n \times m}$ be a dataset and $S_{n \times k}$ be the reduced dataset. In order to have a combined solution, we have to run t algorithms, where $t > 1$, and each algorithm selects from X a subset of features $\mathbf{f} = \{f_1, f_2, ..., f_l\}$, where $l \leq n$. Based on this, one can reduce a dataset using the features indicated by the algorithms, considering that the general results from feature selection algorithms are, in general, just the indexes of the features to be selected.

In order to perform the voting using the selected features found by the t algorithms, we need to compute the relevance of each feature to those algorithms. The relevance, in this context, is inversely proportional to its position in the selected feature vector. So, the relevance of the f_i feature to the j-th algorithm can defined as:

$$r_{ij} = \frac{1}{p} \tag{1}$$

where p is the position of the feature in the solution found by the j algorithm. For example, if a feature is the first choice of an algorithm, its relevance is equals to one. If it appears in the fourth position, then its relevance is 0.25. Using this strategy we consider not only the presence of a feature in the DR output, but its importance to the whole process.

Then, For each one of the l features selected by the algorithms, we have to compute its voting factor:

$$v_i = \sum_{j=1}^{t} r_{ij} \tag{2}$$

where r_{ij} is the relevance of the feature f_i to the j-th algorithm. In other words, in order to compute the total relevance of one feature with respect to all algorithms, we have to sum the individuals relevance of the feature to each algorithm. After this step, we finally select the k (reduced number) features with highest v values to have the more relevant features for all t algorithms and build the reduced dataset S.

3   Materials and Methods

In this section we show all the algorithms used for reducing dimensionality and to perform the classification task as well as the datasets used in the experiments.

3.1   Dimension Reduction Algorithms

As we have mentioned in Sect. 1, Mutual Information based algorithms have a high potential to perform feature selection specially when compared to more traditional methods. So, in order to test our combination approach, we followed the approach used in [9] and selected nine Mutual Information based algorithms for our analysis, including the author's algorithm Spectral relaxation global Conditional Mutual Information (SPEC_CMI). As they turned public their Matlab®toolbox implementations[1], we have used it to run our experiments. The following algorithms were used: Maximum relevance (maxRel), Minimum redundancy maximum relevance (MRMR), Minimum redundancy (minRed), Quadratic programming feature selection (QPFS), Mutual information quotient (MIQ), Maximum relevance minimum total redundancy (MRMTR), Spectral relaxation global Conditional

---

[1] avaliable at http://www.mathworks.com/matlabcentral/fileexchange/47129-informa tion-theoretic-feature-selection.

Mutual Information (SPEC_CMI), Conditional mutual information minimization (CMIM), Conditional Infomax Feature Extraction (CIFE)

All the algorithms were set with default parameters. More details about the mentioned algorithms can be found in [9]. The combination algorithm was used to ensemble all the solutions to produce a single output. We used the simple algorithm showed in Sect. 2.

We chose three values to the number of features to be selected (mentioned as target dimension): 2, 3 and $\sqrt{n}$, where n is the number of samples of the dataset. The first two values refers to dimensions people uses to plot the data aiming the visualization. The $\sqrt{n}$ is a larger value used to collect more information about the data and to reduce the effects of the curse of dimensionality, ensuring that there is always more samples than features.

3.2   Classification Algorithms

We used two classification algorithms: Support Vector Machines (SVM) [6], and k Nearest Neighbor (k-NN) [6]. They were chosen because they are widely used in machine learning community and each one has a distinct approach to find the best solution. With this, we tried to cover distinct heuristics to classification and to avoid a possible bias to a specific approach.

To run the algorithms, we used the Weka software [5] with all parameters set to default. We are aware that a fine tuning of parameters would probably lead to better results, but the number of variables handled in the experiments was already too high. As the main purpose of this paper is to analyse the feature selection algorithms and the combination method, giving the same settings to all should be enough.

In order to achieve more robust results, we used a 10-fold-cross-validation approach for each classification algorithm. We also ran each algorithm 10 times and computed the average results and the respective standard deviation.

3.3   Databases

In our experiments, we used five datasets from distinct natures. With the exception of Lung Cancer [3], all datasets where collected at the UCI machine learning repository [8]. Those datasets were also used in some papers with similar purposes.

The datasets were selected aiming to cover different ranges of number of samples and features. The main characteristics of each dataset are presented in Table 1, where n is the number of samples, C is the number of classes and d is the number of features (dimensionality).

LSVT dataset [13] is composed of 126 sustained vowel /a/ phonations features with 310 dysphonia measures aiming to do a characterization of speech signals of Parkinson Disease subjects. Lung Cancer is a gene expression dataset used in [3] to study malignant pleural mesothelioma (MPM) and adenocarcinoma (ADCA) of the lung. There are 181 tissue samples (31 MPM and 150 ADCA), each sample

Table 1. Datasets descripton.

Dataset	n	C	Dist. of Classes	d
LSVT	126	2	42,84	310
Lung Cancer	181	2	31,150	12533
Semeion Digits	1593	10	161,158,162,159,159,161,159,161,158,155	256
Connectionist Bench	208	2	97,111	60
Ionosphere	351	2	126,225	32

is described by 12533 genes. The Semeion Digits dataset [8] contains 1593 0-9 handwritten digits of 80 persons, each one represented by 256 Boolean values (corresponding to a binarized 16×16 image). Connectionist Bench dataset [4] was created from 208 patterns of sonar signals that bounced off metal cylinders (111 samples) or rocks (97 samples) in several distinct angles. The Ionosphere dataset [12] is composed of 351 radar returns from the ionosphere divided as either suitable for further analysis or not.

4   Results and Discussion

In this section we will show the results from our experiments. As mentioned in Sect. 3, we ran two different classification algorithms, Support Vector Machine (SVM) and k Nearest Neighbors (k-NN), for five datasets (LSVT, Lung Cancer, Semeion Digits, Connectionist Bench and Ionosphere). We also ran the same classification algorithms to the reduced datasets (with 2 features, 3 features and $\sqrt{n}$ features) using the nine distinct algorithm described in Sect. 3.1 and the combination method.

Table 2 shows the results for the original datasets. As expected, there is no better solution in terms of best classification algorithm for all datasets. If we analyse the absolute mean value, we can see that SVM has better performance than k-NN in the first three dataset and the k-NN is better in the last two.

Table 2. Results for the original datasets.

Dataset	SVM		k-NN	
	Mean	Stdev	Mean	Stdev
LSVT	84.530	9.139	75.880	12.486
Lung Cancer	99.390	1,739	95.190	4.141
Semeion Digits	93.630	1.910	91.490	1.951
Connectionist Bench	76.600	8.267	86.170	8.450
Ionosphere	84.020	5.350	87.160	4.961

Tables 3, 4, 5, 6 and 7 presents the results for the five datasets after the feature selection. In each table, it is showed the two classification algorithms in the first row (CA), the three possible target dimensions (TD) in the second row and the next nine rows refers to the DR algorithms used in the experiments (DRA) while the tenth row presents the combination method proposed in this paper.

If we compare the performance of classification algorithms after feature selection, we can see that, in general, the larger is the target dimension the better is the result. This behavior is valid for the DR algorithms and it is reflected in the proposed combination method. However, except for Semeion Digits dataset, the difference is less than it could be expected. This could happened due to the nature of datasets which concentrate the most valuable information in two or

Table 3. Results after feature selection for dataset LSVT.

CA	SVM						k-NN					
TD	2D		3D		$\sqrt{n}$		2D		3D		$\sqrt{n}$	
DRA	Mean	Std	Mean	Std	Mean	Std	Mean	Std	Mean	Std	Mean	Std
maxRel	65.9	3.6	65.9	3.6	83.4	8.0	72.8	10.0	71.6	11.4	83.5	9.9
MRMR	65.8	3.9	65.8	3.9	83.2	10.0	71.4	12.0	75.8	11.3	72.6	12.3
mimRed	65.8	3.9	65.8	3.9	83.2	10.0	71.4	12.0	75.8	11.3	72.6	12.3
QPFS	76.9	8.6	80.7	9.1	83.8	8.3	76.5	10.7	80.2	11.1	82.3	9.4
MIQ	77.2	8.5	84.2	8.1	86.3	8.8	82.1	9.2	81.2	10.4	81.8	9.6
MRMTR	77.2	8.5	77.5	8.6	85.0	8.8	82.1	9.2	84.8	9.2	86.5	8.4
SPEC_CMI	78.5	9.2	80.2	8.3	81.0	8.4	78.5	8.8	79.6	9.0	80.9	9.2
CMIM	77.2	8.5	77.5	8.7	86.4	8.1	82.1	9.2	74.9	11.1	80.7	9.8
CIFE	77.2	8.5	76.4	9.0	78.7	9.1	82.1	9.2	78.6	10.3	78.5	10.6
Combination	77.2	8.5	77.5	8.6	83.8	8.5	82.1	9.2	84.8	9.2	84.6	8.7

Table 4. Results after feature selection for dataset Lung Cancer.

CA	SVM						k-NN					
TD	2D		3D		$\sqrt{n}$		2D		3D		$\sqrt{n}$	
DRA	Mean	Std	Mean	Std	Mean	Std	Mean	Std	Mean	Std	Mean	Std
maxRel	93.5	4.3	95.1	3.8	99.5	1.7	97.8	3.0	98.5	2.6	99.5	1.7
MRMR	95.0	4.0	97.2	3.7	99.0	2.2	97.4	3.4	98.3	2.6	99.0	2.1
mimRed	92.9	4.6	93.2	4.5	93.4	4.5	96.8	3.9	95.6	4.3	93.0	4.9
QPFS	95.6	4.1	96.1	4.1	99.5	1.7	97.6	3.7	98.3	3.3	99.5	1.7
MIQ	93.0	4.5	92.6	4.4	98.9	2.2	97.2	3.7	95.9	4.0	99.5	1.7
MRMTR	94.0	4.4	96.2	3.8	99.5	1.7	98.1	2.7	98.9	2.2	99.5	1.7
SPEC_CMI	95.0	4.2	97.7	3.3	98.9	2.2	98.4	3.0	99.2	2.1	98.9	2.2
CMIM	94.0	4.4	96.7	3.4	99.5	1.7	98.1	2.7	99.0	2.2	99.5	1.7
CIFE	94.0	4.4	94.9	4.1	96.0	4.1	98.1	2.7	98.4	2.6	95.3	4.3
Combination	97.3	3.7	97.7	3.3	99.5	1.7	98.6	2.6	99.2	2.1	99.5	1.7

Table 5. Results after feature selection for dataset Semeion Digits.

CA	SVM						k-NN					
TD	2D		3D		$\sqrt{n}$		2D		3D		$\sqrt{n}$	
DRA	Mean	Std	Mean	Std	Mean	Std	Mean	Std	Mean	Std	Mean	Std
maxRel	23.7	1.7	27.4	2.3	72.6	3.4	23.9	1.7	28.2	2.3	71.2	3.6
MRMR	34.3	1.5	40.8	2.7	75.6	3.2	34.3	1.5	40.6	2.7	75.0	3.3
mimRed	23.2	2.2	26.1	2.2	79.7	3.1	23.1	2.2	26.1	2.6	78.0	2.9
QPFS	23.2	1.5	27.6	2.3	83.8	2.6	23.2	1.4	27.6	2.3	78.6	2.6
MIQ	23.2	2.2	26.1	2.2	84.8	2.7	23.1	2.2	26.1	2.6	84.3	2.7
MRMTR	34.3	1.5	40.8	2.7	73.4	3.2	34.3	1.5	40.6	2.7	71.9	3.6
SPEC_CMI	23.7	1.7	27.4	2.3	73.3	3.6	23.9	1.7	28.2	2.3	71.5	3.3
CMIM	34.3	1.5	40.8	2.7	85.3	2.8	34.3	1.5	40.6	2.7	84.7	2.7
CIFE	34.3	1.5	40.8	2.7	71.0	3.3	34.3	1.5	40.6	2.7	70.3	3.0
Combination	34.3	1.5	37.4	2.8	79.1	3.2	34.3	1.5	37.5	2.4	77.7	2.8

Table 6. Results after feature selection for dataset Connectionist Bench.

CA	SVM						k-NN					
TD	2D		3D		$\sqrt{n}$		2D		3D		$\sqrt{n}$	
DRA	Mean	Std	Mean	Std	Mean	Std	Mean	Std	Mean	Std	Mean	Std
maxRel	75.3	9.2	75.2	10.3	77.9	8.9	68.6	9.0	68.2	9.4	81.5	8.1
MRMR	70.8	10.5	71.8	10.3	79.4	8.0	67.1	9.8	69.9	10.6	80.5	9.0
mimRed	72.4	10.0	73.4	9.6	76.2	9.2	60.5	10.4	59.1	9.4	73.7	9.5
QPFS	75.3	9.2	74.1	9.0	77.7	8.5	68.6	9.0	71.1	8.7	83.3	7.7
MIQ	72.4	10.0	71.9	9.1	78.9	8.2	60.5	10.4	65.7	9.6	79.7	9.0
MRMTR	73.2	10.6	75.0	9.7	77.2	8.4	68.6	9.5	75.4	8.8	86.9	7.3
SPEC_CMI	75.3	9.2	75.2	10.3	77.4	8.4	68.6	9.0	68.2	9.4	80.1	7.8
CMIM	73.2	10.6	70.3	10.7	79.2	8.5	68.6	9.5	69.7	9.5	88.7	6.9
CIFE	73.2	10.6	72.1	9.4	78.5	8.9	68.6	9.5	73.7	9.8	84.1	7.8
Combination	75.3	9.2	75.0	9.7	78.8	7.6	68.6	9.0	75.4	8.8	80.9	8.4

three features (and the DR algorithms were efficient to capture that) or to the number of features we used as target dimension. From Table 8 we can see that this is not directly related to the proportion of original number of features. For intance, the Ionhosphere dataset using $\sqrt{n}$ features has more than 50 % of the original features and the increase in performance is only small. On the other hand Semeion Digits is the dataset with most significant difference between the smallest and largest target dimension (2D and 40D) and the difference of performance in classification is very noticeable.

In terms of impact on classification algorithms, in the context of this paper, we can see that there is no better technique to perform feature selection for all algorithms, datasets or target dimensions. If one specific DR algorithm performs better for one dataset, it is likely that it will not be the best to another.

Table 7. Results after feature selection for dataset Ionosphere.

CA	SVM						k-NN					
TD	2D		3D		$\sqrt{n}$		2D		3D		$\sqrt{n}$	
DRA	Mean	Std	Mean	Std	Mean	Std	Mean	Std	Mean	Std	Mean	Std
maxRel	79.4	6.0	79.0	6.2	85.7	5.1	82.3	5.6	87.2	6.0	86.6	5.4
MRMR	80.8	5.6	82.0	5.4	82.4	5.7	85.0	5.8	86.9	4.6	89.3	4.9
mimRed	82.2	5.5	82.1	5.5	83.6	5.5	86.9	5.0	87.4	4.9	87.5	5.0
QPFS	79.4	6.0	82.0	5.3	84.4	5.3	82.3	5.6	86.0	5.1	88.4	4.7
MIQ	80.8	5.6	82.0	5.4	85.0	5.5	85.0	5.8	86.9	4.6	87.4	5.4
MRMTR	81.8	5.7	80.4	5.8	83.9	5.6	85.5	5.8	88.5	5.5	87.2	5.0
SPEC_CMI	73.7	5.2	74.1	5.1	83.9	5.6	85.1	5.5	89.0	5.6	85.9	5.1
CMIM	81.8	5.7	82.5	5.5	84.5	5.7	85.5	5.8	86.6	5.6	88.0	4.9
CIFE	81.8	5.7	80.4	5.8	83.9	5.7	85.5	5.8	88.5	5.5	86.8	5.2
Combination	81.8	5.7	79.0	6.2	83.6	5.5	85.5	5.8	87.2	6.0	86.4	4.9

Table 8. Proportion of target dimension compared to original number of features.

Dataset	n	d	2D	3D	$\sqrt{n}D$
LSVT	126	310	0.65 %	0.97 %	3.62 %
Lung Cancer	181	12533	0.02 %	0.02 %	0.11 %
Semeion	1593	256	0.78 %	1.17 %	15.59 %
Connectionist Bench	208	60	3.33 %	5.00 %	24.04 %
Ionosphere	351	32	6.25 %	9.38 %	58.55 %

So, choosing a feature selection algorithm should be a hard task if a researcher does not have enough information about the whole problem domain or the data.

On the other hand, the proposed combination algorithm delivers more robust solutions to all datasets. If we see the results, we can notice that, for most cases, the combination method performance is in the three highest values. That is, if a researcher looks for more stable solution instead of a fine result, the combination method could be a safer choice.

In Table 9 we show a ranked performance for the combination method in all datasets. We also calculated the mean (with standard deviation), median and mode for this ranking analysis. As we can see (last row and column), for most datasets, our combination approach is delivering similar results to the best DR algorithms, specially if the target dimension is set to very small values, like 2D. Another important result is related to the Lung Cancer dataset, where the combination approach achieved the best result for all cases. This could be very useful for the gene expression community that deals with a extremely number of features and a significant portion of professionals does not have computational skills to investigate the best DR algorithm.

Table 9. Ranking performance of Combination Method.

CA	SVM			k-NN							
TD	2D	3D	sqrt	2D	3D	sqrt					
	Rank	Rank	Rank	Rank	Rank	Rank	Mean	Std	Median	Mode	
LSVT	2	4	5	1	1	2	2.5	1.6	2.0	2.0	4/6
Lung Cancer	1	1	1	1	1	1	1.0	0.0	1.0	1.0	6/6
Semeion Digits	1	5	5	1	5	5	3.7	2.1	5.0	5.0	2/6
Connectionist Bench	1	3	4	1	1	6	2.7	2.1	2.0	1.0	4/6
Ionosphere	2	8	9	2	5	9	5.8	3.3	6.5	2.0	2/6
	5/5	2/5	1/5	5/5	3/5	2/5					

5 Conclusions

In this paper we presented a experimental approach to compare several Mutual Information based feature selection algorithms. We also presented a method to combine the outputs of feature selection algorithms to produce a single solution. Results showed that there is no better algorithm to select features when we deal with distinct datasets, algorithms or target dimensions. Results also showed that selecting larger target dimensions usually leads to better results in classification tasks.

The combination approach has achieved robust performance in terms of delivering solutions similar to the best feature selection algorithms. For most datasets, our approach had similar performance to the best three algorithms. Although the combination approach provided stable results, running several algorithms to combine solutions represents an extra computational cost, at least in the first time, when the voting scheme is created (after that computing cost is actually cheap). In the end, the combination approach could be a safer choice when a researcher does not have enough information about the data or about feature selection algorithms.

For future works, we intend to use approaches similar to the most robust ensemble methods to create a better combination algorithm. Another important investigation is the diversity of methods used to select features. In this paper, we used only Mutual Information based algorithms, which gives us a low level of diversity. Using a set of DR algorithms with distinct heuristics could lead to better results.

Acknowledgments. This paper was partially supported by CNPq Universal Grant no 480997/2013-6 and UFRN scholarship program.

References

1. Battiti, R.: Using mutual information for selecting features in supervised neural net learning. IEEE Trans. Neural Netw. **5**, 537–550 (1994)
2. Gonzalez, R.C., Woods, R.E.: Digital Image Processing, 3rd edn. Prentice-Hall Inc., Upper Saddle River (2006)

3. Gordon, G.J., Jensen, R.V., Hsiao, L.L., Gullans, S.R., Blumenstock, J.E., Ramaswamy, S., Richards, W.G., Sugarbaker, D.J., Bueno, R.: Translation of microarray data into clinically relevant cancer diagnostic tests using gene expression ratios in lung cancer and mesothelioma. Cancer Res. **62**, 4963–4967 (2002)
4. Gorman, P.R., Sejnowski, T.J.: Analysis of hidden units in a layered network trained to classify sonar targets. Neural Netw. **1**(1), 75–89 (1988)
5. Hall, M., Frank, E., Holmes, G., Pfahringer, B., Reutemann, P., Witten, I.H.: The weka data mining software: an update. SIGKDD Explor. Newsl. **11**(1), 10–18 (2009)
6. Jain, A.K., Dubes, R.C.: Algorithms for Clustering Data. Prentice-Hall Inc., Upper Saddle River (1988)
7. Jolliffe, I.: Principal Component Analysis. Springer Series in Statistics. Springer, New York (2002)
8. Lichman, M.: UCI Machine Learning Repository (2013)
9. Nguyen, X.V., Chan, J., Romano, S., Bailey, J.: Effective global approaches for mutual information based feature selection. In: Proceedings of the 20th ACM SIGKDD International Conference on Knowledge Discovery and Data Mining, KDD 2014, pp. 512–521. ACM, New York (2014)
10. Shannon, C.E.: A mathematical theory of communication. Bell Syst. Tech. J. **27**, 379–423 (1948)
11. Shen, Q., Diao, R., Su, P.: Feature selection ensemble. In Voronkov, A. (ed.) Turing-100. The Alan Turing Centenary. EPiC Series in Computing, vol. 10, pp. 289–306. EasyChair (2012)
12. Sigillito, V.G., Wing, S.P., Hutton, L.V., Baker, K.B.: Classification of radar returns from the ionosphere using neural networks. Johns Hopkins APL Tech. Dig. **10**, 262–266 (1989)
13. Tsanas, A., Little, M.A., Fox, C., Ramig, L.O.: Objective automatic assessment of rehabilitative speech treatment in parkinson's disease. IEEE Trans. Neural Syst. Rehabil. Eng. **22**(1), 181–190 (2014)

Two-Class with Oversampling Versus One-Class Classification for Microarray Datasets

Beatriz Pérez-Sánchez$^{(\boxtimes)}$, Oscar Fontenla-Romero,
and Noelia Sánchez-Maroño

Department of Computer Science, Faculty of Informatics, University of A Coruña,
Campus de Elviña s/n, 15071 A Coruña, Spain
{bperezs,ofontenla,nsanchez}@udc.es

Abstract. Microarray datasets are a challenge for classical computational techniques because of the large dimensionality of their feature space front to a reduced number of samples, besides they usually present unbalanced classes. Thanks to this unbalanced situation, in a previous research, the superiority of one-class classification for handling microarray datasets was proved. This paper presents a new study that tries to improve the behavior of the traditional techniques, specifically Support Vector Machines, by considering oversampling techniques. The experimental results achieved demonstrate that despite inclusion of these methods the performance of classical classifiers still remains below one-class approach.

1 Introduction

Microarray datasets are commonly used for cancer diagnosis distinguishing two approaches: binary and multiple classes. Firstly, the binary approach tries to differentiate patients with cancer from healthy persons and, on the other hand, the multiple classes approach tries to distinguish different variants of the same type of cancer. This paper is focused on the first approach and, since unhealthy patients are less common, these datasets are usually unbalanced. The intrinsic characteristics of microarray datasets – large dimensionality of the feature space (usually several thousand of genes) and small number of samples available (often less than a hundred) – restrict the application of classical learning machine techniques. To date, two-class classification methods are mainly used, being Support Vector Machines (SVMs) among the most notable classifiers for this task. However, in the context of microarray classification some authors proposed to use a one-class classification (OCC) for classifying microarrays due to its ability to deal with unbalanced and noisy data [1]. In OCC only instances from one of the classes are available or considered. They are known as *target* objects whereas the other are the *outlier* ones. Using OCC, models are constructed from objects belonging to only one class distribution and are robust when handling inherent data difficulties. In a previous work [2], we compared the behavior of two-class (specifically, SVM) versus OCC over microarray datasets whilst analyzing the effect of feature selection (FS). This experimental study proved the superiority

© Springer International Publishing Switzerland 2016
A.E.P. Villa et al. (Eds.): ICANN 2016, Part II, LNCS 9887, pp. 398–405, 2016.
DOI: 10.1007/978-3-319-44781-0_47

of the one-class approach achieving both a fine performance and a good trade-off between evaluation measures. However, a criticism to this work is that the success of SVM was limited because of the imbalanced problem that could be partially solved by sampling techniques [3]. Therefore, in this paper we present the results of a study where some of these sampling techniques are applied to improve the SVM behavior for classifying the microarray datasets denoting that, even so, OCC is superior.

This paper is structured as follows. In Sect. 2 a brief introduction about sampling techniques is given and the oversampling methods used in this experimental study are introduced. In Sect. 3 the conditions for experimental study are established. In Sect. 4 we compare the behavior of one-class classifiers and two-class methods with sampling techniques for classifying different benchmark microarray datasets, also the results are discussed. Finally, Sect. 5 is devoted to conclusions.

2   Sampling Techniques

From literature, we can find different methods to face imbalanced datasets. Among them, the most commonly employed ones are: oversampling minority class, undersampling majority class, ensemble methods, cost-sensitive learning or asymmetric classification [4]. Undersampling and oversampling are the simplest approaches. The former consists on randomly select a portion of instances from majority class whereas the latter randomly duplicates samples belonging to the minority class. Taking into account that microarray datasets enclose a reduced number of samples, undersampling does not seem a viable alternative as, it may lead to a loss of useful information. Thus, for this preliminary experimental study we focus on oversampling techniques to overcome the limitations associated to unbalanced sets. Specifically we have selected three widely applied algorithms to deal with imbalance distributions:

1. *Resampling* consists on random duplication of instances belonging to the minority class [5].
2. *Synthetic Minority Oversampling Technique* (SMOTE) algorithm generates synthetic or artificial samples by means of the nearest neighbor rule, interpolating new instances instead of duplicating them as in the case of the resampling method [6]. SMOTE does not consider the distribution of minority classes and latent noises in dataset when it generates synthetic examples. To overcome this limitation, Modified SMOTE (MSMOTE) algorithm [7] categorizes the instances belonging to the minority class into three groups according to the label of their nearest neighbors: noise (all of them belong to other classes), safe (when all neighbors belong to the minority class) otherwise, it is considered as border. Then MSMOTE chooses one of the k-nearest neighbor for safe samples and the nearest neighbor for border ones whereas in the case of noise samples the algorithm does nothing.

3. *Critical SMOTE* (CSMOTE) algorithm [4] is an improved version of the MSMOTE method that follows the idea of generating artificial samples employing only a subset of the minority class. In a first phase this algorithm extracts from the class two subsets of patterns: edge and border samples. This categorization is based on the method proposed in [8]. Edge samples define the boundary of the class and they are enough to represent the original dataset when all classes in the dataset are separated. Border samples are carefully picked in the overlapping region between adjacent classes so as to obtain the best decision surface possible. After this categorization, new patters are generated following MSMOTE. For each border sample CSMOTE randomly chooses one of the nearest neighbors whilst for each edge samples the nearest neighbor is picked.

3   Experimental Setup

The aim is to check the suitability of oversampling techniques to improve two-class classification on microarray datasets. These results are compared to those reached by one-class approach. Two of the most up-to-date classifiers are selected: SVMs for two-class classification [9] and Support Vector Data Description (SVDD) [10] as one-class classifier. It is worth mentioning that the OCC is addressed by using both minority and majority class as target concept and oversampling is not applied in any case because it is unnecessary. Next, we establish certain considerations which have been taken into account in the experimental study.

- In order to obtain statistically significant results, 30 simulations were run with the cross-validation technique to tune the parameters of each method, specifically the width parameter in the radial basis function kernel for SVDD and the kernel function (linear, radial basis and polynomial) for SVM.
- For the implementation of classifiers two different toolboxs for Matlab was used. The data description toolbox, DDtools library [11], for SVDD and the Statistics and Machine Learning toolbox for SVM.
- Similarly to our previous study [2], we have applied feature selection methods as a preprocessing step with the aim of discarding irrelevant features/genes while retaining the relevant ones. All these techniques are available in the well-known Weka tool [12], except for mRMR filter, whose implementation is available for *Matlab*.
- To evaluate the goodness of the selected set of genes in terms of accuracy of the classifier it is necessary to have an independent test set with data which have not been seen by neither the feature selection method nor the classifier. The selected data sets come originally distributed into training and test sets, so the training set was employed to perform the feature selection process and posterior classification while the test set was used to evaluate the appropriateness of the selection and the posterior classification.
- For the sake of fair comparison, only the training set is oversampled when using SVM, whereas the test dataset remains the same.

– Finally, a statistical study was conducted to determine whether the results are statistically different. First at all, the normality conditions of each distribution are checked by means of Kolmogorow Smirnov test. As in any case, normal conditions are verified then the non parametric Kruskal-Wallis test was applied.

Datasets, FS methods and evaluation measures employed for experimental study are briefly introduced below.

Datasets characteristics. Breast and Prostate datasets are widely applied due to two main properties: (1) come originally separated in training and test and (2) present more imbalance in the test set. Both datasets are available for download at [13,14]. Table 1 provides for train and test sets the number of attributes (# Atts.), examples (# Ex.) and the percentage of examples for majority (% Ma) and minority (% Min) classes. The last column corresponds to imbalance ratio (IR), a value of 1 indicates balance whereas a large value denotes a high imbalance. As can be seen in Table 1 both datasets present more imbalance in the test set specially in the case of Prostate dataset. *Dataset shift* problem [15] occurs when the joint distribution of inputs and outputs is different between training and test stages, hampering the classification process that may lead to poor performance results. This problem may be caused by different situations, such in Prostate dataset where the test set was extracted from a different experiment. Accordingly, this dataset raises a challenge for machine learning methods. For this reason some classifiers, whose features are selected according to the training set, assign all samples to the majority class.

Table 1. Description of the train and test binary datasets.

Dataset	# Atts.	Train				Test			
		# Ex	% Min	% Maj	IR	# Ex	% Min	% Maj	IR
Breast	24.481	78	43,59	56,41	1,29	19	36,84	63,16	1,71
Prostate	12.600	102	49,02	50,98	1,04	34	26,47	73,53	2,78

FS methods. Seven classical FS methods widely used in this field are selected: Correlation-based FS (CFS) [16], Fast Correlation-Based Filter (FCBF) [17], INTERACT algorithm [18], Information Gain (IG) [19], ReliefF [20], minimum Redundancy Maximum Relevance (mRMR) [21] and Support Vector Machine based on Recursive Feature Elimination (SVM-RFE) [22]. All of them, with the exception of the last one, correspond to the filter methods that rely on the general characteristics of the training data to select feature independent of any predictor. The three first CFS, FCBF and INTERACT return a subset of features. Thus, from the original 24,481 attributes of Breast dataset 130, 99 and 102 are selected respectively. While in the case of Prostate, 89, 77 and 73 are chosen from the 12,600 initial features. An ordered ranking of the features is obtained by the four last (IG, ReliefF, mRMR and SVM-RFE). For simplicity we introduce the performance keeping the top 10 and top 50 features. Finally, SVM-RFE is the most famous embedded method to specifically deal with gene selection for cancer classification. This method iteratively trains a SVM classifier with the current set of features and basing on its internal parameters the least important are removing.

Evaluation measures. For a binary classification problem, accuracy indicates how well the system predicts both categories. However accuracy is inappropriate when the prior class probabilities are very different since it does not consider misclassification costs and therefore, it is sensitive to class skews and it is biased in favor of the majority class. Then, alternative measures should be considered. The true positive rate (recall or sensitivity) is the percentage of correctly classified positive instances (e.g. the rate of cancer patients who are correctly identified as having cancer). The true negative rate (specificity) is the percentage of correctly classified negative examples (e.g. the rate of healthy patients who are correctly classify as not having cancer). The ideal predictor should be 100 % specific and 100 % sensitive. Regarding OCC, it should be mentioned that sensitivity and specificity measures are always calculated considering as negative the healthy samples and as positive the cancer ones.

4   Experimental Results

In this section the results achieved in the Breast and Prostate datasets are introduced. Table 2 shows the results obtained by SVM and SVDD classifiers, specifically Accuracy (Acc), Sensitivity (Se) and Specificity (Sp) are used to assess their performance. In the case of SVDD we introduce the results reached by using both classes (majority and minority) as the target concept in training process. Regarding SVM we include the results obtained by using resampling, SMOTE and CSMOTE as oversampling techniques. Each column represents one of the three performance measures while rows indicate the FS methods, the last row provides the results when no FS method is applied. To facilitate the analysis of the results, best values (statistically speaking) of each performance measures for each dataset are marked in bold.

Firstly, we focus on SVM with oversampling methods. At first glance, it seems that the behavior of the SVM is similar independently of the oversampling technique. An ideal predictor should be 100 % sensitive and 100 % specific but Table 2 shows that SVM tends towards one of the classes. Comparing to the original results (without oversampling) introduced in [2], it can be seen that the inclusion of oversampling methods lead to particular performance improvements without an outstanding enhancement in the trade-off between Se and Sp.

Regarding OCC, SVDD overcomes the results obtained by SVM showing important differences. In order to know if such differences are significant a statistical study was conducted. As it was previously commented, for each performance measure, FS method and dataset the best values are marked in bold face.

Table 2. Results for SVM (with oversampling techniques) and SVDD classifiers on Breast and Prostate datasets.

	FS method	Acc					Se					Sp				
		SVM[a]	SVM[b]	SVM[c]	SVDD Min	SVDD Maj	SVM[a]	SVM[b]	SVM[c]	SVDD Min	SVDD Maj	SVM[a]	SVM[b]	SVM[c]	SVDD Min	SVDD Maj
Breast	CFS	0.52	0.58	0.57	0.62	0.65	0.32	0.25	0.24	0.49	0.56	0.64	0.77	0.76	0.83	0.80
	FCBF	0.63	0.58	0.58	0.70	0.70	0.09	0.16	0.14	0.72	0.73	0.94	0.83	0.83	0.67	0.65
	INT	0.58	0.57	0.59	0.71	0.71	0.13	0.16	0.17	0.74	0.74	0.84	0.80	0.83	0.66	0.67
	IG-10	0.54	0.54	0.53	0.67	0.67	0.39	0.31	0.32	0.63	0.63	0.63	0.67	0.65	0.74	0.74
	IG-50	0.52	0.54	0.56	0.74	0.73	0.35	0.26	0.26	0.80	0.79	0.62	0.71	0.73	0.64	0.62
	ReliefF-10	0.48	0.49	0.51	0.79	0.79	0.52	0.47	0.49	0.75	0.75	0.46	0.51	0.52	0.86	0.86
	ReliefF-50	0.49	0.51	0.55	0.74	0.73	0.54	0.37	0.39	0.69	0.67	0.46	0.59	0.64	0.84	0.83
	SVM-RFE-10	0.50	0.52	0.52	0.89	0.89	0.57	0.49	0.51	0.90	0.89	0.47	0.53	0.53	0.87	0.87
	SVM-RFE-50	0.42	0.48	0.49	0.84	0.84	0.57	0.55	0.53	0.84	0.84	0.33	0.44	0.46	0.84	0.83
	mRMR-10	0.49	0.49	0.49	0.76	0.74	0.46	0.47	0.46	0.78	0.76	0.50	0.51	0.51	0.73	0.72
	mRMR-50	0.53	0.56	0.56	0.76	0.76	0.41	0.25	0.26	0.81	0.80	0.61	0.74	0.73	0.68	0.68
	no FS	0.47	0.55	0.56	0.63	0.62	0.57	0.27	0.28	0.46	0.47	0.42	0.72	0.72	0.91	0.92
Prostate	CFS	0.59	0.59	0.58	0.97	0.97	0.29	0.29	0.26	0.97	0.97	0.69	0.69	0.69	1.00	1.00
	FCBF	0.62	0.67	0.63	0.92	0.92	0.16	0.26	0.18	0.90	0.89	0.78	0.82	0.79	0.99	0.99
	INT	0.65	0.66	0.66	0.96	0.96	0.13	0.14	0.14	0.94	0.94	0.84	0.85	0.85	1.00	1.00
	IG-10	0.60	0.57	0.59	0.94	0.95	0.32	0.28	0.27	0.92	0.94	0.71	0.68	0.69	0.98	0.97
	IG-50	0.64	0.65	0.65	0.99	0.99	0.19	0.20	0.16	0.99	0.98	0.80	0.81	0.83	1.00	0.99
	ReliefF-10	0.61	0.61	0.59	0.93	0.93	0.25	0.25	0.23	0.91	0.91	0.74	0.74	0.73	1.00	1.00
	ReliefF-50	0.68	0.68	0.69	0.96	0.96	0.13	0.12	0.14	0.94	0.94	0.88	0.88	0.89	0.99	0.99
	SVM-RFE-10	0.64	0.62	0.61	0.87	0.87	0.27	0.24	0.23	0.86	0.86	0.77	0.76	0.75	0.91	0.90
	SVM-RFE-50	0.63	0.62	0.64	0.96	0.96	0.22	0.20	0.23	0.95	0.95	0.78	0.77	0.79	1.00	1.00
	mRMR-10	0.62	0.63	0.62	0.94	0.96	0.18	0.21	0.21	0.93	0.95	0.77	0.78	0.77	0.97	0.99
	mRMR-50	0.63	0.62	0.62	0.94	0.94	0.25	0.23	0.23	0.91	0.91	0.77	0.76	0.76	1.00	1.00
	no FS	0.61	0.59	0.62	0.93	0.88	0.13	0.26	0.28	0.91	0.84	0.78	0.71	0.75	1.00	1.00

[a] SVM corresponds to SVM with resampling technique.
[b] SVM corresponds to SVM with SMOTE technique.
[c] SVM corresponds to SVM with CSMOTE technique.

Only for Breast set, SVM obtains (in some cases) a higher value in the Sp measure, however in all cases SVDD achieves the best value of Acc and Se and also balanced values for Se and Sp. Finally two issues should be pointed out. On one hand, FS not only may lead to better performance results, specially in the case of Breast (for instance, see the differences between SVM-RFE-10 and the last row for this dataset) but also to significantly reduce the computational and time requirements. On the other hand, as it was previously remarked SVDD allows using minority or majority class as the target class in the training process and both exhibit a good performance. Even when the provided results are not statistically distinct, SVDD can remain the best results depending on the specific application. Since the aim of this work was to compare SVM and SVDD, there is no statistically study to compare the application or not of FS methods. However, considering FS or not, and either the minority or majority class, SVDD achieves the best performance results.

5   Conclusions

Imbalanced datasets are very common in real world for example for the diagnosis of a disease as cancer, becoming an important challenge for machine learning field. In this context, the classifiers tend towards the majority class achieving poor performance results. In a previous work we compare the results obtained by one and two class classifiers, SVDD and SVM respectively, on two microarray datasets. SVDD significantly overcame the SVM achieving a fine global performance. In this paper we include oversampling techniques to avoid the effects associated with imbalanced distributions and improve the performance of the SVM classifiers. Despite our initial idea the experimental results show that such modification does not enhance significantly the behavior of the SVM that still remains below SVDD. It is possible that this fact is caused by the peculiarities of the selected datasets. For this reason, we have in mind to extend this study including more imbalanced datasets (with higher IR) and more complex oversampling techniques to ensure the supremacy shown by the OCC in this preliminary study.

Acknowledgments. This work has been supported in part by the Secretaría de Estado de Investigación of the Spanish Government (Grant TIN2015-65069-C2-1-R), and by the Xunta de Galicia (Grant GRC2014/035) with the European Union FEDER funds.

References

1. Krawczyk, B.: Combining one-class support vector machines for microarray classification. In: Federated Conference on Computer Science and Information Systems (FedCSIS 2013), pp. 83–89 (2013)
2. Pérez-Sánchez, B., Fontenla-Romero, O., Sánchez-Maroño, N.: One-class classification for microarray datasets with feature selection. In: Iliadis, L., Jayne, C. (eds.) EANN 2015. CCIS, vol. 517, pp. 325–334. Springer, Heidelberg (2015). doi:10.1007/978-3-319-23983-5_30

3. Akbani, R., Kwek, S.S., Japkowicz, N.: Applying support vector machines to imbalanced datasets. In: Boulicaut, J.-F., Esposito, F., Giannotti, F., Pedreschi, D. (eds.) ECML 2004. LNCS (LNAI), vol. 3201, pp. 39–50. Springer, Heidelberg (2004)
4. Nanni, L., Fantozzi, C., Lazzarini, N.: Coupling different methods for overcoming the class imbalance problem. Neurocomputing **158**, 48–61 (2015)
5. Wilson, D.L.: Asymptotic properties of nearest neighbor rules using edited data. IEEE Trans. Syst. Man, Cybern. B, Cybern. **SMC–2**(3), 408–421 (1972)
6. Chawla, N.V., Bowyer, K.W., Hall, L.O., Kegelmeyer, W.P.: SMOTE: Synthetic Minority Oversampling Technique. J. Artif. Intell. Res. **16**, 321–357 (2002)
7. Hu, S., Liang, Y., Ma, L., He, Y.: MSMOTE: improving classification performance when training data is imbalanced. In: 2nd International Workshop on Computer Science and Engineering (IWCSE 2009), vol. 2, pp. 13–17 (2009)
8. Li, Y., Maguire, L.: Selecting critical patterns based on local geometrical and statistical information. IEEE Trans. Pattern Anal. Mach. Intell **33**(6), 1189–1201 (2011)
9. Vapnik, V.: Statistical Learning Theory. Wiley, New York (1998)
10. Tax, D.M.J., Duin, R.P.W.: Support vector data description. Mach. Learn. **54**, 45–66 (2004)
11. Tax, D.M.J.: DDtools, the data description toolbox for matlab, Delft University of Technology (2005)
12. Hall, M., Frank, E., Holmes, G., Pfahringer, B., Reutemann, P., Witten, I.H.: The WEKA data mining software: an update. ACM SIGKDD Explor. Newsl. **11**(1), 10–18 (2009)
13. Kent Ridge Bio-Medical Dataset. http://datam.i2r.a-star.edu.sg/datasets/krbd. Accessed Feb 2016
14. Microarray Cancers, Plymouth University. http://www.tech.plym.ac.uk/spmc/links/bioinformatics/microarray/microarray_cancers.html. Accessed Feb 2016
15. Moreno-Torres, J.G., Raeder, T., Alaiz-Rodríguez, R., Chawla, N.V., Herrera, F.: A unifying view on dataset shift in classification. Pattern Recogn. **45**(1), 521–530 (2012)
16. Hall, M.: Correlation-Based Feature Selection for Machine Learning. Ph.D. Thesis (1999)
17. Yu, L., Liu, H.: Feature selection for high-dimensional data: a fast correlation-based filter solution. In: 20th International Conference on Machine Learning (ICML 2003), pp. 856–863 (2003)
18. Zhao, Z., Liu, H.: Searching for interacting features. In: 20th International Joint Conference on Artifical Intelligence (IJCAI 2007), pp. 1156–1161 (2007)
19. Hall, M., Smith, L.: Practical feature subset selection for machine learning. In: 21st Australasian Computer Science Conference (ACSC 1998), pp. 181–191 (1998)
20. Kononenko, I.: Estimating attributes: analysis and extensions of RELIEF. In: Bergadano, F., De Raedt, L. (eds.) ECML-94. LNCS, vol. 784, pp. 171–182. Springer, Heidelberg (1994)
21. Peng, H., Long, F., Ding, C.: Feature selection based on mutual information: criteria of max-dependency, max-relevance, and min-redundancy. IEEE Trans. Pattern Anal. Mach. Intell **27**, 1226–1238 (2005)
22. Guyon, I., Weston, J., Barnhill, S., Vapnik, V., Cristianini, N.: Gene selection for cancer classification using support vector machines. Mach. Learn. **46**(1–3), 389–422 (2002)

Polar Sine Based Siamese Neural Network for Gesture Recognition

Samuel Berlemont[1(✉)], Grégoire Lefebvre[1], Stefan Duffner[2], and Christophe Garcia[2]

[1] Orange Labs, R&D, Grenoble, France
{samuel.berlemont,gregoire.lefebvre}@orange.com
[2] LIRIS, UMR 5205 CNRS, INSA-Lyon, 69621 Villeurbanne, France
{stefan.duffner,christophe.garcia}@liris.cnrs.fr

Abstract. Our work focuses on metric learning between gesture sample signatures using Siamese Neural Networks (SNN), which aims at modeling semantic relations between classes to extract discriminative features. Our contribution is the notion of polar sine which enables a redefinition of the angular problem. Our final proposal improves inertial gesture classification in two challenging test scenarios, with respective average classification rates of 0.934 ± 0.011 and 0.776 ± 0.025.

Keywords: Siamese neural network · Metric learning · Polar sine · Gesture recognition

1 Introduction

As consumer devices become more and more ubiquitous, new interaction solutions are required. In recent years, new sensors called MicroElectroMechanical Systems (MEM) were popularized thanks to their small sizes and low production costs. Two kinds of gestures can be considered for different applications. On the one hand, static gestures correspond to a specific state, described by a unique set of features, with, in the context of Smartphones, a "phone-to-ear" posture for instance. On the other hand, dynamic gestures are more complex, since they are described by a time-series of inertial signals, such as the "picking-up" movement when the user is ready to take a call. Thus, in this study, we explore inertial-based gesture recognition on Smartphones, where gestures holding a semantic value are drawn in the air with the device in hand.

Based on accelerometer and gyrometer data, three main approaches exist. The earliest methods suggest to model the temporal structure of a gesture class, with Hidden Markov Models (HMM) [10]; while another approach consists in matching gestures with reference instances, using a non-linear distance measure generally based on Dynamic Time Warping (DTW) [1]. Finally, features can be extracted from gesture signals in order to train specific classifiers, such as Support Vector Machines (SVM) [11].

© Springer International Publishing Switzerland 2016
A.E.P. Villa et al. (Eds.): ICANN 2016, Part II, LNCS 9887, pp. 406–414, 2016.
DOI: 10.1007/978-3-319-44781-0_48

Our work focuses thus on metric learning between gesture sample signatures using Siamese Neural Networks (SNN) [3], which aims at modeling semantic relations between classes to extract discriminative features, applied to the Single Feed Forward Neural Network (SFNN). Contrary to some popular versions of this algorithm, we opt for a strategy that does not require additional class-separating-parameter fine tuning during training. After a preprocessing step where the data is filtered and normalized spatially and temporally, the SNN is trained from sets of samples, composed of similar and dissimilar examples, to compute a higher-level representation of the gesture, where features are collinear for similar gestures, and orthogonal for dissimilar ones. As opposed to the classical input set selection strategies, using similar or dissimilar pairs, or {reference, similar, dissimilar} triplets, we propose to include samples from every available dissimilar classes, resulting in a better structuring of the output space. Moreover, the notion of polar sine enables a redefinition of the angular problem by maximizing a normalized volume induced by the outputs of the reference and dissimilar samples, which results in a non-linear discriminant analysis similar to independant component analysis.

This paper is organized as follows. Section 2 presents related works on SNN. In Sect. 3, we explain our contributions with a new SNN objective function. Then, Sect. 4 describes our results for gesture recognition. Finally, our conclusions and perspectives are drawn.

2   Related Studies on SNN

2.1   Training Set Selection

A SNN is trained to project multiple samples coherently. Two identical neural networks with shared weights W take simultaneously two input samples $\mathbf{X_1}$ and $\mathbf{X_2}$ to compute the error relative to a cosine-based objective function, thanks to the respective outputs $\mathbf{O_{X_1}}$ and $\mathbf{O_{X_2}}$ (see Fig. 1a). The resulting application of the network depends on the kind of knowledge about similarities one expects. In problems such as face or signature verification [2–4,8], the similarity between samples depends on their origin, and the network allows to determine the genuineness of a test sample with a binary classification. In cases involving the learning of a mapping that is robust to specific transformations [6], similar samples differ by slight rotations or translations. However, similarities can be more abstract concepts, such as same documents in different languages [13]. The most common representation consists in a binary relation based on pairs: given two samples $\mathbf{X_1}$ and $\mathbf{X_2}$, the $(\mathbf{X_1}, \mathbf{X_2})$ pair similarity is determined by a tag, which takes two different values whether the relation is similar or dissimilar. However, knowledge about semantic similarities can take more complex forms. Lefebvre *et al.* [8] expand the information about expected neighborhoods with triplets $(\mathbf{R}, \mathbf{P}, \mathbf{N})$, composed of a reference sample $\mathbf{R}$ for each known relation, with $\mathbf{P}$ a *positive* sample forming a genuine pair with $\mathbf{R}$, while $\mathbf{N}$, the *negative* sample, is the member of an impostor pair. Similarities are then represented as much as dissimilarities. With these different knowledge representations presenting multiple samples to a set of weight-sharing sub-networks, it is necessary to study new objective functions in order to define how semantic relations will be reflected in the output space.

2.2   Objective Function

The contrastive loss layer objective function aims at computing a similarity metric between the higher-level features extracted from multiple input patterns. Thus, this discriminative distance is trained to get smaller for similar patterns, and higher for dissimilar ones. It takes two forms, respectively bringing together and pushing away features from similar and dissimilar pair of patterns. Given two samples $\mathbf{X_1}$ and $\mathbf{X_2}$, two main similarity measures are used: the cosine similarity, based on the cosine value between these two samples $\cos(\mathbf{X_1}, \mathbf{X_2}) = \frac{\mathbf{X_1}.\mathbf{X_2}}{\|\mathbf{X_1}\|.\|\mathbf{X_2}\|}$; and the Euclidean similarity $d(\mathbf{X_1}, \mathbf{X_2}) = \|\mathbf{O_{X_1}} - \mathbf{O_{X_2}}\|_2$. In this study, we focus on cosine-based objective functions. A cosine objective function aims at learning a non-linear cosine similarity metric, whether it is expressed specifically, in the form of multiple targets, or relatively, by pair scores ranking. The cosine similarity metric is defined as:

$$cos_{sim}(\mathbf{X_1}, \mathbf{X_2}) = 1 - \cos(\mathbf{X_1}, \mathbf{X_2}) \tag{1}$$

Square Error Objective. One approach comes from the original use of the square error objective function for the SFNN. Given a network with weights W and two samples $\mathbf{X_1}$ and $\mathbf{X_2}$, a target $t_{\mathbf{X_1 X_2}}$ is defined for the cosine value between the two respective output vectors $\mathbf{O_{X_1}}$ and $\mathbf{O_{X_2}}$. In [3], Bromley *et al.* set this target to 1 if for a similar pair, and -1 otherwise. Given the similarity label Y and the weights W of the network, the error E_W for any pair defines:

$$E_W(X_1, X_2, Y) = (t_{\mathbf{X_1 X_2}}(Y) - \cos(\mathbf{O_{X_1}}, \mathbf{O_{X_2}}))^2 \tag{2}$$

Triangular Similarity Metric. Zheng *et al.* [14] imply these same targets. Given Y the numerical label for the $(\mathbf{X_1}, \mathbf{X_2})$ pair, acting as the target $t_{\mathbf{O_{X_1} O_{X_2}}}$ and respectively equal to 1 and -1 for similar and dissimilar pairs; the triangular inequality imposes:

$$\|\mathbf{O_{X_1}}\| + \|\mathbf{O_{X_2}}\| - \|\mathbf{C}\| \geq 0, \; with \; \mathbf{C}(\mathbf{X_1}, \mathbf{X_2}, \mathbf{Y}) = \mathbf{O_{X_1}} + Y.\mathbf{O_{X_2}} \tag{3}$$

After adding norm constraints to prevent a degeneration towards a null projection, the final objective function becomes:

$$E_W(X_1, X_2, Y) = \|\mathbf{O_{X_1}}\| + \|\mathbf{O_{X_2}}\| - \|\mathbf{C}(\mathbf{X_1}, \mathbf{X_2}, \mathbf{Y})\| + 0.5(1 - \|\mathbf{X_1}\|)^2$$
$$+ 0.5(1 - \|\mathbf{X_2}\|)^2 = 0.5\|\mathbf{O_{X_1}}\|^2 + 0.5\|\mathbf{O_{X_2}}\|^2 - \|\mathbf{C}(\mathbf{X_1}, \mathbf{X_2}, \mathbf{Y})\| + 1 \tag{4}$$

Deviance Cost Function. Inspired by the common loss functions such as square or exponential losses, Yi *et al.* [12] opt for the binomial deviance. Since their Siamese architecture does not necessarily share weights between sub-networks, let B_1 and B_2 be the respective functions associated to both sub-networks, and $B_1(\mathbf{X_1})$ and $B_2(\mathbf{X_2})$ be the projections of the samples of a pair, we get:

$$E_W(X_1, X_2, Y) = \ln(\exp^{-2Y.cos(B_1(\mathbf{X_1}), B_2(\mathbf{X_2}))} + 1) \qquad (5)$$

Triplet Similarity Objective. Lefebvre *et al.* [8] generalize the Square Error Objective by using simultaneously targets for genuine and impostor pairs. Samples outputs from similar classes are collinear while outputs from different classes tend to be orthogonal, which translates as a target equal to 1 for similar pairs and 0 for dissimilar ones. Let $(\mathbf{R}, \mathbf{P}, \mathbf{N})$ be a triplet, with a reference sample $\mathbf{R}$, a positive sample $\mathbf{P}$ forming a similar pair with $\mathbf{R}$, and a negative sample $\mathbf{N}$, forming a dissimilar pair with $\mathbf{R}$, we get:

$$E_W(\mathbf{R}, \mathbf{P}, \mathbf{N}) = (1 - cos(\mathbf{O_R}, \mathbf{O_P}))^2 + (0 - cos(\mathbf{O_R}, \mathbf{O_N}))^2. \qquad (6)$$

3 Our Contributions - SNN-psine

3.1 Training Set Selection Strategy

Every training set selection strategy for a Siamese network consists in defining a certain number of similar and dissimilar pairs, deemed representative of the global relationships within the data. This generally induces a bias, since it is not possible to ensure a perfect coverage for every relationship. For this reason, we first propose a unified approach for multi-class problems. Let $C = \{C_1, .., C_K\}$ be the set of classes represented in the training data, $\mathbf{O_{R_k}}$ the output vector of the reference sample $\mathbf{R_k}$ from the class C_k presented to the model for update, $\mathbf{O_{P_k}}$ the output of a different sample $\mathbf{P_k}$ from the same class, and $\mathbf{O_{N_l}}$ the output of a sample $\mathbf{N_l}$ from another class C_l. In order to keep symmetric roles for every class and optimize the efficiency of every update, we propose here to minimize an error criterion for training tuples $T_k = \{\mathbf{R_k}, \mathbf{P_k}, \{\mathbf{N_l}, l = 1..K, l \neq k\}\}$ involving one reference sample from the class C_k, one positive sample and one negative sample from every other class. This leads us to the definition of the SNN-cos, relying on the following cost function. The total error estimation for a training set T_k, $E_W(T_k)$, becomes:

$$E_W(T_k) = (1 - cos(\mathbf{O_{R_k}}, \mathbf{O_{P_k}}))^2 + \sum_{l=1, l \neq k}^{K} (0 - cos(O_{R_k}, O_{N_l}))^2. \qquad (7)$$

3.2 Objective Function Reformulation

While the cosine allows for a correlation estimation between two vectors in any Euclidean space of finite dimension, it is sensible to consider another function which would measure dissimilarities, like the sine in 2D. In the following, we propose a reformulation of the objective function based on a higher-dimensional dissimilarity measure, the polar sine. Lerman *et al.* [9] define the *polar sine (PolarSine)* for a set $V = \{v_1, \ldots, v_n\}$ of m-dimensional $(m > n)$ linearly independent vectors, forming the columns of the matrix $\mathbf{A} = \begin{bmatrix} \mathbf{v}_1 \ \mathbf{v}_2 \ \cdots \ \mathbf{v}_n \end{bmatrix}$ and its transpose $A^\top$:

$$PolarSine(\mathbf{v}_1, \ldots, \mathbf{v}_n) = \frac{\sqrt{\det(A^T.A)}}{\prod_{i=1}^{n} \|\mathbf{v_i}\|} \tag{8}$$

As a measure of a regularized hyper-volume, the polar sine acts as another similarity metric, more precisely as a dissimilarity metric. However, in order to prevent numerical instabilities during the training process and make the metric value independent from the size of the set of vectors, we propose a redefinition of the Polar Sine for learning angles. In the following, we call this adaptation the *Polar Sine Metric (psine)*. Given $\mathbf{A_{norm}} = \begin{bmatrix} \frac{\mathbf{v_1}}{\|\mathbf{v_1}\|} \ \frac{\mathbf{v_2}}{\|\mathbf{v_2}\|} \ \cdots \ \frac{\mathbf{v_n}}{\|\mathbf{v_n}\|} \end{bmatrix}$ and $\mathbf{S} = \mathbf{A_{norm}}^\top.\mathbf{A_{norm}}$, i.e. $\mathbf{S}(i,j) = \cos(\mathbf{v_i}, \mathbf{v_j})$, the polar sine metric equals to:

$$psine(\mathbf{A}) = \sqrt[n]{\det(\mathbf{S})}. \tag{9}$$

Thus, optimizing the polar sine metric corresponds to assigning a target equal to 0 to the cosine between every available pair of different vectors drawn in $T_k \setminus \{O_{P_k}\}$. This comprehensive representation actually holds more information than our original objective function which aimed at assigning zero-cosine-values only for pairs between the reference and negative outputs. Furthermore, this approach is easily scalable to any number of classes. With two comparable similarity estimators, whose values are comprised between 0 and 1, it is now possible to redefine the objective function for our training sets T_k (see Fig. 1b):

$$E_W(T_k) = (1 - \cos(\mathbf{O_{R_k}}, \mathbf{O_{P_k}}))^2 + (1 - psine(\mathbf{O_{R_k}}, \mathbf{O_{N_1}}, \ldots, \mathbf{O_{N_K}}))^2. \tag{10}$$

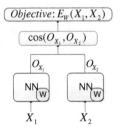

(a) Original SNN architecture.

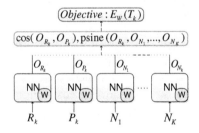

(b) Our SNN proposal.

Fig. 1. Comparison between the original and the proposed architectures. The original SNN processes pair similarity with two weight-sharing NNs and a cosine based objective, while our proposal handles comprehensive class relationships with a combination of cosine and psine metrics.

4 Experiments

4.1 Database

Using the same data and process as [5,7], both proving that neural approaches are suited to the gesture recognition problematic, two datasets were formed, based on the accelerometer and gyrometer data from the Android Samsung Nexus S device, sampled at 40 Hz. The first dataset, named DB1, contains 40 repetitions of 14 different classes performed by a single individual, for a total of 720 records. Conversely, DB2 contains 5 repetitions of these 14 gesture classes performed by 22 individuals, for a total of 1540 records. DB2 corresponds to an open world testing with multiple users. The 14 classes in DB2 encompass gestures with different complexities. They are composed of linear gestures, with horizontal (flick North, South, East, West) and vertical (flick Up, Down) translations; curvilinear gestures (clockwise and counter-clockwise circles, alpha, heart, N and Z letters, a pick gesture towards, and a throw gesture away from the user).

4.2 Protocols

The classification results rely on 4 protocols, named C1 to C4, covering different real application settings: C1, based on DB1, covers the closed-world application with a single user in a context of a personalization paradigm, with 5 randomly selected samples per class for training, and 16 samples for testing; C2, based on DB2, corresponds to a multi-user, closed-world application. Every user is represented in the training data, with 2 samples per class and per user used for training, and the 3 remaining samples for testing; C3, based on DB2, consists in open-world problem, where a comprehensive user representation is not possible: training is performed on every sample from 17 users, while testing is carried out on the samples of the 5 remaining users; C4, based on DB2, is the most challenging scenario, testing the generalization capabilities of each model, with one user used as a training reference and the samples from the 21 remaining users used for tests. Each protocol is repeated 10 times so as to minimize the influence of the training and testing data selection.

The performance of our SNN-psine is compared to the following methods: our SFNN classifies the 270-feature vectors from 45-neuron hidden layer with a hyperbolic tangent activation function, and a 14-neuron "softmax" output layer; our SNN-cos and SNN-psine share the same architecture, and classify with a KNN (K=1) the outputs of a SNN from 270-feature vectors, with 45-neuron hidden layer with a hyperbolic tangent activation function, and a 80-neuron "linear" output.

4.3 Results

Protocol C1: The general performance comparisons between the main models for gesture recognition are presented in Table 1. Every version of the SNN show a comparable result (i.e. 98.8 % for SNN-cos and 98.7 % for SNN-psine). These are the highest scores for neural-based methods, which proves the coherence of the learnt projections. Indeed, both SNN results overcome the SFNN average classification rate of 97.8 %.

Protocol C2: The SNN-cos shows the best accuracy for protocol C2 of 96.9 %, closely followed by SNN-psine with 96.8 %, proving that the SNN performs well even when multiple, different gesture dynamics are involved. Once again, the SFNN obtains a lower score of 94.5 %. A closer study of one confusion matrix for the SNN-psine shows small confusions between "N" and "Up", and "Alpha" and "Heart", which are indeed similar gestures. Moreover, an understandable confusion between the vertical, upwards, gestures "Up" and "Pick" appears. An analysis of the source of these errors shows that all of these samples belong to a unique user. Thus, this phenomenon underlines the fact that some users may have a really specific way of performing gestures, which, combined with the imprecision of the sensors, may result in a great difficulty to manage them with a single, general model not specifically trained for these singletons.

Protocol C3: This protocol amplifies the difficulties encountered with C2. The SNN-psine and SNN-cos take advantage of the bigger training dataset with an accuracy of 93.4 %. Once again, the SFNN performance is lower, with 90.5 %. In that case, the SNN-psine shows a high symmetric confusion between "Pick" and "Up". It also handles badly the gesture "Throw". Indeed, this gesture, which consists in an arc away from the user, brought about fears of actually throwing the device, resulting in the highest disparities between users.

Protocol C4: Finally, this protocol presents the highest challenge for these methods, with a single user data for training. As a consequence, the SNN-psine and SNN-cos overtake the SFNN, with respective accuracies of 77.6 % and 77.5 % against 74.4 %. The flaws identified above are amplified. The "Alpha" and "Clockwise" gestures are still confused. Moreover, the "Throw" gesture still shows the highest variability among users, representing 25 % of the total number of errors, with heavy confusions with the "Tap" and "FlickN" gestures.

Table 1. Recognition rates on our 4 protocols.

	C1	C2	C3	C4
SFNN	0.978 ± 0.010	0.954 ± 0.006	0.905 ± 0.010	0.744 ± 0.040
SNN-cos	$\mathbf{0.988} \pm 0.005$	$\mathbf{0.969} \pm 0.007$	0.934 ± 0.013	0.775 ± 0.032
SNN-psine	0.987 ± 0.011	0.968 ± 0.006	$\mathbf{0.934} \pm 0.011$	$\mathbf{0.776} \pm 0.025$

Table 2. Complexities and times for one update (in ms) on protocol C4.

	Complexity	Number of relationships	Training time for C4 ($N_c = 14$)
cos	$\mathcal{O}(N_c)$	N_c	$2.61779 \pm 1.03648.10^{-1}$
psine	$\mathcal{O}(N_c^{\log_2 7})$	$N_c(N_c - 1)/2 + 1$	$3.21632 \pm 1.79093.10^{-1}$

Consequently, our SNN-psine contribution is a very challenging solution on the 4 protocols, and even better for C3 and C4 protocols. Nevertheless, some limitations are identified, with confusions between gestures where one can be identified as a part of the other. Moreover, the complexity for the SNN-psine error computation, compared to the complexity for the SNN-cos in Table 2[1], implies a trade-off between class relationships which has to be taken into account. However, parallelizable matrix computations allow for a limited repercussion on training times for SNN-psine, with an effective 23 % update time increase for the protocol C4 compared to the SNN-cos.

5 Conclusion and Perspectives

In this study, we first propose an adaptation of the Siamese strategy to a multi-class classification context for a stochastic training. We propose a unified similarity function, the Polar Sine Metric, which offers a comprehensive representation of dissimilarity relationships within the training set. The Polar Sine Metric proposes a matrix approach to describe relationships, and relies on a determinant to compute the final dissimilarity for a set of samples. The complexity evaluation implies $0.5N_c(N_c-1)+1$ relationships in the cost function per update given a reference sample, with N_c the number of classes. Thus, the training set sizes should be taken into account for future research, so as to study the trade-off between accuracy and complexity when the number of classes increases.

References

1. Akl, A., Valaee, S.: Accelerometer-based gesture recognition via dynamic-time warping, affinity propagation, & compressive sensing. In: ICASSP (2010)
2. Berlemont, S., Lefebvre, G., Duffner, S., Garcia, C.: Siamese neural network based similarity metric for inertial gesture classification and rejection. In: AFGR (2015)
3. Bromley, J., Guyon, I., Lecun, Y., Sackinger, E., Shah, R.: Signature verification using a "Siamese" time delay neural network. In: NIPS (1994)
4. Chopra, S., Hadsell, R., LeCun, Y.: Learning a similarity metric discriminatively, with application to face verification. In: CVPR, vol. 1, pp. 539–546. IEEE (2005)
5. Duffner, S., Berlemont, S., Lefebvre, G., Garcia, C.: 3d gesture classification with convolutional neural networks. In: ICASSP, pp. 5432–5436. IEEE (2014)
6. Hadsell, R., Chopra, S., LeCun, Y.: Dimensionality reduction by learning an invariant mapping. In: CVPR (2006)
7. Lefebvre, G., Berlemont, S., Mamalet, F., Garcia, C.: BLSTM-RNN based 3D gesture classification. In: Mladenov, V., Koprinkova-Hristova, P., Palm, G., Villa, A.E.P., Appollini, B., Kasabov, N. (eds.) ICANN 2013. LNCS, vol. 8131, pp. 381–388. Springer, Heidelberg (2013)
8. Lefebvre, G., Garcia, C.: Learning a bag of features based nonlinear metric for facial similarity. In: AVSS, pp. 238–243. IEEE (2013)

---

[1] Computations are performed on an Intel© Core™ i7-4800MQ processor at 2.70 GHz.

9. Lerman, G., Whitehouse, J.T.: On d-dimensional d-semimetrics and simplex-type inequalities for high-dimensional sine functions. J. Approx. Theory **156**(1), 52–81 (2009)
10. Pylvänäinen, T.: Accelerometer based gesture recognition using continuous HMMs. In: Marques, J.S., Pérez de la Blanca, N., Pina, P. (eds.) IbPRIA 2005. LNCS, vol. 3522, pp. 639–646. Springer, Heidelberg (2005)
11. Wu, J., Pan, G., Zhang, D., Qi, G., Li, S.: Gesture recognition with a 3-D accelerometer. In: Zhang, D., Portmann, M., Tan, A.-H., Indulska, J. (eds.) UIC 2009. LNCS, vol. 5585, pp. 25–38. Springer, Heidelberg (2009)
12. Yi, D., Lei, Z., Liao, S., Li, S.Z.: Deep metric learning for person re-identification. In: ICPR, pp. 34–39. IEEE (2014)
13. Yih, W.-T., Toutanova, K., Platt, J.C., Meek, C.: Learning discriminative projections for text similarity measures. In: CoNLL, pp. 247–256. Association for Computational Linguistics (2011)
14. Zheng, L., Idrissi, K., Garcia, C., Duffner, S., Baskurt, A.: Triangular similarity metric learning for face verification. In: AFGR (2015)

Day Types Identification of Algerian Electricity Load Using an Image Based Two-Stage Approach

Kheir Eddine Farfar[✉] and Mohamed Tarek Khadir

LabGED, Computer Science Department, Badji Mokhtar University, Po-Box 12,
23000 Annaba, Algeria
{kfarfar,khadir}@labged.net

Abstract. Short term electricity load forecasting is one of the main concerns for electricity producers in regular system planning, where electricity demand is influenced by the day type among other factors that must be identified before modeling to ensure good load balance. This paper proposes a two-stage approach for identifying day types based on an image of the daily load curve. In the first stage, a set of day classes of load profiles using K-Means clustering algorithm is created, while in the second stage, the Time-Series Visualization method is used to build a classification model able to assign different days to the existing classes, detecting visual characteristics from daily load data curves. This classification model could be used in the forecasting process either by including the day-type as an input or by modeling each day-type independently.

Keywords: Time series · Deep learning · Autoencoders · K-Means · Load forecasting

1   Introduction

Short Term Load Forecasting (STLF) plays an important role for the day-to-day operations in energy management systems. It provides input data for contingency analysis and load flow studies in order to control any technological or economical risks [1].

In general, electrical load time series are complex, they exhibit non-stationary behavior and depend, in addition to its historical data, on many exogenous random factors especially seasonal and weather changes, making the forecasting task difficult [2]. Electric load follows similar daily and weekly variations during the year, and consequently understanding energy consumption patterns is beneficial to design and validate a STLF model in terms of accuracy measurement, where a special attention must be given to distinguish load behaviors which depend on varying social and industrial activities and weather conditions [1].

Forecasting is considered an important yet complex process. Different prediction models can be designed for each day type [3] and there exists numerous techniques and research work that have been applied on data originating from

© Springer International Publishing Switzerland 2016
A.E.P. Villa et al. (Eds.): ICANN 2016, Part II, LNCS 9887, pp. 415–422, 2016.
DOI: 10.1007/978-3-319-44781-0_49

several countries. One can cite Artificial Neural Network (ANN) [4] used with pattern recognition theory to choose load sets that represent a similar day. An ANN approach is also proposed for next day load curve forecasting based on similarity in [5] with the advantage of dealing with seasonal changes, weekends and special days.

Ran Li et al. [6] used hierarchical clustering and K-means to cluster substations into groups based on the shape of the monitored load profile in order to develop low voltage network templates. Daily consumption patterns in industrial parks have been analyzed in [7] by applying a Self-Organizing Map (SOM) and have accurately identified behavior patterns in a completely unsupervised fashion. SOM is also used in [8] to identify the separate day-types in Algerian data and have been combined with K-means clustering algorithm for a better classes identification in [9].

Recently, deep neural networks have shown promises for modelling static data across fields such as object recognition and applying them to time-series data are gaining increasing attention [10]. In this paper, the daily load curves of Algerian electricity load are grouped using K-Means clustering algorithm to create load pattern classes. The classficiation method of Time-Series Visualization (TSV) [11] is then used to build a classifier that detects visual characteristics from daily load data curves to assign different load patterns to existing classes benefiting from recent advances in deep neural networks architectures.

2   Approach Architecture

The objective of this study is to build a day-types classifier, in order to help build efficient forecasting STLF models for dispatching operators, toward optimising energy production and consumption. The proposed approach is based on a combination of clustering and classification as illustrated in Fig. 1, the following two main stages can be distinguished:

2.1   Clustering

The Algerian electric load is characterized, among others, by the upward linear trend that reflects the increasing economic activity [9]. In this stage, some preprocessing was performed on the collected data, in order to only keep the amount of change in consumption between daily hours, removing the trend. To perform that, difference operator are first applied to the time series x, to obtain a new series x', that is normalized around the value 0, whose value at time t is the difference between $x(t+1)$ and $x(t)$.

A centroid-based clustering K-means, using the Lloyd algorithm [12], is then applied. The approach consists in an iterative algorithm with the objective of minimizing the sum of Euclidean distances from each data point to its cluster centroid as expressed in Eq. 1.

$$\varphi = \sum_{k=1}^{K} \sum_{i=1}^{M} \min_{c \in C} d^2(x_i - c_k) \tag{1}$$

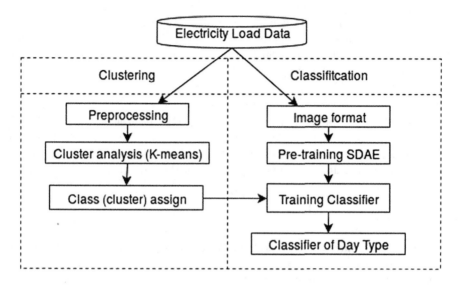

Fig. 1. Flow chart of the approach

Where φ is the potential of a cluster c chosen from a set of possible clusters C, M is the number of data observations, and $d^2(...)$ is the square of the Euclidean distance between a data observation x_i and its corresponding cluster centroid c_k, and K denotes the number of clusters that needs to be specified in advance.

To select a preferable number of clusters, we conducted clustering for different number of clusters and looked at the cost function within the cluster as well based on previous studies [9]. The groupings generated by the clustering algorithm are used as target categories for the classification process in the second stage of this approach.

2.2 Time-Series Classification

In this stage, a similar methodology to the one that is proposed by Chen Qian et al. [11] named time series visualitation (TSV) for the classification of time series, which is based on the good representation learnt from curves of time-series data. This approach is inspired by the intuitiveness for humans to identify the similarity of temporal series by curves instead of looking at raw data. This method involves learning a Stacked Auto-encoders (SAE) to classify the picture representation of the time series curve.

In addition, to overcome difficulties in learning deep models and to reach a better generalization result, greedy layer pre-training algorithm using unsupervised training appears to play predominantly a regularization role in preparing the weights of the network [13], and the Denoising Auto-encoders (DAE) shows that partial corruption of the input pattern yields to extract robust features of input data [14].

Therefore, each DAE hidden layer in the proposed model computes an encoded version of it's input, where a percentage p of randomly chosen elements are forced to be 0. The activation function is $sigmoid(x) = \frac{1}{1+e^{-x}}$ so hidden layer activations are given by:

$$h(\dot{x}) = sigmoid(b + W\dot{x})$$

Being $\dot{x}$ the corrupted input, b the bias and W the weights of DAE. And the output of each pre-trained layer is $g(h(\dot{x})) = sigmoid(b' + W'h(\dot{x}))$. Then, each DAE is trained in order to minimizes the mean squared error (MSE) as expressed in Eq. 2, being $x_{i,j}$ the component i of the pattern j.

$$MSE = \sum_{j=1}^{N} \sum_{i=1}^{M} (\dot{x}_{i,j} - x_{i,j})^2 \tag{2}$$

Once all layers have been pre-trained, the ouput layer is added and the whole neural network is trained to classify day-types using classes given in clustering stage, by minimizing the cost function softmax given in Eq. 3.

$$P(Y = i|x, W, b) = softmax_i(Wx + b) = \frac{e^{W_i x + b_i}}{\sum_j e^{W_j x + b_j}} \tag{3}$$

3   Time Series Visualisation for Load Data

In this section the proposed approach is applied on data that representing the Algerian hourly electric load for a three years period (2010–2012). For the second stage purpose, every 24 samples are transformed into an image that shows grayscale curve of the electric load during that day, each image is of size 30-by-30 pixels. These images are then, randomly separated into three partitions: the training data (60 %) for the creation of the model, validation data (20 %) for the optimization of hyperparameters to avoid overfittig and the last one for testing (20 %), respectively, in order asses the model quality.

Applying deep neural networks, on the created images, requires tunning different parameters, therefore, to decide on the number of units of the SDAE, the suitable values of learning rates and noise mask, Random search is used, as it is known for being more effective in searching a larger, less promising configuration space than grid search [15]. Table 1 shows the different combination of parameters which we used in different experimental setup for SDAE.

25 experiments were performed for each number of hidden layers (1, 2, 3), where the number of epochs for supervised tuning phase is set to 800, number of epochs for unsupervised pretraining of SDAE is 30. Pre-training stops if ever the MSE do not decreased by a 10^{-2} in the last 5 epochs. To view the capacity of DAE as a method for feature extraction, an ANN model without pretraining is also used to compare the results.

The size of input vectors for each model is equal to 900 and the outputs of each model is a softmax layer to assign a probability of belonging to each class, where K-means clustering algorithm assign each day load curve to a specific class.

Table 1. Parameters used in different experimental setup of SDAE. Symbol U means uniformly sampled.

Parameter	Range	Comment
Number of hidden nodes	$U(5, 200)$	Number of hidden nodes are unfixed across the hidden layers
Learning rates for unsupervised pretraining of SDAE	$U(10^{-3}, 0.3)$	
Learning rates for supervised tunning phase	$U(10^{-3}, 0.3)$	
Noise mask	$U(2\%, 40\%)$	Percentage of inputs that would be randomly set to zero

4 Results

In the first stage, for the given number of 4 clusters, the visualization of ten random days of each cluster in Fig. 2 shows curve features similarity between the days that are in same cluster and dissimilarity with days belonging to other clusters.

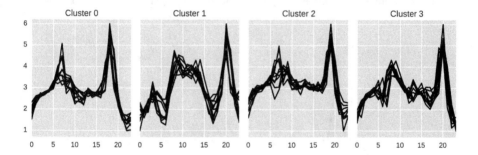

Fig. 2. Visualization of ten random observations of each class

To identify each cluster (class), days of each class are grouped by week days and months. The monthly grouping (Fig. 3b) shows that Class 3 covers almost all the observations of May and the Class 0 contains most of the days of March. In addition, Class 1 groups the months of summer and Class 2 groups the months of winter. This observations shows a relationship between the day-type and the seasonal variations. Therefore, grouping by day of week in Fig. 3a do not show any dominance of a particular day.

In the second stage, the best model for each hyper-parameter is selected based on the validation error, both types of neural network model (with and without pretraining) have given almost similar performances. Where the best system topology, regarding to validation set performance is given by an SDAE model with two hidden layers of 6 and 18 hidden units. This model gave 0.05 as a validation error and 0.11 on the test set. The Fig. 4 shows learning and validation errors in the corresponding experiment where we can see that the model falls into overfitting after about epoch 600.

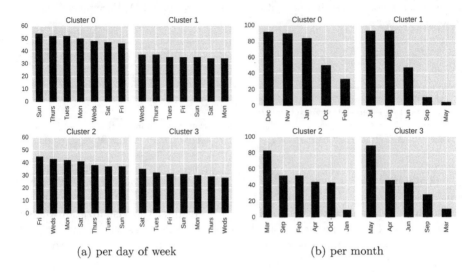

(a) per day of week   (b) per month

Fig. 3. Number of observations per day of week and per month in each class

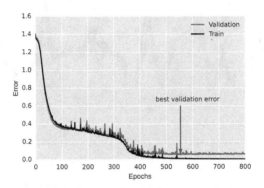

Fig. 4. Plot of learning and validation errors in the experiment of the selected model

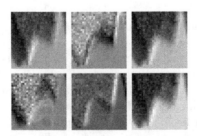

Fig. 5. Visualization of first hidden layer weights of the selected model

The best model is given using 35 % as amount of masking noise, learning rate for unsupervised pretraining equal to 0.11 and learning rate for supervised tunning set to 0.09. This combination of parameters shows the ability of DAE to extract visual characteristics of curves with a sufficient level of corruption at the input layer as illustrated in Fig. 5.

5 Conclusion

In this paper we have proposed an image based two-stage approach for day types identification, where K-Means clustering algorithm is used to define a set of day classes of load profiles. Then, pretraining of Denoising Auto-encoders are used to carry deep Artificial Neural Network training able to assign different days to the existing classes. The experiments show that DAE are able to extract visual characteristics of curves and their generalization performance is better compared to an ANN without pretraining. Future research will focus on STLF that involve the results of this day types identification either by including the day-type as an input or by modeling each day-type independently.

Acknowledgments. We would like to thank Sonelgaz (Algeria's national electricity and gas company) for providing three years of electricity data for this project.

References

1. Kyriakides, E., Polycarpou, M.: Short term electric load forecasting: a tutorial. In: Chen, K., Wang, L. (eds.) Trends in Neural Computation. SCI, vol. 35, pp. 391–418. Springer, Heidelberg (2007)
2. Hippert, H.S., Pedreira, C.E., Souza, R.C.: Neural networks for short-term load forecasting: a review and evaluation. IEEE Trans. Power Syst. **16**(1), 44–55 (2001)
3. Fay, D., Ringwood, J.V., Condon, M., Kelly, M.: 24-h electrical load dataa sequential or partitioned time series? Neurocomputing **55**(3), 469–498 (2003)
4. Dai, W., Wang, P.: Application of pattern recognition and artificial neural network to load forecasting in electric power system. In: Third International Conference on Natural Computation, ICNC 2007, vol. 1, pp. 381–385. IEEE (2007)
5. Senjyu, H.S., Senjyu, T., Sakihara, H., Tamaki, Y., Uezato, K.: Next-day load curve forecasting using neural network based on similarity. Electr. Power Compon. Syst. **29**(10), 939–948 (2001)
6. Li, R., Gu, C., Li, F., Shaddick, G., Dale, M.: Development of low voltage network templatespart i: substation clustering and classification. IEEE Trans. Power Syst. **30**(6), 3036–3044 (2015)
7. Hernández, L., Baladrón, C., Aguiar, J.M., Carro, B., Sánchez-Esguevillas, A.: Classification and clustering of electricity demand patterns in industrial parks. Energies **5**(12), 5215–5228 (2012)
8. Khadir, M.T., Fay, D., Boughrira, A.: Day type identification for algerian electricity load using kohonen maps. Trans. Eng. Comput. Technol. **15**, 296–300 (2006)
9. Tarek, K.M., Farouk, B., Sofiane, K.: Kohonen Maps Combined to K-means in a Two Level Strategy for Time Series ClusteringApplication to Meteorological and Electricity Load Data. INTECH Open Access Publisher (2010)

10. Längkvist, M., Karlsson, L., Loutfi, A.: A review of unsupervised feature learning and deep learning for time-series modeling. Pattern Recogn. Lett. **42**, 11–24 (2014)
11. Qian, C., Wang, Y., Guo, L.: A novel method based on data visual autoencoding for time-series classification. In: Deng, Z., Li, H. (eds.) Proceedings of the 2015 Chinese Intelligent Automation Conference. LNEE, vol. 336, pp. 97–104. Springer, Heidelberg (2015)
12. Lloyd, S.P.: Least squares quantization in pcm. IEEE Trans. Inf. Theor. **28**(2), 129–137 (1982)
13. Erhan, D., Bengio, Y., Courville, A., Manzagol, P.A., Vincent, P., Bengio, S.: Why does unsupervised pretraining help deep learning? J. Mach. Learn. Res. **11**, 625–660 (2010)
14. Vincent, P., Larochelle, H., Bengio, Y., Manzagol, P.A.: Extracting and composing robust features with denoising autoencoders. In: Proceedings of the 25th International Conference on Machine learning, pp. 1096–1103. ACM (2008)
15. Bergstra, J., Bengio, Y.: Random search for hyper-parameter optimization. J. Mach. Learn. Res. **13**(1), 281–305 (2012)

SMS Spam Filtering Using Probabilistic Topic Modelling and Stacked Denoising Autoencoder

Noura Al Moubayed[(✉)], Toby Breckon, Peter Matthews,
and A. Stephen McGough

School of Engineering and Computing Sciences,
Durham University, Durham DH1 3LE, UK
{noura.al-moubayed,toby.breckon,peter.matthews,
stephen.mcgough}@durham.ac.uk

Abstract. In This paper we present a novel approach to spam filtering and demonstrate its applicability with respect to SMS messages. Our approach requires minimum features engineering and a small set of labelled data samples. Features are extracted using topic modelling based on latent Dirichlet allocation, and then a comprehensive data model is created using a Stacked Denoising Autoencoder (SDA). Topic modelling summarises the data providing ease of use and high interpretability by visualising the topics using word clouds. Given that the SMS messages can be regarded as either spam (unwanted) or ham (wanted), the SDA is able to model the messages and accurately discriminate between the two classes without the need for a pre-labelled training set. The results are compared against the state-of-the-art spam detection algorithms with our proposed approach achieving over 97 % accuracy which compares favourably to the best reported algorithms presented in the literature.

1 Introduction

Short Messaging Service (SMS) applications are the most widely used applications on smart phones [16] where 97 % of surveyed users in the report used SMS at least once during the survey. People worldwide were expected to send 8.3 trillion text messages on 2013 alone [14]. The large volume of SMS traffic is opening up an opportunity for spammers to move from email to SMS spamming [7].

Prior research has shown that the most effective approach for spam filtering is to perform the threat analysis on the message content level [5]. The SMS problem is in principle very similar to email spam filtering [2,9]. However, SMS differs mainly due to the nature of SMS messaging itself: (1) SMS is capped at 160 characters. (2) Users normally write an idiosyncratic language subset with abbreviations, bad spelling, SMS slang, and internet acronyms. Despite this most filters use standard feature extraction methods such as direct N-gram character-based and word-based tokenisation [6]. Supervised and unsupervised machine learning techniques are commonly trained using a collection of labelled messages of spam and non-spam (usually referred to as ham) [5]. The trained model is then used to predict labels of previously unseen messages.

© Springer International Publishing Switzerland 2016
A.E.P. Villa et al. (Eds.): ICANN 2016, Part II, LNCS 9887, pp. 423–430, 2016.
DOI: 10.1007/978-3-319-44781-0_50

In this work we use a recently developed text mining method, that of probabilistic topic modelling [18], to extract the hidden topics that are statistically related to SMS. Topic modelling has the advantage of handling seamlessly and robustly any text size [18]. The topics generated per SMS are then used by an unsupervised deep learning approach, stacked denoising auto-encoders (SDA) [19], to build a data model. To increase separation between ham and spam the reconstruction error of the built SDA model is used as features that are passed to a Fisher's linear discriminate analysis (FDA)[15] to classify data into spam and ham. The results achieved using this approach are comparable with the best reported in the literature.

2   SMS Spam Filtering

The first step in a machine learning based SMS spam filter is feature extraction/engineering. The classifier must effectively utilise these features for discrimination of spam and ham. This is by no means a unique problem for spam filtering, however, the limited available text per SMS makes the feature space sparse. This means that the samples, from the input space, are fewer and further apart, thus significantly reducing the data that the classifier has to work with [5]. Hidalgo et al. [6] suggested the use of different features including: normalised words, character bi- and tri-grams and word bi-grams. A novel approach based on Stylometry, i.e. the statistical analysis of linguistic style, was presented in [17], with the goal of identifying spam message from the style by which those messages were written. In their review of email spam filtering, [9] reported that the bag of words was the most common feature used in the literature. However, they argue that the greatest disadvantage of this approach was that the features are fixed and can not be updated as the data changes and the nature of spam threat changes. The extracted features tend to be high dimensional requiring some sort of feature selection, or dimensionality reduction techniques [5,6,17].

After the features are extracted and selected, the machine learning method can be trained to classify the available data into spam and ham. Early work suggested the use of both supervised machine learning methods, e.g. SVM [20], and unsupervised methods, e.g. k-NN [11]. Hidalgo et al. [6] evaluated a number of spam filtering methods and concluded that SVMs are the most suitable classification approaches. As the number of spam samples in any dataset is much smaller than that of ham samples, any classifier must take this into consideration otherwise there is a serious risk of over-fitting the model to one class (usually ham). To address this issue a Bayesian approach to a Naive Bayes based classifier was used [12]. This approach penalises false positives more ensuring balanced performance for ham and spam and higher spam precision.

3   Methods

The most commonly used methods for SMS feature extraction suffer from three main disadvantages: (1) the number of resulting features are usually high requiring the use of a feature selection method (2) the features can be very sparse due to the limited size of SMS (3) the selected features are normally hard-coded in the system and hence are very hard to adapt to emerging spam patterns. To address these issues we have opted to use probabilistic topic modelling [18], a text mining technique that models latent patterns in the messages, that models latent patterns in the text. This approach automatically identifies topics within a set of messages and assigns each message to a set of topics. The approach only requires the maximum number of topics to be set. The messages are distributed among a small number of topics minimising the effect of sparsity. The most importantly topic modelling can work adaptively. Topic modelling also requires only basic pre-processing steps: tokenisation and stop words removal.

Due to the limited availability of labelled training data, unsupervised learning is the most realistic approach for real-life applications. [8,21] surveyed the unsupervised outlier detection algorithms. Here we use an unsupervised deep neural network: stacked denoising autoencoders [19] (SDA). SDAs are usually pre-trained using an unsupervised approach and then a supervised method is used for fine-tuning. In our approach we only utilise the pre-trained stage with the reconstruction error of a data sample given the model used as a surrogate measure of how well the sample is represented by the model and hence is exploited to identify outliers (e.g. spam).

3.1 Probabilistic Topic Modeling

Topic modelling [18] is a text mining tool that can identify latent text patterns in a documents contents, handling large volumes of corpuses regardless of the size of the individual documents. It describes, in statistical terms, how words in documents are generated based on a pre-defined number of topics using a statistical sampling technique. A commonly used topic modelling method is Latent Dirichlet Allocation (LDA) [4]. In LDA the documents are represented by a pre-defined number of topics where each topic is a hidden variable characterised by a nominal distribution over a fixed dictionary. LDA represents each document as a mixture of different topics with prior assumptions about their distribution. A topic may occur in different documents with a different probability and a word may occur in several topics with a different probabilities. A complete description of LDA can be found in [4]. Let V be a vocabulary consisting of a set of words, T is a set of k topics and n documents of arbitrary length. For every topic z a distribution φ_z on V is sampled from a known probability distribution (Dirichlet function [13]). Gibbs sampling is normally used for inference in LDA. LDA estimates the distribution $p(z|w)$ for $z \in T^P$, $w \in V^P$ where P denotes the set of word positions in the documents.

3.2 Stacked Denoising Autoencoder

The main advantage of the unsupervised deep learning is the utilisation of the previously considered useless masses of unlabelled data that are easy to obtain in order to achieve better understanding of emerging patterns in the data. Unsupervised deep learning is capable of extracting high level feature representations of complex structured data outperforming approaches based on handcrafted features [3].

An autoencoder (*AE*) consists of a visible input layer, and a hidden layer. During learning the AE goes through two phases: (1) construct phase which maps the input data into the hidden layer (2) reconstruct phase which maps back the hidden layer's data into the input layer. The model converges when the reconstruction error between input and output is minimum. *AE* normally use tied (constrained) weights for regularisation [3]. This constrains the parameter search space and reduces the number of parameters to learn: W, also known as the weight matrix. The constructed representation of the input x, can be defined as $y = S(Wx + a)$ and the reconstructed representation of y can be defined as $z = S(W'y + b)$, where W' is the transpose of W, and $S(\bullet)$ is a sigmoid function $(S(x) = \frac{1}{1+e^{-x}})$. The reconstruction error is measured using squared error: $L(x, z) = \| x - z \|^2$. The model is then optimised to find the W that minimises L.

To avoid over-fitting, i.e. learning the identify function, and reduce information redundancy in the input features we use a Denoising Autoencoder (DA) [19]. DA is a stochastic version of the AE that corrupts the input data by adding noise, allowing for more variance in the input space and hence better generalisation of the model. In this paper we adopt the Masking Noise corruption forcing a fraction of the input layer units (chosen randomly) to have a weight of 0.

Stacked Denoising Autoencoder (SDA) is the deep version of a single DA, where the output of one DA is the input to the following one. The network is then trained layer by layer. Figure 1 illustrates the SDA architecture. The arrows indicate the direction of information flow. During construction the data flows from the input layer up in the hierarchy to the top layer. For reconstruction the data flows back from the top through the hidden layers down to the input layer where the reconstructed data is compared with the input data and the overall reconstruction error (RE) is calculated.

3.3 Outlier Detection

Reconstruction error is a measure of how well SDA models the presented sample at the input layer. A high RE suggests poor modelling of the input sample while a small RE is an indication of accurate representation of the input. RE among layers is only used during unsupervised pre-training to optimise the model parameters. Similar to [10]In this work we utilise overall RE as a measure for detecting outliers with the novel application of spam detection. As the majority of available data is ham SDA will model them more accurately than spam. In other words, spam will have higher RE than ham making it easier to discriminate the two sets (Fig. 2B) using simple linear classifiers like FDA [15].

4   Experiments and Results

The SMS spam data was collected and first presented in [1]. The data contains 5574 messages: 747(13.40 %) labelled as spam and 4827(86.60 %) labelled as ham.

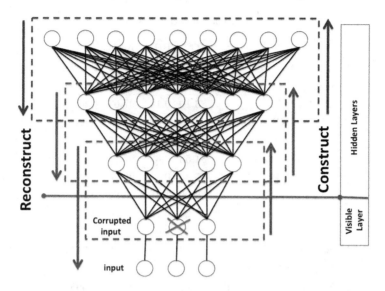

Fig. 1. A sample SDA model architecture. The crossed node in the input layer represents data corruption.

First the text content of the messages is tokenised, and stop words are removed. No stemming is applied to the data as this may affect the interpretability of the topic modelling results. The pre-processed text is then used to build a dictionary and bag of words which are passed to LDA to generate the topic model. Ham contains a wide range of topics that are irrelevant to the discrimination between spam and ham. Hence, only data labelled as spam was employed in building the topic model. A maximum of 60 topics were used. This was the optimal value identified after varying the maximum number of topics between 10 and 100. After the model was built all the messages (ham and spam) were passed to the model producing a 60-feature vector per message, where a feature i is the probability of that message j contains topic i.

SDA uses an input layer of 60 units with two hidden layers of 100, and 150 units respectively. All units use sigmoid activation functions with the learning rate is set to 0.1 and corruption rate of 30 %. The learning algorithm runs for 100 epochs. The learnt model is then used to calculate RE for each message, followed by FDA classification. To properly evaluate the performance of the methods a 10-fold cross validation approach was used. For each fold the training data was used to build a topic model and generate the feature vectors for training and testing data. SDA is built using the training features and REs are used to train an FDA which was then tested on RE of the testing set. This process is repeated 10 times and the average accuracies are reported.

Figure 2 plots the histogram and fitted non-parametric probability density function with a normal kernel for ham and spam. The figure clearly shows a high separability between the two classes using SDA, while a principal component

Table 1. Classification results.

Classifier	SC%	BH%	Acc%	MCC%
TM+SDA	85.59	0.62	97.51	0.899
Logistic Reg. + tok2	95.48	2.09	97.59	0.899
SVM + tok1	83.10	0.18	97.64	0.893
Boosted NB + tok2	84.48	0.53	97.50	0.887
SMO + tok2	82.91	0.29	97.50	0.887
Boosted C4.5 + tok2	81.53	0.62	97.05	0.865
MDL + tok1	75.44	0.35	96.26	0.826
PART + tok2	78.00	1.45	95.87	0.810
Random Forest + tok2	65.23	0.12	95.36	0.782
C4.5 + tok2	75.25	2.08	95.00	0.770
Bern NB + tok1	54.03	0.00	94.00	0.711
MN TF NB + tok1	52.06	0.00	93.74	0.697
MN Bool NB + tok1	51.87	0.00	93.72	0.695
1NN + tok2	43.81	0.00	92.70	0.636
Basic NB + tok1	48.53	1.42	92.05	0.600
Gauss NB + tok1	47.54	1.39	91.95	0.594
1Flex NB + tok1	47.35	2.77	90.72	0.536
Boolean NB + tok1	98.04	26.01	77.13	0.507
3NN + tok2	23.77	0.00	90.10	0.462
EM + tok2	17.09	4.18	85.54	0.185
TR	0.00	0.00	86.95	-

analysis (PCA) approach fails. It shows the ability of SDA to build a model for ham data resulting in small REs, while it does not fit the spam data as well resulting in higher REs.

Our cross-validated approach results in F-score = 90.13 ± 3.4 (mean ± standard deviation), Precision = 95.47 ± 1.9, and Recall = 85.58 ± 6.0. However to keep with the evaluation metrics reported in the literature [1] we also report the overall cross validated classification accuracy (Acc%), the Spam Caught accuracy (SC %), Blocked Ham accuracy (BH%), and Mathews Correlation Coefficient (MCC%). Table 1 presents our results as TM+SDA along with the commonly used methods in the literature [1] ordered by MCC%.

Interestingly, comparing the results to those produced using a supervised SDA, i.e. by stacking an additional logistic regression layer, the real advantage of using the unsupervised approach is further revealed. Using the supervised SDA the classifier suffers from a classic over-fitting problem associated with imbalanced training data with ham classification accuracy at 100 % but with a spam classification accuracy at 0 %. To examine the generalisation of the results

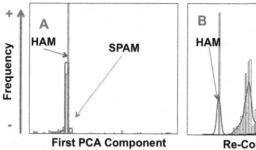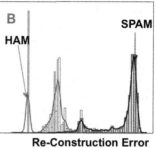

Fig. 2. A. Distribution of first PCA component of both ham and spam data. B. Distribution of reconstruction errors for ham and spam.

to different datasets. We used the DIT SMS spam dataset described in [5]. The dataset includes 1353 spam SMS text messages without any Ham data. Following the authors solution of embedding the spam data with an independent set containing Ham, we embedded the dataset within the dataset used above. Our approach results in F-score = 99.52 %, Precision= 99.34 %, Recall = 99.91 %, Ham accuracy= 99.43 %, and Spam accuracy= 99.28 %.

4.1 Conclusions

This paper presents a novel approach for SMS spam filtering using recent advances in text mining and unsupervised outlier detection based on deep learning.

SDA was presented as an unsupervised technique to model the extracted topic modelling features. SDA is demonstrated here to successfully separate between ham and spam using the structure in the data alone without the need for any labelling. The novelty of our approach is to use reconstruction errors produced by SDA to increase separability between ham and spam. FDA classifier trained on RE is then very effective in classifying the two classes. The accuracy achieved by the proposed system is comparable to the best results reported in the literature (using logistic regression (LR)). Although LR scores higher than ours on spam caught, it scores worse on ham blocked. As SDA is completely unsupervised, the approach is scalable to large unlabelled data sets and requires only a small subset to be labelled for FDA training.

References

1. Almeida, T.A., Hidalgo, J.M.G., Yamakami, A.: Contributions to the study of sms spam filtering: new collection and results. In: Proceedings of the 11th ACM Symposium on Document Engineering, pp. 259–262. ACM (2011)
2. Almeida, T.A., Yamakami, A.: Facing the spammers: a very effective approach to avoid junk e-mails. Expert Syst. Appl. **39**(7), 6557–6561 (2012)

3. Bengio, Y., Courville, A.C., Vincent, P.: Unsupervised feature learning and deep learning: a review and new perspectives, vol. 1 (2012). CoRR, abs/1206.5538
4. Blei, D.M., Ng, A.Y., Jordan, M.I.: Latent dirichlet allocation. J. mach. Learn. Res. **3**, 993–1022 (2003)
5. Delany, S.J., Buckley, M., Greene, D.: Sms spam filtering: methods and data. Expert Syst. Appl. **39**(10), 9899–9908 (2012)
6. Gómez Hidalgo, J.M., Bringas, G.C., Sánz, E.P., García, F.C.: Content based sms spam filtering. In: Proceedings of the 2006 ACM Symposium on Document Engineering, pp. 107–114. ACM (2006)
7. Groupe Speciale Mobile Association (GSMA): SMS spams and mobile messaging attacks - introduction, trends and examples (2011)
8. Gupta, M., Gao, J., Aggarwal, C., Han, J.: Outlier detection for temporal data. Synth. Lect. Data Min. Knowl. Discov. **5**(1), 1–129 (2014)
9. Guzella, T.S., Caminhas, W.M.: A review of machine learning approaches to spam filtering. Expert Syst. Appl. **36**(7), 10206–10222 (2009)
10. Hawkins, S., He, H., Williams, G.J., Baxter, R.A.: Outlier detection using replicator neural networks. In: Kambayashi, Y., Winiwarter, W., Arikawa, M. (eds.) DaWaK 2002. LNCS, vol. 2454, pp. 170–180. Springer, Heidelberg (2002)
11. Healy, M., Delany, S.J., Zamolotskikh, A.: An assessment of case base reasoning for short text message classification. In: Conference papers, p. 42 (2004)
12. Jie, H., Bei, H., Wenjing, P.: A bayesian approach for text filter on 3g network. In: 2010 6th International Conference on Wireless Communications Networking and Mobile Computing (WiCOM), pp. 1–5. IEEE (2010)
13. Johnson, N.L., Kotz, S., Balakrishnan, N.: Continuous Multivariate Distributions, volume 1, Models and Applications, vol. 59. Wiley, New York (2002)
14. PortioResearch: Mobile Messaging Futures 2013–2017 (2013)
15. Scholkopft, B., Mullert, K.R.: Fisher discriminant analysis with kernels. Neural Netw. sig. proc. IX **1**, 1 (1999)
16. Smith, A.: The Smartphone Difference. Pew Research Center, Washington (2015)
17. Sohn, D.N., Lee, J.T., Rim, H.C.: The contribution of stylistic information to content-based mobile spam filtering. In: Proceedings of the ACL-IJCNLP 2009 Conference Short Papers, pp. 321–324. Association for Computational Linguistics (2009)
18. Steyvers, M., Griffiths, T.: Latent Semantic Analysis: A Road to Meaning, Chapter Probabilistic Topic Models. Laurence Erlbaum, Hillsdale (2007)
19. Vincent, P., Larochelle, H., Lajoie, I., Bengio, Y., Manzagol, P.A.: Stacked denoising autoencoders: Learning useful representations in a deep network with a local denoising criterion. J. Mach. Learn. Res. **11**, 3371–3408 (2010)
20. Xiang, Y., Chowdhury, M., Ali, S.: Filtering mobile spam by support vector machine. In: CSITeA 2004: Third International Conference on Computer Sciences, Software Engineering, Information Technology, E-Business and Applications, pp. 1–4. International Society for Computers and Their Applications (ISCA) (2004)
21. Zimek, A., Schubert, E., Kriegel, H.P.: A survey on unsupervised outlier detection in high-dimensional numerical data. Stat. Anal. Data Min. **5**(5), 363–387 (2012)

Improving MDLSTM for Offline Arabic Handwriting Recognition Using Dropout at Different Positions

Rania Maalej[1]([✉]) and Monji Kherallah[2]

[1] Research Group on Intelligent Machines,
National School of Engineers of Sfax, Sfax University, Sfax, Tunisia
rania.mlj@gmail.com
[2] Faculty of Sciences, Sfax University, Sfax, Tunisia
monji.kherallah@enis.rnu.tn

Abstract. RNN and LSTM are now a state-of-the-art technology that provide a very good performance on different machine learning tasks as handwritten Arabic word recognition. This field remains an on-going research problem due to its cursive appearance, the variety of writers and the diversity of styles. In this work, we propose a new offline Arabic handwriting recognition system based on a particular RNN named the MDLSTM on which we propose to apply dropout technique in different positions such as before, after or inside the MDLSTM layers. This regularization technique has the advantages of preventing our system against overfitting problem and reducing the error recognition rate. We carried out experiments on the well-known IFN/ENIT Database.

Keywords: Dropout · LSTM · MDLSTM · Offline Arabic handwriting recognition

1 Introduction

Recurrent Neural Networks (RNN) are among the most powerful sequence learners. In particular, The Long Short Term Memory (LSTM) has achieved remarkable success in various machine learning tasks including language modeling [1], speech recognition [2], machine translation [3], image captioning [4]. LSTM overcomes the problem of vanishing and exploding gradients of traditional RNNs. These units have been shown to give the state of the art performance on handwriting recognition, they have been used as a stacked bidirectional LSTM for online recognition [5] and as a stacked Multidirectionnal LSTM for the offline task [6], the later system has bien tested on the IFN/ENIT corpus [7]. But with the huge number of parameters, overfitting can occur. In order to protect the network against this problem, dropout is applied in different positions. This technique consists in temporarily removing some units from the network. Those removed units are randomly selected only during the training stage. This regularization can improve network performance and significantly reduce the error rate.

© Springer International Publishing Switzerland 2016
A.E.P. Villa et al. (Eds.): ICANN 2016, Part II, LNCS 9887, pp. 431–438, 2016.
DOI: 10.1007/978-3-319-44781-0_51

This paper is organized as follows. Section 2 presents relevant previous works. Section 3 describes our contribution and in Sect. 4 we report on experiment results. Finally, conclusion and future work are drawn in Sect. 5.

2   Related Work

Six major steps are the bases of the traditional procedure of recognition: image acquisition, pre-processing, segmentation, feature extraction, classification and post processing. It is obvious that considerable time and expertise are a must for the feature extraction stage because it has to be redesigned for each alphabet. We suggest a trained system on pixel data in order to overcome this complex step. It is evident that this type of system submitted into holistic approaches, possesses the same difficulty degree to recognize a number of languages. Likewise, the major interest to use these raw images in training stage is their capability to learn the visual and the sequential aspect of cursive handwriting concurrently as well.

In the last years, the majority of researches carried out have been based on either HMM [8] or on the combination of HMM with neural networks [9]. Although being successful, HMM possesses some cons like both its poor discrimination and the shortage of strength to handle the long-term dependencies in sequences as they follow a first-order equation. The suitable solution adapted by some researchers was the use of Recurrent Neural Networks RNN [5]. In fact, RNNs prove their efficiency for modeling times series. They can be trained discriminatively and they do not require a prior knowledge of data. The use of Recurrent Neural Networks RNN [5] was the perfect solution followed by several researches. Indeed, RNNs showed their effectiveness to model times series. They are able to be trained discriminatively and they do not need a prior knowledge of data. However, RNNs are unable to bear the vanishing gradient and the burden of exploding. Luckily, these problems can be worked out with a particular node called the Long Short-Term Memory (LSTM) which holds better outcomes either in speech recognition [10] or in online handwriting recognition [11]. For the latter field, Bidirectional LSTM was suggested as it offers the possibility to integrate context in both sides of each given letter in the input sequence. For offline handwriting recognition, this architecture is not the suitable option as the input data is not one-dimensional anymore. Consequently, we tend to choose the application of the MDLSTM.

Combining a Multi-Dimensional Recurrent Neural Network (MDRNN) with the LSTM nodes is the concept of Multidimensional Long Short Term Memory (MDLSTM) [12, 13] which is a recurrent network where many connections substituted a single recurrent connection so that we can represent all spatio-temporal dimensions of input data. Although MDLSTM's success, overfitting can occur on this network because of the large number of hidden layers and also due to the enormous number of parameters. We can overcome this inconvenience by using dropout [13] consisting of removing some units, which are arbitrarily chosen only during the training stage, from the network momentarily. This regularization is able to better both the network performance and significantly decrease error rate as well.

Table 1. Error recognition rate reduced with dropout

Authors	Network	Dataset	Error rate reduction w/dropout
Maalej et al. [18]	BLSTM	ADAB	8.12 %
Maalej et al. [19]	MDLSTM	IFN/ENIT	4.88 %

We noted that dropout was both successfully practiced with several types of deep neural networks proving to be a significant improvement for a recognition rate [14–17] and triumphantly exploited in RNN, mainly in BLSTM. Likewise, it has proven its efficiency by minimizing label error rate by more than 8 % on ADAB Dataset for the online Arabic handwriting recognition [18] and by more than 4.88 % on IFN/ENIT for the offline Arabic handwriting [19] (Table 1).

In previous systems based on RNN [17–19], dropout was practiced on only some layers that were unable to be fully-connected so that one does not harm the recurrent connections and mainly one can keep the RNN able to model long input sequences. In this Work, as done before, some units in other positions in MDLSTM network were dropped before, after or inside the MDLSTM layers.

3   System Overview

In this section, the architecture of the offline Arabic handwriting recognition system based on MDLSTM and CTC is presented (see Fig. 1). Being a robust method, MDLSTM allows a flexible modeling of this multidimensional context by giving recurrent connections for every spatio-temporal dimensions existing in the input data. These connections strengthen MDLSTM against local distortion in image input (e.g. rotation, shears …). The principal issue of this method is how to gain one-dimensional label sequences from the two-dimensional images. Consequently, we suggest to push data through a hierarchy of MDLSTM layers as well as sub-samples windows added

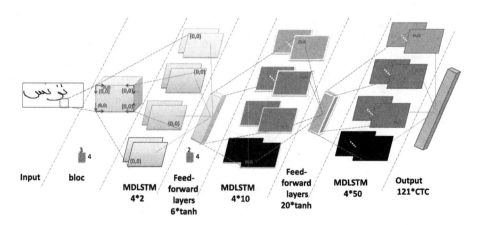

Fig. 1. Architecture of recognition system based on MDLSTM

after each level so that we can incrementally collapse the two-dimensional images into one-dimensional sequences to be finally labeled by the output layers.

To prevent our network from overfitting, dropout is applied at different positions, for implementation, we add dropout layers at different locations around MDLSTM layers. Dropout layers return the same input except at dropped nodes that return null. In our system, 50 % of nodes are randomly dropped. Figure 2 shows dropout layer added before MDLSTM layers, in this case we choose to drop the same input units for all directions.

However Fig. 3 illustrates dropout layer added after MDLSTM layers, and in Fig. 4 dropped units are shown inside MDLSTM layers.

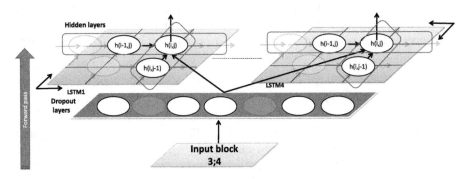

Fig. 2. Dropout applied before MDLSTM layers

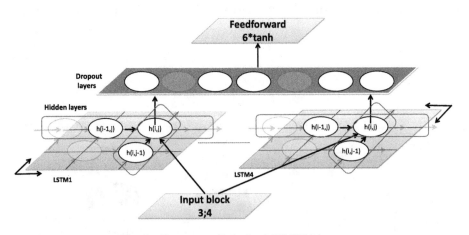

Fig. 3. Dropout applied after MDLSTM layers

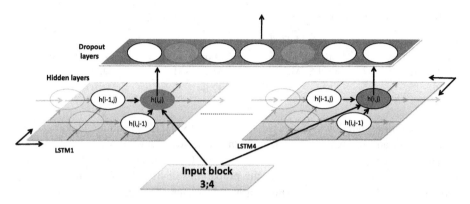

Fig. 4. Dropout applied inside MDLSTM layers

4 Experiments Results

IFN/ENIT Database [7], with 32492 images of Arabic words written by more than 1000 writers are used to validate our system. Those words are 937 Tunisian town/village names. IFN/ENIT Database is divided in 5 sets (see Table 2) and it was triumphantly exploited by more than 50 research groups as well in Offline Arabic handwriting recognition competition in ICDAR 2009 [20].

Our system is trained with 19724 words gathered in *set a*, *set b* and *set c*, however we use *set d* and *set e*, that contains 12768 words, for testing.

Some network's parameters are fixed either automatically or Hand-Tuned. In fact, we fix three levels for the network hierarchy which are separated by two feedforward layers with the tanh activation function (see Fig. 1). Each level of the MDLSTM hierarchy contained four hidden layers for our two-dimensional data. Theses hidden layers were recurrently connected, indeed all input units are connected to the all hidden units and all hidden units are connected to both output units and hidden units. For these LSTM units, gate activation function is the logistic sigmoid, while the cell input and output functions are both tanh, for more details, we refer the reader to [21]. Regarding the online steepest descent was used for training with a momentum of 0.9 and a learning rate of 1e−4. The number of LSTM blocks are: 2 blocks in the first level, 10 blocks in the second level and 50 blocks in the third level. The sizes of the two feedforward layers separating the hidden levels are 6 and 20. And the dimensions of the

Table 2. The IFN/ENIT database

Sets	Words	Characters
a	6537	51984
b	6710	53862
c	6477	52155
d	6735	54166
e	6033	45169
TOTAL	32492	257336

Table 3. Dropout's effect in label error rate tested on different positions around MDLSTM

Label error rate (%) on the IFN/ENIT database			
Dropout before MDLSTM	Dropout inside MDLSTM	Dropout after MDLSTM	MDLSTM w/o Dropout
11.62	11.88	12.09	16.97

three subsampling windows, expressed as a list like (3, 4), (3, 4) and (2, 4), those value are the width and the height of corresponding window.

The output layers are based especially on the CTC method [22]. This technique involves a Softmax layer to compute the probability distribution $P_{r(k|t)}$ for each step throughout the input sequence. This distribution covers the 120 Target labels incremented by one extra blank symbol to represent a non-output. So, in total, the size of this Softmax layer achieves 121. At every timestep the network chooses to emit a label or not. All these decisions define a distribution over alignments between the input and target sequences. Afterwards, and due to forward-backward algorithm, CTC sum over all possible alignments and finally it normalizes probability $P_{r(z|x)}$ of the target sequence given the input sequence. Thus CTC is the best choice for unsegmented cursive handwriting recognition.

The error measure used as the early-stopping criterion on the validation set is the label error rate. So convergence is achieved when the label error rate on a validation set does not decrease by more than a threshold for a given number of iterations. So the training stops if the label error rate did not considerably decrease for 20 epochs.

Dropout is employed to regularize the network's parameters and it was found to boost its performance. Dropout is tested in different places in network, after, before and inside each LSTM layers. According to [13, 23] the best dropout rate, that results in the maximum amount of regularization, is equal to 0.5.

After training, we test our best obtained network with *set d* and *set e*, we get, as mentioned in Table 3, an impressive label error rate which does not exceed 11.62 % when dropout is applied before MDLSTM layers compared to 11.88 % obtained with the same architecture when some units are dropped inside the MDLSTM layers, and 12.09 when dropout layer are added after MDLSTM layers. All those results are better than those found without applying dropout during training.

5   Conclusion

In this paper, we have proposed to improve a powerful offline Arabic handwriting recognizer based on MDLSTM. For that, we have opted for a successfully regularization method called Dropout and we have presented how it can be applied on MDLSTM network. Dropout consists in temporarily removing some units from the network. So, we have tested this technique by zeroing some units in different positions in the network, such as before, after or inside the MDLSTM layers.

Experimental results show that applying dropout before the MDLSTM layers gives best results and it has successfully improve network performance by both preventing it from overfitting problem and significantly reducing the label error rate by more than

5.35 %. As well, we have also achieved good results when dropout is added after or inside MDLSTM layers. However, both randomly dropping out some units during training and repeatedly sampling a random subset of input feature make training stage much slower. So, as future work, we aim to show how to do fast dropout [24, 25] training on MDLSTM network.

References

1. Sundermeyer, M., Schlüter, R., Ney, H.: LSTM neural networks for language modeling. In: INTERSPEECH, pp. 194–197, September 2012
2. Sak, H., Senior, A.W., Beaufays, F.: Long short-term memory recurrent neural network architectures for large scale acoustic modeling. In: INTERSPEECH, pp. 338–342, September 2014
3. Sutskever, I., Vinyals, O., Le, Q.V.: Sequence to sequence learning with neural networks. In: Advances in Neural Information Processing Systems, pp. 3104–3112 (2014)
4. Vinyals, O., Toshev, A., Bengio, S., Erhan, D.: Show and tell: a neural image caption generator. In: Proceedings of the IEEE Conference on Computer Vision and Pattern Recognition, pp. 3156–3164 (2015)
5. Graves, A., Liwicki, M., Bunke, H., Schmidhuber, J., Fernández, S.: Unconstrained on-line handwriting recognition with recurrent neural networks. In: Advances in Neural Information Processing Systems, pp. 577–584 (2008)
6. Graves, A.: Offline arabic handwriting recognition with multidimensional recurrent neural networks. In: Märgner, V., El Abed, H. (eds.) Guide to OCR for Arabic Scripts, pp. 297–313. Springer, London (2012)
7. Pechwitz, M., Maddouri, S.S., Märgner, V., Ellouze, N., Amiri, H.: IFN/ENIT-database of handwritten Arabic words. In: Proceedings of the CIFED, vol. 2, pp. 127–136, October 2002
8. Slimane, F., Zayene, O., Kanoun, S., Alimi, A.M., Hennebert, J., Ingold, R.: New features for complex Arabic fonts in cascading recognition system. In: 2012 21st International Conference on Pattern Recognition (ICPR), pp. 738–741. IEEE, November 2012
9. Dreuw, P., Doetsch, P., Plahl, C., Ney, H.: Hierarchical hybrid MLP/HMM or rather MLP features for a discriminatively trained gaussian HMM: a comparison for offline handwriting recognition. In: 2011 18th IEEE International Conference on Image Processing (ICIP), pp. 3541–3544. IEEE, September 2011
10. Graves, A., Mohamed, A.R., Hinton, G.: Speech recognition with deep recurrent neural networks. In: 2013 IEEE International Conference on Acoustics, Speech and Signal Processing (ICASSP), pp. 6645–6649. IEEE, May 2013
11. Kozielski, M., Doetsch, P., Ney, H.: Improvements in RWTH's system for off-line handwriting recognition. In: 2013 12th International Conference on Document Analysis and Recognition (ICDAR), pp. 935–939. IEEE, August 2013
12. Graves, A.: Supervised sequence labelling, pp. 5–13. Springer, Heidelberg (2012)
13. Hinton, G.E., Srivastava, N., Krizhevsky, A., Sutskever, I., Salakhutdinov, R.R.: Improving neural networks by preventing co-adaptation of feature detectors (2012). arXiv preprint: arXiv:1207.0580
14. Srivastava, N., Hinton, G., Krizhevsky, A., Sutskever, I., Salakhutdinov, R.: Dropout: a simple way to prevent neural networks from overfitting. J. Mach. Learn. Res. **15**(1), 1929–1958 (2014)

15. Miao, Y., Metze, F.: Improving low-resource CD-DNN-HMM using dropout and multilingual DNN training (2013)
16. Zhang, S., Bao, Y., Zhou, P., Jiang, H., Dai, L.: Improving deep neural networks for LVCSR using dropout and shrinking structure. In: 2014 IEEE International Conference on Acoustics, Speech and Signal Processing (ICASSP), pp. 6849–6853. IEEE, May 2014
17. Pham, V., Bluche, T., Kermorvant, C., Louradour, J.: Dropout improves recurrent neural networks for handwriting recognition. In: 2014 14th International Conference on Frontiers in Handwriting Recognition (ICFHR), pp. 285–290. IEEE, September 2014
18. Maalej, R., Tagougui, N., Kherallah, M.: Online Arabic handwriting recognition with dropout applied in deep recurrent neural networks. In: 2016 12th IAPR International Workshop on Document Analysis Systems (DAS), pp. 418–421. IEEE, April 2016
19. Maalej, R., Tagougui, N., Kherallah, M.: Recognition of handwritten Arabic words with dropout applied in MDLSTM. In: Campilho, A., Karray, F. (eds.) ICIAR 2016. LNCS, vol. 9730, pp. 746–752. Springer, Heidelberg (2016). doi:10.1007/978-3-319-41501-7_83
20. El Abed, H., Märgner, V.: ICDAR 2009-Arabic handwriting recognition competition. Int. J. Doc. Anal. Recogn. (IJDAR) 14(1), 3–13 (2011)
21. Hochreiter, S., Schmidhuber, J.: Long short-term memory. Neural Comput. 9(8), 1735–1780 (1997)
22. Graves, A., Fernández, S., Gomez, F., Schmidhuber, J.: Connectionist temporal classification: labelling unsegmented sequence data with recurrent neural networks, June 2006
23. Baldi, P., Sadowski, P.J.: Understanding dropout. In: Advances in Neural Information Processing Systems, pp. 2814–2822 (2013)
24. Wang, S.I., Manning, C.D.: Fast dropout training. In: ICML, vol. 2, pp. 118–126 (2013)
25. Bayer, J., Osendorfer, C., Korhammer, D., Chen, N., Urban, S., van der Smagt, P.: On fast dropout and its applicability to recurrent networks (2013). arXiv preprint: arXiv:1311.0701

A Neural Network Model for Solving the Feature Correspondence Problem

Ala Aboudib$^{(\boxtimes)}$, Vincent Gripon, and Gilles Coppin

Lab-STICC UMR CNRS 6285, Télécom Bretagne, Technopôle Brest-Iroise CS 83818, 29238 Brest Cedex 3, France
{ala.aboudib,vincent.gripon,gilles.coppin}@telecom-bretagne.eu

Abstract. Finding correspondences between image features is a fundamental question in computer vision. Many models in literature have proposed to view this as a graph matching problem whose solution can be approximated using optimization principles. In this paper, we propose a different treatment of this problem from a neural network perspective. We present a new model for matching features inspired by the architecture of a recently introduced neural network. We show that by using popular neural network principles like max-pooling, k-winners-take-all and iterative processing, we obtain a better accuracy at matching features in cluttered environments. The proposed solution is accompanied by an experimental evaluation and is compared to state-of-the-art models.

Keywords: Artificial neural networks · Feature matching · Graph matching · Iterative processing · Max-pooling

1 Introduction

Establishing correspondences between two sets of visual features is a fundamental problem in computer vision. Solving this problem is essential to many visual processing tasks. This includes feature tracking [10], object discovery [11], structure from motion [17], stereo matching [20], image classification [8] and many other applications. An early class of algorithms consisted in matching features based on the similarity of their descriptor vectors. Such similarity can be obtained using simple metrics such as euclidean or hamming distances for example [19]. While such methods are still widely popular, their ability to find correct matches becomes obsolete in more complex situations such as in the presence of multiple instances of the object whose features are to be matched, or in the case of matching two different objects that belong to the same class, or in the presence of clutter.

Early attempts to address this problem consisted in taking the geometric consistency between features into account. This includes methods such as

This work was supported by the European Research Council under the European Union's Seventh Framework Program (FP7/2007-2013) / ERC grant agreement n° 290901.

A.E.P. Villa et al. (Eds.): ICANN 2016, Part II, LNCS 9887, pp. 439–446, 2016.
DOI: 10.1007/978-3-319-44781-0_52

RANSAC [6] and ICP [2]. These methods assume that the deformations undergone by an object are rigid, i.e., they are governed by some form of a parametric transformation (e.g. planar affine or epipolar). However, these methods are not adapted to non-rigid transformations which are very common in natural images.

To address non-rigid transformations, a class of models emerged in the last two decades that applied graph matching techniques (GM) to the correspondence problem [4,12,22]. These methods formulate the matching problem as an optimization procedure of a well-defined objective function. This function takes individual feature similarity into account, as well as other geometric constraints such as pairwise feature affinity measures [12], or even higher order measures [21]. Little effort, however, was devoted to seeking a potential neural network model for solving the graph matching problem. We think that this is an interesting question from an algorithmic point of view, as well as for researchers interested in Marr's third level of analysis that seeks possible neural mechanisms for implementing vision algorithms [14]. While the present paper addresses this level of analysis, we do not pretend providing a real bio-mimetic solution. We hope that our approach be a step forward for vision research seeking biological inspiration.

The main contribution of our work is to introduce an artificial neural network (ANN) model for addressing the feature correspondence problem. This model is adapted from the sparse clustered neural network designed by Gripon and Berrou in [9], which is a generalization of the Palm-Wilshaw neural network [18]. The main *advantage* of the proposed matching algorithm is its better robustness against clutter compared to state-of-the-art. However, when no clutter is present, which is argued to be a less interesting case, the proposed algorithm only gives a comparable or a less matching accuracy. Another advantage is that our approach implements a cooperative algorithm, meaning that each neuron needs only to know about the activity of a few neighboring neurons, which allows for the algorithm to be run in parallel.

The rest of this paper is organized in four sections. In Sect. 2, a brief overview of state-of-the-art algorithms proposed for solving the correspondence problem is presented. The architecture of the neural network along with the algorithm we propose are presented in Sect. 3. The performance of the proposed model is evaluated in Sect. 4 and compared to some other algorithms. Section 5 is a conclusion.

2   Related Work

As mentioned earlier, feature correspondence can be viewed as a graph matching (GM) problem, which is traditionally formulated as a quadratic assignment problem (QAP) known to be NP-hard. Its solution is usually approximated by optimizing an objective function with relaxed constraints [12,21,22]. However, there were some attempts to approximate this optimization procedure by applying an iterative process without defining an explicit objective to optimize [3–5,7]. These attempts date back to as early as Marr's cooperative algorithm for solving the stereo matching problem [14]. It provided an insight on how iterative algorithms can be used to tackle difficult vision problems using only local information.

Max-pooling matching (MPM) introduced by Cho *et al.* in [3] is one recent example of such iterative algorithms. It applies max-pooling to preserve important information while discarding irrelevant details making it more robust in the presence of outliers. Some other methods that use a similar iterative approach include re-weighted random walk matching (RRWM) [4], balanced graph matching [5] and more [7].

Our approach is similar to MPM in that it applies max-pooling to discard irrelevant details. Unlike MPM, pooling is not only applied among features of one image but also in the second one. Another major difference is that the final discretization step is replaced by a non-linear activation function applied at each iteration and a winner-take-all (WTA) applied at the end, which is akin to local inhibition observed among neural assemblies [16].

In the following section, we describe our ANN model and specify the details of the matching algorithm it implements. We use a similar terminology as in [3] in order to highlight the similarities and differences between the two algorithms, and to show where the proposed model is positioned relative to the state-of-the-art.

3 The Proposed Model

Feature correspondence is formulated as the problem of matching a graph $\mathcal{G} = (\mathcal{V}, \mathcal{E})$ to a sub-graph of $\mathcal{G}' = (\mathcal{V}', \mathcal{E}')$, where $\mathcal{E}$, $\mathcal{E}'$ are the sets of graph edges, and $\mathcal{V}$, $\mathcal{V}'$ are sets of nodes. Graph $\mathcal{G}$ represents an object with its features as nodes in $\mathcal{V}$. The same holds for $\mathcal{G}'$ except that it might be representing a scene including other objects than the one we are seeking to match.

We define an assignment matrix $\mathbf{X} \in \{0,1\}^{n \times n'}$, where n and n' denote the number of nodes in $\mathcal{V}$ and $\mathcal{V}'$, respectively. We only set $\mathbf{X}_{ia} = 1$ when a feature $v_i \in \mathcal{V}$ matches another $v_a \in \mathcal{V}'$. We shall use a column-wise vectorized version of $\mathbf{X}$ that we denote $\mathbf{x} \in \{0,1\}^{nn'}$.

We also define a unary similarity function $s_V(v_i, v_a')$ to describe similarities among descriptor vectors of features in $\mathcal{V}$ and $\mathcal{V}'$, and a pairwise similarity function $s_E(e_{ij}, e_{ab}')$ with $e_{ij} \in \mathcal{E}$ and $e_{ab}' \in \mathcal{E}'$ as in [3,12]. We use these functions to define a unary affinity vector $\mathbf{y}_{ia} = s_V(v_i, v_a')$ with $\mathbf{y} \in \mathbb{R}^{nn'}$, and a pairwise similarity matrix $\mathbf{A} \in \mathbb{R}^{nn' \times nn'}$ as:

$$\mathbf{A}_{ia;jb} = \begin{cases} s_E(e_{ij}, e_{ab}') & \text{if } i \neq j \text{ and } a \neq b. \\ 0 & \text{otherwise.} \end{cases} \tag{1}$$

Notice from (1) that $\mathbf{A}$ is a symmetric matrix, and that elements of its main diagonal are always set to zero. The main diagonal does not hold the unary similarity values as in most traditional algorithms [3,12]. These values are stored in the vector $\mathbf{y}$.

The neural network we propose for solving the correspondence problem is constructed on the graph captured by the affinity matrix $\mathbf{A}$, as in the example of Fig. 1. The architecture of this network is adapted from the sparse clustered network (SCN) [9] which was proposed as a generalization of Palm-Wilshaw networks [18].

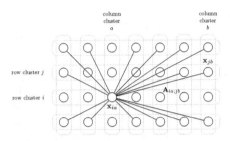

Fig. 1. The architecture of the proposed neural network.

The network grid structure depicted in Fig. 1 corresponds to the 2D configuration of the assignment matrix $\mathbf{X}$. As in SCNs, we impose a grouping configuration on the network neurons in the form of clusters; neurons of the same row are grouped into one cluster, and the same holds for neurons of the same column. Thus, each neuron belongs to two clusters as shown in Fig. 1. Within each cluster, a WTA activation constraint is imposed; only one neuron per cluster can be active at the end of the network activity with a binary activation level (0 or 1) captured by $\mathbf{X}$ as in [9]. However, during the network activity, and before $\mathbf{X}$ reaches its final state, this constraint is relaxed into a k-winners-take-all (kWTA) constraint, and we allow $\mathbf{X}$ to temporarily contain real values. The connections between neurons are captured by the pairwise affinity matrix $\mathbf{A}$, and as we notice from (1), no connections exists between neurons of the same cluster ($\mathbf{A}_{ia} = 0$) as in SCNs.

The WTA and kWTA constraints we impose within clusters are meant to encourage the one-to-one matching constraint between features in $\mathcal{V}$ and $\mathcal{V}'$. From a biological perspective, this is akin to the local competition among neural assemblies enforced by short inhibitory synaptic connections [16].

The network activity starts by assigning to each neuron its unary affinity value ($\mathbf{X}_{ia} \leftarrow \mathbf{y}_{ia}$). Then, within each row cluster, every neuron receives the max-pooled propagated activity of all other neurons to which it connects as in [1,3]:

$$\mathbf{x}_{ia}^{t+1} \leftarrow \mathbf{x}_{ia}^{t} \sum_{j \in \mathcal{V}} \max_{b \in \mathcal{V}'} \mathbf{x}_{jb}^{t} \mathbf{A}_{ia;jb}, \qquad (2)$$

where the superscript t denotes the current iteration. The activity values within this cluster are then normalized to their maximum, and a kWTA operation is applied:

$$\mathbf{x}_{ia}^{t+1} \longleftarrow \mathbf{x}_{ia}^{t} h(\mathbf{x}_{ia}^{t} - \tau) : a \in \mathcal{V}', \qquad (3)$$

where $h(.)$ is the unit step function and $\tau \in [0,1]$ is the kWTA activation threshold. Another iteration is then applied, this time on column clusters. We alternate between row-wise and column-wise iterations until the convergence of $\mathbf{X}$ or until a fixed maximum number of iterations it attained. Notice that for row clusters, max-pooling and kWTA are applied row-wise, while they are applied column-wise for column clusters.

Finally, an activation threshold is applied, where only neurons with a maximal activation value ($\mathbf{x}_{ia} = 1$) are kept active while others are deactivated ($\mathbf{x}_{ia} \leftarrow 0$). A WTA operation is then applied within every row and column cluster; if more than one neuron is active in a given cluster, they are all deactivated and no winner is declared. This is equivalent to imposing an 'at most' one-to-one matching constraint from $\mathcal{V}$ to $\mathcal{V}'$. The complete matching process we propose is described in Algorithm (1).

Algorithm 1. Proposed matching algorithm.

input : Pairwise affinity matrix $\mathbf{A}$, Unary similarity vector $\mathbf{y}$
output: Assignment vector $\mathbf{x}$
$\mathbf{x} \longleftarrow \mathbf{y}$
repeat
  foreach $i \in \mathcal{V}$ **do**
    foreach $a \in \mathcal{V}'$ **do**
      $\mathbf{x}_{ia}^{t+1} \leftarrow \mathbf{x}_{ia}^{t} \sum_{j \in \mathcal{V}} \max_{b \in \mathcal{V}'} \mathbf{x}_{jb}^{t} \mathbf{A}_{ia;jb}$
    $\mathbf{x}_{ia}^{t+1} \longleftarrow \frac{\mathbf{x}_{ia}^{t+1}}{\max_{a \in \mathcal{V}'} \mathbf{x}_{ia}^{t+1}} : a \in \mathcal{V}'$
    $\mathbf{x}_{ia}^{t+1} \longleftarrow \mathbf{x}_{ia}^{t+1} h(\mathbf{x}_{ia}^{t+1} - \tau) : a \in \mathcal{V}'$
  $\mathbf{x}_{ia}^{t} \longleftarrow \mathbf{x}_{ia}^{t+1}$
  foreach $a \in \mathcal{V}'$ **do**
    foreach $i \in \mathcal{V}$ **do**
      $\mathbf{x}_{ia}^{t+1} \leftarrow \mathbf{x}_{ia}^{t} \sum_{b \in \mathcal{V}'} \max_{j \in \mathcal{V}} \mathbf{x}_{jb}^{t} \mathbf{A}_{ia;jb}$
    $\mathbf{x}_{ia}^{t+1} \longleftarrow \frac{\mathbf{x}_{ia}^{t+1}}{\max_{i \in \mathcal{V}} \mathbf{x}_{ia}^{t+1}} : i \in \mathcal{V}$
    $\mathbf{x}_{ia}^{t+1} \longleftarrow \mathbf{x}_{ia}^{t+1} h(\mathbf{x}_{ia}^{t+1} - \tau) : i \in \mathcal{V}$
until $\mathbf{x}$ converges OR last iteration attained
$\mathbf{x}_{ia} \leftarrow \delta_{1}^{\mathbf{x}_{ia}} : i \in \mathcal{V}$ and $a \in \mathcal{V}'$ #δ is the Kronecker delta.
WTA: Zero all rows and columns in $\mathbf{X}$ with
more than one non-zero element.

To sum up, the network behavior consists in each neuron adding up its input signals, which are the max-pooled weighted activities of other neurons. Then, a non-linear activation function is applied to this neuron, taking into account the activity level of other members of its cluster. This is akin to the classic accumulate-and-fire neuron model of McCulloch-Pitts [15].

4 Experimental Evaluation

In order to evaluate our model, we compare its matching accuracy against a number of state-of-the-art models on a synthetic benchmark. Synthetic datasets are typically used for assessing performance of matching algorithms because they allow better control of test parameters.

The synthetic dataset is built as follows. Two graphs $\mathcal{G} = \{\mathcal{V}, \mathcal{E}\}$ and $\mathcal{G}' = \{\mathcal{V}', \mathcal{E}'\}$ are constructed, where $\mathcal{V}, \mathcal{V}' \subset \mathbb{R}^2$ and $\mathcal{E}, \mathcal{E}' \subset \mathbb{R}$. Then, n_{in} points that we call inliers are generated from a uniform random distribution on $[0, 1]^2$, and are added to $\mathcal{V}$. These inliers are also copied to $\mathcal{V}'$ after the addition of a Gaussian noise $\mathcal{N}(0, \sigma^2)$. After that, we add n_{out} outliers, generated from the same uniform random distribution $[0, 1]^2$, to each of $\mathcal{V}$ and $\mathcal{V}'$. Pairwise similarities are computed as follows:

$$s_E(e_{ij}, e'_{ab}) = \exp(-|\|v_i - v_j\| - \|v'_a - v'_b\||). \qquad (4)$$

Unary similarities are always set to one $s_V(v_i, v'_a) = 1$ so that points are matched using only their pairwise geometric information. The kWTA activation threshold is set to $\tau = 0.98$ in all of our experiments. We noticed that in most cases, convergence is attained after 5 to 10 iterations. However, as in [3], a theoretical guarantee for convergence is not yet proved but is worth exploring.

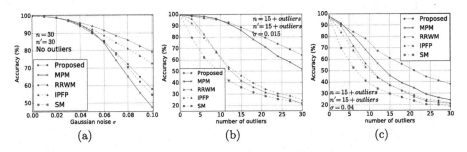

Fig. 2. Experimental comparison of the proposed model's accuracy with several state-of-the-art models on a synthetic dataset. In (a), no outliers are present, and the standard deviation σ of the Gaussian noise is varied. In (b) and (c), the number of outliers is varied for a fixed value of σ. The same number of outliers shown on the horizontal axis is added to both sets $\mathcal{V}$ and $\mathcal{V}'$.

We compare our model to MPM [3], RRWM [4], IPFP [13] and SM [12]. We are only interested in finding matches between inliers in $\mathcal{V}$ and $\mathcal{V}'$, outliers are used to represent clutter. We use the models' mean accuracy as a convenient performance criterion. Accuracy is measured as the ratio of the number of correct matches to the total number of inliers. Comparisons results are shown in Fig. 2. We notice that in the presence of outliers, our model's accuracy becomes significantly better than other models' as the number of outliers increases. This is an interesting property since clutter and deformation are ubiquitous in natural images. This robustness is due to the max-pooling and the kWTA operations that we apply to reduce the effect of false matches on the final result. Notice also that accuracy of our model is still higher than MPM's and SM's when no outliers are present, but lower than that of RRWM and IPFP. However, as stated in [3], comparing accuracies in the absence of outliers is a less realistic situation as outliers are almost always present in natural images, and robustness against clutter is essential in such situations.

5 Conclusion and Future Work

In this paper, we proposed a new approach for treating the feature correspondence problem using artificial neural network. We compared our model to state-of-the-art algorithms, and showed that it enjoys a higher robustness to outliers thanks to the application of max-pooling and kWTA operations, and to alternating rows and columns during iterations. This robustness to outliers is an essential property for matching objects in cluttered scenes. Further development of our model will include searching for a better way of choosing final matches than zeroing rows and columns of the assignment matrix containing more than one winner. We think that it is a simple but a brutal procedure that might be excluding some good matches. We shall also test the performance of the model in the context of natural images, which would give a more precise evaluation of the advantage of using this neural network model for solving the correspondence problem.

References

1. Aboudib, A., Gripon, V., Jiang, X.: A study of retrieval algorithms of sparse messages in networks of neural cliques. In: COGNITIVE 2014: The 6th International Conference on Advanced Cognitive Technologies and Applications, pp. 140–146. Venise, Italy, May 2014. https://hal.archives-ouvertes.fr/hal-01058303
2. Besl, P.J., McKay, N.D.: Method for registration of 3-d shapes. In: Robotics-DL Tentative, pp. 586–606. International Society for Optics and Photonics (1992)
3. Cho, M., Sun, J., Duchenne, O., Ponce, J.: Finding matches in a haystack: a max-pooling strategy for graph matching in the presence of outliers. In: IEEE Conference on Computer Vision and Pattern Recognition (CVPR), pp. 2091–2098 (2014)
4. Cho, M., Lee, J., Lee, K.M.: Reweighted random walks for graph matching. In: Daniilidis, K., Maragos, P., Paragios, N. (eds.) ECCV 2010, Part V. LNCS, vol. 6315, pp. 492–505. Springer, Heidelberg (2010)
5. Cour, T., Srinivasan, P., Shi, J.: Balanced graph matching. In: Schölkopf, B., Platt, J.C., Hoffman, T. (eds.) Advances in Neural Information Processing Systems 19, pp. 313–320. MIT Press (2007). http://papers.nips.cc/paper/2960-balanced-graph-matching.pdf
6. Fischler, M.A., Bolles, R.C.: Random sample consensus: a paradigm for model fitting with applications to image analysis and automated cartography. Commun. ACM **24**(6), 381–395 (1981)
7. Gold, S., Rangarajan, A.: A graduated assignment algorithm for graph matching. IEEE Trans. Pattern Anal. Mach. Intell. **18**(4), 377–388 (1996). http://dx.doi.org/10.1109/34.491619
8. Grauman, K., Darrell, T.: The pyramid match kernel: discriminative classification with sets of image features. In: Tenth IEEE International Conference on Computer Vision (ICCV 2005), vol. 2, pp. 1458–1465, October 2005

9. Gripon, V., Berrou, C.: Sparse neural networks with large learning diversity. IEEE Trans. Neural Netw. **22**(7), 1087–1096 (2011)
10. Jiang, H., Yu, S.X., Martin, D.R.: Linear scale and rotation invariant matching. IEEE Trans. Pattern Anal. Mach. Intell. **33**(7), 1339–1355 (2011)
11. Leordeanu, M., Collins, R.: Unsupervised learning of object features from video sequences. In: IEEE Conference on Computer Vision and Pattern Recognition (CVPR 2005), vol. 1, pp. 1142–1149, June 2005
12. Leordeanu, M., Hebert, M.: A spectral technique for correspondence problems using pairwise constraints. In: Tenth IEEE International Conference on Computer Vision (ICCV 2005), vol. 2, pp. 1482–1489, October 2005
13. Leordeanu, M., Hebert, M., Sukthankar, R.: An integer projected fixed point method for graph matching and map inference. In: Advances in Neural Information Processing Systems, pp. 1114–1122 (2009)
14. Marr, D.: Vision: A Computational Investigation into the Human Representation and Processing of Visual Information. Henry Holt and Co., Inc., New York (1982)
15. McCulloch, W.S., Pitts, W.: A logical calculus of the ideas immanent in nervous activity. Bull. Math. Biophys. **5**(4), 115–133 (1943)
16. Mountcastle, V.B.: The columnar organization of the neocortex. Brain **120**(4), 701–722 (1997)
17. Rothganger, F., Lazebnik, S., Schmid, C., Ponce, J.: Segmenting, modeling, and matching video clips containing multiple moving objects. IEEE Trans. Pattern Anal. Mach. Intell. **29**(3), 477–491 (2007)
18. Schwenker, F., Sommer, F., Palm, G.: Iterative retrieval of sparsely coded associative memory patterns. Neural Netw. **9**(3), 445–455 (1996). http://www.sciencedirect.com/science/article/pii/0893608095001123
19. Szeliski, R.: Computer Vision: Algorithms and Applications. Springer Science & Business Media, London (2010)
20. Tuytelaars, T., Gool, L.V.: Wide baseline stereo matching based on local, affinely invariant regions. In: British Machine Vision Conference (BMVC 2000), pp. 412–425 (2000)
21. Zass, R., Shashua, A.: Probabilistic graph and hypergraph matching. In: IEEE Conference on Computer Vision and Pattern Recognition (CVPR 2008), pp. 1–8, June 2008
22. Zhou, F., la Torre, F.D.: Factorized graph matching. In: IEEE Conference on Computer Vision and Pattern Recognition (CVPR 2012), pp. 127–134, June 2012

The Performance of a Biologically Plausible Model of Visual Attention to Localize Objects in a Virtual Reality

Amirhossein Jamalian$^{(\boxtimes)}$, Frederik Beuth, and Fred H. Hamker

Artificial Intelligence, Chemnitz University of Technology,
Strasse der Nationen 62, 09111 Chemnitz, Germany
amirhossein.jamalian@informatik.tu-chemnitz.de

Abstract. Visual attention, as a smart mechanism to reduce the computational complexity of scene understanding, is the basis of several computational models of object detection, recognition and localization. In this paper, for the first time, the robustness of a biologically-constrained model of visual attention (with the capability of object recognition and localization) against large object variations of a visual search task in virtual reality is demonstrated. The model is based on rate coded neural networks and uses both bottom-up and top-down approaches to recognize and localize learned objects concurrently. Furthermore, the virtual reality is very similar to real-world scenes in which a human-like neuro-cognitive agent can recognize and localize 15 different objects regardless of scaling, point of view and orientation. The simulation results show the neuro-cognitive agent performs the visual search task correctly in approximately 85.4 % of scenarios.

Keywords: Computational neuroscience · Object localization · Object recognition · Virtual reality · Visual attention · Visual search

1 Introduction

Several tasks require looking for a certain object in the environment. This is known as *visual search* in the literature. In such a task, the typical human knows what exactly she/he is looking for. This predefined knowledge of the searched object stimulates a *top-down* signal in her/his brain [1], called *feature-based attention*. It originates in the *prefrontal cortex (PFC)* region (which could be considered as the object memory) and is given to the object recognition pathway of the brain which is known as *ventral stream* (Fig. 1). This pathway starts in the primary visual cortex (V1), continues through the fourth visual cortex (V4) and reaches the inferior temporal cortex (IT). The processing of the ventral stream is modulated by the frontal eye field (FEF).

Computational models of visual attention simulate the processing in the brain to different degrees. The simplest approaches are *bottom-up saliency models* [2], which simulate simple features as located in V1 to calculate a saliency map. This map indicates regions of the visual field containing the most information. This approach is often combined with top-down attention towards simple features to favor target relevant features (*top-down saliency models*, [2]). One step further goes through

© Springer International Publishing Switzerland 2016
A.E.P. Villa et al. (Eds.): ICANN 2016, Part II, LNCS 9887, pp. 447–454, 2016.
DOI: 10.1007/978-3-319-44781-0_53

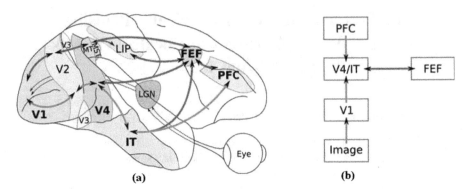

Fig. 1. (a) Primates' Visual Attention System [4]. The green arrows show the Ventral Stream and the blue arrows correspond to the Dorsal Stream, which process the type and location of an object respectively. Bottom-up processing is denoted by arrows from left to right and top-down processing (mediated by attention) by arrows from right to left. (b) Areas and connections which are simulated in this attention model. They are printed in bold in (a). (Color figure online)

proto-object-based models that define spatial regions belonging to one object (the proto-objects) in the saliency map [3]. Finally, there are *neuro-computational models* simulating the attentional processing of the brain, in which feature-based and spatial attention are closely entangled and thus operate in parallel. *Feature-based attention amplifies* the activation of neurons that encode the searched object (and suppress the others), while *spatial attention* amplifies the neurons regarding their location information. This process iterates until the location of the target would be encoded in a spatial map (FEF). Due to their parallel nature, they are called iterative [3] or holistic attention models [4].

However, such neuro-computational models have been typically developed for psychophysical experiments using very simple stimuli, and thus cannot deal with real-world objects. Hence, our aim is to further develop such models for making them applicable to real-world scenarios. A few models have been already demonstrated with real-world objects [4–9]. Yet, they have mostly used static input material. Only two studies have used 3D environments, but merely very simple ones, like three objects in a robotic setup [5] or cubic objects in a black-background virtual reality (VR) [6]. Hence, a next step towards a real-world application would be to benchmark such models in a more complex VR setup. Therefore, in this work, the performance of our model in a VR is evaluated.

In neuro-computational models, objects are encoded typically by neurons representing a specific view (view-tuned neurons); as such cells have been found in area IT [10]. In theory, this approach can encode objects under any kind of transformation. We have previously demonstrated this for objects under different rotations [4–6], different disparities [5], and small difference in the scaling [5]. Here, we will benchmark some of the remaining transformations, i.e. larger changes in the scaling and different views of the object (top versus side view). We have chosen these kinds of transformations as they occur when a virtual agent walks towards objects located on a table, which seems a plausible scenario for VR and real-world applications.

We now present the further development of our biologically-plausible model of visual attention, in particular how it is customized to work in the VR and how object representations are created by a novel learning algorithm, called *One-shot Learning*.

2 Model Structure and Functionality

2.1 Overview of the Model

This model builds upon previous integrative attention models like Hamker (2005) [8]. The present version [4] is based on a recently developed cortical microcircuit model of attention, which replicates many neurophysiological data sets of attention [11]. This and the other biological foundations of the model are explained in the original publication, while we give here only a functional overview. The model simulates the ventral stream pathway in primates' visual system (see Fig. 1(a) as well as the frontal eye field (FEF) and the prefrontal cortex (PFC). The diagram of the model is depicted in Fig. 2. Its input is an RGB image that is firstly processed by a model of the primary visual cortex (V1), whose cells encode oriented edges, red-green and blue-yellow color contrasts. Afterwards, this activity is fed to a higher visual area (HVA) encoding object views. HVA represents high-level visual areas like V4 (fourth visual cortex) and IT (inferior temporal cortex). These object-view maps are constructed via convolutions of receptive fields of V1 layer neurons (as pre-synaptic layer) by a pre-generated weight matrix, calculated offline by the one-shot learning procedure (next section).

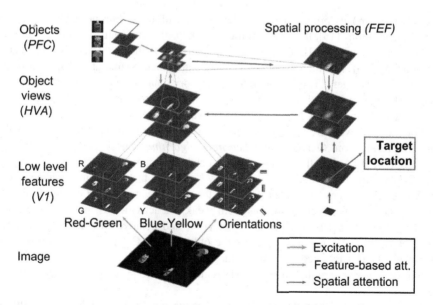

Fig. 2. The model of visual attention [4]. The processing is illustrated at the task to localize the "bottle", indicated by the red cross. See main text for details. (Color figure online)

During the search for an object, a top-down feature-based attention signal is sent from PFC to HVA. This signal contains the encoded features or views of the searched target object. Applying the attention signal, neurons encoding the corresponding object-views will be more excited in comparison to the others, while local inhibitory connections suppress views belonging to other objects. This pattern of activity will be send to the FEF for further spatial selection.

The FEF region is split into three parts, according to its neurophysiological cell properties: FEF-Visual (FEF-v), FEF-visiomovement (FEF-vm) and FEF-Movement (FEF-m). FEF-v is a kind of saliency map and contains the places where the target is probably located. FEF-vm is responsible for focusing neuronal activity at the target location. Additionally, this map projects back to visual areas (HVA), forming a recurrent loop from which spatial attention emerges. This kind of attention does not only excite the activity of the neurons in HVA around the target location, but also suppress the activity of the other neurons to decrease the effect of distractors. This cycle iterates until a saccade plan is completed, indicated by the fact that the neurons in the FEF-m layer reach a threshold. This activity blob indicates the location of the target in the image.

The model has been benchmarked in a task with up to 100 objects (COIL-100 database, [12]) and three background classes [4] and achieved an object localization accuracy of 92 % on black, of 71 % on noisy, and of 42 % on real-world backgrounds.

2.2   Model Customization for VR

The VR used in this project has been developed within the European Union project "Spatial Cognition" [13]. It is part of a framework to simulate neuro-cognitive agents in a virtual environment [14]. This framework consists of the VR (based on the game engine Unity [15]) in which the agent is placed, and a neuro-simulator [16] to simulate the "brain" of an agent. The VR provides all sensory data to the agent like stereoscopic images (from which we use the left eye here), collisions, etc., while the agent can execute actions in the VR like rotating eyes, walking, etc.

For the VR, we developed a simple and straight-forward algorithm to learn the object representation. Our *One-shot Learning algorithm* creates an object view representation in HVA directly from a stimulus patch showing the object under this view. For this, the stimulus is firstly processed by V1 and then the algorithm calculated from this V1 activity pattern (cell index i) directly the weight matrix of a HVA cell (index j). The method creates negative weights from weak V1 activities as these represent V1 features which do not appear in the object view, and positive weights from high V1 activities as these V1 features represent the object view (Eq. 1). The amount of negative weights is calibrated per view independently via the parameter v_j. A higher amount of negative weights tunes the HVA neuron more specifically to its preferred view.

Normally, the method would learn the background in the patch along with the object. Yet, this is a problem when the objects appear very small at the patch, i.e. for farer distances, as the resulting object presentations would mainly encode the background. To solve this problem, we introduce a spatial selection mask S. The mask contains binary elements and allows selecting only a spatial part of the patch for learning. We choose five different circular masks, each one for one learned distance. Finally, the weights are normalized so that if the same stimulus appears again, the HVA neuron reacts for it maximally (here chosen as 1) (Eq. 2).

$$A_{\{i,j\}} = f\left(r_i^{V1}, v_j\right) \cdot S, \quad \text{with: } f(r, v) = \begin{cases} -(v - r)^2, r < v \\ (r - v)^2, r \geq v \end{cases} \tag{1}$$

$$w_{\{i,j\}} = A_{\{i,j\}} / \sum_{\{i'\}} A_{\{i'j\}} \cdot r_{\{i'\}}^{V1} \tag{2}$$

Customizing the model for this VR, we learned firstly 15 different objects with the One-shot Learning algorithm (Fig. 3(a). We used 12 differently rotated views of each object (every 30°), and 5 different distances between the agent and the target object. Hence, for each object, the model has $12 \times 5 = 60$ views in HVA. Selected views and distances of a typical object (the green racing car) are depicted in Fig. 3b. Since the total number of learned objects is 15, HVA has $15 \times 60 = 900$ view-related and PFC 15 object neurons. Besides, the VR stimuli have finer structures than the previously used COIL stimuli. To recognize them, we reduced the receptive field size in V1 (from 19 to 9 pixels) and the spatial pooling factor (from 10:1 to 6:1).

3   Simulation Results in VR

We tested the model in the VR at 3000 test scenes, whereby each scene contains at least 3 different objects under a variation of transformations: arbitrary rotations, arbitrary agent-object distances, and nine randomly-chosen positions on the table. In relation to this test set, the training set contains the objects under 12 fixed rotations (every 30°), 5 fixed distances (every 0.5 units in the VR), and at the center position. This training set was used for learning the object representation and was completely separated from the test data. In each of the 3000 test scenes, every of the three objects were considered one time as target (searched object) while the others would be the distractors, resulting in over 9000 localization tasks. On average, the model can localize the searched object in

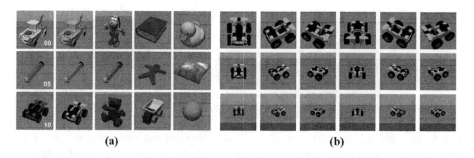

(a)   (b)

Fig. 3. (a) The 15 target objects in Virtual Reality. (b) Six selected views of a typical object (the green racing car) at the nearest, middle, and farthest distance. (Color figure online)

approximately 180–200 steps (each step is the simulation of one millisecond in primates' brain). In Fig. 4, we depicted the result for one typical case.

The performance of the model at the 3000 test scenes is illustrated in Fig. 5a as a confusion matrix. Such a matrix illustrates for each presented target object (Y-axis) the object that has been selected by the model (X-axis). As it can be seen in this figure, in 85.4 % of the cases the model can localize the target correctly (the saccade landed within the object borders or not more than a half object away). Low accuracy values under 50 % are illustrated in red to show mislocalizations. In the matrix, the horizontal axis denotes the localized object or two special cases: B and No. The case B (Background) indicates that one non-sense point in the background was selected instead of the target, and the case No (No-localization) indicates that no location was selected because the model did not converge on any object location including background.

Figure 5b illustrates the object localization accuracy of the model for five different distances between the agent and the objects on the table. Due to the varying distances, the target object (and all others) appears under different scaling and viewpoints, thus we evaluate the robustness of the object localization against these object transformations. Besides the scaling, the viewpoint also changes as the agent looks from half-top to the objects at the closest distance and from the side at the farthest distances. It can be seen

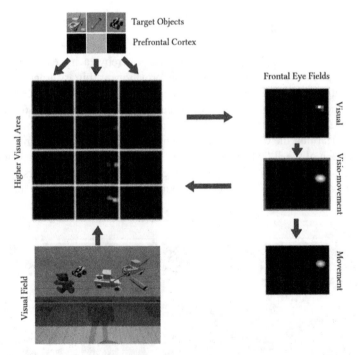

Fig. 4. The searched target (blue pencil) has been recognized and localized at the end of the simulation (indicated by a red circle). Every column of the higher visual area (HVA) is regarded to one object (as depicted in prefrontal cortex), showing four exemplary views. (Color figure online)

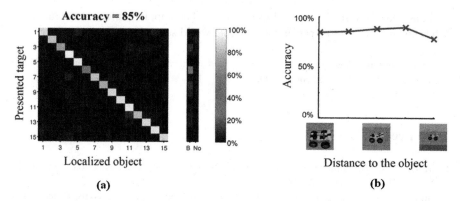

Fig. 5. (a) Performance of the model at 9000 localization tasks. (b) Performance dependent on the distance between agent and the object on the table, whereby the left side denotes the closest distance and the right side the farthest.

that the accuracy is quite stable for the fourth closest distances, showing the robustness of the object localization against changing viewpoints and scaling. The only exception is the farthest distance as the object appears very small (about 15 × 15 pixels). In this case, the accuracy of the model drops. However, it is still 78 % which is quite acceptable regarding its scale.

4 Conclusion, Limitations and Future Works

Here, the performance of a biologically-plausible model of visual attention with the capability of object recognition and localization in a VR has been demonstrated. The model used both bottom-up and top-down approaches in an iterative fashion to perform its visual search task based on an offline supervised learning phase called one-shot learning. In principle, the one-shot learning is easier to use, faster and has a better performance in comparison with previous attempt [5], but produces object representations with more cells. Thus, it is suitable to use in scenarios with a limited number of objects. In the VR, the human-like neuro-cognitive agent can perform the visual search task for 15 different objects in various rotations, places, viewpoints, and scales. The simulation results show that the agent is able to recognize and localize the objects correctly in 85.4 % of cases out of 3000 different scenes as visual search scenarios. It is the first time that such performance evaluation, in presence of multi scaling and viewpoints in VR, is performed. The performance of this model in comparison with similar model [5] which has been evaluated on COIL-100 dataset with real-world background is remarkably better (85.4 % versus 42 %). Although current approach and the old one [5] has been evaluated based on different datasets, we expect the new one would have a better performance on COIL-100 as well, since in COIL-100 all scenes are constructed by objects with same scales. In other words, the new approach performs the task better even in more complicated scenarios. Hence, its performance should be better on COIL-100 dataset as well. However, we would compare them on same datasets, COIL-100 as well as VR, as one of our future works. Besides, we will attempt to implement the model on iCub robot and evaluate its performance in real-world scenarios.

Acknowledgement. This work has been supported by the European Union project "Spatial Cognition" under grant agreement no 600785.

References

1. Miller, E.K., Buschman, T.J.: Cortical circuits for the control of attention. Curr. Opin. Neurobiol. **23**(2), 216–222 (2013)
2. Borji, A., Itti, L.: State-of-the-art in visual attention modelling. IEEE Trans. Pattern Anal. Mach. Intell. (PAMI) **35**(1), 185–207 (2013)
3. Jamalian, A., Hamker, F.H.: Biologically-inspired models for attentive robot vision: a review. In: Innovative Research in Attention Modeling and Computer Vision Applications, pp. 69–98. Information Science Reference, Hershey (2016)
4. Beuth, F., Hamker, F.H.: Attention as cognitive, holistic control of the visual system. In: Workshop of New Challenges in Neural Computation (NCNC 2015), Aachen (2015a)
5. Antonelli, M., Gibaldi, A., Beuth, F., Duran, A.J., Canessa, A., Chessa, M., Solari, F., del Pobil, A.P., Hamker, F., Chinellato, E., Sabatini, S.P.: A hierarchical system for a distributed representation of the peripersonal space of a humanoid robot. IEEE Trans. Auton. Ment. Dev. **6**(4), 259–273 (2014)
6. Beuth, F., Wiltschut, J., Hamker, F.H.: Attentive stereoscopic object recognition. In: Workshop of New Challenges in Neural Computation (NCNC 2010) (2010)
7. Chikkerur, S., Serre, T., Tan, C., Poggio, T.: What and where: a bayesian inference theory of attention. Vision Res. **50**(22), 2233–2247 (2010)
8. Hamker, F.H.: The emergence of attention by population-based inference and its role in distributed processing and cognitive control of vision. Comput. Vis. Image Underst. **100** (1-2), 64–106 (2005)
9. Walther, D.B., Koch, C.: Attention in hierarchical models of object recognition. Prog. Brain Res. **165**, 57–78 (2007)
10. Logothetis, N.K., Pauls, J., Poggio, T.: Shape representation in the inferior temporal cortex of monkeys. Curr. Biol. **5**(5), 552–563 (1995)
11. Beuth, F., Hamker, F.H.: A mechanistic cortical microcircuit of attention for amplification, normalization and suppression. Vision Res. **116**(B), 241–257 (2015b)
12. Nene, S.A., Nayar, S. K., Murase, H.: Columbia Object Image Library (COIL-100), CUCS-006-96. Technical report (1996)
13. Hamker, F.H.: Spatial Cognition of humans and brain-like artificial agents. Künstliche Intelligenz **29**, 83–88 (2015)
14. http://www.tu-chemnitz.de/informatik/KI/projects/agents-vr/index.php
15. https://unity3d.com/
16. Vitay, J., Dinkelbach, H.Ü., Hamker, F.H.: ANNarchy: a code generation approach to neural simulations on parallel hardware. Front. Neuroinformatics **9**, 1–20 (2015)

Pose-Invariant Object Recognition
for Event-Based Vision with Slow-ELM

Rohan Ghosh[(✉)], Tang Siyi, Mahdi Rasouli, Nitish V. Thakor,
and Sunil L. Kukreja

Singapore Institute for Neurotechnology, National University of Singapore,
Singapore, Singapore
rghosh92@gmail.com, tangsy935@gmail.com, mahdi.rasouli@gmail.com,
sinapsedirector@gmail.com, sunilkukreja.sinapse@gmail.com

Abstract. Neuromorphic image sensors produce activity-driven spiking output at every pixel. These low-power consuming imagers which encode visual change information in the form of spikes help reduce computational overhead and realize complex real-time systems; object recognition and pose-estimation to name a few. However, there exists a lack of algorithms in event-based vision aimed towards capturing invariance to transformations. In this work, we propose a methodology for recognizing objects invariant to their pose with the Dynamic Vision Sensor (DVS). A novel slow-ELM architecture is proposed which combines the effectiveness of Extreme Learning Machines and Slow Feature Analysis. The system, tested on an Intel Core i5-4590 CPU, can perform $10,000$ classifications per second and achieves 1% classification error for 8 objects with views accumulated over $90°$ of 2D pose.

Keywords: Neuromorphic vision · Slow feature analysis · Extreme learning machines · Object recognition

1 Introduction

Conventional frame-based sensors capture intensity values of the whole pixel array at fixed time intervals. In contrast, asynchronous imagers remove the notion of a frame by essentially being responsive to intensity changes at an almost continual time-scale. As an example, the Dynamic Vision Sensor (DVS) elicits a spike event at a pixel when the pixel records a relative change in intensity. With their sparse, non-redundant input data stream only capturing salient moving edges, computational burden is reduced by only computing with the *active events* at any time as in [1]. For object recognition this points to faster inference as highlighted in [2], wherein a few spikes acquired from moving objects enable the architecture to estimate object class. The high temporal resolution of $\approx 1\,\mu\text{s}$ also allows for accurate pose-estimation in real-time when the underlying edge-structure of the object is known as shown in [3].

This work proposes a method for pose-invariant object recognition with event-based visual data. Like in [4] where separate eigen-faces were found

© Springer International Publishing Switzerland 2016
A.E.P. Villa et al. (Eds.): ICANN 2016, Part II, LNCS 9887, pp. 455–462, 2016.
DOI: 10.1007/978-3-319-44781-0_54

pertaining to each pose, each object class is subdivided into multiple pose-specific classes. Here we use a variant of Extreme Learning Machines [5] for classification. ELMs have shown a faster way of training neural networks, exhibiting universal approximation capabilities with their random projection based feedforward model. Our approach involves an ELM architecture with excess hidden random projections. Since not all random projections are useful for classification, we proceed to add a layer that separates the noisy and irrelevant subspaces of the projections, stripping the feature vector to a much smaller dimensional space. Quantifying the utility of a projection is not easy, but however slow feature analysis (SFA, [6,7]) proposes a simple way of arriving at informative and invariant features. For frame-based vision, SFA has been successfully applied before to learn pose-invariant features in [8]. The slowness principle targets only smoothly changing features with time, and can therefore be used to derive feature spaces which are robust to transformations. By recording data linearly varying over 2D-pose, we are able to apply the slowness principle in arriving at robust, time-supervised features. Furthermore, our constant event number sampling of events introduced in [9] allows a consistent object representation which enhances recognition performance. The slow-ELM architecture proposed therefore learns to identify robust features from the recorded data exhibiting gradual 2D pose transformations of objects.

As the DVS only responds to changes, one can only expect spikes generated by the object edges when either the object or the camera is in motion. Thereby, the invariance of our classifier performance to speed is demonstrated, along with quantifying the amount of multi-pose-view information needed to make reliable class estimates. Our Slow-ELM learner shows a considerable improvement in classification performance compared to the standard ELM, achieving 1 % error with 8 objects, with their 2D pose views spanning 90 degrees. Compared to the principal components based projections as used in P-ELM [10], slow projections are found to give better recognition estimates. Furthermore, the system is capable of classifying 10^4 times per second, allowing real-time operation. For frame-based vision such high speeds are of not much use due to the 30 FPS input itself, unless there are other computational modules involved which benefit from fast classification. However, for event based vision the high temporal resolution essentially means a frame rate of $\approx 15,000$, which emphasizes the importance of fast computational modules.

2   Methods

The algorithm consists of four steps: Spatiotemporal region of interest (ROI) estimation; slow-ELM; pose-specific labelling; multi-view object class estimation.

2.1   Spatiotemporal ROI Estimation

This section describes our method for estimating the temporal and the spatial ROI for acquiring events. To obtain temporal ROI we employ the constant event

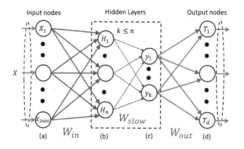

Fig. 1. The Slow-ELM architecture. The transformation represented by the matrix W_{slow} only preserves the slowly changing projections of H. W_{in} correspond to the Gaussian randomized weights as in conventional ELM. W_{out} is learnt between the projected signal and the output vectors.

number approach used in our previous work in [9] which maintains event structure w.r.t change of speed. Similar to [9], a rectangular spatial ROI is obtained by considering a certain fraction of the events on each side (up, down, left, and right) of the centroid of the extracted events. Once the current spatio-temporal ROI events have been obtained, we disregard the temporal differences between those events and form a purely spatial binary image. In contrast to [9], however, we add a smoothness prior to the way the ROIs change through time. This involves only including the events which are lesser than a threshold distance to the previous spatial ROI's edges. The image formed by the pixels within the ROI is then resized to a square image of a fixed size before passing on as an input to the slow-ELM.

2.2   Slow-ELM

We have training samples $\{(x_i, t_i)\}_{i=1}^N$, where $(x_i)_{i=1}^N$ are the binary images obtained from the ROIs. t_i is the target object class vector assigned to x_i. Every dimension of x_i is scaled to the range $[-1,1]$ before passing onto the ELM. The entries of the input layer weights are initialized randomnly according to the normal distribution $N(0,1)$. The n hidden neuron values in H_i are computed via adding a sigmoidal non-linearity f onto the random projections as follows

$$H_i = f(W_{in}^T x_i) \qquad (1)$$

Now the SFA algorithm elaborated in [6] is applied, which finds uncorrelated linear projections of H_i as expressed by the projection matrix W_{slow} :

$$Y_i = W_{slow}^T H_i \qquad (2)$$

The elements of W_{slow} are found according to the SFA optimization. In particular SFA looks for projections which minimize:

$$\langle (\Delta y_j)^2 \rangle \qquad (3)$$

Under the constraints:

$$\langle y_j \rangle = 0 \tag{4}$$

$$\langle y_j^2 \rangle = 1 \tag{5}$$

$$\langle y_i y_j \rangle = 0, i \neq j \tag{6}$$

$\langle y \rangle$ denotes the expectation of y over time, in our case being the average value of the projection across all classes. The unit variance condition ensures projections stay informative. $\langle (\Delta y_j)^2 \rangle$ is the squared energy of the difference of a projection over two consecutive instances of input (difference energy). In our experiments, two consecutive instances of input only differ in the 2D-pose of the object. As noted in [6], these slow features can be obtained simply by sphering the data followed by finding the lowest eigenvalues of the difference data Δy. As the hidden neuron vector H is n-dimensional, W_{slow} will be an (nxn) matrix with each column being a projection found through SFA. Since SFA returns the projections in order of decreasing difference energies we only keep the first k columns of W_{slow}.

2.3   Pose-Specific Labelling

Every object data captured is categorized differently according to the 2D pose range it belongs in as we record from all viewpoints across 360° (Fig. 2a). In particular, we take 8 uniform partitions of the 2D pose: (0°–45°), (45°–90°), ... (315°–360°). So with m objects, we have 8 m classes. The algorithm up to this point remains unsupervised as the only learning happens for finding the entries of W_{slow}. As shown in Fig. 1 the final layer is learnt through the regularized least squares algorithm shown in [11]. For each training sample x_i, we extract the slow projections Y_i through the aforementioned steps. Now the supervised RLS algorithm estimates the linear mapping W_{out} between Y_i and t_i:

$$W_{out} = (\frac{I}{C} + Y^T Y)^{-1} Y^T T \tag{7}$$

Here $Y = [Y_1, Y_2, ..., Y_N]$ and $T = [t_1, t_2, ..., t_N]^T$. The parameter C controls the tradeoff between the regularization and the error term. Higher the value of C, lesser the smoothness constraint on the weights and therefore higher the chance of over-fitting the data. Given the input to the final layer Y_i we finally obtain the estimated output vector t_i^{est}:

$$t_i^{est} = W_{out}^T Y_i \tag{8}$$

The class estimate is then the object for which one of its pose-specific class has the maximum value across all 8 m classes in t_i^{est}.

2.4   Multi-view Object Class Estimation

This describes the method used to estimate object class when multiple input data $(X_1, X_2, ..., X_p)$ derived from many view-points of a single object is presented to the classifier. Since we record the event data with the object smoothly changing in pose, $(X_1, X_2, ..., X_p)$ are the successive instances of the event-structure as the object rotates. The estimated object class is the one receiving the maximum number of votes across the p samples, where the ith vote cast is to the object category inferred by the slow-ELM for X_i.

3   Experimental Setup

As the DVS only responds to changes in the scene, the experimental setup consisted of a rotating platform on which an object was placed. Such a setup however makes the pixels near the centre of rotation generate lesser spike-events than the pixels near the edge. To avoid this motion intensity bias, the objects were placed near the edge of the platform (as shown in Fig. 2a). For each object, the event data was captured as the platform was rotated over 6π radians, thus uniformly covering the range of 2D-pose. The experiment was repeated for two elevations (10 cm and 40 cm) of the camera, similar to what was done in [12], and across 3 different distances from the platform centre (30 cm, 45 cm, 60 cm). For each configuration, object data was recorded for 3 different angular velocities of the platform, with a total of 8 objects. Thus a total of 18 recordings were obtained. The objects chosen were: camera, cup, computer mouse, pen, mobile phone, scissors, spectacle and bottle. The output weight matrix learns a 64-class classification problem.

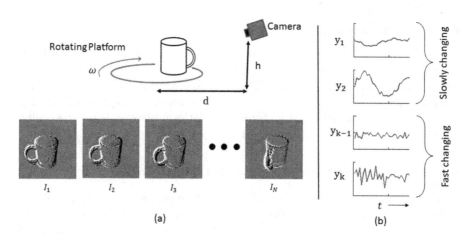

Fig. 2. (a) shows the experimental setup along with sample framed event data (I_1 to I_N) for the rotating cup object. The recording is repeated for 3 values of distance d and two different heights h of the camera, each time with 3 motor speeds of rotation ω. (b) shows the contrast between the slowly changing and fast changing projections in response to the rotating object.

4   Results and Discussion

Out of the 18 recordings, 9 were used for testing (40 cm elevation) and the other 9 for training (10 cm elevation). Not every object had the same number of data, as they generated spikes at different event rates. Therefore for an unbiased estimate of performance, testing data for the classes having lesser examples were duplicated randomly to ensure equal instances of each class. After duplication, each class had approximately 2700 samples. The image extracted from the ROI is resized to a 60×60 image, input as a 3600 dimensional vector to the ELM. W_{in} is chosen such that H has 3000 projections. We try a range of values of k, i.e. the dimensionality of the final vector y input to the classification layer.

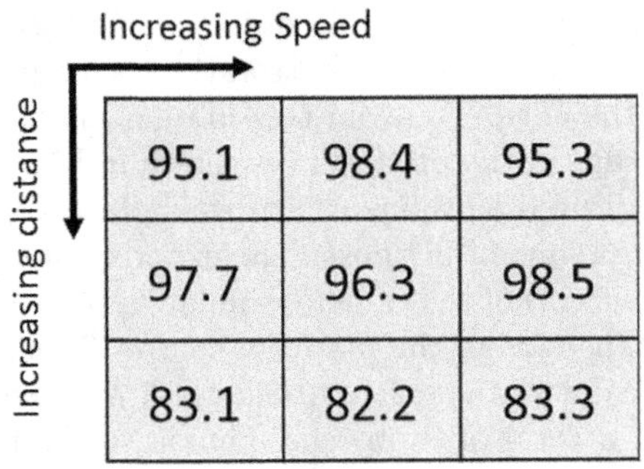

Increasing Speed

Increasing distance

95.1	98.4	95.3
97.7	96.3	98.5
83.1	82.2	83.3

Fig. 3. Recognition accuracy across 3 different speeds and distances.

4.1   Performance with Varying Speed and Distance

Shown in Fig. 3 is the effect of changing speeds and distance of the platform on the accuracy. The accuracy remains high for distances $d = 30$ and 45 cm, but drops abruptly for $d = 60$ cm. This indicates that the classes become less separable quickly as the distance to the object is increased beyond a limit. The effect with varying speed of the motor of the platform however is not discernible which indicates the invariance to speed changes.

4.2   Comparing SFA with Other Selection Methods

Figure 4a demonstrates how slow-ELM compares in performance with traditional ELM and other variants, as a function of the number of projections used for learning. In particular, we compare slow-ELM (our approach), P-ELM [10], conventional ELM and fast varying features (with the projections maximizing Eq. 3). The figure clearly demonstrates that SFA based projections give the best recognition accuracies ($\approx 93\%$). In contrast, the FAST features perform very near to chance itself (14 %, chance is $100/64 = 15\%$). This suggests that fast, fluctuating features do not provide abstract category information essential for classification.

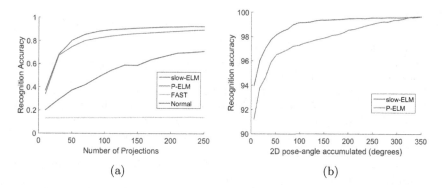

Fig. 4. (a) Recognition Accuracy for varying number of k selected projections, shown for the different selection criteria mentioned in Sect. 4.2 (b) Recognition accuracy for slow-ELM and P-ELM on aggregated data from successive viewpoints spanning different range of 2D-pose

4.3   Multi-pose View Object Recognition

Here the method described in Sect. 2.4 is used to arrive at class estimates with event-data accumulated across changing pose as the objects rotate. Precisely, we quantify the recognition accuracy when event data spread out in different range of 2D pose is available. This is averaged across all possible starting 2D-poses of the objects. Figure 4b compares the recognition accuracy for both SFA and PCA based projections. It can be seen that SFA quickly reaches a low error rate (1 %) in classification with only 90 degrees of pose information whereas PCA requires 280 degrees to achieve the same error.

5   Conclusion

This work presents a system capable of recognizing objects from a real-time feed of spike-events and capable of generating accurate class estimates by combining information from successive views varying in object pose. Apart from the low computation time which allows upto 10^4 classifications per second, the training time is also considerably lesser than the state-of-the-art Convolutional Neural Networks. The speed invariance and the partial scale invariance (object distance) of the classifier has been demonstrated. A novel slow-ELM architecture has been proposed to extract features invariant to pose changes.

Acknowledgements. This work is supported by a NPRP grant from the Qatar National Research Fund under the grant No. NPRP 7-673-2-251. The statements made herein are solely the responsibility of the authors.

462   R. Ghosh et al.

References

1. Ni, Z., Bolopion, A., Agnus, J., Benosman, R., Regnier, S.: Asynchronous event-based visual shape tracking for stable haptic feedback in microrobotics. IEEE Trans. Robot. **28**(5), 1081–1089 (2012)
2. Perez-Carrasco, J.A., Zhao, B., Serrano, C., Acha, B., Serrano-Gotarredona, T., Chen, S., Linares-Barranco, B.: Mapping from frame-driven to frame-free event-driven vision systems by low-rate rate coding and coincidence processing-application to feedforward convnets. IEEE Trans. Pattern Anal. Mach. Intell. **35**(11), 2706–2719 (2013)
3. Valeiras, D.R., Orchard, G., Ieng, S.H., Benosman, R.B.: Neuromorphic event-based 3d pose estimation. Front. Neurosci. **9**, 522 (2015)
4. Huang, F.J., Zhang, H.J., Chen, T., Zhou, Z.: Pose invariant face recognition. Institute of Electrical and Electronics Engineers Inc., March 2000
5. Huang, G.B., Zhu, Q.Y., Siew, C.K.: Extreme learning machine: theory and applications. Neurocomputing **70**(13), 489–501 (2006). Neural Networks Selected Papers from the 7th Brazilian Symposium on Neural Networks
6. Wiskott, L., Sejnowski, T.: Slow feature analysis: unsupervised learning of invariances. Neural Comput. **14**(4), 715–770 (2002)
7. Berkes, P., Wiskott, L.: Slow feature analysis yields a rich repertoire of complex cell properties. J. Vis. **5**(6), 9 (2005)
8. Franzius, M., Wilbert, N., Wiskott, L.: Invariant object recognition with slow feature analysis. In: Kůrková, V., Neruda, R., Koutník, J. (eds.) ICANN 2008, Part I. LNCS, vol. 5163, pp. 961–970. Springer, Heidelberg (2008)
9. Ghosh, R., Mishra, A., Orchard, G., Thakor, N.V.: Real-time object recognition and orientation estimation using an event-based camera and CNN. In: Biomedical Circuits and Systems Conference (BioCAS), October 2014, pp. 544–547. IEEE (2014)
10. Zhang, H., Yin, Y., Zhang, S., Sun, C.: An improved ELM algorithm based on PCA technique. In: Proceedings of ELM-2014, Volume 2: Applications, pp. 95–104. Springer International Publishing, Cham (2015)
11. Huang, G.B., Zhou, H., Ding, X., Zhang, R.: Extreme learning machine for regression and multiclass classification. IEEE Trans. Syst. Man Cybern. Part B Cybern. **42**(2), 513–529 (2012)
12. Thomas, A., Ferrar, V., Leibe, B., Tuytelaars, T., Schiel, B., Van Gool, L.: Towards multi-view object class detection. In: 2006 IEEE Computer Society Conference on Computer Vision and Pattern Recognition, vol. 2, pp. 1589–1596 (2006)

Learning V4 Curvature Cell Populations from Sparse Endstopped Cells

Antonio Rodríguez-Sánchez[1]([✉]), Sabine Oberleiter[1], Hanchen Xiong[2], and Justus Piater[1]

[1] Institute of Computer Science, Universität Innsbruck, Innsbruck, Austria
{antonio.rodriguez-sanchez,justus.piater}@uibk.ac.at,
sabine.oberleiter@student.uibk.ac.at
[2] Search Team, Zalando SE, Berlin, Germany
hanchen.xiong@zalando.de
https://iis.uibk.ac.at

Abstract. We investigate in this paper the capabilities of learning sparse representations from model cells that respond to curvatures. Sparse coding has been successful at generating receptive fields similar to those of simples cells in area V1 from natural images. We are interested here in neurons from intermediate areas, such as V2 and V4. Neurons on those areas are known to respond to corners and curvatures. Endstopped cells (also known as hypercomplex) are hypothesized to be selective to curvatures and are greatly represented in area V2. We propose here a sparse coding learning approach where the input is not images, nor simple cells, but curvature selective cells. We show that by learning a sparse code of endstopped cells we can obtain different degrees of curvature representations.

Keywords: Sparse coding · Endstopped cells · Curvature · Restricted Boltzmann Machine

1 Introduction

New techniques and machines as well as much dedication from neuroscientists have provided big advances in the knowledge of the nervous system and the brain since the first works more than a century ago by Ramón y Cajal. The part of the brain involved in the analysis of visual information is the visual cortex.

The visual cortex seems to be organized into areas where neurons perform similar tasks. The first Scientists to shed some light on how visual information may be processed in the visual cortex were Hubel and Wiesel [1]. They found three different types of cells present in area V1 of the monkey visual cortex: (i) simple cells, which were selective to the orientation of lines and bars; (ii) complex cells, which have a similar selectivity, but unlike in simple cells, their response is independent on where the line or bar lies inside receptive field; and finally (iii) hypercomplex cells (also known as endstopped) would respond

© Springer International Publishing Switzerland 2016
A.E.P. Villa et al. (Eds.): ICANN 2016, Part II, LNCS 9887, pp. 463–471, 2016.
DOI: 10.1007/978-3-319-44781-0_55

to the end of a bar or a line. Continuing along the *object recognition pathway*, neurons in V2 - where endstopped cells have a high presence - respond to contours [2]. When we reach V4, cells are selective to local curvatures in such a way, that groups of those cells can be considered to encode shapes [3]. Fukushima's Neocognitron [4] was the first model inspired on neurons of the visual cortex, the focus was mainly in the first two V1 neuronal types, namely simple and complex cells. Most of the models up to date main focus has been these two types of cells, learning shape contours through a configuration of Gabor-like responses as in the popular HMAX or even in more recent models [5]. Fortunately, endstoppedcells have not been completely neglected, successfully encoding contours and curvatures [6].

In addition to their selectivity, another important characteristic of cells in the visual cortex appears when we consider their activation patterns as a neuronal population. That characteristic is *sparsity*, meaning that the fraction of neurons from a population that is activated by a certain stimulus should be relatively small. Olshausen [7] showed that by implementing this concept through a learning mechanism to natural images, receptive fields very similar to those of V1 simple cells would be obtained. Even though sparsity and selectivity may be related, sparsity does not necessarily imply selectivity [8].

Over the years many learning approaches have been presented that learn sparse representations, mostly applied to natural images and thus obtaining receptive fields - with increasing degree of similarity - to V1 simple cells. More recently, Restricted Boltzmann Machines (RBM) [9] have become popular as a sparse coding learning approach [10–13].

In most sparsity learning approaches, the input to the learning approach are pixel images. We propose here to implement a sparsity learning approach, but where the input are not images nor Gabor-like filter responses, instead, the input will be the response of neurons that are selective to curvatures. The neurons for such a task are endstopped neurons [6,14]. The choosen learning approach is the diversity RBM by Xiong and colleagues [15], which showed to reach high degrees of both, selectivity and sparsity, in a unified learning approach.

In Sect. 2 we will describe the chosen model to encode curvatures as well as the sparsity approach. Section 3 will present our experimental setup and results. We finish with our conclusions in Sect. 4.

2 Methods

2.1 Modeling Cells Selective to Curvatures

Our aim is to obtain cells that are selective to curvatures. In the introduction we discussed that a biologically plausible candidate are endstopped cells. The inspiration to obtain such cells comes from a recent hierarchical and biologically-plausible model of shape representation [6]. Such model obtains cells that are selective to shapes. It does so, by modeling cells that are selective to curvature at the intermediate layers of the model. Thus, we will not follow the aforementioned model completely but the aspects of it where we can obtain curvature selective cells.

The input are images. Which are then analyzed by a set of Difference of Gaussian filters at different scales and orientations:

$$DoG(x,y)_{s,\theta} = \frac{1}{2\pi\sigma_{x_1}\sigma_y}e^{-\frac{1}{2}\left(\left(\frac{x'}{\sigma_{x_1}}\right)^2 + \left(\frac{y'}{\sigma_y}\right)^2\right)} - \frac{1}{2\pi\sigma_{x_2}\sigma_y}e^{-\frac{1}{2}\left(\left(\frac{x'}{\sigma_{x_2}}\right)^2 + \left(\frac{y'}{\sigma_y}\right)^2\right)}$$

$$x' = x\cos(\theta) + y\sin(\theta)$$
$$y' = -x\sin(\theta) + y\cos(\theta)$$

(1)

where σ_y is the height and σ_{x_1} and σ_{x_2} are the width of each Gaussian function. θ is their orientation. At each position in an image there will be N_s different scales s (provided by the parameters σ_y, σ_{x_1} and σ_{x_2}) and N_θ orientations θ. This configuration gives rise to $N_\theta \times N_s$ such filters at each location. The next step is to combine these filter responses - which resemble V1 simple cell responses - into complex cells (CC below). One hypothesis on how complex cells achieve translation invariance (its main characteristic) is that they may be the result of the addition of simple cells along the axis perpendicular to their orientation [16]:

$$CC_{s,\theta} = \sum_{i=1}^{n} c_i\phi(DoG_{i,s,\theta})$$

(2)

For i laterally displaced filters having the same orientation θ selectivity at the same scale s. c_i is a Gaussian weight inversely proportional to the distance of the displaced filter to the center (Fig. 1a). Finally, endstopped cells may be the result from the difference between a simple cell and two displaced complex cells [17]. When simple and complex cells whose orientation selectivity is the same, we can obtain endstopped cells (EC) that are selective to different degrees of curvature and its *sign* (the direction of the tangent along the curve) [18]:

$$EC_{s,\theta,type} = \Phi[c_{DoG}\phi(DoG_{s,\theta}) - (c_a\phi(CC^a{}_{s,\theta^a}) + c_b\phi(CC^b{}_{s,\theta^b}))]$$

(3)

$$\Phi(x) = \frac{1 - e^{-x/\rho}}{1 + 1/\Gamma e^{-x/\rho}}$$

(4)

c_c, c_a and c_b are the gains for the simple (DoG) and the two complex (displaced) cells (Fig. 1a). DoG, CC^a and CC^b are the responses of the simple cell (at the center) and the two complex displaced cells respectively. ϕ is a rectification function, where any value less that 0 is set to 0. Φ is another rectification function of the sigmoid type, where Γ and ρ are rectification parameters. Values for all the parameters of the model will be given in Sect. 3.1. s and θ are a specific scale and orientation as before. Depending on the orientation of the complex cells with respect to the center cell we have two types of endstopped cells (types A and B in Fig. 1a). When $\theta = \theta^a = \theta^b$, it is type A, and the endstopped cell is selective to the degree of the curvature (sharp, medium, broad, ...). When $\theta \neq \theta^a \neq \theta^b$, we have a cell that is selective to the *sign* of the curvature (type B). A usual setup of this latter one is when $\theta^a = \theta + 45°$ and $\theta^b = \theta + 135°$, its opposite would be a cell where $\theta^a = \theta + 135°$ and $\theta^b = \theta + 45°$ (we could identify the former with the positive sign, and the latter with the negative sign).

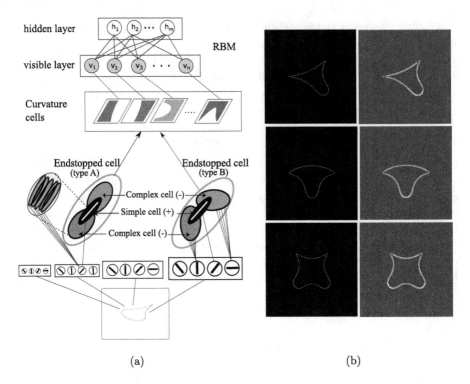

(a)   (b)

Fig. 1. (a) Model of learning sparse curvature neuronal population (see text for details). b) Responses from curvature neurons (right) to stimuli from [3] (left). Colors represent different curvature neurons. (Color figure online)

Finally, a curvature cell ($CurvC$) is the convergence of the types A and B endstopped cells. In order to select the most selective curvature cell to a specific curved area, we first select the type A endstopped cell providing the maximum response. We then select the sign of the cell given by the corresponding type B endstopped cell (which of the two opposite sign type B cells has a higher value).

$$s^*, \theta^* = \arg\max_{s,\theta} EC_{s,\theta,typeA} \tag{5}$$

$$CurvC = \arg\max_{sign} EC_{s^*,\theta^*,typeB^{sign}} \tag{6}$$

For more details on this model, please refer to [6].

2.2 Learning a Sparse Representation of Curvature Cells

There are previous studies that learn simple cell receptive fields through the use of RBMs, either enforcing sparsity or selectivity. For our learning endstopped cell receptive field learning we choose a recent approach that combines both [15]. Next, we briefly explain such learning approach.

The restricted Boltzmann machine (RBM, Fig. 1a) is a two-layer, is a "restricted version" of the Boltzmann machine where there are only inter-connections between a hidden layer and a visible layer. The input data is N_v dimensional (for the $\mathbf{v}$ units in the visible layer). In the hidden layer there exist N_h stochastic binary variables $\mathbf{h}$. The joint probability of $\{\mathbf{v}, \mathbf{h}\}$ is:

$$p(\mathbf{v}, \mathbf{h}) = \frac{1}{\mathbf{Z}} \exp(-E(\mathbf{v}, \mathbf{h})) \qquad E(\mathbf{v}, \mathbf{h}) = -\mathbf{v}^\top \mathbf{W} \mathbf{h} - \mathbf{h}^\top \mathbf{b} - \mathbf{v}^\top \mathbf{c} \qquad (7)$$

where $\mathbf{W} \in \mathbb{R}^{N_v \times N_h}$ is the matrix of symmetric weights, $\mathbf{b} \in \mathbb{R}^{N_h \times 1}$ and $\mathbf{c} \in \mathbb{R}^{N_v \times 1}$ are biases for hidden unites and visible units respectively. $\mathbf{Z} = \sum_{\mathbf{v}, \mathbf{h}} \exp(-E(\mathbf{v}, \mathbf{h}))$ is the partition function for normalization.

Given training data $\mathcal{D} = \{\mathbf{v}^{(l)}\}_{l=1}^{L}$, an RBM can be learned by maximizing the average log-likelihood of $\mathcal{D}$:

$$\mathbf{W}^* = \arg \max_{\mathbf{W}} \mathcal{L}(\mathcal{D}) = \arg \max_{\mathbf{W}} \frac{1}{L} \sum_{l=1}^{L} \left(\log \sum_{\mathbf{h}} p(\mathbf{v}^{(l)}, \mathbf{h}) \right) \qquad (8)$$

Since the log-likelihood is concave with respect to $\mathbf{W}, \mathbf{b}, \mathbf{c}$, based on (7), *gradient ascent* can be applied on (8) by computing the gradient of $\mathcal{L}(\mathcal{D})$. Direct computation of the gradien involves a large number of Markov chain Monte Carlo (MCMC) iterations to reach equilibrium, thus in practice we compute an approximation through contrastive divergence (CD) [9] and the gradient is approximated as:

$$\nabla_{\mathbf{W}} \hat{\mathcal{L}}(\mathcal{D}) = \frac{1}{L} \sum_{l=1}^{L} \left[\mathbf{v}^{(l)} p(\mathbf{h}^{(l)+} | \mathbf{v}^{(l)})^\top - p(\mathbf{v}^{(l)-} | \mathbf{h}^{(l)+}) p(\mathbf{h}^{(l)-} | \mathbf{v}^{(l)-})^\top \right] \qquad (9)$$

where $\mathbf{h}^{(l)+}$ denotes the inferred hidden vector from the lth observed data point $\mathbf{v}^{(l)}$, and $\mathbf{v}^{(l)-}, \mathbf{h}^{(l)-}$ are vectors after one-step block Gibbs sampling.

In order to achieve sparsity and selectivity, we introduce a prior on $\mathbf{W}$, which will represent neurons receptive fields [15]. To this end, we diversify the columns of $\mathbf{W}$ by minimizing the *square cosine similarities* among the columns of $\mathbf{W}$:

$$\arg \min_{\mathbf{W}} \sum_{j=1}^{N_h} \sum_{k \neq j}^{N_h} \left\| \frac{\mathbf{W}_{\cdot,j}^\top \mathbf{W}_{\cdot,k}}{\|\mathbf{W}_{\cdot,j}\| \|\mathbf{W}_{\cdot,k}\|} \right\|^2 \qquad (10)$$

Sparsity and selectivity are expected to be enhanced simultaneously by using this diversity-induced bias (10). We can define the prior probability distribution over parameters $p(\mathbf{W})$ as

$$p(\mathbf{W}) \propto \exp \left(-\lambda \cdot \sum_{j=1}^{N_h} \sum_{k \neq j}^{N_h} \left\| \frac{\mathbf{W}_{\cdot,j}^\top \mathbf{W}_{\cdot,k}}{\|\mathbf{W}_{\cdot,j}\| \|\mathbf{W}_{\cdot,k}\|} \right\|^2 \right). \qquad (11)$$

Then, the parameters can be estimated via maximum a posteriori (MAP) and since the optimization problem is concave with respect to $\mathbf{W}$, we can employ gradient ascent to solve it and derive an iterative update of $\mathbf{W}$ as

$$\mathbf{W}_{\cdot,j}^{t+1} = \mathbf{W}_{\cdot,j}^{t} + \nabla_{\mathbf{W}}\hat{\mathcal{L}}(\mathcal{D}) - 2\lambda \left(\sum_{k \neq j}^{N_h} (\mathbf{W}_{\cdot,k} \otimes \mathbf{W}_{\cdot,k}) + C\frac{||\mathbf{W}_{\cdot,j}|| - 1}{||\mathbf{W}_{\cdot,j}||}\mathbf{I}_{N_v} \right) \mathbf{W}_{\cdot,j}$$

(12)

where $\otimes$ denotes the outer product between vectors, and $\mathbf{I}_{N_v}$ is a $N_v \times N_v$ identity matrix. In (12) we can see that the iterative update of $\mathbf{W}$ is composed of two parts, where the first is the gradient of the log-likelihood while the second is the gradient of the log prior.

3   Experimental Evaluation

3.1   Setup

Image sizes were 400×400 pixels. For our experiments, we used 12 orientations and 4 different sizes (40, 60, 88 and 120 pixels) for the Difference of Gaussian filters. c Values (Eq. 3) for the complex neurons were from the smaller to the larger scales: $c_a = c_b = \{1.5, 1.25, 1, 3\}$, $c_{DoG} = 1$. The parameters for the rectification function (Eq. 4) were $\Gamma = 0.01$ and ρ is the maximum response of the set of neurons for a given scale divided by 8.5. T hese values follow from the model tuning in [6]. 4 endstopped cells type A responded to curvatures from very sharp to very broad and we used two different opposite sign type B endstopped cells. This setup then, provided 8 curvature cells. Curvature cell values were normalized to be in the range $\{0,1\}$. The responses of curvature cells were thinned as to fit the width of the original stimuli. The visible units (v) for the RBM corresponded to the normalized curvature values at each position p. These responses provided the input to the RBM which consisted of patches from the curvature cell responses of 14×14 pixels. The RBM consisted of $N_v = 196$ (to fit the size of small image patches), and N_h is 200, $i.e.$ 200 hidden units.

3.2   Stimuli

Pasupathy and Connor [3] recorded the responses of 109 neurons to 366 different shapes. The stimuli were constructed combining convex and concave boundary elements to form closed shapes. Boundary elements include sharp convex angles, and medium and high convex and concave curvatures. Figure 1b shows some examples of this stimuli as well as the responses from curvature cells. We used these stimuli to train the model.

3.3   Results and Discussion

Figure 2 shows the results of the learnt sparse curvature population from the curvature selective cells. The first two figures used a λ (Eqs. 11, 12) value of 0.01 at two different learning stages: after 1000 and 5000 iterations. For the last figure, we used a value of $\lambda = 0.05$. These results show that we can learn a curvature selective population from a stimuli that was created with the aim to evaluate the selectivity of cells to shapes in area V4 of the visual cortex. We highlighted some cells with different colors that are selective to different degrees of curvatures in the second learnt population (Fig. 2b): blue for sharp curvatures, green medium-sharp, orange for medium-broad and red for broad curvatures.

In a closer inspection, if we compare the results from Fig. 2a and b (1000 vs 5000 iterations) it can be seen that as the learning goes on, the representation of sharp and medium-sharp curvatures becomes larger than the broader classes. Continuing with this line of thought, we further evaluated the method by extracting the peak curvatures in order to compare with the curvature population reported in [3] (Fig. 7B). For this aim, each curvature cell was thinned such as to only the a white curve would appear. Then, the curvature at each point was extracted by approximating the gradient. The maximum curvature along with the standard deviation were extracted for each cell, following [3]. Results are shown in Fig. 3. We can see that the sparse representation follows a representation towards acute curvatures as in Fig. 7B of [3]. Although it can also

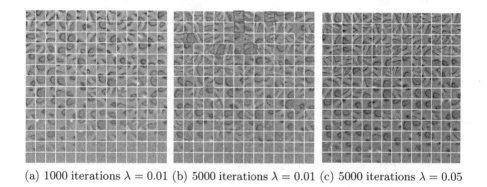

(a) 1000 iterations $\lambda = 0.01$ (b) 5000 iterations $\lambda = 0.01$ (c) 5000 iterations $\lambda = 0.05$

Fig. 2. Results after different learning stages and values of λ

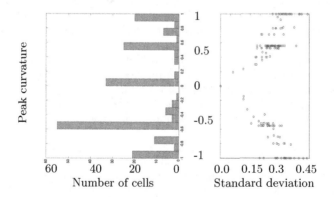

Fig. 3. Curvature population (compare with biological data: Fig. 7B from [3])

be observed that there is larger representation in our approach of zero curvatures than the ones obtained in the neurophysiological study of Pasupathy and Connor. The main source of zero curvature values for is the last rows obtained with our representation (Fig. 2), where the curvature values are not so clear and get assigned 0 using our curvature value extraction approach. We hope to fix this problem in future work by imposing a better prior such that there is less non-definite curvature cells in the last rows of our representation.

4 Conclusions

Instead of images, the input to our sparse coding approach were responses from endstopped cells that were combined into curvature cells. Thus, we do not learn Gabor-like receptive fields, but curvature-like receptive fields. We used a stimuli that was created with the aim to evaluate the selectivity of cells to curvatures in area V4 of the visual cortex to train our system. Our results show that our approach can in fact learn populations of curvature selective cells. Our approach is also in accordance to Carlson and colleagues [19] where they found a higher representation of acute curvatures in V4 neural populations, a fact that could be simulated by enforcing sparse coding. In that work, the presence of acute curvatures was even larger than in our sparse representation, since they used natural images. It would be interesting for future work to test our approach with a large set of natural images.

References

1. Hubel, D., Wiesel, T.: Receptive fields and functional architecture of monkey striate cortex. J. Physiol. **195**(1), 215–243 (1968)
2. von der Heydt, R., Peterhans, E., Baumgartner, G.: Illusory contours and cortical neuron responses. Science **224**(4654), 1260–1262 (1984)
3. Pasupathy, A., Connor, C.: Shape representation in area V4: position-specific tuning for boundary conformation. J. Neurophysiol. **86**(5), 2505–2519 (2001)
4. Fukushima, K.: Neocognitron: a self organizing neural network model for a mechanism of pattern recognition unaffected by shift in position. Biol. Cybern. **36**(4), 193–202 (1980)
5. Wei, H., Dong, Z.: V4 neural network model for visual saliency and discriminative local representation of shapes. In: 2014 International Joint Conference on Neural Networks (IJCNN), pp. 3420–3427. IEEE (2014)
6. Rodríguez-Sánchez, A., Tsotsos, J.: The roles of endstopped and curvature tuned computations in a hierarchical representation of 2D shape. PLoS ONE **7**(8), 1–13 (2012)
7. Olshausen, B.A., Field, D.J.: Sparse coding with an overcomplete basis set: a strategy employed by V1? Vision Res. **37**, 3311–3325 (1997)
8. Willmore, B., Tolhurst, D.: Characterising the sparseness of neural codes. Netw. Comput. Neural Syst. **12**, 255–270 (2001)
9. Hinton, G.E., Salakhutdinov, R.R.: Reducing the dimensionality of data with neural networks. Science **313**(5786), 504–507 (2006)

10. Lee, H. , Ekanadham, C. , Ng, A.Y.: Sparse deep belief net model for visual area V2. In: Advances in Neural Information Processing Systems, pp. 873–880 (2008)
11. Luo, H., Shen, R., Niu, C., Ullrich, C.: Sparse group restricted boltzmann machines. In: AAAI (2011)
12. Goh, H., Thome, N., Cord, M.: Biasing restricted Boltzmann machines to manipulate latent selectivity and sparsity. In: NIPS Workshop on Deep Learning and Unsupervised Feature Learning (2010)
13. Xiong, H., Szedmak, S., Rodríguez-Sánchez, A., Piater, J.: Towards sparsity and selectivity: Bayesian learning of restricted Boltzmann machine for early visual features. In: Wermter, S., Weber, C., Duch, W., Honkela, T., Koprinkova-Hristova, P., Magg, S., Palm, G., Villa, A.E.P. (eds.) ICANN 2014. LNCS, vol. 8681, pp. 419–426. Springer, Heidelberg (2014)
14. Rodríguez-Sánchez, A., Tsotsos, J.: The importance of intermediate representations for the modeling of 2D shape detection: endstopping and curvature tuned computations. In: CVPR, pp. 4321–4326 (2011)
15. Xiong, H., Rodríguez-Sánchez, A., Szedmak, S., Piater, J.: Diversity priors for learning early visual features. Front. Comput. Neurosci. 9(104), September 2015
16. Spitzer, H., Hochstein, S.: A complex-cell receptive-field model. J. Neurophysiol. 53(5), 1266–1286 (1985)
17. Kato, H., Bishop, P., Orban, G.: Hypeercomplex and simple/complex cells classifications in cat striate cortex. J. Neurophysiol. 41(5), 1071–1095 (1978)
18. Dobbins, A.: Difference models of visual cortical neurons. Ph.D. Dissertation, Department of Electrical Engineering. McGill University (1992)
19. Carlson, E.T., Rasquinha, R.J., Zhang, K., Connor, C.E.: A sparse object coding scheme in area V4. Curr. Biol. 21(4), 288–293 (2011)

Recognition of Transitive Actions
with Hierarchical Neural Network Learning

Luiza Mici$^{(\boxtimes)}$, German I. Parisi, and Stefan Wermter

Department of Informatics, University of Hamburg,
Vogt-Koelln-Strasse 30, 22527 Hamburg, Germany
{mici,parisi,wermter}@informatik.uni-hamburg.de
http://www.informatik.uni-hamburg.de/WTM/

Abstract. The recognition of actions that involve the use of objects has remained a challenging task. In this paper, we present a hierarchical self-organizing neural architecture for learning to recognize transitive actions from RGB-D videos. We process separately body poses extracted from depth map sequences and object features from RGB images. These cues are subsequently integrated to learn action–object mappings in a self-organized manner in order to overcome the visual ambiguities introduced by the processing of body postures alone. Experimental results on a dataset of daily actions show that the integration of action–object pairs significantly increases classification performance.

Keywords: Action recognition · Self-organization · Hierarchical learning

1 Introduction

The ability to understand others' actions represents a crucial feature of the human visual system that fosters learning and social interactions in natural environments. In particular, the recognition of transitive actions (actions that involve the interaction with a target object) is an important part of human daily activities. Therefore, computational approaches for the recognition of transitive actions are a desirable feature of assistive systems able to interact with people in real-world scenarios. While humans possess an outstanding capability to easily extract and reason about abstract concepts such as the goal of actions and the interaction with objects, this capability has remained an open challenge for computational models of action recognition.

The study of transitive actions such as grasping and holding has often been the focus of research in neuroscience and psychology [1–3], especially after the discovery of the mirror neuron system [3]. It has been shown that a specific set of neurons in the mammalian brain shows selective tuning during the observation of actions for which an internal motor representation is present in the nervous system. Moreover, the response of these neurons differs in case the action is mimicked, i.e. the target object is absent. Neurophysiological studies suggest

© Springer International Publishing Switzerland 2016
A.E.P. Villa et al. (Eds.): ICANN 2016, Part II, LNCS 9887, pp. 472–479, 2016.
DOI: 10.1007/978-3-319-44781-0_56

that only when information about the object identity is added to the semantic information about the action, then the actions of other individuals can be completely understood [4]. Together, these results provide an interesting framework that has motivated research work in the field of artificial vision systems and machine learning towards the recognition of action–object mappings (e.g., [5–8]). From the computational perspective, an important question can be posed on the potential links between representations of body postures and manipulated objects involved in the learning of transitive actions and, in particular, on the way these two representations can be integrated.

In this paper, we present a hierarchical, self-organizing neural architecture that learns to recognize transitive actions from RGB-D videos containing daily activities. Unlike our previous work [9], we use self-organizing neural networks motivated by the fact that specific areas of the visual system organize according to the distribution of the inputs [12]. Furthermore, extended models of hierarchical self-organization enable the learning of inherent spatio-temporal dependencies of time-varying input such as body motion sequences [10]. The proposed architecture consists of two main network streams processing separately feature representations of body postures and manipulated objects. The last layer, where the two streams are integrated, combines the information for developing action–object mappings in a self-organized manner. We evaluate our architecture with a dataset of RGB-D videos containing daily actions. We present and discuss our results on this dataset showing that the identity of objects plays a fundamental role for the effective recognition of actions.

2 Neural Architecture

The proposed architecture is based on self-organizing neural networks that are capable of learning inherent topological relations of the input space in an unsupervised fashion. An overview of the architecture is depicted in Fig. 1.

2.1 Self-organizing Maps

Self-organizing maps are neural networks inspired by biological input-driven self-organization [11] and they have been successfully applied to a number of learning tasks [12]. It consists of a 2-dimensional grid of units (neurons), each associated with a weight vector of the same dimension of the input space. The learning is performed by adapting these weights to better encode a submanifold of the input space. Given an input vector $\mathbf{x}_i$, this is done by calculating a best-matching unit $b \in A$, where A is the set of map nodes:

$$b = arg \min_{n \in A} ||\mathbf{x} - \mathbf{w}_n||. \tag{1}$$

Then, the weight vector $\mathbf{w}_b$ is moved closer to the input by a fraction that decreases over time, as are nodes that are in the neighborhood of the winner:

$$\mathbf{w}_b(t + 1) = \mathbf{w}_b(t) + \eta(t) \cdot h_b(t) \cdot [\mathbf{x}(t) - \mathbf{w}_b(t)], \tag{2}$$

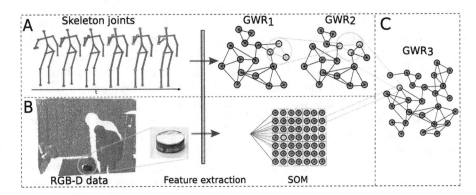

Fig. 1. Overview of the proposed architecture. (A) Processing for the body postures: a set of local features that encode the posture of upper body limbs are extracted and fed to the 2-layered neural architecture with GWR networks. (B) The input for the object recognition module is the RGB image of the object: the region of interest is automatically extracted through a point cloud-based table top segmentation. Objects are represented as compact feature vectors and are fed to a SOM network. (C) The last layer learns the combinations of body postures and objects involved in an action.

where $h_b(t)$ is the neighborhood function that defines the spatial neighbors of the winning neuron and $\eta(t)$ is a decreasing learning rate. In this way, the neurons in the map are organized preserving the topological properties of the input, i.e. similar inputs are mapped to neurons that are near to each other in the map.

The presence of noise in terms of outliers in the input data can have a negative influence on the formation of topological representations using SOMs. Such an issue is better addressed by growing models of self-organizing networks.

2.2   Growing When Required Networks

The Growing When Required network (GWR) [16] is a growing extension of self-organizing networks with competitive Hebbian learning. The GWR has the ability to create neurons and connections between them to incrementally map the topology of the input data distribution. Unlike the well-known Growing Neural Gas (GNG) [17], where the network grows at a constant rate, the GWR has a growth rate as a function of the overall network activation w.r.t. the input.

The GWR network starts with a set A of two nodes with random weights $\mathbf{w}_1$ and $\mathbf{w}_2$ in the input space. At each iteration, the algorithm is given an input $\mathbf{x}(t)$ and the two closest neurons b and s in A are found (Eq. 1). If the connection (b,s) does not exist, it is created. The activity of the best-matching neuron is computed as $a = \exp(-||\mathbf{x} - \mathbf{w}_b||)$. If the activity is lower than a pre-defined threshold a_T and the firing counter of the neuron is under the firing threshold h_T, then a new neuron is created with weight $\mathbf{w}_r = (\mathbf{w}_b + \mathbf{x}(t))/2$. The firing rate threshold parameter makes sure that neurons are sufficiently trained before inserting new ones. The edge between b and s is removed and the edges (r,b)

and (r, s) are created. If a new neuron is not added, the weights of the winning neuron and its neighbours are moved towards the input by a fraction of $\epsilon \cdot h$, with $0 < \epsilon < 1$ and h being the firing counter of the neuron. The firing counters are reduced and the age of the edges are increased. The algorithm stops when a given criterion is met, e.g., a maximum network size. The insertion threshold a_T modulates the amount of generalization i.e. how much discrepancy we want to tolerate between the resulting prototype neurons and the input space. The connection-age mechanism leads to neurons being removed if rarely used.

2.3 Learning Sequences of Body Postures

Our study focuses on articulated motion of the upper body limbs during daily activities such as picking up, drinking, eating, and talking on phone. The set of raw full-body joints positions in real-world coordinates does not supply a significant representation of such actions. Therefore, we compute the relative position of upper limbs w.r.t. the head and body center to obtain translation-invariant coordinates. We use the skeletal quads features that are local features built upon the concept of geometric hashing and have shown promising results for the recognition of actions and hand gestures [13]. Given a quadruple of body joints positions in real-world coordinates $X = [x_1, x_2, x_3, x_4]$ with $x \in R^3$, a local coordinate system is built by making x_1 the origin and mapping x_2 onto the vector $[1, 1, 1]^T$. The position of the other two points x_3 and x_4 calculated w.r.t. the local coordinate system are concatenated in a 6-dimensional vector which is the quadruple compact descriptor. In this way, we obtain a lower-dimensional descriptor which is also invariant to translation, scale and body rotation. We select two quadruple of joints: [*center torso, neck, left hand, left elbow*] and [*center torso, neck, right hand, right elbow*], meaning that the positions of the hands and elbows are encoded with respect to the torso center and neck. The latter is chosen instead of the head position due to noisy tracking of the head caused by occlusions during actions such as eating and drinking.

For the recognition of body motion sequences, we train a hierarchical GWR architecture (Fig. 1A). This approach has been shown to be more suitable than SOM for learning a set of actions from features based on noisy tracked skeletons [10]. We first train the GWR_1 network with the sequences of body postures. After the training is completed, the GWR_2 network is trained with neural activation trajectories from GWR_1. Thus, for each input sample $\mathbf{x}_i$, the best-matching neuron in GWR_1 network is computed as in Eq. 1. The weights of the neurons activated within a temporal sliding window of length q are concatenated and fed as input to GWR_2. The input data for training GWR_2 is of the form:

$$\psi(\mathbf{x}_i) = \{b(\mathbf{x}_i), b(\mathbf{x}_{i-1}), ..., b(\mathbf{x}_{i-q+1}), i \in [q..m]\}, \tag{3}$$

where m is the number of training samples. While the first network learns a set of prototype body postures, the second network will learn temporally-ordered prototype sequences from q consecutive samples. Therefore, the positive recognition of action segments occurs only when neurons along the hierarchy are activated in the correct order.

2.4 Object Recognition

For the representation of objects, we use SIFT features [14] that yield invariance
to translation, rotation and scaling transformations and, to some extent, robustness to occlusions. For the problem of object category recognition, experimental
results have shown that better classification performance is achieved by computing *dense* SIFT descriptors on regular grids across each image. Since objects will
be compared to each other through vectorial metrics such as the Euclidean distance, we compute a fixed-dimensional vectorial representation of each image by
performing quantization followed by an encoding step. For this purpose, we chose
the vector of locally aggregated descriptors (VLAD) [15]. Unlike the bag of features (BoF) approach, these descriptors do not apply hard-assignment of SIFT
features from an image to the closest code-vectors, i.e. visual words. Instead,
they compute and trace the differences between them, leading to a resulting
feature vector with a higher discriminative power.

For learning objects, we train a SOM network on a set of objects extracted
from RGB action sequences (Fig. 1B). We attach symbolic labels to each neuron
based on the majority of input samples that have matched with each neuron
during the training phase. At recognition time, for each input image the best-
matching neuron from the trained network (Eq. 1) will be computed. In this way,
the knowledge of the category of objects can be transferred to the higher layer
of the architecture in the form of a symbolic label.

2.5 Classification of Transitive Actions

Up to this point, the architecture has learned temporally-ordered prototype body
posture sequences and the identity of objects. The highest network in hierarchy
GWR_3 should integrate the information from the converging streams and learn
action–object mappings (Fig. 1C). For this purpose, we compute a new dataset
by merging the activations trajectories from the preceding GWR_2 network and
the object's symbolic label from the SOM. The resulting training data consists
of pairs ϕ_u of the following form:

$$\phi_u = \{b(\psi(\mathbf{x}_i)), ..., b(\psi(\mathbf{x}_{i-q-1})), l_b(\mathbf{y}), \mathbf{x}_i \in A, \mathbf{y} \in O, u \in [q..m-q]\}, \qquad (4)$$

where $l_b(\mathbf{y})$ represents the label attached to the best-matching neuron of the
object recognition module for the object input $\mathbf{y}$. Furthermore, each neuron is
assigned with an action label adopting the same labelling strategy as in SOM,
meaning that neurons take the label of the best-matching input samples. After
the training of GWR_3 is completed, each neuron will encode a prototype segment
of the action in terms of action–object pairs.

3 Experimental Results

3.1 Data Collection

The setup of the experiments and the data collection were planned having in
mind the role of the objects' identity in distinguishing the actions, in particular

Picking up   **Talking on phone**   **Eating**   **Drinking**

Fig. 2. Examples of sequences of skeleton joints taken from our action dataset.

when the sole body motion information may not be sufficient to unequivocally classify an action. Therefore, we collected a dataset of the following daily activities: *picking up*, *drinking* (from a mug or can), *eating* (cookies) and *talking on a phone*. The variety of style with which the actions were performed across different subjects and their similarities in body posture highlight the importance of the object's identity for their effective classification. The actions were performed by 6 participants that were given no explicit indication on the purpose of the experiments nor an explanation on how to perform the actions in order to avoid biased execution.

The dataset was collected with an Asus Xtion depth sensor that provides a synchronized RGB-D image (color and depth map). The tracking of skeleton joints was computed with the OpenNI framework (Fig. 2). Action labels were manually annotated from ground truth of sequence frames and were cross checked by two different individuals. We added a mirrored version of all action samples to obtain invariance to actions performed with either the right or the left hand. The depth sensor was also used for acquiring the objects dataset. Since object recognition should be reliable regardless of objects' perspective, RGB images were acquired with the camera positioned in two different heights and from objects in different views with respect to the sensor. Object labels were manually annotated for the training sequences, and the labels output from the object recognition module were used for the test sequences.

3.2   Training and Evaluation

In order to evaluate the generalization capabilities of our architecture, we conducted experiments with 10-fold cross-validation, meaning that data was split into 10 random subdivisions of 60 % for training and 40 % for testing. The results reported in this paper have been averaged over the 10 folds.

We determined empirically the following GWR training parameters: learning step sizes $\epsilon_b = 0.1$, $\epsilon_n = 0.01$, firing threshold $h_T = 0.1$, insertion thresholds $a_T = \{0.5, 0.4, 0.3\}$ (for each network respectively), maximum age $a_{max} = 100$, initial strength $h_0 = 1$, $\tau_b = 0.3$ and $\tau_n = 0.1$ as constants controlling the behaviour of the curve reducing the winning nodes' firing counter. Each GWR network was trained for 50 epochs over the whole actions dataset. The number of neurons reached in each GWR network given a training set with ≈ 18.600 frames were ≈ 480 for GWR_1, ≈ 600 for GWR_2, while for GWR_3 the number varied from ≈ 700 to ≈ 1000 depending on the inclusion or exclusion of the objects (as explained in Fig. 3). For the SOM training we used a 20×20 map of

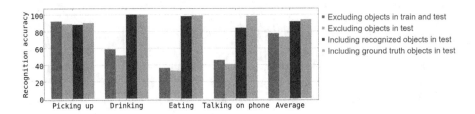

Fig. 3. Evaluation of the recognition accuracy on the test data set under the conditions indicated in the legend.

units organized in a hexagonal topology, a Gaussian neighbouring function and batch training of 50 epochs over the objects dataset.

We evaluated the recognition accuracy of the architecture under three conditions: (1) completely excluding the object identity in both training and testing, (2) including the objects in training while excluding them in testing phase, and (3) no exclusion in both phases. In the third case the label given by the SOM-based object classifier was used during testing. Further experiments were run using the objects' ground-truth labels for comparison. The results are reported in Fig. 3, where it is possible to see a significant improvement of the action classification performance for the third condition. When the objects *can* and *mug* are interchanged by the objects' classifier, the final classification accuracy of the action *drinking* is not affected – this is a desirable generalization capability of our architecture. Furthermore, the relatively low recognition rates in the second condition suggest that the identity of the object is crucial for distinguishing between the actions *drinking*, *eating* and *talking on phone*, while for the action *picking up* the situation does not vary drastically in either case.

4   Conclusions and Future Work

We presented a hierarchical self-organizing architecture for the learning of action–object mappings from RGB-D videos. The architecture consists of two separate pathways that process body action features and object features in parallel and subsequently it integrates prototypes of actions and the identity of objects being used. A GWR-based learning algorithm is used to learn action sequences, since it can deal better with the presence of noise in the tracked skeleton data. Experimental results have shown that the proposed integration of body actions and objects significantly increases the classification accuracy of action sequences.

The obtained results motivate the evaluation of our framework on a wider number of actions and a more complex scenario, e.g. requiring the use of the same object across different actions. Furthermore, we are working on the extension of the proposed approach for robot experiments towards the recognition of goal-oriented actions and intentions based on the interaction with the environment.

Acknowledgments. This research was partially supported by the Transregio TRR169 on Crossmodal Learning, by the DAAD German Academic Exchange Service for the Cognitive Assistive Systems project (Kz:A/13/94748), and the Hamburg Landesforschungsförderung.

References

1. Fleischer, F., Caggiano, V., Thier, P., Giese, M.A.: Physiologically inspired model for the visual recognition of transitive hand actions. J. Neurosci. **33**(15), 6563–6580 (2013)
2. Nelissen, K., Luppino, G., Vanduffel, W., Rizzolatti, G., Orban, G.: Observing others: multiple action representation in frontal lobe. Science **310**, 332–336 (2005)
3. Gallese, V., Fadiga, L., Fogassi, L., Rizzolatti, G.: Action recognition in premotor cortex. Brain **2**, 593–609 (1996)
4. Saxe, R., Carey, S., Kanwisher, N.: Understanding other minds: linking developmental psychology and functional neuroimaging. Annu. Rev. Psychol. **55**, 87–124 (2004)
5. Gupta, A., Davis, L.S.: Objects in action: an approach for combining action understanding and object perception. In: IEEE CVPR 2007, pp. 1–8 (2007)
6. Koppula, H.S., Gupta, R., Saxena, A.: Learning human activities and object affordances from RGB-D videos. Int. J. Robot. Res. **32**(8), 951–970 (2013)
7. Yao, B., Fei-Fei, L.: Modeling mutual context of object and human pose in human-object interaction activities. In: IEEE CVPR 2010, pp. 17–24 (2010)
8. Kjellström, H., Romero, J., Kragíc, D.: Visual object-action recognition: inferring object affordances from human demonstration. Comput. Vis. Image Underst. **115**(1), 81–90 (2011)
9. Mici, L., Hinaut, X., Wermter, S.: Activity recognition with echo state networks using 3D body joints and objects category. In: ESANN, Belgium, pp. 465–470 (2016)
10. Parisi, G.I., Weber, C., Wermter, S.: Self-organizing neural integration of pose-motion features for human action recognition. Front. Neurorobot. **9**(3), 14 (2015)
11. Kohonen, T.: The self-organizing map. Proc. IEEE **78**(9), 1464–1480 (1990)
12. Miikkulainen, R., Bednar, J.A., Choe, Y., Sirosh, J.: Computational Maps in the Visual Cortex. Springer Science & Business Media, New York (2006)
13. Evangelidis, G., Gurkirt, S., Radu, H.: Skeletal quads: human action recognition using joint quadruples. In: ICPR (2014)
14. Lowe, D.G.: Distinctive image features from scale-invariant keypoints. Int. J. Comput. Vision **60**(2), 91–110 (2004)
15. Jégou, H., Douze, M., Schmid, C., Pérez, P.: Aggregating local descriptors into a compact image representation. In: IEEE CVPR 2010, pp. 3304–3311 (2010)
16. Marsland, S., Shapiro, J., Nehmzow, U.: A self-organising network that grows when required. Neural Netw. **15**(8), 1041–1058 (2002)
17. Fritzke, B.: A growing neural gas network learns topologies. Adv. Neural Inf. Process. Syst. **7**, 625–632 (1995)

Rotation-Invariant Restricted Boltzmann Machine Using Shared Gradient Filters

Mario Valerio Giuffrida[1,2]($\boxtimes$) and Sotirios A. Tsaftaris[1,2]

[1] IMT Scuola Alti Studi Lucca, PRIAn, Lucca, Italy
valerio.giuffrida@imtlucca.it
[2] School of Engineering, University of Edinburgh, Edinburgh, UK
s.tsaftaris@ac.ed.uk

Abstract. Finding suitable features has been an essential problem in computer vision. We focus on Restricted Boltzmann Machines (RBMs), which, despite their versatility, cannot accommodate transformations that may occur in the scene. As a result, several approaches have been proposed that consider a set of transformations, which are used to either augment the training set or transform the actual learned filters. In this paper, we propose the *Explicit Rotation-Invariant Restricted Boltzmann Machine*, which exploits prior information coming from the dominant orientation of images. Our model extends the standard RBM, by adding a suitable number of weight matrices, associated with each dominant gradient. We show that our approach is able to learn rotation-invariant features, comparing it with the classic formulation of RBM on the MNIST benchmark dataset. Overall, requiring less hidden units, our method learns compact features, which are robust to rotations.

Keywords: Rotation invariance · Restricted Boltzmann Machine · Explicit invariance · Shared filters

1 Introduction

It is widely known that a crucial problem in image understanding is to find suitable features for the task at hand. Hand-crafted descriptors were able to provide adequate representations, but they rely on specific structures in the scene and could not accommodate certain nuisance factors properly. Hence, extensive efforts in learning image representations have been done in the past years, demonstrating that machine learning approaches are able to outperform hand-crafted descriptors [23]. Examples of learned features are e.g. vocabulary learning [5], sparse coding [15], Gaussian mixture models [1], neural networks [2].

Neural networks (NNs) are graphical models, where nodes in a graph are connected with weighted connections and parameters are determined via optimisation algorithms. The *Restricted Boltzmann Machine* (RBM) has recently gained popularity, mainly because of its applications to deep learning [2,12]. RBM is a generative NN constituted by a bipartite graph, which sides are referred to *visible*

© Springer International Publishing Switzerland 2016
A.E.P. Villa et al. (Eds.): ICANN 2016, Part II, LNCS 9887, pp. 480–488, 2016.
DOI: 10.1007/978-3-319-44781-0_57

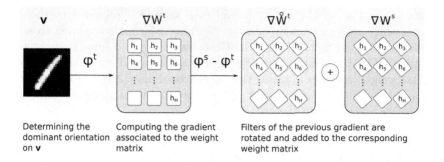

v $\qquad \nabla W^t \qquad \qquad \nabla \mathring{W}^t \qquad \qquad \nabla W^s$

φ^t

$\varphi^s - \varphi^t$

Determining the	Computing the gradient	Filters of the previous gradient are
dominant orientation	associated to the weight	rotated and added to the corresponding
on **v**	matrix	weight matrix

Fig. 1. The dominant orientation φ^t is determined for the provided image and is used to compute the gradient $\nabla W^{(t)}$. The contribution of this gradient is shared amongst the other weight matrices $\nabla W^{(s)}$, $s = 1, 2, \ldots, S$, $t \neq s$, rotating the learned filters by the angle $\varphi^s - \varphi^t$ to generate the $\nabla \mathring{W}^{(t)}$ term.

layer and *hidden layer* respectively. The set of parameters within the RBM are optimised via the *Contrastive Divergence* (CD) algorithm [11]. Although RBMs can achieve satisfactory results [4], their use in shallow networks (namely few layers) cannot accommodate complex variability occurring in the scene [20]. To this end, the *Deep Belief Network* (DBN) was proposed in [14], which is constituted by several stacked RBMs. Albeit DBN have been shown to achieve some translation invariance, they may not well accommodate other nuisance factors (e.g. rotation).

In fact, several modifications of the original RBM formulation have been recently proposed, achieving certain transformation invariance. In [21], a transformation invariant RBM is proposed, where images are subjected to a predefined set of transformations. In [13] an RBM that learns equivariant features is proposed, whereby adding a new variable to be inferred within the hidden units, this variable is then used to rotate learned weights accordingly. In [19], a rotation (invariant) Convolutional RBM is proposed. The marginal probability of RBM is extended with a Markov Random Field, including transformed versions of input images. In [20], an additional step of the backpropagation algorithm used to train DBN is introduced, where the weights are transformed and the entire network is trained again. In [3], the authors propose an RBM where input images are divided into non-overlapping blocks. Then, patches are extracted on SIFT keypoints [18] and subsequently rotated and scaled accordingly. Despite their progress, the aforementioned methods share the following drawbacks: either they are limited to the set of transformations considered within the model, or they involve deep networks in the hope of learning better transformation invariant features [13,20,21], albeit increasing computational demand.

In this paper instead we present the *Explicit Rotation-Invariant Restricted Boltzmann Machine* (ERI-RBM), which can model the nuisance caused by rotated versions of the same pattern, without actually applying any transformation to the data. Our method considers a set of weight matrices (similar concept as in C-RBM [16]) and each sample is provided to the visible layer with its dominant orientation [3]. This information is used to select a particular weight matrix during the Gibbs sampling to compute gradients of parameters. The contribution given by the new update gradients is shared among the other weight matrices, rotating the filters accordingly [20] (cf. Fig. 1). Experiments on MNIST-rot show superior performance to several baseline benchmarks and a recent method from the literature.

Our contributions are multi-fold: (i) rotation is treated explicitly, without rotating the image patterns, in contrast to for example [21]; (ii) we adopt a shallow model using a limited amount of additional weight matrices, instead of deep architectures [17]; (iii) we share the contribution coming from a weight matrix with the other ones, rotating the learned filters by suitable angles.

This paper is organised as follows. Section 2 describes the proposed Explicit Rotation-Invariant Restricted Boltzmann Machine. In Sect. 3, we present experimental results, whereas Sect. 4 concludes the manuscript.

2   Explicit Rotation-Invariant RBM (ERI-RBM)

In this section, we discuss how to embed the concept of rotation-invariance explicitly in the RBM formulation. Since input patterns are images, we will assume that neurones in the visible layer are arranged in matrix form of size $w \times h = d$, width and height respectively. Each row in the weight matrix W, connecting visible units to hidden units, is a d-dimensional vector. Therefore, each row in W can also be arranged in matrix form of size $w \times h$. Henceforth, we will refer to rows in the weight matrix W as *learned filters* and rows in ∇W as *update filters*, which is the gradient computed during the Contrastive Divergence algorithm.

2.1   Proposed Model

Let Φ be a set of evenly distanced angles $\Phi = \{\varphi_1, \varphi_2, \dots, \varphi_S\}$, such that for any $i \le j \implies \varphi_i \le \varphi_j$. In our model, we augment the number of weight matrices $W \in \mathbb{R}^{H \times V \times S}$, such that every angle φ_s is associated to a matrix $W^{(s)}$. Here, H is the number of hidden units, V the number of visible units, and S is the number of angles. In addition, each weight matrix has an associated bias vector $\boldsymbol{b}^{(s)}$. Hence, we rewrite the energy function characterising the standard Restricted Boltzmann Machine formulation as follows:

$$E(\boldsymbol{v}, \boldsymbol{h}; s) = -\boldsymbol{h}^T W^{(s)} \boldsymbol{v} - \boldsymbol{c}^T \boldsymbol{v} - \left[\boldsymbol{b}^{(s)}\right]^T \boldsymbol{h}, \qquad (1)$$

where $W^{(s)}$ is the s-th weight matrix, $\boldsymbol{b}^{(s)}$ is the bias vector for the hidden layer associated to $W^{(s)}$, with $s = 1, 2, \dots, S$, and $\boldsymbol{c}$ is the bias vector for the visible layer. The index s is uniquely determined on each input image $\boldsymbol{v}$, and will be discussed thoroughly in Sect. 2.2. Because of the modification in (1), all the equations involved in the CD algorithm have to be rewritten. Specifically, the conditional probabilities become:

$$p(h_k = 1|\boldsymbol{v}; s) = \sigma\left(b_k^{(s)} + \boldsymbol{W}_{k,\bullet}^{(s)}\boldsymbol{v}\right), \tag{2}$$

$$p(v_j = 1|\boldsymbol{h}; s) = \sigma\left(c_j + \boldsymbol{h}^T\boldsymbol{W}_{\bullet,j}^{(s)}\right). \tag{3}$$

During the optimisation algorithm, an image $\boldsymbol{v}$ with dominant orientation φ_s is provided to the Gibbs sampling. After a sufficient number of alternating computations of (2) and (3), the gradient $\nabla W^{(s)}$ can be computed, whose contribution is shared with the remaining matrices in W. To update $\nabla W^{(t)}$, $1 \leq t \leq S$, $t \neq s$, we transform the update filters in $\nabla W^{(s)}$ which are then added to the t-th gradient. Specifically, since we can represent rows in $\nabla W^{(s)}$ as images, they can be rotated by an angle $\theta = \phi_t - \phi_s$. Therefore, we define a new *shared update filter* term $\nabla \mathring{W}^{(t)}$, such that

$$\nabla\mathring{W}^{(t)} = R_\theta(\nabla W^{(s)}) \equiv \begin{pmatrix} R_\theta\left(\nabla W_{1,\bullet}^{(s)}\right) \\ R_\theta\left(\nabla W_{2,\bullet}^{(s)}\right) \\ \vdots \\ R_\theta\left(\nabla W_{H,\bullet}^{(s)}\right) \end{pmatrix}. \tag{4}$$

where $R_\theta = [\cos\theta \; -\sin\theta; \sin\theta \; \cos\theta]$ defines the 2D rotation matrix by an angle θ. This operation may generate filters bigger than the input layers and we crop them such that the filter size remains $w \times h$. At this point, the final expression for the gradient $\nabla W^{(s)}$ is updated as follows:

$$\nabla W^{(s)} := \nabla W^{(s)} + \nabla\mathring{W}^{(s)}. \tag{5}$$

Note that (5) will be utilised within the Stochastic Gradient Descent step of the CD algorithm. Therefore, $\nabla W^{(s)}$ will be multiplied by a learning rate η that typically has values set in the order of 10^{-3} (further details are discussed in [10]). Hence, any side effects originating from pixel interpolation are minimised, precisely because of the small η. Gradients $\nabla b^{(s)}$ are computed as described in [11], using samples $\boldsymbol{v}$ with the associated dominant orientation φ_s.

2.2   Finding the Dominant Angle and Corresponding s Index

Each image $\boldsymbol{v}$ is associated to an angle φ_s, determined by the histogram of oriented gradients from $\boldsymbol{v}$ [6]. Derivatives along the x and y directions are computed and the angle of each gradient vector can be determined. All the vectors are accumulated into a histogram with S bins and the angle ψ with the highest frequency is found. Formally, the index $s = \text{argmax}_j\varphi_j$, such that $\varphi_j \leq \psi$, $\varphi_j \in \Phi$. Figure 2 shows graphically those steps: from the original image pattern (a), derivatives are computed using Sobel filters (b). Subsequently, we build the weighted histogram of oriented gradients and the angle with the highest

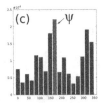

Fig. 2. Computation of the dominant orientation for a sample image taken from the MNIST dataset: (a) original sample, (b) gradients of the image, (c) histogram of oriented gradients with highlighted mode ψ, (d) sample rotated by ψ degree. The region marked by a green ellipse corresponds to the same portion of the number 3 in the original and rotated image. Observe the differences due to image interpolation introduced during rotation.

frequency ψ is selected (c). We highlight in red the 9-th bin of the histogram, hence $s = 9$ for the illustrated example. In (d) we report a rotated version of the sample image by ψ degree to show the deleterious effect of image interpolation.

Since strong edges near image boundaries may bias the estimation of the dominant gradient, the magnitude of the corresponding vectors is weighted with a Gaussian kernel, with $\sigma = \frac{min\{w,h\}}{5}$ (width and height of v respectively), such that central gradients contribute more than those at the boundaries. (We found this value covers evenly the entire image without exceeding its size.)

3   Experimental Results

Setup: We used the MNIST-rot dataset[1] [14], containing $10,000$ images for training, $2,000$ for validation, and $50,000$ for testing. This dataset is derived from the MNIST dataset, where samples were rotated by random angles. To enable comparison with other methods, for consistency, we kept this dataset splitting, and we did not perform cross-validation (that could have provided variances for statistical analysis). Since each image contains several non-zero entries close to 0, we threshold them at a value $\tau = 0.3$. We compare ERI-RBM with several informative baselines and a recent invariant method. *Classical RBM:* We trained a standard Bernoulli Restricted Boltzmann Machine and compared results with our Explicit Rotation-Invariant RBM. *Dominant RBM (D-RBM):* We built a simplified model that learns an RBM for each dominant orientation, splitting the training set into S partitions, associated to a different RBM (i.e., we have S independent RBMs). *Oriented RBM (O-RBM):* We pre-process the dataset by aligning all images according to their dominant orientation to a reference orientation and train a single RBM. *TI-RBM:* We also compared with the method in [21], using the authors implementation[2]. Extracted features are provided to the following classifiers: linear and RBF SVM [22], softmax [9], and K-NN [7].

---

[1] Available at http://www.iro.umontreal.ca/~lisa/twiki/bin/view.cgi/Public/DeepVs ShallowComparisonICML2007.

[2] Available at https://github.com/kihyuks/icml2012_tirbm.

Table 1. Testing accuracies of standard RBM, Dominant RBM, Oriented RBM, TI-RBM [21], and our proposed ERI-RBM.

	RBF SVM C=10, $\gamma = 0.1$	Linear SVM C=0.1	Softmax	K-NN K = 3
RBM (H = 100)	87.37 %	59.27 %	57.80 %	82.69 %
D-RBM (H = 100, S = 4)	83.44 %	58.95 %	56.80 %	78.84 %
D-RBM (H = 100, S = 9)	79.18 %	53.62 %	50.76 %	73.56 %
D-RBM (H = 100, S = 18)	69.84 %	49.20 %	46.58 %	63.61 %
O-RBM (H = 100 S = 18)	87.37 %	58.99 %	57.80 %	82.69 %
ERI-RBM (H = 100, S = 4)	78.49 %	60.27 %	58.31 %	74.97 %
ERI-RBM (H = 100, S = 9)	91.27 %	74.87 %	73.02 %	88.48 %
ERI-RBM (H = 100, S = 18)	**92.08 %**	**77.69 %**	**75.84 %**	**89.34 %**
TI-RBM [21] (H = 100, S = 18)	80.63 %	69.10 %	68.20 %	73.60 %

Parameters: We set the number of hidden units to $H = 100$, while progressively increased the number of bins S, used to generate the histogram of orientations. Following the instructions in [10], we set the learning rate $\eta = 10^{-3}$, the Contrastive Divergence algorithm is iterated up to 200 epochs, and a constant momentum $\alpha = 0.9$ was used. The parameters for SVM were found using logarithmic grid search and best values are reported in Table 1. We set arbitrary $K = 3$ for the K-NN, using the Euclidean distance as metric. For TI-RBM [21], a set of $K = S$ transformations are considered, which is each associated with an array of H hidden units, while a single weight matrix W is considered. The final representation used during inference is obtained by max-pooling. To make the comparison to ERI-RBM fair, for TI-RBM the sparsity term was disabled, and we set the number of hidden units to $H = 100$.

Discussion: We report our results in Table 1 and we noticed that nonlinear SVM gave the best performance in all the cases. The baseline is given by RBM with an accuracy of 87 %. Tests using D-RBM show a gradual loss of accuracy as the number of dominant orientations S is increased. This behaviour can be attributed to the lack of information sharing amongst the RBMs, since they were each trained independently with less data (per RBM). Overall, our proposed model outperforms the baseline RBM ($S \geq 9$). At $S = 4$, ERI-RBM has a loss of performance, because of the coarse quantization of the 2π space: angles 0°, 90°, 180°, and 270° will have orthogonal rotations when shared update filters are computed for neighbour matrices, causing the propagation of sharp rotations that do not contribute much. As the number of S increases, ERI-RBM has a +13 % of improvement, showing that our model is able to learn rotation-invariant features. This is also displayed in Fig. 3, showing learned filters when $S = 9$. O-RBM shows no improvement compared to RBM, demonstrating that the contribution provided by the shared update filters increases the

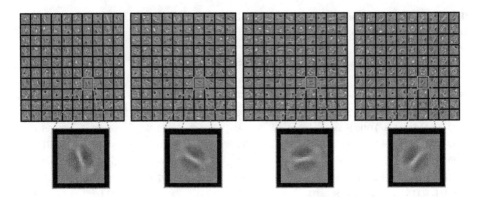

Fig. 3. Filters learned by our ERI-RBM at $S = 9$. We highlight a filter that appears at rotations 0°, 40°, 80°, and 120°, showing that our model learns rotation-invariant filters. The remaining weight matrices are omitted for brevity.

discriminative power of the final representation. Note that we also trained classical RBM with $H = 1000$, noticing an improvement of 2 %, still lower than ERI-RBM. Finally, using the same experimental setup, ERI-RBM outperformed [21] by +12 % in testing accuracy. (These results are different from those reported in [21] since sparsity is not present and we used less units.) Our approach does rely on the determination of orientation, which could be seen as a limitation. Preliminary results (not shown for brevity), obtained by artificially perturbing the orientation estimate, show that we are tolerant to such errors up to ±4 bins off on the original estimate. This remains to be confirmed in images with cluttered background.

4   Conclusions

In this paper we proposed the *Explicit Rotation-Invariant Restricted Boltz-mann Machine* (ERI-RBM). Current approaches do not address the problem of rotation-invariance directly, but use a predefined set of transformations to transform either the input images [19,21] or the learned filters [13,20]. We were inspired by these approaches to modify the RBM learning process, such that to learn invariant features without taking into account all possible transformations, which is demanding and may propagate noise due to pixel interpolations.

Our ERI-RBM utilises the dominant gradient of input images in order to select the best set of filters to optimise. We find the corresponding gradients efficiently and update the filters in a process where information is shared across the different filters, minimising thus any effects of interpolation. Overall, our model learns rotation-invariant features and achieves an accuracy of 92 % in the MNIST-rot dataset. Comparisons with several baselines and approaches from the literature showed superior performance in a common experimental setup. Moreover, comparing to the deep architecture of [8] and the results on MNIST-rot,

ERI-RBM reached similar performance using just 100 of hidden units compared to the 500 in [8]. In conclusion, ERI-RBM is able to learn rotation-invariant features in an unsupervised fashion, with a reduced number of hidden units, within a shallow network.

Acknowledgements. We thank NVIDIA corporation for providing us a Titan X GPU.

References

1. Agarwal, A., Triggs, B.: Hyperfeatures – multilevel local coding for visual recognition. In: Leonardis, A., Bischof, H., Pinz, A. (eds.) ECCV 2006, Part I. LNCS, vol. 3951, pp. 30–43. Springer, Heidelberg (2006)
2. Arel, I., Rose, D.C., Karnowski, T.P.: Deep machine learning - a new frontier in artificial intelligence research. IEEE Comput. Intell. Mag. **5**(4), 13–18 (2010)
3. Cheng, D., Sun, T., Jiang, X., Wang, S.: Unsupervised feature learning using Markov deep belief network. In: 2013 IEEE International Conference on Image Processing, pp. 260–264, No. 20120073110053. IEEE (2013)
4. Coates, A., Arbor, A., Ng, A.Y.: An analysis of single-layer networks in unsupervised feature learning. In: AISTATS, pp. 215–223 (2011)
5. Csurka, G., Dance, C.R., Fan, L., Willamowski, J., Bray, C.: Visual categorization with bags of keypoints. In: Proceedings of the ECCV International Workshop on Statistical Learning in Computer Vision, pp. 59–74 (2004)
6. Dalal, N., Triggs, B.: Histograms of oriented gradients for human detection. In: Proceedings of the IEEE CVPR, vol. 1, pp. 886–893 (2005)
7. Dasarathy, B.: Nearest Neighbor (NN) Norms: NN Pattern Classification Techniques. IEEE Computer Society Press, Los Alamitos (1991)
8. Gens, R., Domingos, P.M.: Deep symmetry networks. In: NIPS, pp. 2537–2545. Curran Associates, Inc. (2014)
9. Hastie, T., Tibshirani, R., Friedman, J.: The Elements of Statistical Learning. Springer Series in Statistics, vol. 1, 2nd edn. Springer, New York (2009)
10. Hinton, G.: A Practical Guide to Training Restricted Boltzmann Machines, 2nd edn. Springer, Berlin (2012)
11. Hinton, G.E.: Training products of experts by minimizing contrastive divergence. Neural Comput. **14**(8), 1771–1800 (2002)
12. Hinton, G.E., Osindero, S., Teh, Y.W.: A fast learning algorithm for deep belief nets. Neural Comput. **18**(7), 1527–1554 (2006)
13. Kivinen, J.J., Williams, C.K.I.: Transformation equivariant boltzmann machines. In: Honkela, T. (ed.) ICANN 2011, Part I. LNCS, vol. 6791, pp. 1–9. Springer, Heidelberg (2011)
14. Larochelle, H., Erhan, D., Courville, A., Bergstra, J., Bengio, Y.: An empirical evaluation of deep architectures on problems with many factors of variation. In: Proceedings of the 24th ICML, pp. 473–480 (2007)
15. Lee, H., Battle, A., Raina, R., Ng, A.Y.: Efficient sparse coding algorithms. In: Advances in Neural Information Processing Systems, pp. 801–808 (2006)
16. Lee, H., Ekanadham, C., Ng, A.Y.: Sparse deep belief net model for visual area V2. In: Advances in Neural Information Processing Systems, pp. 873–880 (2008)
17. Lee, H., Grosse, R., Ranganath, R., Ng, A.Y.: Convolutional deep belief networks for scalable unsupervised learning of hierarchical representations. In: ICML (2009)

18. Lowe, D.G.: Object recognition from local scale-invariant features. In: ICCV (1999)
19. Schmidt, U., Roth, S.: Learning rotation-aware features: from invariant priors to equivariant descriptors. In: Proceedings of the IEEE CVPR, pp. 2050–2057 (2012)
20. Shou, Z., Zhang, Y., Cai, H.J.: A study of transformation-invariances of deep belief networks. In: IJCNN, pp. 1–8. IEEE (2013)
21. Sohn, K., Lee, H.: Learning invariant representations with local transformations. In: Proceedings of the 29th ICML, pp. 1311–1318 (2012)
22. Vapnik, V.: Statistical Learning Theory. Wiley, New York (1998)
23. Wei, X., Phung, S.L., Bouzerdoum, A.: Visual descriptors for scene categorization: experimental evaluation. Artif. Intell. Rev. **45**(3), 1–36 (2015)

Improving Robustness of Slow Feature Analysis Based Localization Using Loop Closure Events

Benjamin Metka[1]([✉]), Mathias Franzius[2], and Ute Bauer-Wersing[1]

[1] Frankfurt University of Applied Sciences,
Nibelungenplatz 1, 60318 Frankfurt am Main, Germany
bmetka@fb2.fra-uas.de
[2] Honda Research Institute Europe GmbH,
Carl-Legien-Straße 30, 63073 Offenbach, Germany

Abstract. Hierarchical Slow Feature Analysis (SFA) extracts a spatial representation of the environment by directly processing images from a training run and has been shown to enable self-localization of a mobile robot by encoding its position as slowly varying features. However, in real world outdoor scenarios other variables, like global illumination or location of dynamic objects, might vary on an equal or slower time scale than the position of the robot. To prevent encoding of said variables we propose to restructure the temporal order of training samples based on loop closures in the trajectory. Every time the robot passes by a previously visited place, former recorded images are re-inserted to increase temporal variation of environmental variables. Hence, it is a feedback signal enforcing the model to produce similar outputs due to its slowness objective. Experiments in a simulated outdoor environment demonstrate increased robustness especially for changing lighting conditions.

Keywords: Self-localization · Slow feature analysis · Long-term robustness · Loop closure detection · Omnidirectional vision

1 Introduction

Self-localization is a prerequisite for autonomous mobile robots executing tasks in a spatial environment. The problem of simultaneous localization and mapping (SLAM) has been studied extensively. Recent geometric approaches estimate the motion of the camera and the depth of the scene from consecutive frames based on feature correspondences or semi-direct image alignment [1,2]. Despite the impressive results demonstrated by these approaches, visual localization and mapping in long-term outdoor scenarios remains a challenging problem due to different lighting conditions, cast shadows, dynamic elements or seasonal effects. The model for SFA-localization is based on the principle of slowness learning [3–5]. It is inspired by the observation that primary sensory signals, like the values of individual pixel, usually change on a faster timescale than the embedded high level information, such as the position of observed objects. Extracting slowly varying features from quickly changing sensory signals thus should

© Springer International Publishing Switzerland 2016
A.E.P. Villa et al. (Eds.): ICANN 2016, Part II, LNCS 9887, pp. 489–496, 2016.
DOI: 10.1007/978-3-319-44781-0_58

yield the underlying abstract information. It has been shown that a hierarchical SFA-network can model place and head direction cells [6], reflecting spatial information in the brain of rodents, and enable localization of a mobile robot in outdoor environments [7] by directly processing the high dimensional visual input. After an offline learning phase localization is instantaneous and absolute since SFA-outputs are computed from a single sample. Despite the good localization results the learned representation are likely only valid for short periods of time when the image statistics are similar to the training. Here we extend the model using loop closures in the trajectory to restructure the training data for improved robustness. Images from loop closures, representing the same place under different environmental conditions, are re-inserted in the temporally ordered image sequence. This increases temporal variation of environmental effects and is a feedback signal for the SFA-model that has to find functions producing a similar output due to its slowness objective.

2   Model for SFA Localization

2.1   Slow Feature Analysis and Orientation Invariance

SFA as introduced in [8] transforms a multidimensional time series $x(t)$ to slowly varying output signals. The objective is to find instantaneous scalar input-output functions $g_j(x)$ such that the output signals $y_j(t) := g_j(x(t))$ minimize $\Delta(y_j) := \langle \dot{y}_j^2 \rangle_t$ under the constraints $\langle y_j \rangle_t = 0$ (zero mean), $\langle y_j^2 \rangle_t = 1$ (unit variance), $\forall i < j : \langle y_i y_j \rangle_t = 0$ (decorrelation and order) with $\langle \cdot \rangle_t$ and $\dot{y}$ indicating temporal averaging and the derivative of y, respectively. The Δ-value is a measure of the temporal slowness of the signal $y_j(t)$, so small Δ-values indicate slowly varying signals. The constraints avoid the trivial constant solution and ensure that different functions g code for different aspects of the input. We use the MDP [9] implementation of SFA, which is based on solving a generalized eigenvalue problem. For the task of self-localization, we want to find functions that encode the robot's position as slowly varying features and are invariant w.r.t. its orientation. The information encoded in the learned slow features depends on the statistics of the training data. To achieve orientation invariance, the orientation of the robot has to change on a faster timescale than its position. We use an omnidirectional mirror as a feasible realization to simulate additional robot rotation, by shifting a sliding window over the periodic panoramic images.

2.2   Self-localization and Learned Representations

The high dimensional visual input is processed by a hierarchical network made of several converging layers. In our standard approach [7] layers are trained subsequently with all training images in temporal order of their recording. A single node per layer is trained with stimuli from all node locations in its layer and replicated throughout the layer after training. The model is shown in Fig. 1. The learned spatial representations are analyzed qualitatively by plotting the color coded eight slowest SFA-outputs $f_{1...8}$ over all positions. In case of strong spatial coding a clear gradient along the coordinate axis should be visible in the spatial firing maps of the first two units. Maps of higher units show a mixture of the first two units or higher modes. For a quantitative analysis we compute a regression function from the SFA-outputs to the ground truth coordinates and apply it to slow features extracted from images of a separate test set.

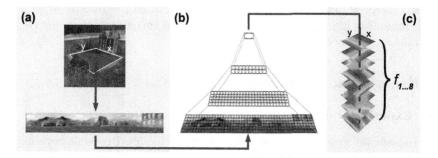

Fig. 1. Model architecture. (a) The views from a certain position (x, y) are steadily captured and transformed to a panoramic view. (b) The view is processed by the network. Each layer consists of overlapping SFA-nodes arranged on a regular grid. Each node performs linear SFA for dimensionality reduction followed by a quadratic SFA for slow feature extraction. The output layer is a single node, whose eight slowest outputs $y_j(t)$ are the orientation invariant encoding of the location. (c) The color coded SFA-outputs $f_{1...8}$ over all positions, so-called *spatial firing maps*, ideally show characteristic gradients along the coordinate axes and look the same independent of the specific orientation.

2.3 Extending the Model Using Feedback from Loop Closures

Since the SFA-model processes raw pixel values the learned representations are susceptible to appearance changes of the environment varying on an equal or slower timescale than the position of the robot. We use invariance learning, which is the basis of SFA, to learn representations that are not affected by environmental changes during the training phase. Loop closure detections allow to re-insert images of the same place, with a possibly different appearance, in the temporal sequence of training images thereby increasing the timescale of environmental effects. Further it is a feedback signal for the SFA-model, because its objective is to find functions that produce similar outputs for temporally close training samples.

Loop Closure Detection. To validate the feasibility of the approach we first use ground truth information to identify loop closures. A positive match requires that the spatial distance between the match candidates is smaller than a predefined threshold and that there is a minimum temporal gap between them. In real world scenarios, where no ground truth is available, loop closures can be identified using image information. A common approach is the bag of words (BOW) model describing each image by the occurrences of visual words from a dictionary (e.g. [10]). Here we created a vocabulary of 1500 visual words using Surf-Features [11]. Loop closure matches are then determined comparing the distance between visual word histograms.

Training Using Feedback. The SFA-model is trained with the temporally ordered images like in the standard approach. In case of a loop closure match, the past image is aligned to the current one by finding the relative orientation which minimizes the image distance. The aligned image is then re-inserted in the training sequence.

3   Experimental Results

3.1   Experimental Setup

Experiments are conducted in a simulated park like environment covering an area of 16×18. Images from the simulated omnidirectional camera are captured with a resolution of 500×500 pixel and transformed to panoramic views with a size of 600×55 pixel. The training and test trajectory consist of 1773 and 1090 poses that evenly cover the area. Crossings in the training trajectory improve spatial coding of the SFA-model and enable the extended model to get feedback from loop closures. The trajectories and the 62 loop closures determined from ground truth information are illustrated in Fig. 2.

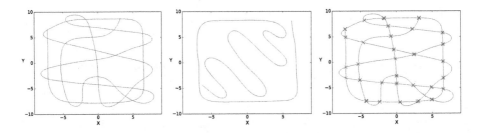

Fig. 2. Left: Training trajectory, Middle: Test trajectory, Right: Loop closures

3.2   Localization in a Static Environment

Initially we compare the standard and the extended model in a static environment to give reference under optimal conditions and to investigate the effect of using feedback from loop closures.

Results. Since the feedback only slightly changes the distribution of visited places, resulting representations of both models are nearly identical, leading to the conclusion that using feedback does not deteriorate performance. Spatial firing maps of the first two units, shown in Fig. 3a and c, show clear gradients along the coordinate axis. Units three and four are mixtures of the first two units. Estimated trajectories illustrated in Fig. 3b and d are close to the ground truth with mean Euclidean deviations of 0.24 and 0.23, respectively.

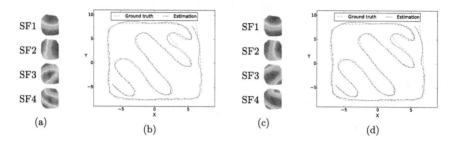

Fig. 3. Results in the static environment. Spatial firing maps of the standard (a) and extended model (c) show strong spatial coding. Estimated trajectories of the respective models in (b) and (c) are close to the ground truth.

3.3   Localization with Changing Light

In this experiment we investigate the effect of changing lighting conditions on the localization performance of the standard model and validate the feasibility of the feedback mechanism for improved robustness. The intensity of an artificial point light is increased over the training run leading to non-trivial illumination changes. Light intensity is thus the slowest varying latent variable embedded in the image statistics. Training images illustrating the effect are shown in Fig. 4.

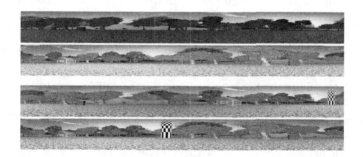

Fig. 4. Environmental effects. First and last image of the training sequences. Top: The effect on the appearance of increasing light intensity over the run, Bottom: A textured cylinder is moved along a circle around the training area.

Results. The quality of the spatial representations learned by the standard model is clearly deteriorated by the changing light intensity. Spatial coding is not observable in the spatial firing maps shown in Fig. 5a, while at least some position information is contained in the SFA-units since the estimated trajectory is not random (see Fig. 5b). The mean Euclidean deviation from the ground truth is 2.4. Using feedback from the loop closures enables the SFA-model to become more invariant against changing light intensity. Spatial firing maps illustrated in Fig. 5c show a clear gradient along the coordinate axis for SFA-units one and two, while units three and four are mixtures of the first two units. The mean Euclidean deviation from ground truth amounts to 0.49. The estimated trajectory can be seen in Fig. 5d.

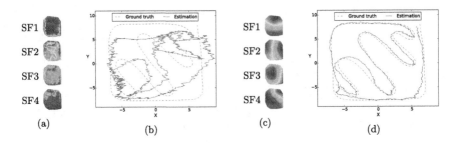

Fig. 5. Results with changing light. (a) Spatial firing maps from the standard SFA-model show no spatial coding. (b) Localization performance is deteriorated but not random which indicates at least weak position coding. (c) Characteristic gradients along the coordinate axis in the spatial firing maps of first two units from the extended model suggest good spatial coding. (d) Localization accuracy clearly improves with the extended model.

3.4   Localization with a Dynamic Object

In this experiment we investigate the effect of a dynamic object. A textured cylinder is moved along a circle around the training area performing one circumnavigation during the training phase so that its location is the slowest changing variable. Figure 4 shows the first and last image containing the dynamic object.

Results. The effect of the dynamic object on the resulting representations is not as big as expected. Spatial firing maps of the first two SFA-units from both models, shown in Fig. 6a and c, show gradients along the coordinate axis. Accuracy of the estimated trajectories is only slightly worse than in the static environment as both models achieve a mean Euclidean deviation of 0.29. Estimated trajectories of both models are shown in Fig. 6b and d. The dynamic object seems to produce local noise only but no high level information about its position is encoded in the SFA-units.

3.5   Localization Using Feedback from BOW Loop Closures

Ground truth loop closures used in the previous experiments have a mean Euclidean distance of 0.06 between match candidates. In this experiment we

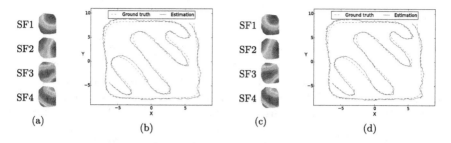

Fig. 6. Results with a dynamic object. Spatial firing maps from the standard model (a) and maps of the model using feedback (c) are nearly identical showing clear gradients along the coordinate axis. Estimated trajectory of the standard model (b) and the extended model (d) are close to the ground truth.

use a bag of words model for loop closure detection. Defining 0.1 as the maximum Euclidean distance for a positive match results in a mean average precision of 0.52. The 54 accepted matches with a mean Euclidean distance of 0.27 are depicted in Fig. 7a. The experiment is performed on the data set featuring changing light intensity since the effect of using the feedback was clearly visible.

Results. The imprecise loop closures interfere the quality of the resulting representations. The effect of the changing light intensity is visible in the spatial firing maps in Fig. 7b. First two units show a gradient along the coordinate axis but are not as smooth as in the experiment using ground truth matches. Units three and four are clearly influenced by the changing environmental variable. The localization accuracy is interfered accordingly with a mean Euclidean deviation of 0.9. Nonetheless, this is a big improvement compared to the standard model with a mean deviation of 2.4. The estimated trajectory is shown in Fig. 7c.

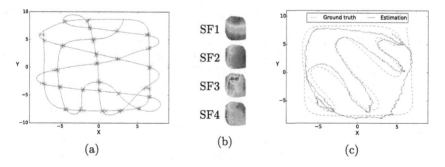

Fig. 7. Results with changing light using feedback from BOW loop closures. (a) Loop closures determined by matching visual word histograms. (b) Spatial firing maps suggest position coding in the first two units while units three and four show the influence of changing light intensity. (c) Localization performance clearly surpasses the standard model while deviations are larger compared to the model using ground truth loop closures.

4 Conclusion

We presented an extension of the biologically motivated model for SFA-localization using feedback from loop closures to improve robustness. Re-inserting images of the same place from the past in the temporally ordered image stream increases variation of environmental effects and is a feedback signal for the SFA-learning algorithm regarding its slowness objective. We have shown that feedback from loop closures improves robustness especially for changing lighting conditions. Experiments with loop closure matches from a BOW-model suggest the applicability of the model in real world scenarios. An elaborate solution to deal with imprecise loop closures could be the use of a weighted SFA-formulation, as described in [12,13], with training samples organized in a graph where the connecting edges represent their similarity regarding the labels.

References

1. Mur-Artal, R., Montiel, J.M.M., Tardós, J.D.: ORB-SLAM: a versatile and accurate monocular SLAM system. CoRR abs/1502.00956 (2015)
2. Engel, J., Schöps, T., Cremers, D.: LSD-SLAM: large-scale direct monocular SLAM. In: Fleet, D., Pajdla, T., Schiele, B., Tuytelaars, T. (eds.) ECCV 2014, Part II. LNCS, vol. 8690, pp. 834–849. Springer, Heidelberg (2014)
3. Földiák, P.: Learning invariance from transformation sequences. Neural Comput. **3**(2), 194–200 (1991)
4. Stone, J., Bray, A.: A learning rule for extracting spatio-temporal invariances. Netw. Comput. Neural Syst. **6**(3), 429–436 (1995)
5. Körding, K.P., Kayser, C., Einhäuser, W., König, P.: How are complex cell properties adapted to the statistics of natural stimuli? J. Neurophysiol. **91**(1), 206–212 (2004)
6. Franzius, M., Sprekeler, H., Wiskott, L.: Slowness and sparseness lead to place, head-direction, and spatial-view cells. PLoS Comput. Biol. **3**(8), 1–18 (2007)
7. Metka, B., Franzius, M., Bauer-Wersing, U.: Outdoor self-localization of a mobile robot using slow feature analysis. In: Lee, M., Hirose, A., Hou, Z.-G., Kil, R.M. (eds.) ICONIP 2013. LNCS, vol. 8226, pp. 249–256. Springer, Heidelberg (2013)
8. Wiskott, L., Sejnowski, T.: Slow feature analysis: unsupervised learning of invariances. Neural comput. **14**(4), 715–770 (2002)
9. Zito, T., Wilbert, N., Wiskott, L., Berkes, P.: Modular toolkit for data processing (mdp): a python data processing framework. Front. Neuroinform. **2**(8) (2009)
10. Cummins, M., Newman, P.: Highly scalable appearance-only SLAM - FAB-MAP 2.0. RSS, USA (2009)
11. Bay, H., Tuytelaars, T., Van Gool, L.: SURF: speeded up robust features. In: Leonardis, A., Bischof, H., Pinz, A. (eds.) ECCV 2006, Part I. LNCS, vol. 3951, pp. 404–417. Springer, Heidelberg (2006)
12. Escalante, A.N., Wiskott, L.: How to solve classification and regression problems on high-dimensional data with a supervised extension of slow feature analysis. J. Mach. Learn. Res. **14**(1), 3683–3719 (2013)
13. Escalante, A.N., Wiskott, L.: Improved graph-based SFA: information preservation complements the slowness principle. CoRR abs/1601.03945 (2016)

Self-Organizing Map
for the Curvature-Constrained Traveling
Salesman Problem

Jan Faigl$^{(\boxtimes)}$ and Petr Váňa

Department of Computer Science, Czech Technical University in Prague, Technická 2,
166 27 Prague 6, Czech Republic
{faiglj,vanapet1}@fel.cvut.cz

Abstract. In this paper, we consider a challenging variant of the traveling salesman problem (TSP) where it is requested to determine the shortest closed curvature-constrained path to visit a set of given locations. The problem is called the Dubins traveling salesman problem in literature and its main difficulty arises from the fact that it is necessary to determine the sequence of visits to the locations together with particular headings of the vehicle at the locations. We propose to apply principles of unsupervised learning of the self-organizing map to simultaneously determine the sequence of the visits together with the headings. A feasibility of the proposed approach is supported by an extensive evaluation and comparison to existing solutions. The presented results indicate that the proposed approach provides competitive solutions to existing heuristics, especially in dense problems, where the optimal sequence of the visits cannot be determined as a solution of the Euclidean TSP.

1 Introduction

A problem of finding a shortest closed path to visit a given set of locations can be formalized as the traveling salesman problem (TSP) for which several approaches have been proposed [4]. The basic variant of the TSP is the Euclidean TSP where locations are placed in a plane and each pair of the locations can be connected by a straight line segment with the length computed as the Euclidean distance between the locations. Although this problem formulation addresses many practical problems [4], it does not fit surveillance missions with curvature-constrained vehicles such as aircraft, for which the shortest path connecting two locations depends on the particular headings of the vehicle at the locations.

Optimal path planning for a vehicle with a constant forward velocity and limited turning radius ρ has been studied by Dubins who showed that the optimal path connecting two locations with prescribed headings is one of the six possible maneuvers [5]. The optimal maneuver can be determined analytically and it is called Dubins maneuver where the motion model is called the Dubins vehicle. However, the analytic solution does not allow to directly solve the so-called Dubins traveling salesman problem (DTSP), which stands to find a shortest

© Springer International Publishing Switzerland 2016
A.E.P. Villa et al. (Eds.): ICANN 2016, Part II, LNCS 9887, pp. 497–505, 2016.
DOI: 10.1007/978-3-319-44781-0_59

closed path for the Dubins vehicle to visit a given set of locations [11]. It is because each heading can be selected from the interval $\langle 0, 2\pi \rangle$ and the total length of the shortest path visiting the locations depends on the headings and also on the order of their visits. Therefore, it is necessary to determine both the headings and sequence of visits to the locations in the DTSP.

Three fundamental approaches for the DTSP can be found in literature. The first are methods based on a solution of the Euclidean TSP (ETSP) with the relaxed curvature constraint that include approximate algorithms with a relatively high approximation ratios [9] and heuristic algorithms such as the Alternating algorithm (AA) [12] or Local iterative optimization (LIO) [14]. Heuristics provide relatively good results in instances with locations far from each other, for which the solution of the ETSP provides optimal or close to optimal sequence in the DTSP. Moreover, for locations with mutual distance longer than 4ρ, the optimal headings for a given sequence can be found by convex optimization [7]. Therefore, it seems that instances with dense locations are more challenging, since it is necessary to simultaneously determine the optimal sequence and paginationbreak headings.

Two additional types of approaches are sampling-based methods [10] and evolutionary techniques such as genetic [15] and memetic [16] algorithms that consider particular values of possible headings at each location and solve the sequencing part of the problem. Sampling-based methods need a prescribed discretization of the headings and address the DTSP as the Generalized Asymmetric TSP which is transformed into the Asymmetric TSP [10] that can be solved optimally by the Concorde solver [2]. Although sampling-based approaches are able to provide high quality solutions, they become quickly computationally intractable for increasing number of locations and samples. On the other hand, evolutionary methods provide the first feasible solutions relatively quickly, which is then further improved if more computational time is available.

In this paper, we consider principles of existing self-organizing map (SOM) approaches for the TSP [1,6,13] to address challenges of the DTSP. The main difficulty of applying SOM to the DTSP is in computation of the best matching unit, which needs to respect the locations and headings regarding the previous and next waypoints in the tour. The proposed SOM for the DTSP encodes expected headings at the locations into the network structure and heading values are refined during the unsupervised learning. Although the proposed approach does not provide optimal solution of the DTSP, which has been also observed in SOM for the ETSP [3], it provides better results than simple existing heuristics [12,14] in problems where the optimal sequence of the visits is not the same as the optimal solution of the underlying ETSP. Moreover, the proposed SOM provides competitive results to the existing Memetic algorithm [16] with the computational time limited to 1 h while SOM is significantly faster.

2   Problem Statement

The motivation of the addressed curvature-constrained traveling salesman problem is a solution of the surveillance missions with a fixed-wing aerial vehicle that is modeled as the Dubins vehicle with the minimum turning radius ρ and constant forward velocity v. The state of the vehicle q is a triplet $q = (x, y, \theta)$ from the special Euclidean group $q \in SE(2)$, where (x, y) is the vehicle position in a plane and $\theta \in \mathbb{S}^1$ is the vehicle heading at (x, y). The model can be formally described as:

$$\begin{bmatrix} \dot{x} \\ \dot{y} \\ \dot{\theta} \end{bmatrix} = v \begin{bmatrix} \cos \theta \\ \sin \theta \\ \frac{u}{\rho} \end{bmatrix}, \quad |u| \leq 1, \tag{1}$$

where u is the control input. For simplicity and without loss of generality, we consider $v = 1$ and $\rho = 1$ in the rest of the paper.

In surveillance missions, the Dubins vehicle is requested to visit a set of n locations $P = \{p_1, \ldots, p_n\}$, $p_i \in \mathbb{R}^2$ by a closed path. Therefore, the problem stands to determine a sequence of visits to the locations together with the vehicle's heading at each location $p_i \in P$ [8]. The problem can be formally described as follows. Let $\Sigma = (\sigma_1, \ldots, \sigma_n)$ be an ordered permutation of $\{1, \ldots, n\}$ and $\mathcal{P}$ be a projection from $SE(2)$ to $\mathbb{R}^2$ such that $\mathcal{P}(q_i) = (x_i, y_i)$, where q_i is an element of $SE(2)$ whose projection is the location $p_i = (x_i, y_i)$. The problem is to determine the minimum length tour that visits every location $p_i \in P$ while satisfying the constraints of the Dubins vehicle (1). This is an optimization problem over all possible permutations Σ and headings $\Theta = \{\theta_{\sigma_1}, \theta_{\sigma_2}, \ldots, \theta_{\sigma_n}\}$ in the states $(q_{\sigma_1}, q_{\sigma_2}, \ldots, q_{\sigma_n})$ such that $q_{\sigma_i} = (p_{\sigma_i}, \theta_{\sigma_i})$:

$$minimize_{\Sigma, \Theta} \sum_{i=1}^{n-1} \mathcal{L}(q_{\sigma_i}, q_{\sigma_{i+1}}) + \mathcal{L}(q_{\sigma_n}, q_{\sigma_1}) \tag{2}$$

$$subject\ to\ q_i = (p_i, \theta_i)\ i = 1, \ldots, n, \tag{3}$$

where $\mathcal{L}(q_{\sigma_i}, q_{\sigma_j})$ is the length of the shortest possible path (Dubins maneuver) for the Dubins vehicle (1) between the states q_{σ_i} and q_{σ_j}.

3   Proposed Self-Organizing Map for the DTSP

The proposed unsupervised learning procedure builds on existing self-organizing maps for the Euclidean TSP [6,13]. SOM for the TSP is two-layer neural network which maps the input space $\mathbb{R}^2$ into an array of output units. The input of the network are the locations to be visited $P = \{p_1, \ldots, p_n\}$, $p_i \in \mathbb{R}^2$, while neurons $\mathcal{N}$ represent particular states of the Dubins vehicle in $SE(2)$, $\mathcal{N} = \{\nu_1, \ldots, \nu_m\}$, where $\nu_i \in SE(2)$ and we use $m = 2n$ according to [13].

Similarly to SOM for the ETSP, connected neurons form a ring representing a closed path in the input space. Since the sequence is prescribed by the output layer and each neuron has associated heading, it is straightforward to determine the optimal curvature-constrained path for the Dubins vehicle (1) using analytic solution of the optimal Dubins maneuvers [5].

In contrast to the solution of the ETSP, we need to adapt not only neuron weights to the locations P but we also need an adaptation rule to adjust the headings at the locations. It is known that the distance function $\mathcal{L}$ of the Dubins maneuvers is sensitive to headings, especially for two close locations. Therefore, in addition to the main heading θ_i associated to each neuron ν_i, we consider up to $2k$ headings around θ_i according to the neighbouring function $f(\sigma, d)$, where d is the distance in the number of nodes and σ is the learning gain. These headings may be considered as additional neurons; however, they are utilized only in the evaluation of the winner and in the local improvement of the solution of the DTSP represented by the ring. Based on the empirical evaluation, $k = 12$ provides a suitable tradeoff between the solution quality and computational requirements.

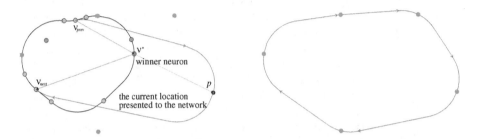

Fig. 1. Example of winner selection (left) and the final found solution (right). The locations to be visited are represented by green disks, the neurons are in blue and they are connected into a ring by Dubins maneuvers (black curve). The green straight line segment connects the current winner with its location $p \in P$ while the selected previous ν_{prev} and next ν_{next} neurons of the winner are highlighted by the blue segments. The red curve (left) is the Dubins path used for the selection of the winner neuron. (Color figure online)

The key idea of the proposed SOM for the DTSP is the winner selection that considers headings and also the length of the Dubins path. The winner ν_i^* for $p \in P$ is selected as the best matching unit according to the distance computed as the length of the two Dubins maneuvers connecting ν_{prev} with the state (p, θ_i) and (p, θ_i) with ν_{next}, where θ_i is the heading of ν_i^*. The neurons ν_{prev} and ν_{next} represent the previous and next neighbouring neurons of ν_i, i.e., $prev < i$ and $next > i$, and they are determined according to the neighbouring function $f(\sigma, d)$ as the farthest neighbors for which $f(\sigma, d) \geq 10^{-4}$. It has been empirically observed that such a selection of ν_{prev} and ν_{next} provides better results than the immediate neighbouring neurons. Besides, σ is decreasing after each learning epoch and, therefore, in later epochs, the immediate neurons are utilized which further support stabilization of the network. An example of the relation between the winner, neighbouring neurons, and the presented location to the network is visualized in Fig. 1.

Let headings associated to $\nu_i \in \mathcal{N}$ be $\Theta_i = \{\theta_i^{-k}, \theta_i^{-k+1} \ldots, \theta_i, \theta_i^k, \ldots, \theta_i^k\}$ then, the winner neuron ν^* is selected with the heading θ according to:

$$(\nu^*, \theta) = \operatorname{argmin}_{\nu_i \in \mathcal{N}, \nu_i \notin \mathcal{I}, \theta \in \Theta_i} \mathcal{L}(\nu_{prev}, (p, \theta)) + \mathcal{L}((p, \theta), \nu_{next}), \qquad (4)$$

where $\mathcal{I}$ denotes all neurons selected as winners in the current epoch. After that, the winner ν^* is adapted towards p and its main heading is set to θ. The neighbouring neurons are also adapted towards p, but only using the position as in the standard SOM for the ETSP. The neighbouring function $f(\sigma, d) = exp(-d^2/\sigma^2)$ for $d < 0.2m$, and $f(\sigma, d) = 0$ otherwise, is used for the adaptation.

Finally, to further improve convergence of the network and selection of the most suitable headings at the locations P, we update the main headings of the current winners after each learning epoch, i.e., after complete presentation of all locations P to the network. Since each location p has a unique winner, the order of winners in the output layer prescribes the sequence of visits to the locations. We consider the associated headings to the winners and construct all possible feasible Dubins paths connecting the locations P in the sequence defined by the winners. The best heading for each winner is determined by a forward search, which time complexity can be bounded by $O(nk^3)$. In comparison to the winner selection with the time complexity $O(n^2k)$, this is negligible since $k \ll n$. Beside improving the headings at the winners, this also provides a feasible solution of the DTSP at the end of each learning epoch. The selection of the winners, their adaptation and ring regeneration is repeated until the solution is not improving or after reaching the maximal number of learning epochs. The overall adaptation procedure is summarized as follows.

1. *Initialization:* For n locations P and the Dubins vehicle with the minimal turning radius ρ, create $2n$ nodes around the centroid of P equidistantly placed on a circle with the radius ρ. The learning gain σ is set to $\sigma = 12.41n + 0.06$, the learning rate $\mu = 0.6$, and the gain decreasing rate $\alpha = 0.1$ according to [13]. The epoch counter i is set to 1, $i = 1$.
2. *Randomizing:* Create a random permutation of the locations $\Pi(P)$.
3. *Learning epoch*: Clear inhibited neurons $\mathcal{I} = \emptyset$ and for each $p \in \Pi(P)$
   (a) *Select winner* ν^* and its heading θ for $p \in \Pi(P)$ using (4).
   (b) *Adapt* the winner and its neighbouring nodes to p using $f(\sigma, d)$ and update headings of the winner according to the selected value θ.
   (c) *Update* the inhibited neurons $\mathcal{I} = \mathcal{I} \cup \{\nu_i^*\}$.
4. *Ring regeneration:* Update headings of the current winners from the shortest Dubins path for the sequence of the locations defined by the winners in the ring and their associated headings.
5. *Update the learning gain and epoch counter:* $\sigma = \sigma(1 - \alpha)$, $i = i + 1$.
6. *Termination condition:* If solution is not improving or $i > i_{max}$ Stop the adaptation. Otherwise go to Step 2.
7. *Construct the final Dubins path* from the last winners and their headings.

An example of the final found solution is depicted in Fig. 1. Evaluation results and comparison with existing approaches are reported in the next section.

4 Experimental Results

The proposed SOM for the DTSP has been evaluated in several randomly generated problems with different numbers of locations n and mutual distances between the locations. We consider a relative density d of the n locations and the minimal turning radius ρ and generate the locations inside squared area with the side $s = (\rho\sqrt{n})/d$. In particular, we consider 20 instances for each $n \in \{10, 20, 50, 70, 100\}$ and $d \in \{0.3, 0.5, 1.0, 1.3, 1.7, 2.0\}$, which gives 600 different problem instances in total.

The performance of the proposed SOM algorithm has been compared with the AA [12] and LIO [14] heuristics and Memetic algorithm [16]. To evaluate the performance of the algorithms in so many instances, we consider the solution quality as the average ratio R_L of the particular path length to the reference path length L_{ref} and its standard deviation σ_R. Because optimal solution of the DTSP is not available, we consider the best found solution from all the solutions as L_{ref}. For providing high quality reference solutions, we consider the Memetic algorithm [16] with the computational time limited to one hour. On the other hand, for comparison with SOM and heuristics, we limit the computational time to 100 s to make the computational requirements of the Memetic algorithm competitive to SOM. Notice, AA and LIO are deterministic algorithms, while SOM is stochastic. Therefore, we performed 20 trials for SOM and each problem, which gives 13 800 trials in total. Only a single trial is performed by the Memetic algorithm to provide an overview of its convergence speed.

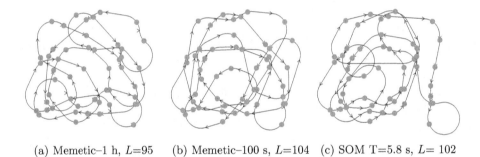

(a) Memetic–1 h, L=95   (b) Memetic–100 s, L=104   (c) SOM T=5.8 s, L= 102

Fig. 2. Selected found solutions for the same problem with $n = 50$ locations and $d = 1.0$

All the algorithms have been implemented in C++ and executed on a single core of the iCore7 CPU running at 3.4 GHz with 16 GB RAM and thus, the presented required computational times can directly compared.[1] The results are listed in Table 1, where R'_L is the average ratio of the best found solution for each problem from 20 trials. The standard deviation for R'_L is always less than 0.1 and typically around 0.05. Selected found solutions are shown in Fig. 2.

The fastest algorithms are the heuristics that provide a solution in less than one second, which includes optimal solution of the underlying ETSP by the Concorde [2]. Although the AA and LIO algorithms provides relatively good results

---

[1] Reference solutions provided by the Memetic algorithm with 1 h computational time has been found using a computational grid to decrease real time requirements.

Table 1. Average ratio of the solution length in the DTSP instances

d	n	ETSP-AA [12]			ETSP-LIO [14]			Memetic[a]		Proposed			
		R_L	σ_R	T [ms]	R_L	σ_R	T [ms]	R_L	σ_R	R_L	σ_R	T [s]	R'_L
0.3	10	1.35	0.14	3.7	1.32	0.15	9.4	**1.04**	0.06	1.11	0.10	0.5	1.00
	20	1.38	0.11	9.0	1.26	0.08	21.9	**1.07**	0.04	1.12	0.07	1.6	1.01
	50	1.35	0.11	52.7	1.27	0.08	148.0	**1.10**	0.06	**1.10**	0.06	7.2	1.01
	70	1.47	0.60	202.0	1.27	0.06	237.3	1.14	0.05	**1.08**	0.05	13.5	1.01
	100	1.31	0.06	346.5	1.24	0.05	641.8	1.23	0.04	**1.07**	0.05	26.2	1.00
0.5	10	1.65	0.20	4.7	1.73	0.31	11.5	**1.09**	0.09	1.23	0.16	0.5	1.02
	20	1.61	0.13	10.5	1.73	0.23	31.2	**1.10**	0.08	1.20	0.11	1.5	1.03
	50	1.71	0.54	60.9	1.68	0.08	145.7	**1.10**	0.05	1.14	0.07	7.4	1.03
	70	1.68	0.54	258.2	1.65	0.10	500.0	1.14	0.04	**1.11**	0.06	13.5	1.01
	100	1.50	0.05	766.8	1.63	0.10	587.9	1.23	0.05	**1.09**	0.05	25.8	1.01
1.0	10	1.72	0.21	6.6	2.33	0.27	14.8	**1.12**	0.14	1.29	0.18	0.4	1.06
	20	1.97	0.15	18.4	2.57	0.14	34.0	**1.11**	0.10	1.25	0.13	1.5	1.05
	50	1.94	0.11	93.4	2.63	0.16	174.2	**1.12**	0.06	1.17	0.08	7.3	1.03
	70	1.94	0.06	440.2	2.70	0.15	585.5	1.21	0.07	**1.14**	0.06	13.1	1.03
	100	1.93	0.07	332.8	2.63	0.12	537.9	1.31	0.06	**1.11**	0.06	25.1	1.01
1.3	10	1.64	0.17	7.0	2.35	0.22	14.8	**1.12**	0.10	1.29	0.15	0.4	1.04
	20	1.97	0.14	19.7	2.73	0.29	42.8	**1.12**	0.08	1.28	0.13	1.3	1.08
	50	2.09	0.10	113.7	3.04	0.11	183.8	**1.13**	0.07	1.18	0.08	7.0	1.04
	70	2.12	0.09	194.1	3.13	0.16	332.0	1.24	0.06	**1.14**	0.07	12.8	1.01
	100	2.05	0.07	443.0	2.97	0.11	540.6	1.32	0.06	**1.10**	0.06	24.4	1.00
1.7	10	1.56	0.15	6.6	2.31	0.28	11.7	**1.12**	0.11	1.30	0.17	0.4	1.07
	20	1.80	0.17	19.5	2.79	0.26	36.7	**1.10**	0.10	1.31	0.14	1.2	1.12
	50	2.16	0.12	90.6	3.34	0.21	174.2	**1.17**	0.07	1.20	0.10	6.7	1.05
	70	2.16	0.11	275.4	3.36	0.19	359.8	1.21	0.05	**1.15**	0.07	12.4	1.02
	100	2.24	0.11	354.3	3.46	0.19	554.3	1.33	0.06	**1.11**	0.07	23.7	1.00
2.0	10	1.40	0.08	7.8	2.17	0.18	13.7	**1.11**	0.11	1.26	0.13	0.4	1.06
	20	1.69	0.13	19.5	2.64	0.23	38.7	**1.09**	0.07	1.32	0.13	1.2	1.12
	50	2.11	0.15	120.7	3.36	0.23	268.4	**1.16**	0.10	1.25	0.11	6.5	1.10
	70	2.21	0.10	222.5	3.46	0.15	345.7	1.22	0.08	**1.16**	0.08	12.2	1.03
	100	2.25	0.10	339.5	3.59	0.19	541.0	1.33	0.07	**1.11**	0.06	23.6	1.00

[a]Computational time of the Memetic algorithm [16] has been limited to 100 s

for sparse problems, i.e., $d = 0.3$, with increasing density, the solution quality is quickly decreased. The proposed SOM does not provide competitive results to the Memetic algorithm for sparse problems. However, with increasing density of the locations, SOM solutions are competitive with the Memetic algorithm with the running time limited to 100 s, while SOM provides solutions in less than 30 s.

5 Conclusion

We proposed probably the first SOM-based solution of the Dubins traveling salesman problem which includes challenges of the underlying combinatorial TSP with the continuous optimization of the headings at the locations. Although the results do not show significantly better solutions of SOM than a more computationally demanding Memetic algorithm, the results support feasibility of the proposed idea and better scalability for larger and denser problems.

The distance of the farthest neurons utilized in the winner selection influences how close the solution is to the underlying ETSP, which provides better results for sparse problems, or the adaptation is more focused on optimization of the headings. In this paper, we consider dense problems regarding the motivation of surveillance planning, because we aim to further deploy the proposed solver in more general problems with continuous sensing, i.e., sensing along the path and not only in a finite set of locations. This problem can be considered as the TSP with Neighborhoods, where SOM already exhibits its flexibility [6] for problems without curvature-constrained paths. The proposed SOM for the DTSP is an initial building block for solving this more general problem.

Acknowledgments. The presented work has been supported by the Czech Science Foundation (GAČR) under research project No. 16-24206S.

Computational resources were provided by the MetaCentrum under the program LM2010005 and the CERIT-SC under the program Centre CERIT Scientific Cloud, part of the Operational Program Research and Development for Innovations, Reg. No. CZ.1.05/3.2.00/08.0144.

References

1. Angéniol, B., de la Vaubois, C., Texier, J.Y.L.: Self-organizing feature maps and the travelling salesman problem. Neural Netw. **1**, 289–293 (1988)
2. Applegate, D., Bixby, R., Chvátal, V., Cook, W.: Concorde tsp solver (2003). [cited 22 Jan 2016]
3. Cochrane, E.M., Beasley, J.E.: The co-adaptive neural network approach to the Euclidean travelling salesman problem. Neural Netw. **16**(10), 1499–1525 (2003)
4. Cook, W.: In Pursuit of the Traveling Salesman: Mathematics at the Limits of Computation. Princeton University Press (2012)
5. Dubins, L.E.: On curves of minimal length with a constraint on average curvature, and with prescribed initial and terminal positions and tangents. Am. J. Math. **79**, 497–516 (1957)
6. Faigl, J., Přeučil, L.: Self-organizing map for the multi-goal path planning with polygonal goals. In: Honkela, T. (ed.) ICANN 2011, Part I. LNCS, vol. 6791, pp. 85–92. Springer, Heidelberg (2011)
7. Goaoc, X., Kim, H.S., Lazard, S.: Bounded-curvature shortest paths through a sequence of points using convex optimization. SIAM J. Comput. **42**(2), 662–684 (2013)
8. Le Ny, J., Feron, E., Frazzoli, E.: On the dubins traveling salesman problem. IEEE Trans. Autom. Control **57**(1), 265–270 (2012)

9. Oberlin, P., Rathinam, S., Darbha, S.: Today's traveling salesman problem. IEEE Robot. Autom. Mag. **17**(4), 70–77 (2010)
10. Obermeyer, K.J., Oberlin, P., Darbha, S.: Sampling-based path planning for a visual reconnaissance unmanned air vehicle. J. Guidance Control Dynamics **35**(2), 619–631 (2012)
11. Savla, K., Frazzoli, E., Bullo, F.: Traveling salesperson problems for the Dubins vehicle. IEEE Trans. Autom. Control **53**(6), 1378–1391 (2008)
12. Savla, K., Frazzoli, E., Bullo, F.: On the point-to-point and traveling salesperson problems for Dubins' vehicle. In: Proceedings of the American Control Conference, pp. 786–791. IEEE (2005)
13. Somhom, S., Modares, A., Enkawa, T.: A self-organising model for the travelling salesman problem. J. Oper. Res. Soc. **48**, 919–928 (1997)
14. Váňa, P., Faigl, J.: On the dubins traveling salesman problem with neighborhoods. In: International Conference on Intelligent Robots and Systems, pp. 4029–4034 (2015)
15. Yu, X., Hung, J.: A genetic algorithm for the dubins traveling salesman problem. In: IEEE International Symposium on Industrial Electronics, pp. 1256–1261 (2012)
16. Zhang, X., Chen, J., Xin, B., Peng, Z.: A memetic algorithm for path planning of curvature-constrained UAVs performing surveillance of multiple ground targets. Chin. J. Aeronaut. **27**(3), 622–633 (2014)

Non-negative Kernel Sparse Coding for the Analysis of Motion Data

Babak Hosseini[(✉)], Felix Hülsmann, Mario Botsch, and Barbara Hammer

CITEC Centre of Excellence, Bielefeld University, Bielefeld, Germany
`bhosseini@techfak.uni-bielefeld.de`

Abstract. We are interested in a decomposition of motion data into a sparse linear combination of base functions which enable efficient data processing. We combine two prominent frameworks: dynamic time warping (DTW), which offers particularly successful pairwise motion data comparison, and sparse coding (SC), which enables an automatic decomposition of vectorial data into a sparse linear combination of base vectors. We enhance SC via efficient kernelization which extends its application domain to general similarity data such as offered by DTW, and its restriction to non-negative linear representations of signals and base vectors in order to guarantee a meaningful dictionary. We also implemented the proposed method in a classification framework and evaluated its performance on various motion capture benchmark data sets.

Keywords: Kernel sparse coding · Motion analysis · Classification · Interpretable models · Dynamic time warping

1 Introduction

Ubiquitous sensors such as Microsoft's Kinect, video cameras, and motion capture systems cause an increasing availability of human motion data as digital signals. However, it remains a challenge how to automate semantic search in motion data bases, unless such data are labeled manually. In this contribution we investigate in how far natural priors such as sparsity allow an automatic extraction of semantically meaningful entities based on the given data alone.

We hypothesize that semantics is mirrored by recurring signals, which are present in semantically similar motion data, and it is possible to infer such signals from given data based on their property that they allow a particularly efficient description of the signals. We will rely on two techniques which have proven successful in such settings: (1) Dynamic Time Warping (DTW) that enables an efficient grouping of time series of different lengths according to their semantic similarity, incorporating invariance to small temporal shift and distortion [13]. (2) Sparse Coding (SC), which extracts a dictionary from a given data set and enables a sparse linear representation of the signals based thereon [2]. The resulting dictionary elements constitute an interface based on which semantic search becomes possible: signals which decompose into the same dictionary elements have a large semantic overlap.

© Springer International Publishing Switzerland 2016
A.E.P. Villa et al. (Eds.): ICANN 2016, Part II, LNCS 9887, pp. 506–514, 2016.
DOI: 10.1007/978-3-319-44781-0_60

Classical SC deals with vectorial data. To combine it with DTW, we will resort to a kernel version of SC [15]. Several approaches apply SC for motion data, but they provide unreasonable base functions and linear combinations due to negative coefficients [7]. We will extend kernel SC to a non-negative version, and we will demonstrate its accuracy for various motion capture benchmark data sets.

2   Non Negative Kernel Sparse Coding

Sparse coding for *vectorial data* represents every measurement y^i from a set of measurements via a sparse representation $y^i = \mathbf{D}x^i$ with a dictionary matrix $\mathbf{D}$ of basic primitives, which are shared by all measurements, and sparse coefficients x^i, which describe how the observation y^i is generated by the basic primitives. In our setting, we deal with motion data instead, i.e. data are given as *time-series* $Y^i = (y^i(1)...y^i(T)) \in (\mathbb{R}^n)^*$ of possibly varying length T. We assume that a kernel is given for such time series (such as the DTW kernel), denoted as $\mathcal{K}(Y^i, Y^j) = \Phi(Y^i)^\top \Phi(Y^j)$ with feature map Φ. In the feature space, sparse coding problem becomes $\Phi(Y^i) = \Phi(\mathbf{D})x^i$, where $\Phi(\mathbf{D})$ is the dictionary matrix in the feature space.

Usually, the feature map Φ is not available, hence this problem cannot be solved directly. We follow the approach as proposed in [15]: we choose the dictionary as linear combinations of data $\Phi(\mathbf{D}) = \Phi(\mathbf{Y})\mathbf{A}$ with coefficient matrix $\mathbf{A}$. Often, $\mathbf{A}$ is chosen as an unconstrained matrix. However, we are interested in semantically meaningful features, i.e. dictionary elements should have the characteristics of motion signals and they should act as representatives for different motion groups. For this reason, we impose two constraints on $\mathbf{A}$ and x^i: The coefficient vector x^i, in addition to its sparseness, must be non-negative, such that motion signals are constructed from the dictionary elements as a meaningful mixtures of motions. For the same reason, the coefficient matrix $\mathbf{A}$ must be non negative, and the formation of meaningful groups of dictionaries is enforced by the sparsity of $\mathbf{A}$ by minimizing its L_1 norm. Hence sparse coding becomes the following optimization problem, where $\mathbf{Y}$ refers to all observed sequences and $\mathbf{X}$ to its respective matrix of coefficients:

$$\min_{\mathbf{X},\mathbf{A}} \|\Phi(\mathbf{Y}) - \Phi(\mathbf{Y})\mathbf{A}\mathbf{X}\|_F^2 + (\|\mathbf{A}\|_1)^2$$
$$\text{s.t} \quad \|\mathbf{X}_i\|_0 \leq T, \quad a_{ij} \geq 0, \quad x_{ij} \geq 0 \quad \forall i,j \tag{1}$$

T limits the sparsity of the resulting SC. In order to solve this optimization problem (Eq. 1), we use alternating optimization of the sparse coefficients and the dictionary. These two steps are realized by "Non-Negative Kernel Orthogonal Matching Pursuit (NNKOMP)" and "Non-Negative Kernel dictionary learning", described subsequently.

2.1   Non-negative Kernel OMP

KNNOMP optimizes the coefficients $\mathbf{X}$ in (Eq. 1) assuming a fixed dictionary characterized by coefficients $\mathbf{A}$. NNKOMP is based on the kernel OMP algorithm as proposed in [15], but enforcing non-negativity of the components. For this purpose, when adding non-zero coefficients in a greedy way in the kernel OMP, dictionary atoms with maximum *positive* correlation to the remaining residual error are selected. After selecting a new non-zero component based, coefficients $\mathbf{X}_i$ are optimized by the Non-negative least square algorithm (K-NNLS).

$$\min_{\mathbf{X}_i} \|\Phi(\mathbf{Y}_i) - \Phi(\mathbf{Y})\mathbf{A}\mathbf{X}_i\|_2^2 \quad \text{s.t} \quad \mathbf{X}_i \geq 0, \quad \|\mathbf{X}_i\|_0 \leq T \qquad (2)$$

For the K-NNLS method we use the active set "lsqnonneg" optimization algorithm from [14], and we kernelize the parts that calculate the intermediate solution point and the gradient based on the variables selected in the passive set. As a result, the output of the K-NNLS would be used as the solution in the intermediate step of the NNKOMP algorithm.

2.2   Non-negative Dictionary Update

As the second part of our algorithm, we want to find the best dictionary $\Phi(\mathbf{Y})\mathbf{A}$ which minimizes (Eq. 1) while using the obtained coefficients $\mathbf{X}$ as the output of NNKOMP in the previous section. Based on [15], the error function $\|\Phi(\mathbf{Y}) - \Phi(\mathbf{Y})\mathbf{A}\mathbf{X}\|_F^2$ can be re-formulated as:

$$\|\Phi(\mathbf{Y})\mathbf{E}_j - \Phi(\mathbf{Y})\mathbf{A}_j\mathbf{X}^j\|_F^2 \; ; \quad \mathbf{E}_j = (\mathbf{I} - \sum_{i \neq j}\mathbf{A}_i\mathbf{X}^i) \qquad (3)$$

$\Phi(\mathbf{Y})\mathbf{E}_j$ is the reconstruction error using all the dictionary columns except $\mathbf{A}_j$ and along with corresponding coefficients $\mathbf{X}$ which were estimated by NNKMOP. Therefore, the dictionary can be updated through solving the (Eq. 3) for each $\mathbf{A}_j$. As an important constraint we have to take into account that the optimal dictionary should be used along with non-negative coefficients $\mathbf{X}$. Accordingly we formulate (Eq. 3) as the following alternating optimization set:

$$\min_{\mathbf{X}^j}\|\Phi(\mathbf{Y})\mathbf{E}_j - \Phi(\mathbf{Y})\mathbf{A}_j\mathbf{X}^j\|_F^2 \quad \text{s.t} \quad \mathbf{X}^j \geq 0 \qquad (4)$$

$$\min_{\mathbf{A}_j}\|\Phi(\mathbf{Y})\mathbf{E}_j - \Phi(\mathbf{Y})\mathbf{A}_j\mathbf{X}^j\|_F^2 + \|\mathbf{A}_j\|_1^2 \quad \text{s.t} \quad \mathbf{A}_j \geq 0 \qquad (5)$$

In order to solve (Eq. 4), we used the large-scale non-negative least squares algorithm from [10] which can be easily extended to a kernel version that fits to (Eq. 4).

NN-Kernel FISTA: In order to solve the optimization problem in (Eq. 5), we devised the non-negative kernel FISTA algorithm (NN-K-FISTA) which is a combination of the projected gradient technique [9] and the Shrinkage-Thresholding method [3]. We kernelize [3], by calculating $f(\mathbf{A}_j)$ and $\nabla f(\mathbf{a})$ for the objective function f based on the Mercer kernel's inner product property; the shrinkage function is substituted with $\tau_l(x) = (x - l)(\text{sgn}(x - l) + 1)/2$. As the last step in the dictionary update part, we normalize the dictionary coefficients such that $\|\Phi(\mathbf{Y})\mathbf{A}_j\|_2^2 = 1$.

2.3 Label Consistent NN-KSC Classifier

The proposed non-negative kernel sparse coding framework will be used as a semantic encoding scheme for the observed motion data. In addition, we will evaluate the ability to base a classifier on top of the proposed coding scheme, as follows: We extend the label-consistent sparse coding as proposed in [4,6]. In the latter, kernelized KSVD has been used. We assume a labeling is present, $\mathbf{H}$ is the label matrix of training data where $\mathbf{H}(i,j) = 1$ if $\mathbf{Y}_j$ is contained in class i. In addition, we choose the matrix $\mathbf{Q}$ such that $\mathbf{Q}_j = \mathbf{Q}_i$ if $\{\mathbf{Y}_j, \mathbf{Y}_i\}$ are in the same class. The objective of sparse coding is now extended to enforce that coefficients $\mathbf{X}_i$ and $\mathbf{X}_j$ are similar for data in the same class, weighted by α. Further, base functions tend to accumulate coefficients for exemplars of one class, weighted by β.

$$\min_{X,D} \|\Phi(\mathbf{Y}) - \Phi(\mathbf{Y})\mathbf{A}\mathbf{X}\|_F^2 + \alpha\|\mathbf{Q} - \mathbf{Q}\mathbf{A}\mathbf{X}\|_F^2 + \beta\|\mathbf{H} - \mathbf{H}\mathbf{A}\mathbf{X}\|_F^2 + \|\mathbf{A}\|_1^2$$
$$\text{s.t}\quad \|\mathbf{X}_i\|_0 \leq T, \ \forall i = 1...N., \quad a_{ij} \geq 0, \quad x_{ij} \geq 0 \tag{6}$$

The optimization of this objective relates to a change of the kernel matrix as $\widetilde{\mathcal{K}}(\mathbf{Y}_i, \mathbf{Y}_i) = \mathcal{K}(\mathbf{Y}_i, \mathbf{Y}_j) + \alpha\langle\mathbf{Q}_i, \mathbf{Q}_j\rangle + \beta\langle\mathbf{H}_i, \mathbf{H}_j\rangle$. Using the new $\widetilde{\mathcal{K}}$ as the kernel function, (Eq. 6) can be solved by the proposed NNKSC algorithm. The parameters α and β control the trade-off between the reconstruction error and the classification accuracy. After optimizing the dictionary matrix $\mathbf{A}$, the NNKOMP (Eq. 2) can be used to find sparse codes $\mathbf{X}$. This induces a labeling of the data via $l^i = \text{argmax}_j|\mathbf{H}(\cdot, j)\mathbf{A}\mathbf{X}_i|$.

Furthermore, we are interested in having each column of $\mathbf{A}$ related to only one class of data. Doing so, we can partition $\mathbf{A}$ into separate class-specific dictionaries which will result in having specific prototypes and dictionary for each class of data. Therefore, in NN-K-FISTA algorithm the shrinkage-Threshold will be applied to only those elements of $\mathbf{A}_j$ related to data from classes with lower contributions in $\mathbf{A}_j$ (via updating the value of $\mathbf{H}\mathbf{A}_j$ after (Eq. 4)).

3 Datasets and Experiments

In this section we compare the proposed LC-NNKSC algorithm with other baselines on a few benchmarks. All datasets carry motion signals. Hence, first, we use the DTW algorithm to calculate a distance matrix $\mathbf{D}$ for the given samples. This is converted to a similarity matrix $\mathbf{K}$ using the Gaussian kernel $\mathcal{K}(x, y) = exp(-\frac{\|x-y\|^2}{\sigma})$. A valid Gram matrix results therefor by setting all its negative eigenvalues to zero (clipping). For the comparison, we choose the following methods:

LC-K-KSVD: We use a classification based on Kernel KSVD which has been proposed in [4]; this approach is closely related to the proposed NNKSC as regards its overall structure and objective.

k**NN:** We use the k-Nearest Neighbor classifier ($k = 3$) as a base line example, with which we classify the data samples based on the pairwise DTW distances.

Kernel-Kmeans: As another similar kernel based method, we apply the Kernel K-means clustering [12] to find m (equal to size of dictionary $\mathbf{A}$) cluster prototypes. Afterward, the distance of each validation data $\mathbf{Y}_i$ to all prototypes would be calculated as $D_i = \text{diag}(E^\top \mathcal{K}(Y,Y)E) - 2\mathcal{K}(\mathbf{Y}_i,Y)E + \mathcal{K}(\mathbf{Y}_i,\mathbf{Y}_i)$, where E is the normalized cluster assignment matrix based on [12]. After passing D into a Gaussian function to convert it to a normalized similarity matrix and keeping the first T biggest elements for each data, the result has a similar structure to $\mathbf{X}$ in the NNKSC algorithm. Then we feed the coefficients into a multi-class linear SVM in order to classify the validation data.

Affinity Propagation: We chose Affinity Propagation algorithm [5] as an approach which selects prototypes from the data samples in a clustering manner. There, the gram matrix would be used as the similarity matrix, and the class labels of validation data would be determined based on the closest neighboring prototype to each data sample.

Kernel PCA: As the last method for the comparison, we use the kernel-PCA approach from [11] to project the DTW based gram matrix $\mathcal{K}$ into M dimension space resulting in data vectors X. We apply a multi-class linear SVM to classify the generated data vectors.

In order to prevent local optima, for each method, we repeat the same experiment with 10 different initial points (or initial dictionaries) and we choose the one with the best result for the comparison.

3.1   Evaluation Criteria

Classification: We measure the correct classification rate as the first metric to evaluate the performance of the algorithms. Each dataset is randomly split into train, test and the validation parts with 50 %, 25 % and 25 % number of data respectively, and the learning process of the dictionary is stopped according to the increases in error curve of the test data. Finally, the classification accuracy and other measures are calculated based on the validation data.

Reconstruction Error: Among the utilized methods, only LC-NNKSC and LC-KKSVD belong to a sparse coding framework and provide a reconstruction error (Eq. 2) as a measure of their accuracy in a sparse representation of the data.

Class Based Sparsity: In addition, because another important concern of our framework is to provide sparse representation for the data, we also consider the level of sparseness for the coefficients $\mathbf{X}$. So in order to measure the sparseness in the classification framework we consider SP_i as the number of non-zero elements in $\sum_{k \in Class_i} |\mathbf{X}_k|$ for each class of the data, and we present the best and the worst SP_i for each algorithm.

Dictionary Sparseness: Furthermore, to study the dictionary interpretability, we calculate the relevance of each dictionary atom d_j to the data classes. We can find the contribution of each data class in $\mathbf{D}_j$ via $c = \mathbf{H}\mathbf{A}_i$ where $\mathbf{H}$ is the class label matrix as in (Eq. 6). Then the dictionary sparseness is measured as $DS = c_x / \sum c_k$ where c_x is the biggest element in c.

3.2   Datasets

CMU Motion Dataset: We use the Human motion capture dataset from the CMU graphics laboratory [1], which was captured by a Vicon infra-red system. We combined the movement data of subject 86 from the dataset which is a combination of 9 different types of human movements such as "walking", "running", "clapping",.... Then the data is segmented in order to brake down the long movements into smaller segments as single periods of each type of motion. Consequently, we obtain 9 classes of data with 10 sample per class, and for implementing LC-NNKSC we used $\alpha = 1$ and $\beta = 5$.

Cricket Umpire's Signals: For our classification experiment we use Cricket Umpire's Signal data provided in [8]. This dataset contains 180 sample of data from 12 different classes of umpire signals related to the cricket game. In order to perform the sparse coding classification we choose $\alpha = 0.5$ and $\beta = 1$.

Articulatory Words: The articulatory words dataset is the facial (ex. lips and tongue) movement signals captured via EMA sensors [17]. The dataset is used to categorize 25 classes of different words uttered by the subjects in total 575 sample of data. For this dataset we choose $\alpha = 0.2$ and $\beta = 0.5$.

Squat Dataset: The squat dataset is gathered in our institute as a part of the large-scale intelligent coaching project. The data is a set of squat movements performed by three sport coaches while being captured by the optical MOCAP system [16]. Each squat is segmented into three movement primitives "preparation", "going down" and "comming up", which generates 87 sample of data and 9 class labels together with the coach labels. Classification of this dataset is performed while using 1 and 0.2 as the α and β respectively.

3.3   Classification Results

For all the 4 dataset we choose the number of dictionary elements $\mathbf{A_i}$ as twice as the number of total classes. As a rule of thumb, we assume the data in each class can be reconstructed with a low error using only 2 atoms related to that class. We use the same value as the number of prototypes and the mapping dimension in K-Kmeans and K-PCA respectively. Also for the NNKSC and the LC-KKSVD algorithms we choose the sparsity limit $T = 4$ to see how the algorithm is going to use these 2 additional redundancy levels for the dictionary learning and the reconstruction.

In Table 1, the classification result are provided. We can see that for all datasets the proposed algorithm achieved the highest classification accuracy among the evaluated methods; however for Cricket and Words datasets the LC-KKSVD provided similar accuracy rates to LC-NNKSC (83.33 % and 97.33 %) while having smaller reconstruction errors due to the non-negative restrictions.

Table 1. Classification accuracy (%) and the reconstruction error (%) from applying the selected methods on the chosen datasets

	CMU		Cricket signals		Articulatory words		Squat	
	Acc	Rec. Err	Acc	Rec. Err	Acc	Rec. Err	Acc	Rec. Err
LC-NNKSC	90.91	4.17	83.33	11.07	97.33	14.52	100	0.14
LC-KKSVD	86.36	7.44	83.33	10.1	97.33	7.8	85	3.4
K-Means+SVM	68	–	56.25	–	90	–	81	–
Affinity P	90.1	–	68.75	–	92	–	100	–
K-PCA+SVM	50	–	56.25	–	60.66	–	37	–
kNN	86.36	–	79.16	–	96.66	–	100	–

Also in some of the datasets, the affinity propagation and the kNN managed to obtain performance levels equal to the proposed method, for example both have 100 % classification accuracy for CMU dataset; nevertheless they do not provide any reconstruction model for the data in comparison to the sparse coding framework.

Table 2 brings the sparsity analysis of the results, as the best and the worst measures (bDS, wDS) for the relevance of dictionary elements to the classes, as well as the best and worst number of class based sparsity (bSP, bSP). According to the Table 2, LC-NNKSC provide models for the datasets with better sparseness regarding both the dictionary atoms and the class data reconstruction. For all datasets, it defines each dictionary atom using the data of a single class which results in almost 100 % dictionary sparseness. For the squat data the algorithm managed to reconstruct the data of each class using only one specific atom (wSP = bSP = 1), meaning that only half of the dictionary is needed to model this data with NNKSC. Also, due to the value of wSP in Cricket and Words data (4 and 3 respectively), apparently there exist classes which require more than 2 dictionary atoms to be reconstructed and categorized efficiently.

The LC-KKSVD too has a high classification accuracy for Cricket and Words data, but this performance is lower than Affinity Propagation in the other 2 datasets. Furthermore, from the sparseness point of view, it is outperformed even by Affinity propagation by providing lower class based sparsity.

Table 2. The best and worst class based sparseness (bSP and wSP), and the best and worst dictionary sparseness (bDS(%) and wDS(%)) for the different selected approaches

	CMU				Cricket signals				Articulatory words				Squat dataset			
	bSP	wSP	bDS	wDS	bSP	wSP	bDS	wDS	bSP	wSP	bDS	wDS	bSP	wSP	bDS	wDS
LC-NNKSC	1	2	100	100	1	4	100	100	1	3	100	98.1	1	1	100	100
LC-KKSVD	5	9	100	76	5	13	100	44	5	16	100	56	3	8	100	87
Affinity P	4	6	–	–	6	4	–	–	5	11	–	–	4	5	–	–
K-Means	4	17	100	50	5	27	100	16	5	50	100	50	4	12	100	60

4 Conclusion

In this paper we presented a non-negative kernel based sparse coding approach for modeling and classification of motion data. According to the results, the non-negative approach provides much sparser representation for the data comparing to the conventional Kernel SC method, using fewer number of prototypes to reconstruct the motion signals. Additionally, where it is possible the LC-NNKSC approach forces dictionary elements to be created using positive linear combination of data only from individual classes. Doing so, the obtained dictionary can be easily broken down to class based dictionaries as separate prototype-based models for each class of data. In addition these sub-dictionaries can be used as a warm start in further classification tasks even when there is different combination of classes. All together, the LC-NNKSC classifier provides dictionary prototypes and sparse coefficients which are more class based consistent and makes it possible to have individual models for reconstruction of each class of data as well as for its classification.

Based on the strength of this method in constructing prototype based models for the motion data, there is a considerable potential for future works on the clustering and designing generative models of motion data using this framework or its variants.

Acknowledgment. This research was supported by the Cluster of Excellence Cognitive Interaction Technology 'CITEC' (EXC 277) at Bielefeld University, which is funded by the German Research Foundation (DFG).

References

1. Carnegie-mellon mocap database, March 2007. http://mocap.cs.cmu.edu/
2. Aharon, M., Elad, M., Bruckstein, A.: K-SVD: an algorithm for designing overcomplete dictionaries for sparse representation. IEEE Trans. Sig. Process. **54**(11), 4311–4322 (2006)
3. Beck, A., Teboulle, M.: A fast iterative shrinkage-thresholding algorithm for linear inverse problems. Society **2**(1), 183–202 (2009)
4. Chen, Z., Zuo, W., Hu, Q., Lin, L.: Kernel sparse representation for time series classification. Inf. Sci. **292**, 15–26 (2015)
5. Guan, R., Shi, X., Marchese, M., Yang, C., Liang, Y.: Text clustering with seeds affinity propagation. IEEE Trans. Knowl. Data Eng. **23**(4), 627–637 (2011)
6. Jiang, Z., Lin, Z., Davis, L.S.: Label consistent K-SVD: learning a discriminative dictionary for recognition. IEEE Trans. Pattern Anal. Mach. Intell. **35**(11), 2651–2664 (2013)
7. Kim, T., Shakhnarovich, G., Urtasun, R.: Sparse coding for learning interpretable spatio-temporal primitives. In: Advances in Neural Information Processing Systems, pp. 1117–1125 (2010)
8. Ko, M.H., West, G., Venkatesh, S., Kumar, M.: Online context recognition in multisensor systems using dynamic time warping. In: Proceedings of the 2005 International Conference on Intelligent Sensors, Sensor Networks and Information Processing Conference, 2005, pp. 283–288. IEEE (2005)

9. Lin, C.J.: Projected gradient methods for nonnegative matrix factorization. Neural Comput. **19**(10), 2756–2779 (2007)

10. Mark, H.V.B., Michael, R.K.: Fast algorithm for the solution of large-scale non-negativity-constrained least squares problems. J. Chemom. **18**(10), 441–450 (2004). doi:10.1002/cem.889

11. Schölkopf, B., Smola, A., Müller, K.R.: Kernel principal component analysis. In: Gerstner, W., Hasler, M., Germond, A., Nicoud, J.-D. (eds.) ICANN 1997. LNCS, vol. 1327, pp. 583–588. Springer, Heidelberg (1997)

12. Shawe-Taylor, J., Cristianini, N.: Kernel Methods for Pattern Analysis. Cambridge University Press, New York (2004)

13. Shokoohi-Yekta, M., Hu, B., Jin, H., Wang, J., Keogh, E.: On the non-trivial generalization of dynamic time warping to the multi-dimensional case. In: SDM (2015)

14. Shure, L.: Brief history of nonnegative least squares in matlab. Blog (2006). http://blogs.mathworks.com/loren

15. Van Nguyen, H., Patel, V.M., Nasrabadi, N.M., Chellappa, R.: Design of non-linear kernel dictionaries for object recognition. IEEE Trans. Image Process. **22**(12), 5123–5135 (2013)

16. Waltemate, T., Hülsmann, F., Pfeiffer, T., Kopp, S., Botsch, M.: Realizing a low-latency virtual reality environment for motor learning. In: Proceedings of the 21st ACM Symposium on Virtual Reality Software and Technology, pp. 139–147. ACM (2015)

17. Wang, J., Samal, A., Green, J.R.: Preliminary test of a real-time, interactive silent speech interface based on electromagnetic articulograph (2014)

Effect of Neural Controller on Adaptive Cruise Control

Arden Kuyumcu$^{(\boxtimes)}$ and Neslihan Serap Şengör

Istanbul Technical University, ITU Ayazağa Campus, Maslak,
34469 Istanbul, Turkey
{kuyumcua,sengorn}@itu.edu.tr
http://www.itu.edu.tr

Abstract. Adaptive cruise control is a system which controls a vehicle equipped with radars and a control unit to maintain either velocity of the vehicle or the distance between the preceding vehicle. The basic principle of this system is to read and interpret the radar measurement to determine the required actuating signals and apply these signals to reach the desired goal. In this work, the control is accomplished using a feed-forward artificial neural network, and its role is discussed. All the system is modelled in MATLAB/SIMULINK environment, and the main contribution of this work is to show the applicability of artificial neural network structure to an engineering problem at system level.

Keywords: Vehicle · Adaptive cruise control · Artificial neural network · MATLAB · Controller

1 Introduction

Nowadays autonomous driving has taken attention by engineers and commercial companies. Autonomous indicates that a computer based controller should control the vehicle in a proper manner. Main intentions of the modern autonomous vehicles are comfort and safety. In order to provide these features, the vehicle must recognize its environment and act accordingly. Thus, the controller controls the vehicle by sending actuating signals to the mechanical actuator which changes the dynamical condition of the vehicle by investigating its environment with sensors equipped around the vehicle.

The controller can be modelled or created in many ways in any part of the vehicle, here the technology of Adaptive Cruise Control (ACC) is considered and a controller is added to control the autonomous behaviour. ACC is a system that gathers the preceding car (here after *leading vehicle (LV)*) velocity and the distance between the ACC equipped car (here after *host vehicle (HV)*) and LV, then by processing these data, it sends required signal to the throttle or brake actuators in order to achieve the desired goal. These goals can be either to keep the desired distance between two vehicles or to reach the maximum velocity point adjusted by the driver. ACC system requires some mathematical models or

© Springer International Publishing Switzerland 2016
A.E.P. Villa et al. (Eds.): ICANN 2016, Part II, LNCS 9887, pp. 515–522, 2016.
DOI: 10.1007/978-3-319-44781-0_61

maps of the vehicle and the engine so that it can be able to decide what should the actuating signals be. Thus, like inaccuracies in most of the mathematical models, vehicle dynamics and engine model with power train loss etc. can cause inaccurate actuating signals. In order to prevent that in the system modelled in [1] a PI controller is utilized to correct the required actuating throttle signal obtained mainly by the vehicle engine inverse map.

In this work, PI controller is exchanged by a Artificial Neural Network (ANN) to correct the throttle signal. PI controllers requires coefficients to be set beforehand and adjusted accordingly to fit all the situations. Unlike PI controllers, ANN has the capability of learning and changing the coefficients based on the information provided to it. These abilities make ANN adaptive to the changing situations. All the superiorities of the ANN makes it worth to be built as a controller for the automatic systems. ANN is first mentioned in [2] as a controller and is used in many control applications [3,4]. ANN is also considered as an ACC controller in [5–7]. The ANN structure considered here as controller is a simple feed-forward structure and works online adapting its parameter values to provide a better throttle signal.

In order to investigate the effect of ANN controller on ACC, ACC system is modelled in MATLAB/SIMULINK environment using a very basic vehicle dynamic model considering some assumptions and then ANN is integrated into it by modelling it directly with simple SIMULINK blocks. At the beginning ACC is modelled with a basic equation and then some noise and delays for the dynamic actuators are added for further investigations. The effect of ANN is considered also both in the absence and presence of white noise added to the throttle actuator.

2   Adaptive Cruise Control

ACC controller is modelled in order to read the data from vehicle radar system mounted in front of the vehicle and interpreted accordingly. Radar reading is used to determine the switching between two modes allowed by the ACC system: spacing control and velocity control. Therefore, in order to simulate the readings, controller behaviours and vehicle dynamics a model is created as in Fig. 1.

The method of ACC utilized in this work is based on the work in [1]. Making some assumptions mentioned in [1] for the vehicle dynamics leads to one single equation which describes the vehicle longitudinal dynamics. So, it is assumed that, vehicle clutch is always connected. Meaning that there is no torque interruption and time delay in order to shift gear and there is no tire slip. Then the equation describing the longitudinal dynamics can be written as following;

$$T_e R_g - (T_b + M_{rr} + hF_a + mgh sin\theta) = \beta a. \tag{1}$$

Where T_e is engine, T_b is brake, M_{rr} is rolling resistance, hF_a is aerodynamic and final term is road gradient torque acting on the vehicle.

Equation 1 shows that net torque acting on a vehicle tire is equal to lamped inertia times acceleration of the vehicle. All the quantities denoted in equations

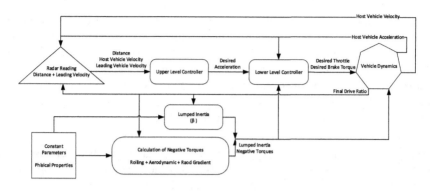

Fig. 1. Main SIMULINK model of the ACC system.

along with the parameter values are given in Table 1. In [1], Eq. 1 is inconsistent and miswritten and it is corrected here. This equation is manipulated in order to get the desired variable by leaving it alone in left side of the equation. That variable will be either torque required for the desired acceleration or acceleration provided by torques. Lumped inertia (β) consist of all the inertial parameters of the vehicle defined in Eq. 2 along with the final drive ration (R_g).

$$\beta = \frac{J_e + R_g^2 \left(J_{wr} + J_{wf} + mh^2 \right)}{R_g h}. \tag{2}$$

ACC reads radar data and feed them into upper controller. Upper controller can be followed from Fig. 2(a). It has two modes and determines whether it will switch into spacing control or velocity control. If it does not detect any vehicle

Table 1. Parameters

Parameter	Definition	Value	Unit
J_e	Inertia of Engine	0.16	kgm^2
J_{wr}, J_{wf}	Inertia of Rear and Front Axle	5.15	kgm^2
C_a	Aerodynamic Drag Coefficient	0.30	
K_1		0.5	
K_2		0.5	
K_3		0.00007	
$Radar\,Range$		100	m
t_{gap}	Time Gap	1.5	s
Δ	Inter Vehicular Distance	5	m
θ	Road Gradient	0	rad
m	Vehicle Mass	1650	kg
h	Tire Radius	0.3	m

within the radar limits it uses directly velocity control, in case it detects a vehicle, it reads the velocity of LV and determines required acceleration to achieve the desired goal. By comparing two accelerations calculated by velocity and spacing control, it provides the minimum acceleration required for the control. Acceleration (a_1) required to achieve the desired maximum velocity (v_d) is obtained as follow,

$$a_1 = K_1 \cdot (v_d - v_h). \tag{3}$$

Desired acceleration (a_2) required for the spacing control is obtained by considering the desired time gap (t_{gap}) and distance (Δ) to be kept in case both vehicles are completely stopped. The desired distance (S_d) and acceleration are calculated in the spacing control block as following.

$$S_d = \Delta + (v_h \cdot t_{gap}) \tag{4}$$

$$a_2 = K_2 \cdot (v_l - v_h) + K_3 \cdot (S_d - S_a). \tag{5}$$

Where v_l is velocity of LV and S_a is the actual inter vehicular distance.

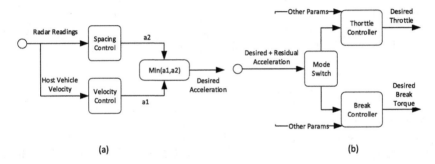

(a)   (b)

Fig. 2. The details of two controllers denoted in Fig. 1 (a) Upper level controller. (b) Lower level controller

After the calculation of desired acceleration (a_{des}), lower level controller gets the data and determines whether throttle control or brake control should be applied by comparing the desired acceleration and the residual acceleration (a_{res}) which is the acceleration when there is no torque component created by any input. It should be mentioned that there is a torque T_{ect} provided by the engine and the resistances even there is no throttle or brake commands. Thus the a_{res} can be calculated as follow where $T_e = T_b = 0$,

$$a_{res} = \frac{T_{ect}R_g - M_{rr} + hF_a + mgh\sin\theta}{\beta}. \tag{6}$$

Then comparison is made by adding small hysteresis h_{yst} and decision is made as follow,

$$\begin{aligned} a_{des} - a_{res} > h_{yst} &\longrightarrow \text{Throttle control} \\ a_{res} - a_{des} > h_{yst} &\longrightarrow \text{Brake control.} \end{aligned} \tag{7}$$

and modelled as in Fig. 2(b). In this figure desired acceleration is used to obtain the required engine torque by using Eq. 1 and feeding obtained torque into inverse engine map gives the required throttle position which is sent to the engine controller and engine generates the torque. The engine and brake system dynamics are considered as first order systems, roughly and by setting response time to 0.1 s gives a transfer function representation.

In the throttle control block, there was an additional PI controller in [1] which is intended to correct the throttle position caused by the inaccuracies in engine map and inverse of it. It is intended to compensate difference between the desired and actual acceleration of the vehicle. That PI controller is exchanged by a ANN controller in this work in order to see the effects of it in an ACC system.

3   ANN Controller

ANN is considered here as a controller which adapts its weights to minimize the difference between desired acceleration and the vehicle's acceleration. ANN which is implemented into the throttle control block is designed to build a relation between the desired acceleration and the torque applied to the vehicle in order to effect the dynamics of the vehicle. All this is shown in Fig. 3(a).

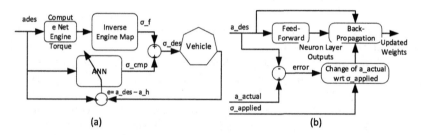

Fig. 3. ANN controller integration into throttle control (a). ANN controller design (b).

ANN is consist of two main blocks where the signal flows forward and takes the outputs from all the layers using the current weight values. Calculated outputs are used in order to calculate the local gradients and to generate new weights. Very basic mathematical description of the multilayer ANN can be described as follows,

$$v_k^i = W^i x^{i-1}, \qquad y^i = \varphi(v^i). \tag{8}$$

where, x is an input vector to a layer i, W^i is denotes the weight between two successive layers, v^i is applied to an activation function defined by φ is sigmoid function in hidden layers and linear function in the output layer and y^i is the layer output. In ACC controller, position of throttle can vary between 0 to 100 percent, so the activation function for the output layer is taken as linear function.

To update the weights, local gradients for each layer should be calculated. Equation 12 shows the calculation explicitly for the output layer. Since the calculated error is not the output of the controller but the output of the vehicle itself the local gradient for the output layer is adjusted as follows,

$$\delta^0 = -\left(a_{des} - a_{actual}\right) \frac{a_{actual} - a_{actual-1}}{\sigma_{des} - \sigma_{des-1}} \tag{9}$$

$$\boldsymbol{\delta}^2 = \left(\boldsymbol{W}^2 \delta^0\right) . \varphi'(\boldsymbol{v}^i) \tag{10}$$

These gradients are used to update the weights as follows with the contribution of learning rate η and the momentum term μ,

$$\boldsymbol{W}^i\left(k+1\right) = \boldsymbol{W}^i\left(k\right) - \eta \boldsymbol{\delta}^i \boldsymbol{y}^{i-1} + \mu \left[\boldsymbol{W}^i\left(k\right) - \boldsymbol{W}^i\left(k-1\right)\right] \tag{11}$$

In order to implement Back-Propagation shown in Fig. 3(b) directly as MATLAB codes to the system implemented, MATLAB Fcn blocks are used. For updating weights, there are variables that are needed from previous steps to calculate the outcome, so Memory block is used to handle this problem.

4   Simulation Results

Two different vehicles were implemented as a velocity profile like in Fig. 4 and positions of them were obtained by integrating the velocities with the initial positions shown in Fig. 5. Solid and sharp line in Fig. 4 indicates the velocity of the LV read by the HV and upper two lines inf Fig. 5 indicates two LVs position. There are four different analysis in each figure. Two of them were carried on without ANN controller and there are two analyses where white noise added into throttle system. Adding noise, clearly does not affect the vehicle behaviour very much, since the actual acceleration output is integrated once to get the velocity and twice to get the position and its effect is smoothed out.

The behavior of the system without ANN controller can be followed in Fig. 4 with dashed lines and this case has some delays. Solid lines have some little offset compared with the dashed ones which means ACC with ANN provides more quick response to change in radar reading and allows the HV to adapt quickly to the behavior of the LV or it shifts mode accordingly to reach maximum velocity. One can see that, two lines cross each other in Fig. 5 at approximately in 140th s indicating that a second car changes its lane interrupting the LV and HV by becoming a new LV and HV successfully follows the new one after the interruption. This is indicated in Fig. 4 as a drop in velocity to 50 km/h which is the velocity of the second LV.

Figure 6 shows the distance read by the HV in each configuration. Solid lines indicates the ANN controller effect on ACC system. It can be said that ANN allows the HV to follow the LV more closely.

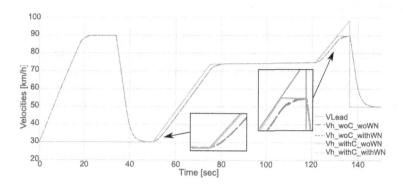

Fig. 4. Velocities of the leading and host vehicles with and without ANN controller and white noise.

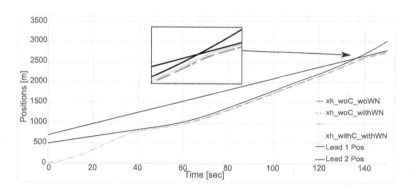

Fig. 5. Positions of the leading and host vehicles with and without ANN controller and white noise.

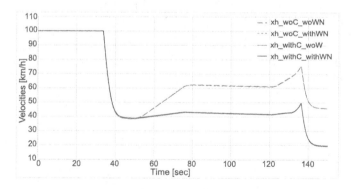

Fig. 6. Distances between the leading and host vehicles with and without ANN controller and white noise.

5   Conclusion and Discussion

The main objective of this work was to implement an ANN controller modelled in SIMULINK and integrate it into a vehicle control system. This has been done successfully and it is shown that ANN can provide fast response and narrow vehicular distance for the ACC system. The ACC system can be further improved, considering the biological facts and by implementing biomimetic cruise controllers [9,10].

References

1. Eyisi, E., Zhang, Z., Koutsoukos, X., Porter, J., Karsai, G., Sztipanovits, J.: Model-based control design and integration of cyberphysical systems: an adaptive cruise control case study. J. Control Sci. Eng. **2013**, 1 (2013)
2. Narendra, K.S., Parthasarathy, K.: Identification and control of dynamical systems using neural networks. IEEE Trans. Neural Netw. **1**(1), 4–27 (1990)
3. Spall, J.C., Cristion, J.A.: A neural network controller for systems with unmodeled dynamics with applications to wastewater treatment. IEEE Trans. Syst. Man Cybern. Part B Cybern. **27**(3), 369–375 (1997)
4. Khalid, M., Omatu, S.: A neural network controller for a temperature control system. IEEE Control Syst. **12**(3), 58–64 (1992)
5. Desjardins, C., Chaib-draa, B.: Cooperative adaptive cruise control: a reinforcement learning approach. IEEE Trans. Intell. Transp. Syst. **12**(4), 1248–1260 (2011)
6. Onieva, E., Godoy, J., Villagra, J., Milanes, V., Peeez, J.: On-line learning of a fuzzy controller for a precise vehicle cruise control system. Expert Syst. Appl. **40**(4), 1046–1053 (2013)
7. Dermann, S., Isermann, R.: Nonlinear distance and cruise control for passenger cars. In: Proceedings of the 1995 American Control Conference, vol. 5, pp. 3081–3085. IEEE (1995)
8. Haykin, S., Network, N.: A comprehensive foundation. Neural Netw. **2** (2004)
9. Pata, D.S., Escuredo, A., Lallée, S., Verschure, P.F.M.J.: Hippocampal based model reveals the distinct roles of dentate gyrus and CA3 during robotic spatial navigation. In: Duff, A., Lepora, N.F., Mura, A., Prescott, T.J., Verschure, P.F.M.J. (eds.) Living Machines 2014. LNCS, vol. 8608, pp. 273–283. Springer, Heidelberg (2014)
10. Maffei, G., Santos-Pata, D., Marcos, E., Sanchez-Fibla, M., Verschure, P.F.: An embodied biologically constrained model of foraging: from classical and operant conditioning to adaptive real-world behavior in DAC-X. Neural Netw. **72**, 88–108 (2015)

Intelligent Speech-Based Interactive Communication Between Mobile Cranes and Their Human Operators

Maciej Majewski$^{(\boxtimes)}$ and Wojciech Kacalak

Faculty of Mechanical Engineering, Koszalin University of Technology,
Raclawicka 15-17, 75-620 Koszalin, Poland
{maciej.majewski,wojciech.kacalak}@tu.koszalin.pl

Abstract. In this paper, an overview of human-machine interactive communication for controlling lifting devices is presented, covering also the integration with vision and sensorial systems. Following a general concept, and motivation towards intelligent human-machine communication through artificial neural networks, selected methods are proposed, which provide further directions both of recent as well as of future research on human-machine interaction. The aim of the experimental research is to design a prototype of an innovative interaction system, equipped with a speech interface in a natural language, augmented reality and interactive manipulators with force feedback. The presented research offers the possibility of motivating and inspiring further development of the intelligent speech interaction system and methods that have been elaborated in this paper.

Keywords: Intelligent interface · Neural networks · Interactive system · Speech communication · Intelligent control · Natural language processing

1 The Design of an Innovative Human-Machine Interface

The most up-to-date artificial intelligence-based technologies find their application in the process of designing modern systems for controlling and supervising machines. An example are vision systems - machine vision, augmented reality, voice communication as well as interactive controllers providing force feedback. The design and implementation of intelligent human-machine interactive communication systems is an important field of applied research. Recent advances in development of prototypes of human-machine speech-based interfaces are described in articles in [1–3].

The presented research involves the development of a system for controlling a mobile crane, equipped with a vision and sensorial system, interactive manipulators with force feedback, as well as a system for bi-directional voice communication through speech and natural language between an operator and the controlled lifting device [4]. The system is considered intelligent, because it is capable of learning from previous commands to reduce human errors.

© Springer International Publishing Switzerland 2016
A.E.P. Villa et al. (Eds.): ICANN 2016, Part II, LNCS 9887, pp. 523–530, 2016.
DOI: 10.1007/978-3-319-44781-0_62

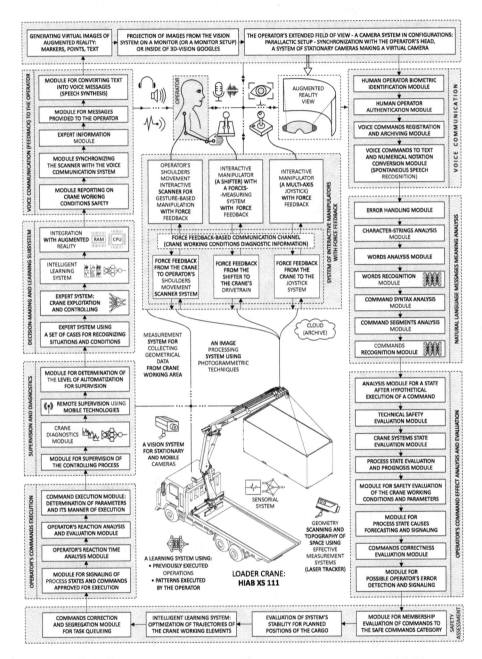

Fig. 1. Designed structure of an innovative system for interaction of the loader crane (Hiab XS 111) with its operator equipped with a speech interface, vision and sensorial systems, and interactive manipulators with force feedback.

The ARSC (Augmented Reality & Smart Control) prototype control system uses: intelligent visual-aid systems based on augmented reality, interactive manipulation systems providing force feedback, as well as natural-language voice communication techniques. We propose a new concept which consists of a novel approach to these systems, with particular emphasis on their ability to be truly flexible, adaptive, human error-tolerant, and supportive both of human-operators and data processing systems. The concept specifies integration of a system for natural-language communication with a visual and sensorial system.

The proposed interactive system (Fig. 1) contains many specialized modules and it is divided into the following subsystems: a subsystem for voice communication between a human-operator and the mobile crane, a subsystem for natural language meaning analysis, a subsystem for operator's command effect analysis and evaluation, a subsystem for command safety assessment, a subsystem for command execution, a subsystem of supervision and diagnostics, a subsystem of decision-making and learning, a subsystem of interactive manipulators with force feedback, and a visual and sensorial subsystem. The novelty of the system also consists of inclusion of several adaptive layers in the spoken natural language command interface for human biometric identification, speech recognition, word recognition, sentence syntax and segment analysis, command analysis and recognition, command effect analysis and safety assessment, process supervision and human reaction assessment.

2 Meaning Analysis of Commands and Messages

The concept of the ARSC system includes a subsystem of recognition of speech commands in a natural language using patterns and antipatterns of commands, which is presented in Fig. 2.

In the subsystem, the speech signal is converted to text and numerical values by the continuous speech recognition module. After a successful utterance recognition, a text command in a natural language is further processed. Individual words treated as isolated components of the text are subsequently processed with the modules for lexical analysis, tokenization and parsing. After the text analysis, the letters grouped in segments are processed by the word analysis module. In the next stage, the analyzed word segments are inputs of the neural network for recognizing words. The network uses a training file containing also words and is trained to recognize words as command components, with words represented by output neurons.

In the meaning analysis process of text commands (Fig. 3A) in a natural language, the meaning analysis of words as command or message components is performed. The recognized words are transferred to the command syntax analysis module which uses command segment patterns. It analyses commands and identifies them as segments with regards to meaning, and also codes commands as vectors. They are sent to the command segment analysis module using encoded command segment patterns. The commands become inputs of the command recognition module. The module uses a 3-layer Hamming network to classify the

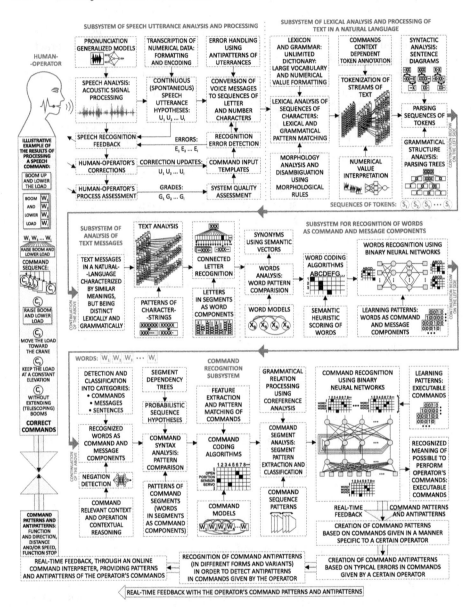

Fig. 2. A concept of a system of recognition of speech commands in a natural language using patterns and antipatterns of commands.

command and find its meaning (Fig. 3B). The neural network of this module uses a training file with meaningful executable commands.

The proposed method for meaning analysis of words, commands and messages uses binary neural networks (Fig. 3A and B) for natural language

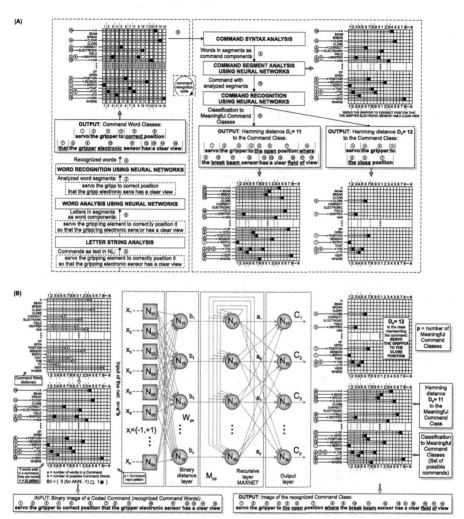

Fig. 3. (A) Block diagram of a meaning analysis cycle of an exemplary command, (B) Illustrative example of recognition of commands using binary neural networks.

understanding. The motivation behind using this type of neural networks for meaning analysis [5] is that they offer an advantage of simple binarization of words, commands and sentences, as well as very fast training and run-time response. The cycle of meaning analysis for an exemplary command is presented in Fig. 3A. The proposed concept of processing of words and messages enables a variety of analyses of the spoken commands in a natural language.

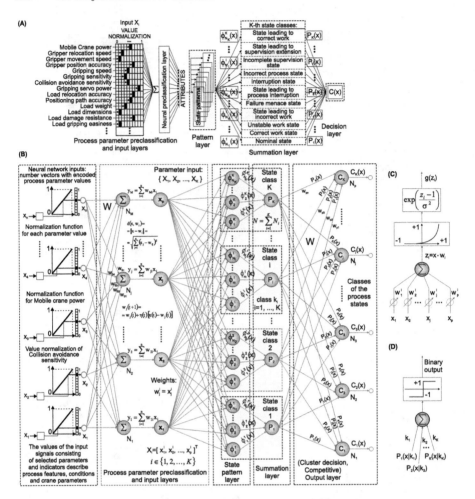

Fig. 4. (A) Hybrid neural model of effect analysis and safety assessment of commands in a cargo manipulation process, (B) The architecture of the hybrid neural network used, (C) Neuron of the pattern layer, (D) Neuron of the output layer.

3   Effect Analysis and Safety Assessment of Commands

The problem of effect analysis and safety assessment of commands can be solved with hybrid neural networks. The proposed method (Fig. 4A) uses developed hybrid multilayer neural networks consisting of a modified probabilistic network combined with a single layer classifier. The probabilistic network is interesting, because it is possible to implement and develop numerous enhancements, extensions, and generalizations of the original model [6]. The effect analysis and safety assessment of commands is based on information on features, conditions and parameters of the cargo positioning process. The developed hybrid network

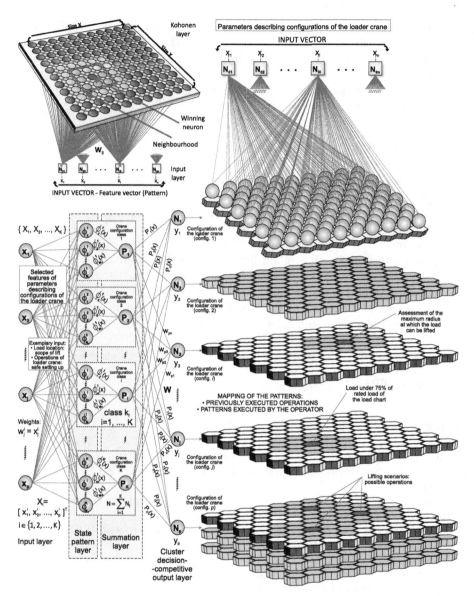

Fig. 5. Proposed learning systems using previously executed operations and patterns executed by the operator.

(Fig. 4B, C and D) is applied for classification of the cargo manipulation process state.

The proposed innovative speech interface is equipped with learning systems using previously executed operations and patterns executed by the operator. The developed learning systems are based on proposed hybrid neural networks

(Fig. 5) consisting of self-organizing feature maps (Kohonen networks [7]) combined with a probabilistic classifier. The inputs of the hybrid networks contain selected features of the parameters describing configurations of the loader crane. The outputs represent individual configurations of the crane which provide self-organizing feature maps of the previously executed operations and patterns executed by the operator.

4   Conclusions and Perspectives

The designed interaction system is equipped with the most modern artificial intelligence-based technologies: voice communication, vision systems, augmented reality and interactive manipulators with force feedback. Modern control and supervision systems allow to efficiently and securely transfer, and precisely place materials, products and fragile cargo. The proposed design of the innovative AR speech interface for controlling lifting devices has been based on hybrid neural network architectures. The design can be considered as an attempt to create a new standard of the intelligent system for execution, control, supervision and optimization of effective and flexible cargo manipulation processes using communication by speech and natural language.

Acknowledgements. This project is financed by the National Centre for Research and Development, Poland (NCBiR), under the Applied Research Programme - Grant agreement No. PBS3/A6/28/2015.

References

1. Kacalak, W., Majewski, M., Budniak, Z.: Interactive systems for designing machine elements and assemblies. Manag. Prod. Eng. Rev. **6**(3), 21–34 (2015). De Gruyter Open
2. Kumar, A., Metze, F., Kam, M.: Enabling the rapid development and adoption of speech-user interfaces. Computer **47**(1), 40–47 (2014). IEEE
3. Ortiz, C.L.: The road to natural conversational speech interfaces. IEEE Internet Comput. **18**(2), 74–78 (2014). IEEE
4. Majewski, M., Kacalak, W.: Intelligent speech interaction of devices and human operators. In: Silhavy, R., et al. (eds.) CSOC 2016. AISC, vol. 465, pp. 471–482. Springer, Switzerland (2016)
5. Majewski, M., Zurada, J.M.: Sentence recognition using artificial neural networks. Knowl. Based Syst. **21**(7), 629–635 (2008). Elsevier
6. Specht, D.F.: Probabilistic neural networks. Neural Netw. **3**(1), 109–118 (1990). Elsevier
7. Kohonen, T.: Self-Organization and Associative Memory. Springer, Heidelberg (1984)

Short Papers

Orthogonal Permutation Linear Unit Activation Function (OPLU)

Artem Chernodub and Dimitri Nowicki

Center for Cybernetics, Institute of MMS of NASU,
42 Glushkova Ave., Kiev 03187, Ukraine
a.chernodub@gmail.com, nowicki@nnteam.org.ua

Abstract. Orthogonal initialization of weight matrices is a promising trick for training deep convolutional [3] and recurrent neural networks [2]. In linear case it leads to faithful propagation of gradients through many layers [4] and preventing the vanishing/exploding gradient problem because of norm-preserving properties of orthogonal mappings. We propose a novel Orthogonal Permutation Linear Unit (OPLU) activation function that implements non-linear piece-wise orthogonal mappings based on permutations. For each pair of neuron's inputs $\{a_i, a_j\}$ we get a pair of outputs $\{z_i, z_j\}$ as follows: if $a_i \geq a_j$ then $\left(z_i \ z_j \right)^T = \left(a_i \ a_j \right)^T$ else $\left(z_i \ z_j \right)^T = \left(a_j \ a_i \right)^T$. It is straightforward to implement and very computationally efficient. A sufficient condition for strict preservation of the norm of backpropagated gradients is orthogonality of Jacobian matrices $\frac{\partial \mathbf{z}^{(n)}}{\partial \mathbf{z}^{(n-1)}}$ where n is layer's number. OPLU acts pairwise on layer's outputs and its derivative is an orthogonal operator at every point. OPLU activation function ensures norm preservation of gradients backpropagated through the non-linearity. This approach is promising the training of deep, extra deep, and recurrent neural networks thanks to strong and clear mathematical justification that guarantees strict norm preservation for unlimited number of layers if their weight matrices are orthogonal. We tested it on two toy problems namely MNIST and Adding problem for convolutional and simple recurrent networks respectively. It shows similar performance to tanh and ReLU. Exploring of its potential and limitations for real-life problems is a subject of our future research. For details, please see our full paper at [1].

Keywords: Orthogonal initialization · Vanishing gradient effect · Simple recurrent networks

References

1. Chernodub, A., Nowicki, D.: Norm-preserving orthogonal permutation linear unit activation functions (oplu). arXiv preprint arXiv:1604.02313 (2016)
2. Henaff, M., Szlam, A., LeCun, Y.: Orthogonal rnns and long-memory tasks. arXiv preprint arXiv:1602.06662 (2016)

© Springer International Publishing Switzerland 2016
A.E.P. Villa et al. (Eds.): ICANN 2016, Part II, LNCS 9887, pp. 533–534, 2016.
DOI: 10.1007/978-3-319-44781-0

3. Mishkin, D., Matas, J.: All you need is a good init. arXiv preprint arXiv:1511.06422 (2015)
4. Saxe, A.M., McClelland, J.L., Ganguli, S.: Exact solutions to the nonlinear dynamics of learning in deep linear neural networks. arXiv preprint arXiv:1312.6120 (2013)

Smartphone Based Human Activity and Postural Transition Classification with Deep Stacked Autoencoder Networks

Luke Hicks$^{(\boxtimes)}$, Yih-Ling Hedley, Mark Elshaw,
Abdulrahman Altahhan, and Vasile Palade

Faculty of Engineering, Environment and Computing, Coventry University,
Coventry, UK
ab3062@coventry.ac.uk
http://www.coventry.ac.uk/

Abstract. Human activity recognition (HAR) is a prominent research area attracting considerable interest in recent years. The use of Body Sensor Networks has enabled researchers to collect user data on which machine learning techniques can be employed for modelling and classification tasks. More recently, smartphones with inertial sensors allow the collection of user activity data. With environments becoming increasingly connected through the Internet of Things (IoT) and the development of smart buildings, data can be meticulously collected to identify patterns of human activity. Health care is an area of great interest focussing on activity based classification research for the promotion of wellbeing, with research centers engaging with individuals in a real world context to improve caregiving [1]. We have conducted experiments to understand how the application of machine learning, specifically Deep Stacked Autoencoder Networks (DSAN), along with traditional models including the Multi-layer Perceptron, Radial Basis Function Neural Network and Support Vector Machine for comparison, perform in presenting a solution to the HAR problem. The research analyses data collected from smartphones in order to classify between motion based activities including walking, running, and transitional actions such as moving from a sitting to standing position [2]. Results show that the DSAN outperforms traditional models with an increase in classification accuracy. A Deep Reinforcement learning approach is considered for future investigation into human behaviour recognition and prediction in smart environments in order to improve classification performance.

Keywords: Human activity recognition · Machine learning · Artificial neural networks · Deep learning

© Springer International Publishing Switzerland 2016
A.E.P. Villa et al. (Eds.): ICANN 2016, Part II, LNCS 9887, pp. 535–536, 2016.
DOI: 10.1007/978-3-319-44781-0

References

1. Doyle, J., Caprani, N., Bond, R.: Older adults attitudes to self-management of health and wellness through smart home data. In: Proceedings of the 9th International Conference on Pervasive Computing Technologies for Healthcare (2015)
2. Reyes-Ortiz, J.-L., Oneto, L., Sam, A., Parra, X., Anguita, D.: Transition-Aware Human Activity Recognition Using Smartphones. Springer, Neurocomputing (2015)

Accuracies and Number of Rules Extracted Using the Re-RX Algorithm Family from a Pareto-Optimal Perspective

Yoichi Hayashi[1]([✉]), Guido Bologna[2], and Riku Hashiguchi[1]

[1] Department of Computer Science, Meiji University,
Kawasaki 214-8571, Japan
hayashiy@cs.meiji.ac.jp, teitei117udonge3711@yahoo.co.jp
[2] University of Applied Science of Western Switzerland,
Rue de la Prairie 4, 1202 Geneva, Switzerland
Guido.Bologna@hesge.ch

Abstract. The Recursive-Rule eXtraction (Re-RX) algorithm family includes the Re-RX algorithm, the Re-RX algorithm with both discrete and continuous attributes (Continuous Re-RX [1]), the Re-RX algorithm with J48graft [2], Re-RX with J48graft combined with Sampling Selection Techniques (Sampling Re-RX with J48graft [4]), and the Re-RX algorithm with a trained neural network (Sampling Re-RX [3]). In this study, we compare the performance of the Re-RX algorithm family with various previous algorithms. One issue that always remains important in rule extraction is Pareto optimality, or in other words, an ideally balanced trade-off. In rule extraction, the trade-off is between the classification accuracy and interpretability of extracted rules. Our goal is to obtain a wider viable region for the Pareto optimal curve that will enable improvements in both the accuracy and interpretability of extracted rules. We vividly demonstrate Pareto-optimal curves between the accuracies and number of rules obtained for German and Australian datasets by 10 runs of 10-fold cross validation of the Re-RX algorithm family and those obtained using other algorithms. The Re-RX algorithm family has proven effective for extracting concise and interpretable rules from medical [1, 2, 4] and financial [3] datasets.

References

1. Hayashi, Y., Nakano, S., Fujisawa, S.: Use of the recursive-rule extraction algorithm with continuous attributes to improve diagnostic accuracy in thyroid disease. Inform. Med. Unlocked **1**, 1–8 (2016)
2. Hayashi, Y., Nakano, S.: Use of a recursive-rule extraction algorithm with J48graft to archive highly accurate and concise rule extraction from a large breast cancer dataset. Inform. Med. Unlocked **1**, 9–16

© Springer International Publishing Switzerland 2016
A.E.P. Villa et al. (Eds.): ICANN 2016, Part II, LNCS 9887, pp. 537–538, 2016.
DOI: 10.1007/978-3-319-44781-0

3. Setiono, R., Azcarraga, A., Hayashi, Y.: Using sample selection to improve accuracy and simplicity of rules extracted from neural networks. Int. J. Comp. Intel. Appl. **14**, 1550021 (2015)
4. Hayashi, Y., Yukita, S.: Rule extraction using recursive-rule extraction algorithm with J48graft with sampling selection techniques for the diagnosis of type 2 diabetes mellitus in the pima Indian dataset. Inform. Med. Unlocked (IMU) **2**, 92–104 (2016)

Finding an Hidden Common Partition in Duplex Structure-Function Brain Networks

Casimiro Pio Carrino[1]([⊠]) and Sebastiano Stramaglia[2]

[1] Physics Department, University of Turin, 10125 Turin, Torino, Italy
casimiro.carrino@edu.unito.it
[2] Physics Department, University of Bari and INFN, 70126 Bari, Italy
sebastiano.stramaglia@ba.infn.it

Abstract. We investigate the intricate relationship between human brain structure and function from a complex networks perspective. Indeed, several works in neuroimaging data analysis indicate the presence of robust partitions in both structural and functional networks, thus confirming that these two networks are interdependent. The function acts on the structure in virtue of the mechanism of neural plasticity, and conversely the structure acts on the function by means of topological constraints. In the attempt to understand this relation, we focus on groups of nodes making a comparison among structural and functional neural networks by exploiting their hierarchical modular organization. With respect to traditional methods in the community detection framework, we have developed a novel approach which allow us to figure out a common skeleton shared by structure and function in brain network. Using this, a new, and optimal common partition, can be extracted from duplex structure-function networks. Specifically, an algorithm, based on a probabilistic network model, has been developed to design an unsupervised multi-layer community detection. Hence, a numerical implementation has been rooted on the Expectation-Maximization technique (**EM**) to perform statistical inference on real brain data. We tested our algorithm on structural connectivity (**SC**) and resting state functional connectivity networks (**rsFC**) extracted from 12 healthy patients. Furthermore, we define a novel network measure called Cross-Modularity X, suitable to quantify the grade of similarity between two layers partitions. Finally, in order to validate our clustering algorithm, we use this quantity to make a comparison with classical single-layer community detection methods. As main result we obtain that the correlations between structural and functional networks are improved when the comparison has been made at the level of our extracted partition.

Keywords: Complex networks · Multi-layer community detection · Statistical inference · Neural networks

Reference

1. Diez, I., Bonifazi, P., Escudero, I., Mateos, B., Muoz, M.A., Stramaglia, S., Cortes, J.M.: A novel brain partition highlights the modular skeleton shared by structure and function. Sci. Rep. **5** (2015)

© Springer International Publishing Switzerland 2016
A.E.P. Villa et al. (Eds.): ICANN 2016, Part II, LNCS 9887, p. 539, 2016.
DOI: 10.1007/978-3-319-44781-0

A Novel Quasi-Newton-Based Training Using Nesterov's Accelerated Gradient for Neural Networks

Hiroshi Ninomiya[✉]

Department of Information Science, Shonan Institute of Technology, Fujisawa, Japan
ninomiya@info.shonan-it.ac.jp

Abstract. Neural networks have been recognized as a useful tool for the function approximation problems with high-nonlinearity [1]. Training is the most important step in developing a neural network model. Gradient based algorithms are popularly used for the training. The popular methods are first-order methods so called Steepest Gradient (SG), Classical Momentum (CM), Nesterov's Accelerated Gradient (NAG) methods and a more dedicated method such as RPROP. On the other hand, quasi-Newton (QN) method which is one of the most efficient optimization techniques with super-linear convergence is also widely utilized for more complicated problems. However, when applied to highly nonlinear function modeling, the above methods even QN still converges too slowly and optimization error cannot be effectively reduced within finite time.

This paper describes a novel acceleration technique of QN using Nesterov's accelerated gradient [2]. The proposed algorithm is referred to as Nesterov's accelerated quasi-Newton (NAQ) method. The update equation of the approximated matrix of Hessian is mathematically derived from the quadratic approximation of error function. The Hessian is approximated using both of the normal gradient and the Nesterov's accelerated one in NAQ. NAQ is a technique for accelerating QN that accumulates an update vector in directions of persistent reduction in the objective across iterations. As a result, the iteration during the NAQ training can be shortened without loss of the strong ability to search a global minimum in QN. The proposed algorithm is demonstrated through the computer simulations for the benchmark problems with high-nonlinearity compared with SG, CM, NAG, RPROP and QN. From the simulation results it is shown that NAQ is faster than the conventional methods without compromising quality of training solutions.

Keywords: Neural networks · Training algorithm · Nesterov's accelerated gradient method · Quasi-Newton method

References

1. Haykin, S.: Neural Networks and Learning Machines. Pearson (2009)
2. Sutskever, I., Martens, J., Dahl, G., Hinton, G.: On the importance of initialization and momentum in deep learning. In: Proceedings of the ICML 2013 (2013)

© Springer International Publishing Switzerland 2016
A.E.P. Villa et al. (Eds.): ICANN 2016, Part II, LNCS 9887, p. 540, 2016.
DOI: 10.1007/978-3-319-44781-0

Use of Ensemble Approach and Stacked Generalization for Neural Network Prediction of Geomagnetic Dst Index

Vladimir Shiroky$^{(\boxtimes)}$, Irina Myagkova, and Sergey Dolenko

D.V.Skobeltsyn Institute of Nuclear Physics,
M.V.Lomonosov Moscow State University, Moscow, Russia
{shiroky,irina,dolenko}@srd.sinp.msu.ru

Abstract. The Earth's magnetosphere is a complex dynamic system whose state is hard to predict due to its dependence on solar wind, interplanetary magnetic field, and on its own recent history. Neural networks are able to construct a non-linear function mapping all these factors to future values of geomagnetic Dst index, which is usually used to characterize the degree of disturbance of the Earth's magnetosphere. The prediction horizon considered in this study ranges from 1 to 12 h.

The study considers ensemble approach, combining perceptron type base neural networks in a simple ensemble by averaging their predictions, and stacked generalization approach, feeding the predictions of the base networks to the inputs of special supervisor neural networks and combining the latter in a simple committee by averaging their predictions.

For small prediction horizons (up to 3 h), the statistical indexes of predictors are very good - the multiple determination coefficient exceeds 0.88. With increasing prediction horizon, the complexity of the problem monotonously increases, causing a drastic drop in the performance indexes. ANN models outperform the trivial model (prediction = latest value) completely. The preceding study of the authors [1] for a similar task demonstrated that ANN (with small simple ensemble and without stacked generalization) also outperformed such powerful data analysis methods as Partial Least Squares and Group Method of Data Handling.

Using stacked generalization approach, even over identical MLPs differing only by weights initialization and the order of presentation of samples, yields additional gain in prediction quality. This gain increases with increasing complexity of the task either with increasing prediction horizon, or if the statistical indexes are measured on more complicated cases for disturbed magnetosphere (magnetic storms with large absolute values of the predicted Dst index).

This study was supported by RFBR grant no.14-01-00293-a.

Keywords: Time series · Prediction · Prediction horizon · Earth's magnetosphere · Committee of predictors · Ensemble · Stacked generalization

Reference

1. Efitorov, A., et al.: Advances in Intelligent Systems and Computing, vol. 449, pp. 281–287. Springer (2016)

© Springer International Publishing Switzerland 2016
A.E.P. Villa et al. (Eds.): ICANN 2016, Part II, LNCS 9887, p. 541, 2016.
DOI: 10.1007/978-3-319-44781-0

Artificial Neural Network for the Urinary Lithiasis Type Identification

Yasmina Nozha Mekki[1]([✉]), Nadir Farah[1], Abdelatif Boutefnouchet[2], and KheirEddine Chettibi[2]

[1] LABGED Laboratory, Computer Science Department, Badji Mokhtar University, BP 12, 23000 Annaba, Algeria
[2] Faculty of Medicine, Badji Mokhtar University, 23000 Annaba, Algeria

Abstract. Nowadays, it is widely admitted that urolithiasis has become a frequent disease [1]. The most famous epidemiological study has pointed out the existence of numerous types of calculus, as a function of some morphological and constitutional intrinsic characteristics [2]. Determination of urinary calculi types is hence important to set suitable diet or treatment and consequently, to limit risks of renal function deterioration and relapse. Several parameters, that should characterize both the stone composition and the patient's profile, have been used in the classification process (age, gender, region, background, calculi composition...). In a first step, a statistical treatment of more than six hundred (600) experimental data has been carried out in order to perform an adequate interpretation of the obtained results and hence, to adopt the most suitable algorithm. Afterward, several models have been tested and compared i.e., the artificial neural network multi layer perceptron (MLP) trained with both Broyden-Fletcher-Goldfarb-Shanno (BFGS) [3] and the standard back propagation [4] error learning algorithm, as well as the support vector machine (SVM), with different kernels [5], in order to identify the calculi types, according to their compositions and patient's profile. These latter represent twenty-two (22) entry features used in the classification process. Preliminary results show that MLP (BFGS) was the best model for the urolithiasis type identification, regarding to its lowest error rate.

Keywords: Artificial neural network · Comparative study · Urinary lithiasis · Type identification

References

1. Daudon, M., Trawer, O., Jungers, P.: Lithiase Urinaire. Lavoisier (2012)
2. Daudon, M., Bader, C.A., Jungers, P.: Urinary calculi: review of classification methods and correlations with etiology. Scanning Microsc. **7**, 1081–1106 (1993)
3. Liu, D.C., Nocedal, J.: On the limited memory BFGS method for large scale optimiza-tion. Math. Program. **45**(1–3), 503–528 (1989)

A.E.P. Villa et al. (Eds.): ICANN 2016, Part II, LNCS 9887, pp. 542–543, 2016.
DOI: 10.1007/978-3-319-44781-0

4. Robert, H.-N.: Theory of the backpropagation neural network. In: International Joint Conference on Neural Networks, IJCNN, pp. 593–605. IEEE (1989)
5. Vladimir, V.: The Nature of Statistical Learning Theory. Springer Science & Business Media (2013)

Artificial Neural Network-Based Modeling for Multi-scroll Chaotic Systems

Mohammed Amin Khelifa$^{(\boxtimes)}$ and Abdelkrim Boukabou

Department of Electronics, Jijel University, BP 98 Ouled Aissa, Jijel 18000, Algeria
khe.amine88@gmail.com, aboukabou@gmail.com

Abstract. Chaotic systems have been widely studied and applied in many real-world applications and laboratory experiments such as electronic circuits, secure communication, smart grids, power systems protection, and so on [1]. The design and circuit implementation of multi-scroll chaotic systems have been a subject of increasing interest due to their potential applications in various chaos-based technologies and information systems. Recent investigations discussing the control, modeling and synchronization problems of multi-scroll chaotic systems are mentioned in [2, 3].

This paper considers the problem of developing an adaptive neural network (NN) for constructing models that incorporate a prior knowledge in the form of differential equations for multi-scroll chaotic systems. For this purpose, we represent the results of the use of multi-layer feed-forward back-propagation neural network to model some well-known multi-scroll chaotic systems, especially, the n-scroll Chua's circuit and the multi-scroll Chen system. The specified neural network is trained with the system model extracted from the time series. The Levenberg-Marquardt (LM) algorithm is used as the training function to update weights and biases values according to LM optimization. Further, in common with other NN-based researches, the hidden layers and the number of their neurons are selected via trial-and-error method. The capability of the adaptive neural network to approximate this type of chaotic systems is confirmed by numerical simulations.

Keywords: Artificial neural networks · Chaotic behavior · LM optimization · Multi-scroll systems

References

1. Banerjee, S., Mitra, M., Rondoni, L.: Applicationsof Chaos and Nonlinear Dynamics in Engineering, vol 2. Springer-Verlag, Berlin Heidelberg (2014)
2. Khelifa, M.A., Boukabou, A.: Control of UPOs ofunknown chaotic systems via ANN. In: Wermter, S., Weber, C., Duch, W., Honkela, T., Koprinkova-Hristova, P., Magg, S., Palm, G., Villa, A.E.P. (eds.) ICANN 2014, LNCS 8681, pp. 627-634. Springer-International Publishing, Switzerland (2014)
3. Khelifa, M.A., Boukabou, A.: Design of anintelligent prediction-based neural network controller formulti-scroll chaotic systems. Appl. Intell., 1–15 (2016)

© Springer International Publishing Switzerland 2016
A.E.P. Villa et al. (Eds.): ICANN 2016, Part II, LNCS 9887, p. 544, 2016.
DOI: 10.1007/978-3-319-44781-0

Detailed Remote Sensing of High Resolution Planetary Images by Artificial Neural Network

Marzieh Foroutan$^{(\boxtimes)}$

University of Calgary, Calgary, Canada
foroutam@ucalgary.ca

Abstract. Increasing the application of high resolution spatial data such as high resolution satellite or Unmanned Aerial Vehicle (UAV) images from Earth as well as High Resolution Imaging Science Experiment (HiRISE) images from Mars makes it necessary to develop automated techniques capable of extracting their detailed information. Furthermore, model validation based on multi-temporal images in different Environmental management issues and geophysical problems such as climate change effects demand more precise imagery-processing in remote sensing discipline. This study intends to develop a methodology based on Artificial Neural Network (ANN) algorithm to achieve the automatic extraction of small footprints from these high resolution images in order to facilitate and speed up image analysis along with the improvement of the results accuracy. Mapping different types of micro-landforms, such as aeolian, glacier and volcanic minor features, and extracting their morphometric and pattern information on planets is challenging because of their small footprint on satellite images and their large numbers or high density in small areas. Unfortunately available feature extraction modules of remote sensing software don't work properly for the size of these features. Previous studies traced and digitized small features manually (e.g. [1]). This proposal intends to create a framework based on an unsupervised ANN algorithm to automatize outlining these features and extracting their metrics. ANN algorithm characteristics such as learning ability, abstraction with topology preservation, and visualization can be applied to complex tasks in different disciplines (e.g. [2, 3]). In this study HiRISE images from Mars as well as UAV images from Earth are used as preliminary data and other layers will be extracted from selective filters. Different settings have been examined for the best which captures small linear feature outlines most accurately from these high quality satellite images. We intend to make our framework and module applicable and adjustable for all types of high resolution images. This methodology with its high accuracy can save a lot time and ease quantitative studies in different Earth and Planetary science researches.

References

1. Fenton, L.K., Michaels, T.I., Chojnacki, M.: Late amazonian aeolian features, gradation, wind regimes, and sediment state in the vicinity of the Mars exploration rover opportunity, meridiani planum, Mars. Aeolian Res. **16**, 75–99 (2015)

© Springer International Publishing Switzerland 2016
A.E.P. Villa et al. (Eds.): ICANN 2016, Part II, LNCS 9887, pp. 545–546, 2016.
DOI: 10.1007/978-3-319-44781-0

2. Kohonen, T.: Self Organizing Maps, 3rd edn. Springer, New York (2001)
3. Marini, F., Zupan, J., Mageri, A.L.: Class-modeling using Kohonen artificial neural networks. Analytica Chimica Acta **544**, 306–314 (2005)

Sentiment Analysis Using Extreme Learning Machine with Linear Kernel

Shangdi Sun and Xiaodong Gu$^{(\boxtimes)}$

Department of Electronic Engineering, Fudan University, Shanghai, China
{sdsun14,xdgu}@fudan.edu.cn

Abstract. Sentiment classification is one of the hot research topics currently and Support Vector Machine (SVM) is usually used as the baseline method. In our research, Linear Kernel Extreme Learning Machine (Linear kernel ELM) has been applied firstly to the sentiment classification and it is compared with SVM on widely used sentiment (RT-2K) and subjectivity/objective (Subj.) datasets. Furthermore, we build our datasets (Amazon Smartphone Review, ASR), an unbalanced dataset of product reviews with pre-defined 12 aspects. All the 2561 sentences belong to at least one aspect and every sentence is labeled as positive or negative sentiment. Therefore, ASR could be used in both sentiment classification at sentence level and aspect-based opinion summarization at aspect level. ELM is a standard single layer feedforward neural network(SLFN) and it is not required to tune the parameters of the hidden nodes [1]. Inspired by the successful use for sentiment analysis of SVM with linear kernel [2], we apply ELM with linear kernel to our three tasks. Meanwhile, the hidden node weights equal to sample values with zero bias. We use the bag-of-words model to test the robustness of SVM and linear kernel ELM through three different global term weighting schemes respectively [3].

Table 1. Experimental results on three datasets

	RT-2K(1000,1000)			Subj.(5000,5000)			ASR(1731,830)		
	ELM	SVM	+/-	ELM	SVM	+/-	ELM	SVM	+/-
Boolean	87.20	87.25	−0.05	91.82	91.12	+0.70	82.53	81.66	+0.87
IDF	87.75	87.40	+0.35	92.40	91.58	+0.82	83.12	83.48	−0.36
DSIDF	86.80	87.05	−0.25	92.65	91.88	+0.67	82.85	82.69	+0.16
DBIDF	87.60	87.80	−0.20	92.74	91.95	+0.79	82.93	83.05	−0.12
Average	87.34	87.38	−0.04	92.40	91.63	+0.77	82.86	82.72	+0.14

The experimental results show that the accuracy of linear kernel ELM is higher on the large dataset (Subj.), and is roughly the same as that of SVM on the small dataset (RT-2K). Linear kernel ELM is also a competitive sentiment classification approach on the unbalanced dataset(ASR).

Keywords: Sentiment classification · Linear kernel · ELM

© Springer International Publishing Switzerland 2016
A.E.P. Villa et al. (Eds.): ICANN 2016, Part II, LNCS 9887, pp. 547–548, 2016.
DOI: 10.1007/978-3-319-44781-0

References

1. Huang, G.B., et al.: Universal approximation using incremental constructive feed-forward networks with random hidden nodes. IEEE Trans. Neural Netw. **17**(4), 879–892 (2006)
2. Wang, S., Manning, C.: Baselines and bigrams: simple, good sentiment and topic classification. In: Proceedings of ACL, pp. 90–94 (2012)
3. Paltoglou, G., Thelwall, M.: A study of information retrieval weighting schemes for sentiment analysis. In: Proceedings of ACL, pp. 1386–1395 (2010)

Neural Network with Local Receptive Fields for Illumination Effects

Alejandro Lerer[(⊠)], Matthias S. Keil, and Hans Supèr

Basic Psychology Department, Faculty for Pshycology, University of Barcelona (UB),
Passeig de la Vall D'Hebron 171, 08035 Barcelona, Spain
alelerer@hotmail.com, matskeil@ub.edu
http://www.ub.edu/viscagroup

Abstract. Little is known about how or whether dedicated neurons of the visual cortex encode gradual changes of luminance (GcL). We approach this question computationally, where we describe possible advantages for explicitly encoding GcL, and explain how corresponding putative neurons could be used for estimating the illumination direction. With this objective, we compiled three sets of intrinsic images (IIs) by extracting low and high spatial frequencies from natural images. The third set contains the full frequency range. Each set of IIs was subsequently whitened with the ZCA transformation, and dictionaries with receptive fields (RFs) were learnt from each set via unsupervised learning. In the end we used the dictionaries for comparing the encoding efficiency of natural images, and found that GcL could be encoded by dedicated neurons about three times more efficient in terms of energy expenditure than with neurons that respond to the full or high spatial frequency range. Furthermore, the RFs of the three dictionaries can classify image features (ROC curves with close to 0.95 area under curve), into reflectance-related or sharp changes in luminance and gradual changes in luminance. We also propose a utility of GcL neurons for estimating the local or global direction of illumination within a visual scene, where we used the maximum a posteriori estimator (MAP) and minimum mean square error estimator (MMSE).

Keywords: Illumination · Shading · Reflectance · Receptive fields

© Springer International Publishing Switzerland 2016
A.E.P. Villa et al. (Eds.): ICANN 2016, Part II, LNCS 9887, p. 549, 2016.
DOI: 10.1007/978-3-319-44781-0

ROS Based Autonomous Control
of a Humanoid Robot

Ganesh Kumar Kalyani[✉], Zhijun Yang, Vaibhav Gandhi,
and Tao Geng

Middlesex University, London, UK
Gk434@live.mdx.ac.uk, {Z.Yang,V.Gandhi}@mdx.ac.uk

Abstract. This paper demonstrates how to control a Bioloid humanoid robot using a BeagleBone Black (BBB) and Robot Operating System (ROS). ROS works as a development framework in synchrony with the BBB and integrates the robotic functions as a whole. Individual AX-12A Dynamixel servo motors and sensors are used to control the robot movement, so that it walks with reasonable balance and gait (cf. Fig. 1 and a demonstration video in [1]).

The two-legged robot is constructed using 12 servos, resulting in 12 degree of freedom (DOF). USB2Dynamixel connector is used to operate the Dynamixel actuators through the Wi-Fi interface of the BBB [2]. Position of the Dynamixel AX-12A servos is obtained using inbuilt encoders. A Gyro sensor is mounted around the centre of the robot, which supports in balancing the robot. One infrared (IR) sensor mounted on the robot's chest is used to detect obstacles. Additional libraries are added from ROS, thereby enabling the BBB to work with a Wi-Fi adaptor and a USB camera. When the robot is moving forward, if the IR sensors detect presence of an obstacle, then further movement of the robot is stopped. Additionally, an alarm is raised by flickering of the LEDs mounted on the BBB. The gyro sensor also sends data to the BBB, and these sensor

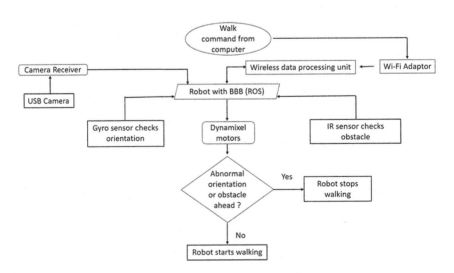

Fig. 1. Functional components of the robot

© Springer International Publishing Switzerland 2016
A.E.P. Villa et al. (Eds.): ICANN 2016, Part II, LNCS 9887, pp. 550–551, 2016.
DOI: 10.1007/978-3-319-44781-0

parameters are updated once in every 500 ms. This dynamic model is used as a building block to actuate the motors mounted on the leg, thereby resulting in a swing-stance period of the legs for further movement [3].

This study has the potential to enhance the capability of the Bioloid humanoid robot. The inbuilt RoboPlus software of the Robotis Bioloid robot is meant for easy programming, but it has limited universal applicability. Therefore, in the work presented here, this software has been replaced by ROS, along with a python script for a universal acceptability towards autonomous control of the Bioloid humanoid robot.

References

1. https://www.youtube.com/watch?v=9N0LkQyjW7U&feature=youtu.be
2. ROBOTIS e-Manual v1.25.00, v1.27.00, ROBOTIS 12-06-2015
3. Yang, Z.: Dynamic control of walking leg joints: a building block model perspective. In: ICNC 2011, pp. 459–463

A Robotic Implementation of Drosophila Larvae Chemotaxis

Daniel Malagarriga[✉], Ivica Slavkov, James Sharpe, and Matthieu Louis

Centre for Genomic Regulation (CRG),
The Barcelona Institute of Science and Technology, Barcelona, Spain
daniel.malagarriga@crg.eu

Abstract. The fruit fly Drosophila melanogaster larvae demonstrate an exquisite ability to track and exploit changes in sensory conditions to locate food and stay away from danger. Among other features, D. melanogaster larvae are capable of locating attractive odour sources by means of a sophisticated navigational algorithm, which directs stereotypical behavioural responses consisting in sequences of runs, stops, lateral casts, directed turns and weathervaning or laterally biased runs. By studying the neural-circuit computations underpinning larval taxis, we are seeking to understand the neural implementation of goal-oriented behaviours and learning. During the past decade, considerable efforts have been dedicated to measuring and modelling Drosophila chemotaxis, and to relate this behaviour to the general problems of sensory encoding and olfactory learning. Modelling approaches usually entail a discretization of a complex behaviour into elementary behavioural states (or actions). According to this framework, sensorimotor control is analysed in terms of state transitions probabilities modulated by the integration of changes in sensory stimuli. Quantitative hypothesis have then been tested in agent-based simulations. Here, we reproduce larval behaviours by using an agent-based algorithmic approach to larval chemotactic performance, which we implement into an artificial system of small robots. Specifically, we use the so-called kilobots, a robotic platform for which we also have an adequate simulator. We model the process of odour source tracking, exemplary of larval explorations as well as other stereotypical demeanour. Since kilobots are designed for general exploration and modelling of swarms and swarm behaviour we plan to further use them for implementation of other types of larval behaviour, besides odour source tracking. In conclusion, our results provide a basis for a potential application of larval chemotactic behaviour to engineered artificial systems for optimal source location.

Keywords: Drosophila melanogaster · Chemotaxis · Robotics · Decision making · Kilobot

© Springer International Publishing Switzerland 2016
A.E.P. Villa et al. (Eds.): ICANN 2016, Part II, LNCS 9887, p. 552, 2016.
DOI: 10.1007/978-3-319-44781-0

Author Index